THE WHITNEYS *

John Whitney (1583 – 1673)

James Scollay Whitney (1811 – 1878)
m. (1836) Laurinda Collins (1810 – 1908)

Mary A. Whitney (1837 – ?)
Henry Melville Whitney (1839 – 1923)————————
m. (1878) Margaret F. Green (1856 – ?)————————

William Collins Whitney (1841 – 1904)
m. 1. (1869) Flora Payne (1842 – 1893,
daughter of Mary Perry &, Henry B. Payne)

m. 2. (1896) Edith May Randolph (c. 1859 – 1899)
Susan C. Whitney (1845 – 1939)————————————
m. (1867) Henry Farnum Dimock (1842 – 1911)————————
Henrietta P. Whitney (1847 – ?)
Laurinda (or Lilly) C. Whitney (1852 – 1946)————————————
m. (1875) Charles Tracy Barney (1851 – 1907)————————

Leonora Payne Whitney (died at birth, c. 1870)

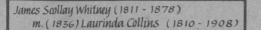

(1896)   HARRY (baptised HENRY) PAYNE WHITNEY (1872 – 1930)

Pauline Payne Whitney (1874 – 1916)————————————
m. (1895) Almeric Hugh Paget (1861 – 1949)————————
(William) Payne Whitney (1876 – 1927)————————————
m. (1902) Helen Hay (1876 – 1944)————————————
Olive Payne Whitney (1878 – 1883)
Dorothy Payne Whitney (1887 – 1968)————————————
m. 1. (1911) William Dickerman Straight (1880 – 1918)————————
m. 2. (1925) Leonard Knight Elmhirst (1893 – 1974)————————

Flora Payne Whitney (1897 –   )————————————
m. 1 (1920) Roderick Tower (1892 – 1961)————————————
m. 2. (1927) G. Macculloch Miller (1887 – 1972)————————————
Cornelius Vanderbilt Whitney (1899 –   )————————————
m. 1. (1923) Marie Norton (1903 – 1970)————————————
m. 2. (1931) Gwladys Crosby Hopkins (1905 –   )————————
m. 3. (1941) Eleanor Searle (1915 –   )————————
m. 4. (1958) Marie Louise Schroeder Hosford (1925 –   )————————
Barbara Whitney (1903 –   )————————————
m. 1. (1924) Barklie McKee Henry (1902 – 1966)————————
m. 2. (1947) Samuel Anderson Peck (1904 – 1960)————————
m. 3. (1960) George William Headley III (1908 –   )————————

Gertrude Vanderbilt Whitney

Also by B. H. Friedman

Fiction

CIRCLES

YARBOROUGH

WHISPERS

MUSEUM

ALMOST A LIFE

Nonfiction, including monographs

SCHOOL OF NEW YORK: SOME YOUNGER ARTISTS
(edited and introduced)

ROBERT GOODNOUGH
(with Barbara Guest)

LEE KRASNER

JACKSON POLLOCK: ENERGY MADE VISIBLE

ALFONSO OSSORIO

SALVATORE SCARPITTA

Gertrude Vanderbilt Whitney

a biography by B. H. FRIEDMAN

with the research collaboration of
Flora Miller Irving

DOUBLEDAY & COMPANY, INC.
GARDEN CITY, NEW YORK
1978

Library of Congress Catalog Card Number 77–26524
ISBN: 0-385-12994-7
Copyright © 1978 by B. H. FRIEDMAN
BOOK DESIGN BY BENTE HAMANN

First Edition

To Abby, Daisy, and Jackson
with much love
and with many apologies
for so many hours
spent with Gertrude
away from you

Preface
and
Acknowledgments

A full history of the Vanderbilt and Whitney families would fill many volumes covering all of American history from colonial times to the present. I have therefore restricted myself as much as possible to the life of Gertrude Vanderbilt Whitney, emphasizing only those aspects of genealogy necessary to clarify her situation and her husband's. For background on the Vanderbilt family I have used mainly *Commodore Cornelius Vanderbilt, Sophia Johnson Vanderbilt, and Their Decendants*, compiled through 1972 by Verley Archer, published by Vanderbilt University; *Commodore Vanderbilt* by Wheaton J. Lane; *The Glitter and the Gold* by Consuelo Vanderbilt Balsan, formerly Duchess of Marlborough; and standard reference works such as the Dictionary of American Biography, Notable American Women, Who's Who, and the Social Register, as well as contemporary newspapers and periodicals. For Whitney family background I have used substantially the same reference sources, plus Henry Melville's *The Ancestry of John Whitney*, F. C. Pierce's *The Descendants of John Whitney*, and Mark D. Hirsch's thorough and detailed biography *William C. Whitney: Modern Warwick* in the "American Political Leaders" series under the general editorship of Allan Nevins.

However, for material on Gertrude Vanderbilt Whitney herself I have gone almost entirely to her journals, logs, correspondence, photograph albums, scrapbooks, and memorabilia; published and unpublished fiction, poetry, criticism, and drama; and drawings and sculpture—all with a view to emphasizing the quotidian as much as the more broadly historical aspects of her life. This would have been impossible without the co-operation of her devoted daughter Flora Whitney Miller and granddaughter Flora Miller Irving, to both of whom I owe a great debt. In addition, Flora Irving helped organize, chronologize, and catalogue much of the material her grandmother and mother had saved, arranged for me to meet various members of her family and to visit the homes in which her grandmother lived and the studios in which she worked, and performed many jobs of research, including the recovery of lost or mislaid documents. In all of this she and I were ably assisted by Julia Garretson Strand, Tamara Tovey, Jean Reynolds, and Claire Mozel. Although I consider myself responsible for the text of this book and for any mistakes of fact or interpretation which may have gotten into it, Flora Irving, as research collaborator, wishes to share responsibility for any such mistakes.

She also made available to me, with the consent of the author, a short biography of Gertrude Vanderbilt Whitney by Stuart Preston. Though he gave permission to use the material in his unpublished and now abandoned text, I have chosen rather to refer to it only as a check list against what I might otherwise have missed; for its usefulness in this way I am grateful. In the same way, *A History of the Whitney Museum of American Art, 1930–1954,* the unpublished New York University dissertation of Dr. Daty Healy was extremely valuable. I thank her for making her impeccable scholarship available. I also appreciate the generous co-operation of the Whitney Museum itself, not only for permitting the use of its archives but for the time and help given by Lloyd Goodrich and John I. H. Baur, former directors; the late Margaret McKellar, former registrar; Nancy McGary, present registrar; Jennifer Russell, curatorial assistant; Anita Duquette, rights and reproduction; Libby Seaberg, librarian; and Susan Lieberman, library assistant.

Karolyn Gould, who is presently working on a biography of Gertrude Whitney's sister-in-law Dorothy Whitney Straight Elmhirst, has been generous in sharing her research and making rare documents available. Many thanks are also due to Flora Irving's husband Michael, whose professional knowledge of architecture and great experience in sailing were very useful and whose support and interest throughout the project were extremely meaningful to his wife as well as to me. Similarly, Flora Irving's cousin Shirley C. Burden's interest in this book and his ability as a photographer made it possible for us to call on him again and again to restore and/or rephotograph damaged or faded pictures, many of which appear more clearly here than in their originals. There is no way to thank him sufficiently for the time and painstaking care he has contributed. Rory McEwen has, throughout this project, been my faithful British correspondent, patiently answering queries on everything from death certificates to descriptions of English homes. He, too, I can't thank enough. And, not quite finally, John I. H. Baur, in addition to other help, read my first draft, and Louis Auchincloss read galleys. Both made many valuable suggestions, which I greatly appreciate.

For various contributions, including permission to quote family letters, Flora Irving and I also want to thank Charles Francis Adams, Ivan Albright, John Winthrop Aldrich, Archibald S. Alexander, Doris Alexander, Harry Amdur, Carley Paxton Angell, Marie Elizabeth Appleton, Willy Arnheim, Peggy Bacon, Ivor Balding, Nicole Barbier, David Bergamini, Kathleen and the late Dr. Herbert M. Bergamini, John D. Bergamini, Henry Bergé, Isabel Bishop, Patricia L. Bodak, James Bonar, Edward L. Bowen, Joseph Brala, Susanne Brendel, John C. Broderick, Alexander Brook, W. Douglas Burden, Luther C. Burnett, Alan Burnham, Nathaniel Burt, Barbara Byrnes, Jane Canfield, Philip Carroll, M. Etienne Caux (*Maire de la ville de Saint-Nazaire*), William A. V. Cecil, Laura L. Chace, Butler Coleman, Ruth Collins, Gerta Henry Conner, J. R. Conner, Beatrice Straight Cookson, Ann T. Corliss, Ralston Crawford, Frank L. Crocker, Harry C. Cushing IV, Howard G. Cushing, Andrew Dasburg, Jacques Davidson, Jean Davidson, Erica Davies, Monica Borglum Davies, Barbara Debs, Anne d'Harnoncourt, Peter Dzwonkoski, Gwladys Hopkins Elliott, John Ellis, Louelle W. Felt, Rep. Millicent Fenwick, Ruth Ferguson, Comdr. J. B. Finkelstein, John J. Fletcher, Frank M. Foley, R. Buckminster Fuller, Mayor Richard H Fulton, John A. Gable, Richard Gachot, Donald C. Gallup, Diane Girvin, Edith Goodrich, Robert Graham, Bradley Gramprey, James F. Greene, Kenneth M. Greene, Katherine Gregory, Frederick W. Guardabassi, Jennison Hammond, Caroline J. Hartwell, Marshall Haseltine, Barbara Whitney Headley, Morrison Heckscher, W. Barklie Henry, G. B. Higgonbotham, Sohei Hohri, Damaris S. Horan, Joseph H. Hunt, Charles P. Hurd, Fiona Irving, Macculloch Miller Irving, Fred Keefe, Clarence M. Kelley, Thomas Smith Kelly, Everett Raymond Kinstler, Lincoln Kirstein, Carol Knauss, Robert W. Kraus Kopf, Henry A. La Farge, Eleanor Lambert, Monique Laurent, Shiela Burden Lawrence, Pamela Tower LeBoutillier, Janet Lehr, John C. Leslie, Helen Hoyt Lewis, R. W. B. Lewis, Nancy C. Little, Nancy Whitney Lutz, Mary C. McGreenery, Alexander McIlvaine, Frank McMahon, Anne F. Malone, Mabel S. Marsh, Mercedes Matter, David L. Miller, Leverett S. Miller, Thea Morgan, Robert Moses, Mary Murphy, John J. Murray, Reuben Nakian, Kalman Noselson, Edna O'Connell, Edwin Olsen, Katherine Osgood, Monique Panaggio, Betty Parsons, the late Catherine Hunt Paxton, Anthony Peluso, George W. Pepper III, Gladys Széchényi Peterson, Wesley H. Poling, Homan Potterton, Beatrice Gilman Proske, Cynthia Quimby, Louis A. Rachow, the late Helen Appleton Read, Henry Hope Reed, Jeanne M. Rengstorff, Robin Richardson, Daniel Robbins, Ilonka Rogers, John Russell, Richard S. Salant, Rafael Sardá, Judith A. Schiff, Catherine Schmidt, Barbara Sicherman, Kipp Soldwedel, Claire A. Stein, Sally Ann Stewart, Michael Straight, Whitney Straight, Robert Strawbridge, W. A. Swanberg, Sylvia Széchényi Szápáry, Reginald B. Taylor, Gladys Roberts Thomas, Lately Thomas, Whitney Tower, Samuel Untermyer II, William Henry Vanderbilt III, Kirk Varnedoe, Mary Ward, the late Katherine Warren, Phelps Warren,

Robert Penn Warren, Whitney Warren, Jr., Alice Weaver, Cornelius Vanderbilt Whitney, Marjorie F. and Helm George Wilde, Helen T. Williamson, Brooks Wright, Walter W. Wright.

I must, too, express some regrets: Except for early letters, mostly from Gertrude's husband Harry Payne Whitney to her, there is comparatively little documentation on him and therefore the possibility of some diminution of his life. There is also the possibility of diminution of their three children's lives. All of them are living, and I have therefore protected their privacy to an extent I have not protected that of their parents. Finally, within the family, I regret, though I fully understand, the unwillingness of Gloria Vanderbilt Cooper to present her side of the custody case involving her. It was a very painful experience for all parties concerned—her, her mother, and her aunt Gertrude. I have relied largely on court records, newspaper and magazine accounts, Gertrude's letters and Line-A-Days, and two autobiographies by Gloria's mother, *Without Prejudice* and *Double Exposure* (written with her twin sister). Outside the family, I have not given the attention I might have to Juliana Force, director of the Whitney Museum until her death in 1948. She would be a suitable subject for a separate biography. Meanwhile, the chronological facts which appear here are drawn from a memoir written by her nephew Carl Rieser, who is depositing this and Juliana Force Papers with the Archives of American Art, Smithsonian Institution. I am grateful to Mr. Rieser for his permission to use the memoir and to quote from his aunt's letters. However, I believe that in my book more details concerning Mrs. Force's life and the operation of the Whitney Museum itself would be disproportionate. I have not tried to write a full history of the museum—Dr. Healy has done that.

The above emphasizes my desire to write about Gertrude Whitney from her point of view—and as much as possible in her own words. Her writing, a small fraction of which I've used here, is quite comparable quantitatively to that of many professional writers. Given this enormous bulk of words, it seems to me both misleading and pretentious to include a long bibliography listing books from which I've used only a phrase or a paragraph. Instead, I include all essential bibliographical sources within the text, and I have also kept footnotes to a minimum. Quotations from Gertrude Whitney are mostly as written by her. However, especially with journals that were done hurriedly, I have corrected spelling and occasionally added punctuation where necessary for clarity.

In conclusion, I may owe the reader a few words about myself. Though I have been a trustee of the Whitney Museum since 1961 and have known many members of the Whitney family since then, I have written this book as an independent author trying to be as objective as possible. In 1965, I wrote most of a novel called *Museum*, a large part of which appeared in *Quarterly Review of Literature* in 1968, though the entire book was not published until 1974. That novel about a family museum, though valid in itself, is fiction and was completed before I had seen any of the documentation concerning Gertrude Whitney. In 1975, another novel of mine, *Almost a Life*, was published three years after writing *Jackson Pollock: Energy Made Visible* and is a direct fictional response to that experience. I have not changed my opinions expressed in *Almost a Life*. I still think that fiction can be complete and "definitive," that biography can never be, and that at best it is an attempt at the solution to an unsolvable mystery. As Nicola Chiarmonte writes about Luigi Pirandello's *Clothing the Naked*, "for present day consciousness in general, human beings elude any finality of judgment and the real truth, for each, consists only in a destiny."

B.H.F.

PART ONE

Coming Out

Introduction

In 1875, when Gertrude Vanderbilt was born, she was the eldest daughter of the eldest son of the richest American family. That meant being born to hereditary celebrity at a time when "society" (established wealth, not necessarily very long established) produced most of America's stars and superstars, a time when not even the great personalities of theater and opera and literature appeared in newspapers and magazines as frequently as the often overlapping categories of business leaders and inventors. There was then no Hollywood, no radio, no television. The great sportsmen were those in Gertrude's own social circle, many in her own family, sailing their yachts, racing their horses, riding their polo ponies, hunting foxes, and shooting their own wild game. The great political powers, if not elected officials, came often from her own milieu. During her formative years and well into her maturity, there was hardly a week or even a day when she did not read in the popular press about the members of her family, their close friends, their business and professional associates. Then as now, the public's curiosity about wealth and its concomitant power was insatiable. The very rich had no private events, neither weddings nor funerals, neither joys nor sorrows. Money, an abstraction of energy (often inherited), seemed more an abstraction of fantasy. With money the rich acted out the dreams of the poor; with it anything seemed possible and celebrity itself enchanted. The outer limits of this dream had been realized —the stone walls or iron fences of huge homes in the city and in resorts and seasonal colonies; the ease of travel here and abroad; the possessions imported from faraway times and places; the servants, mostly imported too; the anything-money-can-buy. Except in such comparatively unpopular visions as those of Henry James and Henry Adams, only the inner limits of the dream had not been dreamed of—the emptiness there, the frequent hollowness of possessions and of celebrity itself (so long before that particular mythic reality of Hollywood, radio, slick magazines, and the rest).

3

Gertrude Vanderbilt was among the first to have to face celebrity, her specifically American kind, and to question it, and ultimately, in a different form, to succumb to it. Long before the publication of James's *The American Scene* or Adams' *Education* she wrote dozens of journals in which she presented her struggle between the materialistic and the idealistic, between the realistic and the romantic, between the public and the private, between a dozen dichotomies of American life. These journals say more about her life than does her outward social history, which was mostly in tension between private and public needs; or her sculpture, which, though competent, was never fully realized because of a similar tension; or even her career as the greatest single patron of contemporary American art, a patronage which, again, drew energy away from her own work and toward public service. Her grandfather William H. Vanderbilt said, "The public be damned." She could never have said that—perhaps, as we'll see, not even he did—but, especially in her journals, she said, "The private be saved," said this as a young girl, as a mature woman, as a comparatively old lady—all through her life, and always against the odds of her particular situation and heredity.

≈

Toward the end of 1893, at the age of eighteen, Gertrude opens a black leather-bound gold-stamped notebook purchased in Paris, turns past the marbleized end paper, and begins writing:

My History

I was born on the 9th of January 1875.

My parents had lost their eldest child, a daughter [Alice], a short time before my birth. Two boys remained, one four years old [William], the other, one [Cornelius]. We lived in New York. I presume I was an ordinary child. They say I had curly black hair and was advanced for my age. Myself I do not remember. Not quite three years later I had another little brother who was called Alfred Gwynne.

One of the first things I remember was how I longed to be a boy. I was four years old when unable to resist the temptation longer I secreted myself in my mother's room and proceeded to cut off my curls. This it seemed to me was what distinguished me most from my brothers; they said only girls had curls, so mine were sacrificed and all I gained was a severe punishment. We went abroad in 1880 and some incidents of the trip I will never forget.

It was only after we came back that I began noticing things more distinctly. I would wonder why my cousins did certain things I never did and why everything my parents did and said was more right than what anyone else's parents did or said. Then we had scarlet fever, but just before that I had another little brother [Reginald], and of course I longed more than ever to be a boy. But even though Fate had given me this burden to bear I certainly rebelled at it by letting my actions be entirely those of a boy.

Time passed. We were educated at home first. Then the older boys went to school, while Alfred and I had a governess. I cannot remember when I first realized who I was. It must have been very slowly brought about, this realization, for I can put my finger on no time when it burst upon me. At any rate when I was eleven I knew perfectly that my father was talked of all over, that his name was known throughout the world, that I, simply because I was his daughter, would be talked about when I grew up, and that there were lots of things I could not do simply because I was Miss Vanderbilt. At first I felt as if I could not stand this. That I should have to go through life being pointed at, having my actions talked about, seemed too hard. That I should be courted and made a friend of simply because I was who I was, was unbearable to me. I longed to be someone else, to be liked only for myself, to live quietly and happily without the burden that goes with riches. Of course time made all this easier to bear, and when I was eighteen I felt as if I could hold my head up under it, and that I would act my part well for God had put me there, just where I was, and if He had not meant me to have strength to go through He would never have put me where I was. So I became to a certain extent reconciled to my lot. If I was liked for my worldly possessions, why I gave nothing in return and lost the respect I might have had for the person. It was a simple arrangement and for anyone as self-centered as myself it was not such a hard one. For let me tell you I had friends in spite of the terrible obstacle which stood in our way. There were girls who liked me for myself, I know it. I was not altogether unlovable, I think.

I remember so well one day Mama had told me something which will come into this History later and then she said, "You will have a very interesting and amusing life and all kinds of 'aspirants.'" It was that which first gave me the idea of writing my history. I thought other girls might like to hear of me and my life. . . .

I am not going to tell you much about myself until I was eighteen because my childhood passed almost without incident . . . and then came a very sad time after I lost my eldest brother [William] which I would rather not dwell upon. Before this I had a little sister [Gladys], eleven years younger than myself. My delight when she was born was quite beyond description, and it never for a moment died away. She was the only person to whom I showed my affection and the consequence was I called her all the pet names my imagination could invent and showered upon her kisses and caresses without number. When she was very young the greatest pleasure of my day was to put her to bed and I watched the expression of her face so that I could tell the thoughts that passed in her little brain.

I was always reserved, too much so, they said, and I froze people up if I did not want to be intimate with them until they actually became afraid of me. I had a way of hiding my feelings so completely that even my best friends, those who knew me best, could not tell what was passing within me. Speaking of best friends makes me think that I always said I had none, and perhaps it was true. My first real friend was Alice Blight. I think she loved me as much as I loved her. Sometimes I used to imagine it was not for myself she loved me and then I think I was the most unhappy girl that ever breathed. . . .

Her *History* continues. There is her second real friendship—with Esther Hunt. There are trips to Europe. There are, in her late teens, the first men she meets. But all of this is covered less retrospectively and summarily in later journals. Near the bottom of the forty-ninth handwritten page, about a third of the way through the notebook, this *History* ends, Gertrude's voice fades—but lingers. One can still hear it—cultivated, modulated, privileged—like that of a Henry James heroine. One knows, for example, that the accent falls heavily on the second syllable of *Mama*. However, this long quotation not only introduces a voice, speaking in various moods through a period of time, but also introduces many of the themes which will be amplified and complexly intermingled throughout Gertrude's life: positive and negative aspects of Family, Wealth, Society, Love. . . . Love —again and again in overlapping notebooks, journals, diaries, letters, autobiographical fictions, autobiographical writings of all kinds (some pseudonymous), she will ask in one way or another if Society or if a particular individual, as with Alice Blight, loves her for herself.

The one important general theme which is not explicitly stated in this autobiography covering her first nineteen years is that of Art, which deserves to be capitalized as much as if not more than any of the other themes of her life. Yet art is there between the lines, in the very act of privately writing, speaking her *History*. From early on Gertrude records the significance she attaches to her experience. Surviving journals and diaries begin at the age of ten, the earliest of these under the pen name "Jane Philipper." Not only are school composition books saved, but school themes of which she is proud and passages of poetry and prose which move her are transcribed into elegant notebooks, scrapbooks, address books, whatever comes to hand.

When she meets new people she records them too, sometimes in brief characterizations, sometimes in quickly sketched pictures, sometimes both. There are whole books filled with dinner-party seating arrangements, drawings of round tables, oval tables, square tables, oblong tables, with the names of guests as carefully placed on her diagrams as were the guests themselves at dinner, names written small when parties were large, large when they were small. Not just in youth but all her life she will save letters, telegrams, invitations, greeting cards, calling cards, place cards, dance cards. . . . Her hoarding of experience—her instinct for preservation, transcription, transmutation—is not restricted to what we call "the real world." She records dreams, fantasies (some fictionalized, some not), imaginary letters and replies. In short, she tries to save everything, life itself as it runs by. At the same time as she expresses doubts about herself, her being, she asserts herself, hour after hour, by writing and sometimes sketching. At the same time as she says "my childhood passed almost without incident" she records one incident after another.

So, granting the theme of Art—at this time the more compulsive aspects of it, anyway—you have been introduced to Gertrude Vanderbilt. Now look at her physically. At nineteen she has reached her full height of five feet eight inches, tall by today's standards and comparatively even taller then. She is slim, elegant, "willowy." She stands erect as she has been taught but there is nothing overbearing about her posture. Her long neck and torso lean forward from her small waist as she talks to intimates. With others she seems literally to back off, to arch away, expressing that reserve she has commented on in her *History*. Her hair is lighter than in childhood, brown now and soft, wavy rather than curly. Her eyes are green, mysterious, vulnerable, set far apart above a long straight nose, deep philtrum, sensuous lips, slightly recessive chin. Her face, like her body, is long, a mixture of strength and delicacy. Her beauty is aristocratic. Indeed, she is like her handwriting. It, too, is a mixture of strength and delicacy. It moves smoothly and easily, interrupted most noticeably by the long decisive crossings of *t*'s (mistakable for underlinings of words above) and the definite downward strokes of those letters which drop below the line. She minds her *p*'s and *q*'s but also her *f*'s, *g*'s, *j*'s, *y*'s, and *z*'s.

When Gertrude wrote her *History* there would have been as little need as she herself found to speak of her family background. Her name spoke then for itself. But today it is one of many names. There are newer fortunes—greater in dollars if not in buying power. The Vanderbilts are part of history, the subject of several books. Since Gertrude, and not her family, is our subject, a few pages of background, rather than another book, will suffice.

⪻ Vanderbilt Background

Jan Aertsen van der bilt (of the Manor of Bilt, near Zeyst, Holland) emigrated to New Amsterdam in the mid-seventeenth century. In 1667 he settled in Flatbush where the family remained until his grandson Jacob moved to Port Richmond, Staten Island, early in the eighteenth century. From there his grandson Cornelius Vander Bilt moved to a large farm at Stapleton, Staten Island, where he and his wife Phebe Hand, a strong, almost masculinely handsome and energetic woman of better-educated English stock, struggled to raise a family. Cornelius Van Derbilt, Jr. (as he preferred to write his name before its further and final consolidation) was born May 27, 1794, the fourth child of nine born to this sixth generation of poor Dutch farmers.

This Cornelius (never again Jr.), combining the strong physique of his father and the rugged, sharp features of his mother, would radically change the economic situation in his family. As a boy, growing up on the farm and on the Staten Island waterfront, he had tremendous vitality. His dark blue eyes, his hawklike nose, his strong mouth and chin, even the mop of wild blond hair all seemed to exude energy. At eleven he stopped going to school. Just over six feet tall, he was strong enough to become his father's regular helper on the farm and to assist him with some boating in New York Harbor. Within two years he was supervising the lightering of a ship; at sixteen he bought a sailboat for a hundred dollars and began ferrying passengers and freight between Staten Island and New York; and at eighteen, during the War of 1812, he had several boats under his command and received a government contract to provision New York Harbor forts. Except for money he gave to his family, he invested the rest in more ships, and at the age of nineteen determined to marry his cousin and neighbor Sophia Johnson.

There were parental objections based on elementary knowledge of eugenics but, since Cornelius was by now the family's principal breadwinner, his will prevailed. Through the busy summer and fall, while running his small shipping business, he helped his father on the farm, with the understanding that when the harvest was in and the cold weather came he would marry Sophia and devote his time to shipping. The large Vanderbilt clan gathered at the Johnson farmhouse the night of December 19, 1813, for a wedding dinner, after which he took his bride to a small house he had rented near the Stapleton landing. There was no honeymoon. Early the next morning he was at the dock in one of his flat-bottomed sailing barges.

That first morning was like the rest. Cornelius worked long days, usually starting at sunrise and ending late at night, and sometimes, when on a particular job, commanding his small fleet of ships on voyages that lasted a week or more. Sophia ran their small home frugally and began having children just over a year after they were married. Phebe, born early in 1815, was the first; twelve more followed in fairly rapid succession. But about the time of Phebe's birth Cornelius had already built his first large schooner, for service to Long Island Sound, and by 1816 two larger ones for coastal trade. Commanding the largest of the three, he shipped cargo for others and traded for his own account on the Hudson River and along the coast from New England to Charleston.

In 1818 he sold his ships and went to work for Thomas Gibbons as captain of a steam ferry between New Brunswick, New Jersey, and New York City, fighting the steam-navigation monopoly which had been granted to Robert Fulton. In New Brunswick, Cornelius and Sophia converted a rundown tavern into Bellona Hall, a hotel soon famous for good food and service to travelers between New York and Philadelphia. While she ran the hotel, Cornelius reconditioned Gibbons' one ferry, formed a tough, hard-working crew, and within a year had the ferry showing a profit which was invested in a larger steamer, the *Bellona*, a mobile advertisement for the hotel. The New York monopoly sued Gibbons, fought with Cornelius and his crew, and tried unsuccessfully to arrest him every time he entered New York waters. While Gibbons battled in court, Cornelius kept the new big ferry running. In 1824 the United States Supreme Court ruled that the Fulton monopoly was illegal.

During the eleven years Cornelius was with Gibbons he greatly enlarged his employer's business by building a total of eight steamers and by developing Delaware as well as Hudson River lines. At the same time he greatly enlarged his own experience and capital. By 1829 he was worth close to half a million dollars and was ready to go into the steamboat business on his own. Against Sophia's wishes, he sold Bellona Hall and moved his family to New York City. There, having learned how to fight ruthlessly against entrenched steamship lines, he started a rate war against Daniel Drew's Peekskill line. When the fare to Peekskill dropped to twelve and a half cents, Drew sold out to Cornelius, who then used similar tactics against the more powerful Hudson River Association, serving Albany. Soon the association paid him to withdraw from competition for ten years, and he invested this payment in establishing lines on Long Island Sound and to Providence and Boston.

His worth had now substantially passed the half-million mark, but that in itself was not enough to make a favorable impression on New York's exclusive society. Local bankers and businessmen admired his clear broad vision, his toughness and courage, his reputation (their own experience now) for making a bargain and sticking to it. But these direct, blunt qualities showed themselves also in coarse manners and speech. He was loud. He chewed tobacco. He used the slang and profanity of the wharves. As Henry Adams writes in *The Education*, Cornelius was "not ornamental" and "lacked social charm." What was admired in business was characterized in drawing rooms as "pushy" and "cheeky." So in the late thirties he built a mansion on Staten Island and in 1840 returned there with his family.

During the next half dozen years, as the business prospered and his steamers became increasingly more comfortable and elegant, the cold reception by Manhattan society must have gnawed at him. In 1846 he launched the first *Vanderbilt*, as luxurious as any of the "floating palaces," and in the same year, again despite Sophia's protests, he began construction of a large town house in Manhattan at Washington Place. The "Commodore," as he came to be called, was now very visibly a millionaire.

Sophia continued to resist relocation. The Commodore continued to build. When the house was ready early the following year and she refused to move, he had her committed to a private insane asylum. She was not released until the spring when she went to their new house.

The Commodore's business grew almost organically, imperceptibly, as steamers were added to his lines and dollars to his fortune. One million. Two (probably). Three (possibly). . . . There are no accurate records. . . . And then, in 1849, a rush—toward gold. . . . And he saw his greatest opportunity thus far.

Before the end of 1849 passengers and freight were going to California by way of Panama, crossing the isthmus on muleback. The Commodore proposed a shorter and consequently cheaper route via Nicaragua—west on the San Juan River to Lake Nicaragua and then preferably by canal or, if the additional financing was not available, by road to the Pacific. He formed the American Atlantic and Pacific Ship Canal Company and sought the necessary outside financing, first in New York and then in London. When those millions were not forthcoming, he gambled his own fortune, settling for a road rather than a more efficient but much more costly canal. As soon as he obtained a charter from the Nicaraguan government, he began construction of eight steamers; east-coast, west-coast, and lake docks; and a twelve-mile macadam road. Though the job was vast and necessitated improving the channel of the San Juan River, Vanderbilt made all of the major decisions, personally supervised most of the details, and soon had his steamers running from New York and, later, from New Orleans as well.

Profits came in so quickly that by late 1852, at the age of fifty-eight, he decided to build a private ship and take the first vacation of his life; a four-month trip abroad with most of his immediate family (Sophia, seven

of nine daughters, two of three surviving sons, various in-laws, two grandchildren) and a few friends, including a medical doctor and the Rev. Dr.
Choules, who would act as chaplain and chronicler. As Choules describes
it—in *The Cruise of the Steam Yacht North Star; a narrative of the Excursion of Mr. Vanderbilt's Party to England, Russia, Denmark, France,
Spain, Italy, Malta, Turkey, Madeira, etc.*—the 2,500-ton, 270-foot yacht
with its three principal Louis XV salons and ten staterooms "combine all
that is required to insure comfort and elegance . . . a noble specimen of
American mechanical skill."

Before leaving (May 19, 1853), the Commodore resigned as president
of the company and, while gone, his managers manipulated the stock and
gained control. In the fall when he returned, the Commodore wrote a
short letter:

> Gentlemen:
> You have undertaken to cheat me. I will not sue you—the law
> takes too long. I will ruin you.

It took him several months of shrewd stock manipulation of his own to
regain control, but then—with the American adventurer William Walker,
who had taken over Nicaragua—his managers got the government to re-
scind the company's charter and to appropriate its assets. The Commodore sent agents to Central America who formed an alliance of Hon-
duras, El Salvador, Guatemala, and Costa Rica—all finally backed by the
United States Navy—to destroy Walker and reclaim the property.

The fight behind the scenes on Wall Street, and in Washington as well
as in Central America itself, took almost four years. When it was over, the
Commodore, sixty-three now and just as tough and energetic as ever, nego-
tiated a deal with the two great Panama-route carriers. For $40,000 per
month (later increased to $56,000) and for $400,000 outright in payment
for the *North Star*, he would discontinue his Nicaragua line. He wanted,
anyway, to concentrate on what he thought would be the more lucrative
Atlantic trade and built three more ships including another *Vanderbilt*,
his largest, fastest, and best equipped to date. The Atlantic line didn't
prove to be as profitable as he had hoped. At the beginning of the Civil
War he sold it for $3,000,000, except for the *Vanderbilt*, which he con-
verted to a warship and loaned to the navy while chartering other ships to
it. Many of these turned out to be unseaworthy. Yet, when the Senate
voted a resolution of censure, his name was removed from it, and at about
the same time—not probably by simple coincidence—the "loan" of the
Vanderbilt was accepted by the government as a gift, recognized by a gold
medal, inscribed from "A Grateful Country to her Generous Son."

Until the war, the Commodore had delegated no business affairs to his
boys. Indeed, George, his youngest, healthiest, and favorite son, was to die
as a result of battle exposure. His second son, Cornelius Jeremiah, notably

absent on the 1853 cruise of the *North Star*, was a pitiful epileptic, a debt-ridden gambler, a "ne'er-do-well" in the terminology of the day. The Commodore once said, "I'd give a hundred dollars if I had never called him 'Corneel.'" And his eldest son, William Henry, had offended his dynamic father by being a sickly child and then by marrying at the age of nineteen. Though the Commodore himself had married at this age, he had been in good health and was already succeeding in business. Furthermore, the Commodore, nearly a millionaire at the time of William's marriage, had seen no prospects for his son in marrying Maria Louisa Kissam, the daughter of a poor, though refined, Brooklyn clergyman. When William's health continued to decline after marriage, the Commodore bought him and Louisa a 70-acre farm at New Dorp, Staten Island. There, almost exiled, they raised a family of four sons and four daughters and, to his father's surprise, William, with considerable help from his wife, managed the farm profitably and increased its size to 350 acres. Even more surprising was a request from William shortly before the Civil War that the Commodore use his influence to have William appointed receiver of the small bankrupt Staten Island Railroad, which William then succeeded in rehabilitating.

During 1862 the Commodore himself began investing heavily in railroad stock, putting proceeds from his shipping business into the New York & Harlem, whose stock was then selling cheap. By 1863 he controlled this railroad, persuaded the City Council to let him extend streetcar tracks to the Battery, watched the stock rise then, and even more when he had himself elected president of the company. Now his old enemy Daniel Drew plotted to have the extension rescinded and to sell the stock short. He had seemingly forgotten about the Commodore's courage—fortified now by enormous economic power. The Commodore bought all the shares that were offered, drove up the price, and forced Drew to settle. In 1864, he made William vice-president of the railroad and, in effect, vice-president of all his business activities, and bought him a home on Fifth Avenue. So, at the age of forty-three, his eldest son was finally recognized as heir apparent, though he was not given full executive power until the last eight months of the Commodore's remaining thirteen years, years devoted to a series of railroad take-overs and mergers.

In 1868 Sophia died and the following year, at the age of seventy-five, the Commodore married a Mobile, Alabama, belle with the unlikely name of Frank Armstrong Crawford, a great-granddaughter of Samuel Hand, brother of the Commodore's mother. Soon thereafter he completed the merger of the New York Central and Hudson River railroads, leased the Harlem Railroad to it, and in 1872 increased the capital stock by $42,000,000—stockwatering on a grand scale! Now William urged him to extend their rail system to Chicago. This he did. An empire had been created, so powerful that during the panic of 1873 the Commodore was able to help stabilize the economy by continuing payment of New York Central dividends and by beginning the construction of Grand Central Terminal in New York City—not, however, without getting the city to pay half the cost of viaduct and open-cut approaches to the station. During this period (November 11, 1869) the diarist George Templeton Strong comments on the unveiling at the Hudson River Railroad Depot of Ernest Plassman's "Vanderbilt Bronze" (one hundred and fifty feet long and thirty feet high in which the Commodore stands in a fur-lined overcoat): ". . . he is a millionaire of millionaires. And, therefore, we bow down before him, and worship him, with a hideous group of molten images, with himself for a central figure, at a cost of $800,000. These be thy Gods, O Israel!" (The Commodore now stands alone before Grand Central Station at the top of the Park Avenue ramp.)

When the Commodore died on January 4, 1877, he was surrounded by his family. He calmly bade children and grandchildren good-by, requested that the Grand Central Depot not be draped in mourning, and then listened as his young wife led the group in singing his favorite hymn, "Show Pity, Lord." He left more than $100,000,000, of which about $90,000,000 went to William; $7,500,000 to William's four sons ($5,000,000 to the eldest, Cornelius, the Commodore's favorite); about $500,000 to each of his surviving daughters; $500,000 in cash. 2,000 shares of New York Central stock, and his New York home to his second wife; and $200,000 to Cornelius Jeremiah. Women were, thus, treated only slightly better than charities, to which there were no substantial bequests; indeed during his life the only such gift ($1,000,000) was to Central University in Nashville, Tennessee, renamed Vanderbilt University in 1875 when the two-part gift was completed.* Of the slightly less than nine years left to William Henry Vanderbilt, it took over two to settle the Commodore's estate. Cornelius Jeremiah and two of his sisters contested the will, which, though upheld in court, was settled privately by William, who gave each of his eight sisters another $500,000 and guaranteed Cornelius Jeremiah the income from $1,000,000 (not paid for long, as he committed suicide five years later, the first recorded skeleton in the Vanderbilt family closet).

The great railroad strike of 1877 occurred soon after the Commodore's death. When New York Central employees refused to join the strike William rewarded his trainmen and laborers by distributing $100,000 among them. He was off to a constructive start in management and, like his father, believed in the improvement of working conditions, equipment, and service. Quickly he also began further strengthening the New York Central system by more mergers. In 1879, when the Hepburn Report on

---

* In a public letter to Commodore Vanderbilt (*Packard's Monthly Magazine*, March 1869), Mark Twain wrote: "All I wish to urge you now, is that you crush out your native instincts and do something worthy of praise. . . . Go boldly, proudly, nobly, and give four dollars to some worthy charity."

rate discrimination and other abuses in the management of New York State-chartered railroads was published, he foresaw the coming reform and regulation of too tightly controlled railroads and, through J. P. Morgan, sold 250,000 shares of New York Central stock to European investors in order to broaden its distribution without depressing the American market.

His concern for public image was evident in his second Fifth Avenue home, built soon after his father's death and quickly filled with paintings, sculpture, and objets d'art; in the gilded neo-Byzantine mausoleum, approximately ninety feet square and sixty high, designed by Richard Morris Hunt and situated on a private "plot" of eleven acres adjoining the main Moravian Church cemetery in New Dorp; and in his many philanthropies. Not only did he give generously to Vanderbilt University, St. Bartholomew's Episcopal Church, the Moravian Church at New Dorp, and the College of Physicians and Surgeons, but he made other less institutional, though substantial, gifts such as $103,732 to cover the cost of moving the Thothmes III (misnamed "Cleopatra's Needle") obelisk (224 tons, 69½ feet high) from Egypt to New York City's Central Park, and the forgiveness of a $150,000 debt of Ulysses S. Grant's (secured by Grant's swords, medals, works of art, gifts from foreign governments, etc.). It is ironic, therefore, that W. H. Vanderbilt is today best remembered (in Bartlett, in Mencken, and elsewhere) for having said, "The public be damned"—the way his words were reported in the Chicago *Daily News* following his refusal to grant an interview, though members of his family say he was told, "Mr. Vanderbilt, your public demands an interview," to which he replied, "*My* public be damned."

By 1883, two years before his death, William had doubled the family fortune, to about $200,000,000. (That is, about a billion dollars in current consumer purchasing power; and this figure takes into account neither the even more extreme increase in the cost of pure services, including servants, nor the numerous taxes that have been increased or introduced in the past ninety-five years.) Now, in failing health, William delegated his two eldest sons, Cornelius and William Kissam, both of whom had been active in the business since before the Commodore's death, to take over its leadership. When William Henry died in 1885, he left $10,000,000 to each of his eight children—four sons, Cornelius, William Kissam, Frederick William, and George Washington, and four daughters, Margaret Louisa (Mrs. Elliott F. Shepard), Emily Thorn (Mrs. William D. Sloane), Florence Adele (Mrs. H. McKown Twombly), Lila or Eliza Osgood (Mrs. William Seward Webb)—all family names which will appear frequently in Gertrude's life, as recorded in *My History* and her other journals. To Cornelius he gave an additional $2,000,000 and $1,000,000 in trust for Cornelius' eldest son, William. Substantially more than $1,000,000 was left to the institutions he had given to during his life plus other missions, churches, hospitals, the Y.M.C.A., and the Metropolitan

Museum of Art. To his wife he left his home, the art in it, and an annuity of $200,000. Though he had treated the women in his family far better than his father had, there was still more than $100,000,000 remaining, and this was divided equally between his two eldest sons.

Cornelius, Gertrude's father, was the harder worker of the two and became, until his death, the head of the family. Many mornings he was at his desk at the Grand Central Building before any of his clerks. There he carefully analyzed the reports of the family's various corporations and directed investments. Yet, occupied as he was with business meetings, he spent almost as much time on philanthropic activities. He was a trustee of several hospitals, including the College of Physicians and Surgeons, to which he and his three brothers added the Vanderbilt Clinic and a sister, Mrs. William D. Sloane, gave a maternity wing. He was a trustee of Columbia University, the General Theological Seminary, and the Cathedral of St. John the Divine; a manager of the Domestic and Foreign Missionary Society of the Protestant Episcopal Church; chairman of the executive committee of the Metropolitan Museum of Art, to which his most famous gift was Rosa Bonheur's *The Horse Fair*. He founded and built the clubhouse for the Railroad Branch of the Y.M.C.A. He was a warden of and generous contributor to St. Bartholomew's Church. (It was at a church meeting there that he met his wife.) The list could go on.

William K., like his brother, was born on their father's farm on Staten Island and was given a rather sketchy education until joining the management of the railroad at an early age. He was not as interested in business as his brother and, goaded by his socially ambitious wife, Alva Murray Smith of Mobile, was much more interested in society, including horse breeding, with its emphasis on bloodlines. For example, in 1879, primarily for the Horse Show, he bought the property at 26th Street and Madison Avenue that had been the New York Central's southern terminus before 42nd Street and was, in 1873, replaced by P. T. Barnum's Monster Classical and Geological Hippodrome and then Gilmore's Garden. William K. called it Madison Square Garden, the name which has stuck through three subsequent buildings under different ownership at this location and two others.

However, although his father, too, had made considerable progress in penetrating aloof New York society, the family was still not accepted by the Astors and others of the innermost circle and longest-established wealth until March 26, 1883, when the William K. Vanderbilts gave a costume ball for the opening of their new mansion—"a little Château de Blois," Alva called it—designed by Richard Morris Hunt, at Fifth Avenue and 52nd Street. Miss Caroline Astor, certain she would be invited, planned a quadrille for her friends preceding the ball. When Alva heard of this she told a mutual friend she was sorry she could not invite Miss Astor since her mother had never paid a call. Now, finally, Mrs. Astor called. The ball was reported on the front page of the *Times* and was probably the most extravagant given in New York until that time. Costumes for it cost about $155,000, champagne and other refreshments $65,000, flowers $11,000. Gertrude's father came as Louis XVI in a *habit de cour* with breeches of fawn-colored brocade, trimmed with sterling silver lace; a jabot, similarly trimmed; and a diamond-hilted sword. Her mother, as "Electric Light," was more dazzling still, in white satin trimmed with diamonds and a headdress of feathers and diamonds. In a famous photograph taken at the ball Mrs. Vanderbilt holds an electric torch above her head, possibly parodying the Statue of Liberty, then, though three years from completion, already under construction and well known to New Yorkers. Gertrude and her two older brothers were among the few children who made an appearance—she as a rose, in pink tulle, with a satin overdress of green leaves, a waist of green satin, and a headdress of white satin, fashioned like a bouquet holder; her brothers as Sinbad the Sailor and a young courtier. Thus, two generations after the Commodore had founded their fortune, the Vanderbilts were now social as well as economic news. Four years later, when Mrs. Astor's List was supplanted by the Social Register, the Vanderbilts were in it.

This, then, is the world in which Gertrude grew up. She was only two when her great-grandfather died; three when her father moved from a town house at 72 Park Avenue to the much larger French Renaissance château (later renovated and still further enlarged) on the westerly blockfront between 57th and 58th streets on Fifth Avenue; ten when her grandfather died. The past was almost forgotten. She was the daughter of Cornelius Vanderbilt II, *the* Cornelius Vanderbilt now, philanthropist and chairman of the New York Central; the niece of William K., another philanthropist (most actively involved with the Metropolitan Opera and other "social" activities), a sportsman particularly interested in horse racing and yachting, and number two man at the railroad. These men and their younger brothers and wealthy sisters were the paternal relatives she knew while growing up. Her mother, born Alice Claypoole Gwynne, was the daughter of Abram Gwynne, a prominent Cincinnati lawyer who came from a more modest family, of Welsh descent, which had settled in that city in the early nineteenth century. However, Alice's grandmother was a Claypool (the *e* seems to have been added later), the daughter of Captain Abraham Claypool, a Revolutionary War veteran and an original member of the Society of the Cincinnati, who claimed descent from Oliver Cromwell and, more verifiable, though distant relationship to the American romantic painter Washington Allston. However, it was not toward the Gwynnes or the Claypooles, any more than toward Aunt Alva's Southern Smiths that Gertrude looked for her identity. She knew that men controlled the economic power in her family. Her mother and Aunt Alva might have their social and cultural aspirations, but their husbands paid the bills for their expression. As Gertrude wrote in her *History*, she "longed to be a boy." That little *History*—later so much expanded in her other writings and, still later, in her sculpture—is, indeed, a clue to the inheritance of some of her great-grandfather's energy, from which, through three generations, the self-confidence of the self-made man had to a large extent been filtered out. He, at least, had known that people loved (or hated) him for himself.

Now, after these three generations, the energy which the Commodore had directed into creative productivity was being channeled largely into custodianship. Gertrude's grandfather, William H., and his eldest sons, her father and her uncle, had been neither forced nor willing to take the risks that the Commodore had taken. To their Dutch Protestant tradition of industry and piety there had already been added a sense of Puritan prudence and social service. As to Gertrude herself and her brothers and sisters, energy must have seemed to be hung on walls, placed on pedestals, locked in vaults, closets, chests—and, for her particularly, in albums and diaries. Despite having inherited more of the Commodore's energy than any of her siblings, she too would feel pressured initially into patterns of prudent custodianship and tame social service. And having inherited "success," she would spend much of her life attempting to redefine it *as a woman.*

≈ *Introduction Continued*

Gertrude Vanderbilt's situation is that of a girl who, like Edith Wharton's fictional Gwen Van Osburgh in *The House of Mirth*, "has always been told that there is no one richer than her father." However, Mrs. Wharton's character had "guileless confidence"—Gertrude, as we have seen, does not.

At the age of ten she is writing a *Story and Poetry Book* "by Jane Philipper," a recurrent pseudonym which suggests the taking of a boy's name in its comparative form, "more than Philip." A year or two later Gertrude is Beatrice, the "languorous" invalid daughter of a rich New York banker whose son, her brother, was "stolen" and never recovered. In "A Midnight Ride," written while crossing to London the next year, the fourteen-year-old daughter of a seamstress must ride through a stormy night to fetch the doctor for her little brother. She catches cold and is unconscious for five years: the period of time that separates Gertrude in real life from her own little brother Regi (as well as her eldest brother

William). And the following spring, in Paris, a separation of five years occurs again in the story of two sisters—Dove, seventeen; Bess, twelve—who live separate lives in the same house, as ordered by their father, a coarse and angry widower who visits them only occasionally. Dove petitions him for a reunion with Bess, when their father is with a youth who asks for a kiss. Dove refuses. Her father tells the youth to take as many kisses as he wants. Dove stabs herself with a stiletto hidden in her bosom. . . .

Most of these romantic fantasies are placed within the context of mundane Line-A-Day journals, but Gertrude is no less romantic when she attempts essays. One, written in November 1889, the fall after her story about Dove, is in a separate notebook and entitled "The Only Happiness." She states her theme: "We are put into the world, each one of us, with a heart, a soul and a body, and we are told to make what we can out of them. Sometimes the body has the biggest share, sometimes the heart, and seldom the soul." After seven pages on the rarity of Soul, she moves on to her real theme:

All men are brutes. They love women purely for the pleasure they derive from them. A pleasure of senses or a pleasure of flattery. As soon as they have drunk their fill of these, the woman is cast aside. . . . I once knew a man who was devotedly attached to his wife. Before they were married they loved each other to the verge of distraction, and for a while after the honeymoon the affection lasted. Then the woman, who was amusing and entertaining on a slight acquaintance and rather pretty into the bargain, became dull and lost some of her good looks. It was not that she did not entertain the man, but she failed to amuse him just as she had before. It led to a divorce. And yet it was all so simple and might so easily have been avoided. But for this fatal characteristic of mankind.

Enough for now of fragmented fantasy and abstract soul searching. From the spring of 1890 on, in Gertrude's fifteenth year, the record becomes more specific and complete.

⇜ *1890*

APRIL 28

Something has happened. At least, it has not happened yet, but it is going to happen, and I have been told, although it is still a secret.

I never suspected it, for all along Mama and Papa have said that

we were *not* going to Europe, but now, as you can guess, we are!!!!!!!
And the Saturday after next. That will be the 10th of May. I was so
surprised, I did not know what to do. But find I am perfectly
delighted. I have always longed to go for four or five weeks, and that
is just what we are going to do. I can scarcely believe it! It is too good
to be true! I don't really know just why I am so perfectly delighted, I
can hardly understand myself! I suppose it is because I love the trip
(the ocean) and then Paris! And the idea of a change! Oh! I cannot
possibly express my delight!!!!!!!!!! Enough! Calm yourself! This will
never do! You must, of course, take it as all things come.

This subject occupied all my thought this morning at school, which
did not help my lessons any, you may be sure.

I took a walk with Pauline [Whitney] this afternoon, and she afterwards came to see me a little while here. Of course, I could not tell
her yet, although I felt like it. I have told no one.

The entry—on one of a half dozen loose sheets placed inside the
187-page journal Gertrude keeps this summer—is, like what follows, a mixture of Gertrude's enthusiasm, self-awareness, and discipline in confiding
to a diary rather than to Pauline, her friend who lives just across 57th
Street.

As always, the Vanderbilts travel in style. They have five deck cabins on
the *Umbria*, four of them new and never previously occupied. Mr. and
Mrs. Vanderbilt use two; Gertrude's younger brothers, Alfred and Regi,
share one (her older brothers are not along on this trip); Fräulein and the
baby, four-year-old Gladys, share another; and Gertrude has one to herself
—"the prettiest," she thinks, noting the blue stuff three quarters of the
way up the walls, the narrow strip of white wood, and then pink stuff to
the white ceiling; the sofa, the wardrobe "really very big for the ship," the
bureau, the looking glass, the washstand. Once settled, Gertrude spends
"the morning in trying to get acquainted with the people. I do not mean
to speak to them, for that Mama never lets one do, but just to study them
without being noticed and to name them." Naming people is one of many
similar games she plays throughout her life. She names one Tom the Piper
"because he smokes a pipe! (Ridiculous!)," another Dr. de Tray "because
he is just like a doctor and that name sounds like him," another Mr.
Whitewash "because his shoes look as though they were whitewashed,"
and still another the Colonel "because he is just, or very much, like
O. Payne," the treasurer of Standard Oil, Oliver Hazard Payne, an uncle
of Gertrude's friend Pauline Whitney and a frequent visitor to the
Whitney home across the street.

Just as on previous voyages, each day Gertrude records the weather and
the number of nautical miles the ship has progressed. She plays Old Maid
and other games with her father and brothers, walks the deck with them,
watches the men play cricket on the steerage deck, reads a great deal, par-

ticularly enjoying Rider Haggard's *King Solomon's Mines* and Captain King's *Between the Lines*, lent to her by Alonzo Potter, the son of the Vanderbilts' friends Bishop and Mrs. Henry Codman Potter, who are aboard. Whether the ocean is calm or rough, Gertrude feels fine and sympathizes with Fräulein, who is often seasick.

May 17, a beautiful, extremely calm Saturday, "the last day has come and I cannot say I am really glad. The ship always has a sort of attraction for me (I think I know why, too, but it is a secret)." Based on this journal and others, we can guess that, though carefully supervised aboard ship, she has a greater sense of freedom than at home, a sense of contact with the outside world, strangers, men.

Because the *Umbria* cannot cross the bar twenty miles from Liverpool, a special tug meets the Vanderbilts and the Potters and takes them to the Adelphic Hotel where they have a good dinner ("Everything tastes so nice after the steamer") and then board a private railroad car so they can go right to bed and wake up the next morning in London. There they stay at the Bristol for two days, visit an obscure chapel, Herbert House, Moore & Burgess' minstrel show, do some shopping, and Gertrude goes to Truffet's "to have my head shampooed and it was very well done."

They are ready for Paris, which, as Gertrude says, "greets them with a smile." Now they stay at the elegant, *art nouveau* Hotel Bristol, a sister establishment of the one in London. Gertrude's cousins Adele and Emily Sloane visit her almost immediately upon arrival. "They are just the same. Do not seem to have grown or changed in the least." Gertrude wants to grow. Her parents want her to grow. They arrange for her to take lessons—"only two hours a day, which certainly is not hard compared with what we had in New York. The time passed very quickly. . . ."

The rest of the day is spent in sightseeing of all kinds, mostly with Fräulein and Alfred and Regi. On the second day at the Nouveau Cirque they see the famous dancer Chocolat (remembered now from Toulouse-Lautrec posters) and the trapezist La Belle Geraldine, who does "all sorts of dreadful things. She was really quite pretty and seemed much too nice for the part she took." The next day after lessons she goes shopping with Adele, Emily, and their pretty French governess. Gertrude finds the Paris stores "very attractive, much more so than those in America and even in London." In the afternoon they go for a drive in the Bois.

Saturday she has no lessons. She spends the morning at the Salon, studying paintings and making detailed notes on each. The one she likes best is by Bouguereau, of two beggar girls, one about twelve, the other several years older, Gertrude's own age, with a sad expression in her eyes. Again and again, as Gertrude responds to the paintings in the Salon—a girl in bed reading a book, another reading the newspaper, another flirting with two old men at a café, another abandoned with "a shawl drawn around her shivering form," clasping a mandolin which "seemed her only friend now"—we feel her identification with the subjects, particularly sad young women.

Sunday the family goes to the new American Church on the Avenue de l'Alma. There the minister, Mr. Morgan, "preaches a nice sermon on the personality of The Holy Ghost." Gertrude likes the choir too, "especially one boy who sang alone and has a sweet, touching voice." In short, she likes Paris.

Days and weeks of lessons, walks, rides, shopping, sightseeing, entertainments, and writing daily journal entries go by quickly. The family takes little Gladys to the Hippodrome circus and the zoo and the Punch and Judy show in the Tuileries. Gertrude, to her surprise, likes the Louvre as well as the Salon. She is charmed by the "beautiful, sweet, serious face" of the Venus de Milo. "But nicer than this was the picture of *La Cruche Cassée* by Greuze. It is of the girl with the broken pot on her arm. The expression of her little mouth and sad eyes is too sweet, and can never be copied by half. The picture of *Mme. Vigée-LeBrun* and her little girl, painted by herself, is also lovely. The faces are both so sweet. There were other pictures I liked too, but none so well as those two."

Gertrude may not be ready to appreciate greater, less anecdotal art in the Louvre, but in her many visits to churches her taste is surer. She singles out La Sainte Chapelle as "really, without exaggeration, perfect; and considering it was built in the 14th century, it seems more than perfect, for if they did such things then, what is to be done now?"

She takes photographs in Fontainebleau, Versailles, wherever she goes. On the Eiffel Tower, completed for the Paris Fair of 1889, she and Alfred are shocked to have their film confiscated, so that, like other tourists, they must buy picture postcards. Though a typical tourist purchase, there can be little doubt that the colossal tower, like the Statue of Liberty (for which Eiffel designed the inside structure)—both monuments such perfect expressions of late nineteenth-century optimism, materialism, and pomposity—makes a lasting impression on Gertrude, influencing her later desire to make monuments of her own. Another revealing, though less typical, purchase, "added to [her] things to think about, and to travel with," are "two sweet little birds," which will accompany her during this trip, as the fictional "Dove" has in her imagination, and as other real birds will during most of her life.

On June 8, Pauline Whitney arrives in Paris after a week in London. Since Fräulein is just leaving for a visit to her family in Berlin, Gertrude has dinner alone with Pauline and her governess.

> I enjoyed it very much, that is, the whole evening. I am afraid I will not see P. for a good while as she expects to stay abroad with her governess alone for two years. . . . We talked about the fine pictures and other articles which belonged to Grandpa and now to Grandma.

I had no idea [Grandpa] had such fine things. I knew of course they were very expensive etc., but I hardly thought them such as she said.

The next day the Vanderbilts leave Paris for London. Gertrude is "Sad, yes I did feel as badly as though it was my native city. . . . Jack and Jill (my birds) were very good travelers but naturally rather frightened at the cars and boat. I feel dreadfully that they should have to live in the little bit of a cage I bought them in, and now that I am in London I intend to buy a large cage. . . ." This she does and is "delighted to have the pleasure of taking them out of the little cage. . . ."

In London, morning tutoring is resumed, and shopping, and sightseeing. Gertrude enjoys the zoo, Madame Tussaud's, the panorama of the Battle of Waterloo ("If [Napoleon*] had been tall, he would have been outwardly *perfect*"), but mostly St. Paul's. It, like Sainte Chapelle, is "truly beautiful."

They start the trip home June 21 and soon Gertrude is again naming passengers, reading (the *Pickwick Papers* now), and recording the day's run. The steerage passengers dance for money, and when they finish "give three cheers for the cabin passengers and then for Mr. Vanderbilt. It was very amusing." So the trip goes until finally the family is met in New York Harbor by a private tug which takes them to 42nd Street where carriages are waiting to take them to a sleeping car at Grand Central Station, but "at Newport instead of seeing our carriages waiting for us there were but a few cabs . . . the telegrams which papa sent the evening before did not arrive. . . . Everything was quiet, showing that we were not expected." Gertrude finds her brother Cornelius, who had arrived the previous night, and has "the pleasure, if so it might be called," of announcing their arrival. She is more excited to see that her dog Sancho recognizes her and wags his tail without stopping and, at the stable, that her favorite horses Virginia and Kitty are looking splendid. Though the family's trunks will not arrive until the next day, her father insists that she accompany him to church. There she greets the Blights, the Shermans, and Edith Cushing and in the afternoon takes a walk with Alice and Edith Blight and Sybil Sherman. Europe seems already far behind.

Once in Newport (112 pages after the start of this journal), she is so busily settled in her "ordinary life" that she no longer finds "it necessary to write every day," but Sundays she has plenty of time. From July 6 through September 14 she reviews each week. She plays tennis with Sybil, visits with the Blights, drives Kitty, rides Virginia. "It is so nice now I can

* This is the first of many worshipful references to Napoleon by Gertrude and her friends. In *The Hero in America*, Dixon Wecter observes: "Napoleon figures as the hero *par excellence* in a great deal of [the Gilded Age] success literature; his care for detail, brilliant audacity, and mastery over men are held up as the perfect go-getting ideal."

drive and ride both the same day." On July 4 there are fireworks and the next day a drive with the entire family to their farm outside Newport for strawberries and ice cream. Another day she and fifteen girls, chaperoned by the Winthrops and the Kernochans, go on an outing to Gooseberry Island and after lunch climb the rocks there. And sometimes she walks with a friend along the cliffs in front of The Breakers† and the other great homes along Ocean Drive. But almost every day she drives and rides and frequently plays tennis and goes swimming at Bailey's Beach, the most "social" beach in the East. Harry Whitney, Pauline's attractive older brother and a neighbor here as in New York, visits her brother Bill several times but she has "only seen him to bow to." "J." Burden, another attractive young man, she meets twice riding—"he bows beautifully." She takes painting lessons with Sybil on Thursdays and sewing lessons at the cottage on Saturdays and, as always, on Sunday there's church. Sybil "is almost the only girl Mama likes me to go with, and certainly the only one I care to, as I cannot go with the older girls." Thus the weeks fly by, but not without time for romantic fantasies, which the budding young lady confides to her journal in French. For example, there's "*Songe d'une Nuit d'Été*" or "A Dream of a Summer Night":

> I was alone one summer night, curled in a hammock suspended between two trees. My memory took flight far into the past, and I dreamed of those I had loved and those I loved still.
>
> I saw the past as in a mirage and in it this girl who I could distinguish but not recognize as myself. I saw loved ones come as if to touch me, I held their hands, seized them in order never to let them leave me; but alas! The shapes that seemed so real were only elusive memories which flew, sad and fearful, at the light touch of reality. They disappeared, leaving me alone, alone in the world! Can one live without those one loves?

She might have asked, too, if one can live *with* those one loves. A week later this question is asked implicitly, if abortively: ". . . no matter how nice a time I have had something happens that spoils it all. I have tried to hide it a little but could not, it seems, for Mama told me I was sulky, etc., etc. I cannot repeat all the things even to you, dear old book whom nobody reads. It is enough to say I am unhappy. I will not talk any more about it, but—well, nothing." She returns to riding and bathing. She watches a hunt and a polo match. She insists she "ought to be happy."

In mid-August her parents give a garden party. From the piazza of the main house, a rug flanked by an arbor of potted palms extends to a large turkey-red tent "shedding a reddish tinge on the ground." In this tent there is a buffet of ices, cakes, sandwiches; in two smaller tents, tables and

† Cornelius Vanderbilt's first home in Newport, not to be confused with the later, more elaborate house built in 1892, on the same 12½-acre Ochre Point site.

chairs. The surrounding trees are decked with hollyhocks. Mrs. Vanderbilt stands next to a bench beneath the palms receiving her guests. Near her there is a group of mandolin players and farther off, behind the large tent, a full orchestra. From the piazza Gertrude observes: "The music carried by the breeze was enchanting, and as the ladies in their pretty light costumes walked on the lawn it almost seemed like fairyland. The gentlemen were less romantic, but could not possibly be done without, at least, so I daresay, the young ladies thought." She goes on to describe "all the beauties of the [social] season." However, she "did not go much among the people, but still some people who came on the piazza where I was I was forced to talk to." The only conversation which she records is one with a Mr. Phiney who had been aboard ship with her the previous year. He says, "You have grown, yes, a good deal." In her journal she comments, "I hate to be told that."

So much for a typical garden party. Less than a week later there is a dance. August 18, the Newport *Morning Journal* runs the following item which Gertrude carefully pastes into her journal:

> All society is agog with open-mouthed wonderment as to the outcome of the ball to be given at The Breakers tomorrow night by Mrs. Cornelius Vanderbilt. A special electric plant has been erected to illuminate the dancing hall and reception rooms, and the use of gorgeously-colored globes will make a charming effect.
>
> The east balcony has been extended fifty-four feet, making a grand promenade twenty-four by fifty-four feet broad. This will be enclosed in turkey-red canvas. Costly rugs will decorate the floor and the roof will be of specially prepared costly teak wood.
>
> Landers, the expert decorator, has carte blanche as to expenditure and is spreading himself for the grandest affair he has ever had in hand.
>
> The south piazza will be transformed into an oriental vision of beauty by the aid of plants, gayly-colored lanterns and tropical plants. The water's edge and borders of all flower-beds will also be visions of beauty and radiance.
>
> As regards the favors direct from Paris not a soul knows their nature except the fair hostess, who unpacked them herself in privacy. It is to be the grandest affair ever given this side of the Atlantic, and a royal scene is safely predicted.

The *Morning Journal*'s expectations, expressed in repeated superlatives, are justified by long accounts of the party in the same paper the next day and in Gertrude's weekly journal entry—sixteen pages, including another French composition. In it she imagines a young man and his dancing partner drifting off all alone to a little sofa under a great palm where they can express "*l'amour pur, innocent et immortel.*" She adds in English, "A heart that feels [love] is not a child's but has grown with the love into a woman's." Though she is, of course, speaking of her own heart, the heart of a woman, she is still treated like a child, like all the children of high society who have not yet "come out," moved up chronologically to the age of eighteen or nineteen.

At five o'clock she watches white and blue hydrangeas and geraniums being put up around the hall and the favors from Paris being placed on racks—tambourines and mandolins tied with ribbons, gold epaulettes, tortoise back-hair combs trimmed with silver, dungeon keys colored to look like iron and each containing a souvenir ring, simulated Eastern daggers, little dolls to be pinned on, hand-painted fans. . . . Almost immediately after an early supper the children go to their rooms to rest—Gertrude to Alfred's, as hers is to be used as a cloakroom for the ladies.

After a two-hour nap she awakens and dresses hurriedly. "I could hear the music quite distinctly and it made me long to see people dance as long as I could not do so myself." At eleven, sitting with Fräulein and Elsa, the nurse of the younger children: "The hall was rather full yet not crowded, a few couples were waltzing almost gliding around the room, the ladies' soft, light dresses swinging slightly, and their pretty faces all smiles and happiness. The men, some good dancers, others bad, led their graceful partners around and listened, some gravely, others smilingly, to the cheerful, nonsensical talk of the vain creatures at their sides.

"Those who were not dancing were standing about the room talking. Some ladies had managed to keep two men, while others were unfortunate enough to have none. Some flirted dreadfully, others were reserved and pleasant, but all seemed entirely at ease. Some men who did not dance, and who considered themselves woman haters, stood in one corner with not courage enough to address one of the other sex. But still they gazed and followed some particular *one* with their eyes, if in no other way. . . . I knew almost all the people, that is the principal ones. . . . I loved to watch who the men talked most to, and whether the girls liked some better than others, and if they showed it. All this was most interesting to me . . . for I wondered how I should do when I went out."

Gertrude does not say who "the principal ones" are. Their identity is as much taken for granted by now as that of her own family, but the *Morning Journal* selects a few from among those seated at three large tables and twenty-seven small ones; "a full list would require at least a column." At the head of its list are "Ward and Mrs. McAllister," (Samuel) Ward McAllister being the great social arbiter of the period, author of the concept that there are "only about four hundred people in New York Society," and, like Mrs. Astor, a member of the innermost circle which accepted the Vanderbilts just seven years ago. The McAllisters are followed by Mr. and Mrs. William C. Whitney, Mr. and Mrs. Frederick William Vanderbilt, Mrs. W. Astor, Mrs. Paran Stevens, Mr. and Mrs. William

Waldorf Astor, Mr. R. K. Wilson, Julian Potter, Prince Galitizin, Mr. T. N. Howard, J. J. Van Alen, Hollis Hunnewell, Grafton Cushing, John Jacob Astor, Charles Havemeyer, Mrs. Townsend Burden, Miss Charlotte Winthrop, Miss Knowlton, Miss Hargous—names, like most in Newport society, that need not be individually identified; collectively they represent one thing: established wealth.

Supper is served at twelve-thirty. "People do not as a rule eat very much at such an hour, so [it] did not last very long." Mrs. Blight, the mother of Gertrude's friends, talks with her for a short time, as do Emma and Elsa, two sisters, and then Hollis Hunnewell looking for Elsa. Gertrude knows who he is but as she has not been presented to him she "did not of course look around. . . . I heard him say very low: 'Won't you introduce me to Miss Vanderbilt?' "

Elsa performs the introduction. Gertrude turns, bows, smiles slightly. He says, "It's very nice up here."

"Yes," Gertrude replies, "but I suppose it is still nicer downstairs."

Gertrude looks at him a moment. He looks at her and "gives a little laugh as much as to say 'you know more than I thought.' He is not handsome but has something decidedly nice in his face."

That is all—but, for Gertrude, seemingly the high point of the party and worth three pages of her journal. The dancing continues. "At 3:45 almost everyone had gone, so I went up and danced around the hall by myself until the music stopped, the hum of conversation died away, and the hall and the whole house was deserted."

Sometimes, as even on the day of the dance, Gertrude takes a walk with her beautiful cousin Consuelo Vanderbilt, two years younger and the daughter of Aunt Alva and Uncle William. Aunt Alva is very strict with Consuelo. She must wear tightly laced corsets and skirts that almost touch the ground. Her dresses have high whalebone collars. Even going to Bailey's Beach, Consuelo wears gloves and carries a parasol. She is tutored for more hours per day than Gertrude and while doing her lessons has to wear a metal brace to improve her posture. By comparison, as the summer ends with more of the activities that have preceded the dance, Gertrude's life sounds almost informal. One Sunday she and the entire family drive to the church near the farm outside Newport, picnic there and gather wild blackberries. On other days they ride to the hunt, watch polo matches, or go to tennis at the Casino in Newport, that wonderful shingled and latticed McKim, Mead & White structure founded ten years before by James Gordon Bennett, the colorful owner of the New York *Herald*. As Gertrude sits there one morning with two girl friends, one of the senior Astors tells her that he saw her in the gallery the night of the dance.

"You will be out soon, I suppose," he says.

"Yes, quite soon."

"About four years?"

"Yes, three or four years."
"Doesn't the time seem very long?"
"No, time passes so quickly, it will soon be here."

⇐

The time does pass quickly, even in the quiet of Newport after the social season has passed. The riding continues, and excursions to the farm,
and now, in mid-September, a more distant but brief excursion to Bar
Harbor, Maine, with her parents. There they visit Grandma, William H.
Vanderbilt's widow, now almost seventy, staying with her youngest son,
Gertrude's uncle George, who, though almost twenty-eight, still lives with
her most of the year in New York. During the first stage of the journey, as
far as Boston, "There was no drawing room car on the train, but it is
almost more fun in the others as there are people of different kinds to
watch. But no one of special interest was there, so I buried myself in
[Wilkie Collins' mystery novel] *The Woman in White,* which is certainly
not hard."

As they drive through the Boston streets Gertrude is struck by the
crowds of men, "each occupied with some thought of his own, unmindful
of the others. I wondered what sort of a home they were all hurrying to."
She imagines some where "cruel, unloving wives . . . wait . . . to demand
money" and others where "loving wives . . . wait . . . with impatience,
and run to meet [their husbands] with a smile and a kiss, and sit down
with them to a simple but dainty meal." Gertrude is reminded of Bryant's
poem "The Crowded Street":

> How fast the flitting figures come!
> The mild, the fierce, the stony face;
> Some bright with thoughtless smiles, and some
> Where secret tears have left their trace.

At the station—crowded, like the streets, but with women as well as
men—Mr. and Mrs. Vanderbilt are met by Fred Jones, a tall, attractive
friend who "does not seem married" until Gertrude hears "Mama say
something about Mrs. Jones." Jones amuses them through dinner, after
which Gertrude retires to her berth in "Papa's car . . . the last on the
train." From there, as they leave the city, she can see "the dark outlines of
the trees against the sky" and "once in a while a lonely light." The crowds
in Boston have depressed her and now the bleak landscape does too. She
tries to think of other things but can think only of the contrast between
all this and the last wonderful voyage to Europe.

The approach to Bar Harbor itself is also a disappointment for Gertrude. There's fog over Frenchman's Bay, scattered with the Porcupine Islands, "which seem to be completely made of rocks . . . thousands of pine
trees growing right down to the very edge." At Bar Harbor it is raining so

28

that the rubber sides of Uncle George's buckboard must be fastened down. Gertrude can see only mud and pines. The rain continues. Gertrude reads, plays cards, is taught billiards by a house guest of Uncle George's. It is still raining the next morning but they decide to do some sightseeing all the same. Finally the rain stops, the fog lifts and, with it, Gertrude's spirits. She responds to the mountains and islands she can now really see and to the fresh loveliness of the woods after the rain and, perhaps most of all, to the waves breaking on the rocks.

The next day, their last in Bar Harbor, is beautiful. The sun shines brightly on the water, reminding Gertrude of Newport. Not only she but "Uncle George was in a state of excitement. . . . He showed it by almost squashing Grandma when he kissed her good morning, jumping around like a child, and pulling my hair. He informed us we were to go out on his boat." Aboard the 69-foot steam launch, they have a perfect day which ends when they return to their private car on the train back to Boston. Stimulated by contact with nature, how different Gertrude's mood is. The sky, seen from her berth, is now filled with moonlight, the Milky Way, and bright stars. She feels she "had been away from Newport for years."

Yet, though we know she has visited another landscape and responded to it, there has been hardly a word in response to her notoriously pious grandmother or, except for his enthusiasm about the boat ride, to Uncle George. The reader of Gertrude's journals would never guess that George Washington Vanderbilt was by far the most individualistic and best educated of her uncles and aunts, a man who spoke eight languages and read several others and who had studied architecture, forestry, and landscape gardening. Just the year before Gertrude's visit—it must have come up in conversation—he had begun to buy the 130,000 acres of Appalachian property south and southwest of Asheville, North Carolina, where he would pioneer in agriculture, forestry, and ecology and work with the architect Richard Morris Hunt and the landscapist Frederick Law Olmsted to build Biltmore, considered by some the finest country house in America and by most the one conceived with the greatest sense of social responsibility. But to Gertrude he is only her father's youngest brother, unassociated with the management of the New York Central, a bit childish; his adventurous sort of custodianship is as yet lost on her.

≈

In postseason Newport Gertrude remains quietly occupied with her close-knit group of friends and cousins. Sybil Sherman and she plan an evening of tableaux at the Burdens', but Gertrude's mother won't let her participate because of her age. Her "first real friend" Alice Blight, whose mother is more permissive, is the greatest success of the evening, "very nearly perfect [as Night], all dressed in black with a diamond in her hair." After ice cream and cake, the girls dance and play games and have what one of them describes as "a regular girls' romp." Another afternoon Gertrude, Sybil Sherman, Evelyn Burden, Marie Winthrop, and Edith Blight play Truth. After "the usual questions about 'your best boy' and love letters . . . Sybil asked who was the prettiest girl of our age in Newport. Most of us thought Alice Blight the prettiest, but Sybil insisted Edith Blight and I were. . . . Naturally, this is not so. Then we asked Sybil whom she considered the handsomest and, after a good deal of persuasion, she said, 'Evelyn Burden and you, Gertrude.' . . . I fear I am getting vain, but Sybil says I am not stupid enough to care. I hope it is true."

By October, Gertrude and Sybil are receiving regular tutorial instruction from a Mr. Langley, nine to eleven weekday mornings, and painting lessons several afternoons a week. These studies and her compositions and journals as well as sports, games, and occasional hikes keep Gertrude busy. Her contact with boys is limited. On one outing with her younger brothers Alfred and Regi and some friends she "was to kiss the boy I liked best in the carriage. This I naturally refused, and Willie W. came to my rescue saying I was to kiss Alfred and that was enough." The children return home late. Papa is waiting in the hall. "Why are you so late?" he asks. Mama, upstairs, hears him, asks the same question, forbids them to go to the farm again. "Mama was angry and Papa sorry." At supper Gertrude asks her brothers, "Why don't they wait until the next day so as not to spoil all the pleasure?" Within a few days Gertrude is in more trouble with Mama. Having caught a slight cold, she has been told to do no more riding until the cold is gone. When she thinks it is gone she goes out riding with Alfred.

"What, you rode!" Mama says. "When I told you not to, you naughty, naughty child."

Gertrude feels "just like laughing."

"You did it because you thought I would not know," Mama continues.

"Why I just told you I had ridden. I am sure I did not have to."

". . . for a punishment, you shall not ride for a week."

But Mama is not through. The next day, while talking to Regi about the Bible, she says, "and do you know what God hates most in any person? . . . A lie, and I am very glad to say that none of you—*boys* have ever told one."

Gertrude is "struck" by "the full force of what [her mother] had said." She remembers an earlier incident, "an old, old story," of falling out of a hayloft and breaking her arm. Her mother has told her many times that she had forbidden Gertrude to go up into the loft. Gertrude insists that she had not been forbidden, had not deliberately disobeyed her mother, and now her mother still thinks she's a liar. Gertrude leaves the room "utterly bewildered." She cries herself to sleep, stifling her sobs to prevent anyone from hearing them. "And so Mama thinks a lie is hanging over me more than a year, and I am too proud to confess it. Oh! Thank God I am not so proud as that. He knows all, and someday all will be made clear."

Gertrude does not consciously deceive others, but often she deceives herself. Through the autumn she develops more and more of a crush on her tutor, Mr. Langley. One mid-October evening he schedules a lecture on astronomy. Gertrude listens with "Baby," four-year-old Gladys, sitting "with her head on my shoulder, her little hands in mine, and my arms around her." Mr. Langley is "lovely . . . a little more serious than usual, and would look down, then up, directly at you, with *his* eyes. . . . After the lecture . . . when I told Fräulein I thought him so nice, she laughed. I said it was far too serious a matter to laugh about. Then she said I must stop it. This, I knew, was beyond my power. Ha! Ha! That sounds as though I was in love, and I don't want this old book to be deceived. Mr. Langley is married! So when I wish to fall in love, I will choose someone more adapted to the purpose."

A few weeks later, during an English lesson, Sybil and Gertrude bicker, Sybil calls Gertrude "a donkey, a stupid animal."

LANGLEY: "Now a donkey is not such a bad beast."

GERTRUDE: "No, not by any means. They are very useful, and you might be perfectly contented if you were anywhere near so useful."

SYBIL: "Oh, Gertrude."

Langley laughs. They get on the subject of flirtation.

GERTRUDE: "Oh, that's all right."

SYBIL: "You seem to know a lot about it."

GERTRUDE: "Certainly."

LANGLEY: "Now I don't think Miss Vanderbilt is so bad, you might take her for something better."

GERTRUDE: "Why, I don't think it is so bad."

SYBIL: "Oh, Gertrude."

"Then followed a story about how dreadful it was to play with love. Now, this I believe as much as anyone else, if not more, and agreed. But I could not keep from saying to Mr. Langley directly, looking him right in the face, 'Now, do you think there is any harm in just a very little flirtation?' He had a smile on his face and a strange look in his eyes I had never seen before. I could almost have flirted with him."

Gertrude adds: "In the conversation above [immediately preceding the last paragraph], where Sybil and I apparently quarreled, we were only playing."

In November there are many adieux. First Sybil, to whom Gertrude says, "*Fare thee well for I must leave thee, do not let this parting grieve thee, but remember that the best of friends must part.*" "The other girls

31

laughed, but Sybil looked pleased. Then we stood and watched the *Eolus* get farther and farther away, and a sad, almost lonely feeling crept into my heart. Sybil had gone!" Another friend, Daisy Post, leaves next, and then the Blights. Gertrude goes to say good-by. "I stayed a little while and then Alice walked home with me. Edith was tired so we were alone. We spoke of ordinary things, of Sybil and how, before she really knew me, she had asked Alice if I was so awfully nice."

ALICE: "I told her she would find it out for herself, just wait and see. And she found it out."

"When we got to the front door I asked (Alice) to come in, but she said it was getting too late. Then we kissed, only once, but when Alice looked at me there were tears in her eyes and she would not look at me again although I tried to make her. I called something out as she was leaving the house, but her only answer was 'yes,' not a glance, she was walking with her head down. Oh Alice! You may think I don't like you any more, but you are mistaken, yes very much so."

During her last two weeks in Newport, with her closest friends gone and William and Cornelius away at school, Gertrude spends most of her time riding with her younger brothers and once, on a weekend, with Papa. One evening the children entertain their parents with a German play they have been studying with Fräulein, Alfred taking the part of an eighteen-year-old girl, Gertrude and Regi playing old lady friends. But mostly now Gertrude spends her time anticipating New York. "I feel sadder and sadder. It is such a different life . . . always on the go." Finally it is time to say her last good-by—to Mr. Langley. "We shook hands and he kept mine in his quite a while. He said he had enjoyed the lessons very much and he hoped to see me again next year. Of course I said I hoped so."

The *Eolus* is almost empty. Mr. Vanderbilt and the children and Fräulein go directly from it to Mr. Vanderbilt's private car on the train. Gertrude reads and writes. She is at Grand Central Depot before she knows it. The rest of the weekend, except for a "splendid" sermon by Dr. Greer on Sunday morning and a walk that afternoon, is spent unpacking.

Monday morning, November 24, she starts her second year of formal, as opposed to tutorial, education, having missed two full months of school. She leaves home earlier than necessary to get to "The Brearley" by eight-thirty, walking quickly with Fräulein down Fifth Avenue to 44th Street and then a few doors west to No. 17. "I met no one I knew, much to my disappointment. Jenny Howard was the only girl I knew already there, and I talked with her until Sybil came. The moment I saw her I rushed up and gave her a kiss. Ethel Davies was close by and I shook hands heartily with her. The other girls all arrived one by one and they all (for politeness, of course) said they were very glad to see me back."

The daily schedule of prayers, English, history, French, mathematics, and science begins. Gertrude does very well in recitations, particularly in

English and French, less well in written examinations. But school has hardly begun for her before the Thanksgiving holiday. That Thursday she and her parents go to church and in the afternoon she, Mama, and Baby ride in their open carriage in Central Park. Baby steals the show: "a perfect beauty" in an enormous greenish-gray plush hat and coat, both trimmed with feathers and lined with pink silk. As always, Gladys brings out Gertrude's most maternal feelings. "That child is the sunshine of the house. She is like the queen rose in a garden." Gertrude expands on these sentiments in a poem to "Queen Rose Bud" beginning "Thou bringest sun and merry laugh with thy smile and kiss."

The rest of the day she and her mother spend decorating the dining room for a post-football game dinner to which her eldest brother Bill has invited some twenty friends from Yale. Gertrude cuts and fringes blue ribbon while her mother, using white ink, writes the menu and guests' names on the pieces of ribbon. They place a small blue tablecloth at the center of the table over a white one extending to the outside and arrange a centerpiece and sideboard decorations of violets and other blue flowers and ferns. The candles are blue. A small flag with a Y on it is hung from the mantelpiece in the dining room and a large one over the mantel in the hall and still another over the outside door. Everything is ready.

At about six Gertrude hears the clatter of horses' hoofs, looks out, and sees a large coach stop at the Whitneys' across the street. There are cheers and hurrahs, with the voice of Pauline Whitney's older brother Harry, another Yale man, sounding above all the voices. Gertrude knows that Yale has won. Ten minutes later Bill's coach arrives. He and his friends cheer at the Yale flag over the door. Gertrude watches them enter the dining room, hears them sing songs during dinner, watches them and the Whitney party leave for theater.

"What fun boys do have, when I think of it. They can do just about what they like, and girls, especially myself, cannot do one thing. Not go out alone, or have a jolly time at college." Gertrude's complaint is by now familiar and, indeed, justified. However, now only a little over a month from her sixteenth birthday, she concludes differently from before: "Still, with all this, I had rather be a girl. Strange."

Friday: Macy's to buy Christmas presents for poor children in Newport. Saturday afternoon: the opera, "a new one [*Tannhäuser*] . . . rather sacrilegious." Sunday: Dr. Greer's "very interesting sermon on evolution." Monday: the return to school; a pen-and-ink drawing lesson in the afternoon. Tuesday: the resumption of dancing class. . . . On some days Gertrude misses school because of a cold, on others because of the weather. There is more shopping at Macy's; a Saturday morning at F.A.O. Schwarz where she buys toys for Alfred, Regi, and Baby; another opera—*The Huguenots*—to which she goes with her friend Esther Hunt. . . . "I really have so much to do, with school, and studying, and music, and drawing,

and walking, and Christmas things, and dancing, and writing, and thinking, that I feel as though I had no time to spare and if for a minute I find
myself idle I feel it is a waste of very precious time. I have not been able
to read one book since I have been here and do not intend to till the
Christmas holidays, then I can feast on them."

⇐ *1891*

We do not know how much reading Gertrude does now. Either a volume of her journal has been lost or she is too busy to write during the holidays and the next three months—probably the former, since she keeps
compulsively at her journal during other periods of extreme activity. In either case, she begins a new volume dated Monday, March 30, 1891, during
the Easter recess from school. That morning she takes an enjoyable drive
with Papa, visits Sybil, and takes a walk in the afternoon along "streets
still full of gay Easter people." In the evening, while she writes, Bill is having another of his dinner parties, this one for "young girls and fellows."
Tuesday, as usual, she has dancing school. She wears her white dress and
some lilies of the valley. The flowers are pressed between the pages of the
journal. Nothing has changed in three months.

Bill returns to Yale, Cornelius must remain home to study, and the rest
of the family leaves on Wednesday for Lakewood, New Jersey. The pattern
is familiar: a ferry, Mr. Vanderbilt's private car on the train, being met
with an omnibus by the manager of the new hotel, "an enormous red
brick building, holding about 600 people. But there are only about 325
now, so that we have very nice rooms and are extremely comfortably settled."

Lakewood is not Europe. Except for "pines, pines, pines," it is not even
Bar Harbor. After a week Gertrude returns eagerly to school. There her favorite teacher, Miss Winsor, tells her how impressed she has been by Gertrude's composition on Bulwer-Lyttons' "A Strange Story." "She said it
was very good indeed, better than anything I had ever written and it had
some excellent qualities. Of course, I was very glad and looked so." For
Gertrude, much in need of appreciation and encouragement, this is perhaps the high point in the few weeks of school remaining before the family goes off to Europe.

Once again there is concentrated touring, but this year London is followed by Brussels. There at the Wiertz Museum—dedicated entirely to the historical, mythological, and allegorical works of this popular nineteenth-century Belgian painter—Gertrude is particularly moved by *Napoleon in Hell*. "Awful! I turned away in disgust. They are offering him human raw flesh to eat, and he stands, his beautiful brow drawn together in a frown, his arms crossed over his chest, in disdain." When she and her family visit the Waterloo battlefield, Gertrude identifies even more strongly with her childhood hero Napoleon. She imagines him "seated on his beautiful (black) charger, looking at each move, considering each step before acting. And then the end, oh how had he taken it, how could such a proud man stand such a defeat. I could see the struggling soldiers, the streams of blood; hear the roar of the guns, and the shouts of the men, each wild with the excitement of war. The mound ['226 steps to go up,' she notes earlier] was built by the women who carried the earth from the fields to build something in memory of those who died so nobly for their country."

In Brussels, in Cologne (where the family goes next), and then in Leipzig, in Dresden, everywhere, Gertrude is impressed by monuments of all kinds—to saints as well as soldiers. Not only does she believe that lives must be commemorated and monumentalized in stone, in bronze, in oil portraits but that she must remonumentalize them by daily recording and cataloguing in her journal. Yet, if life itself is not enough, neither is monumentality in itself: the monument must be beautiful. In Dresden, she says outright what had been only suggested two weeks before while looking at a Sargent in London: "Most of Rubens is to me too clumsy, his style is not ideal enough." And of work by Rubens' pupils and imitators she observes that some is "so exaggerated as to be positively disgusting (sometimes worse). But I must say that when I went away I did not have a very clear idea of what I had seen." More graspable are the porcelain figures she sees a few days later at a factory in Meissen. There she is fascinated by the way the clay is shaped, baked, glazed, painted, and polished. "So much is done by hand that, as you see the men and women working over it, you do not think it expensive any more."

As has happened sometimes in New York, Gertrude is in school for just a few days (her last three in Dresden). There her most exotic classmate is Flora Rosenthal, "an American Jew . . . who is quite nice," but Gertrude never gets to know her. The family moves too soon to Switzerland and then Vienna where she has some contact with another Jew, the family's *valet de place* or guide, "a curiosity . . . fat and not tall, with trousers that are twice too wide for him—his walk—imagine a large frog dressed in a light suit with a white waistcoat walking with his back to you, look at this creature and you will find very little difference. He is a Jew—with a Jew's nose, a Jew's hair, etc." As the family tours Vienna, " 'The Frog' walked on ahead, waving his hat in his hand and wobbling from foot to foot, making the most ludicrous picture you can imagine." The prejudice expressed in these quotations is not surprising, considering Gertrude's background, sheltered from all but the "right" rich families and their Gentile servants. It will take about sixteen years and a good deal of suffering and real "coming out" before she is able, partially at least, to abandon anti-Semitism and other aspects of social, economic, ethnic, and religious bigotry. And if, even then, she continues to feel more comfortable and secure with her "own sort" than with outsiders, she will still have gone a long way in accepting the precedence of talent over social rank.

Though most of Gertrude's aesthetic responses are to art and architecture, when the family leaves Vienna for the mountain spa in Bad Ischl, near Salzburg, she is very excited by the scenery and remembers a "dream of the first evening we had thought of coming abroad. . . . I saw in Ischl the place of my dream and my imagination. These mountains, I could almost identify them, the evening quiet—everything, in fact, from the song of the birds to the occupations which we would daily perform." These occupations are swimming (during hours when men are not in "the tank"), driving, and mostly walking. After a week or so the family splits up, leaving Baby and a nurse at Bad Ischl while the rest go to Venice from which Papa and the boys will go on to Turkey and Greece and then reunite with the women in Vienna.

In Venice, too, Gertrude responds to the beauty of the scenery—natural as well as man-made. As always the guidebook sights—building by building, statue by statue, painting by painting—are ticked off, but more important to her are the magic of canals and gondolas, the look of old stone, the light reflected in the water, feeding the doves at the Piazza San Marco, the music everywhere, day and night. Even when "the music itself was not so good . . . it was everything together!"

For "good music," Gertrude will have to wait until the family returns to Germany during the last weeks of vacation. After a brief tour of Nuremberg (the Iron Maiden and other instruments of torture in the Old Castle, Dürer's house), they proceed to Bayreuth and, almost immediately upon arrival, go to *Tannhäuser*. Though her older brother Cornelius tires during the opera and returns to the hotel, Gertrude lasts through the final act and its song to the evening star which she used to play on the piano. "I did not lose much time in getting to bed." The next morning the family visits the palace just outside the city and Wagner's house and grave in its garden. Then Gertrude rests for *Parsifal*—so much longer and more challenging, especially for a sixteen-year-old. It is not surprising that she finds parts of the opera "very slow" and that the outline of its libretto in her journal is joyless. As Nietzsche had written (*The Gay Science*, 1882), "My objections to the music of Wagner are physiological objections: why should I try to dress them up in aesthetic formulas?" Though Gertrude will be a patroness of the opera and spend many nights of her life there, Wagner will never be one of her favorite composers. She prefers work that is shorter and more romantic (with a small *r*).

⇐ *1892*

Again there is a gap in Gertrude's record, this time one of over a year and four months. Among her papers there are fragmented clues concerning her activity—retrospective compositions on the previous summer's travels; essays on European history and brief sketches of important historical figures; a generalized description of the ocean and another of a specific day at sea; a similarly generalized description of a summer's day in Newport and another of a specific day in mid-September when everybody leaves except for her family and a few others; bits of fiction, including a story about Violet, a young lady who lives in the country with her father and his maiden sister, and who goes to sit for her portrait by a dashing, broad-shouldered artist. Finally, there is Gertrude's 1891–92 report book from Brearley:

OCTOBER: Whole number of school days 21. Absent 21 times;

NOVEMBER. Whole number of school days 17. Absent 17 times;

DECEMBER. Whole number of school days 18. Absent 2 times; excused 2 times; late 0 times; excused 0 times.

From December until May, each monthly page of the book is signed by Laura Wheeler (who has replaced Miss Winsor as "Teacher in charge"), by J(ames) G(reenleaf) Croswell, A.B., "Head Master," and by A(lice) G(wynne) Vanderbilt, "Parent or Guardian." Now, Gertrude is seldom absent and again never late. Not until May is Mrs. Vanderbilt's signature missing beneath the others, despite the injunction "Please return this book to school promptly."

It is not, then, difficult to reconstruct the broad outlines of the year: the private tutoring and even more private compositions in Newport; the return to New York about the beginning of December; the prayers and five basic subjects at Brearley; the dancing class, piano lessons, and "physical culture," all after school; the holidays when her brother William, and now Cornelius too, are home from Yale. . . .

Yes, most of the academic year is routine, but during Easter vacation

William, then twenty-one and just finishing his junior year at Yale, contracts typhoid fever. Though brought to New York on May 6 and treated by Dr. James W. McLane and other celebrated physicians, after a brief rally he dies at the Vanderbilts' Fifth Avenue home late Monday night May 23, with McLane in attendance; parents, brothers, and sisters at his bedside—even Gladys, then only six. The death of Cornelius Vanderbilt's eldest and favorite child is one of the greatest griefs that he has ever had to bear, and of course it affects not only him but the rest of the family. Gertrude, though not as close to Bill as to her younger brothers, feels the gloom that descends on their house, a gloom (referred to in her *History*) that she "would rather not dwell upon," though in a subsequent autobiographical scrap, "The Story of a Child," she writes of her "oldest brother who had all the brains of the family."

Bill's death and funeral—both covered in detail by the newspapers—are sad reminders of his popularity and promise. At St. Paul's he had been stroke of the school crew. At Yale he had become a member of Psi Upsilon fraternity (from which the name of Gertrude's subsequent Psi Club "Girls Chapter" may have derived) and would have been elected to Skull and Bones, had he not been ill at the time. In the past few months, since attaining his majority and receiving the income from the trust left to him by his grandfather, he had joined the Knickerbocker, New York Yacht, Seawanhaka Corinthian, Racquet and Tennis, and Westchester Polo and Riding clubs; and had purchased a forty-six foot sloop, intending to put it in commission during the summer.

Friday morning at nine, the Rev. Dr. David H. Greer conducts a brief service for the family at home. Then they go to St. Bartholomew's, where a huge crowd has formed—strangers as well as friends—including eighty-six Yale students who have come down on two special trains with Yale President Dwight and several professors. The funeral procession is led by honorary pallbearers, including Bill's roommate Moses Taylor and friends Alonzo Potter and Harry P. Whitney of Yale and James ("J.") A. Burden and Columbus Baldwin of Harvard, followed by the entire family—all the Gwynnes as well as Vanderbilts, except for a few in distant places—and finally ten New York servants walking two by two. After services, the coffin is taken by the family to the foot of West 42nd Street where it is put on a ferryboat and transported to the Moravian Cemetery at New Dorp, Staten Island. The family proceeds past the old graveyard, containing the bodies of some distant relatives and an abandoned, comparatively small mausoleum built by Commodore Vanderbilt for his parents, himself, his wife, and children, from which they have all been moved to the seventy-two crypt tomb, the size of a very large town house, built by William H. Vanderbilt. There, Bill's coffin is placed to rest forever with only those direct descendants of the Commodore's parents who have the last name Vanderbilt. Other branches of the family have plots adjoining the mausoleum which, until the Great Depression, is watched, as it has been since Bill's grandfather built it, day and night by guards who punch a clock every quarter hour, and its parklike setting is maintained by eight grounds keepers.

For the Vanderbilts, as for all of those whom the etiquette books of the day call "people of refinement and standing," the mourning period is rigidly long—not less than two years of the proper dark clothes, black furs, and simple jewelry, and the same period of comparatively restricted travel and social activity. Thus, during this summer mostly in Newport (and the following one), Cornelius Vanderbilt and his family live quietly, avoiding society rather than seeking it.

Toward the end of the present year they must face another, though less grievous, blow. On November 25, during the cold windy afternoon, a fire, started by a defect in the overworked heating system of The Breakers, moves quickly through the 160-foot brick and wood-frame Queen Anne mansion, so quickly that it is miraculous the occupants survive. Mr. and Mrs. Vanderbilt are at the time receiving a call from "Mr. and Mrs. E. R. Wharton" (almost certainly Edward R. Wharton, and his wife Edith, thirteen years his junior, whose life will frequently, if never intimately, intersect Gertrude's). Cornelius has left for Yale the previous morning. His younger brothers are out driving. The whereabouts of Gertrude and Gladys are unknown. Everyone is frantic except for the girls, who come running across the lawn just as the head coachman is about to go into the burning building.

The loss is estimated at $700,000, including tapestries, antique furniture, silverware, and linens. Mr. Vanderbilt accepts this philosphically, thankful that no one has been injured, and blaming no one, though the Fire Department has been slow and the water pressure inadequate. Indeed the fire may have been a blessing. It gives Mr. and Mrs. Vanderbilt, him in particular, a distraction from grief. Only two months before William's illness, the remodeling and enlargement of 1 West 57th Street had begun under the supervision of the architect George B. Post, to provide such missing amenities as a ballroom (65 feet long by 50 wide by 35 high). Now, and for the next two and a half years, the Vanderbilts will work closely with another, even more distinguished architect, Post's teacher, Richard Morris Hunt, who has just completed Marble House, a Newport "cottage," for Cornelius' brother William K. Planning their own new home, visiting comparable ones, selecting suitable construction materials and interior furnishings will occupy much of their time and result in the most elaborate summer house in the United States, a several-million-dollar Italian Renaissance palace, grander even than Marble House.

And by late January, though less directly involved with the construction, Mr. Vanderbilt has still another building job under way—a 120-student dormitory at Yale in memory of Bill, for which no price is specified in the contract, so that it will be a fitting memorial to his eldest son.

≈

Seven months after her brother's death, Gertrude begins a new journal in a tone far more brusque, disjointed, and self-critical than what we have become accustomed to.

DECEMBER 27th
Speak to Alice [Blight] about the cloak. Write on description of Queen Elizabeth.

DECEMBER 28th
Don't think so much of "Life." Be careful who you confide in.

DECEMBER 31st
Complexion only good point in exterior. Cold and distant. Have a very good opinion of yourself. Change! Reform before it is too late. A World of Doubt. Make good resolutions for the next year and keep them. Don't forget to write every bad thing anyone tells you.

≈ *1893*

Except for the January 3 notation "History/Prayer book and Hymnal (small)/Novels" and the January 15 summary of a sermon by Dr. Greer which leads to an awkward religious poem of her own, ending "For gold is God, and heaven/ is in, yes, in all men," Gertrude does not resume writing regularly in her journal until January 18.

Thus far there has been little there about boys and men—occasionally the coded initials of a boy who does not figure importantly in her life or the name of an older man such as Mr. Langley on whom she has a passing crush. But now, suddenly, although she has not yet come out, is not yet supposed to think about such things, entire pages of her journal are filled with the initials of boys she sees at dancing class or while ice skating in Central Park—all usually followed by self-reproach. For example, after two such lists on January 18 and 19, there's this:

You should be ashamed of yourself for thinking about the above at all. A girl of your age and so little able to control her thoughts, and but a short time ago you were congratulating yourself . . . that such subjects were quite beneath you, only because you had no occasion to think of them. I am ashamed of you, yes, do you hear, you have not the control and what is more you have not conquered but have been conquered. You have not grown, not by any means, you are weak, foolish and young, so there. Remember this, read it every day. When you think yourself attractive look in the glass. . . .

She still cannot believe that boys are interested in her for herself. More important is the praise of Miss Winsor, now her English teacher. "When she said she was going to read three [essays] I wondered if mine ['Poetry for Children'] would be one. I feared it would not, yet I hoped it would. When the first began and it was not mine, I lost a little hope. The second, I felt my hands grow cold, the third, I recognized. I was relieved, pleased and proud." The next day, after listing the initials of six boys she sees in the morning and seven in the afternoon, she writes: "I still rejoice when I think of yesterday." And the next: "I have still that feeling of pleasure when I think of Friday." But now she tells herself, "You must not think too much of it. The girls may not have succeeded well with the subject, therefore it is not much, mine being best. It certainly sounded a good deal better when it was read, but that may have been only to myself!! Conceit. I do care what Miss Winsor thinks about me anyway."

The need for recognition is intense and competitive and will be increasingly so as Gertrude grows older. So will be the need to denigrate herself when she wins the recognition which she so desperately wants. In February the lists continue and then toward the end of the month: "Another snare for your conceit. Photographs. Keep cool, show yourself above your equals, that is young girls, by not caring. Be indifferent. Thereby deceive the others. Marie Hamilton said today, someone said 'You were very handsome and had a beautiful complexion.' Don't believe it, she said it to get on the right side of you. Someone else said, not very long ago, I was stupid." And some five weeks later: "Have come to the conclusion seriously that G.V. is *dull.*"

In mid-April Gertrude composes a long imaginary letter "what I sometimes think I should like to write":

Dear Miss Winsor,

You will be very surprised to get this long letter from me, no doubt, and will wonder what I can have to say to you.

In the first place, I must tell you that I should never have troubled you by telling you how fond I am of you unless I had thought that it would be good for me and it might lead to so much more.

There is no use going back to the time when I first went to the Brearley and met you, but I must tell you that ever since then I have had the same feelings toward you. I know only too well that you disliked me, that you even made fun of me, and that it amused you to see me when I blushed and stammered. Why I did not hate you I am sure I do not know. It was not my imagination which made me imagine this, if you have forgotten all about me in those old days, for the other girls would laugh and say, "Oh yes, Miss Winsor always asks you when she knows you do not know, and she takes great delight in your blushes." This cannot interest you, in fact my letter will not interest you, except that I suppose we all, from a feeling of vanity, like to be cared for by others. You know me, I think, pretty well from my compositions. Some people might read them and not do so, but from your criticism I can often see that you fully grasp my ideas. I know you less, but still I am sure that we would sympathize in certain things.

You are most likely thinking now, "Why, what is she driving at? Have all my talks on Rhetoric done so little for her, that she cannot even make a clear point?" But whether you think in reading my letter of its literary value, its clearness in reference to rhetoric, or the meaning which lies below all these cold words, I am afraid it will not change me. You see, you have to do with a stubborn kind of girl who, when she once likes, will not be changed in spite of her feeling not being in the slightest degree returned. Miss Winsor, I do not want you to feel now that you must write to me and say it's very good of me or any such conventionalities, I hate them as much as I do anything which interferes with our good prospects in life. If I thought that because I am Gertrude Vanderbilt it made any difference to you in the way you treated me, I would be more unhappy than if I never saw you again. For then I could keep the memory of one whom I consider noble, and in the other case I would never believe in human nature again. I know to some this does make a difference, makes all the difference in the world, but there are a few, I know there are, who don't care, like myself. I wonder is it wrong to wish that all those worldly things did not exist, for I do often. I then think that those who are worth loving do not care about them and would not be influenced by them.

The reason I have written you this little is this. I don't tell my thoughts or feelings to anyone and for five years I have kept my affection for you quiet. The girls know I like you, but that is all. I don't air my feelings anyway and don't approve of people who do. But I wanted you to know how it was. I hope you have not been bored, and that you will believe in the sincerity of everything I have said. It need make no difference in our relation toward each other, but you will understand that I am not exactly the same as all the other girls. I don't ask you to think of me or to do anything else, only please don't forget that you are to me as few others and as no one at school. You may say, "But you don't know me. You have never spoken to me much alone." Yes, yes this is all true, but why does sympathy exist? Why we none of us know. You, who do not care for me, who has not even a thought for Gertrude, please forgive my having written and believe me always

Yours
Gertrude

P.S. I will never trouble you again this way.

Then Gertrude writes the imaginary reply, "What I always think I should like to have her answer":

Dear Gertrude,

I was surprised and pained to get your letter. I know you well enough to know that you would not have written me if you had not really felt what you said, perhaps more. Your dislike for conventionalities prevents my saying anything I do not thoroughly mean. I take as conclusion to your letter that you would like to know me better, and I can say that I have often thought, but especially in reading certain of your compositions, that I would like to know you better.

We wish that Gertrude had sent her letter and that Miss Winsor had replied, or that she had simply told Miss Winsor, or anyone, her thoughts and feelings. Surely then Gertrude's life would have been different, but of course she herself would have had to have been different. She is what she is, torn between her need for love and her proud refusal to ask for it, her need to express herself and her inhibited secrecy in doing so. Her journals are full of imaginary letters, and among her papers are many actual letters, often those most felt, which were never sent. This is the world of Henry James and Edith Wharton, where everything is felt but sometimes too little said and done directly, and where that very lack of direct communication often results in tragedy. We are reminded again of Mrs. Wharton's *House of Mirth* (that painfully appropriate and ironic title), in which Lily Bart would have been saved, had she been able to speak, really speak, to Lawrence Selden. Miss Bart, like Miss Vanderbilt, is proud, beautiful, "not exactly the same as all the other girls," more talented, more sensitive, more aware of the conflict between the worldly and unworldly satisfactions of life. Miss Bart can rationalize her behavior in terms of the worldly things she lacks, Miss Vanderbilt in terms of the superabundance of those she possesses. Gertrude wishes, only wishes, "that all those worldly things did not exist."

❧

During the late spring and early summer the Vanderbilts go to Europe with Richard Morris Hunt (about to receive the Gold Medal of the Royal Institute of British Architects), his wife, and two of their children, Joe and Esther, she almost exactly Gertrude's age, at least as well traveled, and probably more sophisticated, having been exposed since early childhood to a social circle of intellectuals and artists (including her uncle William Morris Hunt). No doubt one of the reasons for the trip is to select furnishings for The Breakers, though there is no record of just what the Vanderbilts buy. There are, however, published newspaper accounts that Gertrude is engaged to the son of Prince Borghese, "the oldest family probably in existence. This was very interesting news of course to me, and the family laughed and then we all forgot about it." When the Vanderbilts and the Hunts return Gertrude begins two more journals. The first, *People I Meet*, subtitled "People met for the first time, where met, first impressions. Private, if you please." begins August 9: "Mr. Livingston Hunt at Mrs. [Richard Morris] Hunt's. Rather quiet, sick looking. Not very much character. Guess at age—29." The entry is typical of what follows during the next eleven months. The entries, about 230 of them, always start with a name and a place, almost always indicate who performed the introduction, and almost always, too, attempt a quick guess at character and age. The second journal, *My Letting-Off-Steam Book*, will be, as she writes in its "Prelude," "a mixture of fact and fiction, of people and thoughts and anything else which happens to strike me."

She starts (August 17, in a house the Vanderbilts have rented until the new one is ready) with a charming initial letter of two ladies shaking hands in the shape of an H " '[H]ow do you do,' the people say down at the beach, 'is the water cold today?' and they shake hands 'a la 400' and then sit down and begin talking. Suddenly one of your friends goes by in her bathing suit and you immediately discuss her. . . . It's a very undressed atmosphere . . . but no one seems to care, so I suppose it is all right. . . ."

The next day Gertrude begins a short story called "Arabella's Two Proposals," about the daughter of "the strictest of mothers," during "her first season out." Arabella and her friends are about to meet Lord Warren and his friends when the story breaks off "(To be continued)." It never is. Instead, Gertrude draws another initial letter, this one of an erect tiny-waisted, I-shaped girl playing tennis: "[I]t is not often that a young girl gets a chance to act as if she were a fellow (I don't mean to say I have had any such chance, not much), but when she does I think she should make the most of it. Men have a so much jollier time in the world. But I intend to make the most of being a girl and be very undignified, not a bit sedate, although Mama, I know, thinks dignity a prime factor."

And the day after that Gertrude goes on what she calls "a spree, you see, I so seldom do anything out of the ordinary." She and Esther Hunt intend going to the hunt but when it is called off at the last moment they and six friends—Ethel Davies, her cousin Miss Rochester, her brother

Fred Davies, Bobbie Gerry, and the Bishop brothers—decide, anyway, to
drive in that direction. The girls in their carriages, the boys on horseback,
all end up at the Davies farm—unchaperoned. "I am quite sure Miss
Rochester was a little shocked, not that we did anything. . . ." The "not
at all good-looking, prim, shy" Alice Rochester must have felt left out in
relation to Gertrude, Esther, and Ethel—all three tall and attractive, all
three founders less than a week before of the secret Psi Club, with its
typed constitution containing nineteen regulations, the last of which
reads: "That the club be for the sake of enjoying ourselves." It is a radical
rule and one with which the in-group seems as uncomfortable as Miss
Rochester. The Sunday following the spree Gertrude writes: "I am restless, cannot keep quiet and want to be on the go. This all comes from
having enjoyed myself lately. If I had not been made a member of the Psi
or gone to the beach, I might sit at home all the afternoon, reading or
writing, and be perfectly happy." Her guilt mounts. She decides to spend
the time profitably by doing a story. It is called "My Own True Love" and
is written from the point of view of Jack, a lover seemingly rejected by
Alice but accepted at the end. "His arms were about her and she, with her
head on his shoulder, was whispering in his ear: 'Jack, I love you.'"

Gertrude draws a disciplined line across the page and writes beneath it:
"Three-quarters of an hour very agreeably spent with Jack and Alice." The
most remarkable thing about "My Own True Love" (about 770 words) is
the speed at which she writes it. (Even earlier, at fourteen, Gertrude has
noted on a forty-line poem that she has written it in fifteen minutes. Allowing for the poor quality of these particular works, that is still fast by
any standard and helps explain the survival of more than a million words
by Gertrude, with perhaps another million lost or destroyed.)

In late August the Vanderbilts visit Bar Harbor again, this time to visit
Gertrude's aunt Margaret and uncle Elliott Shepard. Gertrude returns
with a poem to her cousin Elliott Shepard, Jr., ending:

> He was smiling
> She was blushing
> Both contented, both quite happy
> Both lives full of spooning bliss
> While old Moon, he feels quite silly
> As these foolish sweethearts kiss!

She writes "a Sunday sermon" to herself; "I care for nobody, no not I, and
nobody cares for me. . . . A fine motto to have! A fine text! . . ." For six
pages she questions the meaning of love. "How often I think, love, love if
you can, and just as often I find I can't, so make believe I don't want
to. . . . I want to learn, I am waiting, blindfolded and alone, come—
come, you who have already learnt, teach me that I may taste [love's]

fruits and live!" As often, she ends her entry, her "Sunday sermon," with a poem, this one, like her life now, an intense mixture of longing for both the sacred and profane:

> Oh teach me how to love thee
> Thou great, though all unknown
> Oh teach me how to die for thee
> To love thee, thee alone.
> Oh teach me how to feel toward thee
> That great and heavenly bliss
> Oh teach me how to worship thee
> Oh teach me how to kiss.

❦

Gertrude's sexual frustration will continue to intensify during her teens and, indeed, until her marriage. In her very sheltered and restrictive environment there is little chance for release. Contact with boys must be chaperoned. Kisses are sisterly, cousinly, chaste. There is some release of sexual energy in the much freer social contact with girls; some in riding, swimming, hiking, and other sports; some in the incessant keeping of journals. Though Gertrude has had tender loving relationships with several girls—Sybil Sherman, Daisy Post, Alice Blight, Cousin Adele Sloane, and most recently Ethel Davies—her relationship with Esther Hunt begins now to go further; further, perhaps, than Gertrude wants or is able to deal with; further, surely, than her mother wants.

Early in September, after going for a long drive with Esther and returning home late, Mama calls Gertrude into the parlor, questions her "in a terrific tone," and "as if very, very much provoked," forbids her going to Esther Hunt's again for a month. Gertrude asks why. "Because I don't like the way you act—with her." Gertrude can say nothing. She leaves, goes to her room, locks the door, cries, determines not to "show [her] feelings that evening downstairs," and writes a letter to Esther. At dinner Gertrude "managed to talk, to appear natural, to take interest in what was being said, and not to let my feelings be seen." Her mother asks, "What time did you go out to drive?" Gertrude answers calmly, "Early, at four, and we took the wrong road coming back." The next morning "when Mama said she took back what she said about going to Esther's, I was hardly surprised. I felt sure I was in the right and I think that is what made me act as I did, and that is what Mama must have seen." Yes, Mama must realize that the punishment has been harsh and that, beneath the calm acceptance of it, Gertrude is very upset, but Mama has also begun to suspect, if only intuitively, something else that Gertrude doesn't yet see and can never fully face or talk about: Esther is in love with her, really in love, so passionately and completely that it will make Gertrude's relationships with other girls seem like the "crushes" they are and those with boys—to date and even until marriage—seem, by comparison, like child's play.

During the rest of September and all of October, Gertrude sees a great deal of Esther as well as other friends. Fred Davies, who had been along on that "spree" a few weeks before, confesses his love for Gertrude, but once he has done so Gertrude, in turn, confesses—to her journal, as always —"it has made a little difference . . . somehow I don't like Fred as much as I did." She continues to analyze her feelings and his and comes to the conclusion that "it is not worth so much thought or trouble." It is easier to leave the specific case of Fred and once again attempt a more general "Essay on Love." "Love is the source of all earthly happiness, yet it comes and goes in the short space of a day. How explain this mystery?" She tries for two pages, admitting finally, as she has before: "I find myself perfectly incapable of writing on this subject."

Yet two days later she can listen with perfect sympathy to the schoolboy confessions of Esther's younger brother Herbert, contrast her understanding of his problems with her mother's lack of understanding, and then write this prayer:

Oh, God, hear me I pray Thee, let me never forget my feelings when I was a child, when I was a girl, so that, if it is Thy will that I should live and marry and have children, I may know what they think and sympathize with them and know what they feel and need without their telling me. And I pray that never by word or deed I may offend them. Oh, God, who art so good and so forgiving, grant me this that I may bring happiness and not sorrow into the lives of all the young about me. For Jesus Christ's sake. Amen.

Gertrude lists some of her grievances, the grievances of a child (almost nineteen now): to "sit by and hear your best friend [Esther] picked to pieces or the fact of your having three letters in the same week from the same girl laughed at and mockingly alluded to. Listen to your friend being called a runner after rich girls, with a knowing look in your direction, or 'dear so-and-so' spoken of before other people in a tone which says more than words can express. . . . If I have children of my own, they will tell me everything because they know I will understand and sympathize, yes, if my prayer is granted, I will live over my youth with them and God will help me, for He is good. I know He is, I am sure He is."

Gertrude describes an etching, perhaps real, perhaps imaginary, called "The Kiss" in 231 words (counted and recorded by herself and, needless to say, correct), another called "Life" in "about 339." It ends: "The maiden, who sat with Life and would sit there forever, answered, 'My name is Love.'" She writes a letter to a girl friend named Sally, saying good-by (again everyone is leaving Newport), and transcribes it in her

47

journal. She writes and writes until the beginning of October when she and her family go to the World's Columbian Exposition in Chicago. Esther and her family are there too, as Richard Morris Hunt has done the much-publicized Administration Building for it. There is no indication of how much Gertrude sees Esther in Chicago, or of Gertrude's specific response to the fair itself. It "was beautiful and grand and everything else, but I don't feel as if I could give you any idea of it even if I did sit down and write page after page about it, which I don't intend to do." However, the fair's flamboyant architecture and monuments as well as its general sense of vitality and theatricality make a strong impression on Gertrude, one that will last all her life.

When Gertrude returns to Newport, she finds Sally's reply, "the most perfect letter ever written," and she asks herself, "Can the heart not be big enough to hold two friendships? I like Esther far, far more than I used to. Do I love her?—that is the question. I think, no, I am almost sure I love Sally, but Esther? . . . I know I am perfectly happy to sit hand in hand with Esther and not say anything, but does that mean very much? I know so painfully little of love that I cannot tell you. I know, though, that I have felt a thrill run through and through me when I touched Sally's hand. Does that mean much? . . . It frightened me somehow. . . . I look into the future and imagine I see myself, grown up and out. I meet a man. I love him. He is attentive to me for my money. He proposes, makes me believe he loves me. I accept, since I love him. We are married. Now, since money is secure, he shows me that he does not love me. I love him still and am wretchedly unhappy. We lead separate lives, he going his way, I mine. And thus we grow old."

A week after returning from Chicago, Gertrude asks Esther to fill in the blanks on the printed pages of an ornately decorated Victorian book, purchased in London two years before and not until recently offered to anyone.

CONFESSIONS,
An Album to Record Opinions,
Thoughts, Feelings, Ideas, Peculiarities, Impressions,
Characteristics of Friends, & c.

As Esther carefully writes her answers to the printed questions, there are many hints concerning her and her relationship to Gertrude:

Your favourite virtue. Frankness. Constancy.

Your favourite qualities in man. Honesty.

Your favourite qualities in woman. Truthfulness.

Your favourite occupation. Dancing. Driving with_____

Your chief characteristic. And when she was nice she was very very nice, and when she was bad she was horrid.

Your idea of happiness. At present, something only you know.

Your idea of misery. To love someone and not have them love you.

Your favourite colour and flower. Violet. [Gertrude's too.]

If not yourself, who would you be? 7/22 [Perhaps the date of something significant that happened on their return from Europe this past summer.]

Where would you like to live? New York. Newport.

Your favourite prose authors. Dickens. Walter Besant. Edna Lyall [novelist and ardent supporter of women's emancipation].

Your favourite poets. Tennyson. Wordsworth.

Your favourite painters and composers. Wagner.

Your favourite heroes in real life. Napoleon. [Again, Gertrude's too, and that of most of their friends.]

Your favourite heroines in real life. Marie Antoinette. Jeanne D'Arc.

Your favourite heroes in fiction. Donovan [the eponymous hero of Edna Lyall's best-known novel].

Your favourite heroines in fiction. [none]

Your favourite food and drink. Spiders and Honey.

Your favourite names. Gertrude. Violet. Jack. Richard.

Your pet aversion: Affectation.

What characters in history do you most dislike? Henry VIII.

What is your present state of mind? Rather undecided.

For what fault have you most toleration? Temper. Jealousy.

Your favourite motto. Honesty is the best policy.

Esther leaves Newport for New York by mid-October and on November 2 Gertrude does. This year, Gertrude's last at Brearley, she has a "modified regime." As Head Master Croswell explains, "She is at a point where a little further attention to her English will make a great difference in the form and finish of her written work. . . . This gives me an opportunity to say that I felt her presence in my class a genuine gain to myself. She is an inspiring pupil; and will be very soon without doubt a high minded and intelligent woman."

Gertrude writes in her *History*—now just begun, to the partial neglect of her day-to-day journal: "I was to have come out that winter but of course did not. I only went to dinners. The same 2d of November I came from the country I went to my cousin Emily Sloane's coming out tea and it was the first thing I went to. Of course I was frightened, it was my nature to be, but all the same I enjoyed it in a sort of half and half way. When I first went into the room I felt as if I did not know a soul. Fortunately I had Cornelius to turn to, for he had come with me and was even more scared than I was. But soon some girls came up and Willie Sloane (a college fellow) and Mr. Sands, who by the way is very nice, and several others. So altogether it might have been worse. What I felt very much was knowing so few people. Then it seemed strange meeting people I had always looked up to, on an equal footing."

❧

There is nothing in Gertrude's journal about her newly enlarged New York home, but much in the newspapers and magazines where it is now accurately described as "the largest dwelling-house occupied by a single family in the city of New York." Not only has the property been extended to include land formerly occupied by five town houses on 58th Street, but the entire ground floor has been opened up so that its 57th Street entrance —still decorated as formerly with sculpture and family reliefs by Saint-Gaudens—leads to a grand hall, 40 by 50 feet with a ceiling height of 35 feet, all of Caen stone, handled in the style of the Château de Blois. On Fifth Avenue, starting at the 57th Street corner, there is the library, small salon, large Louis XV salon, and water color room; on the west side of the hall, Mr. Vanderbilt's office, Moorish smoking room, dining room, and breakfast room. Except for the office and breakfast room, all of these can be opened into each other. In addition there is a new 58th Street entrance to the ballroom with a circular porte-cochere, for which wrought-iron gates 16 feet high are presently being fabricated in France.

Though the Vanderbilts cannot really use this vast, social space until the coming spring, when Bill will have been dead for two years, for Gertrude already the social pace quickens, the social world unfolds. There is no more peeking at it from piazzas and galleries, as three years earlier. From now on, for the next three years, she is in it, deeply immersed.

After more than a month of not writing in her journal she addresses it: "Poor neglected book, I only write here to put down a little list I should like to make subjects of conversation for tonight. Uncle George, Mr. Lorey, and Belmont Tiffany are coming. I am anxious, frightened, subdued, and feel that I shall be utterly bereft of ideas. So I make this list while I have a little left in me.

GENERAL: The Newport Opera House. Irving. The Horse Show.

UNCLE G.: Biltmore.

MR. L.: Was Paris the same as ever?

MR. T.: Jeannie."

There are more lists of guests and topics of conversation, both often much longer; more anxiety, presumably greater. She meets dozens of "suitable" young men, many of them friends of her dead brother Bill. She observes that she has made "a heap of good [even if premature, New Year's] resolutions" but "a very poor beginning as far as keeping them goes," feeling "as if I were becoming a society girl and it is breaking my heart. Ha! Ha! You know that I like it so much. . . ." However, not until a dinner at Aunt Emily Sloane's, followed by the opera, is she somewhat smitten. That night she has "such a perfectly, delightfully, supremely nice time" as she has "never had before. Lots of nice people came into the box . . . and Mr. [Reginald] Ronalds was nicer than words can express. He is going to be at the Cushings', so of course I look forward to that above all the other dinners now." Immediately after these words there is another so-called "Etching—Love." This one is surely imaginary. The figures in the etching speak. When the girl accuses the man of not listening, he answers: " 'I heard, I heard only three words repeated over and over again. And it was my soul that felt them. I love you, I love you, that is what I heard. Darling.' He had her in his arms and, with their lips meeting, he told her, but not in words, what he had heard and what he would never cease to hear."

Within a few days the imagined dialogue becomes more realistic. "What I would like to say to R.R.: 'You know, I find I am entirely mistaken about thinking all men were alike. Do you remember I said so the other night? . . .' " And within a few more days one supposes it is not imagined at all:

He: "Do you live in the country much?"

She: "In summer. What makes you ask?"

He: "You have such pink cheeks."

She: "I wish you would not say it, I dislike them especially."

He: "You are fishing."

She: "I am not, I am perfectly in earnest. I dislike them very, very."

He: "And red lips, do you dislike them too?"

And:

He: "Your carriage comes for you here, does it not?"

She: "Yes, and my maid meets me, you know."

He: "I wonder why everyone is so formal. Now wouldn't it be nice if I could just take you home, you know. We'd call a hansom, jump in and be off."

She: "Yes, wouldn't it. But we couldn't, could we?"

He: "I am afraid not."

She: "How much nicer it would be. If only someone would start the fashion, everyone else would follow."

He: "Yes, but who would start?"

After these bits of dialogue Gertrude once again comments guiltily and ambivalently: "I am getting to be quite crazy about going out. I almost, not quite, wish I were going out every night. It is so delightful at first, it's like drinking, I should think. First it is only a great pleasure, then it is looked forward to, longed for, thirsted after and died without. You do other things, you must, but the memory of it is there always. It becomes the main part of the life, the root of all your evil actions. At last it becomes your life and you sacrifice your character and love for it."

Gertrude never comments on the wealth or background of her beaux. Within her circle these things are taken for granted; are, indeed, the basis for admission into it. Reginald Ronalds is typical. On his mother's side he is a Lorillard, of the tobacco Lorillards, who go to the same resorts and belong to the same clubs as the Vanderbilts. Regi has graduated from Yale ('86); is about ten years older than Gertrude; has no definite occupation and needs none; is, in short, as acceptable as—really no more and no less than—the others she will meet during the coming year, those about whom we will furnish a few details only if the men are important to Gertrude now or later in her life. For Gertrude, their names—as for all aristocrats, even in a democracy—are their sufficient identities.

✍ *1894*

The lists of dinner party guests, often including Mr. Ronalds, begin again. The night of Gertrude's nineteenth birthday she is at the Reids', a few nights later, at the Cushings', then at the Webbs', then at the Sloanes', then at the Taylors'. . . . Ninety-two dinner parties, dances, and/or evenings at the opera will be listed in her *Dinner Book* for this winter season which will cause the abandonment of her *History,* the crowding of *People I Meet,* and a very sporadic pattern in *My Letting-Off-Steam Book* and subsequent journals. Often when she is introduced to yet another eligible bachelor, she asks her journal if "he talked to me because I am Miss Vanderbilt." To one such fellow (nameless in her journal) she writes an imaginary letter, reminding herself in so doing of Mr. Toots in Dickens' *Dombey and Son.* The letter is as long as the one to Miss Winsor, and the questions Gertrude asks in it are similar to those she has asked, or wanted to ask, Mr. Ronalds—for example, "Can you imagine this—if it were only the fashion, if we could take a long walk after dark, together, alone?"

A month and a half later, two days before Easter, she is still thinking of the mysterious new bachelor and writes her fantasy reply from him—or perhaps a composite of him and Mr. Ronalds and still more recent acquaintances. It is headed "How I imagine a Love Letter to be" and begins: "Dearest, Why should I write and tell you what you already know? It is to be sure you understood that one look of mine tonight. How I hated all that crowd, I would have given ten years of my life to have been alone with you then. . . ." What the one look means is explained in a proposal at the end of three climactic pages: "My own precious Gertrude, will you give me the right to lead you through life in my arms?" He gives her until five o'clock to decide.

"What I imagine to happen after," she heads the next installment of this journal entry. "Gertrude had never been so nervous in the whole course of her life, she could not sit still in the same place for five consecutive seconds. Half a dozen times she had been on the point of sending him a line, and twenty times at least she had written him imaginary letters which she had not the faintest intention of sending. . . ." She puts the finishing touches to her toilet, still has half an hour to wait, does nothing in doing much—opens every book in the room, plays with every photograph, sits in every chair, finally selects a low footstool at the window, thinking, "How could he care for me? I am not very pretty or very attractive or very nice, and he, he—"

"Mr. Jack Capes," as she "will call the imaginary person," is announced. She makes further preparations, combs her hair, adjusts her tea gown, wonders if the servant is "suspicious about the brightness of her eyes." She leaves her room, thinks how long the hall is, then (as she nears the library) how short! He says her name "passionately, yet low." She says his, extending her hands. "Jack drew the hands he held about his neck, clasped his own arms about Gertrude's body and strained her to him. Every nerve in them thrilled, every fibre felt that touch; she thought of heaven and he of life. Then their lips met and Jack robbed them of their innocence."

Easter Sunday it rains. Gertrude is driven to and from church, feeling "really sorry for all the people who have clothes to show off." In the afternoon she sits in her room, writing, "I wonder if people call on Easter?" She lists those who might, coming soon to Mr. Ronalds. "He was here Sunday before last, so of course he will not come again today. Perhaps next Sunday. Last time he let two Sundays pass between his visits. I wish he would come tomorrow afternoon (I think Mama may go away for the day) not because I don't want her to know, but I think it would be nice to see him alone." She remembers his last visit, the "date" they set up to meet when she would be riding with a friend in Central Park, that brief unsatisfactory meeting itself, and another a week later. . . . She looks forward to dinner and theater with the Sands the next night. Charles and Robert Sands, who have recently lost their parents, are living with their oldest sister, about thirty. Gertrude has seen the brothers at several dinners and at the opera. "Mama says she supposes I will be the only one. Oh my, if I am, sorrow. . . ." Tuesday her brother Alfred will be coming home from school. "I am so glad, it seems ages since I saw him last. He must have lots to tell me, and I have lots to tell him."

Gertrude's mind moves forward and backward in time, writing page after page in her journal until "it is five o'clock. Oh joy, that means no one. Perhaps we are not receiving, I never thought of that. This is Easter and where have my thoughts been all day? Not where they should have, certainly. . . . I am getting worse instead of better. . . . I am wicked and it does not make very much difference to me. . . ." She thinks of another dinner she will be going to on Thursday, at the Gerrys', and resolves to describe it in detail: "something of the conversation, and of the people's clothes and anything and everything that takes place. In books the descriptions of dinner parties are very interesting. . . ."

The next day she adds, "After all we had two visitors yesterday, Mr. Cushing and Mr. Munn. I had never met this latter before . . . about 34, good looking and very attractive manners. I want to know more about him, something of his back history. . . . [As with] most men, a woman who flattered him would have complete control over him. . . ." Though Mr. Munn will not assume a significant role in Gertrude's life (and Mr. Cushing will), there is significance in this first statement of the theme of control over men and the suggestion of manipulating them, which now and in the future counterbalances her frequent previous fantasies of total passivity.

Gertrude never describes the dinner party at the Gerrys' the way they do "in books," but there is an interesting, if brief, description of "a little dinner" at home the night before, one about which she had been rather doubtful, but which turned out extremely nice. Here is the table:

	Mama	Mr. Cottenet	
	R. Baldwin	Miss Delafield	
	Alice Shepard	Henry Clews	
	F. Polk	G.V.	
	E. Hunt	H. Whitney	
	H. Robbins	M. Strong	
	C. Evans	C.V. Jr.	

They came in by degrees of course, and we sat or stood around until dinner was announced, then Neily [C.V., Jr.] went for Miss Strong and we paired off. As we went into dinner I said to Harry [Whitney]: "I expected to see you appear tonight in a sweater" (you see, the fellows had been telling me tales about him), and after that, of course we got on beautifully. We talked some about old times, the snow fight where I was the last to give in and had the snow stuffed down my neck, etc. The whole evening was enjoyable and led to a ride with Harry Robbins on Thursday.

Though Esther Hunt has been at this dinner and a few others during the winter, her presence has been merely listed, not felt. Now, four days after the dinner, Gertrude has something to unburden herself of. She begins, hesitates for nine more days, and says it—at last—to her journal. "What I should like to have out and done with once and for all":

MAMA: It is enough, Gertrude, you know I cannot stand those people, they run after you, oh Esther is such a friend, she is so fond of you. Now I wish it to stop. You are not to go there any more, I will not have it. (Silence and apparently no impression created on my part.) Do you hear me? Esther has no bringing up, I will not have you running there all the time and her coming here and staying till I don't know what hour.

G.V.: Of course, you can prevent my going to see her, but if you think you can change my opinion of her you are mistaken, that's all there is about it. Because the Hunts are not quite swell enough, of course they are not worth having anything to do with. I know perfectly well that you have been trying for over a year to prejudice me against Esther. You have said about as many disagreeable things about her as you dared to, and the best of it is you have imagined you were influencing me. You think you can twist me round your finger, and let me tell you that the only thing you have succeeded in making me do is in telling you less and less about myself and my affairs, and something else which I think I had better not say. If you want to suspect everyone you can, that is no reason for my doing so. I am old enough to make my own friends. Because I have seemed to agree with you is no sign that I did. I used to think it was my duty to do in almost everything as you wanted me to, now I think I am old enough to do more as I want and I am going to speak my opinions hereafter and not only think them. You may call me undutiful and all that sort of thing, but if you will take a child the wrong way, I think you have to suffer. I know I have no right to say that, but it is true, and I know Alfred feels the same way about it. That is why we have never told you more. Other children tell their parents almost everything. I never did. Now it's all out, it's been there so long I knew it had to come sometime. Thank goodness it is over.

It is not over. Nor, again, is it possible to believe that Mrs. Vanderbilt really objects to Esther Hunt's background and upbringing. Esther's family is in the Social Register. It comes, on both sides, from early colonial stock—earlier than that of the Vanderbilts—rich even in the eighteenth century. Richard Morris Hunt has been educated at the Boston Latin School and in Geneva and Paris, where he went to the Beaux Arts and then continued his study of architecture for nine years. His mother, his sister Jane and, most important, his brother William Morris Hunt were all distinguished painters. By the late 1860s Richard was fully established as one of the leading architects of the period. Not only had he designed the Fifth Avenue mansion in which the William K. Vanderbilts were accepted into society by the Astors, as well as several other Vanderbilt homes and their family mausoleum, but also New York or Newport homes for John Jacob Astor himself, Elbridge T. Gerry, Ogden Goelet, and Oliver H. P. Belmont. . . . His institutional work included the main portion of the Metropolitan Museum, the base of the Statue of Liberty, the Lenox Library, the Scroll and Key Club at Yale, the National Observatory in Washington. . . . He was one of the founders of the American Institute of Architects, served on the fine arts jury of many expositions (most recently the World's Columbian Exposition), and in 1892 received an honorary LL.D. degree from Harvard, the first artist/architect so honored. . . . The list of his accomplishments and honors could go on and on. It is enough to emphasize that his credentials, Esther's family background, should have been acceptable to Mrs. Vanderbilt; indeed had been, to both her and her husband at least twice when selecting an architect to do their homes, with all that implies concerning an intimate and sociable client-patron relationship. What the rather puritanical Mrs. Vanderbilt can object to is the cultivated and hedonistic, even vaguely European and bohemian, style of the Hunt family—exactly, we suspect, the very style that seems romantic and exotic to Gertrude.

Finally, in Gertrude's journal the Gerry dinner list appears—bare, without conversation, without clothing. Among the fourteen guests, besides "G.V.," are "R. Ronalds" and "R. Sands"—just names. Through April and into May the lists continue, interspersed with "A Dream" of a woman married to an older man she does not really love; a passage copied from *Romeo and Juliet* addressed to "Sweet Gertrude"; an essay on "The Romans and Greeks in reference to ourselves" ("We skim over the degrading in [the Greeks'] lives from a natural instinct of protection. They are of personal interest to us and we don't like to have our personal friends' faults dwelt upon"); a more specific essay on "My First Day in the Country under Certain Circumstances" describing a luncheon in Flushing at which she meets Count Hans Lierstorpff, "who has the reputation of coming over here to marry an heiress, but as yet I think there is no prospect of his getting one. . . ." The days and nights speed by, leaving a wake of ink.

It is again time for Europe, Gertrude's "first season in London." Two weeks after arriving there, Gertrude writes this letter—a real one now—and transcribes it in her journal (with pen-and-ink illustrations):

Dear Miss Winsor,

I know you are very busy just now so I did not wait to hear from you before writing as I suppose I should have done.

London is the same as ever. It has rained more or less every day since we have been here, and that misty cloud still hangs over the city threatening a fog every moment. But I find it is quite a different thing being here as a child and being here as a grown-up person. The people and their customs interest me, and though London is the same, it is quite different to me. As you have been here you know just about how one's time is spent. There are some very good exhibitions of pictures now that I am sure would interest you. One especially in Grafton Street called *Fair Woman* and, although the women are not all fair, there are lots of lovely portraits by Sir J. Reynolds, Romney, and others. I wish you could see them, they are so beautiful and interesting. The Royal Academy this year does not seem as good as usual but it may only be the contrast to these other galleries that makes it appear less good. You know an English dance is so different from ours. I went to one last night and it was such a pretty sight as it was very "smart" and a good many of the Royalties were there. So people were very much dressed up and wore their most beautiful jewels and best gowns. And as for the dancing I really wondered how anyone enjoyed it. I am crazy on the subject myself, but when it came to being twirled round and round and round at the rate of 25 twirls a second, I considered it more a duty than a pleasure. Then the way your partner first comes for you, then dances with you, then takes you to a nice quiet corner and talks to you, but the moment the next dance begins either takes you back to your chaperon or to your next partner, is all very strange because so different from the American custom.

This is the day of the Derby and we are going down as it is quite a sight.

I got some of the books whose names you gave me and am going to begin reading in the *Social Life in Greece* every day. The Americans over here are without number and I am surprised there is anyone at all left in America.

I hope you will not be too busy all June to write me.

June 22, after three more weeks, Gertrude is deep within the London whirl:

Such a gay and delightful time as I have been having lately. Ah me, if I were getting spoilt as people who don't know me say I am! Sad indeed. I must tell you about Ascot, spoiled or not spoiled, I really enjoyed the second day there very much. Of course, I take it for granted you know what Ascot is, and how the people wear their best clothes and, in fact, don't care beans about the races but care everything about each other. On Thursday we went to lunch at the Bachelors' Club and before lunch we saw a good many people we knew—the Burns, Captain Dawson, the Martins, Colonel Larkin, others, and Lord Garwick whom I had met once a little while before. He said he would come back after lunch and take me on the stand. So we had hardly come from lunch when he appeared and together we went off. I was prepared to enjoy myself and I did. A little description of Lord G. might interest you. He is a tall, fashionable looking, young man of about 27. He has lightish yellow red hair, a little moustache to match, and blue eyes. His face is rather red, but he is good looking on the whole. We got on very well together. I was in the mood to make an effort to be nice and he seemed to be as well. So we kept up almost a steady flow of talk. First we talked of the Martins and Cravens, and then of Scotland, and fishing, and shooting, horse racing, America, the season, the people, and I got him to talk about himself. Yes, get a man to talk about himself and, unless something is radically the matter, you will get on beautifully. Of course, these subjects led to others and altogether it is seldom I have enjoyed that sort of thing so much. You see, we were in something of a crowd most of the time and I knew no one and was practically quite alone with Lord G., so I had not the slightest feeling of shyness. We must have been there three quarters of an hour and it was fun. I must tell you that a few days after I met him at dinner, he and his mother and father, whom we do not know, left cards. Mama returned the call, of course, and on Wednesday (I met him Friday) we received a formal invitation to luncheon from the Earl and Countess of Mar (Papa and Mama). Of course, Mama and Papa laughed and laughed and Mama, who had told Mrs. Martin (where I met Lord G.) of the call, also told her of the note and asked her advice. This was on Thursday at Ascot. Mrs. Martin, however, only laughed and did not give any advice. So Mama next questioned Lord Cork who knows everyone and is a very swell old gentleman. He said no, he would not accept. This took place while I was off with Lord G. on the stand. Mama took Lord Cork's advice and regretted the invitation (previous engagement) as soon as we reached the hotel that afternoon (six o'clock). The next morning when I came in to breakfast, Mama and Papa suddenly broke into fits of laughter. I could not imagine what was up, so said: "Well, what's the matter?" And they told me. It seems the Mars had written again and wanted us to lunch on Thursday or Friday!! Ha, ha. So I joined in the laugh and Mama said to please me: "What have you done to him, Gertrude?" and Papa said: "Why, I am afraid of you," and I laughed and answered: "I am afraid I am not the attraction." Which I fear is really the case. I wonder what it will all lead to. Those things mean so much more here. Perhaps Mama and Papa Mar want to have a look at us. This is how I explain the matter now. They are poor (that I know) and have always wanted Lord G. to marry money. We appear upon the scene, Lord G. finds me not very disagreeable or ugly, well brought up, and his family jumps at the chance. Possibly Lord G. thinks he might rather like me in time, but nothing rash must be done, the family must be inspected before Lord G. commits himself in the least, so we are asked to be inspected. Oh how amusing, a scene fit for a book! Imagine—the house in upper B— Street, the drawing room, not very large but very home-like. We arrive on Thursday. We have had a good laugh in the carriage or now we should never have such straight faces. We are not the first, fortunately, but it is rather a small house, there will not be many guests. Mama leads the way, looking very dignified and stylish and everything nice. I come next, my knees knocking together, but outwardly calm, dressed in something light and becoming. Papa brings up the rear, as handsome and distinguished looking as ever. What a trio! Ha, ha, and the trio we confront at the door—what is that? The Countess of Mar—an elderly lady with gray hair, a black silk dress, a little lace cap on her head, dignified yet small. The Earl of Mar—a tall, oldish man, slightly bent with age and having old fashioned manners. Piercing eyes that seem to see into you. And Lord Garwick—we know what he is like. We talk of the weather, of Ascot a little, a few people are introduced, a few more arrive, then lunch is announced and we file in. Ha, ha! How I laugh in my inside, how we laugh, it is impossible to meet Mama's or Papa's eyes, impossible. Papa entertains the Countess with conversation on the theatres, etc. Mama discusses something else equally interesting, the other guests amuse each other as best they can, while Lord G. and I continue our conversation of the other day. There are enough people, and there is enough talking to prevent anyone else overhearing the conversation. Every once in a while when I look up I see the Earl taking Papa in from head to foot with his piercing eyes, or meet his eye and he again turns and continues his meal. Yes, truly a scene fit for a book! But what is the opinion of these worthy people who have thus showered upon us their hospitality? That is indeed an important question, and I try and form an idea from the expressions of our hosts. The Countess is evidently pleased. She had not expected to find us so thoroughly well bred. She had thought we would be like those dreadful Americans who talk loud and through their noses. Ah me, this is a relief, she thinks, and she shows it on the face. Mama she immediately respects and, as she is a lady herself, reads the perfect lady in Mama. And as for poor little me, she has the bad taste to think me not bad, but rather nice on the whole, as a few people have before. It is impossible from the Earl's face to see what he thinks, nothing is written there, only one feels he is taking one all in. I wonder how far from this picture the truth will be. I await Thursday with impatience.

JUNE 23D

My interest grows each day. At least it is going to be an excitement. Oh how I laugh when I think of it. And now an important factor steps in. We may not sail on Saturday. Of course, if we do it leaves too little time for anything serious to take place, but suppose we stay two weeks longer! What may not happen in two weeks?! I am too imaginative, that is what's the matter.

JUNE 24TH

The doctor says Regi may only have a cold. In that case, of course we sail on Saturday.

Ah me, what complications. Amusement must be had out of something. Here the people all take things in such cold blood that I feel as if I must do something really and truly bad, as if I must shock somebody. The steam has kept in too long this time, my pen cannot be the only outlet for it—or the machinery will break. I would be willing to walk the streets on my head if it were possible, or to eat peaches all the way down Bond Street, or anything else equally dreadful, but that is out of the question so I must think of something else. I know in my inmost heart what I should like to do. How I should love to shock Lord G. Oh how I wish I would meet him somewhere alone—quite alone—entirely alone this time, on a sofa together. Say at an evening party somewhere, and instead of asking me to go on the stand, ask me to go in the conservatory. Ah! —I would do everything in my power to make him like me. I would talk about himself, I would gently flatter him, I would try and amuse him, I would be frank and open with him to make him think I was taking him into my confidence. I would tease him about some unknown, yes, who was she? Ah, I thought I knew, a fair girl with pink cheeks whom I had seen him talk to at Ascot. He need not say it was not, I know better. I would ask him what it felt like to be in love, and laughingly ask him how often he had lost his appetite for some fair lady. I would describe to him with many gestures what I imagined it was like—a thrill—a slow, creeping, powerful sensation, taking heart and soul in its possession! I would lean towards him as I told him this, lower my voice and will him with all my might to thrill, to feel my presence. I would then sink back and see how all this had affected him. I would see what had made the most impression, the attention to his own interests, the flattery, the teasing, or the confidence, and whichever it was I would pursue that method till the end. Would I succeed? Oh give me but the chance to try, give me the solitude and the Lord [G.] and—you will see, dear old book, little confidence that you have in me, I think I would. The chances are ten to one against my having that chance, but if I have it! Believe me I will make the most of it. Oh how carefully I will watch what he likes best, what rubs him the wrong way. I will go so far as to take the most tremendous interest in his little finger. I will not omit to ask him how it happened that he became a little deaf in one ear. I will laugh at all his jokes and myself try to make him laugh with accounts of whatever I may think of. If I don't succeed—why then there must be something radically wrong with me. You say all that would not be shocking to him. No, but if all that had no effect I would try the shocking scheme. I would stuff him about America, I would tell him all the liberties we girls have, I would say it was so long now that I had not had an evening stroll with a man, so long, oh how I missed it, and I would sigh and describe an imaginary stroll I had in New York. I would arrange it so that at this point he must offer to take me for a stroll. Ah me! I would carry out the farce as long as possible, we would plan where we were to meet, where we would go, we would talk over what people would say, and then when we got on dangerous ground, as we most likely would, I would burst out laughing and tell him I had been fibbing as hard as possible, and pick up the American girls out of the dust where I had thrown them. It would be fun, at least it would make him laugh, he could not be bored talking about himself, and altogether we would have a different time from what he would have with an English girl. Vain, vain dreams, never to be realized, even were I to have the chance my stupid self would interfere. Oh why have I any self except what I should have? But the dream haunts me, torments me, makes me long at least for the opportunity. To make a man feel for me, thrill for me, long for me, worship me, care for a little while once for me, this, in my present mood, seems happiness. . . .

If Alfred were only with me tonight how much I would have to tell him! Poor boy, it is good for him he is not. It's only the excitement that makes me feel this way, and I know when the time arrives I shall be so frightened that I won't be able to open my mouth. Consequently I must think of something now, each day I will make a little list each time I think of it. Here goes to begin with:

1. The last day of Ascot.
2. The party I said I was going to at the Corks.
3. You said you were a little deaf in one ear, just how did it happen?
4. The Maharaja and his customs.
5. Are you going to the Bentinck dance?
6. What *have* you been doing since I saw you last?
7. I suppose you are longing for the season to be over here to get to your shooting, etc.
8. St. Margaret's. Where do you go to church?
9. Tell me something about English girls. I have not met one.
10. Do you read much? What kind of books?
11. Are you superstitious?
12. Character reading by hand or face.

JUNE 25TH

Another day gone, now we know Regi is sick [measles] and we cannot possibly sail on Saturday. We have to wait over a week or two, but then suppose I get sick too! I don't like to say what it is even to you, so I will call it "it." I have never had "it," but oh how I pray for Mama's and Papa's sake, as well as my own, I may be spared.

JUNE 26TH

"A Vanderbilt, and oh a Miss Vanderbilt—this will bring to light all the fortune hunters," the people I suppose say. "What! She is to be at the Bentincks' "—oh I hate it so I can't go on.

JUNE 27TH

As the hours pass my interest grows. Mama will not be able to go tomorrow, I think, so my picture will be slightly changed. I will be the one to lead the way and to be dignified, etc. For some reasons I am glad, I don't mean that in a disagreeable way at all, but it does put me not quite at my ease when Mama is there.

New Dresses this year. . . .

There follows a detailed list of thirty-two outfits, beginning with "Light blue crepon, white spots, trimmed with yellow (yellow hat)," after which are totals within each color category. Blue and pink, eight each, are her preferred colors.

It is evening, 9:50, and I am waiting for the time to come to dress to go to a reception. My hair has been carefully arranged by the hairdresser so I cannot lie down. I come to you for solace. How I long for excitement, for emotions, provided they are of the right sort. I realize tonight how true it is what Mrs. H. Ward says in *Marcella*—a man chooses the path that gives him the most thrill. That is what I want, I want someone to make me feel, feel this is indeed life. Understand, I don't want to fall in love, that would be both bothersome and useless. But I want for a little while to live completely. We fall so easily into a semi-conscious state, when we don't get anything out of life, we simply exist. If I could but thrill tonight for a few moments, for one blissful second, how happy I should be. See something, hear something, feel something to make me thrill through my whole being.

I can count the thrills of my life, they are so few and far between. Once it was when Sally (dear old Sally whom I don't care very much for now) took my hand. Again when Esther kissed me, and, I am ashamed now to confess it, when Mr. [Frank] Crowninshield [then an apprentice book publisher and later a fashionable magazine editor and patron of the arts] was talking to me that night at the Hunts. Strange now when I think of it, Mr. R[onalds] never made me thrill, once he made me feel all queer, but it was not a thrill. Take these three instances, the cause is not the same decidedly. I may have loved the two first, I certainly did not care much for the third. Why then did he make me feel that way? Sometimes I have thrilled at the opera when some beautiful note was sung and most often of all I have thrilled in my dreams. That dream I put down here (April 14th) made me thrill, that is why I wrote of it. Oct 15th [Esther again] is another instance when I spoke from the same cause. And Feb. 2nd and 4th are other entries [the anonymous bachelor].

I must certainly get a lock for this book, and I must also not forget to leave special instructions, in case I die suddenly, this is to be destroyed unread. When one uses such a book as a letter off of steam you understand it is private. . . .

JUNE 28th

It's over! It's over! It's over—and—and, oh where shall I begin, what shall I say. Well, the best thing is to tell you everything, everything. Ha, ha. In some ways it was so strikingly like my picture that I started and shook myself mentally as if I were dreaming. We started from the hotel at 7 minutes before 2 and reached the house a little after the appointed time. Papa thought we were late and so, though by the time we arrived we had laughed a great deal, we were very serious and subdued. A good many servants, it struck me, were standing about in the hall and we were taken upstairs after leaving our parasols. I did indeed feel shaky but, to tell the truth, was not thinking about myself, there were so many other things to think of. Our trio was as I described, theirs was slightly different. Yes, slightly. Though Lady Mar had on the black silk dress I felt sure she would, she was a remarkably young looking woman to be Lord G.'s mother. She is good looking and has light brown hair. Lord Mar is a little man and not tall as I imagined. His eye is not piercing, but he is rather old-fashioned. To go on—when we got in the room there were, besides our hosts, I think two men and a lady. I am not at all sure for I was naturally on the lookout only for the hosts. When this young looking woman stepped forward to receive us I could hardly believe my eyes. We shook hands all round. Mama was introduced by the Countess to a lady seated on the sofa, Papa talked to the Earl, and Lord G. fell to my share. I said right away so there was no awkward pause: "Did you go to Ascot again on Friday?" and we had quite a little conversation. More people arrived and finally, it seemed ages I must confess, lunch was announced. We were 12 in all and we filed down the stairs one by one. At the lunch table there were cards so we had no trouble in finding our seats. My fate was between a Lady somebody and Lord Garwick. And lunch began. Oh, if I could draw! Then you would see the whole affair. I would make everything a little exaggerated. There would be seated the Earl between two ferocious looking elderly ladies. Strict. English to the backbone. There would be Mama succeeding so wonderfully in concealing her real feelings that she appeared as unconcerned as to what was going on opposite as if I were no relative or even acquaintance. And Papa? Being entertained by the hostess but casting furtive glances at poor me across the table. Of course, Lord G. would be the center of interest. He would be bending over me in a half devoted, half terrified position, and I would be as unconcerned as you please. But this is exaggerated, and I must go on with the truth. For my part, I got on very well, yes very. We talked of Scotland, and Lord G. gave me a vivid description of a lovely trip and went so far as to say he would make out the whole plan and send it to me. Of course, I said oh no, it would give him too much trouble, etc., but he still insisted and we talked it all over, and finally he said "Oh, may I come and see you when you get back and hear all about it?" and I said: "Certainly, I should be very glad to see you." And he said: "Oh, may I call and see you?" and I said "Of course, I will be delighted to see you." And then I laughed in my inside but to him I smiled a little and he went on talking about Scotland. And then we talked of this, that and the other and by that time lunch was over and the females filed upstairs. Oh how funny, how ludicrously funny it was. When the men came up we only stayed a little while. Lord G. said a few words, walked downstairs with us, and when we got to the door I looked around to say good-bye (I had already said it once) but he was not there. I was on the step when suddenly a voice arrested me—it was Lord G.'s. "Won't you take this rose?" he said and presented me with a beautiful red rose. I scarcely had any breath left but I managed to say audibly: "Oh thank you, what a beautiful color." We then shook hands and parted—. As soon as we turned the corner we all burst into fits of laughter, fits really; for a little while we could not speak.

Though the *Letting-Off-Steam Book* ends here (coinciding with the final abandonment of her much more summary *History*), Gertrude still has a lot of men to meet and a lot of steam to let off concerning them, much of it to be expressed aggressively, as with Lord Garwick, in manipulation and teasing, based on her continuing insecurity and self-defensiveness. She is still trying to get used to being Miss Vanderbilt.

☙

Despite the family's precautions, Gertrude catches the measles from her brother and in mid-July, while recuperating, begins a new journal. At this time a Mr. Peal calls. "Mama and Papa were both out and I have never had such a satisfactory call." They talk about the differences between British and American society, and Gertrude "explained how, as there were so few people in American society, there could be no sets." He asks pointedly if she advises him to go to America, and she replies, "there may not be as many people as usual there, in fact I know there won't; but there may not be any more next year." In short, though she encourages him to visit, she makes it clear that American society is in Europe.

This incident she recognizes as "trifling. . . . One does not forget the main facts but there are always little words that are forgotten or looks or smiles." She remembers a dinner party during the past winter which she now wishes she had described in more detail. Mr. Ronalds "was so nice I could not resist. It was wrong, I daresay, but I could not help myself. It was as if he had tried to mesmerize me and I did not want to resist. I let him go on and on, saying things and looking things, until I think it went a little to my head. It was like champagne. Then the dinner came to an end and that put a stop to it. I was not the one to stop it as I should have been. . . . I have learned something since then. You! What have you learned? How I could make a man get flirtatious. I could watch him, study him, and work on his feelings. I could even make him rather like me by taking much interest in him personally and talking about him. That is a good deal to have learned. I am going to try it as soon as possible too. You will see how it works."

By the end of the month the family has returned from London to Newport, where Gertrude will have every opportunity to test her new skill in handling men. She hears that Mr. Ronalds will soon arrive. "I shall have to make a list and learn it by heart as I did before, for fear all ideas forsake me." It includes all the obvious topics concerning his summer and hers and extends to such questions as "Have you taken up bicycle riding? Do you approve of it for women?" Finally Gertrude sees Mr. Ronalds at the landing just before she is to leave on a yachting party. She barely has time to shake hands and say "how d'y'do," no time for lists, but the next day they are to meet at a dinner party at the Cushings'.

"I gathered my fan, gloves and handkerchief together and turned to see that I looked all right before leaving. I had thought sometimes that I was a little pretty. I was looking perhaps better than usual, but I was hideous. The green dress made like an old fashioned picture dress, which should have been becoming, was the only pretty thing about me. I wondered why I did not break the glass. Papa stood at the foot of the stairs and told me to hurry up, I would be late. I knew better." As they drive to the Cushings', Gertrude repeats ten to twelve times a prayer she made up long ago and says every night before going to bed: "Oh, God, give me grace and strength to do what is right and to look to Thee for help in all things."

Mr. Cushing greets Gertrude: "You are like the rest of your family, prompt."

"Yes," Gertrude replies, "when Papa has anything to do with my getting off, I am always the first. He stands in the hall with his watch in his hand."

Finally Mr. Ronalds speaks: "Your brother took your photograph this morning on the beach, did you know?"

"I know," Gertrude replies furiously, "he had no right to do such a thing."

They all laugh, and Edith Cushing asks, "As you were going in bathing?"

"No, worse still, as I was coming out."

We can almost see the suit clinging to Gertrude's tall handsome figure and almost see her blush as she reports her humiliation. She is as unwilling to accept her beauty on the beach that morning as in the mirror this evening. She really thinks that Mr. Ronalds would prefer to hear her list of topics, which she has barely the opportunity to get into before the evening is over. "How long would it be before I saw him again? I knew I would see his back at church, but was that all?"

It is. She sits behind him for an hour and a half, and he says only good morning "coming out of church, he was talking to Mama." However, that afternoon he calls, and Gertrude gets through more of her list. He asks if she is going on the Gerrys' moonlight sail: "The deck, you know, is to be all lighted up." She replies, "I will tell Mama that, perhaps that will influence her." Then they talk about golf and he gives her some pointers.

August rushes on, filled with dinners, dances, yachting, riding, swimming, golf. Count Reventhau and Count Castigliane appear, Count Lierstorpff reappears. Gertrude's affections shift somewhat from Regi Ronalds to Charlie and Bobby Sands, mostly to Bobby. And Harry Whitney begins to emerge as a close friend in whom she can confide, with the understanding that what is said will not be repeated to his sister—her friend Pauline. At the Brooks' in late August, Harry is her dinner partner, and Gertrude tells him what a good time she has been having.

"You will always have a good time because even when your looks give out you will still be a great heiress."

("No one else would have said it—I was delighted," Gertrude adds in her journal.)

"I am glad you are so frank," Gertrude says, looking at him intently.

"I don't think I ever need say things to you I do not mean."

"No, exactly. What is the good of having old friends, if they do not say what they mean?"

"I will always tell you the truth."

"Will you really? Always? Then if I ever want to ask you anything, you will tell me exactly what your opinion is?"

"Yes. Then that is an agreement; and if I don't want to tell you, I will say so."

"Agreed."

"I like that."

"And I have perfect trust and confidence in you."

After dinner Esther Hunt, who was seated too far from Gertrude to permit conversation, compliments her on her looks.

"It's happiness," Gertrude says, laughing. (In her journal she now adds, "I only told her I had enjoyed myself. No one could quite have understood how, so I said no more.")

The importance to Gertrude of her understanding with Harry becomes increasingly evident. She has spent two mornings on the beach with his friend Rawlins L. Cottenet, but has "not yet quite made him out. Either there is nothing at all to him or there is a great deal indeed. There is no inbetween for him, I think. Harry is a great friend of his and that makes me think there is much underneath. I told Harry that night at the Brooks that I judged men from whether they have many men friends, not from whether they have many girl friends, and he said: 'You have started out with the right ideas,' and I was glad he said it because, though I knew it to be true, I liked to have him acknowledge it. He is so strong and true, Harry, one can look up to him in everything. I wish he would tell me things. He always makes me feel as if I must tell him everything. And he is interested too. He cannot act what he does not feel. I wish I could see him often, but he has gone away now and will not be back again. I care more about his opinion than anyone else's. It makes me feel happy whenever I think of our agreement. I mean to ask him things whenever I feel like it. I should like to ask him something now, but am afraid. It is this—"

Once again Gertrude resorts to an imaginary letter. Once again she begins insecurely and self-defensively: "Dear Harry, Do you remember the night at Mrs. Brooks' when you took me into dinner and we made that agreement? I hope you have not forgotten it. . . ." And once again she states her theme, warming to it with this young man from a family at least as distinguished as her own and very rich, though not *as* rich (none is): "I am an heiress—consequently I know perfectly well there are lots of men who would be attentive to me simply on account of that. When I first fully realized that to be the case I was terribly unhappy and wished I might be a poor girl so that people would only like me for myself. Now I have become used to the thought and I face it boldly, as I must, and try to make the most of it. What I want to know is this—do you think it possible for anyone to love me for myself entirely? That the money would—no, could—make no difference? That anyone in all the world would not care for the money but would care as much as his life for me?" The theme is further elaborated upon, the letter continues for another page, and is signed "Your true friend/Gertrude."

She knows that sending such a letter would be "impossible. . . . It would sound funny, to say the least, and rather fishing." Instead she writes yet another imaginary letter, this one passionate, addressed to "Dearest _____." Though possibly connected with the letter to Harry (". . . you had entered into my life and taken possession of my soul. Someday you will take possession of everything that is mine, my worldly goods and my self"), the blank is more likely an imaginary composite, since Gertrude ends by saying that if she sees "_____ tomorrow I will be able to tell you how deep [my love] is," and Harry has already left Newport.

September 5, three days after the long journal entry containing its two imaginary letters, Gertrude begins a separate book of characterizations called *People* (not to be confused with *People I Meet*, which is now abandoned). It could more accurately have been called *Men*—it contains no women. She introduces the volume with two pages of generalizations. "People are the most interesting study in the world. . . . We are apt to divide people into classes, to put them under heads or to think them all very nearly alike. It is impossible to class people. No two individuals in the world are enough alike to go in the same class. How wonderful it is when one thinks of it, because there are comparatively few characteristics divided between us; still we manage so to place them together that a different result is obtained each time. In studying people remember that the wise judge by little things." The admonition is presumably to herself. Yet despite it, the characterizations of her male friends, mostly suitors, are broad and contain virtually no physical description. Among the initial portraits (those actually written on September 5) is:

HARRY WHITNEY: You give the impression of being thoroughly trustworthy. You are so truthful and frank that it is refreshing to be with you. You may be too much so to succeed very well in business. You cannot fail to have many friends, you will certainly have enemies as well. [This characterization, a particularly short one, will, like many in the book, be added to during the next two years.]

Though Gertrude is concentrating on men and considering them as prospective husbands, Esther Hunt is still concentrating on Gertrude, who, in mid-September, writes: "I don't know what is the matter, I feel so queerly. No one cares for me except Esther, no one takes any interest in me." The truth is that many men are very interested in her and she in them—among the most prominent at this time: Moses Taylor, her dead brother Bill's roommate at Yale and, like him, the grandson of a railroad capitalist; Lloyd Warren, a well-connected young architect; and Howard Cushing, a sensitive academic painter, about six years older than Gertrude, who is frequently listed along with his cousin Edith and other members of his prominent Newport family at Gertrude's dinner parties. By the end of September, Gertrude has made charts in her journal, recording, hour by hour, the time spent with "Mo" and with "Mr. Warren," and by the beginning of October, when Regi Ronalds is due to arrive in Newport, she compares his eyes with "three other sets of eyes that are attractive besides his to me. Those are Howard Cushing's, they are so cold and distant; Mo Taylor's, they are so warm and true; and Lloyd Warren's, they are so deep and changeable. R. Ronalds' are passionate, tender, but they might be false, I wish they were true."

The comparisons continue; the hours with Mo accumulate, total more than those with any of her other suitors. Pauline Whitney—accompanied by a maid and her brother Harry—comes to visit Gertrude. Harry immediately goes to see Mo.

> . . . I should like to have a talk with Harry alone. Why did he go off to Mo? Why didn't he go off with me? He did not want to, child, as if anyone under the sun did. How anyone can see anything in you I am sure I don't know. You are only nice looking, you are not one bit entertaining or amusing, you are stupid, you are conceited, and you are tiresome, you are weak, you are characterless, you are cold and reserved, small and narrow minded, ignorant and unwilling to learn, you think you are always in the right, you are shy and foolish, your waist is big, your hands and arms badly formed, your features out of proportion, your face red, your legs long, now—what have you to say for yourself?
> I have something to say in spite of all that. You know my hair is curly, my mouth small and red, my complexion very good, my movements graceful, my expression sweet.

She does not defend her hands, which everyone else finds exquisitely well shaped. No, she has already been too kind to herself. Masochistically she piles on more abuse:

> Stop, that is nothing, you exaggerate. Your hair is curly but not a pretty color, simply a dull brown. Your mouth may be small and red but it is weak, your complexion is too red and spotty, you are not graceful, your expression, when you have any, is stupid.
> My voice, then, it is said to be silvery?
> Yes, perhaps by some idle talker who wanted to flatter you.

With Harry gone, after a brief visit and one "nice talk," Gertrude focuses more completely on Mo. Again the recorded hours with him accumulate. Before a brief trip to Connecticut, she writes him an imaginary letter:

> . . . Oh, Mo, I will miss you very much. Miss passing you in the street, miss knowing you are not very far off and we may meet any moment. . . . Now why can't I send you this letter, just as it is, in-

stead of writing it here where you will never, never see it? And why can't you answer it in just the same spirit it was written, the spirit of truth? Why are there so many conventionalities? If we could only be above them, or below them, or whatever it is, so that we might be to each other as we really are, not as we appear to strangers. . . . I wish I could see into you for a second. I don't mean to let myself get fond of you, I mean very fond, because it would not pay. You would not get fond of me and I would be the one to suffer. . . .

The impossibility of a free and open relationship with Mo, or with any of the men she knows, tortures Gertrude. She feels an "extreme blueness. It is Esther perhaps. I loved her more yesterday afternoon than I have ever done before. I felt more thrill at her touch, more happiness in her kiss." Not only are these intimacies with Esther possible—permitted, except from Mrs. Vanderbilt's viewpoint—but intimacies of correspondence too. As a woman, Esther can write tenderly and lovingly to Gertrude, addressing her as "Dearest" or "My Dearest," quoting poetry, signing "Yours/" or "Your/Esther." She can write as none of Gertrude's male suitors can permit himself to.

For about a year Gertrude, Esther, and Mo (who is fond of Esther too) will be a romantic triangle, the first of several such triangles involving Esther, in which no one except Esther fully understands what is happening. The first Saturday in November these three—along with Mrs. Vanderbilt, her sister Cettie Shepherd, Cornelius, Jr., Mrs. Taylor, Romold Dahlgren, and Lispenard Stewart (a practicing lawyer, twenty years older than Gertrude, who represents his mother's family interests in the Rhinelander estate)—all go to Providence in Mr. Vanderbilt's private car for the Yale-Brown football game. They are met by three carriages. Mrs. Vanderbilt takes Esther and Mo in hers, as if taking special charge of them. In Providence they are met by Frank Andrews, another Newport summer resident (from a prominent Washington, D.C., family) whom Gertrude has met the previous September through Mo's sister Netta and described then as "Fussy, so-so looking, affected accent, frivolous, not much character, 27." Gertrude has not changed her mind and describes him now as "awful indeed. He imagines, or sees fit to let me imagine, he is in love with me." And yet (many words later): "If I wanted, I could make him propose in less than a week."

However, once again the Newport postseason is over—prematurely for Gertrude, who has an attack of jaundice which interferes with the possibility of a proposal from Frank as well as normal farewells to Mo. When she recovers, the family returns to New York by way of Boston and Concord to visit Alfred at St. Paul's. In anticipation of the return, Gertrude writes: "I don't think it good to see too much only of one person . . . it is dangerous. Foolish! I do believe, however, in platonic friendship. . . . What I should like most next winter . . . would be to have, say, three men friends of whom I would see a great deal. . . . Mo would do for one. Now let us think of the others. Harry Whitney would be just the thing, but he is going away, alas. . . ."

On the train from Boston, "shaking so I can hardly write," Gertrude thinks that "the only way to enjoy [life] most is to have other interests besides the social ones. If I could have some interest, some purpose that would furnish me with thought matter, but not take more time than I would have to spare, it would be so nice. . . . How would it do to write a book! You could be plotting and planning all day long and you could write, say, an hour and a half or two hours a day on it. Choose a subject which really interests you and which must be read up on and weave about it a romance, not sentimental or trifling, but of real, true live people. Let it be different from the majority of books—original and fresh. Do your very best by it. Put all that is best in you in the book, no platitudes, but daring thought, the kind that will be laughed at by certain people but will be read. Don't do anything in a hurry, don't mind rewriting, correcting or taking pains over. Study human nature for your characters. Have a rhetoric by you. Write in short, crisp sentences. Don't be afraid to put your own thoughts down, they are the thoughts of the world. Have an ideal which you strive to reach, don't let that ideal be another book, but something in you. Oh! If I could but do this. But you can, of course it will fall very short of your ideal, but try to make something of it—and then show it to Miss Winsor." (*A Foreign Experience*, an unfinished novel begun about now, is based at least partly on the Vanderbilt family's adventures abroad with Lord Garwick and others.)

In New York, there is little time to spare. Mr. Andrews pursues Gertrude. Mo comes down from New Haven. Regi Ronalds and Bronson Winthrop (another attorney, this one about ten years older than Gertrude, and a descendant of the governor of Massachusetts Bay Colony) are invited by the Vanderbilts to dinner and the opera. "At least 24 men came in the box (of all ages) so you can imagine it was fun. . . ." Friday, November 30, Gertrude goes to the opera again, and Saturday to Regi Ronalds' football party. It is only the beginning of December. Through the month, dinners, dances, and the opera follow each other almost night after night. When there is no "event," Gertrude makes visits or receives visitors, and one night there is a musicale at Uncle George's, one night a concert. No wonder there are only lists of the events themselves and the names of those who attend them, the now familiar names. In the journal, the days seem suddenly empty, so focused are they on the nights—the invitations, the thank-you notes, the visits to couturiers and hatmakers and hairdressers—that Gertrude barely has time for an occasional ride in Central Park or a visit to an art gallery. By the end of the year, after just a month and one week in New York, she is bored—by Mo as well as by almost everyone else.

⇐ *1895*

An exception is Esther. Early in 1895—perhaps for Gertrude's twentieth birthday—Esther gives her a leather-bound album with the silver initials "G.V." mounted on the cover and the inscription:

To my Gertrude

To see her is to love her,
And love but her forever,
For Nature made her what she is
And never made another.

I have gathered a posie of other men's flowers, and nothing but the thread that binds them is my own—

from
Esther

On the face of each of the sixty pages (and sometimes on the back as well) Esther has transcribed an anthology of love poems extending from the Elizabethans to the Victorians and including also a few of the French Romantics. This is but one labor of love. There is also a short birthday poem and two days later a very long letter in which she chides Gertrude for not telling Mo's sister Netta that she (Gertrude) likes Esther

. . . better than any other girl—Why if you like her to know that I like you best don't you like her to know that you like me best? Gertrude dearest, I love you so entirely that if I thought you really liked anyone else more than you do me, I do not know what I should do. . . . Sweetheart, I wonder if you really know how much you are to me—Do you ever feel blue for me and does your heart ever ache for me? Gertrude, answer this letter in the evening when you have gone up to bed and keep it before you—I love you and I would give *anything* in this world if you were only Gertrude—anything but Vanderbilt—Somehow I always feel as if your Mother thought you were too good for anyone to know well because of this and yet there are many things that equal money, more than equal it, but America seems given over to nothing but this—Please take this in the right way, my Gertrude, if you are to be open with me, I am going to be entirely so with you—I want you now, all the time, I slept with your letter in my hand under my pillow, I mean the one about not coming for you etc.—I had already ordered the violets and I sent up to Miss Fadden's and told her not to send them—Think she sent me a bunch of violets this morning as a present, I had just come in from the dentist and found them and your letter—Bless you, my own Sweetheart, it gave me so much so much pleasure, I have read it three times and only had it—four hours—Think of coming to see you when I was not allowed to, I was good wasn't I?—I took Kitty for a drive Friday afternoon and then went to see Netta, as I had promised to, I did not feel like her, Gertrude, I will not let her hold my hand if you mind, I don't care and I don't like you to hold anyone's, really I don't, anyhow you can't kiss anyone the way you kiss me, Dearest, you couldn't, you never want to, do you? Gertrude, I love you too much to be teased. You have been my one great pleasure this summer and the only thing I did not like was your not telling me more about yourself, now it will be different, and my Darling, we shall keep it different. What you tell me is too sacred for me to think of repeating, you know this—Do you like Charlotte Barnes so very much? Please say you don't *love* her. . . . I wish you would have regular days for me, and that you would keep to them like a lesson—Every other day is not enough but this is all you will do—No one need know, not one girl. . . .

You might just as well be abroad for all I see of you—Do you care anymore? Or were you only pretending—This morning I spent at home waiting for you and this afternoon I have stayed in till four, hoping you would come—I could not go to you because you did not ask me to—Gertrude, really I love you, and I thought you were never going to do these thoughtless things anymore. . . . Dearest, can you come to me to-morrow morning—I must see you—Unless of course you do not care—Gertrude, you cannot know how much I love you—

Also early in the year—it is dated "1895 to All Time" and may have been intended as an additional birthday present or a New Year's gift— Esther sends Gertrude a "little book of [eight] love letters" for "sometime when you are tired or blue." Though the theme is consistent, the variations are remarkably inventive, ranging from near-abstract generalizations to very intense physicality. An example of the latter:

My Darling—
It is when the lights are out and when I am all alone and all is quiet, that most I want you—Then, if you could only come to me and lie beside me and let my arms enfold you, and let me feel your dear head so near to me, that to reach my heaven I only had to lean a little more towards you and draw you closer—Your mouth—Gertrude, your mouth someday will drive my crazy, I kiss it softly at first, per-

haps shortly too, then for longer, then somehow I want you all, entirely, and almost I care not if I hurt you—then gently again, because I am sorry—So I love, even worship you—

Esther—

What is Gertrude's reaction to all this? Obviously she is not aloof. She sees Esther a great deal. She responds to many of her letters. She, too, sends gifts. However, even having just one side of the correspondence, it is clear that Gertrude sees Esther and writes to her less often than Esther wants, many times only after supplication. Furthermore, in Esther's letters there are frequent references to dates broken by Gertrude, appointments not kept, letters unanswered, what, in general, Esther calls "thoughtless things." But are they "thoughtless" or carefully, defensively thought out? We can only guess at how frightened Gertrude may have become as Esther's passion intensifies. We may wonder, too, as Esther does in her long letter, if Gertrude really knows how much she is to her friend. And, finally (knowing that there is no "finally," that the possibilities are infinite), we may ask how much Mama's objections to the relationship stimulate Gertrude's rebelliousness and assertion of independence. For whatever reasons, both conscious and unconscious, there is no question that Gertrude teases Esther, alternately encouraging and discouraging her, in much the same way Gertrude teases her other suitors; and of these there continue to be many.

On her birthday Gertrude writes: "Alas, I am out of my teens today! Alas, I am no more very young. Alas, when a girl is twenty she is on the road to being an old maid."

Ten days later Gertrude's engagement to Moses Taylor is reported on the front page of the *World* as "rumored in club circles." The rumor is quickly denied in the evening papers. The next day Gertrude turns to Miss Winsor in her "tiny little room, oh so delightfully cozy and well fixed" where they talk mostly of "society," and a few days later, perhaps still looking for answers, Gertrude does "something I ought not to have done." She goes with her maid to see a fortuneteller—recommended by Mr. Lawrence—on Eighth Avenue, above a saloon. The trip by hansom, the wait in the parlor, the apprehension, the furnishings are all described in detail. Finally a Negress bids Gertrude enter the bedroom where she is told to take off her gloves, shuffle the cards, and make a wish. Gertrude wishes she "would have as good a time next winter as I was having this." The fortuneteller says Gertrude's wish will come true and then proceeds to read the cards. Gertrude concentrates hard, later recording six pages of what the woman says. Much of it, having to do with wealth, education, et cetera, is obvious from Gertrude's manner and appearance, but some things must have struck Gertrude as more intuitive, even if safe, fortune-telling guesses: "You are before the public in some way. . . . Have you thought of adopting a profession? . . . You have great facility for using your fingers. . . . There is a young man who loves you *very, very* much and wants to marry you. . . . There is another man who is studying law and who likes you very much. You are connected with horses in your life . . . You will have two proposals very soon. You will be married in a year from now. There is a lady who is very fond of you and would do anything for you. . . ."

≈

The Vanderbilts have been planning a trip to Europe in mid-February, but on the last day of January Marguerite Shepard, aged fourteen, "the youngest child of Papa's oldest sister," dies of pneumonia, and two weeks later Cornelius breaks out with the measles at college. The trip is postponed, Gertrude "disappointed and at the same time delighted," because since the death of her cousin she has been seeing a lot of Bobby Sands. Indeed she is supposed to go to a dance with him the night after Marguerite's death and writes to him so he can get another partner. He replies with a sympathetic note, followed by violets and then a condolence call. "That night I could not sleep. From 1:30 to 5:30 I lay and thought and my thoughts would not let me sleep." Though we don't know Gertrude's exact thoughts, they are surely centered on Marguerite's death, on Bobby Sands's "more than ordinary niceness," and, once again, on Esther Hunt.

During the next few weeks, before the Vanderbilts' departure for Europe, Bobby Sands acts as a go-between for Esther and Gertrude at the same time as Esther plays this role for Gertrude. For example, Sands takes Gertrude to a small jeweler on Broadway where she orders "a locket made for Esther with my photo in it and one for me with hers." He also sees to the details of delivering the photographs to the jeweler and having the bill sent to him so Gertrude won't be embarrassed with her mother. Simultaneously Gertrude meets him at Esther's for unchaperoned walks. On one walk (not emanating from Esther's but from a luncheon at the home of Sands's sister, Mrs. Havemeyer) Gertrude dismisses her maid and she and Sands go up Fifth Avenue to the Metropolitan Museum. "As we looked over the same catalogue together, as we stood near together, nearer perhaps than was positively necessary, and talked about the warm or cold color in some landscape, I was very happy and sometimes a thrill passed through me. How Mr. Sands felt I cannot tell for sure. I know that his eyes had a strange look in them and that at times he was quite peculiar. Once we sat down to look at some picture together and while I fumbled through two or three catalogues to find it, he sat as if dazed. Oh! Can it be—no, no, I dare not think so. . . ."

That night, again, she cannot sleep. "I got up at last and made up my mind to take something to make me sleep. The only thing I had was a pill that I take when I am unwell and have pain. It has morphine in it and always makes me sleep. Well, it had that effect and others too that were not as agreeable. I feel rather miserably today. That accounts, I suppose, for my blueness." In the morning Esther arrives with a letter from Sands asking when he can see Gertrude. As much as Gertrude wants to see him, she has Esther write that "Miss V. can't make any arrangement about seeing you today as she is very busy." However, Gertrude permits Esther herself to advise Sands to call late in the afternoon but to do as he thinks best. Gertrude spends a good part of the afternoon writing a dialogue with her journal:

BOOK: . . . Remember he will like you all the better for having difficulties in the way.

GERTRUDE: Yes, I will remember. Your advice is good. I will tell him how fond of Mo I am. I will apparently be talking perfectly freely —as if he were a good friend indeed—and I will try and make him jealous. If he cares at all he will be.

BOOK: Good. Only remember you don't care.

GERTRUDE: No, I don't care.

BOOK: Repeat it to yourself as you go down in the little elevator. Over and over again—I don't care—I don't care—

Mr. Sands doesn't come that day but sends pink roses with a letter. "Enough to say I wrote him he could walk up from Miss Hunt's with me the next day." Sands is hesitant about calling too often. The day after this walk he sends a bunch of violets with "best wishes," and the next day more roses, "white this time, all snow white. The letter that accompanied them said business had prevented his coming. I did not believe it. He wanted to see if I cared. . . ."

Between visits and communications from Bobby Sands and Mo Taylor and until the family's departure, Gertrude attracts many other suitors— principally Mr. Cottenet, Mr. Lawrence, and Mr. Harrison—but she writes most lengthily in her journal, about Bobby Sands's acceptability, saying she has "not been able to make out much" about what her mother thinks of him, nor does she think Mama "knows at all that I care in the least. . . . Cornelius does not like him, I am almost sure, but then he does not know him, the same with Alfred." Gertrude doesn't say what her father thinks about Sands. With him she focuses on herself: "I am sure Papa hates me. Perhaps not exactly that, but he does not like me. I don't know what I have done, but I think it is more what I have not done. He does not think anything I do is right, he thinks me still nothing but a child and—lots more, I know it, I feel it. My instinct tells me it is so, and a woman's instinct is right. I am a woman now, I know that too. I have changed lately, perhaps Papa feels *that* and it may be what he does not like."

Gertrude looks back to her entry, before the winter began, and sees how far short of her plans she has fallen: "How about the book—how about the study it was going to bring you, the change of thought it was going to suggest? How about all this? It was then only a phantom of the imagination, ah me, child, you would have done better had you followed the higher instincts within you. And how have your days been spent—tell me? Put it down in black and white and then you will see the waste of time it shows. Well, here—breakfast often, very often, upstairs. At ten, after a dinner; none at all, often after a dance since I was not called till one. What was left of the morning was divided into two parts, one answering notes, the other walking. After lunch came a little practicing or reading, but very little, say half an hour, then out with Mama, calling, or down to see Esther with my maid, or to the Skating Club, or to see someone else. Home at about five when there were almost always visits and then just time to dress for dinner at eight."

That is the last entry Gertrude has time to make before the family—all except Cornelius, Jr., and Alfred—is aboard ship. There, on Cunard stationery, she describes her last hectic day in New York. It is a condensation or recapitulation of the past three months. Gertrude has a music lesson right after breakfast. Then, while her maid is busy packing, Gertrude goes alone ("extraordinary for me") to see Esther. ". . . we fixed ourselves comfortably on the sofa for a nice long stay. I don't say talk because sometimes we hardly speak at all. Esther puts her arm about my waist and I put my head on her shoulder and we are happy. But Tuesday morning we were more talkative than usual. We remembered all the time, though we tried to forget, that it would be six weeks before we saw each other again. Esther insisted upon my staying to lunch and at last I consented, then after she came up with me in the omnibus. When we got to the house she came in really to say good-bye. It was twenty minutes past three when she left. I had made an engagement to walk with Mr. Sands at three-thirty."

Gertrude has made the date for this hour because she expects her mother to be out. But Mama is home and Gertrude decides to wait downstairs so she and Sands can leave unseen. She waits in her black dress, jacket, hat, and sable. Sands is late. At three-forty Gertrude has just made up her mind to visit Miss Winsor when Sands appears, looking tense, and Gertrude thinks maybe she would have done better to visit Miss Winsor. However, once they leave the house and walk into Central Park, Sands relaxes.

"How did you get away?" he asks.

"Oh, it was such fun." She laughs and explains "a little," but now Gertrude becomes somewhat tense and self-conscious. "I suppose you don't see two well dressed people often walking along the little paths of the park unless something is up." Men seem to be scrutinizing them, women to be glancing knowingly at each other and making remarks. As they return

Sands gives Gertrude a gold pencil which she does not want to accept but cannot give any reason not to. Gertrude pays him twenty dollars for the lockets. He asks if he may write to her in Europe. Yes, she replies, she would be glad to hear from him but is a very bad correspondent herself. "Not allowed to write?" No answer. At the house, Sands decides he had better not come in since there are several carriages outside the door. He will see her, anyway, that night at Winkie Cutting's dinner party.

Mrs. Vanderbilt is downstairs receiving visitors. Gertrude goes up to her own room to finish packing until a little after five when Mo arrives. They talk, he wishes her a pleasant trip, they shake hands. "I said something, I don't know exactly what, and he left. How a few short weeks can change things. I think (I am not sure) I am the same to Mo as I used to be, but he is not the same to me. Not that I ever came near loving him, oh no, but still he was most in my thoughts."

Gertrude is in her room again, with Gladys now, when the butler asks if she will see Mr. Lawrence.

"Yes," Gertrude replies.

"But, Sister," Gladys exclaims, "you won't have time to dress, and it's one of those old long stayers."

"I will send him away in ten minutes," Gertrude says, rehooking her dress and smoothing her hair.

She tries, but Mr. Lawrence, overcome with emotion, barely able to speak, clings to her outstretched hand. Finally she gets rid of him, dresses, goes to the Cuttings', says good-bye again to Bobby Sands. With last-minute packing, it is two before she gets to bed.

The next morning, aboard Cunard's R(oyal) M(ail) S(teamer) *Lucania*, where, as sometimes in the past, the printed List of Saloon Passengers is dominated by Vanderbilts—

Mr. Cornelius Vanderbilt,
and Manservant.
Mrs. Vanderbilt,
and Maid.
Miss Vanderbilt,
and Maid.
Mr. R. C. Vanderbilt.
Miss G. M. Vanderbilt,
Maid,
and Special Stewardess.

—Gertrude is surrounded by flowers from friends including, of course, Bobby Sands, who, the steward tells her, has sent a box for every day of the crossing. Gertrude records the kind of flower for each day of the uneventful trip:

. . . violets, white roses, orchids, violets, red roses . . . it was a good idea and really thoughtful of him, don't you think so, old book?

Thoughtful—humph—yes—rather.

What do you mean by looking so wise?

Oh, well I guess you know as well as I do. What did your family say to this?

Again, no answer.

The family spends a week in London, a day in Paris, and then goes to Nice by train, "the whole of a sleeping car (really for eighteen people) for which Papa paid 3,000 francs." In Nice, Gertrude receives her first mail from the States. She is disappointed that there is no letter from Mr. Sands but tries to convince herself that she doesn't care. There are, among other letters not recorded, two from "faithful" Esther, and a proposal from the persistent but peripheral Mr. Lawrence.

Gertrude writes in her journal that this letter "finished the comedy or tragedy, whichever you choose to call it." Among her papers she saves the draft of her reply (with the one sentence shown here in parentheses, actually crossed out):

Dear Mr. Lawrence,

Your letter which I have just received pains me extremely, for while I appreciate very highly the compliment you pay me, I must tell you that my feelings for you are those of a friend only. I have never thought of you in any other light. (This must be my excuse if my manner has in any way misled you.) I hope we may still & always be friends although nothing more. What you have said to me I consider sacred, it will never be repeated.

Believe me

Sincerely yours
G. Vanderbilt

As the family moves from Nice to Geneva to Florence, Gertrude still waits in vain for word from Mr. Sands and turns increasingly toward her little sister Gladys, who "seems to love me more every day. If it were possible to love more, my affection for her would be increasing, but it is not. My whole heart and soul are wrapped up in her. I sometimes think that is why I don't care more for Esther. Oh, I wish I did, I wish I could, but it's impossible. I really try and when we are together a great deal I think I really do love her, but when we are separated—that is the test—I find my heart is not always warm. Sometimes for a day or so she does not come into my thoughts. . . .

"When Alice and I were great friends it was when we were apart that I felt most how I loved her. Well, love is not a thing that can be trifled with, or made to take one course or another. Certainly that is one thing

I have learned from experience. I love Miss Winsor, I am sure. I love Gladys with all my heart and soul, and Alfred too. Love, love, what is it anyway? I told Esther I would write a book for her of quotations that I thought appropriate to her, but I can't. Am I really changeable? Oh no. It's that I really did not care.

"When I have Gladys in my arms and press her against my heart I know what love is, at least I know how it feels to love tenderly, truly, deeply, sincerely. My love for her can never change, and when I see how she comes to me in her little troubles or when she is tired and puts two tender arms around my neck and her head on my breast, it makes me feel that here is the pleasure of my life, here is someone who needs and loves to have me. Esther does too, I must not forget it. She needs me now, needs me to be happy. Oh, God has given me much in this world to be thankful for, yet, why can't I love Esther? Forgive."

Late in March Gertrude writes that she "might just as well be in New York for all I tell you about my travels. It's disgraceful. One would think I was not interested in all I see. I am most deeply interested. I love sightseeing and read the guidebooks and look at the objects with care and appreciation. To prove this to you, from memory I will tell you what I saw yesterday. . . ." She begins with the streets, neither narrow enough to be interesting nor wide enough to be impressive. She compares Italian civilization with that of Germany. She describes the Church of Santa Croce, on a square of the same name, where a statue of Dante was erected in 1865. After two pages, she stops in the middle of a sentence. We feel her relief as well as our own, and we begin to feel that, though she still has the now occasional need to prove the contrary, traveling for her is finally becoming more than cataloguing.

As Gertrude "faces home" she attempts writing a story. It is as fragmentary and incomplete as her description of Florence, and yet again we feel that she is maturing, that she knows she doesn't *have* to write, that she is allowed to enjoy Paris. "Paris once more! I have nothing to tell you just now, my mind is turned the wrong way." But, of course, for this moment it is turned the right way—toward Paris. There what gives her the most pleasure is seeing Howard Cushing, who is continuing his art studies at the Académie Julien. He has tried unsuccessfully to communicate with the Vanderbilts but meets Gertrude by accident at the Louvre.

He was copying a picture by Velasquez and standing way in the corner of one of the big rooms. He had come forward as if he was not quite sure if it was myself, but it attracted my attention and I went over to him with my hand extended. I was truly glad to see him and he really seemed glad to see me. We had such a nice little talk, very little indeed it was. He said how sorry he was not to have seen me and said he had a sort of feeling I would come to the Louvre. And I asked him about his work and he told me he had eight pictures in the Salon and he is coming back to Newport the 1st of June. He seemed sorry when I told him I would be in Lenox all June, but he said, "You will be back just in time for the bathing," which of course led to our talking and laughing about last year's bathing. We spoke of Adele's engagement [to J. Burden], he asked about it, and a few more things and then I felt I must go. He said again how sorry he was about not having seen me more and spoke of lunching with him in his studio and I said—till Newport then—and we shook hands and I left.

The Vanderbilts have been abroad for about six weeks. In London on their way home, a forwarded letter from Robert Sands finally arrives just before Gertrude joins her family for breakfast.

PAPA: "That letter came this morning in another envelope marked 'Immediate and Important' and I had to give a receipt for it. . . . Who is it from?"

GERTRUDE ("innocently"): "Why it looks like Mr. Sands's hand-writing. Let me see."

At this moment something is passed to Gertrude and she puts the letter on the table.

MAMA: "Yes, let's see."

Mrs. Vanderbilt tears open the envelope and seems to be doing more than look at the signature.

GERTRUDE: "Here, I can look. I suppose I have a right to read my own letters."

MAMA (having turned the last page): "Yes, it is Mr. Sands."

Gertrude reads the twelve pages, full of gossip—several references to Esther and to how much she misses Gertrude; a description of the eighteenth birthday party of Gertrude's cousin Consuelo, including seating lists very much like those in Gertrude's journals and the rather pointed report that after supper Mo Taylor "devoted himself to Miss Livingston"; the "universal topic of conversation," the marriage of Anna Gould to Count Boni de Castellane ("One would have thought that the son or daughter of an American Emperor was being married"); activities of the Strollers (formerly the Columbia College Dramatic Club) with which Sands is associated. . . . The letter is signed "very sincerely yours, Robert G. Sands." It was "apparently written to be read by anyone—even Mama," who later in the morning asks, "Was it a letter like the one you had a short time ago?" Gertrude, understanding the reference to Mr. Lawrence's proposal, says, "No, no, of course not. It was just New York news."

⇌

A Mr. Evans—"nice looking and amusing," age thirty-five—adds interest to the return passage, if only because he is able to spend much time on deck alone with Gertrude while Mama sleeps late in the morning and while Papa naps in the afternoon. However, at times Gladys would "perch herself on the chair next to me and listen to what we were saying out of her sharp little ears." At other times, when Evans is being most chivalrous —wishing, for example, that a storm will delay their arrival—Gertrude wonders if he has made up his mind "to do his best with the heiress." And at still other times, while they sit silently watching the ocean, she is imagining "when and how I would meet Mr. Sands for the first time when I came back."

She does not have a long wait to find out. The Sunday after they return the callers begin arriving—Mr. Cushing (just back from Europe a little before her), Mr. Ronalds, Mr. Sands . . . When Gertrude hears his name announced she doesn't "know what Mr. Cushing was saying. I know he was talking and I was apparently listening. Mr. Sands shook hands with Mama first, who was by the tea table. I was off in the middle of the room. We shook hands. He was pale, I don't know what I was. One of the men with Mama left, Mr. Sands joined that group." More visitors arrive: the indefatigable Mr. Lawrence, Mr. William Jay Schieffelin (who is married to Louise, the second eldest of Gertrude's Shepard cousins). . . . "The end of it was I did not see Mr. Sands a minute alone." He remedies this the next day with a blooming azalea and an invitation to the opera. When Gertrude accepts, violets arrive. At the opera they talk through an act and afterward, while waiting for the carriage, their eyes meet in operatic intimacy. Gertrude knows that Bobby Sands loves her and is quite sure she doesn't love him. This is confirmed the following night at the Gerrys' when she has a very enjoyable time with Mo Taylor but is aware always of Bobby Sands watching her, looking at her lovingly. She doesn't know what to do, feels that she is being led into doing an unkind thing. "To let a man propose when he has shown you in a thousand ways that he loves you, and then throw him over is, to say the least, unkind. Conclusion—you must stop it this minute! There is no time to spare. . . . Don't see him tomorrow when he comes. Don't make any other engagement to see him. Don't look at him. Don't think of him. Don't talk to him."

Despite these resolutions Gertrude does nothing, and her ambivalence intensifies. A few days later she is "Saved! Saved from a terrible calamity" when Mr. Sands sends her a telegram from Philadelphia saying he has been delayed there and cannot call. Her problem seems to have solved itself. She goes off gaily to a dinner party at the Burdens'. ". . . I never had a better time in my life. I lost my heart to Mr. [James] Appleton who was so nice that I believe in the whole world there is no one quite as nice. . . . He is the best looking man I have ever known and he is simply a brick. . . ." The superlatives roll on, but as usual background is taken for granted: heir to the Waltham watch fortune, Harvard '88, outstanding American breeder of beagle hounds. Mr. Rawlins Cottenet is also "extremely nice," his background, also undescribed, less typical: unlike most of the Vanderbilt circle, except for Howard Cushing, Cottenet is already dedicated to the arts—a fine musician who plays several instruments, composes songs, and has a profound knowledge of opera. And there's Mo, whom she wishes she "could see [her] way clear with." There's a whole world of men, dozens she has met, dozens she will yet meet. In this frame of mind she is less concerned about unkindness to Bobby Sands: "Shall I run [him] to the death and then tell him I thought it was only friendship between us, or shall I put a stop to the hunt halfway and spoil the sport?" She softens, rephrases the question: "Shall I be heartless enough to cause him more pain than is absolutely necessary? I believe he loves me truly. I know it. I saw it in his eyes, and his nature is a deep and passionate one, so he loves with all his strength. It's too late to change that now, only the sooner you let him see it's hopeless for him the better. Will he have the right to accuse you of encouraging him? I can say I thought it was friendship, but—well—I did up to a certain point and I didn't know my own mind. If the worst comes to the worst, I will tell him all. But that would give him hope. No, I will say I once thought I might care, I found out it was impossible. But if you thought *once* you might care, couldn't you think so again? No, never. That would be my final answer and it would make me feel so badly that—well that—nothing. It's half past three. I don't see why Mo does not come. Oh, Mo—the very idea of having him make love to me is abominable. I could not stand it. I could *never, never love Mo. Never.* I wish all the world could see that last sentence and know it comes from the bottom of my heart and also know that I could never marry without love. I couldn't. Absolutely. I wonder if Mr. Sands came back to New York this morning or if he stayed over Sunday in Philadelphia. If he did he is sure to come tomorrow afternoon which is just what I don't want."

Gertrude works herself up into more and more of a state. She "can't sit still and read . . . can't write for ten minutes without getting the fidgets," laughs happily one day and cries the next. "The idea of *my* crying. I am the most self-possessed individual in the world as far as that goes, as a general rule. Sunday evening I almost died I was so blue, Monday I almost gave up, and Sunday I lay flat on the floor on my back and put out all the lights and the tears would come. I fear I am thinking too much about myself. Monday afternoon I told Mama a good many things I have not before and, oh dear me, last night I could eat *nothing* for dinner. This morning I was too unrestful to stay home, or to go out in the ordinary way. I

83

wandered off by myself in the Park and sat on the benches and forgot myself in watching the children."

April grinds on—sometimes painfully, sometimes happily—and Gertrude is passive. She receives Mr. Sands but also Mr. Evans, Mr. Cottenet, Mr. Whitehouse, Mo (the only one of these suitors she calls by his first name). . . . Mr. Lawrence sails to Europe for his health. . . . Finally, on the last day of the month, she sounds convincingly through with Mr. Sands: "I have now completely recovered from the attack of the 'Sands' which I had quite badly. I don't know whether it just happened that J. Burden [who this year marries Gertrude's cousin Adele Sloane] told me some things about Mr. Sands as he would about anyone, or whether he had heard something. At any rate, he took away the very things I admired in Mr. Sands." Whatever Burden confides must come to Gertrude less as a revelation than as a convenient excuse for breaking off the relationship. She herself says, "It showed I never cared very much or I should certainly not have changed my mind so easily."

As Sands's presence recedes, fades with a last bunch of violets, other friends and suitors, some old, some new, move into the foreground. Rollie Cottenet invites Gertrude and Mo and J. and Adele to visit him and his mother for a day of riding in the country. "The world has begun to say— what—'Adele and J., Gertrude and Mo!' But I don't care. We are friends and I should not let it make any difference.". . . Mr. McVickar, a married man in his early thirties, "has suddenly taken it into his head to be very nice to me. . . . I can't understand it because he evidently does not want to get anything out of me, being a married man there is nothing to get. If he is hard up for a flirtation I am the last person in the world for him to try it on." Yet while riding, "he went so far as to tell me I made him forget he was married!". . . The spring is filled with horseback riding: "Monday, Harry Robbins; Tuesday, Mo Taylor; Wednesday, Regi Ronalds—" The list breaks off and she writes, "I am desperately gone on Mr. Appleton. . . . I don't care about anyone else in the world at present." She confides to him "about being crazy to ride a bicycle and not being allowed to." He makes the necessary arrangements. The next day she writes:

Dear Mr. Appleton:
I want to tell you I have decided the [bicycle] party we were talking of last night is utterly and entirely *out of the question.* How I could for a moment have thought of it seriously I really don't see. Suppose I was discovered! Besides, I think it might be wrong. Please forget I ever mentioned the subject and Believe Me

Sincerely Yours
G.V.

As these men move into Gertrude's life and as Bobby Sands fades from it, what of Esther, who has so often depended on him as a go-between? At Easter she and Gertrude have exchanged gifts and that day Esther writes:

My Dearest,
 This is the first time I use my most beautiful new pen! I am sure it will be kept very busy writing to you; in one way it will be the same as my old pen, it will always want to. I love you too, my dearest Gertrude—

But by May 7, Gertrude writes in her journal: "I promised Esther to go down and see her this morning, but it's so hot I don't know whether I shall have the courage. It's such a long pull." All the way down to Washington Square! The next day Gertrude writes: "I did not go down to see Esther yesterday and did not send her a note. Ah me. It's so warm I should love to be in the country. In three weeks and a few days we will be in Lenox. Think how lovely! I am so lazy, I can't do anything at all but loaf." She sketches a cupid in her notebook and then continues writing: "If this little fellow would keep himself more out of the way I might be able to accomplish more, but there he hovers and refuses to move on."

How he hovers all through May—over the heads of Jimmie Appleton, Regi Ronalds, Harry Robbins, Robert Livingston ("Livy") Beeckman, Worthington ("Worthie") Whitehouse, Rollie Cottenet, Willie Field, Phil Lydig, and, of course, Mo Taylor. At the end of the month the Vanderbilts visit the Sloanes in Lenox (by now almost as fashionable a summer resort as Newport and about on a par with Bar Harbor), visit Alfred at school in Concord, and go to Newport to check on construction progress of the new Breakers, which will be ready in July. When they return to New York, Gertrude is surprised to find Mr. Sands's name among those who have called in her absence. Now he sends flowers and calls again. Gertrude "could not help right away wanting to hear what he had done and where he had been." However, she does not record this information but, instead, her determination, as often with those she rejects, to make him "a friend." With only slight wavering, this is the course she follows as they meet at a series of weddings and other social events in June. On the first is the Cameron-Tiffany wedding and on the sixth, more important to Gertrude—she is a bridesmaid—that of her cousin Adele Sloane and James Abercrombie ("J.") Burden, heir to the Burden iron fortune. It is probably the largest and most elaborate wedding in Lenox until that date—the list of guests includes "everyone" and the gifts, on display, are "conservatively estimated to have a value of $7,000,000"—yet it is still another wedding, just two weeks later, which Gertrude does not attend, that impresses itself most on her consciousness; that of her cousin Alice Shepard to the "unknown" Mr. Dave Hennen Morris, a premedical student at Harvard. On the day of the news of Alice's elopement Gertrude devotes eleven pages to the "Alice Case" and later in the month an additional four to solving some of its mysteries.

Gertrude begins, "If the world had turned round and gone the wrong way, the turn things have taken could not have surprised me more. Alice Shepard of all people! Alice the saint-like, the angelic. Alice who of all people we thought would be the last to pain or hurt anyone, especially her mother." Gertrude goes on to describe her own mother receiving the telegram: "We could scarcely believe our eyes. Alice—Alice who had left us only a week before [after a visit following the Sloane-Burden wedding]. And Mr. Morris, we had never heard of him! What could it mean! Had the girl gone crazy? Was she going to break her mother's heart?" Gertrude remembers telling Alice jokingly after Adele's wedding how she herself would do things: "After I was engaged and my engagement had been announced, I would wait about a week and then someday when my fiancé and I were out walking we would stop in at a church and just get married and telegraph to the family afterwards." Alice had laughed and seemed to like the idea but said, "Gertrude, you could do that perhaps, but I never could because Mother has had so much trouble [the death of her husband two years before and that of Marguerite, her youngest child, earlier this year]." Then Alice had gone on to tell Gertrude about a man of splendid character, two years older (i.e., twenty-three), whom her mother had liked until finding out who his father was, when she told Alice not to see him again. Gertrude tells her mother all this, emphasizing the humorous context of the conversation. Then they go to Aunt Emily Sloane's for a family meeting where there is nothing really to be done but piece together more of the facts. "Alice met Mr. Morris coming back on the steamer [*Majestic*] last year. His father was head of the Louisiana Lottery and some horse races, therefore Aunt Maggie would have nothing to do with him. He proposed to Alice about Christmas time. Alice . . . accepts him without telling her mother until after. . . . Aunt Maggie says she must break it off immediately. . . . Alice thinks it over, decides to make the sacrifice and writes him breaking off the engagement. He is not at all well. His sister writes to Alice saying if something is not done he cannot live. . . . Aunt Maggie is as firm as ever. . . . Alice decides she will see him and finish everything up. . . . Alice goes to New York . . . [does] just the reverse! . . . Aunt Maggie has a stormy interview with Mr. Morris. . . . Alice goes off with him. . . ."

The day after this account, barely summarized here, Gertrude's journal entry is in a very different mood, a mixture perhaps of guilt associated with Alice's marriage and longing for that state. Gertrude writes about herself in the third person: "When she felt as if some strange new feeling had come into her life she would lean up against the wall and, with her head against the cold wallpaper, would clasp her hands and, in a passionate quiet, stand thus. Yes, the wallpaper was cold compared to the burning heart within her, but it was a comfort to her to stand thus, it made her imagine that perhaps the wall had some life in it and could feel the throbbing of her heart, or hear the little short gasps of breath that escaped her. She would run her hand down the edge of the curtain perhaps and little tiny thrills would run down her back or up her legs till she realized it was only the wall. Then she sighed and thought how foolish she was and left the cold consolation of the wall to fall on her knees and pray."

At the end of June there is a last entry concerning Alice: "She had written since her marriage that she is perfectly happy. Mrs. S[hepard] going out of her head. At times she screams out loud and Edith and Louise [Alice's sisters] have to hold her down."

However, by this time Gertrude has a new interest—Mr. Barnes. As far back as the previous December, when she meets him at the Stokeses', he appears in her journal, but only *en passant*. In mid-June they meet again, by chance, on the Lenox golf course where he helps her to beat her best previous score, going round in 83. That night he enters her *People* book:

JIM BARNES: Interesting, intensely fascinating, clever, entertaining, deep and passionate. This is what strikes one first in you. A man of the world who has seen life and profited by what he has seen is what one thinks next. You are an intense nature, original, forcible and strong; a man to respect; a man to honor, a man to love. If your dealings with the world have made you worldly it is totally against your nature to be so, I do not believe you are so, you are disinterested and true. You could be as tender as you are strong, as dependent on love as you are independent of people's opinions. You take things hard, yet you are a philosopher. You don't take the trouble to get to know many people, or any people if you are not interested in them, and you are reserved in spite of your manner which might lead a casual observer to think the reverse. Your voice, which is deep, musical and vibrating, is the key to yourself. [Like virtually all of Gertrude's suitors, James Barnes has the right background: pre-Revolutionary stock, St. Paul's, Princeton, B.A. '91, M.A. '95) but like only a few— particularly Howard Cushing and Rawlins Cottenet—he too is deeply interested in the arts and has this year published his first book, A *Princetonian*, and is on the staff of *Scribner's* magazine.]

Early in July Mrs. Vanderbilt needs to fill out a dinner party. "Would it do to ask Mr. Barnes?" she asks Gertrude. "Is he the kind of man for a dinner?"

"He is extremely nice," Gertrude replies calmly.

"What is his name? John?"

"I think it is James. I have always heard him called Jim."

His acceptance arrives for the dinner the next night. Gertrude writes, "I never cared so much about my appearance as I did that night. When I went downstairs a few minutes after eight, Tina Winthrop and Mr. Barnes were already there. . . . He said right away 'The golf champion' and with that began a conversation. . . ." Three days later she starts to record, as she has done with just a few other men, "When I have seen Mr. Barnes." So far the list is short:

DECEMBER 8th 1894, Stokes dinner, introduced only.

JUNE 15th 1895, Lenox Golf Links, 1¼ hrs.

JULY 3d 1895, Dinner at Home, 1 hr.

JULY 5th 1895, Stokes dinner, 5 minutes.

JULY 6th " Barnes lunch, 20 "

The next day: ". . . Why have I allowed myself to get in this state? Now I am going away and—and he is the only man in the world I care anything about." Three days later: ". . . I wear the little gold heart [possibly the duplicate of the one she bought Esther] as a sign that my heart is his. . . . I admire, respect and honor him, nothing more. . . . He will be in Newport sometime this summer and he will come to see us. But he does not care for you. No, no—but—well? Oh nothing. You are very changeable. No, I have never cared like this before. Don't talk like that— look back to the entries on April 17, for example [Bobby Sands]. That was different. I never really admired that person or respected him. It was because he cared for me that he occupied so much of my time." The next day: "I know for a fact the following—Mr. Sands has come here [Newport] this summer for the sole purpose of getting me. . . . It was Esther who told me. . . . He wanted to know if I liked him. Esther said—like him, yes, but that was all. . . . And Mo is coming up to spend Sunday. I think to see me. I mean I don't think he would have come if I had not been here. . . . I wonder if when men love it is necessary for them to tell the girl. I mean, if they saw it was useless, could they keep it to themselves? . . . If I were a man, it seems to me . . . I would have to tell the girl. . . . It's evening and I am in bed. I wonder what sort of an evening it is in Lenox and if [Jim Barnes] is dining out. I wonder if he has thought once of me since I have been away. I see him in my mind's eye now. His broad, beautifully shaped figure, his decided features. I hear his voice, the tenderest voice in all the world. Will we meet again or is it only to be 'ships that pass in the night'? I received a signal from him, did he receive one from me?— God willing, I will know someday. Amen." And two days later: "Mama remarked yesterday that I looked so tired—there is only one thing to make me tired now, and that is waiting."

Mr. Barnes has moved to the center of Gertrude's thoughts and dominates her mind so completely that there has not been, and won't be, even a moment for description by her of the Vanderbilts' new summer home. The Breakers is, however, worth at least a few paragraphs.

Richard Morris Hunt has been inspired by his own love of Renaissance architecture (specifically, in this instance, the North Italian villas of Genoa and Turin) and by his client's desire for a home that will be large, solid and, above all, fireproof. There is no timber in the basic structure. Walls are built of stone or brick or tile. Steel beams carry shallow brick arches and the slabs on which are laid finished floors of imported marble, terrazzo, mosaic, tile, and oak parquet (the one flammable concession, along with paneling in a few rooms). Even the heating plant (the cause of the fire in the previous house) is placed several hundred feet from the main house and connected to it by a tunnel, literally large enough to drive a team of horses through.

The seventy-room house is four stories high and approximately 250 by 150 feet, or almost an acre, situated on its magnificent twelve-acre site overlooking the Atlantic. The ground floor, arranged symmetrically around a central great hall rising through the second floor to a height of 45 feet, is, except for Cornelius Vanderbilt's small study, used almost entirely for entertaining. The great hall is finished in carved Caen stone ornamented with marble plaques and columns, gilded cornices bearing the acorn and oak leaf Vanderbilt "crest" (which Alva Vanderbilt had "discovered" a few years earlier when Marble House was built), bronze chandeliers and candelabra, wrought-iron and bronze stair and balcony railings, a 24-by-18-foot seventeenth-century Flemish tapestry, stained-glass skylight, red porphyry vases, hooded Italian fireplace, Della Robbia plaque, Karl Bitter's twin-dolphin fountain under the staircase. . . . There is no need for an inventory of the furniture and oriental rugs. Enough to say that in scale, in quality, in opulence they are consistent with the great hall itself. Nor is there need for a complete inventory of the other ground-floor rooms. The dining room, with its red alabaster columns, crystal chandeliers, carved and painted ceiling, has about the same dimensions as the great hall. However, except for ceiling height, the other rooms, too, are consistent— the antique-paneled reception rooms and family dining room (or breakfast room), the walnut- and leather-paneled library, the morning room decorated with oil paintings of the muses done on silver leaf, the billiard room with its pale green marble walls and mosaic ceiling—these and the large sleeping apartments on the second and third floors and the knowledge, if rarely the sight, of kitchen, pantry, silver vault, and thirty-three servants' rooms in the kitchen wing and in the attic, must all have overwhelmed the contemporary visitor, if not Gertrude herself.

Henry James visits Newport a decade after the opening of The Breakers, having been in England and other parts of Europe for more than twenty years. In *The American Scene* he remembers a time before the nineties when "even the shortness of the Avenue seemed very long, and even its narrowness very wide, and even its shabbiness very promising for the future." Now the "monuments of pecuniary power rise thick and close."

There is no longer "a sense of margin and mystery." In what may be the most famous passage in the book, James sighs, "What an idea, originally, to have seen this miniature spot of earth, where the sea-nymphs on the curved sands, at the worst, might have chanted back to the shepherds, as a mere breeding-ground for white elephants!" He is, in short, shocked by the excessiveness of The Breakers, Marble House, and similar homes, as he is by the excessiveness of America itself. With less poetic passion, less visionary intensity than James's but with more historical distance, the architecture historian Vincent J. Scully, Jr., coolly observes that "a combination of economic and social forces had delivered into [Hunt's] hands a group of appropriate clients."* Yet, like James, he recognizes that The Breakers "moves toward giantism and the grandiose." When these buildings are still young James wonders "what in the world is to be done with them," and answers, "nothing but to let them stand there always, vast and blank, for reminder to those concerned of the prohibited degrees of witlessness, and of the peculiarly awkward vengeances of affronted proportion and discretion." And half a century later Scully answers somewhat more affirmatively, "The Breakers beyond all doubt is the acme of the American palatial mansion of this period, and as such it should continue to be of very great historical interest."

This monument is the home in which Gertrude is spending the summer, a home in which she will never again, as in the former Breakers, have to vacate her bedroom in order to provide space for guests' coats. Her room is at the southeast corner of the second floor. From it she can see the tip of Ochre Point to the south where on stormy days the Atlantic beats against the cliffs and, to the east, more distantly, Sachuest Point; but except for these visual anchors there is mostly a sense of being at sea on an absolutely steady ship. In this room, in mid-July, Gertrude is still thinking about Jim Barnes, waiting for him. There she receives a note from Charlotte Barnes, Jim's sister, which gives her an excuse to write, but before answering the letter she fantasizes in her journal about becoming a governess to the Barnes family. She would do "fancy work" for Mrs. Barnes, bicycling with Mr. Barnes, talking with Charlotte, walking with Nellie, smoking with Sanford, golfing with Jim. "Ha, ha, fine governess!! Take me, eh, Mrs. B.? Yes. Good. Come tomorrow. Dining with Cushings tonight. Wonder who will be there. Jim won't, so what matter."

But the Cushing dinner, with Howard sitting next to her, turns out to be "great fun." So does a small dinner at home, with Howard again, a few nights later. Not till Saturday, at the Cuttings', when Bobby Sands appears and takes her in, does Gertrude record feeling sad again: ". . . something must be done. Wish Mr. S. would spend summer somewhere else, or have everything over. Hangs over me, bothers therefore. Will anyone call

---

* Antoinette F. Downing and Vincent J. Scully, Jr., *The Architectural Heritage of Newport, Rhode Island*, 2nd ed., Rev. (New York, 1967), p. 172.

this afternoon? Yes—he. . . . Still wear gold locket with heart night and day, under low neck dress too."

Jimmie Appleton arrives in Newport. Gertrude receives a letter from Mo Taylor saying he will arrive for the Cup Races. But these arrivals mean little to her. Jimmie's handsomeness is no longer so compelling. Mo, she hopes, is now just a friend, like Howard. No one in Newport can replace Jim Barnes. No one else can command much attention in Gertrude's journal. On August 1 she writes: "Mr. Hunt died yesterday at noon. I saw Esther the day before, sent flowers yesterday. She wrote me a note asking me to stop and see her this afternoon. Of course I will since she wants me."

Finally, a week later, Jim arrives. Gertrude hears from others about the good work he has been doing at St. Bartholomew's Mission. "Of course I think more of him than ever." The next day she has lunch with him and his family. "The table had no cloth and I never ate so much bread in my life." As usual, there's a seating diagram: Mr. and Mrs. Barnes at either end; one side, Sanford, Edith [probably Cushing], a male cousin of Barnes's, F. Ives; the other side, Nellie, Charlotte, Jim, and Gertrude.

> Jim was so nice that day, but then he was always nice. He had the most fascinating way of looking at you and he came once or twice and stood by me, and I *felt* he was there and, did he feel it? No. I appeared, naturally, perfectly horrid. I always do if I especially want to appear well. [The last Barnes lunch] was on the 6th, a month ago and two days. I still wear the little heart night and day. Only once have I forgotten it and then it almost broke my heart. My heart! Which is it —the one that beats so hard in me or the gold one that nestles near me? That hard, cold one cannot be mine and yet I am hard and cold when people I don't care for are about, but not—oh stop.

Jim leaves Newport. Gertrude rides frequently with the very wealthy, considerably older Lispenard Stewart and knows she could marry him if she wanted. "He likes me very much because I am not clever or pushing or poor. He knows I would not marry him for anything except love because I have everything else. And he has always been more or less afraid of that. His feelings are not very deep, he could get to love me as much as was necessary." Thus, except for mentioning his presence at the previous fall's Yale-Brown game, Mr. Stewart enters Gertrude's journal and, in similar fashion, her *People* book too. Frank Andrews doesn't make *People* but he also is in the journal at this time, telling Gertrude he loves her. "I tried to laugh it off, to change the subject, not to take him seriously, but in vain. So I made up my mind to stop it now and forever. I told him no, there was *no* hope. I knew I could never care. Oh my, the conceit of some people. The last man who told me he was in love with me was Mr. Evans on the ship that day—I wonder who the next will be and if he will care as much as these two! Ha, ha, that amuses me."

Gertrude's journal jumps from "August 11th, 12th" to "August 23d"—a short jump but an odd one since she doesn't mention the huge ball given by her parents on August 14: a sort of belated coming-out party "to formally introduce their daughter to society." Though by now close friends of the family are familiar with The Breakers, for most of society—that is, for most of the three hundred or so guests—it is their first look at the interior of the mansion which has been the talk of Newport all summer. Newspaper accounts describe the place in detail, then the ball itself. The New York *Herald* notes that "it was in the grand hall that Mrs. Vanderbilt received with her daughter," that "Mullaly's orchestra and Sherry's Hungarian band alternated in continuous strains of music," that "supper was served on innumerable small tables that were brought in as if by magic, each with its silver ornaments and pink shaded lamps," and that "Lispenard Stewart started off at midnight a spirited cotillion† with Miss Vanderbilt."

As always when a large party is covered in this paper or in others of the time, the rest of the article is names. There are almost all of those we have seen in Gertrude's journal, with Jim Barnes most conspicuously absent. There are representatives of the British and French embassies, the Belgian ministry, and the Spanish legation. Edith and Edward Wharton are present, possibly on their first visit to the property since the former Breakers burned down. And finally, among the names we do not yet know, are those of Mr. and Mrs. Richard T. Wilson, their son Richard, Jr., and their daughter Grace. For now, it is enough to say that Gertrude's older brother Cornelius is strongly attracted to the beautiful Miss Wilson and that the romance which begins this evening will profoundly affect Gertrude's life and that of her family.

When Gertrude resumes writing in her journal on August 23, though the ball is not mentioned, Lispenard Stewart is. That very day the newspapers have Gertrude engaged to him. She feels "provoked," then writes: "Perhaps I will marry him and be through with it. We could go off alone together and travel. He likes traveling. I think it wouldn't be at all bad being alone with him. He is entertaining and amusing, and then it would be nice just sitting by him. I wouldn't even mind if he held my hand sometimes. The other night, when we were sitting on a small sofa together, I thought it would be very nice if everyone vanished and we were alone and he said something nice and I stroked his arm just a little and then—well you know. It was terrible of me to think of it but I

† Lispenard Stewart is one of only half a dozen or so really fashionable cotillion leaders of this period, including at least two other friends or suitors of Gertrude's, Worthington Whitehouse and Craig Wadsworth. These "society men" knew all the most intricate figures, starting (as Dixon Wecter tells us in another important book of his, *The Saga of American Society*) "with a Grand Right and Left to exchange greetings all around" and then following with a basket figure.

couldn't help it and I can imagine us going to Japan together and taking a long railroad journey alone together and stopping at little out of the way places where nobody knew us and where we could do just what we liked and no one would care and talk. Cold blooded child that you are. No, I must talk over a little with someone. Yes, you can think of that but think of the years before you. Trouble and sickness might come to you or perhaps to him. Could you keep to him then, nurse him, respect, love and honor him then? Then again, remember the rights of a husband. If he chose to be affectionate what could prevent him—you certainly not—had you not given him the right—to love you."

There this fantasy ends for the moment but sometime after September 4, the date of her next entry, she inserts a fold of paper on which the fantasy continues:

A big establishment is one thing I will not have. This is in case I should ever marry—

A house to which mine and my husband's friends were *always* welcome. No matter the time or place.

Our house would be rather small, or very small would suit me better, homelike in the true sense of the word, with one delightful library with a divan and easy chairs. That would be a private room for my husband and myself *alone*.

We would travel a great deal without much baggage or any servants.

When we were at home we would ride a great deal, take long walks, have delightful times together, little sprees of all kinds.

I wouldn't care about going out, but we would see our friends in an informal way.

September's entries are mostly lists of those with whom Gertrude goes horseback riding, again familiar names: Rollie Cottenet, Mo Taylor, Lispenard Stewart, Jimmie Appleton. As early as September 16 she writes, "Ah me! The people have left, the place is getting quiet. But what matter." And in October the family makes a trip to Hot Springs, Arkansas. It must have been quiet there too, as Gertrude's only journal entries are "imaginary calculations of things ordered at Doucet." She has a clothing allowance of $5,000 per year, of which half is for winter, half for summer:

Six evening dresses at say an average of $150 each	$ 900
Six day dresses at say an average of $125 each	$ 750
Two jackets and a cape at say $125 each	$ 375
A tea gown at say	$ 150
A saut-de-lit	$ 100
	$2275

She has $225 to go and considers:

Tailor made dress, short skirt at say	$ 100
Three pretty light shirts trimmed with lace	$ 30

Four days later she changes her mind:

White evening dress, roses, I suppose about	$ 150
Velvet shirt waist	$ 65
	$ 215
	$2275
	$2490

Pretty close shave.

When the family returns to Newport, Gertrude receives a note from Mo Taylor fixing a riding date for Saturday and one from his mother asking her to lunch on Sunday. The seating diagram is small and symmetrical: Mr. and Mrs. Taylor at either end; Lispenard Stewart and Netta Taylor on one side; Mo and Gertrude on the other. "Mr. Stewart watched us like cat and dog. . . . Every time Mo looked at me Mr. S. looked at Mo and vice versa." After lunch:

GERTRUDE: "By the way, do you know if Miss Sands is engaged?"

NETTA: "I don't really know."

LISPENARD: "What do *you* think about it?"

GERTRUDE: "I can't say, as I have not even seen them together."

LISPENARD: "Do you think you can tell if you see people together who are engaged?"

GERTRUDE: "Well, I should think you could tell a little."

LISPENARD: "I don't think you can a bit because they are always on the lookout and are even more indifferent than they would otherwise be."

When Gertrude is alone with Lispenard he talks about a new friend, Belle Nelson, and Gertrude is "consumed with jealousy . . . hate[s] her, and him too for that matter." When she is alone with Mo, she "can't quite make out if Mo is in love with me or not. Sometimes I think he is, sometimes not." The next day a letter arrives from Mo in New York which ends her doubt:

52 Wall Street

Oct 28

My dear Gertrude—

When I got home yesterday, I was on the point of coming back and seeing you, but was sure there would be people with you, and I would not be able to ask you a question I have been meaning to ask you for months, but I have been waiting to see what answer I would get, but now cannot wait any longer. You must know Gertrude I have loved you ever since I first met you on my return from around the world, and every day has increased my love, until now I can wait no longer, and must have an answer. I would have waited over today to see you, but really could not.

And since all these newspaper reports . . . I am afraid for your sake to be seen too much with you until we can be seen by all the world.

Oh, Gertrude I cannot tell you how I love you but will if you only will let me, when we meet again.

Please let your heart give me hope, just a little hope that some day we may be the happiest two people in the world—I have been on the point of telling you this several times, but everytime I waited being afraid to get no and losing you forever, but now I cannot wait any longer, and must have an answer, Oh how I hope it will be yes. Yesterday when I was out walking I was on the point of asking you but every time I was not sure and was afraid of losing you, but now I cannot wait any longer and must have an answer, please say Yes!

I am waiting Gertrude with you do not know how much anxiety for your reply, and God grant it is yes. Your eyes which have looked into mine cannot have told me wrong and that you do not care for me, as mine certainly have told you how I love you Gertrude. I am waiting for your reply with anxiety to such an extent I am unable to tell, please say yes—

Ever Yours Most Sincerely until death
Moses Taylor

In a lighter spirit there is this undated verse, presumably written shortly after the letter:

> My dearest Gertrude,
> Please accept these few roses,
> And don't think it rude
> From yours lovingly Moses.
> I'm feeling quite badly,
> So don't make me paler,
> But say yes at once
> And become Mrs. Taylor.

Since it is written in Gertrude's hand on her own stationery, there is no way of knowing whether she simply transcribed it or actually composed it as a fantasied contrast to the heaviness of his conventional proposal. In either case, she addresses herself to the proposal itself and drafts her reply:

Dear Mo,

I cannot possibly tell you how badly your letter made me feel. Was I to blame? That is the thought that haunts me, but how could I have been when what you said surprised me as much as it pained me. I always thought we were such good friends and when the papers began talking it provoked me so because I thought you only cared for me as a friend and that our friendship would now be broken up. I know you have paid me the greatest honor it is in the power of a man to pay a woman, and when I think how unworthy of it I am it makes me hate myself. Mo, I want you for a friend—but it can never be anything more. Forgive me if I have ever made you think more than this. Of course what you have said to me is sacred, no one shall ever know of it, and I hope and pray that you will still be to me the friend whom I trust and want and need to see. It seemed so natural our liking each other. Were you not Willie's best friend and I so often think of all the nice things he used to say about you. It seems as if you must love him almost as much as I do, let this thought keep us together if nothing else will.

Ever Sincerely Yours

Two days later, in her journal, Gertrude comments: "That tells its story and a sad story it is." However, this story, like most, is not completely told. Even as she writes, Mo is replying to her refusal:

My dear Gertrude—
I meant to write you yesterday and tried once or twice but failed, and now I am simply dropping you a line. Of course it is no use to tell you how your letter made me feel, that you can probably understand —As to our being friends even if it was not for Willie's sake, for your own I always will be the best friend you have in the world, if you will let me be, and you can always be sure that I would do anything in the world to help you in any way that I possibly could, but it is no use trying to write you, I cannot write what I mean, I will have to wait until I see you, but one thing you can feel that if you ever want a true friend call on me for anything—

Ever Your Sincere Friend
Moses Taylor

And another two days later, when Gertrude receives Mo's second letter, she writes in her journal: "To think that a year ago at this time I would have given a good deal to have Mo care so—and yet would I, if it had come to the point? I think not." She continues to brood on the situation, *her* situation, so specific and familiar now: "You don't know what the position of an heiress is! You can't imagine. There is no one in all the world who loves her for herself. No one. She cannot do this, that, and the other simply because she is known by sight and will be talked about. Everything she does or says is discussed, everyone she speaks to she is suspected of going to marry, everyone she loves loves her for what she has got, and earth is hell unless she is a fool and then it's heaven. The few people who are not snobs, but the very ones she wants, will not be seen with her because they won't be called worldly. Her friends flatter and praise her to her face, only to criticize and pick her to pieces behind her back. The world points at her and says 'watch what she does, who she likes, who she sees, remember she is an heiress,' and those who seem most to forget this fact are those who really remember it most vividly. The fortune hunter chases her footsteps with protestations of never ending devotion and the true lover (if perchance such a one exists) shuns her society and dares not say the words that tremble on his lips. Of course, worldly goods surround her. She wishes a dress, a jewel, a horse—she has it, but not all the money in the world can buy her a loving heart or a true friend. And so she sits on her throne, her money bags, and society bows to her because her pedestal is solid and firm and she doesn't seem perhaps quite human. But she has a heart just the same and the jeers or praise thrown with bows at her feet cut her and make the hours that should be spent happily pass in dreary succession on and on. Oh! Will they ever end?"

The brooding ceases, for the time being anyway, as fall weddings capture Gertrude's attention as much as those of the previous spring. And, as with her cousin Alice Shepard's marriage to Dave Hennen Morris, it is again a cousin's wedding which Gertrude doesn't attend that excites her interest, the wedding on November 6 in New York of Consuelo Vanderbilt to Charles Richard John Spencer Churchill, the ninth Duke of Marlborough. Of course, this is no elopement. The wedding has been planned for months—and even years according to Consuelo's autobiography, in which she presents herself as a very unwilling eighteen-year-old bride, pressured into the marriage by her mother. However, the idea of an American heiress being pushed, or at least forcefully encouraged, to marry European aristocracy is not what keeps Gertrude and her family in Newport—by now there have been enough such marriages to accept them—but, rather, the recent divorce of Consuelo's parents, Alva and William K. Vanderbilt.

In early March, while Gertrude and the family are in Europe, the divorce decree has been granted to Alva on grounds of her husband's adultery and she has been given custody of the children; Marble House; another country place in Islip, Long Island; and a cash settlement estimated to have been as much as $10,000,000. By April rumors are being published that she and Oliver H. P. Belmont—also divorced, and possibly part Jewish—are going to be married. There is simply no chance of Cornelius Vanderbilt or his family making a public appearance at Consuelo's wedding, not with Alva there and possibly Belmont too. But in Newport they read and hear enough about the wedding. The New York *Times*, like most newspapers, makes it the featured story of the day, occupying two columns of page one, including large pictures of the exquisite bride and elegant groom (though described by Gertrude as "nothing on looks"), and continuing onto all of page two and part of page three. The *Times* says the wedding "was, without exception, the most magnificent ever celebrated in this country." The paper describes the elaborate floral decoration of St. Thomas' Protestant Episcopal Church, the crowds inside and out, the long musical program conducted by Walter Damrosch and the sixty-member Symphony Orchestra. "The only regret that might be expressed is that the near relatives of the bridegroom were not present to witness the marriage of the young Duke to one of America's fairest young women, and that, outside of the bride's immediate family, none of the Vanderbilts were in attendance." Everyone else is—the representatives of the British Embassy, New York Governor Levi P. Morton (formerly congressman, minister to France, and Benjamin Harrison's Vice-President) and his wife and daughters, many Astors (escorted down the aisle by Regi Ronalds, among other ushers), and just about all of New York society, the names that have by now become familiar in Gertrude's journals.

Three days after this wedding Gertrude and her family return to New York for the next one, that of Pauline Whitney and Almeric Hugh Paget, Baron Queensborough. Harry Payne Whitney, Pauline's elder brother, is on the train with the Vanderbilts. Gertrude notes, "Harry Whitney is a brick! There is no doubt about that."

The Whitney-Paget wedding, also at St. Thomas', is as grand as the previous one and as prominently and fully described in the *Times* and elsewhere. The temptation to compare the two weddings is irresistible: "Many persons were eager to see whether the Vanderbilts were out in force, and it was doubtful whether the small black side-whiskers of Cornelius Vanderbilt [Sr.] or the scarlet flowers which waved on the top of Mrs. William K. Vanderbilt's hat caused the louder buzz of conversation." Yes, the Vanderbilts are out in force—Gertrude herself is a bridesmaid, as is her cousin Emily Sloane, and her brother Cornelius is an usher. Moreover, because Pauline's father, William C. Whitney, has been active in public life, especially as President Cleveland's Secretary of the Navy, many nationally prominent guests attend the ceremony, including President and Mrs. Cleveland and two cabinet members and their wives. Even the names of Governor and Mrs. Levi P. Morton and their daughters appear far down a subsequent alphabetical list, with no comment, just after Mr. and Mrs. Dave Hennen Morris. The crowds, the floral decorations, the orchestra (a new one conducted by Nathan Franko), are all described in detail, and so is Harry Whitney, "who seemed to discharge his duties [as an usher] with a keener interest than the others." Gertrude, too, singles him out for attention. The next day she writes only: "The wedding is over. It was nice. Harry is bully and we are going to be friends."

A few days later Gertrude's mother tells her that Colonel Payne, Pauline's and Harry's uncle, says several times at the wedding, "I think your daughter is the loveliest thing. I can't tell you how lovely I think she is." Then he goes on to remark upon how nice Harry is, and Mama informs Gertrude "that if Harry keeps straight, [Colonel Payne] is going to leave him all his money, and he is supposed to be worth about $30,000,000." The innuendo is not lost on Gertrude: "Oh my, how worldly, child, you are getting! . . . my imagination gets the best of me sometimes. I was just thinking, now suppose Harry did ever care for me. I know he *likes* me *very* much now, but there would be no reason to be nice to me if he didn't *really* care. And that is a little daydream I had better put out of my head. It's too dangerous to play with it. I care too much for Harry. Before I knew it I would be over the edge and Harry would not."

As the excitement of Pauline's wedding dies down, Gertrude is caught in other aspects of the New York social whirl. There are two nights at the Horse Show, where the horsemanship is seemingly as incidental to the social intercourse of those sitting in the loges at Madison Square Garden as, on other nights, the opera is at the Metropolitan. At the Mortons', there is a dinner followed by theater, at which both Mo Taylor and Lispenard Stewart are present. "I had always said after you refuse a man of course you can be friends with him. Now I don't know—after a time yes, but . . . [Mo and I sat] together at the theater, that was all, but it was trying, very. Mo looked awfully pale, perhaps it was the light, but was perfectly self-possessed. Evidently he had braced himself for the occasion. . . . What I am afraid of now is that people will notice. Mr. Stewart must have for one."

A day later these thoughts are interrupted by the account of a visit to Charlotte Barnes: "I was in 'Jim's' house today! I mean the house he lives in, and my excitement was—? . . . He does his work at home, I have an idea, and yet I don't know. I sat on the sofa I thought it most likely he sat on, and I took in every detail of the room. It was furnished with tapestry furniture, either old or copied, very beautiful, and had rugs and gilt tables, screens, etc., with true French portières. . . . Louis XV, yet I wouldn't swear to it. There were a few pictures on the walls—good ones—one a Van Marke, I did not like to look too closely at the others." Following this is a diagram of the parlor, with each piece of furniture placed and an X marking the spot on the sofa where Gertrude sat. "Charlotte kept me waiting five minutes . . . I wish she had kept me waiting half an hour, then I could have sat on every chair in the room so as to be sure and make no mistake. Tomorrow, thank goodness, is Sunday and I can be under the same roof with him for an hour and a half, that is if he goes to church. He always went in Lenox. I pray he may do the same here. It's my only chance of seeing him. . . ." Yet other possibilities occur to her. Perhaps the Stokeses will have a dinner and invite both of them. Or Mama will ask him to dinner if Gertrude suggests it. "Bliss. Perhaps I can have him next to me. Oh joy, a thousand times bliss! I wonder if he has ever thought twice of me. I doubt it—I should *love, love* to know, even if he hadn't."

Gertrude leaves the world of real possibilities—at church, at the

Stokeses', in her own home—and, for more than eleven pages, records a "daydream" of riding with Jim every morning for a month or more. After a particularly late ball she arrives as usual at nine-thirty, waits for him, finally gives him up, and starts by herself. At the entrance to the park he overtakes her. He is pale and looks ill. She cannot tell him how concerned she is, how much she loves him. Instead she chats about the previous day's visits, the ball, the dinner. He seems distracted, possibly indifferent, but suddenly interrupts "a little amusing story" of hers.

"You are not feeling well," he says.

". . . I couldn't sleep last night, that's all."

"I couldn't either. . . . You do too much. . . . Three balls this week, a dinner party every night and your rides and calls—it's too much—you will be sick."

"Oh no, indeed, you are the one who is tired. You work while I frivol away the time. . . . Can't you tell me why you are worried?"

"How did you know I was worried?"

To herself Gertrude says: "How did I know it? Oh God, didn't I love him!" To Jim: "You always forget that I know you *very* well."

Gertrude's "power of acting was coming in now. And it's wonderful how a girl can rise to an occasion. He would *never* know there was any other feeling except friendship in my heart for him. Friendship—and I loved him so!"

But of course he will know. The horses play cupid. First Jim's shies, brings him so near that their shoulders touch, and Gertrude "thrills through and through." Then a horse coming quickly from the opposite direction frightens Gertrude's horse, which plunges from side to side and sets off at a gallop. "I didn't feel frightened, I didn't care. My only thought was if I die it will be near *him*. Then his voice said at my elbow. 'Sit quiet and wind the reins around your hands.' It was such a steady voice, oh how I loved him. He was not near enough yet to catch the reins himself. Suddenly my mare gave a bound forward, then to one side, and before I knew it we were both over the edge."

When Gertrude regains consciousness, Jim has her in his arms, is kissing her "white cheeks and forehead," and is saying, "I love you, I love you. Darling, I love you. . . . Where are you hurt?"

"I am not hurt, I am well now," Gertrude replies, kissing him. Then she is taken home, is "sick for a week or so, and after that—I saw him again—and—oh my—what a story! *It's only a dream.*"

We don't know if Gertrude sees Jim at church that particular Sunday. About two weeks pass before she again mentions his name in her journal. Meanwhile she does mention several other callers: "When Lispenard Stewart leaned over to speak to me and pressed his shoulder against mine, it almost undid me entirely. . . ." Bobby Sands "sent the most enormous bunch of violets I have ever seen. Really, I had to carry them to the opera, they were too many to wear." Harry Whitney has explained that he doesn't like calling because it is too formal—one *has to talk* and therefore the conversation is strained—but prefers seeing people when he is smoking and can just speak when the spirit moves him. Gertrude buys a box of cigarettes for him and takes one herself "as if it were a habit. . . ." But by the end of the month these callers, as well as Jim, are all pushed to the background. The new focus of Gertrude's attention is her brother Cornelius.

Against the family's wishes, Cornelius has become increasingly involved with Grace Wilson, the beauty he met the previous summer at Gertrude's belated coming-out party. She admits to being twenty-two, his own age, though she is surely older; and she is the daughter of Richard T. Wilson, a prominent and well-connected banker living on Fifth Avenue, though not one who is in the same financial position as the Vanderbilts (few are). As against these objections, she is attractive, charming, and sophisticated, if perhaps, like her Southern epicurean family, too "worldly," compared with the puritanical Vanderbilts. At the beginning there is teasing disapproval and dissuasion in which Gertrude joins her parents. For example, walking home from church, Cornelius announces that he is lunching out.

"Where?" Gertrude asks.

"At the Goelets'." (They are relatives of Miss Wilson's by marriage.)

"Ah, for Grace Wilson!" Gertrude laughs.

That night at dinner she continues the teasing: "Who was at the lunch?"

"Miss Wilson," Cornelius replies in a very grumpy tone.

"Is that all?"

"Yes."

Gertrude and her mother look at each other and smile. Then Mama says, "She was afraid to have anyone else."

The subject is dropped. Cornelius continues to be "more than usually grumpy." Through the rest of the meal he hardly speaks. We can assume that in the past his patience has been similarly tried, but this evening, a few minutes after the family withdraws to the library, Cornelius says, "Papa, I would like to speak to you and Mama alone in the other room."

"I will go," Gertrude says, getting up and leaving, "terribly excited." She is sure, absolutely sure, that Cornelius is engaged to Miss Wilson.

The next morning at breakfast she asks Mama what happened. Her mother replies in a terribly serious voice, "I cannot tell you."

So, when open conversation is impossible between Gertrude and her parents, she simply "keeps her eyes open"—and her journal. For several days Cornelius is scarcely in the house. He does not come down to breakfast, he is out by ten and not in till late at night. A letter comes for him, marked IMMEDIATE. Gertrude sounds her parents, remarking innocently,

"Why, that looks like Grace Wilson's handwriting." When they say nothing—not even "What can she be writing him about?"—she knows she is on the right track, and a few days later when she hears outsiders talking she is absolutely sure.

At family breakfast the next morning, Cornelius says directly to Gertrude, "I am going to sail tomorrow."

She is speechless, "flabbergasted."

As he is leaving the room, Mama says, "Cornelius, come and kiss me."

He replies, "Well, you needn't be so pleased. I've told Papa."

The next minute Papa puts his head in the door and says to Mama, "Will you come in here a moment, I want to speak to you."

Gertrude is left with her "untouched breakfast. No one had eaten anything that morning."

At dinner Papa asks Gertrude, "Did Neily tell you anything?"

"No."

Gertrude waits, but again the subject is dropped. After dinner she tells Mama her suspicions—her certainties now. Yes, Mama says, Gertrude is right. Cornelius has told them he is engaged. They have tried to break it off. Papa has been to see Mr. Wilson, has told him what he thought of the Wilsons' behavior and that if Grace doesn't give up Cornelius right away it will "alter his prospects." Mama has told Mrs. Wilson the same. There has been talk of waiting a year, of letting Cornelius travel, but the Wilsons "behaved like liars and cheats." *She*, Grace, this corrupt older woman, is herself going abroad in a week!

Gertrude suggests writing to Fred d'Hauteville in London and asking him to see Cornelius and get him away so that when Grace arrives he will not fall immediately under her influence. Mama discusses this idea with Papa. They think well of it. Mama writes the letter. They consider other schemes that are put aside. One is to have a friend of Cornelius' go over and meet him as if by accident, but that might make him suspicious. Another is to telegraph him to come back just after Grace has left, but the family decides he would not obey.

By now Mama is sure that Gertrude, in this situation, is her ally. She tells her daughter that Grace is so unscrupulous that she might even marry Cornelius the next morning before he sails. "There is *nothing* the girl would not do. She is at least 27 . . . has had unbounded experience. Been engaged several times. Tried hard to marry a rich man. Ran after Jack Astor to such an extent that all New York talked about it. Is so diplomatic that even the men are deadly afraid of her. There is nothing she would stop at. There is no one attentive to her, she thinks. Aside from it being a Vanderbilt, it will be her last chance." Mama is told that now all New York says it is "the most dreadful thing of its kind that has ever happened in society." And Gertrude comments: "Oh, I pray he has not married her yet. I fear it is so. His eyes had such a strange look today

[November 27, the day before Cornelius' departure]. He was much more cheerful than he has been for a long time. I feel as if I were living in a book. It's terrible. Mama and Papa have hardly slept the last ten nights. Everything is wrong."

For the next few months Cornelius travels in Europe and in the Near and Middle East, spending much of the time at sea, isolated from Grace Wilson but unable to forget her, becoming increasingly determined to marry her as his parents become equally determined never to permit that. His romance and banishment are fully covered by the press, his health is undermined by rheumatism. . . . Though Gertrude probably knows little or nothing of her wretched grand-uncle Cornelius Jeremiah Vanderbilt, who committed suicide when she was only seven, she senses that her father, like his own grandfather, wishes at times that he had not named his son Cornelius. . . . And there are references to her brother Bill, dead now for almost four years. Doesn't Cornelius understand that when Bill died he, Cornelius, assumed the obligations and responsibilities of the eldest son? Doesn't he understand that "altered prospects" means being cut off, disowned? Hasn't he, like Gertrude, witnessed what Aunt Margaret Shepard went through when Cousin Alice ran off with that Morris fellow? . . . Yes, Cornelius understands, even if he doesn't agree. And Gertrude understands and feels her parents' pain, as she feels her brother's in his occasional letters from overseas. . . . However, in regard to Bill, there may be one thing Cornelius knows which Gertrude doesn't: that Grace has been involved with, perhaps even secretly engaged to, William. This, in terms of Papa's adoration of William, would more completely explain his passionate disapproval of Cornelius' relationship to Grace. . . . Gertrude is determined to do what she can to bring her parents and Neily together again. At the same time she begins to believe that when her turn comes to marry she will present her parents with a suitor totally acceptable to them.

≈

Re-enter Jim Barnes. It is the last day of November and Gertrude is to be his dinner partner at the Sloanes'. She looks forward to this evening as to no previous one. "I fussed so over my appearance that I was late. It took me longer to dress than it has ever taken me in my life. First I took a bath, then I did my hair, and finally I got to my dress. It was an all white one, not a bit of color about it, just a little gold on the waist. I think it's almost the prettiest dress I have ever had. Dinner was announced a few minutes after I got in the room. Mr. Barnes came to me."

"Jim!!" she exclaims (with the double emphasis indicated in her journal).

"I am to have the pleasure."

"How nice."

He offers her his arm. They talk all through dinner. "I started right in with the only thing I could think of on the spur of the moment—my being so late, and how often when you thought you were early you were terribly late, and just the reverse. Oh, how attractive he was, and he didn't seem to mind my foolish remarks. . . . We got on well—oh yes—he seemed interested, even more I thought sometimes, but his manners are so good. I found out a good deal about his tastes, etc., and he has the most splendid character, you cannot possibly imagine. Honorable, true, high, frank, open, lovable—and a thousand other things. Mama herself suggested asking him for dinner and the opera. . . . !! I have never been so happy."

All that subsequent day Gertrude thinks "tonight he will be at the house—tonight I will be near him, I will hear his voice, will look in his eyes, will sit at the same table with him, will breathe the same air that he breathes." Finally the evening arrives. Gertrude wears a green dress. By the time she is ready and goes downstairs, the men of the party are assembled. Mama is talking to Frank Polk and Jim Barnes, Papa and Howard Cushing are in "earnest conversation." Gertrude shakes hands all around, Mabel Gerry arrives (a great-granddaughter of two signers of the Declaration of Independence—on her fathers' side of Elbridge T. Gerry; and on her mother's, of Francis Lewis), the party is complete, and they all go in to dinner, where Mama sits at one end of the table, Papa and Frank Polk at the other, Mabel Gerry and Howard Cushing on one side, Gertrude and Jim on the other. So Gertrude has the opportunity—the "necessity," as she puts it—to talk to Jim and finds him, as always, "absolutely fascinating." When the group divides to take two carriages to the opera, again Gertrude is seated next to Jim, again they talk.

At the opera other men, "piles" of them, call at the Vanderbilt box. Lispenard Stewart asks Gertrude to dine with him and go to the Shotlers' the next night ("Mrs. Witherby was to chaperone"). Gertrude accepts. Worthie Whitehouse makes an engagement to call the next day, Charlie Sands the day after. Gertrude studies her engagements: she is to ride with Lispenard Stewart on Tuesday, with Philip Lydig on Wednesday, with Reginald Ronalds on Thursday. It is a busy week. Mr. McVickar asks her to dine and says he is going to have Beatrice Bend and Laurie Ronalds and two men. He suggests that Jim Barnes could be one. Externally calm, Gertrude replies that that would be very nice. . . . Perhaps Mo Taylor, too, stops at the opera box. There's this, written a few days later: "People used to say . . . after you have refused a man *you like* very much, it's never the same. . . . I don't care for Mo anymore. It's all I can do to be friends with him." Busy as Gertrude is—with both her social life and the recording of it—it is understandable that details and/or the lack of them become confusing at times as she tries to catch up on missed journal entries.

December 8 is a day about which there is no confusion. Again she commemorates first meeting Jim a year ago, then records this Sunday's walk from church down to 36th Street with him and her brother Alfred, bemoans the fact that Jim called on Friday when she was out but remembers that last night at the opera (another unnamed opera) he said that that call didn't count. "Oh bliss, he will come again." There is that to look forward to—and the McVickars' dinner. Meanwhile Gertrude lists "When I have seen 'Jim' continued":

> July 7th, Call, Lenox, 25 min.
> Nov. 24th, Church, 3 min.
> Nov. 30th, Sloane dinner, 1 hr.
> Dec. 2d, Home dinner, 1½ hr.
> Dec. 6th, Opera, 10 min.
> Dec. 8th, Walking from church, 15 min.
>
> Total 3 hrs. 23 min.

A week flashes by, summarized on December 15 (after "This angel of a man, my dear, and what of him? Ha, ha! His wings sprout daily"): Monday, the opera. Tuesday, a fast short ride with Regi Ronalds, a walk with Rollie Cottenet, a "not particularly nice" dinner at the Pomeroys'. Wednesday, a call from Rollie Cottenet and *théâtre en famille*. Thursday, riding with Lispenard Stewart, call by Philip Lydig, "extremely nice" dinner at the Van Rensselaers'. Friday, the opera: "Harry [Whitney] went with us and was a brick." Saturday, selling at a fair in Turkish costume (presumably for some charitable organization) and, finally, that night, the McVickars' dinner.

The dinner is smaller than originally planned—only the McVickars, Beatrice Bend, Gertrude, and Jim. Gertrude is wearing the bridesmaid's dress she wore at Adele Sloane's wedding ("white with just a little green"). Jim takes her in to dinner. Again there is no description of the meal or the other people. But after dinner, as they sit around a table in the dimly lighted back part of the drawing room (diagrammed, as usual), "something happened. I don't know if I ought even to tell you. But still, there is no harm and I tell you he is the only man in the world I have ever allowed to do what I allowed him to. Of necessity, we were very near. He was rather restless and his foot pushed up against mine. First, I moved it away, but it happened again and this time I could not resist. I left it there. And for the rest of the evening we were thus off and on. I would have taken mine away but he always came back, not in a horrid, pushing way— but—oh my God, if I was wrong forgive me. It flashed through me that he might think less of me for it, and imagine I allowed other men to do the same, but when I looked into his face, his eyes, and saw there something that made me almost tremble, I could not resist and I let my foot rest against his to show him my life was his to make or mar, just as he chose. He talked a good deal. He has gone through a good deal, he has suffered. Well, the evening came to an end only too soon—oh God, if it could only have lasted forever—and I went home."

Gertrude looks forward to seeing Jim the next morning after church, but a Mr. Wilkes joins her going out and she can't get rid of him. Jim passes, they say only good morning and make some remarks about a steam carriage they stop to inspect. Then Jim goes downtown and Gertrude continues uptown with Mr. Wilkes, so angry with him she "could have taken his head off. . . . A pleasant frame of mind to be in just after coming out of church."

Sunday afternoon Messrs. G. Sherman, F. Crowninshield, E. Hoffman, A. Livingston, L. Steward, C. Webb, J. Appleton, and R. Ronalds all call. Jim waits till Monday. Though Mama is in the room most of the time, writing a note, Gertrude and he get on very well. Mama asks him if she may send him an invitation to the Assembly. He accepts. And it comes out that he, like Gertrude, will be going to the mid-January "Cinderella dances," so Gertrude knows she will be seeing Jim often. Friday she receives a note from him asking her for the cotillion at the Assembly. "Was already engaged. Oh how sad."

At church the following Sunday there is no Mr. Wilkes to interfere with Jim's walking Gertrude home, and they have thirty-five "bully" minutes alone together, duly recorded in yet another continuation of "When I have seen Jim," after which she notes: "Erskin Hewitt said Jim Barnes made such a clever speech last night at a club, also recited 'Outside Delmonico's Window' extremely well. I love to hear nice things about him. The idea of his paying the slightest attention to me!"

There, on December 22, the journal breaks off until New Year's Eve. However, though not indicated in the journal, on Christmas Day, George Washington Vanderbilt formally opens Biltmore, his country house, planted solidly on 125,000 acres of the Blue Ridge range of the Appalachians, just outside of Asheville, North Carolina. The 250-room house— inspired by such French Renaissance châteaux as Chambord, Chenonceaux, and Blois—is built to impress, to provoke exclamations. Gertrude might have devoted a brief journal entry to it, if not during the hectic festivities of the opening, then at least in the quiet of her father's private railroad car as the family returns to New York. But perhaps she is not as impressed by Biltmore as is most of the world. After all, though the specific architectural style is different from that of The Breakers, Richard Morris Hunt has done this building too—in scale and opulence it is not that different. Still, wouldn't Gertrude notice the specialness of her uncle's library—the 73-by-30-by-34-foot room of a wealthy scholar—containing some 20,000 volumes, mostly on art and architecture and landscape gardening, in the eight languages he knows? And wouldn't she notice the grounds, the inner estate of 11,000 acres magically landscaped by Frederick Law Olmsted in the same naturalistic style as New York City's Central Park, but about thirteen times the size? . . . Whatever the reasons, Gertrude's only surviving account of this trip (except for a diagram in her *Dinner Book* of twenty-seven Vanderbilts, Webbs, Sloanes, Shepards, Twomblys, Kissams, and a more distantly related Barker, all seated at a long table for Christmas dinner) is the draft of a letter to Esther:

December 29th

Dearest,

You will get this letter the same time we arrive home, but no matter, I want to write you.

It has been so delightful down here—so, so much nicer than I thought it would be that I hate the idea of going home. We have walked and ridden and when we were at home sat about together and fooled and I have seldom enjoyed anything as much. Emily [Sloane] has been a little hold-offish, but Lila [Sloane] was dear and we are more fond of each other than ever. Ethel [Kissam] and I moved our quarters yesterday and we are not now near each other. So last night after I had taken off my dress I put on my wrapper and went stealing through the hall to her room. We did not talk very late because we were both tired and of course have seen each other so much that we have not quite so much to say as we used to. Last evening the house party arrived. You know who was coming, so I won't bore you with the list. For the first time we were seated at table and I found myself next to Mr. [William Bradhurst Osgood] Field [whom Lila Sloane will marry in 1902]. We got on like a house afire and he really seemed disappointed when I told him I was going home the next evening. I tried to make the family leave me but it was in vain so the only thing left to do was grin and bear it. Some darkey musicians came in and performed for us after dinner and it was 11:30 when we retired to our rooms. Today only eight people could go to church, so I was good and gave up my seat! To tell the truth I didn't feel very bright yesterday, so thought it was just as well. Mr. Field wanted to take a walk but I had to make all kinds of weak excuses. And now good-bye dear, why didn't you write me once?

Your
Gertrude

On New Year's Eve Gertrude writes: "'95 for the last time. And this year—what has it brought me? I look back to the entry a year ago—poor Mo. The world's a sad place after all. And yet this year has been kind to me, has brought me in contact with 'Jim.' Surely I cannot blame it when it has been so exceeding kind. . . . the whistles beginning the New Year will be here in a few minutes. I pray that this New Year may bring 'Jim' every blessing and happiness—*every* blessing. I see them all at Lenox—at the Stokes'—dancing the New Year in—who is he dancing with?—oh lucky girl! If only for one little moment he would think of me. God, who is all powerful, make him happy. That is my prayer for the New Year. And at Biltmore too they are dancing—bless them all. Help Graham Stokes to get over his love for Emily, and may each one of them have what they most desire. Protect them. Oh God, protect 'Jim.' Forgive me for my weakness, help me to be brave, and I do thank thee for what thou hast put in my life, to love even if it bring me unhappiness. Amen. Amen."

≈ *1896*

The new year begins badly for Gertrude. Owing to the death of a cousin, she cannot go to the Assembly and have supper there with Jim. She writes him a formal note, urging him to call. However, first they meet again at church. On the way home he suggests giving her a small party two weeks hence at an electrical laboratory so that he can show her, her parents, and a few friends the experiments he does, which would presumably—very presumably—impress them more than his writing. Gertrude resolves, "I am going to do nothing but read electricity from now till we go. Two hours a day. I promise it." By the next day, after listing the ten gentlemen who have sent her Christmas or New Year's gifts (a list from which Jim is conspicuously absent, unless he is either of two anonymous men who give her a silver bonbonnière and a bouquet of violets), she has begun her study of electricity. "Imagine me toiling away when I hate the old thing, and I really like to toil. That's the funny part."

It is difficult to imagine anything more foreign to Gertrude's interest than this particular study, but it is, of course, a single aspect of her all-absorbing interest in Jim. We feel Esther Hunt's desperation and frustration as Gertrude becomes more and more distant from her, more and more involved with Jim. The same day Gertrude is "toiling away" on her electrical study and hating it, Esther writes inviting her to dinner on a choice of days when Esther's mother will be in Newport. ". . . I love you and want you—Dearest, we will not go upstairs unless you suggest it and you will act just as you wish—I am waiting for a letter tomorrow morning telling me when I am to see you—Ever yours/Esther." Judging by other documents, including a flurry of undated letters from Esther written during this period, Gertrude either ignores the invitation or refuses it. Six days later she resumes her comments on the study of electricity: "Did you say funny? . . . I think it's the most pathetic thing I have ever heard of for a long time."

The day Gertrude writes this her aunt Alva Vanderbilt and Oliver H. P. Belmont, having been refused by the Episcopal Church because of their respective divorces, finally marry in a civil ceremony performed by New York Mayor W. L. Strong. This is a social event that Gertrude only reads about. More real, more distracting, is the constant parade of callers. Jim visits once, but Harry Whitney drops in frequently from across the street, and his friend Rawlins Cottenet calls at least twice, and so does Philip Lydig. Perhaps Jim Barnes's inattentiveness provokes a comment from Gertrude's mother, perhaps his preoccupation with literature and electrical experiments. Whatever the specific cause, Mama says *something*. On January 17 Gertrude writes:

I shall put it down in black and white or die—I hate her. Her! Who? My mother. Yes, ha ha, I have never allowed myself to say it, to think it scarcely before. Now I know it is true and say it, I would say it to her if she gave me the chance. I am happy, am I not—oh yes, living in an atmosphere of worldliness and suspiciousness—no matter. Well today has made me make up my mind to one thing and that is that I will not try to stop my love for Jim but I will do all in my power to make him love me in return. And if he does I will marry him. I won't take a cent from the family if he can support me quietly and happily. Oh God, riches make more unhappiness than all the poverty in the world. Keep me from being suspicious. Neily I have not seen. Then there will be a row. If it was any girl in the world but Grace Wilson, I would help C.V., Jr., on and on all in my power to help him if I thought they would be happy. I only live at times. Most of my life is simply existence. That is what she tries to make it. There is no more sympathy between us than there is between the table and myself, perhaps less, ha ha. Perhaps less. And I am young and longing and dying for sympathy, for feeling, for human love, and there isn't any for me—none—none. I could almost accept Mr. Sands, who loves me, and let him comfort and help me and love me for a little while. No one ever takes my hand or kisses me now as if they cared. He would. And I don't love him, but then there would be comfort in being loved. Some people think I am cold—cold—oh how my heart burns. Do cold people feel as I do? Tell me, why am I rich—oh if I could only be poor—very, very poor and Jim would love me. But he wouldn't, no matter, he would care for me then as much as he does now. Perhaps more—who knows—not less. I wonder if people ever go crazy just because they have such fits of the blues. Well, it doesn't matter—I won't—I was made to suffer—I know it. And on I shall go. I don't believe I will ever be happy in my life. I will be an old maid— but I won't live at home, and do good among the poor, oh my, such work was never meant for me. I'll do it just the same. Then some day they will say, your money does good even if you don't, and after that I suppose I will die contented. And no one will care, why should they? Not even the poor people because I will leave them my money. Money, money, money, money—Suppose I had accepted Mo. He would have had money too. Oh my—I *am* glad I did not.

The following Sunday, two days later, Gertrude and Jim are again together at church. "I was so penitent. . . . I suppose I shouldn't have seen [Jim] but I did. . . . We [Gertrude's family] were going to stay for communion, so when the people started to go out I took a last look at the back of his head, saw out of the corner of my eye how he turned to open the pew door, and then glued my eyes on my prayer book. I knew I had never seen him stay. I did not look up till everyone had left and then— there he was, the only one remaining in his pew. I feel so deeply and solemnly that it was more than an ordinary pleasure for me to go through the holy service with him. I know he felt very near God too and it seemed to make us nearer each other. I don't think it was wicked to think that way about it. I always feel God in this love of mine. I always pray for Jim —surely there was no harm in it."

Gertrude adds the usual long lists of Sunday callers and of the past and forthcoming weeks' riding companions, then neglects her journal for the next two weeks. There is not a hint in it of what happened with Jim another two days later at the laboratory. However, the evening must have gone well, for the next day she supplements the portrait of Jim she had written in her *People* book the previous June: "There is more to you than to any man. You have had disappointments, but they have not soured you. You are capable of the deepest and most intense feelings. You possess an unlimited supply of magnetism. You have grand and beautiful possibilities in you. You love life, yet you have deep fits of the blues." And there is a letter from Jim asking for the pleasure of taking Gertrude to supper two weeks hence at one of the little Cinderella dances ("more fun than the big ones"). And, finally, once again there is a letter from Esther (dated January 23) in which she complains that "Not so long ago you certainly seemed to love me and now really I might not exist—It is hardly fair to treat me the way you do when you know how much I love you, Gertrude —You always said that if ever you stopped loving me you would tell me, and then you used to say *you* never would—What is it, dear? I want to see you so much, tell me when you will come and see me. . . . Why are you so queer to me? Someone certainly has come between us. . . ." Yes, Jim is there, standing between Gertrude and Esther, between Gertrude and all the long lists of her other suitors, between Gertrude and her own journal. One has the feeling during these periods of Gertrude's silence that she knows no words can express her love and that the lists of callers are just a way of passing time between peeks at Jim, measured always in hours and minutes when what she wants is all eternity.

On February 2, again Gertrude and Jim are at church. Again, coming out, he asks if he may walk with her, and then: "Must you go home right away?" They take a long walk, south down Fifth Avenue, past several Vanderbilt mansions and his own brownstone in 48th Street, all the way to 33rd, then back up Madison, "so much nicer for walking . . . no, not nice—heavenly. We talked as I have imagined we might talk. . . . I know him better now, and he knows me better. He is more than I had anticipated, and yet how can he be more?"

She brings her accounting of time spent with Jim up to date: three hours, twenty-five minutes, including this last forty-five minutes walking. Then: "Harry has been to see me quite often, twice last week. He has a little dog whom I keep very often when he is at law [Columbia Law School]. It's a dear and I send over for him whenever I want." Within another four days there's a further shifting of interest from Jim Barnes to Harry Whitney: "Harry and I are having a desperate flirtation. It's splendid. We understand each other perfectly. Mr. Lydig had a big theater party [followed by supper at Delmonico's where at a table for twenty-four Gertrude is flanked by Phil Lydig's father and Harry Whitney]. It was delightful. Jim is fine. Tonight I go to supper with him. I told Harry all about Jim. He understood. I wouldn't have told him if I hadn't cared for him even more—perhaps than Jim? Who knows? Certainly not I? This book is getting to be the outlet of a crazy mind—crazy is the only word for it."

About now (on an unspecified day in February) Gertrude adds substantially to the three brief sentences on Harry, written in her *People* book back in September of 1894. Then he was "thoroughly trustworthy . . . truthful and frank. . . ." Now she says he is these things and more. For two and a half pages she expands on her initial insights and enthusiasms, modifies some slightly, but mostly expands: ". . . You are thoughtful of other people . . . though you give the impression of not being so. You are wonderfully broad in your views. . . . In certain ways you are not fully developed yet, but you have the strength to crush the bad in you and to bring out all the good. . . . You have a way of putting on a manner that you neither feel nor are, because instinctively you wish to hide something that will not be understood. This does not seem in accordance with the frankness of your nature. . . . You have energy and when you make up your mind nothing will change you. . . ."

Gertrude doesn't yet quite realize that Harry has made up his mind and is putting much of his energy—expressed in increasingly frequent calls, invitations, flowers, notes, attentive and considerate gestures such as the loan of his puppy—into pursuing her. Nor does she quite realize the enormous advantage she has given Harry over Jim by treating Harry as an old family friend and confidant. Throughout these weeks of vacillation, moving further from Jim and toward Harry, Gertrude is torn between moments of tactical consciousness and moments of unbelievable naïveté, but more profoundly she is torn by her lifelong conflict between self-confidence and self-doubt.

Gertrude's vacillation continues:

FEBRUARY 7: I discovered last night that Jim remembered every time we had met, and cared to remember. That he had had imaginary conversations with me, that he wanted to tell me about himself and that he cared to hear about me. He had taken an interest in me from the beginning—oh joy—I loved him last night and—well, it was heavenly. He is coming this afternoon. This afternoon—this afternoon.

FEBRUARY 12: Yes and he came and Mama only stayed a few minutes and then we were alone together and—nothing—everything—nothing—. Harry is fine. He is going to a dance tonight where Jim will be and he is going to tell me everything. I wonder, if I wanted to make Harry care for me, would this be a good way to do it? Last night we had such a nice talk in a little out of the way corner and I leaned back on the cushions and he sort of leaned over me and it was all very nice. I wonder if I could make him care? Sometimes I think "yes," then again I think "impossible."

Harry says he does not think I really care for Jim. He understands how I am attracted towards him, but he still does not think I really care. I frankly said, no, I didn't really think I was in love with him now, but just because I did feel a longing in me I imagined the longing was for him, or something to that effect.

Why can't we always keep our heads when we want them or really need them. Now sit down quietly and think of this problem as if you yourself were not concerned in it. An extremely attractive man—character of Harry, rich, etc.—a girl moderately nice looking and with what some people consider charm, rich, etc.—they are friends—how to make them more?!!

FEBRUARY 18: And so the world goes on. Sunday was my greatest disappointment. I stayed, Jim went away, and there was my only chance of the week gone for seeing him. Oh, doesn't he care, or is there some other reason he keeps away? I got some valentines—some flower offerings, etc. from Mr. Lydig & Mr. Sands. Mr. Stewart sent beautiful flowers Wednesday, also, I think, Friday and again last night before he came to dinner. And I wore them. The most delightful trip—we are going to take [down South] with a party. Imagine, and Harry is one of them. . . .

FEBRUARY 22: And so I made myself think for a little while I didn't care and now—back comes the old pain of longing, of wanting, and of never being able to have. Tomorrow is Sunday—if Jim is not in church I really believe I shall burst out crying in the midst of it all. I have so little control over my feelings, and if I didn't tell Harry only yesterday I had gotten over it and that we could always get over feelings if we wanted to! I wonder if he knew enough about feeling to see the wisdom of that remark.

Whatever he knows about feelings—Gertrude's in particular and, even more particularly, hers in regard to Jim Barnes—the knowledge is greater than she gives Harry credit for. After all, it is only since the turn of the year that he has been actively courting her—or as actively as his health and his law studies permit but, in any case, more actively than she seems at first to realize—and even in that short period of time he has pretty much shifted Gertrude's affections from Jim to himself. In dozens of undated letters—almost all written on heavy, gold-engraved, cream-colored Tiffany note paper, sent by hand to Gertrude across the street—he complains of aches, pains, headaches, fevers. In one he refers to himself as "an invalid," in another as having "bruised the periosteum of the pelvic bone," though remarking in parenthetic irony, "I know that these details must be interesting." At first the letters are addressed always "Dear Gertrude" and signed typically "Yours truly," or "Yours in haste," or "Yours in expectation," or simply "Yours," with "Harry P. Whitney" written out. But by the end of January, though these conventions continue, Harry is lending her the puppy referred to in her journal for specified hours of the day, writing to her more and more frequently, often sending flowers and reserving dances at parties in New York and Long Island. When conditions permit, they ice-skate and sleigh-ride together. There are hints now—at least on Harry's side of the correspondence—of serious intentions and hints, too, of his having confided these to his close friend Rollie Cottenet. But Harry's most revealing letter is one of ten pages written sometime in February:

Dear Gertrude,
    You are a brick—really you are—& you need never be afraid of an insincere "yes" from me.
    Of *course* it is possible for someone to love you simply and entirely for yourself. We have been made to go through an existence here,

God knows for what—it is hard enough & unsatisfactory enough—but there is one, just one, redeeming feature & that is the possibility of love. One cannot argue about this—arguments will not prove or disprove it. One can only *feel* it & be sure of it. The unit of the Creator's Mind is a man & a woman—not only physically but morally, mentally, intellectually, & in every other way. Our *whole* nature yearns for its complement, its other half in every respect. There is no doubt about it. It is the scheme of creation. And we have been given that one chance of happiness here, that is, to find a person who is the complement of our nature. And to make it the greater prize, it has been surrounded by a difficulty greater than any society can impose & which will hold even when the barriers of our present social existence are swept away—and that is our own natures, which feel their greatest need so strongly that they are prone to interpret mere whispers as loud distinct calls. That is why so few people who marry *really* for love really get what they married for—more find that they interpreted in their eagerness something trivial for the "real thing." . . .

Harry expands upon the complementary nature of man and woman as in Genesis 1, a text which has also meant much to his father, as compared with the subordinate role of woman in Genesis 2. Then Harry begins to move in on Jim:

. . . So be careful. It will be easy to make yourself see in Jim what is in your nature's ideal, if you think & brood about him enough. I have seen it in *men* several times while I was at college & was close to their lives & knew their loves. I came very near doing it myself.

There this is enough. Let's *talk* about it. If [I] don't understand anything, I may not have told you anything. We can *surely* talk about it—not at dinners or balls but at the right time & place. Room a little dark.

Because, though I seem young & light hearted, I have been through a good deal & lived perhaps more than my years.

Now about Jim. His mood was artistic—he dilated on the beauties of the streets, the lamps etc. as the mist showed them up. I was not in a mood to see them & was uncharitable enough to call it a "pose" —not knowing his mood or what might have made it. I take it back. About his being "worldly"—I don't know. I said that because he wants me to lunch with him & wants to get up schemes to renew our old acquaintance & in my sour mood I laid it down simply as a way to get at you. See!

I will play with him as much as possible so as to perchance help you. Thank you very much & I repeat, you are a brick.

Yrs truly
Harry P. Whitney

From this letter and others less blatant and Gertrude's own journal entries, it is not difficult to understand how her relationship to Jim becomes undermined by doubts. February 24, Gertrude anxiously awaits a call from Harry's friend Rollie Cottenet because he will by then have met Jim for the first time and she wants to hear his impressions, though doubting that they will be altogether favorable. "He is critical and then he thinks I like Jim which is sure to prejudice Mr. Cottenet [who] cares for me, even cares very much for me, but then he knows it is absolutely impossible for me to care for him. Harry jokes him about it the whole time, even when I am about. They call me Carmen. . . . Harry is a brick. I am going to *make* him care for me when we are off on the trip. *Make* him by being indifferent and oh, various other little tricks that I have learnt in my career. I have been pretty successful so far—and, strange as it may seem, it is not only my money!"

The prospect of the Southern trip—including Harry, perhaps even built around him (by Gertrude's parents with her own encouragement, or vice versa, or both)—is set now and dominates the last few pages of this volume of her journal. After much discussion as to desirability and availability, the men, in addition to Harry, will be Lispenard Stewart, Craig Wadsworth, Philip Lydig, and Dudley Winthrop and "for girls" Edith Bishop, Sybil Sherman, Mabel Gerry, and Helen Morton. Gertrude's sister Gladys, now ten, will be accompanied by a nurse. On Thursday, March 5, the day before leaving, Gertrude writes, "As I am never going to see Mr. Barnes again, I had better put down my When I have seen Mr. B. continued." It is a short list ending with a three-quarter-hour call a month before. The usual total is absent; instead there is only *"The End."* Beneath the emphatic finality of this and running onto the end paper, Gertrude writes: "And from that day forth she neither spoke to him nor so much as saw him, except twice in church. May the gods preserve and keep him and never let him suffer what unwittingly he makes others suffer. We start for the sunny South tomorrow."

On Sunday, only two days after the Vanderbilt party begins its trip to Palm Beach in Mr. Vanderbilt's private "car Number 493" and attendant cars, the New York *Journal* reports the event in the lead story on its society page. Headed "A QUIET LENTEN WEEK IN THE WORLD OF SOCIETY" and illustrated with engravings of "March, in Jersey City" (a snow-covered Wagner coach), "The Vanderbilt Party En Route to Florida" (several members of the party comfortably seated in armchairs being served tea by a steward), and "March, at Palm Beach" (a huge hotel looking out on bright sand and lush palms), the article asks:

. . . what is more natural than that the Vanderbilt car should find itself traveling toward Southern Florida at this wretched season of the year? The only really interesting item of gossip lay in the fact that young Cornelius, Jr. was not in the party. For even this young favorite of fortune has his troubles, and the stern but wise parents' swift, not to say peremptory, nipping in the bud of young love's dream, and the sudden recall home from the presence of the fair but forbidden one, has resulted in a seclusion of himself and his shattered memories in the wintry waste of Newport . . . unhappy and alone since his summary recall from Paris and the presence of his love.

Yes, the progress of young Cornelius' relationship with Grace Wilson is news. Everything the Vanderbilts do is news. Money is news.

Who can say how much wealth is represented in that Wagner coach . . . ? First, of course the host and hostess. Then, Miss Gertrude Vanderbilt, with the prospective dowry of an Empress. Miss Helen Morton, whose father, Governor Levi P. Morton, is certainly not among the poor. . . . Miss Mabel Gerry, too, is a young lady whose name has a golden ring and leads one to think of sound New York realty, widespread and fully improved, which makes up the multi-millionaire [sic] Goelet estate. In the party list, too, occur the names of Miss Sibyl [sic] Sherman, daughter of Mr. and Mrs. Watts Sherman; of Miss Bishop, also well gilded; Lispenard Stewart, again city lots galore with brick and warehouses on top of them; Craig Wadsworth, whose name calls up visions of broad acres of fat wheat lands dotted with mighty oaks and elms in the wide stretch of the fair Genesee. Philip Lydig and Dudley Winthrop, too, have been names of wealth for generations, and then also included in the party last, but not least, I come upon the name of Harry Whitney, with all that means in the way of countless millions of barrels of oil pumped out of our common mother earth by human craft and device transmitted into the wealth which doesn't perish if you only invest it wisely. And of all the alchemists that ever plied the trade since alchemy began never have been more potent ones than Oliver Payne, the Rockefellers, Flaglers et al, of the men who built up the Standard Oil Company, and Harry Whitney is the son of Oliver Payne's pet and deeply mourned sister, and besides William C. Whitney, ex-Secretary of the Navy, and possible Presidential candidate is not himself a poor man, and Harry is his son.

Truly to the cars which bear the Vanderbilt party southward the chariot of Midas would be but a huckster's cart. Although not given to match making, it is shrewdly guessed that Mr. and Mrs. Vanderbilt have arranged their party with thought for the future welfare of several of these young people, and that they are willing to remove every obstacle in the course of true love if all other things are consistent and proper. That we shall have announcements of early Summer weddings with June roses galore is a foregone conclusion.

Two more items concerning the Vanderbilts appear toward the end of the page—one concerning a large theater party given by them the previous

Monday ("A jolly supper followed the play at the house, at Fifth Avenue and Fifty-Seventh Street") and another concerning Mrs. Vanderbilt's patronage of an amateur performance of *Patience* to be given at the Metropolitan on the Nineteenth. . . . By now, even if Gertrude's attitude is ambivalent, she is surely accustomed to the attention of the press and, if she cannot completely accept it, she can at least view it with some detachment. She saves the clipping, sent to her by Craig Wadsworth, but to the central engraving of the party ensconced among the carpeting, paneling, upholstery, and drapery of car 493 she, or possibly he, adds a drawing of a mongoose (his nickname).

The press's view of the excursion is one thing, Gertrude's is another. On April 17, more than a month later, she begins a new volume of her journal: "Strange that I should have finished my other book just as I finished a certain period of my life, and have been all unconscious of the fact. For I did. And now begins a new serious time—when everything has a meaning and life has a different aspect and the world in fact is not what it was. How ridiculous and dime novelish that sounds and yet how much it means. Having made this little introducing so as not to startle you too much by what is coming—I proceed with my story."

She describes going "round in the omnibus to gather up the girls," the way they are dressed, the flowers they are carrying, the arrangement of the five cars behind the engine: first a smoking car, then the men's car separated from the women's by the dining car, and at the end, for the view, the so-called day car. After five pages she comes "to the point": Harry. He has provoked her by not coming near her for a week and so she has been cold and distant to him. During the first day on the train they do not speak unless it is absolutely necessary. In the evening when Gertrude goes to her room she is in such a state that she writes: "Dear Harry, What is the matter? I can't sleep tonight unless I know. G.V." She sends the note by porter. In ten minutes she has an answer. He has not been feeling well all day, has had trouble at home, etc. Gertrude is disappointed in his reply and cries herself to sleep.

The second day is better. In St. Augustine she and Harry lose the rest of the party and sit on the piazza talking, and that night at dinner Harry sits next to her and they have "the sort of conversation it is impossible to repeat. A great deal was meant but an outsider could not possibly have understood. I just began to realize then that perhaps it was not all friendship on Harry's part. . . ."

Sunday is quiet. She and Harry sit together at church. Monday at noon the party starts for Palm Beach. She and Harry excuse themselves and play cards all afternoon. "Cards indeed! I told his fortune, etc. . . . told him to make a wish and I would tell him if it would come true. The answer was—'yes, it will come true but it will not be as nice as you expected. In other words, you will be disappointed.'"

That evening after dinner the train pulls in at Palm Beach and onto a spur leading directly to the grounds of the Hotel Royal Poinciana. The party is conducted to its rooms and then reassembles at a dance going on in the hotel. In the morning Gertrude throws open her blinds. "The hotel is right near the water and in a garden full of palms. You have never beheld anything so exquisite. It did not take long for me to dress and have my breakfast that morning, I can tell you." Various friends in Palm Beach join the party and they go sailing. Not until afternoon, with Mabel Gerry's help, can Gertrude arrange to be alone for a while with Harry, and even then, just as they start walking, Craig Wadsworth joins them and spoils the day. The evening starts the same way. At dinner she is seated between Lispenard Stewart and a Mr. Livingston. "Horrors! After it was over I felt I must get off somewhere, either by myself or with Harry. Harry had had a hard time too and we somehow met and with scarcely a word we got the whole party onto the piazza." There they sit in a row, Gertrude finally next to Harry, and when the others go inside to dance they are "pretty much alone. That is, as much as one can expect to be on a big piazza full of people."

They sit for a while looking at the stars and thinking their own thoughts. In the past, in such a silent situation, Gertrude has always been very comfortable with Harry (and with others to whom she felt close), but not tonight. Several times she tries to start a conversation but Harry says only, "Wasn't thinking about that" or "What difference does it make?" Gertrude knows that she, too, isn't really thinking about *that* (whatever it is), that it makes no difference to her either. After a long silence Gertrude speaks again, not now to make conversation but to reveal herself. She talks about sympathy and getting on with people and, specifically, about wishing that she had a better relationship with Mama. "It is not really anything that we say or do, it is simply that she does not understand. When it is like that, there is no use trying to have an understanding."

Harry turns suddenly toward Gertrude and, though her head is leaning on the back of the chair and she is not looking at him, she feels his eyes on her. "Gertrude, shall we have an understanding?"

Gertrude feels weak, as if she has no strength in her body. She puts her hand to her eyes. She cannot speak.

He leans forward still more. "Shall we, Gertrude? Do you care for me?"

For still another moment Gertrude cannot speak. She feels the strength and power in Harry, turns to him, and gives him her hand, saying only, "Oh, Harry."

He takes her hand—her "poor ugly hand," as she describes it—and kisses it "over and over again and yet over and over," and says, "No, no, Gertrude—it can't be. Oh no, Gertrude." There is joy in his voice. He keeps laughing to himself as they squeeze hands. Later he tells her that he has always cared, that even way back it was never platonic. Gertrude replies that she has really not known he cared like that and that she herself has not known she cared until this very night when he spoke. "I suppose, if I had been like other girls, I would have said 'no' at first even if I really meant 'yes'—but that—well, I just couldn't." They are discussing what their families' reaction to their understanding will be when it is time to leave the piazza.

Craig Wadsworth joins Gertrude and says she looks tired or, rather, as if she has been crying. She admits she is tired and feels dizzy. She sits down for a moment while the others say good night, shakes hands with Harry, and goes to her room with "a queer swimming in my head and a strange joyful feeling at my heart." She does not sleep more than two hours, does not want to sleep, wants only to lie and think.

Of course the next morning she is *really* tired. Again, because others of the party are present, she shakes hands with Harry. They have no chance to speak until they board the train for the next leg of the journey, to Savannah. Then in the smoking car at noon, Harry asks:

"Have you repented?"

"No, have you?"

He looks at her, saying no with his eyes, and tells her that he, too, has not slept the previous night. After lunch they arrange to play cards in the observation room of the day car, but they don't get much card playing done. When there is a chance they hold hands and Harry kisses hers.

"The door was of course open into the hall and some member of the party constantly passing—so even the holding hands was extremely risky . . . but still the strain [of separation earlier in the day] was relieved by having him there with me. . . . I suddenly looked at him and could not take my eyes away. He looked down—I could not. He looked at me again —and for the first time we looked right into each other's eyes and saw each other's soul. Then he leaned forward suddenly and pulled my hands to him. He said: 'Kiss me.' And before I knew it he had leaned over the table and kissed my mouth. A few moments later he said: 'I feel better now.'"

For Gertrude that evening is the hardest of all. She is dead tired, not having slept the night before, but at the same time she is excited and wants to stay awake. When the evening is over at last, Mabel notices that Gertrude looks badly and when Gertrude gets back to her room she herself sees that she is white as a sheet. The next morning she is ill and stays aboard the train while the rest of the party tours Savannah. In the afternoon, on the way to Aiken, she and Harry play cards again— " 'hearts' the party had taken to calling it, and they little knew how correct they were. Harry kissed me again and then he spoke about the strain on us, and if we could only get away from all these people for a little while and just feel that we were alone in the world. He said: "You know it is Leap Year, you will have to arrange it." And I did. And it did not seem forward of me. . . . I loved him—it seemed natural. I suggested our meeting in that car after the rest had gone to their rooms. . . . How did dinner and the evening pass? I scarcely know—with Mr. Wadsworth, I think.

"At last Mama made the move to go and we said goodnight to the men as usual. I looked at Harry and he understood. I murmured, "In ten minutes," but don't know if he heard. There were dangers—I had known it—but what matter. I waited till the car seemed quiet and then walked leisurely down the corridor. I met one maid and in the end car two porters. I looked around as if in search of a book. Looked at the bookshelves, etc. Then went into the back of the car. No one was there! I waited a few moments. Suddenly there was a rap on the door and the next moment Harry came in from that end, saying:

"'I tried to get word to you not to come.'

"'Why?'

"'You ought not to have come. It was too risky. I saw it afterwards. But it's too late now.'"

Harry is out of breath and strange and seems a little wild, but Gertrude goes back to her room. There, Mabel, very worried, awaits her. She goes to bed with Gertrude and they talk. "I don't remember what else happened that night. It was all strange."

In Aiken, where Harry's father owns extensive property, Mabel, Craig, Harry, and Gertrude spend the day together in a buggy, "like children, singing, joking, and amusing ourselves. I had scarcely a word with Harry alone until after we came back." Then, again, they "play cards," but in the evening are trapped with the rest of the party. It is the same the next day on the way back to New York, when once more Mabel gets the others away, and Harry closes the door and for "just one second [they are] quite alone together—"

New York seems different and yet the same. On Sunday Harry spends most of the afternoon with Gertrude, who has announced that she will not receive other callers till after five. Mama is surprised but says nothing. Harry calls again on Monday and Tuesday and then must leave town for two days to go to the funeral of a friend in Baltimore. Though he writes (to "Dearest Gertrude" now), she misses him terribly and by the following Saturday, just a week since returning from the South, they decide to tell their parents—or, more accurately, Gertrude will tell her mother as Mr. Vanderbilt has just the day before left on a three weeks' trip, and Harry will tell his father (his mother has been dead for three years).

"I was trembling a little at the prospect before me—and we amused ourselves imagining the awful things our parents would say. It was a joke and yet—" And yet nothing. Gertrude "knew Mama liked Harry very much because she had said so. . . . Oh, the thrill of happiness when she said nice thing after nice thing about him—and that was before she even suspected." As to Harry, he knows too that his father will wholeheartedly approve of the match. Oh, there may be some talk about his youth (he will be twenty-four in a month) and about completing his law studies, but no more resistance than that. The event will be. So, while awaiting the various formalities, here is an opportunity to fill in some of the Whitney background, especially since Gertrude has felt no more need to do so than with her own family. The Whitney name—like her own and like so many in her journal—is institutional but faceless. It would, she must again have thought, speak for itself. And, like those other names, so it would have in 1896—more loudly then than now.

≼ *Whitney Background*

Like the Vanderbilts, the Whitneys settled in America in the mid-seventeenth century. John Whitney, his wife, and five sons were among 120 passengers aboard the *Elizabeth and Ann* when it arrived in Boston in June 1635. However, the Whitney genealogy can be traced much further back than that of the Vanderbilts, back to Turstin "The Fleming," who followed William the Conqueror into England and is mentioned in the *Domesday Book* of 1086 as an extensive landholder in Hertfordshire and the Marches of Wales. In 1242, Sir Robert de Whitney appears in the *Testa de Nevil* or *Liber Feodorum*, a list of feudal fiefs and fees of knights in Hertfordshire prepared for Henry III. Almost continuously Whitneys represented Hertfordshire in Parliament. By the mid-sixteenth century, with its rising middle class of merchants, manufacturers, and entrepreneurs, Thomas Whitney had moved from Hertfordshire to Westminster. There Thomas' first child, John, was well educated at the Grammar School and became at twenty-one a member of the Merchant Taylors Company, an important guild of "freemen" not restricted to the textile business. After some thirty years of bustling competitive trade in Westminster and later in London itself, subject to increasing Stuart economic restrictions and abuses of personal liberty and parliamentary rights, John purchased licenses for himself and his family to leave for the New World. Unlike the typical Puritan, he seems to have been motivated mainly by a desire for greater freedom and opportunity. His business was solvent, his home was comfortable and, as an Anglican, he had not suffered religious persecution.

He and his family settled a few miles outside of Boston, in Watertown, which had been founded five years earlier by Sir Richard Saltonstall and the Rev. George Phillips. The community of a hundred or so families recognized John's superior education, penmanship, and knowledge of legal documents. His neighbors called him *Mister* Whitney, and on March 3, 1636, he was formally admitted as a freeman by vote of the General Court of Massachusetts Bay. In Watertown he served as selectman, assessor, surveyor, town clerk, and on April 1, 1641, took oath as town constable. During these same years he bought first (in July 1636) a 16-acre homestead and received 50 more acres as his freeman's dividend, then purchased a farm of 120 acres and another parcel of 48 acres, so that even by 1640 his tract of 228 acres was one of the largest in the town "Inventory of Grants and Possessions" and would, in later years, become larger still.

Thus, quickly, here as in England, the Whitney family was established not only in the ownership of real property but in the acceptance of concomitant social responsibility and political or military or constabulary leadership.* Within a few generations Josiah Whitney of Harvard was fighting against the French and Indians and twenty years later, when the siege of Boston began, he was a lieutenant colonel, soon promoted to full colonel in a Massachusetts regiment raised to defend Boston Harbor. By the end of hostilities Josiah was a general and his son, of the same name, an officer. General Josiah Whitney went on to represent Harvard in the General Court, and in 1788 he was a delegate to the Boston convention for ratification of the federal constitution. Though initially he voted against ratification, because he feared federal centralization of power, he supported ratification when the Massachusetts delegation made it conditional upon a Bill of Rights. General Josiah Whitney's anti-federalism undoubtedly influenced later Whitneys in their support of decentralization, states' rights, and the Democratic Party.

A great-grandson of the general, James Scollay Whitney, born in South Deerfield, Massachusetts, in 1811, was the next historically significant member of this branch of the family. Though he went to local schools and joined his father's retail business, he was always actively interested in military affairs and at twenty-four was commissioned brigadier general in the militia. The next year he married Laurinda Collins, a descendant of Governor William Bradford of Plymouth Colony. They settled in nearby Con-

---

* Besides the branch of John Whitney's family with which we will deal here, other outstanding direct descendants include Eli Whitney (1765–1825), the inventor of the cotton gin and the assembly line (for muskets with interchangeable parts); Asa Whitney (1791–1874), the inventor and manufacturer of improved cast-iron railroad car wheels; another Asa Whitney (1797–1872), merchant and pioneer promoter of a Pacific railroad; Josiah Dwight Whitney (1819–96), geologist and chemist; Anne Whitney (1821–1915), sculptor and poet; William Dwight Whitney (1827–94), scholar of Sanskrit and linguistics; James Lyman Whitney (1835–1910), librarian; Myron Whitney (1836–1910), bass singer; and Mary Whitney (1847–1920), astronomer. It is difficult to think of another American family which has distinguished itself in so many fields.

way, a rural town in the Deerfield Hills, where James Whitney built a general store, first in partnership with a brother-in-law, who was later succeeded by Charles Wells, Jr. Whitney & Wells flourished and soon the partnership built a cotton mill for the manufacture of seamless bags. The mill, on the South River, was successful too and demanded much of General James Whitney's energy. However, he found time to be local postmaster, and in 1851 was elected a member of the Massachusetts House and was also appointed sheriff of Franklin County. The same year he was instrumental in obtaining Democratic support for Charles Sumner, running as a Whig candidate for the United States Senate. In 1853, Whitney was a member of the Massachusetts Constitutional Convention and the next year returned to the House, while at the same time obtaining a charter to organize the Conway Bank and helping to establish the Conway Mutual Fire Insurance Company, of which he was the first president. So, by the middle of the nineteenth century, this branch of the Whitney family was, by local standards, rich and powerful. The general's wealth and influence would increase until his death in 1878. By then he was president of both the Metropolitan Steamship Company and the Boston Water Power Company and had for six years been a state senator in Massachusetts and in 1876 and 1878 presided over the Democratic state conventions which nominated Charles Francis Adams for governor and, two years later, Samuel Tilden for President. Yet it remained for one of the general's five children, William Collins Whitney, to push far past local boundaries in both politics and business and to become one of the most powerful Americans of his period.

William C. Whitney, the father of Harry Payne Whitney, traveled a long hard road from Conway to the palatial home on the corner of Fifth Avenue and 57th Street, opposite that of Cornelius Vanderbilt. In Conway he went to the Franklin School and then the Academy. Even during these early years he was a complex young man, attracted to the extroverted social grace of both his parents, particularly the horsemanship of his mother, who could drive a four-horse team as well as any man, and the military and political accomplishments of his father; but attracted also to solitary introspection and study. He was so serious that the family called him "Deacon," and often he sat alone on the bank of the South River where, as he wrote years later to his wife, "my troubles all disappeared." At Conway Academy in 1854 he co-edited the *Students Literary Journal,* written in longhand and bound with blue ribbon. That year President Pierce appointed the general Civilian Superintendent of the National Armory in Springfield, where the Whitneys moved. After two years at the local school, William was keeping a "Book for recording good thoughts borrowed from other men and things." These included "Four things come not back—the spoken word—the past life—the sped arrow—the neglected opportunity" and "Act well your part. There all the honor lies."

Though there had been indications of literary interest, it was not until
William and his brother Henry entered Williston Seminary in Easthamp-
ton in the summer of 1856 that William read the Greek and Latin classics
and became seriously interested in literature, composition, and oratory.
Except for his literary efforts and an aptitude for discussion and debate, he
was only a fair student, but since he wanted to go to West Point, his particular skills and his father's reputation would have been more important
than high marks in Greek and Latin. However, the general became depressed at the thought of William suffering the rigors and risks of an army
career, so depressed that Mrs. Whitney had to visit William at Williston
Seminary and persuade him to forget West Point and choose among Harvard, Yale, and Williams.

William chose Yale and entered in 1859. He was already a commanding
figure—just over six feet tall, with large dark gray eyes, sharp well-formed
features, straight brown hair parted on the left, and a soft mustache extending beyond the corners of his thin firm lips.

Life at Yale was rigorous. The dormitories lacked plumbing, heating,
and adequate lighting. The daily schedule began at six with compulsory
chapel services, then recitation by candlelight, breakfast, another recitation or lecture on either side of lunch, and finally a second chapel service.
The recitations were mostly of the Greek and Latin classics, with even
more emphasis on these than at such preparatory schools as Williston, and
with as few electives. Mathematics, ancient history, rhetoric, logic, philosophy, and morality (ethics) were all taught from appropriate classical
texts. Even in 1860, when the Sheffield Scientific School was inaugurated,
the curriculum was so rigid, so tightly bound to the memorization of texts
rather than experimentation and discussion, that natural philosophy
(hydrostatics, hydraulics, acoustics, electricity, pneumatics, and magnetism) was "taught" in a single term.

It is no surprise that William's academic record was mediocre. He concentrated on and did well in only those subjects that interested him. From
freshman year on he was active in literary and debating societies and from
sophomore year on in boating and boxing clubs. Through these activities
and through the attractiveness of his looks and personality he made and
kept many friends. The closest was Henry Farnam Dimock, his roommate,
whom he had known well since Williston and who would eventually be
his law partner, marry his sister, and become a business associate. Second
closest was Oliver Hazard Payne of Cleveland, with whom Whitney
shared a commitment to Democratic politics and whose sister he would
eventually marry. Slightly less close, but the best debater of the group, was
the future sociologist and economist William Graham Sumner, who along
with Dimock was elected to Phi Beta Kappa in their junior year. Much
later, in a retrospective *History of the Class of 1863*, Sumner states that
Whitney's "position amongst us . . . was, from the first, that of a leader.

He lacked the ambition to excel, which would have driven him to hard and persevering industry. He never distinguished himself in the classroom. He was what, in those days, we called a 'writer and speaker.' . . ." Sumner judges him "easily the man of widest influence in our Class and perhaps the College." Though Whitney didn't make Phi Beta Kappa, he was, like Dimock and Sumner, tapped for Skull and Bones, and Dimock complained about the difficulty of studying due to the continuous procession through their room of Whitney's friends. This early we have a sense of the incipient politician.

Law school was a logical step in this direction. Whitney, along with his friend Dimock, entered Harvard—probably the best law school of the time—in September 1863. Attending ten lectures a week, in one year they took courses in agency and equity jurisprudence, pleading and constitutional law, the *Commentaries* of Blackstone and Kent, insurance evidence and contracts, law of real property, arbitration, will and administration, criminal law. There were also weekly moot courts and semi-annual regular trials before juries of law and/or divinity students, at both of which Whitney excelled in arguing cases. However, at the end of the year he felt that he could more profitably satisfy the two-year bar requirements by clerking in a law office. He went directly to New York, the fastest-growing, most dynamic business center in the States, and Dimock soon joined him there, after visiting a Novia Scotia lead mine in which they both had interests.

Whitney arrived with a letter from his father to Samuel J. Tilden, the prominent Democrat and future governor of New York and presidential candidate, who quickly placed Whitney in the burgeoning law office of Abraham Ricker Lawrence. Lawrence was a good example of how fast a bright ambitious young man could move in New York at this time. Though only thirty-two, he had been assistant corporation counsel from 1853 to 1857 and now had a practice of more corporate work and suits against the city than he could handle. Even in his first year with the firm Whitney assisted Lawrence as an adviser to the Board of Fire Underwriters, attempting to improve the efficiency of the loose political network of volunteer fire companies controlled by "Boss" William Marcy Tweed, who had himself started in politics as a volunteer fireman. Whitney worked on the final draft of the bill put before the New York State legislature "to create a Metropolitan Fire District and especially a Fire Department therein." It was passed March 30, 1865—one of the first great blows to the Tweed Ring. Later that spring Whitney and his friend Dimock, who had been working in another law office, were admitted to the bar, both impressing Elbridge T. Gerry, chairman of the examining committee.

It seemed likely that Whitney and Dimock would quickly form their own law partnership. However, this was delayed for about two years while

Whitney considered joining his father or his brother, both of whom needed help. The general's health was bad and his Metropolitan Steamship Company was in financial trouble. William's brother Henry, who had formed his own steamship company in New York, was then in the South considering the organization of a New Orleans–Mobile line as well as a ship salvage operation and speculation in cotton. Ultimately, Henry lost most of the money he had made in New York and joined General Whitney at home in the Metropolitan Steamship Company. Only then—in 1867, at 17 Wall Street—did Dimock and Whitney open law offices, the partnership that was further strengthened by Dimock's marriage to William's younger sister Susan in September of that year.

Now for the first time in his life Whitney put all his energy and will into his work. In addition to handling New York matters for his father and brother (the Metropolitan Steamship Company ran the "outside route" between Boston and New York), he accepted many kinds of cases —criminal, patent, corporate—researching and preparing them all with great thoroughness. His family and Yale friends, especially Sumner, were surprised by the long hours he now worked and by the ambitiousness he had previously lacked. But for Whitney the law was no longer an end in itself, a body of academic theory; it was a practical path to power.

Oliver Hazard Payne, Whitney's close friend and admirer at Yale, had not stayed to graduate but had instead joined the Union Army. Though during college years Payne had had Whitney to his home in Cleveland, at that time his sister Flora had not been around. She had simply—and accurately—been described as an exceptional young woman, one whom Oliver wanted William to meet. In 1859–60 she was in Cambridge in an experimental seminary for women conducted by Louis Agassiz. From the beginning of 1863 until the end of 1864 she traveled extensively in Europe, North Africa, and the Levant, pursuing her many interests, which included science, archaeology, and languages. During this period her father, Henry B. Payne, one of the wealthiest and most powerful Democrats in Ohio (previously a state senator and later a United States senator), published many of her letters in the Cleveland *Daily Record*. After the Civil War, when Oliver returned a colonel, he kept in touch with Whitney and in February of 1868 introduced his sister to his friend, knowing "That if they met they would fall in love with each other."

"So you are the Will Whitney that I have had held up to me for so many years?" the high-spirited Flora began. The romance moved quickly from the Payne suite at the Fifth Avenue Hotel to dinner that night and the opera a few nights later. When Miss Payne returned to Cleveland they corresponded, and in the spring Whitney visited the Payne home. However, he was discouraged by the presence of another suitor and the courtship dragged until December when Flora came back to New York. There, just before proposing marriage, he wrote to her, asking questions intended to please and impress. Her replies were wittily concise. We can almost see the twinkle in her very pale, intelligent gray eyes:

> Mr. Whitney shall do as he pleases, I don't think a new hat requires a dress coat. . . . The carriage would undoubtedly be a vast ornament to us but as I am in good health, I would suggest that we walk the three steps that lie between the Hotel and the Opera House. . . .

During the engagement period—from December 15, 1868, to October 13, 1869—again and again Whitney felt the need to explain himself, to state his case, however modestly. In April he wrote:

> I do what I do by means of hard work, and you will probably see how long I work over a matter for the small result. . . . All this will make it necessary for me (if I live a life of active professional labor which I wish to, and must) to be a good deal absorbed in labor. . . .

In May:

> I wouldn't do anything else if I could, and if I was sure I could be a first rate lawyer bye and bye, I should consider it the greatest possible success, in a worldly point of view, this life could offer. . . . In New York, a great Lawyer is a Dictator, because you can't buy his brains and experience and stores of legal knowledge anywhere in the market, you must get it from him or not have it at all. He has the confidence and is a repository of the secrets of a great many people, and he makes men and saves them from ruin by the power of his mind. There is the drudgery to go through and the years when you make the amount of business you have the intention to; but bye and bye come the years when you reap the reward of years of your struggling and your work. . . .

Whitney's style was considerably inferior to that of his bride, but despite repetitions (some cut even in these brief passages) and faulty grammar, punctuation, and spelling, it is clear that he knew where he was going. Like the practice of law itself, Flora Payne would help him get there. She, too, was ambitious. Her contacts, through family interests in the iron industry and in oil refining (later merged into Standard Oil, of which Oliver became treasurer), would be very valuable to her husband.

Whitney's legal practice grew. As early as the spring preceding marriage he was able to write Flora, "Today I have been drawing up a bond and mortgage for that notorious gentleman, Cornelius Vanderbilt. . . ." Whitney must have known that over the years he would do other work for Vanderbilt. Yet even attracting a client of this importance was not enough. He wanted to be his own client. During the summer he and his brother Henry speculated heavily in railroad stocks and lost almost all their savings. In late September, just before William's marriage, Henry wrote to him: ". . . I am sorry that those Wall Street devils should have pocketed that little purse of ours, we are *all right* yet and will make them pay it back with interest one of these days. . . .

Though that purse was gone, it was replenished by generous gifts from the Payne family. Flora's father commissioned William's friend, the architect Russell Sturgis, to design and build a town house for the young couple at 74 Park Avenue, in the fashionable Murray Hill section where the Cornelius Vanderbilts then lived too; and her brothers gave her an elaborate diamond necklace.

Now with an attractive, gracious, intelligent wife as his hostess, with her family and social connections added to his own, and with an elegant home in which to entertain, Whitney's law practice began to grow even more rapidly. It was clear already that his particular talents would best serve and be served by corporation law. In 1870 he and Dimock amicably dissolved their partnership, Dimock remaining temporarily New York manager of the Metropolitan Steamship Company, and Whitney joining another ambitious corporation lawyer, Frederick H. Betts (Yale 1864). Again, Whitney was involved with the Vanderbilts—with the old Commodore himself —who wanted a horse railway tunnel under Park Avenue from 34th Street to the new terminal at 42nd Street. Though Whitney represented the residents of Murray Hill in opposing the tunnel, he and the Vanderbilt interests compromised on a ramp and landscaped tunnel, much like what exists today. But this was almost extracurricular. Associated now with Betts, Whitney was by 1871 retained as counsel for two life insurance companies, two railroads, and various industrial companies, and was trustee for the mortgage holders of the Dayton & Union Railroad of Ohio. "We have had ups and downs," he wrote Flora, referring to his financial difficulties during their engagement, "just now we are up."

While Whitney's power, wealth, and prestige increased, so did his interest in politics. As a confirmed Democrat and the son and son-in-law of party leaders in Massachusetts and Ohio, for him in New York this meant reform politics. He allied himself with Samuel J. Tilden in the fight against Tammany and the Tweed Ring, which in two and a half years (January 1869–August 1871) had raised the city's debt from $29,000,000 to $101,000,000, with much of that increase going into the pockets of "Boss" Tweed and his associates. Just before the election of 1871, Whitney was instrumental in forming the Young Men's Democratic Club, which contributed to the tremendous victory of the Apollo Hall (anti-Tammany Hall) faction of the Democratic Party, including Tilden: a victory for clean municipal government. The Tammany survivors were still to be dealt with. In January of the following year the Apollo General Committee held its primaries. Whitney was elected from the Eighteenth Ward and prepared the set of resolutions which became the party platform.

However, Tilden vacillated between outright reform and the need for the Tammany organization and finally decided on the latter course of political expediency. Whitney, at this stage of his political career, was shocked and uncompromising, but years later Henry Adams would lump both him and Tilden among those "men who played the [political] game for ambition or amusement, and played it, as a rule, much better than the professionals, but whose aims were considerably larger than those of the usual player, and who felt no great love for the cheap drudgery of the work." Adams' detachment is Olympian but perhaps not as accurate concerning Whitney's "love for the drudgery of the work" as was the more immediate and intimate picture Flora gave in a letter written during the summer of 1872 to her sister Molly:

> . . . William is *in politics* and the first thing that kind of business does is to take a man away from the bosom of his family. I submit, as I think it is the duty of young men to work when they are called upon in such a time as this. William is a natural politician, and takes to it as a duck to water, and is one of the leaders among the young men. He has made several speeches and has been very highly complimented. He gets invitations almost every day to make addresses around in the Suburbs. It is a good thing for it brings him desirable acquaintances and gives him a reputation that some day when he has leisure for such things will be of use to him. About a hundred committee men are to meet here Wednesday night and you can imagine the pow wow. . . .

It would seem that it was exactly his "love for the drudgery of the work"—his talent for the digestion and organization of details, early evident in law and later in business—combined with his charm and sociability, that attracted him to politics.

It is tempting to go on in detail tracing Whitney's political, professional, and business career—all one, all interlocked—but, excepting the highlights, for our purposes it is more important to emphasize his relationship to his wife and children, particularly to his eldest son Harry, born April 29, 1872, and christened Henry Payne Whitney. In a book of some eight thousand words Flora Whitney described their joy at Harry's birth:

> Never came a Baby into the world, more wanted, with more love ready to welcome him than our Boy. One little life had been given to us before. We had planned and hoped and been ready for it. Fancy had filled our home with Baby cries, and a little cradle had been placed to one side. Then came the agony, and the birth, but the little voice would first be heard in Heaven, and not in the Mother's ears. Our daughter, Leonore, first-born had laid for a moment in her

Mother's arms. She saw the dear little face with the closed eyes, the pretty head—like her Father's—covered with soft brown hair, its tender and perfect little hand. . . .

The passage is typical of Flora, typical of her intense feeling and tough mind that she begin with the loss of her first-born. With her there is no glossing over, no forgetting, and by beginning with the lost Leonore, she makes her happiness and William's at Harry's birth all the greater. Not only in this little journal but in dozens of her own letters and William's it is apparent that they doted on this son. There was simply not the same degree of pleasure in the birth of Pauline (March 21, 1874), or (William) Payne (March 21, 1876), or Olive (January 22, 1878), who died of diphtheria six years later. Perhaps only the birth of their last child, Dorothy (January 23, 1887), excited them as much—partly because she replaced Olive, partly because she came late in their lives. Even in William C. Whitney's various triumphs and defeats—the losses he sustained during the financial panics of the seventies; his aid in the 1874 election of Tilden as governor of New York and in obtaining the presidential nomination for him in 1876, when Tilden lost this disputed election to Hayes; his role as corporation counsel of New York City (1875-82), in which he contested some 3,800 suits inherited from the Tweed Ring and saved the city about $12,000,000; his substantial contribution, particularly in organizational ability, to the campaign and election of Grover Cleveland in 1884 and his subsequent role as Cleveland's Secretary of the Navy (1885-89), when he modernized the fleet and eliminated corrupt bidding and contracting practices; his long and ultimately victorious struggle (allied with Thomas Fortune Ryan and Peter A. B. Widener) for the Broadway street railway franchise—in none of these did he or his wife seem more interested, more emotionally involved than in Harry.

In the early years of their marriage almost all the letters between Flora and William were tender and loving. The first break occurred when William, having urged Flora to write for publication, discovered the manuscript of *Jilting a Minister,* a novel written in the first person and based on her relationship with a suitor prior to marriage. He mistook it for a recent confessional journal and precipitated not the confession of infidelity he feared but that of his wife's long-suppressed frustration in her role of waiting in the background. It was not she who had been unfaithful but he who had been inattentive—that was the point. With her customary passionate objectivity, she wrote in July of 1874:

I knew I was heavy and awkward, and not this last winter a lithe little lady love to caress; but it added to the hurts, and hurts grow into disappointments, and these into indifference, and these into commonplace living, and then the angel of romance folds forever her wings, or turns and finds its waiting by the cradles of the sleeping children. . . . [She reminds William that he criticized a friend for spoiling his wife.] I wanted to say: "Oh! You men who have wives who love you, be careful lest we wives who are not spoiled envy the spoiled wives of the other men." Is it degrading to your severe manhood to stoop to put on your wife's rubbers, to place the stool at her feet, the shawl over her shoulders, to anticipate her whims?

There was a reconciliation and from William no further accusations of infidelity; instead, the reverse. As he continued to travel and be separated from Flora, as inevitably he spent evenings and sometimes afternoons of horseback riding in the company of other women, her list of grievances grew longer, her bitterness mounted. It hardly mattered whether the gossip which reached her was based on fact or fantasy or simply maliciousness, William wasn't around much and when he was she was too often pregnant. As she had predicted "romance folds . . . her wings . . . and finds its waiting by the cradles of the sleeping children." Now the children, too, became a battleground on which the parents could assert their love. When Dorothy was born in early 1887, Harry had been at Groton for almost three years, and Flora and William seemed close again. However, within a year, as Harry, second in his class, began thinking about college, the choice between Yale and Harvard became the occasion for an epistolary battle between his parents. Flora wanted Harry to go to Yale where her brother went without graduating and where William himself did his undergraduate work before going on to Harvard Law School. She wrote that she had "neither sympathy, nor association, nor admiration for Harvard . . . I never heard you advance any argument but the one of there being more gentlemen's sons there than at Yale. As two-thirds of these come from the State of Massachusetts, that did not mean much to me, though I feel that you may have unconsciously a filial feeling. . . ." William was indignant. He had been associated with both institutions and recently investigated both again, had studied the subject of education for twenty-five years, "including the bulky volumes of the Parliamentary Commission. . . . I resented to the last degree when in college the narrowness of Yale College in every way. In religion, it nearly drove us all to the bad—but no matter about that—the instruction was bad, stupid, not stimulating to the mind . . . we learned nothing."

William seemed to have forgotten that his friend Sumner had been instrumental in liberating Yale from the clergy. In any case, his arguments were to no avail. Harry chose Yale and dropped the special study program required for Harvard. Nevertheless, at Groton he remained high in his class and at Yale did even better. There he received oration appointments in his junior and senior years and was elected to Phi Beta Kappa. He was also on the *Yale Daily News* board and the Junior Promenade and Class Supper committees; was a member of Hé Boulé, Psi Upsilon, and Skull and Bones; and had, in his leisure at school and during holidays and vacations, become an excellent horseman, particularly proficient at polo. The list of activities reminds us of those of William C. Whitney. Like him Harry is bright, energetic, sociable, and popular with his classmates. Almost without having him described, we know he is attractive. We hardly have to be told that—again, like his father—he is tall, about six feet; erect in posture, standing or sitting; strong and athletic in physique; and handsome, even more so than his father. Harry's nose is straighter; his blue-gray eyes larger and set farther apart, piercing and observant like his father's but more tender and sensuous, as is his mouth too. Many friends remark on Harry's boyishness, which is emphasized by the way he parts his dark brown hair, almost straight down the middle, just slightly to the left, and by the boisterous enthusiasm of his strong voice and hearty laugh, which we remember from the night, years before, when Gertrude heard him returning home from a Yale football victory.

Yes, there is much about Harry that reminds us of his father, much that seems, superficially at least, an improvement upon him. However, there is one most profound difference: William C. Whitney had to work, had really to struggle, in his early years for his money. Harry was given his. Especially after Flora's death in 1893, as Harry and his father drew closer and closer, there was not only the typical spoiling of a very rich man's son— horses, carriages, theater tickets (fifty one time when Harry came down from Yale)—but an extreme degree of solicitation when Harry was sick and protectiveness when he was well. Frequently, in the correspondence between them, we have the feeling that William wanted only for Harry to have the benefits of his wealth (about $20,000,000) without any of the effort and discomfort he himself had experienced in accumulating it. One even suspects that when William was so strenuously urging Harry to go to Harvard, his own memories of his difficult years at Yale had as much to do with the decision as the alleged educational superiority of Harvard. In short, though Harry has had all the advantages of two exceptionally distinguished parents and their great wealth, he has been prepared better for the leisurely sporting life of a gentleman and the custodianship of wealth than for a committed career from which he could receive satisfaction.

This, then—after a year's travel abroad following graduation from Yale and after beginning study at Columbia Law School—is the young man with whom Gertrude has come to an understanding; her Prince Charming, quite literally trained as such; the Boy Next Door, both now on Fifth Avenue at 57th Street and earlier at Murray Hill. Though the Whitneys are not the economic equals of the Vanderbilts, they have more than enough money, a slightly superior social position, and a more distinguished genealogy. Gertrude is confident that Harry is marrying her for herself. However, she probably does not know how much she reminds Harry of his mother, particularly his mother as both sensitive private journalist and (especially during the Washington years) as brilliant hostess and creator of dreamlike environments—in both these roles, like Gertrude, the materializer of fantasies. And Gertrude surely does not yet know how profoundly these attractive similarities reinforce Harry's identification with his father.

⇌ *1896 Continued*

The afternoon of Saturday, March 21, when Gertrude and Harry have taken a walk and resolved that she will tell her mother and he his father, Harry leaves her at her house and crosses the street to his own. Gertrude enters the parlor. There Mama is chatting with Mr. Harriman, who remains only a short while. When he leaves Gertrude gets up and walks about.

"Where did you go this afternoon?" Mama asks.

Without preparation Gertrude replies, "I am engaged."

"Engaged! Gertrude! Who to?"

"Harry!"

Mama's surprise is beyond words.

"Do you like it?" Gertrude asks.

"Yes. This afternoon?"

"Oh no—a long time ago [exactly a week]—on the trip."

Mama cannot believe it. She kisses Gertrude.

There is no similarly detailed account of Harry's conversation with his father but it must have gone smoothly. Within a few hours Harry begins a letter in ink to Mr. Vanderbilt and after several words decides to draft it in pencil:

Dr. Mr. V.

As you may have suspected, I am in love with Gertrude & have asked her to be my wife. She has consented and has told Mrs. V. so that I write this to tell you of it & to ask for your consent.

I fully appreciate the responsibility of taking Gertrude from a home like hers but will make it my life's duty & pleasure to try to make her happy & feel certain that I shall be able to do so.

I did not realize that you were going away again so soon or I should have found an opportunity to speak to you about it before you started.

Yours truly,

Harry rewrites the letter entirely in ink, spells out the *Vanderbilt* name, changes each ampersand to *and*, then adds a sentence about his love for Gertrude. At two o'clock in the morning he is still writing—but now to Gertrude herself, from his father's country home in Westbury, Long Island:*

. . . I feel so happy, oh so happy. As you say it seems more real & true. It's been more like a dream. I haven't really realized all it meant. It was simply that I loved you & that you loved poor me & that was all. And then when I came to write it down to your father, I had never formulated it before & was afraid to think of it. Oh my precious Gertrude it seems too much.

If I had thought that you were waiting for my letter in such a critical mood I could not have written it. It was not hard. I did not try it until late because I was overflowing with everything else & could not quiet down, I wrote the first quickly, thought that it sounded blunt & added that other sentence. I would rather not have said it, as it seemed to be something just between you & me.

And then the mockery of coming down here. And your regretting making me miss a train. What are trains to minutes with you dearest & you know it. They are my life now & all that I live for & a train, why I didn't think of it twice. It was all happiness at being with you longer.

Goodnight
Ever ever yours
Harry

By Easter Sunday, Gertrude and Harry have told several close friends and relatives but have still neither heard from Mr. Vanderbilt nor agreed on a date for the public announcement of their engagement. On the card accompanying his Easter flowers, Harry writes to Gertrude, "I've told Almeric [Paget, his brother-in-law] but not Polly [his sister Pauline]." But already rumors are circulating. Esther writes to Gertrude the same day: "Dearest, Your thought above all pleased me, and what a beautiful plant —Gertrude, when am I to see you? And are you engaged to Harry Whitney? . . ." By Tuesday, Esther has her answer and writes: ". . . of course I am glad for you but I love you and really I want to see you—/Always

---

* The Westbury area on the north shore of Long Island about twenty-seven miles east of New York is presently divided into Old Westbury (including the Whitney property) and Westbury. Gertrude and Harry generally refer to the property simply as Westbury, though the correct mailing address is Old Westbury; the train station, Roslyn; and the phone, Wheatley Hills. For convenience, we will use "Westbury."

Faithfully/Esther," then adds, "It hurts! And yet I am so glad for you." And by Friday she writes a longer protestation of enduring love, one of many from Esther during the months remaining until Gertrude's marriage:

My very dearest—

The world is a new world since last Tuesday—Somehow I feel as if we were beginning now the friendship of our life, an older and steadier one—Do you feel this? I love you Gertrude, and you must feel that nothing I can ever do for you will be too hard—Dearest, it is my wish to be of use to you—Every night I prayed that there should not be much longer before everything should come out all right—I love to think of you in your great happiness, and with you it always will last—You are the kind to hold anyone to you, and to make them wish to love you more, and know you better—

Yours Faithfully
Esther

However, during this period of awkward private "engagement," Harry is by far Gertrude's most faithful correspondent, writing to her day after day as "Dearest" or sometimes "Dearest Gertrude" and closing these letters too frequently, "In haste." Indeed, now as on the Southern trip, "in haste" is the story of their lives together. Visits are often as short as five or ten minutes, seldom as long as half an hour, and always by appointment from across the street. Everything must be proper and circumspect, even more so than if Harry were an ordinary suitor. After seeing Gertrude one Friday night, he writes:

. . . It was such an unsatisfactory (how I hate that word) way of seeing you—so short that the pleasure of seeing you was all shadowed-over & spoilt by the thought of losing you at the end of the short minutes. . . . It sort of seems as if we were each other's for only a brief moment each day—*then* we seem to be in our own different life & alone together on the "threshold" of our own individual life—something too happy & blessed & beautiful & sweet—and then the rest of the day, strangers—sitting in a distant box, seeing all the men in turn smiled on &, being the only one who is a stranger—who can't go into the box, who can't ride, who can't walk, who can't be asked to dine, who can't even seem neighborly in case of a meeting. . . .

After an evening at the opera Harry is sick once again, this time with an "acute infection" of his eyes—"possibly measles." From bed he dictates to Gertrude through Pauline, who now, like Almeric, knows about the "engagement." She adds this postscript: "Don't be worried about the boy, Gertrude dearest, there is nothing much the matter, I hope, and I will let you know *everything*." Later the same day Harry dictates another letter: "It is not measles!!!!, so eyes are all right!" Again Polly adds a postscript: "What it is to have an angel for a sister!!—If you don't love me after this, you never will! Harry is very much better in body and extremely low in spirits, and wishes that he was married!!"

Although by late April Gertrude's and Harry's closest friends and relatives know about the "engagement" (still placed privately in quotes), there is a larger world, including most of Gertrude's suitors, who have not been informed. For example, on April 20 Jim Barnes sends Gertrude the manuscript of *Stirling*, the beginning of a novel he is working on and has previously "threatened" to show her. Until now there has not been a clue from Gertrude that Jim's interests have shifted from electrical experiments to writing, but her enthusiastic response to his book indicates that he has at last found his calling. Indeed, as he now disappears, partially though not entirely, from her life, it is worth mentioning that within another two or three years he will become a very successful journalist, especially as a war correspondent and travel writer. But now, in response to Gertrude's encouragement he sends another letter: ". . . Do you know that you are the first person who has read *Stirling* so far as it goes? When I have the rest of it finished, should you care to see it, I should be delighted to send it to you. (You may bring it good luck, you know.) Pray do not think that I am so wrapped up in my work that I can't think of anything else. . . ."

Given the epistolary conventions of the day, there is no doubt of Jim's continuing interest. What, we wonder, would Gertrude's reaction have been, had she received it two or three months earlier, before Harry began advising her on her relationship to Jim? Would she have been willing to follow him on the course toward which he is now heading? And if willing to follow, would he really want her to?

Another uninformed suitor is Philip Lydig. During the last week in April he writes her too and complains about an abortive riding date for which Harry was supposed to get him a horse. When Phil arrives at the stable the "horses were all engaged for the afternoon . . . and Harry, although pretending to help me, ostensibly, is, between ourselves, a fraud." But perhaps Harry deserves some sympathy. He is, as he says, "the only one who is a stranger."

Many times he urges Gertrude to announce their engagement and set the wedding date. Why she delays is not entirely clear. There are no journals from mid-April until after marriage, except for a brief retrospective entry, made August 13, and tacked on to the journal dealing mostly with the Southern trip:

> It was some time before we heard from Papa. [His letter of consent is dated April 1, but may have taken a week or so to arrive.] Harry and I saw each other every day, but we had to be very careful on account of people and servants, etc. He used to come and dine quite

often and oh! the evenings we had in Papa's office, and the after-noons and mornings in the library. I hated the idea of announcing the engagement soon and so it was not till the 10th of June that it came out. People were not much surprised, I must say, and everyone thought it delightful, etc.

This, then, seems to describe the compromise made during the many weeks until the engagement is publicly announced. And yet other corre-spondence indicates that Papa's continuing battle with Cornelius, Jr., con-tributes to the delay. Since Neily's return—or, more accurately, recall—from abroad, after reuniting with Grace Wilson in Paris, he has been vir-tually banished from his father's sight and is in poor health. In several let-ters he seeks Gertrude's sympathy and support: "I meant this morning that I should not get married while I was ill, but that I was to be the judge of my being well. Well enough to have someone who cares take care of me, if necessary. So please understand." He goes on to explain that Dr. Draper has, on their parents' instructions, contacted Miss Wilson and told her he shouldn't get married. He is outraged and as determined as ever to marry her. To this letter—or perhaps to another on the same subject—Gertrude replies:

Dear Neily,

I can't say what I want to half the time—the words stick in my throat. Please, please don't announce your engagement now. You may think because I do not say much that I don't really care for you. You may think too that I am as narrow as the others and that I don't un-derstand your point of view. That is not so. I care so much for you that if I were not absolutely sure that you would not be happy I would take your side against the family. I am not narrow and I know how hard your position is and how desperate you feel, but you are not going to do yourself any good by announcing it, and you certainly are going to do Miss Wilson harm. . . . When people are sure of their feelings it is not such a hard thing to wait. You are positive you won't change, you are positive she won't change—why can't you wait? You will say your position is a hard one. True, but not as hard as it will be if you announce this engagement. What could be my object in saying all this if I did not care for you. The family have not asked me to speak to you.

It's four years ago tonight you came down to New York and found Willie dying. He died and you—instead of taking his place—what are you about to do? If you have said you would announce don't think you can't go back on that. If Miss Wilson really cares for you she will not mind waiting. I tell you I know & I am a girl. If you have told Mr. Wilson you will announce it go & tell him tomorrow that you will wait & if he is honorable he will say you are right. . . .

While all this is going on within the Vanderbilt household, Gertrude and Harry begin to prepare guest lists. At the same time, too, they write to each other concerning their anxiety about marriage, and at least twice Harry writes to Gertrude about her superiority to him, his unfitness for her. Frequently, again, he complains of headaches as he divides himself between attentions to Gertrude and to his law studies, and sometimes he goes to Westbury just so he can study. But in May he writes from there in a more exuberantly healthy mood than usual:

FRIDAY—MIDNIGHT

Dearest

Work is over &, as writing makes me seem to be a little nearer to you—almost like talking to you—I will write. But, as it is for my own selfish purpose of being with you, you may not think what things might better have been written nor yet criticise what will be, how trivial soever it may prove.

I have really done pretty fair work this afternoon & tonight. It is curious, but it seems almost as if making up my mind to go away, to make myself work & not to think always about you, really gave my old mind a chance. To-night it has really worked well again. When it came time to come down here, I almost gave it up, but my head had gotten so stuffy, that I finally kept on & had Prince Charming—the finest horse on earth—meet me at Mineola, 7 miles from home, & galloped all the way over the plains. It was dusk, fairly dark before we got home, & the old horse flicked along, snorting with pleasure at every stride (resisting any attempt at steadying him), flying over the little sunken lanes, that cut through the plains in all directions, in & out of the big wave-like hollows & pulling up dancing at the end of it. Oh a great horse & I kept thinking all the time he was galloping along how much you would enjoy him—I know you could ride him, & how queer he will look with a side saddle & what will he think of it. Tommy Hitchcock used to own him & Mrs. H. has always wanted to ride him, as he was the only horse of Tom's that she had not ridden.

He is nervous & high strung &, when Papa rides him now & then, each drives the other crazy. But he is the finest on Earth.

I did not mean to imply in that note this aft. that you mightn't be able to get on without me till Monday. It was all selfish. I was not thinking of your feelings, Dear, though I might have & ought to have. Only of my own.

On Monday—I have exam. in the afternoon—how about ten o'clock? or any other time you say, but say.

Good night, Dearest.
God bless you.
Harry

More typically, though, Harry is irritated by his law studies. He ends one letter: "After working last night & this morning, I believe that I know less than when I started. It is the greatest rot imaginable." Then, as so often: "In haste." In another letter he says he is "going down to the Club to drown my feelings in innumerable cocktails."

The pre-engagement period seems almost as unhappy for Harry as for Neily, who writes Gertrude on June 8: "We have announced 'it' and thus far everyone is pleased. . . . We are going to be married on Thursday [June] 18 and I need not say how much I wish you would be there, but suppose you cannot." We don't know the exact words of Gertrude's reply, although surely she would not be permitted to attend the wedding, but on June 11 Cornelius, Jr., writes to her in a very different tone:

Dear Sister,
Please don't write me like that again. For you know I am positive that I am in the right & I won't change, and I have not the least desire to.

I am as sorry as possible about the row, but it cannot be helped.

All my friends are rallying around me, and people I thought were quite the reverse are enthusiastic so your arguments about public opinion are reversed.

The invitations for our wedding go out today, and I hope sincerely it will be very very quiet & small.

For you know my opinions on that subject.

If we should go to Newport part of the summer, you will be surprised to see how people will treat us. I must stop as I am very hurried.

Your aff. bro.
C.

The same day Neily writes this note, the announcement of his engagement appears (two days late) on the front page of the *Times*, right below that of his sister's engagement to Harry. Except for the sub-headline, the top story is straightforward: "MISS VANDERBILT ENGAGED/She Is to Marry Henry Payne Whitney, the Friend of Her Brothers." The story stresses "the long and intimate association of the two families" and ends: "This engagement has the cordial approval of all the members of each family." In contrast, the longer story, placed below, is headed: "AGAINST MR. VANDERBILT'S WISH/His Son Cornelius Will Marry Miss Grace Wilson Soon." Mr. Wilson is quoted: ". . . Cornelius Vanderbilt, Sr. is opposed to the marriage—on what grounds I do not wish to discuss. It is untrue that my daughter is eight years older than Mr. Vanderbilt. She is twenty-five years old, and he is twenty-three." Cornelius Vanderbilt, Sr., "authorized the statement that 'The engagement of Cornelius Vanderbilt, Jr. to Miss Wilson is against his father's expressed wish.' Mr. Vanderbilt declined to add anything to that sentence, or to say what he would do in regard to allowances to his son or the final allotment of his property. The attentions of young Mr. Vanderbilt to Miss Wilson have been a subject of talk and newspaper notices for several months, and his father's opposition to the match has been known to everybody."

"Miss Wilson's father is a broker and banker. His reputed wealth is "far beyond $1,000,000." His eldest daughter, May Wilson, is married to Ogden Goelet. His eldest son, Marshall Orme Wilson, is married to Caroline Astor, daughter of Mrs. William Astor. Their younger sister, Belle Wilson, is married to Michael H. Herbert, brother of the Earl of Pembroke. With family connections like these, Mr. and Mrs. Wilson's rage at the rejection of their daughter is understandable. (Who do these *nouveaux riches* Vanderbilts think they are?) The Wilsons send out the invitations for June 18, including one to Gertrude. However, within a few days these are followed by a card announcing that

Mr. and Mrs. Wilson are obliged to postpone their daughter's wedding on account of the serious illness of Mr. Cornelius Vanderbilt, Jr.

Neily has had an attack of rheumatic fever, described now as "chronic." The wedding date is "indefinite."

So too, thus far, is Gertrude's and Harry's. William C. Whitney wants Harry to complete his law studies without distraction. The Vanderbilts want no more precipitousness. All three urge the couple to put their wedding off until September. However, even with the engagement announced, Harry still finds their situation "unsatisfactory." Almost always their meetings are in public—at formal dinner parties, balls, operas, dozens of events planned around them by well-meaning friends and relatives but, more literally, surrounding them. Finally, Gertrude and Harry settle on August 25 as being "almost September." Yet despite the many events (scarcer as the summer goes on), Harry spends most of June, July, and August in New York and Long Island, studying, riding, playing golf and polo, sailing, and writing almost every day to Gertrude in Newport. His letters are full of love and of complaints about his studies, missing her, and various physical and/or psychosomatic ailments. In one, dated June 22, he mentions telling some friends that a particular polo match may be his last. Rollie Cottenet's sister says perceptively and, from Harry's viewpoint, irritatingly: "Why I thought you were engaged to sport." Harry devotes the rest of the long letter to assuring Gertrude that she is his only interest in life. . . . For a few days he visits The Rocks, his family's place in Newport, so he can be near Gertrude at The Breakers. . . . In July he visits Whitney property in Lenox, Massachusetts, to see that work is proceeding properly on a house being built for their honeymoon, but nothing is going right and soon he is back in New York with a fever and "sick headache."

During Harry's convalescence, his father reads him a novel by Frank Norris which Harry finds "tiresome and insipid," though Mr. Whitney thinks it "equal to Thackeray." It is partly about a couple who marry too young and discover that their experiment has been a failure. Harry writes Gertrude: "They lacked both of what we decided were essentials—i.e., to love or to care for the same things in life."

As Harry's illness drags on, Gertrude teases him with a letter about Jim Barnes. Harry doesn't find it amusing. Everything seems to be going wrong—his health, the work on the cottage in Lenox, and now her "horrid letter." Harry's only consolation is that his father has arranged to have the head guide from the Whitney camp in the Adirondacks (then some 70,000 acres, later enlarged by another 40,000) come down to Lenox and "put up a couple of Adirondack tents, one for sleeping & one for eating & we can use them for a couple of days while they finish the house. I really rather like the idea. Something more romantic about it. Love me in a tent —not even a cottage."

Harry and Cornelius, Jr., are not the only ones to feel the tension of imminent marriages. In July, Cornelius, Sr., now fifty-six, has a paralytic stroke. After this, on August 3, the day of her brother's rescheduled marriage, Gertrude writes to her cousin and intimate friend (or "playmate," as they call each other) Adele Burden in Paris. With Adele she can be very open. No one has written to her and Harry more enthusiastically and lovingly about their engagement—and about the possibility of a beautiful honeymoon, mostly in Japan like the Burdens' own. And no one is suffering more right now than Adele, whose baby Emily is very sick. Yes, Adele will understand. After expressing great sympathy for Emily's suffering and Adele's helplessness, Gertrude writes:

> I too have been through an anxious time. When they sent for me in Newport to go down and see Papa two days after he had the stroke they did not think he could live, but now he is better and though his recovery is very very slow, the doctors say he will recover. But it will probably be three months before he can stand again, and even then— we don't know. And there are other troubles besides sickness. Today, Adele, Neily is to [be] married. He *knows* it is his behaviour (that of course is private) that gave Papa his stroke, he refused to see him. Never took the trouble to walk across the hall & ask how he was. When he was told Papa's life depended on it he would not say he would even put off the wedding. I used to feel that it would be hard when he married her not to see him, now I don't care, I would go out of my way to avoid him. He is inhuman, crazy. Whatever you want to call it. I don't believe he will ever come in the house again. He won't come without her and that is out of the question. Of course Papa can't be told for months. Thanks, dearest Adele, for writing me

all about Japan when you were so worried about other things. We won't go now. Papa is not well enough. . . .

≈

Letters! Between early April and late August Gertrude and Harry receive and answer several hundred, many drafted and rewritten, some with each other's supervision. There are first the letters to close relatives and friends to whom they want to tell the news before it appears in the paper. Then there are the letters from those who hear from those who have been told. And finally there is the greatest wave from those who read the public announcement. Almost every letter contains the sentiment that the match is perfect, that Gertrude and Harry are made for each other, that they are a pair of bricks. However, the letters are not all mechanically congratulatory. Many are long and nostalgic, requiring thoughtful responses. There is hardly a person mentioned in Gertrude's journals who does not write—and many of them more than once—every girl friend, every suitor, the parents of friends, the friends of her own parents, aunts, uncles, cousins, doctors, lawyers, ministers, teachers (including Miss Winsor and Miss Wheeler of Brearley), and Harry hears from the same categories (including Endicott Peabody of Groton and various teachers at Yale and Columbia) until finally Gertrude, like Harry, is signing "In haste." But this is only the beginning: there are letters to prospective ushers and bridesmaids, there are thank-you notes for gifts, there are relatives to put up in Newport, there are honeymoon arrangements to be made, there are hundreds of details, more of them Gertrude's responsibility than would have been if Mama were not distracted by Papa's illness, about which, in addition to everything else, Gertrude sends frequent encouraging reports to Gladys ("dear little ducky daddles"), who has been sent early from the gloom of 57th Street to The Breakers.

Gertrude has no time for her journal and Harry is harassed by his law studies. Still she can find time to write long letters to Adele and, later, to Esther, who is by then also in Europe. To her, in July, she writes: ". . . I never thought it possible to care for anyone the way I care. Sometimes the way I feel reminds me a little of something *you* have said and I wonder if you ever could have cared for me anything like this way. I am sorry for you if you did. . . . Esther, you must get engaged, you don't know what it is to be absolutely happy until you are."

As to Harry, in what may be his final letter during this premarital period, he notes that Cornelius, Jr., "is married and has started for Saratoga so the papers say. Frank Polk best man. Poor Neily & poor Grace. Still they may fool us all & be happy." This brings to Harry's mind the end of the book by Norris, in which the father (of the young man who has married unhappily) generalizes: " 'Matrimony is a deplorable institution. As a cause of misery I should rank it second only to drink. . . .' " Harry continues: "And he then agrees with you that love & so happiness can only last a year; or two at most. As to women—'Women are only adjuncts of existence, the world belongs to the men. . . .' (Beautiful, is it not?)"

Obviously Gertrude has spoken to Harry about the unequal treatment of women, of which she has been aware since childhood in her own family, among others. Her relationship with Harry is open enough so that he can joke about this. Yet in the joking there is condescension, as there is also in both his and Gertrude's attitude toward other marriages, except for the Burdens'. However veneered with worldly sophistication, there is an underlying naïveté in Gertrude's and Harry's great expectations mixed with a rather smug assurance that their marriage will be better than most people's.

Cornelius' wedding is, of course, front-page news. The world is informed that it is simple—without wedding breakfast; without music; without Vanderbilts, except for Cornelius, Jr., himself. As Gertrude's and Harry's own wedding draws near, there is speculation in the papers as to whether or not the new Mr. and Mrs. Cornelius Vanderbilt, Jr., will be permitted to attend. "Miss Vanderbilt has been ceaseless in her efforts to re-establish peace between the father and son, and during Mr. Vanderbilt's illness is believed to have urged her brother to defer his marriage for at least a year. Unsuccessful in this, she did not give up hope, and as her own wedding day approached is said to have redoubled her efforts to have it a day of family reunion."

Newspaper stories concerning the Vanderbilts and the Whitneys are now almost as frequent as the letters they receive. Most of the stories deal with the imminent wedding. However, since the spring, William C. Whitney's name has appeared often as an important Democratic defender of the gold standard ("sound money") against William J. Bryan's advocacy of "free silver," and he has been urged again and again to seek the presidential nomination. He refuses for many reasons, including his health; the death of his wife who, personally and through the Payne family, had inspired his former political ambitions; and potentially damaging gossip concerning his liaison with Mrs. Edith S. Randolph, the thirty-seven-year-old attractive and socially well-connected widow of a British army captain. Though not a candidate, he works quietly and exhaustingly before and during the Democratic Convention in Chicago in July trying "to save the party." Against his wishes there are WHITNEY FOR PRESIDENT placards at the convention and for a few days before recognition of Bryan's greater popularity, it looks as if Whitney may be drafted.

This is a big story, a public one that fizzles and sputters as William C. Whitney withdraws from politics and before he is on the front pages again when he marries Mrs. Randolph in September. . . . But now, in August, on the Tuesday a week before their own wedding, Gertrude and Harry attend that of Mo Taylor and Edith Bishop, with Gertrude flatteringly seated at the bridal table. . . . The following Saturday, Gertrude gives a dinner at The Breakers in honor of her bridesmaids: her cousins Emily and Lila Sloane and Edith Shepard and her friends—actually the sisters of closer friends—Minnie Taylor and Angelica Gerry. . . . Sunday, Pauline and Almeric Paget give a dinner in honor of Gertrude and Harry . . . . The next night Gertrude's uncle William K. Vanderbilt has a party for the entire bridal party aboard his yacht, the *Valiant*. . . . That is the day before the wedding, and then the floral decorations being installed at The Breakers make the front page:

> . . . The ceremony is to take place in the gold room, or grand salon, and between the groups of twin columns here, which form alcoves, large vases, filled to overflowing with lilies, Augusta Victoria roses, and anchorist amazonica[*sic*], are to stand. Bunches of rare cut flowers will stand about the room in cases. The fireplace is to be banked with fern. A feature of the decoration here will consist of a prie dieu of white sweetpeas and lilies of the valley, on which the bride and bridegroom will kneel. The gray room, where the then Mr. and Mrs. Whitney will receive congratulations, under a canopy of foliage, will be blooming white and pink roses. The grand hall will be charmingly decorated with cascades of fine asparagus and maiden hair ferns, white lilies, hydrangea, pink and white roses, pink and white gladioli, terminating with ruffles of pink and white sweetpeas, and sprays of lily of the valley. There will be twelve of these cascades, and at their bases there will be roses apparently growing. . . .

The article runs ten column inches. We learn that Harry drives to the city clerks' office and takes out the license, giving his age ("twenty-four") and his occupation ("law student") and that of his bride's father ("railroad man"). "It cannot be learned whether or not Mr. Vanderbilt will give his daughter away. . . . He can stand with assistance now, and so, with aid, could take his part of the ceremony. . . ."

The weather in Newport on Tuesday, August 25, is warm but fresh, the skies clear blue and almost cloudless. The newspapers will make much of this meteorological auspiciousness: ". . . if sunshine is a good omen, Mr. and Mrs. Whitney's life will be one of continued pleasure."

The gardeners and florists have finished their work. The halls of The Breakers have become a cool marble conservatory, heavy with the smell of flowers trembling in a gentle breeze from the ocean. There are no mysteries here, except that of vast wealth itself. Everything is exposed. The questions raised by newspapers and magazines are quickly answered as, in the late morning, guests assemble in the grand salon. Yes, because of Mr. Vanderbilt's health, the wedding party will be small—just over sixty, mostly Vanderbilts (the family is much larger than that of the Whitneys), a few very close friends. No, Mr. and Mrs. Cornelius Vanderbilt,

Jr., are not invited. The additional excitement of *that* might be too much
for Cornelius, Sr. Yes, he will take part in the ceremony. After the guests,
sitting in gilded chairs, have listened to Nathan Franko conduct Jensen's
"Wedding March," Wagner's "Prize Song" from *Die Meistersinger*,
Rubinstein's "Melody," Schumann's "Träumerei," and Raff's "Cavatina,"
Mr. Vanderbilt, in a plush-covered invalid's chair, is wheeled into an al-
cove of the salon, smiling and looking less sick than had been feared, his
face tanned from sitting in the sun for a few hours each day. His eyes are
alert and he takes as obviously keen an interest in the proceedings as he
has in the last-minute preparations for the wedding. He has given the
order to turn on the fountains in the grand hall and the surrounding gardens. He has made out checks to each of the indoor and outdoor servants.
Now he studies Harry Whitney and his brother Payne Whitney, the best
man, standing together at the altar. Like Harry, Payne is handsome and
athletic—a member then of the Yale crew and later its captain. The two
young men look almost like twins, dressed in dark frock coats, vicuña
waistcoats, striped gray and black trousers. Harry wears a boutonnière of
gardenias, his brother one of orchids.

The orchestra begins the "Bridal Procession" from *Lohengrin*. The
ushers—Gertrude's youngest brother Regi, a student at St. Paul's, and
Harry's close friends Rollie Cottenet, Columbus Baldwin, Philip Mac-
Millan, and the ubiquitous Frank Polk, Cornelius, Jr.'s best man three
weeks earlier—each wearing a boutonnière of lilies of the valley on his
frock coat, lead the procession. Then come the bridesmaids—Emily, Lila,
Edith, Minnie, and Angelica—wearing gowns of white silk covered by
mousseline and with inserts and fringes of lace, followed by the maids of
honor, Gertrude's ten-year-old sister Gladys and Harry's nine-year-old sister
Dorothy, both dressed similarly to the bridesmaids but performing their
roles as flower girls. Finally, as the bridesmaids part at the altar, Gertrude
appears on the arm of her favorite brother Alfred.

Gertrude is, according to all accounts, a gorgeous bride in her Doucet
gown (incorrectly reported as coming from Worth) of white figured satin
trimmed with lace that "had been in the family for years" and a veil
"which the bride's mother wore on her wedding day." As Gertrude and
Harry meet at the center of the group they are a strikingly handsome couple, both of them tall, erect, and elegant. The Right Reverend Henry C.
Potter, Bishop of New York, performs the ceremony, assisted by George
Magill, rector of the local Trinity Church. When the time comes for Mr.
Vanderbilt to give his daughter away, he does not stand, though he might
have done so with assistance, but reaches up from his wheel chair and
places Gertrude's hand in Harry's. There is the kiss. There is Handel's
"Largo." There is Mendelssohn's recessional "Wedding March." And, as
Gertrude and Harry receive congratulations in the morning room, there is
finally "The Star-Spangled Banner." Franko comments: "It is so rarely

that an American girl of fortune marries one of her countrymen that I thought the selection decidedly in keeping with the occasion."

Just before twelve-thirty, as the wedding breakfast is to be served, Mr. Vanderbilt is wheeled to the elevator and taken up to his room to eat with his mother, Mrs. William H. Vanderbilt, and Dr. McLane, with two nurses in attendance. In a nearby room on the second floor three detectives guard wedding gifts, including most prominently the diamond tiara and necklace he has given his daughter, a diamond cluster from his brother William K. Vanderbilt, a silver tea service from their mother, a set of diamond pins from William C. Whitney, and five strands of matched pearls, valued at $200,000, from Senator Henry B. Payne; bridesmaids' gifts of brooches of diamonds and pearls in the shape of forget-me-nots; and diamond and pearl stickpins for the ushers.

Downstairs in the dining room, at tables set with old silver and Belfast linen and decorated with lilies of the valley, white orchids, and roses, the guests lower their heads as Bishop Potter asks grace. Without further formality the breakfast begins: Melons, Oeufs à l'Estragon en Bellevue, Turbans de Saumon à la Cardinal, Suprême de Dindon, Lima Beans, Chaudfroid de Maubrettes, [*sic*], Tomates Farcis, Céleri Mayonnaise, Pêches Glacées (shaped as wedding bells), Chantilly, Fruit, Gâteaux Bonbons (the wedding cake is served in satin-covered boxes, tied with white silk ribbons, showing the Whitney monogram† in the fold), and Café. Before two o'clock Gertrude and Harry excuse themselves from the bridal table. They go upstairs and change into traveling clothes (she puts on a blue-gray cashmere dress). Then Gertrude gives her father a last kiss and, in the traditional shower of rice and old shoes, she and Harry leave The Breakers. For a few minutes they are alone in the Vanderbilt carriage as it carries them to the station. There, once more, they briefly face a crowd—strangers now—while boarding a special train to Fort Adams where the *Valiant* waits to take them to Providence on the second leg of their trip to Lenox in the Berkshires.

As in so much of Gertrude's life, and Harry's too, the facts—dates, names, places, things—are recorded and catalogued. For the past few hours—and indeed for the past twenty-one and twenty-four years, respectively—it has seemed as if they themselves are no more than these facts, as if they are props or phenomena placed at the top of a social mechanism in which they occupy much more space than most people, and consume many more things, and yet exist in a spirit of accidental or passive privilege. As they sail smoothly toward Providence, one wonders not whether they will go on from there to Japan (Mr. Vanderbilt's health permitting) but whether, given the education, the travel, the culture, the leisure they

---

† Though the Whitneys are entitled to at least sixteen heraldic quarterings, they always use only a W, while the Vanderbilts, who can boast of no such lineage, have invented their acorn and oak-leaf crest.

have had, they will go on to lead satisfying and useful lives. Among their friends and relatives it is generally assumed that Gertrude is destined for no more specific career than society wife, with all that suggests of a properly reared family, gracious entertaining, and the right amount of energy spent on worthy causes. There are, indeed, a few friends, such as Esther and Adele, who have read bits of her fiction and poetry and suspect that she may have a literary career, but this is vague, no more than a possibility and, even as such, more likely to be a hobby or avocation than a profession. For Harry, as a man, the possibilities seem greater. He, like his father, will probably increase the family fortune and use his knowledge of law to build new industrial empires. Again, like his father, he will, no doubt, use property for pleasure—not just Newport, Westbury, Aiken, Bar Harbor, Lenox, the Adirondacks camp, Sheepshead Bay, and Lexington, New Jersey, but new places. With his mind, his charm, his looks—all as good as or better than his father's, and with Gertrude, potentially even richer than Harry's own mother—who knows where he will go? Perhaps someday he will be President. . . .

All these possibilities fill the heady sea air, even as the *Valiant* sails toward Providence. And as with all lives, there are the other possibilities not yet dreamed of, a spectrum of emotion that reaches appreciably no higher than their present joy but sinks to depths of sadness beyond anything in their past experience. Gertrude and Harry don't yet know that a privileged life is no equivalent to an enchanted one, that their destiny is no more certain than that of Gladys and Dorothy, those pretty little flower girls whose lives, at an even younger age, also seem laid out for them but who, like Gertrude surely, and Harry to some extent, will have surprisingly unpredictable careers and considerable pain as well as pleasure. For Gertrude and Harry, as for Gladys and Dorothy, as for everyone, there will come a day when journalism's sunshine, auspicious of "continued pleasure," will seem ironic.

PART TWO

Wedlock

⇜ 1896 Continued Further

For Gertrude marriage is very nearly a rebirth, surely a much more radical change than for today's women of the same age and social position. This is the first time in her life that she and a man have been alone together for a sustained period of time, without parents nearby, or chaperones, or servants. Everything on top of October Mountain—William C. Whitney's recently purchased 8,000-acre preserve some eight miles outside of Lenox—has been planned by Harry and his father to give the honeymoon couple the maximum in isolated, well-guarded privacy. Tourists and sightseers are kept away, servants are kept at a distance. The "Adirondack tent" about which Harry and his father have corresponded is ready, consisting of four rooms, furnished, according to the *Times*, "in old English style . . . the parlor in Delft blue and white . . . the bedroom [in] old mahogany." There, Gertrude and Harry spend their first few nights on October Mountain, until the honeymoon cottage is completed.

Gertrude writes Esther, "The little house we lived in, the smallest and dearest you have ever seen . . . only had two rooms and a piazza, and we did not have a servant within a quarter of a mile. . . . If you ever get married, Esther (which of course you will, and probably very soon too) don't take a maid on your honeymoon. Harry and I really grew dependent on each other. More than that. There is nothing that brings you so close to a person as having to do the little necessities of life together." Not that Gertrude and Harry are really roughing it. Measured by Newport and New York standards, the bedroom and dining/living room are certainly small, though romantically cozy. Both rooms have coal stoves and are comfortably furnished with oriental rugs on the floors and exotic floral fabrics on the walls. In pictures taken by a local photographer neither the brass double bed nor the dining table and sideboard look at all crowded.

Alas, the outside world has a way of moving in on private fantasies. Within a few days, in a series of letters, Mama sends Gertrude her quarterly allowance check, "forgotten" in the excitement of the wedding; advises Gertrude to write a few notes of acknowledgment each day to friends and relatives; asks if she is warm enough and warns her about taking cold; wonders if and when Gertrude wants Car 493; suggests that Gertrude send her laundry to Newport and that she might want Jeanne (Gertrude's personal maid). Of course, these are minor intrusions. More consequential is the news on September 10 that Harry's grandfather, Senator Henry B. Payne, has died the previous day. Mama advises Gertrude not to wear mourning.

Gertrude and Harry have been playing house little more than a week when they leave October Mountain for the funeral in Cleveland, where (as Gertrude also writes Esther), "I met a lot of [Harry's] relations under rather trying circumstances, but they were as sweet as could be." From there they return with Harry's father, his brother Payne, and his brother-in-law Almeric Paget (Pauline is indisposed by pregnancy) to Wheatley Hills in Westbury, the other estate purchased recently by William C. Whitney but one much more important to Gertrude's and Harry's future life.

The Westbury property, 700 acres of woods and meadows (once twenty farms), is further improved than October Mountain. Though Mr. Whitney has not yet built his home—he is renting a neighbor's large white mansion on the crest of a hill overlooking the property—he has, under the supervision of the landscape architects Olmsted, Elliott & Olmsted, cleared portions of the woods and erected a complete stable, 212 by 50 feet, with an enclosed paddock (an all-weather training or exercising track) extending around the building. The stable is heated by its own furnace, and fresh water is pumped from an artesian well by a windmill large enough to take care of future buildings on the property. In addition to a natural forest of 250 acres, six or seven acres have been set aside as an arboreal nursery containing over 6,000 trees, and surrounding the property a mile-and-a-half steeplechase has been built in the character of an English cross-country run, containing brush, water, and stone-wall jumps. For two days Gertrude rides and walks through the estate with Harry and the three male members of his immediate family, and then she and Harry go to visit her family in Newport.

Though so far it has not been the honeymoon they planned, Gertrude and Harry are pleased that her father is recovering well from his stroke and is even walking a little without support. At least, as originally planned, they can go to Japan, and they are thrilled now to receive a telegram from Adele Burden: "GUIDE MATSUDA WILL BE READY FOR YOU. . . ." Gertrude and Harry hurry back to October Mountain for a last week there before leaving for New York on September 29 en route to Vancouver to board the *Empress of India* for Yokohama.

Again the world intrudes. Two days before Gertrude and Harry leave Lenox, William C. Whitney, now in Bar Harbor, scrawls this brief, startling request to his son:

> As these moments are a little summary, I wish if you & Gertrude feel inclined you wd send your good wishes to Mrs. (Arthur) Randolph by wire Tuesday morning. . . .*

* The same day William C. Whitney writes to President Cleveland: ". . . You know how baseless scandals originate and circulate and I therefore wish to say to you and Mrs. Cleveland that the only person from outside our immediate family whom Mrs. Whitney wished to have with her daily and did have with her daily was Mrs. Randolph. This at the end of her life down to the 2nd or 3rd day before she died."

The note misses Harry in Lenox and reaches him in New York, but by then the papers are full of Mr. Whitney's marriage to Mrs. Randolph. Harry reads that less than a dozen invitations have been issued, that a reason for this privacy is the recent death of Senator Payne, that Harry himself and his wife cannot be present because they are en route to Vancouver, that Pauline and Almeric cannot be present because they are in the Adirondacks, where Mrs. Paget's condition forbids traveling, that Payne cannot be present because he is attending classes at Yale. In short, none of Mr. Whitney's family can be present, and yet the bride's brother, Frederic May, ushers, and the bride's children attend her, while Mr. Whitney is attended by the Danish Minister, a comparative stranger. Harry is shocked. His whole family is shocked, shocked the way Gertrude's was when Cornelius, Jr., married Grace Wilson. But with Mrs. Randolph the discrepancy in age is reversed and therefore acceptable, the discrepancy in wealth unimportant. What turns out to be important—with effects ultimately at least as far-reaching as those caused by Cornelius, Jr.'s marriage—is Oliver Payne's irrational worship of his dead sister Flora. Though she has been dead for more than three and a half years, though William has mourned for her and is now fifty-five and particularly alone since Harry's marriage, Oliver cannot forgive William and is, in fact, so offended that he discards their intimate, near-brotherly relationship of thirty-five years. Encouraged in his fanatical devotion to Flora by the failure of the Whitney children—particularly Pauline and Harry, the two eldest—to attend William's wedding, he urges them not to recognize it and suggests, in effect, that he will from now on be more than their closest, richest uncle (richer than William C. Whitney himself)—he will replace their lapsed apostate father; they will be his children and heirs. Oliver is ultimately successful in influencing Pauline and Payne. But Harry, however great his shock and hurt and however great his love for his mother, is too close to his father to be estranged from him. And Dorothy, only nine at this time, is adored by her father and returns that adoration.

Once Harry and Gertrude are aboard the *Empress of India*, Harry writes to his father explaining his feelings:

> Of course your marriage was a great surprise, and when it was all done it seemed harder to get along with even than in the thought of it last winter. . . . The house [2 West 57th Street] is so much Mama's that it's hard enough to think of somebody living in it in her place without adding to that having it opened to entertainment with another hostess. . . .
>
> The wedding being so sudden put us all in an unpleasant light. Everyone naturally thinks that we all were away because we would not be present, and the fact that we did not hear of it till the day before does not help much. Still it may all be as you say, and turn out well.

Harry concludes more cheerfully:

We had a delightful trip across the Continent in Mr. Vanderbilt's car [493] and everything possible was done for us. The Steamer is very comfortable and we have two of the best cabins and seats next to the Captain. So we are well fixed.

The trip to Yokohama takes two weeks. Gertrude and Harry devote much of that time to letter writing, except when he is seasick. As he tells his father in a subsequent letter from Tokyo, "I had three days in my bunk and very few meals at the table. . . . Gertrude did not miss a meal. She is a splendid traveler." Not until two weeks after their arrival does Gertrude open *My Trip Abroad*, a new black leather-bound blank book with gilt-edged pages and the script legend tooled in gold on the cover. Except for the brief August postscript to the previous journal, it has been almost seven months since she has written to herself (and us).

Her rebirth is accompanied, for the moment at least, by regression. She turns to the back of the book and sets up five columns for dates, places, miles, days, hours. The information is tabulated for Newport to Montreal, Montreal to Vancouver, Vancouver to Yokohama, Yokohama to Nikko. From Nikko she writes (in the front of the book now): "This is not to be a journal, only a little notebook. Traveling is not . . . conducive to much writing." She recalls their hurried plans confirmed only a little more than a week before starting, "not much time to gather together trunks and packages, perhaps that is why we only had about fourteen pieces . . . the Burdens . . . told us just what to take. Harry objected to most of the fine dresses I wanted and, as we had only been married six weeks, I came away with lots of useful clothes. The Burdens came before . . . yes, they did. I am beginning to wish they had not . . . we have the same guide they had; we hear the name of Burden. . . ." Once more the world they thought they had left behind seems to be intruding, but now more obviously than before it intrudes because they have brought it with them. In this journal (or non-journal, as Gertrude prefers) there is the usual close observation of strangers and foreigners mixed with condescension toward them. The friendliest couple they have met aboard ship is "distinctly common." The Japanese are too frequently "Japs" and almost always "funny" and "little." In much of this Harry echoes, or perhaps reinforces, Gertrude's prejudices. In the last-quoted letter to his father he writes: "They have very few horses and everyone uses jinrikshas, a sort of immature hansom, with a little Jap for a horse. At first it seemed cruel to go about all day in one, with the poor little man running along between the shafts dripping with perspiration and we used to insist upon two men to each jinriksha; but now we are quite callous and drive around all day with only one man and really with much less thoughtfulness for the locomotive force than if it were a horse."

In Nikko they travel with the Jodrells—a British colonel and M.P., his wife and daughter—a "nice" (i.e., acceptable) family they have met aboard ship. With them they have an easy, polite relationship, sightseeing and examining bargains in furs. But there are some things Gertrude and Harry see that can only be discussed between themselves and even then with difficulty. "There is a species of 'new woman' in this place. She wears trousers, therein her likeness to the 'new woman.' If she is old, it is difficult to tell her from the men. Harry and I had our first discussion on the subject . . . we never came to any conclusion, as of course we did not like to ask."

The days pass in visits to mountain lakes, streams, and waterfalls; pagodas, temples, and tombs—all noted, with distances by riksha, and historical backgrounds where applicable. The tea begins to taste less bitter, new experiences to seem less boring. In Tokyo, Harry says: "Let's take a house and settle here for the winter." Gertrude thinks seriously about it. "There is no doubt . . . we have caught the fever at last. I am pleased. It is not a bad fever to have." However, there is the competing fever of her compulsive tourism, the Burdens' itinerary, their guide, the places that must be seen or at least checked off the list.

Before leaving Tokyo they receive several important communications from home, some in letters, some in cables, some in English-language newspapers, some in all three. Mama is the most frequent correspondent. Her first letters are joyous and gossipy as she reports on the wedding of Gertrude's cousin Edith Shepard to Ernesto Fabbri and, a little later, on Bryan's defeat by McKinley, whose "election is very gratifying to most thoughtful people" (including not only the Republican Vanderbilts but such hard-money Democrats as William C. Whitney). But within a few days the joy turns to sorrow. First, Gertrude's grandmother, Mrs. William Henry Vanderbilt, dies at the Scarborough, New York, home of her daughter Mrs. Shepard, where she had remained since Edith's wedding, and the next day Harry's sister Pauline has a premature baby who dies. Such news spoils the Mikado's garden party—in Harry's words, "the social event of the Japanese Autumn"—though neither he nor Gertrude is too depressed to be amused (and shocked) by the Emperor's wobbly departure, drunk on champagne. But the most important communication, the one that will have the most lasting effect on their own lives, is a cable from William C. Whitney, offering them his house at 2 West 57th Street.

Gertrude and Harry discuss the matter fully and, as he writes to his father, "We would both prefer to start with a smaller house, though in five years we should want a large one." Then he presents what he considers the main objection: "It would be manifestly improper for us to have it (eminently the home of a prominent citizen, which I am *not* at present) and for you to live in some small house. . . ." And its corollary: "Of course if you are well fixed it is an excellent way out of the difficulty. . . . We children would probably have always had an injured feeling and a sense of injustice with the present state of affairs and it might in time make us drift . . . apart, which would never do. Also I fancy that your wife must prefer a house of her own. I am very much attached to the house and of course am pleased with the idea of having it, but it must not be at your expense."

Given William C. Whitney's passion for property, it is not surprising that he expects to be "well fixed" and that, as Gertrude and Harry continue their travels, he is already planning the alteration of 871 Fifth Avenue, a larger house than the one at 57th. As early as November 19, Mama writes Gertrude: "Yesterday I received a letter from Mr. Whitney telling us that he intended giving Harry his house. . . . I need not tell you and Harry how surprised and delighted your Father and I are. . . . I wrote to Mr. W. that your Father told you he would give you a house before he was taken ill and that as that plan is now spoiled, he must at least let your Father furnish it. This will be a pleasant occupation for you if you get to Paris. . . . I think Mr. Whitney is, as always, the best and most indulgent of Fathers. . . . Don't forget to write Mr. Whitney yourself about the house."

Despite Gertrude's lingering objection to the largeness of 2 West 57th Street, she probably writes a gracious note of thanks. Harry, who is not immune to the hereditary love of real estate, writes a long letter—from Kyoto now—not only accepting his father's "decisions" but going on at length about plans for the development of "a sort of Whitney Village" at Lenox. At the same time, by mail Harry is also completing the purchase, as a gift to Gertrude, of the John Knower "cottage" on Bellevue Avenue and The Cliffs in Newport between the homes of Mrs. William Astor and Hermann Oelrichs, a short distance from The Breakers. The waterfront property of slightly over three acres costs $250,000, without remodeling and enlargement, which will start immediately so that the place can be ready by summer.

⮜ *1897*

Among the last letters Gertrude receives in Japan is one from her mother, written just after Christmas and marked DESTROY. It begins routinely with thanks for Christmas presents and for a cable Gertrude has sent and it lists other presents, flowers, and greetings the family has received, including "lots of toys and pretty things" for Gladys and "the most

superb basket of orchids" from Colonel Payne ("He does things roy-
ally!!"). After six pages of Christmas news, as such, Mama writes: "Your
Father went to Communion—up to the chancel rail, I mean—for the first
time & that made him very happy. . . . Cornelius [just home from his
honeymoon abroad, following widespread rumors that Grace has had a
child in Switzerland] has written three letters to him of the sort you might
expect, saying he was sorry Father was ill & that he wanted to come home
& see him. Never saying, however, he was sorry he had acted as he did or
anything to show contrition except that they differed. Your Father got Dr.
McLane to cable him not to come home as he did not wish to see him at
present & an interview would be impossible. . . ."

On the trip from Yokohama to San Francisco, Gertrude, now three
months' pregnant, is miserable and this time, like Harry, frequently sick.
The journal peters out in brief, retrospective entries concerning Japanese
theater, a horseback trip with Harry in the mountains near Fuji, and three
weeks spent in Kyoto during which "Harry went more and more often by
himself." There will be no more journals for several years—at least none
survive—but rather dinner party books and bits of sketchy fiction. As Gertrude and Harry board Car 493, after three days in San Francisco, it seems
that she is hurrying home to have her baby and assume the role of society
matron.

During the spring they half settle in the 57th Street house, intending to
move to Newport as soon as possible so that Gertrude will be comfortably
established there for the birth of her first child. Meanwhile, she makes several trips to see her family, presently in Washington, D.C., and Harry
does some reading in law and a great deal of riding. He also buys a team
of horses—four solid bays with black points—for driving. These he and
Gertrude name Aladdin, Amazon, Aspiration, and Ambition—qualities
necessary for a successful trip through life, the first two signifying Magic
(or Luck) and Strength.

Early in June Harry writes from Newport to his father in Westbury:

> Your fears about my becoming a "dilettante" amuse me. I average
> about eight miles a day on a bicycle and two hours of golf—running
> this place, horse back rides, and some law thrown in.
>
> About polo. I am not going to play in any matches until the Au-
> gust ones here. Gertrude is going to have a baby and though the
> game does not worry her, I don't want to run the risk of being injured
> and having that added care. . . .

A few days later Gertrude drafts a letter to Mrs. Jodrell, the British lady
she and Harry met on their honeymoon: "We have been home now some
time but it does not seem as if I had been settled till now. . . . Then the
houses! Oh those houses! I have fussed over this one [in Newport] & I
wish you could see it. It's very simple and all that, but very comfortable

too. And imagine, I had no sooner gotten things to rights here than those Japanese things arrived. I wonder how yours look in England. I don't like ours in America, except a few things & mostly cheap ones. . . . Were you not glad to get home? And did not the first good meal taste delicious? . . . Mama & Papa have been in London [on their way to Switzerland]. I wish you could have met. Papa is traveling for his health or they would not have gone this summer. I am going to have a baby in August and am not a bit rejoiced [?] as I should be. I don't want to be tied down but Mama has promised to take care of it, so we will be off again soon, I hope. . . ."

At least two of Gertrude's uncles are also in Europe, George and William K. While Uncle George is abroad, President McKinley visits Biltmore, where George's agent refuses entry to newsmen until forced at the President's insistence to capitulate. On the *Valiant*, Uncle William sails to Southampton to pick up his daughter Consuelo and the Duke of Marlborough for a trip to France, Norway, and Russia. . . . There is news, too, from William C. Whitney that a collection of elk, deer, and buffalo has arrived at October Mountain where the different animals have been placed in separate thousand-acre enclosures. But probably none of this means much to Gertrude as she—with her mother, who has just now returned from Switzerland—waits for her baby.

Early the morning of July 29 a girl is born, the first grandchild of the Cornelius Vanderbilts. The *Times* says "it is understood that it is to be named Alice, after Mrs. Vanderbilt," but she is named Flora Payne Whitney, in memory of Harry's mother. In a subsequent story, the papers are inaccurate, too, about a reconciliation between Mrs. Vanderbilt and Cornelius, Jr. Inevitably they have contact during Gertrude's confinement, but there is no real reconciliation, and Mama returns to Switzerland after a two-week stay.

Harry has arranged for a law tutor to come from Amherst to Newport from mid-August until late September and, during that period, even while winning two polo championships with the Meadow Brook team, he studies fairly regularly and is in frequent communication with his father, often by cable. September 24 he wires to Westbury: "ARE YOU USING THE GOOD HOUSE . . . NEAR THE STABLE? CAN WE FIX IT UP AND LIVE THERE NOW?" His father replies that it will take time to fix. Harry wires again the next day: "A GOOD IDEA. WE WILL GO TO THE MOUNTAIN OCTOBER 3 OR 4 FOR TWO WEEKS, THEN WESTBURY. DON'T BOTHER ABOUT WESTBURY HOUSE. I SHALL ATTEND TO IT. DON'T WANT MUCH DONE EXCEPT BATHROOM. WILL BE IN N.Y. TUESDAY FOR LAW EXAMINATION. DON'T EXPECT TO PASS BUT WILL GIVE THEM A TREAT."

We do not know if Harry passes this particular examination, only that Dean Keener of the Columbia Law School considers him "one of the most brilliant students he has known"; that by late fall Harry is admitted to the prestigious law firm of Elihu Root; and that, near the turn of the year, Harry accepts appointment as New York City associate commissioner of statistics, perhaps expecting that, as with his father, law combined with politics will lead to power.

As to Gertrude, except for the trips to Lenox and Westbury, she does none of the traveling she hopes to do and must settle for one "overnight spree" with Adele Burden to Niagara Falls. On this adventure the two young women travel under assumed names in a regular sleeper rather than a private car, only to discover that they have been recognized by a detective at Grand Central Station, "still rather a family affair." He follows them to Buffalo and identifies them there as they register under their false names. The anticlimax is an appropriate ending to a rather anticlimactic year.

⇌ *1898*

As months of law study drag by, cutting into time Harry would rather devote to polo and other sporting and social activities, he loses interest in law, except to the extent it will be helpful in business. He will never complete his course, will never take the bar examination, and finally, after about seventeen months, will resign as associate commissioner, when the Bureau of Municipal Statistics is criticized for not holding a meeting since its founding, Harry having refused to associate with one of his colleagues "for social reasons."

Just as Harry turns away from his seemingly predestined career in law, Gertrude turns at least partly away from hers in "society." Settled now at 2 West 57th Street, on January 10 she and Harry give a supper dance, followed by a cotillion, led by their old friend Craig Wadsworth, for about forty couples. The guests are described in the papers as belonging to "the exclusive set" or "the young married set." Among them are the Cornelius Vanderbilts, Jr., the Pagets, and various cousins. In response to Gertrude's mentioning this and other social events in a letter to her parents and Gladys, all now in Egypt, Mama replies: "It was very awkward for you about the Small Dances. I think you ought not to accept anything or go on any committees were the W[ilson] family are to be & I would not attend those particular Dances if I were you. That family will do everything to make it appear that you side with them & there should be no mistake in letting people see that you do not. Your Father has sent word to

C[ornelius] that he may have the position he formerly filled in the Engineer's Office, saying that 'he does this, not because he & I have changed our opinion of his conduct, but because he had promised it before he was taken ill.' As a promise it had to be kept & that is all."

But despite occasional references in Gertrude's correspondence to social events, their magic is wearing off. It is one thing to attend parties, another to give them, to spend one's time and energy creating the magic while simultaneously dealing with all the complications of family and social politics, and even committees. Ironically, it is Grace Wilson Vanderbilt who will follow in the steps of Mrs. William Astor and Mrs. William K. Vanderbilt as New York's leading hostess. Gertrude will seek—is already, so soon after marriage, seeking—her magic elsewhere, mostly in art and, specifically, in American art. In a journal written about 1912 or a little later, called *Beginning of Autobiography*, she says: "The house I had stepped into after my marriage was furnished, complete and full. Beautiful Renaissance tapestries. Furniture of all the Louis. Old French and Italian paintings hung on the walls. It was the very same atmosphere in which I had been brought up, the very same surroundings. Just as physically I had moved some fifty feet from my father's house into my husband's, so I had moved some fifty feet in feeling, environment, and period. No more than that, and it was a very big jump for me when I began to realize the possibilities of something new in art. . . ."

When she and Harry begin redecorating the house, William C. Whitney introduces them to the artist John La Farge, "a sort of protégé," who has done stained glass windows for his house at 871 Fifth Avenue and similar work, earlier, in Gertrude's parents' Fifth Avenue mansion. She writes that La Farge's studio is "presided over by a secretary and a Jap [assistant] . . . . Mr. La Farge resembled the Jap to such an extent that it was disconcerting. I was much too shy to say anything and when we came away the proud possessors of three [of La Farge's] Japanese watercolors I will never forget the feeling of inadequacy combined with pleasure I experienced—not only in possessing the La Farges but in having had the privilege of meeting so great a man. From then on I took an interest in American art. I began to realize the opportunity I had of acquiring."

≋

In the past two and a half years, since his second marriage and retirement from politics, William C. Whitney has been devoting more and more time to horses. He continues to develop his stables at Westbury and in Aiken. He purchases 67 acres in Brooklyn at Sheepshead Bay, adjacent to the Coney Island Race Track, and there renovates a hundred-and-fifty-year-old mansion for use as a racing lodge. He plans a polo field for Harry on October Mountain. But now, in late February, Harry and Gertrude receive shocking news from Aiken. While riding under a small low bridge, his young second wife, Edith, has broken her neck and become paralyzed. It as as if a curse by Oliver Payne has been visited upon William. He is at once grief-stricken and guilt-ridden, attentive and powerless. He remains at her bedside, summons specialists, but it is almost two months before she can be moved in a specially fitted private car. Newspaper accounts of the journey are heart-rending. When the horse-drawn ambulance leaves the Jersey ferry, William walks beside it, "his right hand resting upon the edge of the open window and his gaze anxiously upon the roadway." On 42nd Street he stops twice to remove obstacles. Between New York and Long Island he hires a ferry and instructs its captain not to bump against the pier. In Westbury he spends night after night reading medical books in a futile attempt to find some cure for Edith's condition that the specialists have overlooked. During these two months and the remaining thirteen in which Edith continues to fight for her life, Gertrude and Harry, as well as his younger sister Dorothy, are very solicitous of William. At this time news from the Vanderbilts is secondary to reports of Edith's condition, that fluctuating graph of hopes and disappointments moving steadily downward to death.

But there is the other news. A letter from Gertrude's father, written from the Grand Hotel in Rome at the end of March, is touching more because of its form than its content. It is a three-page account of travels in and around Naples, in perfect penmanship, dictated by him to twelve-year-old Gladys and signed and dated in his shaky hand, possibly now his left hand. . . . At the end of April, closer to home, Grace has a ten-pound boy named Cornelius Vanderbilt IV. . . . And in May and early June, Mama writes from London, hoping that Gertrude and Harry will attend the wedding there of George Washington Vanderbilt and Edith Stuyvesant Dresser—most of the family will come—but by then Gertrude, Harry, and little Flora are in Westbury in their own house near that of William and the other Edith, and Gertrude is again pregnant.

In a late June letter from Esther—one of many that continue to come through the early years of Gertrude's marriage—Esther writes, "And so you gave up your trip—and why I wonder!" A few weeks later Esther visits Newport, sees Gertrude, and writes again: ". . . you were looking so pretty. . . . How seldom we see each other nowadays! And yet I cannot help feeling that you are nearer to me than anyone—and perhaps the day is coming that you will want me more."

It is impossible to say exactly what Esther senses or what Gertrude may have told her. Probably, though, Gertrude would have expressed various disappointments—in being pregnant so soon again; in being unable to travel (her beloved Paris would have been only a hop from her uncle's wedding in London); in the round of Newport social events where her sister-in-law Grace is already becoming a dominant hostess; and, even this soon, in the frequent absence of Harry, who is continuing to win polo matches and is spending more and more time with his father, both as business confidant and co-enthusiast in all phases of horsemanship.

Again we turn to the retrospective *Beginning of Autobiography:* "As a child I had known an artist called Howard Cushing. After my marriage he took a fancy to me and liked guiding my steps. He had a great gift of sympathy. Someone once described him as a degenerate Puritan, a description I did not understand till very much later. I couldn't free myself from certain feelings. I wanted to work. I was not very happy or satisfied in my life. The more I tried to forget myself in my life the less I succeeded in doing so. I found myself analysing with minute care . . . looking into a future that held neither pleasure nor satisfaction. I had always drawn and painted a little, now I wanted to try modeling. My memory distinctly brings back a dream I had at this time, very distinct. I was in a cellar and modeling the figure of a man. There were a great many difficulties connected with my getting forward with the work."

❧ *1899*

Because of Gertrude's advanced pregnancy, she and Harry do not attend two big social events. On January 6 her parents give a ball for six hundred guests. Having been in Europe the previous winter and in Washington the one before, their first large party in two years is eagerly anticipated. We can imagine Gertrude watching from across the street as familiar carriages pull up—those of her relatives and of such old friends as Mo Taylor, Bobby Sands, Regi Ronalds, and Worthie Whitehouse, the last of whom will lead the cotillion. . . . Three weeks later, a few blocks south, William K. Vanderbilt gives a dance in honor of the Comstock heiress, Virginia ("Birdie") Fair, and her fiancé, William K., Jr. . . . At about the same time Uncle William's house Idle Hour in Oakdale, Long Island, burns down and he commissions Richard Howland Hunt (the son of Richard Morris Hunt) to design another, which will ultimately cost $6,000,000. . . . Yes, as always, the Vanderbilt name is prominently in the papers and once again intertwined with other names we know. . . . Finally, on February 20, Cornelius Vanderbilt Whitney is born, another familiar intertwining of names. This time the newspapers get the child's name right, but Rollie Cottenet, in a note sent with flowers right after the birth of "Sonny," assumes he is to be named "Harry P., Jr."

By early April, Gertrude and Harry are going to parties again. On the fourth they attend the marriage of William K. Vanderbilt, Jr., and Virginia Fair, a Catholic ceremony in the Fifth Avenue mansion of William K., Sr. Alfred and Regi help their father into the house, where he sees but doesn't speak to Cornelius, Jr. On the sixth Gertrude and Harry and her parents are at another Vanderbilt wedding, that of John Henry Hammond and Emily Sloane, at St. Bartholomew's. This time there's no family awkwardness. The Sloanes protect Cornelius, Sr., by not inviting Grace and Cornelius, Jr., and they add to his pleasure by making Gladys a bridesmaid. Gertrude herself is radiant in a gown of elaborately embroidered Chinese crepe with a "ciel bleu" yoke and hat to match. She—along with her mother, her aunt Florence Twombly, her cousin Adele Burden, and Mrs. Stanford White—is named one of the most beautifully dressed women there (meaning anywhere). Papa must have been proud of Gertrude. Later in the month he adds a codicil to his will leaving her an extra $1,000,000.

In May, Gertrude's and Harry's social activity turns sad. On the seventh Edith Whitney finally dies in Westbury. William is at her bedside, as during so much of the past year and a half. With him is the attending physician, Edith's daughter Adelaide Randolph, and Harry and Dorothy. Neither Pauline Paget nor Payne Whitney is present then or at the funeral three days later in Garden City, when three hundred friends and relatives travel there from New York on a special train.

Because of mourning, William and Harry don't go to the Withers Stakes, the Amateur Cup, or the Belmont Stakes, all later in May, and thus miss seeing William's horse Jean Beraud win both Stakes races and his Buela win the Amateur Cup. However, even more than during the previous year, Harry is spending a great deal of time with his father, particularly in connection with Metropolitan Street Railway franchises, and by spring is almost commuting from New York and Westbury to Gertrude in Newport. Once again he is frequently signing his letters "In haste." For example, on June 28 he writes from the Knickerbocker Club:

Dearest

Bad child—why don't you tell me about yourself—how much you were sick & how you feel.

I want to know.

J. [Burden] spent last night with me at Mr. Whitney's house at Westbury & of course got talking & it was 12 o'clock before we knew it.

So this morning I have a nice headache & lots to do. I am fixing to try to get off Tuesday & have till Wednesday.

In haste,
Harry

Or, on Thursday, August 3, he writes from the office of Thomas Fortune Ryan, an associate of the Whitneys in the Metropolitan Street Railway Company:

Dearest

This is an easy day. I got so much through yesterday that I am going on 3 o'clock train to the country [Westbury].

I am sorry your old Gerry dinner was fun. It ought not to have been.

Presents for Flora worry me. I am afraid I shall forget them tomorrow morning [when they are planning her belated birthday party]. Give her my love, also to my big baby.

H.

And Friday, August 11:

Dearest

I know who is the real bad one. I really haven't time & someone else has.

Of course I get five minutes every now & then (like this time) but what is the sense in a rushed off letter when one's mind is on other things.

Rollie came to the country last night & played [the piano] till we all went to sleep. Papa & I played squash racquets & so got some exercise. Today there is a lot to do & I can't get to Newport till Saturday but can stay over Monday I think.

In haste,
Harry

Though we don't have Gertrude's side of the correspondence, if any at this time, she cannot have been happy giving and attending parties for her and Harry's old circle of friends, especially not knowing now whether or not he will show up. The familiar names appear repetitively in her dinner party books. Some, such as Lispenard Stewart, Worthington Whitehouse, Frank Andrews, Mo Taylor, and Regi Ronalds, must by now have meant very little to her. Surely by late summer she is yearning for new faces or, at least, more interesting familiar ones, faces anyway from some less confined world. In Newport, though there is brief contact with Edith Wharton, she has really only her old friend Howard Cushing with whom to discuss art. In late August she invites Jim Barnes, now a well-known journalist, to visit her and Harry. He replies from Lenox:

My dear Mrs. Whitney,

I regret more than I can tell you that it will be impossible for me to go to Newport, or to go anywhere else, for some weeks to come as I am hard at work wrestling with a refractory hero and trying to keep a volatile heroine in order, all of which means that I am busy turning the literary wheel with my nose on the grindstone. It was mighty kind of you to give me that informal and tempting invitation and nothing would have given me a greater pleasure than to have been your and Harry's guest. It is very strange—now and then I catch glimpses of you, but they are only glimpses. Perhaps some day we may actually have ten minutes conversation. I live in hope that a kindly fate will grant it so.

Believe me I am grateful for the kind thought that had you ask me to come to you. I wish I could. Give my best regards to Harry.

Faithfully yours,
James Barnes

Gertrude's search for cultural stimulation is interrupted by the sudden death of her father a few minutes before six, Tuesday morning, September 12. Feeling well on Monday, he—with Mama and Gladys—leaves Newport for New York to attend directors' meetings on Tuesday of the New York Central, the New York and Harlem Railroad, and the Wagner Palace Car Company, intending to return to Newport for a dinner they are giving on Thursday in honor of President Grant's granddaughter Julia and her fiancé Prince Michael Cantacuzene of Russia. Mr. Vanderbilt goes to bed early; so there is no reason for surprise when, before six the following morning, he rings for the servant in attendance. However, the servant finds him writhing in pain. His last words, spoken even before Mrs. Vanderbilt and Gladys can be called, are "I think I am dying—" His wife and daughter enter the room just as the end comes. Later, when the doctors arrive—four of them, including Dr. McLane—they determine that the cause of his death is cerebral hemorrhage. This is confirmed by two coroners, one of whom comments, "One could almost believe it was Julius Caesar that lies there dead. He has perfect Roman features of the most classical type."

It is still early morning when word goes out to the rest of the family. Gertrude and Harry, Cornelius, Jr., and Regi—all in Newport—rush to the city by special train and arrive early in the afternoon. Alfred, who has graduated from Yale in June and is on a round-the-world trip, gets to China on the day his father dies and makes arrangements to return. Of Mr. Vanderbilt's three brothers, both William and Frederick are in the city, the former to attend the directors' meetings. George Washington Vanderbilt is reached at Bar Harbor. Sisters and brothers-in-law are scattered at resorts and in the city, but all are at 57th Street by the end of the day. There, in accordance with Mr. Vanderbilt's wishes, a simple funeral is planned—a service at St. Bartholomew's, burial at New Dorp. A representative of Saint-Gaudens makes a death mask.

For a month and a half newspapers and magazines are full of articles memorializing Cornelius Vanderbilt's accomplishments, especially his philanthropy. At the same time there are many unconfirmed stories about the will, which is dated June 18, 1896, the day on which Cornelius, Jr., had first planned to marry Grace Wilson and his father had cut him off with a direct gift of $500,000 and the income from a trust of $1,000,000. By late October, Cornelius, Jr., begins to dominate news of the family, and it is clear by then that the $70,000,000 estate cannot be settled until Alfred returns. Otherwise, it is rumored, Cornelius intends to contest the will. October 27, Senator Chauncey M. Depew, senior executor of the estate and long-time operating president of the New York Central, issues a statement: "When Alfred Vanderbilt returned home after his father's death he decided, from brotherly affection and for family harmony, to take out of his own inheritance and give to his brother Cornelius a sum sufficient [about $6,000,000] to make the fortune of Cornelius the same as that of his brothers and sisters. This has been accepted in the same spirit."

The next day Cornelius issues his statement: "The agreement has been made to appear as a mere gift. It is really a family settlement or adjustment of the situation, which, I am glad to say, my brother met with fairness. I have nothing further to say. All the negotiations and arrangements were made by my lawyers, Messrs. Carter and Ledyard of 54 Wall Street, in whose hands I left the matter absolutely." And the day after that, in an interview, he denies rumors that he will become a banker, presumably in association with the Wilson family. No, what interests him is railroads, and particularly the corrugated furnace of Engine 947 which he has invented and which is now being used by some of the New York Central systems.

We don't know what Gertrude feels about Cornelius' ambitions to succeed at the New York Central any more than we know what she feels about Grace's ambition to succeed as a hostess. However, we can assume that Gertrude, like Alfred and Regi, must have been irritated by some of his public statements and that at the end of the year this irritation may have been compounded when Justice Fitzsimmons of the City Court scores Cornelius for failing to respond to a summons for jury duty issued in April. Judge Fitzsimmons fines him $100 and comments on his lack of civic responsibility. "As a matter of fact, I don't want men of young Vanderbilt's station. What interest have they in suits for small amounts that they would have to consider here? I might want their fathers, because they earned their money and know its value."

The 1900s are about to begin. In 1899, Veblen's *Theory of the Leisure Class* is published. In 1901, Theodore Roosevelt will become President. In some ways, as historians say, Cornelius Vanderbilt's death "marks the end of an era"—at least for his own family and others like it. Already the Vanderbilt fortune has been fragmented by the size of the family, by disputes, by divorces (though William K.'s has been the most significant to date, there are many more to come), and by extravagance and carelessness.

≈ *1900*

Flora is now two and a half, cheerful and healthy. Sonny, who has been very sick, is well again and is nearly one. Harry, almost twenty-seven, continues to be away frequently, involved as he is with his father's business affairs, including now the very profitable Guggenheim Exploration Company and the New York Electric Vehicle Transportation Company (also profitable before the proven superiority of the gasoline engine), and such quasi businesses as horse racing and rural real estate. He and Gertrude go away together only occasionally, as on a trip in January to his new "shooting box" (a substantial house) in Hickory Valley, Tennessee, where they, the Burdens, Rollie Cottenet, Jimmie Appleton, and other close friends spend a few days hunting and shooting.

However, neither Harry's success in business and sports, nor the children, nor friends are altogether satisfying to Gertrude. At twenty-five, she is restless and needs more. She has resumed her interest in drawing, then attempted small-scale clay modeling, and finally decided that sculpting is what she wants to do—seriously, professionally, and on a large scale. She must have only a good studio and a good teacher and can, of course, afford the best of each. In anticipation of the coming summer at Newport, she has a studio built there at the edge of the property, dramatically placed a dozen steps or so below the top of the cliff with a balcony running from the foot of the stairs to the entrance overhanging the pounding water. And in anticipation of a trip to Europe with Harry, ultimately postponed, Mama writes a letter to Augustus Saint-Gaudens, the foremost American sculptor of his time and one who has worked on several Vanderbilt commissions including relief portraits of Gertrude and her brothers as children: "This will introduce to you my son-in-law and daughter Mr. and Mrs. H. P. Whitney who are to be in Paris for a short stay. They are desirous of seeing your studio and work as Mrs. Whitney has a taste for modeling."

Less imperiously Howard Cushing arranges for her to study with his brother-in-law Hendrik Christian Andersen, just back from Europe. As Gertrude recalls in *Beginning of Autobiography*: "He made colossal figures which no one wanted but which afforded him great pleasure. His looks were delightful. He had distinct muscles in his face, adored Ibsen and had a real talent for teaching. I remember how often he destroyed some misshapen limb I had constructed, telling me how unworthy it was of my possibilities. And though I wept I always came back with faith in my own capacity. . . . While I worked he read Ibsen to me and I began to see how many things in life I knew nothing about. Not that I thought I knew much. I don't think it entered my head to think one way or the other about it. I can remember not looking forward to life. That strikes me as very strange now [i.e., 1912 or later] when I look forward to so many things in life, so many things from day to day." But in 1900, other than sculpture, traveling is about the only thing to which she looks forward. She wants most of all to see, and in many cases re-see, the great sculpture abroad. Travel "appealed so strongly that I wheedled a promise from my husband that if it were possible we would take a trip to Italy, the Mediterranean, Greece and Constantinople in a year and a half."

Hendrik Christian Andersen's name is hardly known today, except to students of Henry James. The Master met him in Rome in 1899 and was attracted to the young, blond, handsome Scandinavian of "magnificent stature" and reminded of his own fictional portrait (written some twenty-five years before) of Roderick Hudson, whom Andersen resembled in name, in physique, and in his desire to make monumental sculptures on such abstract themes as Love, Equality, and Peace. As James's principal biographer Leon Edel tells us, Andersen—a distant relative of Hans Christian Andersen—was born in Bergen, Norway, one of three artistically gifted sons (there was also a daughter about whom less is known) of an alcoholic father and a long-suffering mother. The family settled in a poor but genteel section of Newport where such old and cultured families as the Cushings, the La Farges, and the Howes took an interest in the talented Andersen children. Ultimately Howard Cushing's sister Olivia married the eldest brother Andreas, who became a successful painter. With the help of the Cushings and others, Hendrik went to art school in Boston, to the École des Beaux Arts in Paris, and then to study sculpture in Italy. When James met him in Rome he bought a small bust, entered into correspondence with Hendrik (as passionate on James's side as Esther's letters to Gertrude), and invited him to visit Lamb House, Rye—a visit Hendrik had made just before returning to Newport.

It is not difficult to imagine Gertrude's excitement as Hendrik Andersen instructs her in sculpture and encourages her to make her first large piece —appropriately called *Aspiration*—while at the same time reading to her from Ibsen, reminiscing about his student days in the Latin Quarter in Paris and around the Piazza del Popolo in Rome, and dreaming aloud of the gigantic sculptures he plans to make, whether or not there is a market for them. He is a type she has not known, a free bohemian spirit more concerned about expressing his own dreams than in achieving the worldly success she has been taught to respect and pursue. Despite the enormous discrepancy in their wealth, he has done more, seen more, felt more, retained more than she. She has toured Europe, he has lived there. She has recorded the names of artists and monuments in her journals, he knows these works by heart and has made large pieces of his own. In short—and she must have been painfully conscious of this—until now she has only dabbled in art, he has committed himself to it. It is his life.

As Gertrude admits in her *Beginning of Autobiography:* "I used to be . . . very scared of my emotions. I used to hide behind a curtain and preserve a discreet silence. By force of expressing myself in my work, my shyness has become much less embarrassing. . . . I came to be happy in meeting people with big personalities, especially in my own sphere [in context, meaning sculpture]; and when they let me in and we discussed our own interests I felt as if I had been let into a Secret Society." That Andersen had such a big personality is apparent in another passage of this retrospective autobiography: "It was a hot day in Newport and I had been struggling over the first big figure I ever attempted. Andersen and I went up to the house. As usual he was complaining about my faults. My two kids came into the room. They were very lovely and he sat back and looked at them. 'What is the use of trying to make anything better than that?' he remarked." And somehow it is clear that the remark was intended no more for her than for himself. But nowhere is Andersen's large humanity more apparent than in a letter written (on James's Lamb House stationery) after leaving Newport and returning to Rye:

DECEMBER 1st

Dear Mrs. Whitney,

After six stormy days with high seas, and two dark days of London fog and rain, I find myself in this sweet little town of Rye, in the very beautiful old fashion[ed] house of my dear friend Henry James. But I feel that it is worth a thousand dull and dangerous journeys, to feel that one can at last make a welcome harbour in such a "Paradiso" of good taste. So here I sit before my little fireplace that burns so cheerfully, dreaming out strange figures for the future, and building castles in the air.

I feel so much at home here and the gentleness and goodness of dear Henry James makes me feel so very happy. It is that kind of goodness that a father should give to a son. And all through life I have looked for this kind of love, sympathy and advice; but I have never before found it, as my own poor father lost his reason when I was a young baby—so you must know how much every moment means to me and how every hour counts.

Everything is made beautiful and full of interest around this dear little town. Our long walks over the hills and along the river banks to the sea, and home in the evening twilight, then sitting up until midnight by a cheerful fire, and again wandering through the long beautiful silent corridors of the past, and planning and hoping for the unborn future.

There is something so simple and so strong about Henry James, his large blue eyes and massive head, always so very kind in an honest and real way. His insight is so clear and his judgement so true, and backed up by long years of study and the keenest and most penetrating kind of observation. One cannot help being one's self in his presence. And one feels that all the intellectual activity of the age is as well known to him as though he lived in the heart of New York, London or Paris. His judgement has truth and wisdom and comes from a fountain of goodness and refinement.

I wish it were possible for me to remain with him longer, but I must hurry off to Rome. There I will start at once on my winter's work. I will write to you about the things of interest to me, and send you photographs of anything that I can find that may help you in your sculpture, and I sincerely hope you will work at it. Draw and study anatomy all you can, for in a technical sense it is the foundation of both painting and sculpture, and if you continue to work at the fundamental I know the rest will follow with a strength, grace, and dignity that will be all your own.

It makes little difference who you study with, as long as your instructor is not too *artistic* or *sentimental.*

I do hope the young man at Walthausen's will be able to make the required modifications on your statue, and that you may be able to give this work your personal supervision. Otherwise it may go very poorly. Remember that none of the forms should be sacrificed for the sake of *smoothness,* as the construction will not count on such a large figure unless it appears strong from a distance. Use your own judgement about the modifications and ask the advice of *no one!* as the figure must stand alone, and since it is your first work, let those things that others consider faults be *your faults!* and not subjected to a lot of *assimilated* hysterical and well intended suggestions.

I shudder when I look back and reflect on the vast army of art critics! and art criticism in America! Kindly given, [but] with a deluded sense of the beautiful as well as with an unreflected sense of purpose, misguided seriousness as well as unhesitating and unqualified understanding of accuracy. But the sad part of it all is that, by this, art is to be helped? I wish you would write to me and tell me just how the work goes. And when the time arrives I shall arrange about the Salon. Have Walthausen make very strong casts of *both* figures especially the *one for the Salon.*

I hope the children are strong and well, and that they will continue to be so. I hope you will not forget me and let me slip out of your kind memory. Remember me to Mr. Whitney very kindly, and also to any kind friend that may be good enough to ask for me. I hope I shall see you and Mr. Whitney in Rome, and that you may enjoy a good winter's work, and beg to remain

very sincerely your friend
Hendrik C. Andersen

P.S. I have talked so much to Henry James about you who is so very much in sympathy with your work.

How that postscript must thrill Gertrude. She needs sympathy. True, Harry, much more than members of her own family, encourages her deepening interest in sculpture and understands her need for proper instruction and studios—in New York now, she is already looking for space and another teacher—but it is doubtful that Harry really understands the new seriousness and single-mindedness of her pursuit. To him it may have seemed little more than a hobby or pastime, not appreciably different from, if as serious as, his own interests in horse racing, polo, hunting, yachting, clubs. . . . This past May his father's Kilmarnock has won the Withers; in June, Prince Charles has won the Great American Stakes; and in August, with his father in Europe and Harry representing him, Ballyhoo Bey has won the Futurity and then a week later, just after his father's return, the Flatbush Stakes. . . . Also, during the spring and summer Harry plays polo in Westbury and Newport; appears in horse shows; buys, with his friend H. B. Duryea, *Yankee*, a 106-foot racing yacht, one of four built this year by the great shipbuilder Herreshoff (the others were for Gertrude's brother Cornelius, her uncle W. K. Vanderbilt, and August Belmont). . . . In the fall during the shooting season Harry visits October Mountain and later goes on a hunting trip to Hickory Valley and then on to his father's place in Aiken. . . . To Harry all this must have seemed at least as important as Gertrude's messing about with clay and plaster, keeping herself busy while he is away in the real world, the world one reads about every day in the newspapers.

After Andersen's departure, Gertrude does draw and study anatomy all she can. Using Arthur Thomson's *Handbook of Anatomy for Art Students*, a Victorian manual in which the male sex organs are always obscured, she makes technical notes and does drawing after drawing of bones, full skeletons, musculature, and nudes—all with a view to achieving expression and proportion. But by the end of the year she still does not have a new teacher, though again her mother has been instrumental, however inadvertently, in trying to get her one.

From June until October, Mama has been traveling abroad with Gladys and the Sloanes and Twomblys. In London she is met by Alfred, who introduces her to his future wife Ellen Tuck French, the daughter of the late president of the Manhattan Trust Company; and three days later Regi, too, joins her. Letters from Mama to Gertrude are frequent. In the twenty-two which survive from this period, all on heavily black-bordered stationery, there are items of news about Gertrude's sister, brothers, relatives, and friends, interspersed with many tender memories of Cornelius, beginning on the crossing aboard the steamer *Oceanic:* "It was at first terrible for me to be on the ship without your father. It seemed as if it could not be—his interest in the run and all his pleasure when he was started on one of the frequent trips we made was so vivid that I felt as if I could not stand it, but that of course is to be expected and I made a mistake in not having anticipated it, for I can bear a thing a great deal better if I know it is coming." Then from London there are various communications about the bronze doors she wants installed at St. Bartholomew's in memory of Cornelius. She cables "IF RENWICK IS NOT POSSIBLE . . . EMPLOY WHITE." The architect James Renwick, most famous for designing St. Patrick's Cathedral, is not possible. He has been dead since 1895. Gertrude employs Stanford White. This commission, along with others in the past for the Vanderbilt family, leads White to suggest that perhaps his friend, the sculptor Daniel Chester French, might accept Gertrude as a student. French, then fifty, established his reputation at twenty-three—two years younger than Gertrude is now—with his *The Minuteman* in Concord. Yes, French might be perfect; perhaps, because so much younger, even better than Saint-Gaudens. White writes and French replies:

> I have always declined to ever consider having a pupil in my studio. My quarters are too circumscribed and I am really too busy to give the time that would be demanded but (and please consider this a tribute to you) I *will* consider Mrs. Whitney's flattering wish, at least to the extent of talking to her and finding out what she has in mind. I think it would be best for her to come and see me here, so that she can see the studio as well as me. Will she let me know when to expect her so that I may be sure to be in. I wish you would thank her for the compliment she pays me.

Though White's proposal is ultimately rejected, Andrew O'Connor, a less well known sculptor, executes the reliefs for the center doors under French's supervision and will within a few years become Gertrude's teacher; and French will on occasion be a helpful friend and a sympathetic critic.

But to return to Mama: in late August, having written frequently about the bronze doors, she now communicates the news that George Washington Vanderbilt's wife Edith has just had a baby named Cornelia for Cornelius. "I think it such a touching thing that all the world should pause a moment in contemplation of a brother's love." In September she thanks Gertrude for visiting Cornelius' mausoleum in Staten Island but the bulk of this letter is in response to a photograph Gertrude has sent of

Aspiration, an academic, larger than life-size standing male nude, with arms outstretched, palms upturned, and eyes lifted toward heaven:

". . . to do all that in 10 days is marvelous. The profile view I can judge best. It looks to me quite Greek and I feel sure promises *success.* Do give him a scarf. The fig leaf is so little! . . . What becomes of him when you leave your studio, and how does Harry like him?" In October the two themes continue: "It is terrible to be here without your father. He is really more associated with Paris than with any place, even home, for when here, we were never separated and my whole life was taken up caring for him." And: "I hope your baby is well—do not let him get ill like last year —keep him warm and leave the Statue—what is anything compared with health of those we love."

How does Harry like the sculpture? There are no hints in his letters of 1900. He is absorbed by his activities and his health. For example, he writes from Sheepshead Bay at the end of August:

Dearest

I was glad to get your nice letter. I have been feeling lonely & blue. I was sick for a couple of days & took my temperature every hour or so because I thought I might have typhoid. I was nearly all right by Wednesday night however. Today I have a bad cold & sore throat caught last night because I had no one to take care of me. I will bring your dresses with me. Rollie says they are lovely. I am going to leave here by special train tomorrow & catch the five o'clock to Newport. I want to see Ballyhoo's race.

Papa has engaged Cook's best dahabeah, also best river steamer [for the trip Harry has promised Gertrude] & we can take our choice.

In haste
H.

And in December from Hickory Valley to Gertrude in New York:

Dearest

I leave here tomorrow morning & am sorry to go, with Aiken ahead. I think that this place has done me good. We have worked really hard—up about sunrise every morning & back again in time to dress for dinner dead beat. I meant to write every night but have been too tired to do anything but roll to bed.

We have had splendid shooting & good hunting. Out three times, killed one fox & holed two. I wish you had been here; you would have enjoyed it immensely. Ideal weather. Dearest, I am glad you are doing your duty by the kids & I will be back soon & give you a kiss for it.

Lots of love,
Harry

And a few days later from William C. Whitney's Joye Cottage in Aiken, a rambling mansion occupying much of an entire square at the intersection of Easey Street and Whiskey Road (an address which amuses the family), with stables and a squash court on adjoining property:

Dearest

The last afternoon. We leave tomorrow. I got up at 5 this morning to go hunting, went to the Hitchcocks', found them in bed, having given up the hunt on account of wind. I went back mad to bed & now have a headache.

At this time of year, when nobody is here, Aiken is really very nice. We do what we want & see nobody, because there is nobody to see. Papa expects to spend the winter here after his ball [i.e., after January 4, when he will give a ball at 871 Fifth Avenue, in honor of his niece Helen Tracey Barney, to which four hundred guests have already been invited] & I think our kids had better come back with him. I should like to send a picture of the kids to my aunt Mrs. Dimock for Christmas. Also to my Grandmother—a nice big one of lots of "Sonnys" as she has lots of "Jacks."

Love dearest
Harry

Although these letters of Harry's are typically self-absorbed, he must have been a little more interested in Gertrude's sculpture than they indicate. We know from a Christmas letter of William C. Whitney's that Harry sent him to look at *Aspiration* after it was shipped from Newport to a New York warehouse (or possibly a foundry). It is a very loving letter, though overly optimistic:

Dear Gertrude

You must overlook breaking my word about giving you nothing, but I wanted this Christmas to say how much I value it that Harry has you for his wife.

It is such a lottery as you know & the undeveloped characters of 20 years of age take sudden & fatal twists often & come out in ways fatal to happiness—I have wanted you & Harry to be able to live your lives together these first hard years. When people get over their illusions— & have to be broken into life's hard sides—& it has worked right in this way—that separation from each other has not in your case, as in many cases it does, brought separation of interest one going one way, & another another—

Now you are old enough & strong enough to each do something worth doing & you are bound to do it—You should have seen Mr. Gavin [?] before the figure—in 41st St. I didn't tell him which was yours when we entered & he was struck by this but waited for me to show him yours—Too long to write what he said. I will tell Harry. So

far in life you have both done right & gone on the right course—
Harry may be supposed not to have done much—But wait until he
settles down & you will see what the years of association intimately
with the men like Vreeland & Root & Ryan & others & seeing the inside of it all has done in the way of maturing him—

And dear Gertrude it isn't what either of you have done up to now.
It's what you have escaped that you must think of.

You are not alienated from each other as many are after so many
years of married life. By being together you have acquired tastes in
common—

Neither of you has acquired a bad habit & you are about as unselfish & strong and healthy a couple as the world can show.

You cannot know how much this is to me. I send you a little token
of my sincere love.

Yours
W.C.W.

In this journal-less year there is one last correspondence of Gertrude's to
consider: the final letters from Esther Hunt. Far more realistically than
William C. Whitney, she senses and infers Gertrude's growing separation
of interests from Harry's and her concomitant loneliness. However, as always, Esther implores and Gertrude replies reluctantly. In the spring or
very early summer Gertrude has written from Newport to New York, and
July 9 Esther writes back:

Dearest Gertrude,

It pays really only caring for *one* person the way I do for you,
and your very dear letter makes me feel you also know it is worthwhile—Sometimes it seems to me that most things that are *right* are
hard, and yet one cannot beat about the bush and try and make some
wrongs appear right. I have to worry about you, but indeed I do trust
you—but *don't* drift into writing [presumably, rather than sculpture],
be careful. I love you and you can go on thinking nice things about
me but I know better.—

Yours—
Esther

It would seem, within the context of this letter and previous ones, that
Gertrude has confessed her difficulties and conflicts in pursuing a career in
sculpture while being tied to a husband and children. Perhaps, too, Gertrude has told Esther that the very nature of making sculpture and the
mechanics of a studio regime, as well as a need for the stimulation of
travel, are more difficult in her situation than writing, especially writing in
scraps and jottings as she continues to do. Alas, we don't have Gertrude's
side of the correspondence—we know only that Esther goes abroad later
in July.

From St. Petersburg, on August 7, she writes that Gertrude is constantly in her thoughts even amidst all the tourist attractions, that she longs to hear from her and wishes they "were off together, here, or anywhere." Finally she adds this cryptic postscript: "I do hope you will never return inside of your former Hell with me," which may suggest a return to Gertrude's feelings of guilt about their relationship.

Two weeks later Esther writes from Vienna: "How long it seems since I have heard from you. I see by the Paris Herald that Mr. Whitney has been ill, I do hope nothing serious, and also you gave a lunch in your studio—with success, I am sure." After saying why she likes Vienna better than St. Petersburg and Moscow, she returns to Gertrude: "I feel that things are drifting with you, am I right? I am doing a devil of a lot of thinking!—I would give a good deal for a talk with you. I wonder why you have not written." And finally from the Tyrol, August 31: "I keep on writing to you although I have not heard from you once since landing—I am hoping to find something waiting at Venice next week. . . . How nice it will be to see you again [i.e., when Esther returns]. Yours/Esther." And there her last surviving letter to Gertrude ends. We know nothing more of their correspondence, except that a note must have accompanied the Christmas gift Gertrude gives Esther at the end of the year. A list of presents to fifteen close friends and relatives and eight servants includes "Esther Hunt. Card case"—the same thing she gives to her old friend Lena Morton.

⇜ *1901*

Happy New Year! Happy New Century!

Very early this year, there must have been at least one more note from Gertrude to Esther—this one accompanying a wedding gift. Now, after some five years of tenacious courtship by George Muirson Woolsey, Esther finally decides to marry him. She would not have had to explain to Gertrude who George is—his name has appeared occasionally in her letters—but more important, his family, like Esther's, though not as wealthy as the Vanderbilts or Whitneys, is as aristocratic. George travels in the same society, belongs to the same clubs, including the Knickerbocker. Among the wedding guests at Grace Church in mid-February will be many members of the Vanderbilt and Whitney families. However, conspicuous among the absentees will be Gertrude and Harry. By then he will have made good the previous summer's promise—even improved upon it by almost a year—to take Gertrude on a trip abroad. So Gertrude will be traveling at the time of Esther's wedding just as Esther was, four and a half years earlier, when Gertrude married.

Before leaving on their trip, there are three important family social events—January 2, a dinner for 166 given by Gertrude's mother at Sherry's; January 4, the ball, "New York's first cotillion of the century," given by Harry's father for his niece; and January 14, the marriage in Newport of Alfred, now the head of the House of Vanderbilt, to Ellen French. Predictably, all of these events are lavish, and the wedding presents at the last of them particularly so. To Ellen, Mama gives a diadem and necklace of diamonds, Gertrude and Harry a collarette of diamonds, Regi and Gladys (the maid of honor) three chests of table silver. Of Alfred's immediate family only Grace and Cornelius are missing from the list of givers, but they are also missing from the list of invitees.

The trip has been carefully organized by Harry for his own pleasure as well as Gertrude's. The party will consist initially of one other couple, Adele and J. Burden, of whom Gertrude and he are equally fond; and one bachelor, the congenial, amusing, smartly dressed Jimmie Appleton, a former, peripheral suitor of Gertrude's but a good friend of Harry's as well. sharing many of his interests. Later they will be joined by two more bachelors—in Rome, by Gertrude's old friend and art counselor Howard Cushing and, in Naples (where the boat Harry has chartered will be waiting), by his friend since childhood, the musical, mustachioed, and generally entertaining Rollie Cottenet, also a peripheral suitor of Gertrude's, though one who bowed out quickly for Harry.

In the odd numbers five and seven, suggesting ideal small oriental dinner parties at which no couple need be locked into conversation, there is asymmetry and Victorianism. Just eight days before the initial five leave, aboard the *Oceanic* bound for Southampton, Queen Victoria dies. We wonder if, with the passage of a little time and the advent of the Edwardian epoch, there might not have been single women to join Jimmie aboard ship and to join Howard and Rollie later on in the journey.

Whatever other possibilities might have been, Gertrude is very pleased with those that exist. This is her first crossing of the Atlantic in six years, and for the first time in four (since crossing the Pacific), she writes regularly in her journal, sustaining the effort through two fat volumes, supplemented by retrospective and also fictional accounts of the five-month trip. Even previously dreary London excites her. It is "so big, so much bigger than any place in the world, in fact it is a world itself swallowing up all the lesser ones, and it has swallowed and absorbed me so completely that I feel like an atom of the great city—lost, lost in its meshes, ensnared in its charms and loving it all the time. To give oneself up to it—forgetting all but the tiny present! . . . one of the great charms of the place is its wonderful faculty of wiping out all of one's personality—and therein surely lies our fear of size." And also, she might have added, our respect for it, a positive awe, felt and spoken about by Hendrik Andersen and later increasingly by her too. But returning to a more human scale, she ends her first London entry with a fragmentary paragraph: "A walk, a drive, a bus ride, a little frivolity, a dash of Monet, pleasant companionship and—"

Over the weekend Harry goes reluctantly with her to one play; on Monday sends Jimmie Appleton with her to another while he remains behind with Sir Edward Colebrook, probably discussing business and horses; and on Tuesday she and Jimmie are in the Poets Corner at Westminster Abbey during the evening service: ". . . the place was dimly lighted with lots of dark spots left to be illumined by the imagination. I lit mine with fancies of a future in which the glories of unknown worlds figured. Oh beautiful Gothic arches, how many prayers and longings are you responsible for! The music echoed in a way that made its very dimness seem near, and yet through it all came the conviction that my own imagination was as nothing compared to the reality—had I been able to grasp it. No one knew who we were—or cared perhaps—and we seemed alone with a past that had a thousand voices. But try as I would, I could not quite forget ourselves and therein I lost much of what I might have felt, even while I gained the experience of myself and of him. God seemed no nearer, only the power of the Invisible stronger, and while I listened I seemed to grow *older*. It is surely thus that one ages, all in one moment and yet after the culmination of *all* powers. We drove home in the dark, quiet. I felt overpowered and as if a crisis had been passed."

It is not clear whether Harry remains in London on business or is obliged to return there. Either way, in Paris Gertrude continues to spend much time with Jimmie. They lunch together at the Café Anglais, they shop at the Bon Marché where they are mistaken for husband and wife, they visit the Musée Grevin. When Harry returns he says several times, "You are not in the mood to go to Italy and enjoy it." Gertrude admits— at least to her journal—that she is "certainly in a Paris mood now. A mood of change and lightheartedness, and a mood too of deviltry that is not altogether safe. And yet—well—Harry says too I have not good principles or much either and perhaps he is right again. My conscience is not what it should be—I am in no writing frame of mind tonight—I *feel* too much. Good night. I shall sleep it off no doubt."

The two couples do go on to Rome, while Jimmie lingers for a bit in Paris. In Rome, Harry is overcome by a cold and Gertrude is forced to do much of her sightseeing alone—now really serious study of sculpture, particularly Michelangelo's—until Howard Cushing joins them. With him she visits St. Peter's and as they stand in front of the *Pietà* she feels there is "no one I would rather see beautiful things with than this man. There is that about him which is not only sympathetic but strong and magnetic.

He knows right away what he likes and why he likes it. He picks out from the whole the individual and stamps it in your memory with a few words of force." The two of them visit other sights together and Hendrik Andersen's studio, and Howard writes a parody of a court chronicle—a court "given to wine"—which Gertrude incorporates in her journal. It is a playful piece—a game in which adjectives are applied to nouns and names without knowing their context—of interest only because of the roles in which he casts the characters and the adjectives, probably Gertrude's, which fill the blanks. Gertrude is "The Queen," Harry "The Prince Consort," Jimmy her "Gold Stick," J. and Adele "The Duke and Duchess," and Howard himself "The Caterer." (Later Gertrude will elaborate upon these names and Rollie Cottenet when he appears will have several of his own.) As to the adjectives, the court is described as "dissipated"; the Queen as "devilish . . . frenzied . . . drunken . . . and dissolute"; the Gold Stick as "sensuous" and "amorous"; the Caterer as "degenerate." For now, the Prince Consort is given no epithet but is simply quoted as having said, "Wine from morning till night makes the day peaceful." Yes, it's all very playful and yet it's an introduction to heavy drinking by the court.

Suddenly the journal becomes fragmentary, as if Gertrude has no time for more than notes which she plans to fill out later. A guide named Emmanuel is often with them now. Sometimes the party is in a new red Panhard touring car which Harry has had shipped to Rome, sometimes aboard the *Sheelah*, which he has chartered. Brief entries skip from town to town and island to island. At Mount Athos, Gertrude and Adele are not allowed in the monastery. At another monastery on an island not far from there, they are not even permitted ashore, and when Harry, J., Jimmie, and Rollie return to the ship they find Gertrude and Adele dressed as men. In Bursa, the first capital of the Ottoman Empire, the two women go to the sulphur baths where they "find a large number of nude or semi-nude women lying about on marble slabs! . . . A number of boys ran about among the nude women. Neither they nor the women seemed to care in the least and the boys were some of them about fourteen. It seemed rather strange."

Everywhere Gertrude goes to museums and often tortures herself with invidious comparisons between her own work and that of the past. "How marvelous is a really fine piece of sculpture and how can a person like myself dare to *dabble* in such things! It is a desecration. . . . I feel sometimes that I can never go on with my own work, that I am too old to begin with, that my aim would be too high for my knowledge, and that never, never in the world would I be willing to do mediocre things. . . . Technique takes time and time means the sacrifice of something, and the sacrifice of those things that perhaps cannot be sacrificed—who knows! There are some things that make us terribly unhappy but in the end these very things add a great deal to one's life. . . . The Acropolis, for instance, could not have been to me what it was, nor could I have seen in its silent history what I saw, if it had not been for my life. I came away feeling older and—more at rest."

As Gertrude travels, she spends less and less time on guidebook details; instead, these in the form of pamphlets, brochures, postcards, and photographs are pasted into her journal. There is the other, deeper journey to face, the one into her life and into herself. Mixed with anxiety about a career in art is a presently more profound anxiety about marriage. What really need she sacrifice for art? She is only twenty-six. She has time. She has money. She has rooms of her own and one studio already, with others to come. She has servants to take care of her children. No, these problems are soluble. Harry is more difficult. She loves him still, probably always will, but is increasingly aware of the everwidening gulf that separates their interests. She cannot help but feel rejected by his behavior during the first four and a half years of their marriage, including that on this trip. Indeed this trip is a recapitulation and intensification of the previous years. Harry does not need business or horses or real estate as an excuse to go off by himself, touring in his way, without her; and just as at home, he encourages her, too, to go off and busy herself with art, her hobby as he sees it. As to her own behavior, she must admit that some of it has been provocative. She has flirted with Jimmie Appleton. She has established an intimate and confiding, though more platonic, relationship with Howard Cushing. And she has not been very responsive to Harry or appreciative of the arrangements he has made. Often she chooses to linger as he wants to move on, particularly in that expensive toy of his, the red Panhard. Again and again this journal in two volumes (and the next which will grow out of them) moves from the immediate experience into the past and the future—with or without Harry:

Two nights ago I was in a turmoil. I could scarcely stand the strain. Some of those discussions that we have made me so nervous they nearly killed me. It got so bad, I was rapidly getting crazy. I can't repeat it. Not only the discussion and the way of it, but the cruel things that were said were like knives and cut deep. I only just saved a "disgrazia" which everyone except Harry and J. saw. I came down to my cabin in a state! What does it all lead to? Ah, that is the trouble. It makes it harder all the time to fight the temptations in my life. And I care about the kind of things that were said not because they were said, but because they were said before people. Ah me! Life is complicated and its ways are difficult to understand. Two or three things I know and they are things I don't want to know, and the rest of the things I know nothing about and those are the things I want to understand. Once I was so blind on beautiful subjects that one ought to be blind about, but that is a long time ago.

Around the same time, about halfway through the trip, Harry—
especially Harry but possibly some of the others as well—must have been
in her mind as she writes:

I pity, I pity above all that class of people who have no necessity to
work. They have fallen from the world of action and feeling into a
state of immobility and unrest. They have become inert, both mentally and bodily, also from an emotional standpoint, and they are not
even spared the ignorance of their condition. They consequently become pessimists. What an existence is theirs. They have few friends,
for they have no interests to hold them together. They can scarcely be
called weary of life for they have never tasted it. They drag out a state
as monotonous as it is useless. Their perpetual whine fills the ears of
the man who is living. They grope after they know not what. Finally
they strike a rock and are either dashed to pieces on the reef of scandal, or they become religious fanatics, Christian Scientists, society
leaders or something equally meritorious. Such walks in life are
recruited from the unemployed. The great and grand unemployed—
the dregs of humanity.

This is harsh, even vindictive, prompted no doubt by pain and bitterness. Harry is hardly "inert." Nor does he have "few friends" or "no interests"—he has plenty of both. What Gertrude cannot accept is that neither his real friends nor his real interests are hers (any more than hers are
his) and, more painful still, that she herself is no longer as close or as interesting to him as once. Perhaps she has to reach back in her memory,
past their honeymoon, to where what they had in common, their heritage,
was enough. Aboard the *Sheelah*, cruising now among the Greek islands,
Gertrude's anxiety intensifies. She has filled one journal and begins another pretty much where she left off:
". . . I don't think I understand [sculpture] now any better than when
I first went to Rome. . . . My heart can go so much beyond my mind
that I come away from a museum often with a totally unsatisfied feeling.
These archaic statues strike a very deep note. . . . I feel sometimes that I
never can go on with my own work, that I am too old to begin with, that
my aim would be too high for my knowledge, and that never, never in the
world would I be willing to do mediocre things. . . ." The passage continues, through the need for "time" and "sacrifice," in exactly the same
words she has used earlier; and at the beginning of June, while visiting
a Byzantine church in Parenzo, she feels a "love of [her] fellow beings"
and a "softening" but is as hard as ever on herself: "How I hate myself tonight and all my weaknesses and follies and how I should love to change
places with *anybody*." Before abandoning her journal for a month, except
possibly for undated scraps that are tucked into it, she adds a last paragraph:

"Howard has gone away and I miss him very much. I realize now how he supports and helps me. It is so entirely impossible to think of caring for him except in a platonic way that it makes his help of a kind that I never before experienced. And his feeling for me is so purely platonic that we are really good friends."

On July 2 she skips a couple of blank pages and writes:

"Day after tomorrow, if all goes well, I shall be in Newport with my little kids again. Over five months since I have seen them. The ducks, I wonder if they will have changed much and if Flora will remember me. The angel baby and my little sonny boy—I can hardly wait for Thursday."

The external trip is over but it lingers as no previous one has, returning again and again to Gertrude's mind and to the pages of her journal, where it mixes with the internal trip which extends through her entire life.

Gertrude and Harry go directly to The Breakers. There her mother and the children await them and there they will all remain for a month and a few days while Harry resumes his commutation between Newport and New York and Westbury, before moving into their own "cottage" on Bellevue Avenue. After about two weeks at The Breakers, Gertrude skips a few more pages in her journal and writes:

And now that I have come home and review the trip I find myself in an agony, in a whirl, in a tumult. It seems to me impossible to go on with my existence as . . . before. I have not only been taken out of my ruts, shaken and kicked, but I am still suspended in the air unable to descend, irretrievably changed. Is it the result of the trip, or what is it? Is it merely the great change and that I have not yet dropped onto my feet and found my new level? Perhaps so. Or is it that I am permanently made into a restless, wild person with crazy notions and a dull exterior? Ah, who can say. If that, surely the trip has not been successful. I was always dull, can I have become duller? I was always weak, can I have become weaker? I have read if one was dull there was some hope for one, but I don't believe it. Till kingdom come I shall be dull and till kingdom come I shall rail against it. Why was I made so? I understand what people say and what I read. I have a more logical mind than most women, but—there it stops. I have no faculty of making things sound amusing, I have no eyes for little bright things. I am hopelessly and eternally dull. If I could only forget it, but no it stands by me like a sentinel, guarding me. Oh hated dullness, can I never take you out and lose you? Now take tonight, for example, when I should like to be bright and full of fun and youth, etc. What shall I talk about, what can anyone expect from me, who will want to hear my commonplaces? Think—think when your brain is clear of some subjects, keep repeating them and talk of them, only talk and forget yourself. Now for subjects. P. Lorillard's lady on steamer. Alfred's auto accident. Mary L. Vice's story. Mrs. P. Morris' matelot and mousquetaire story.

Probably at that night's dinner party she will talk about these subjects and others that are acceptably far from her deepest feelings. And she will listen to "new" stories, "new" jokes, "new" gossip—somehow always the same. . . . Cornelius and Grace have acquired Beaulieu, another comfortable cottage in Newport. . . . William C. Whitney's Volodyovski has won the Derby in England. . . . Harry's rating at polo has been increased to eight goals. . . . These and similar topics will dominate the conversation. But Gertrude won't speak of *Aspiration,* which has since June been on exhibition in Buffalo at the Pan-American Exposition. She won't speak of what the recent trip really meant to her, though she will say where they went. She won't speak of her relationship to Harry. These topics are reserved for her journal.

Until the end of August when Gertrude and Harry and the children go to October Mountain (which he leaves to be with his father at the Futurity in Sheepshead Bay), she begins organizing her travel journals and related materials: notes to be fleshed out and really written; other passages that need polishing; travel books and brochures and pamphlets that require study; sketchbooks of her own and one given to her by Howard Cushing, including a pencil portrait of her playing cards; dozens of postcards and photographs. . . . All these, along with a resumption of her modeling, will occupy much of her time during the remainder of 1901, well into 1902, and perhaps even into early 1903. In the back of her mind a literary project is forming, a really complete book about the trip, the joy and the sadness of it, the stimulation and depression, all of it, on the surface and in depth.

Gertrude's creative ambition has matured. Though she is often extremely depressed, she is able now to focus her energy on what she really wants to do. She knows where to find time and what to sacrifice. The number of dinner parties will be reduced. Harry's absences will be increasingly accepted. The new-found hours will be devoted to sculpture and writing. There will even be more time for Flora and Sonny.

As Gertrude plans *Travels in Foreign Countries and in the Mind,* her best, most personal writing to date, she has two deaths to face. The first is public, the assassination of President McKinley while speaking at the Pan-American Exposition, not far from her sculpture. He dies September 14 (to be succeeded by Theodore Roosevelt, the only President during Gertrude's life, until the election of his cousin Franklin, to come from "her world"). Gertrude is, of course, shocked—not only her own family but even Harry's has supported McKinley—but the second death is much more shocking, the loss much more personal. On October 19 in London, Esther Hunt Woolsey dies suddenly of an internal hemorrhage during pregnancy. As with the death of her eldest brother William, it will be years before she can write about it. Then—in 1904, during a bad stretch with Harry—she writes, "I have no friend to talk to now, all is over or dead. My two best friends, the only two people to whom I ever really talked out, have died [Esther Hunt and Lena Morton] and the only two men to whom I talked are as good as dead. One [Howard Cushing] is [recently] married and the other one [Jimmie Appleton] I cannot see intimately anymore. There is my life. I do not make friends easily anyway."

The trip continues, bending around the turn of the year, doubling and even tripling around itself, around Gertrude. At about this time she finally finds a suitable studio in New York (one of the Gibson Studios, named for Charles Dana Gibson, on West 33rd Street); she creates a temporary one in a blacksmith's shop on the property at Westbury; she resumes studying sculpture, now with James Earle Fraser (almost two years younger than Gertrude but famous since the age of seventeen for *The End of the Trail**) and later with Andrew O'Connor; but mostly she "travels . . . in the mind."

Before beginning her ambitious reworked travel book, Gertrude fills many of the empty pages of the second volume of her actual travel journal with notes and rough drafts for "Their Emancipation," the story of a marriage which, after five or six years, collapses, leading to trial separation—a theme which will recur frequently in "fictional" sketches and notebook "fantasies."

In additional fragments at the end of this second volume there is sufficient, less fictionalized evidence that Gertrude and Harry are, in spirit if not in fact, already separated; that he has rejected her; and that she in turn is thinking seriously about other men, more sympathetic to her. Two brief passages will suffice: "You touch me in the semi-darkness and I reach out my hand but I find nothing. Are you gone or do I grope in the wrong direction?" And she remembers again the evening at Westminster Abbey with Jimmie Appleton: "A pulse in my life, a slow fever-burned pulse that no time could efface . . . when two people for a moment, no matter how short, lived a pulse together they were irretrievably linked. . . ." And in with all this are clippings from newspapers and popular magazines on such subjects as "MAKE HOME PLEASANT/Woman Can Very Easily Keep Her Husband Away from Clubs" and "THE EDUCATION OF THE TSARITSA," in which we learn that "Princess Alix of Hesse is a modern woman . . . rides, rows, plays tennis, and enjoys the healthy, hardy outdoor life . . . is an ardent painter and a capital linguist. . . ."

* He will become even more famous in 1913 when the Buffalo/American Indian nickel he designed is circulated.

⇐ *1902*

Having taken the trip, experienced it, gathered materials and, at the end of the previous year, organized them, Gertrude is now writing *Travels in Foreign Countries and in the Mind,* reliving much of 1901 in 1902, telling the same story but telling it with a degree of detachment that makes it a different story, about a different woman, pursuing a different present activity.

Before presenting this more literary and contemplative Gertrude, a few words about the code names in *Travels:* Harry is now called "Fatty" as well as "The Prince Consort," usually with "Fatty" crossed out and "Harry" written above. Gertrude is still sometimes "The Queen"; Adele "The Duchess"; J. still "The Duke" but also "The Power Behind the Throne" or "Iron Works" (probably because of his family business); Howard still "The Caterer" but also "Alice" ("because of a story that is not worth repeating"); Jimmie "The Thug" or "The Gold Stick"; and Rollie "The New Acquisition," "The Little Man," "Siegfried," or "The Dago." To avoid confusion, we will not use nicknames except where necessary in contexts that are clear.

Travels begins with the arrival of Gertrude and Harry in Rome.

[Harry] whose fondness for staying at home was marked . . . indulges in numerous . . . silent observations. [His] travel-loving wife . . . felt the experiment a dangerous one, being both loath to displease and anxious to try [her] wings. . . . One could look forward during a lifetime to the day in which one set foot in one's air castle and yet when that moment came one could be diverted by a draught of air, a finger ache, a shallow smile. With something near a sob I lay down to sleep. Far worse than disappointment in a thing is disappointment in the power to feel that thing; and being of a simple mind it seemed to me that I had lost an ideal somehow by the wayside and that instead of the copious enjoyment I had expected I lay side by side with shattered hope. However, my bed fellow was as fickle as I could desire.

Early the next morning Gertrude leaves the Grand Hotel by herself and goes to St. Peter's where she is overwhelmed by Michelangelo's *Pietà.*

That a mere boy could put into his work that something which later generations would seek in vain. . . . New York, my tiny center, a week at sea, London, Paris all breathed of less than frivolity, less than nonentity, less than actual stupidity—now had come the striking of the clock. The hour was here.

The following day Gertrude goes alone to the Vatican, which "swallows her whole," aesthetically and historically—"the papal throne, the conspiracies within plots, the voices of Art, the music of a thousand lives." She wants now to share Rome with Harry.

"What a day to see the Sistine Chapel!" she says to him.

Harry, referring to a previous visit of his own, replies: "We lay on our backs on cushions in the middle of the floor." That is no longer permitted.

"It must be very uncomfortable, and rather—negligé."

Thus their travel bickering begins—a small version of the larger, deeper opposition in their lives. Often, as now, Harry is spoiled and petulant while Gertrude is goading and maternalistic. They go to the Chapel where it takes Harry some time to get over the disappointment of not lying on the floor. "We have to sit up," he says disconsolately, as Gertrude bathes in "shafts of yellow light . . . coming in through the high windows," thinking "surely life is most wonderful and this place of which it is a copy stands for its glory."

"How do you like *The Last Judgment?*" Harry asks after a while.

"I don't like it," is all Gertrude says.

"I suppose it is wonderful as a study," Harry continues, "but it is so complex and confused. I think it is hideous."

This is not what Gertrude meant, but as so often she reserves that for her writing:

> To me it spoke in no variety of keys and was therefore monotonous. It was like a hag with a past but whose present is a mere breath of what it was. Its wrinkles were deep, its youth over. I might go to it full of sympathy and expectancy, it would never give me back more than a cold stare, an unsatisfied want. But no feeling save one of happiness and enthusiasm can last in the Chapel. The ceiling takes all sting away.

Harry tours in the way Gertrude used to. He ticks off sights and wants to move along, fast. After "miles of picture galleries, acres of churches," he calls out, "Go along there—what's the matter?"

"I can't take in another thing."

"Well, go on anyway," comes the "loud answer."

At the Capitoline Museum they bicker for two full closely written pages about *The Dying Gladiator*. Harry is for it, Gertrude against. She writes, "Such Irish talk could lead to nothing and we approached no nearer to the truth," but again, as with so many of these dialogues, they are being led to something, near to *their* truth, if not to that of *The Dying Gladiator*.

The dialogue is partially interrupted, diffused, and perhaps defused too, by the arrival of the Burdens (who have been on a side trip), soon to be followed by Howard, Jimmie, and finally Rollie. Adele's sensitivity and warmth are a welcome contrast to Harry's and J.'s factuality and coldness. J.'s mere presence—"he advertises himself, what he is, well dressed, well groomed, well educated and well mannered"—suggests "respectability and conventionality." For Gertrude, Howard is more than welcome—he is necessary, "a strange mixture of originality and conventionality . . . with unerring taste . . . and an artistic point of view. . . . He led me into paths that I longed to know and while his hand was upon me I could see beyond the boundaries of nondescript ideas. With his presence in Rome came also a more ethereal point of view."

One moonlit night when the others in the party want to play bridge, Gertrude, "with half of [herself] out of the window," wants to visit the Coliseum. "With as much haste as tact," Howard offers to take her. They enter upon a view in shadow and move "gradually, afraid to shorten one moment of bliss, yet fearing to prolong joy to the point of satiety," to where they "could see the side lit by the moon—and suddenly yet melt-ingly the rows upon rows of seats stood out leaving the rest like a cloud, dark and unfathomable. Does one's heart ever stop beating? Of one thing in that moment I was sure and that was of [Howard's] and my absolute understanding of each other. . . . It was a night for talking, unlike many beautiful nights. . . . I did not want to go back to the heated, crowded room at the hotel, where bridge ruled supreme."

After waiting for the Panhard since coming to Rome, the bright red car finally arrives from France. Harry gives instructions to the chauffeur— "The baskets on the side—you remember, the baskets, they are like this" —and soon the party is off to Hadrian's Villa in Tivoli. On this and many other short trips they always amaze and often frighten the people and animals on the road. The automobile is a new experience. A donkey bucks and dumps its load of eggs. They stop to compensate the driver, then go on again feeling exhilarated by "the rush of wind in [their] faces." Fiesole, Florence, Siena . . . Donatello, Cellini, Titian . . . towns, cities, master-pieces flash by, wine cellars are "investigated." In Siena, Adele runs a high fever, diagnosed as diphtheria by a doctor brought down from Flor-ence, and the pace slows. The doctor recommends that they all be inocu-lated. They ask if that's really necessary.

"No, not necessary, but perhaps better. It is only necessary for the child."

All of them are puzzled and follow the Professori's eyes. They rest on Harry, who later assists the Professori as Gertrude gets her shot. She tells her friends, "The Dago washed me! He scrubbed me. Harry said it left a little white place. Beasts!"

Thinking about Harry's youthful appearance, perhaps in contrast to her own image of herself, Gertrude writes that he is now approaching thirty and might be, judging from looks, some years younger. Strong of limb, deep-chested, inclined to corpulence, with green eyes and a straight nose and an innocent look which his sins have not yet robbed him of. His nature is a strong one and given to many impulses and combined with a brain of unusual activity he might live to do great things. However these very qualities form as well his greatest temptation. By very reason of his facility for learning and adapting himself he stands in danger of not probing deep enough or of being spoiled by fate and the world. Wherever he goes his boyishness, his charm, his brightness, his cleverness insure him a warm reception. He has won mankind from the beginning and therefore has great belief in his powers, yet he takes them simply and without real conceit. He recognizes his abilities without gloating over them, and if he sees no reason for hiding his superiorities it is not that he unduly exaggerates them. His brain is marvelously quick and with discipline could yet do wonders. He has known no discipline. Life has given him all he has asked of it from the beginning. Indulgent parents provided for every wish before it was uttered, it is most wonderful of all that he retains any strength. Cheerful of temperament, with a great fondness and natural adaptability for teasing, he is quick, bright and good company.

This portrait, though more physical and more realistic than the one in her *People* book of 1894–96, is still surprisingly similar. Though Harry has aged and gone slightly to fat, though her expectations for him have somewhat diminished, she has not lost sight of his attractive qualities. His appeal remains strong. It is her own which she doubts. If Harry is sometimes silent or abstracted or rejecting when he is with her, he is at least physically there. It is she, thinking often of herself as a bird, who attempts to fly off.

If one has been surrounded all one's life by a great high fence . . . then when . . . one is liberated from prison one's wings are so inconceivably weak that though one longs to fly one has abrupt falls which are painful. . . . My wings have neither grown nor have they spread. . . . The Anglo-Saxon temperament is the real constructor of high fences and in consequence the clipper and restrictor of wings. . . . What do [the Latin races] know of the inexpressible agony of the "shut in feeling," the perverted self-consciousness of "reserve," the long, drawn out sorrow of the "unutterable"? . . . Though I may feel near to them, how cold my look which seems only to conceal my sympathy. I would rather die than show my real feelings once deeply touched, while they share with the world that which makes them so human and understanding. . . . Love, love is too much. Friendship is enough—less than that—a touch of something that vibrates.

But even friendship, even a touch, are not always there when she wants them. Perhaps, she thinks, her salvation will be in art, which is enduring Artists have

the sublime joy of giving themselves to the world. . . . And yet it is in the expressing that the real joy exists and not so much in the method. How account for the bad pictures painted, the wretched books written, the weak statues constructed unless one takes into account the joy of creation?

Just as sometimes Harry is more "with" Gertrude when she is writing her solitary journal than when he is physically present, so America is with Gertrude in Italy as much as Italy is with Gertrude now, a year or so later, in America.

Would that we practical Americans with our love of money, our unbounded belief in ourselves, could cultivate an eye for the artistic in all phases of life. Not in art alone, though alas we need it sadly there, but in every part of our too full and hurried lives. If we could but rise in the morning artistically, to work or play artistically, to eat, sleep, and love artistically!

But like love, art too sometimes disappoints Gertrude. In Naples, shortly before boarding the *Sheelah*,

for once the Museum failed to touch me. I was carved of stone, I was frozen to ice, I was impenetrable marble. . . . How flat the pictures looked, how expressionless the statues! What were the cold imitations compared to the originals? . . . Live, throbbing people, with hearts and souls and lives before them and experiences behind them! That was all there seemed to be in life just then. [Howard] looked pale in the morning light, but he had a life to live and for him I could turn my head and raise my hand and be happy. [Jimmie] with his kindness and unselfishness was worth more in one second than those affected imitations could be during the course of centuries. The live thing! How I loved all that breathed. I did not look one iota below the surface, but only at [Rollie's] despondent figure and Harry's portly size —it was enough. Dash the pictures! Life, life was the only interest, the only force. Could I for one moment regard a work of art with anything like the interest that a human soul could awaken in me? . . . I wanted to scream out, "Let us go into the streets where people live and struggle and breathe. Why stifle in here with dead things? . . . things?" . . . And soon we went into the living street and a rush of warmth came to me and a love for mankind and a sympathy for all humanity.

In Naples there is one restaurant, Gambino's, visited by Rollie on a previous trip, that has

come to mean the height of perfection. I pictured the place, large, brilliant, the meeting spot of aristocratic and beautiful Naples. Princesses, countesses and all the glittering demi-monde assembled, with here and there a dash of bright uniforms and the wonderful beauty of the Latin race displayed to its greatest advantage. [The group goes there for lunch.] As we took our seats I remarked that a party of German tourists occupied the table next to us. This was a disappointment. [Gertrude had had] visions of how [the Neapolitans] would hate the Waldorf or Delmonicos. [Now she is not so sure as she looks around the] rather small, decidedly rusty . . . half empty . . . very quiet room.

"Where is the band?" she asks Rollie.
He does not hear her. He has a bewildered look.
Howard, who speaks Italian fluently, orders lunch.
Harry scans table after table and Gertrude can see the look of expectancy dying out of his face.

JIMMIE: "Germans . . . common . . . ordinary . . ."
GERTRUDE: "They are not very—beautiful."
HOWARD: "Or very smart."
JIMMIE: "Or very Italian."
HARRY: "They are bum!"

Rollie looks "as if he had built the restaurant, decorated it, provided the customers and was responsible for it all." He tries to explain: "Of course—the reason—and—"
"Where is the music?" Harry interrupts.
"There is no music," replies a waiter who speaks English.
That is final. They concentrate on the food.
"What is this anyway?"
"It tastes of shoe leather."
"For heaven's sake don't touch the butter."
"Oh! Ah! No thank you."
"Is there any plain bread?"
"It's come a long distance."
"How those Germans must love this."
"I don't care if it is bad manners, I can't help it."
"I am hungry."
"Neither, thanks."

And so forth. . . . Another disappointment surely, but with what detachment and good humor Gertrude recreates it. In this vignette—such a typical little travel fiasco—we feel an acceptance of life that is, of course, basic to the acceptance of art as part of life rather than vice versa. And we feel by now, too, a certain anticipation of manners, attitudes, and prejudices that will filter down during the next twenty years or so into "the lost generation," a middle-class stylization of the elitism and freedom—principally economic—of the very rich.

The next day Gertrude and Harry inspect the *Sheelah* to be sure everything will be comfortable for themselves and their party. The Scottish captain has barely started to show them around when Harry falls through a hatch into the hold.

"Harry!" Gertrude screams. There is no answer. "Brandy . . . whiskey . . . something . . ."

A gasp comes from below and a sailor climbs down to assist Harry. Gertrude hangs over the hatchway, waiting. At last Harry's voice, usually so strong but now weak, says, "It's my wind—all right."

Gertrude "breathes again. He staggered up pretty soon and was none the worse for his fall."

The weather turns gorgeous. The sea, Capri, Vesuvius all glow in the sunlight. Even the objects in the archeological museum, dead a few days before, are alive again when Gertrude revisits them. *Psyche* she loves the most. "Though only a fragment, the turn of the head remains; the neck and breast are marvelous examples of that modeling which looks simple but is in reality the most difficult." However, again she turns from the dead museum and focuses now on the living

new acquisition, alias Rollie, alias Siegfried, alias The Dago, alias The Little Man. . . . There is something of all his names in him, from the newness of him to the rather small size of his person. As for Rollie, so the world knows him. Siegfried refers to a certain epoch in his career when German Opera (with capital letters) played a large part. Dago needs no explanation, in a way it absorbs him, for his ancestors were surely Italians and Turks and they have transmitted to him all their charm with a dash of their wickedness.

ROLLIE: "Of course I am Italian, can't you see it?"

HARRY: "If you mean you are like the lazy-good-for-nothing-Dagos in America, yes I can."

ROLLIE smokes on in silence for a moment, then sighs: "That is, unless I am a Turk."

Gertrude comments silently to her book:

Full of moods, musical, poetical and something of a sport, he is a strange combination. He could get so much out of money and it never came his way. One could never imagine him making it, but he missed a vocation in not having it.

Later she thinks again of Harry, Harry who has money, Harry who has everything, Harry who offers everything—except that ultimate communion which perhaps only exists in art and religion. As now she writes about herself in relation to him, we suspect that she may also have in her mind the image of Rodin's *The Kiss* (exhibited and widely publicized four years earlier):

Alone—alone for always. Could love do nothing? Oh yes, something, but it could not step over the last bond, it could not push aside the last veil of the soul, and there lay the sorrow of existence, the knife that cuts in this life. Two people loving each other in all ways, unseparated by the world yet separated—separated though close, closer than all else. *I* can never know his thoughts, *he* can never feel every beat of my heart. And in my mind's eye there arose two tall figures, a man and a woman locked in each other's embrace, and yet—torn by the desire for a yet closer relationship, a relationship that cannot exist while we have bodies that eternally separate us.

They set sail for Sicily.

Howard, probably the most experienced traveler in the group, preaches the advantages of liquor at sea: "You should drink on all occasions, and every kind of drink, especially cocktails—"

GERTRUDE: "Is that what all yachting parties do?"

HOWARD: "If they don't, they should."

JIMMIE: "No wonder they always have a good time."

HOWARD: "You need stimulants at sea—"

As the coast of Italy fades behind them and Capri shimmers ahead, the Scottish steward hands them a menu and suggests that they eat something solid. No, they will go on drinking. They make jokes about a credit for the food they have refused.

Now they are out on the open sea and everyone becomes quiet.

Howard breaks the silence: "I feel very sick. Harry, don't you feel sick?"

Harry screws up his eyes and swallows before answering: "Well, I am afraid it is going to be pretty rough."

HOWARD: "I tell you I feel very sick. I am sure you must feel sick. You know you are a bad sailor."

HARRY: "This is not rough. . . . Have some champagne."

HOWARD: "I am going below. Harry, how do you feel?"

HARRY: "Oh, pretty strong. I will send you some champagne."

JIMMIE: "Poor Howard."

They order more champagne, much to the disapproval of the steward whose "whole air seems to say, 'In Scotland we don't do such things.'"

Soon Rollie is clinging to the rail, groaning, "I told you so, I told you so."

None of the remaining five knows what he told them.

The *Sheelah* shoves on, dipping her head into the sea, rising, shaking from bow to stern.

The steward announces dinner.

HARRY: "I am not hungry. I feel rather tired."

GERTRUDE (starting for the saloon): "Shall I send you anything?"

HARRY (weakly): "No, no nothing. I tell you I am not hungry."

Gertrude and Jimmie eat with the Burdens. The other three have an awful night.

In Palermo everyone revives, even Howard, the sickest and the most abused by the "horrid unsympathetic steward," who kept asking if he wanted anything. "What should I have wanted!"

They wander about the city where Gertrude is particularly moved by the luminous mosaics in the Mon Reale, its cloisters, and "the garden charged with anticipation (like the woman who waits her lover)." In the garden she sits on a moss-covered stone and dreams that a female companion tells her "that the tiny flame which flickers in each heart is a sacred and blessed possession not to be carelessly handled, not to be smothered in worldly goods." In parting the companion speaks of "a brown skinned boy with almond eyes" who will come into Gertrude's life. The dream goes on and on. At first Gertrude is in the woods; then with the boy on the open beach where flies and bugs keep running on her legs and back; then singing in the sea as strange fish begin to follow her, raising their quivering bodies from the water and ogling her.

> Delicious eddies caressed my skin and I knew that nature alone was perfect; but I knew it was a little boy who knows not what it means. . . . I licked my lips for I loved the salty taste. . . . Now again the woods . . . and there I fancied that I saw the-something-that-I-wanted waiting for me. And I said: "Are you full?" And it answered: "I am." And I said: "Are you a watering pot full of water?" And the answer came: "I am." So I . . . took that something-that-I-wanted and I carried it home singing.

The abundant sexual imagery in this dream needs no special interpretation or emphasis, but what must, more generally, be emphasized is that this dream is being redreamed not in Palermo but in the United States as Gertrude writes alone in one of her many private rooms or studies. The latter part of *Travels* contains several such fantasies, stretching into the present and beyond. But now, as in Palermo, Harry is absent. Now, as there and then, though there can be little doubt of Gertrude's enduring attraction to him, there is also little doubt that she is thinking more and more frequently of other possibilities, in life as well as art.

But to return to Sicily—to Taormina—one moonlit night, filled with "an unholy murmuring of voices," Gertrude

imagined myself a woman of fire and of passion with a thousand loves in my heart and a million lovers in my train. I imagined myself with an inexhaustible passion. I walked one night in a garden of orange blossoms and longed with a deadly longing for the arms of my lover. But he did not come and the odor of the oranges and the sight of the golden moon drove me into a frenzy and I sank on the purple ground and wept from passion and anger. And then in the gloom and sorrow I heard a low sound. At first it seemed to me to be the noise of the sea wind, but when I stretched out my arms, lying in the shadow, I felt a form. And low words came to my ears, quivering words of love, and a savage man stretched forth arms of passionate desire to me, and I fainted into his arms and he took me as savage men take their women, and I was happy. And then I remembered—that I was not a woman of fire or of passion, and—I left the window.

In Taormina, Jimmie Appleton leaves the *Sheelah* to return home and the rest of the party sails on to Syracuse and then Tunis. To Gertrude the Arabs are as strange, as foreign as were the Japanese on her honeymoon, and yet how differently, how much more openly she looks now, how she responds to the

harmony of color. . . . Mysterious life, in long limbs, in the far off indifference of pose, in sinewy forms, in dark placid eyes, thick hair, ivory skins filled me with joy. I was attracted by the marvelous incomprehensibility of the mind, the life. From whence came their peace, their calm, their power? To me they were untraveled lands. The elements of pictorial expression were all present, but even when I viewed them they mystified me. How eager to do violence we appear as contrasted to these others. We drive through life with a fury and a vehemence unknown in the East. Our disheveled hair and frantic hands ready to tear and desecrate all, while with self-restraint and tranquility they contemplate life. . . . And always one feels the colorist, the hand of the artist, the splendid folds of drapery and the sincerity of it, and forever making the feeling of remarkable elation.

On a fête day Gertrude and Harry stop at a café to have coffee and vermouth and to study the passing parade. Two Arabs take seats at the table next to them.

One is dressed in pale pink and wears a light blue burnoose. He has almond eyes and he ogles the women as they pass. The other is very tall and pale. He is dressed in white, and a bright orange burnoose hangs loosely from his shoulders. He looks at no one and answers [his friend] in monosyllables. I wonder if he loves unhappily, but Harry says he has taken too much dope.

Of their group only Howard and Rollie respond to the East as she does. Howard fills a notebook with bright sensuous sketches of Arab men and women, and for Rollie "the East possessed the same insoluble mysteries as for me. Every part of it seemed made of some ethereal substance." The distance in responsiveness which Gertrude has come is immense. Yes, she and her friends still use words like Dago and Jap, but compare her portrait of a Jewish dancer in an Arab café with that made a decade earlier in Vienna of her family's Jewish guide. The dancer is "young, impudent, languorous, slim," probably younger than Gertrude but physically not unlike her. Her dance

represents nature, but nature as seen through the eyes of meaning. Here the alluring body, the sense of joy of motion so visible in the girl, the artificial travesty of it and yet the natural expression, all combined to make of it a perfect though momentary work of art. As she danced in that hot, heavy atmosphere amid the impenetrable faces of her kind, the full intoxication of the moment assailed me. She expressed what was more remote than the stars and yet more human than that which stood closest to me. She expressed what seemed more desirable than my ambitions and yet more evasive seemed she than a will-o'-the-wisp. The faint, heady music marked the undulating rhythm of her body. The close yet loose drapery forced to my mind the strength of all passing enjoyments, the luxury of thoughtlessness and the present. Here again was the expression of life and therefore Art. For a moment she seemed satisfied alone with the joy of motion and as one long arm shot above her head and the other slowly felt its way along her undulating body she personified the real instinct of life. And then through the eyes the symbol of her life seemed to come to me, a world such as I chose to make it, untrammelled by the actual.

Gertrude *is* the Jewish dancer. The present intensity of her identification—and this is by no means the only example—is non-existent, or at least unexpressed, in 1891 and 1896 and even on January 30, 1901, when this trip begins. That recently, even with family and close friends, she maintains a rather shy and frightened distance. But now, in giving herself to life, she is ready to give herself to art. Though she feels liberated by the Arabian aesthetic ("In each garment there is a grace, the perception of the proper proportion, the almost imperceptible curve that makes for perfection. And all bears witness of the creative instinct, the born artist"), she is also aware of the poverty around her, the filth, the disease, and probably most of all, the subjugation of women.

> Poor servants, yoked oxen, straining to pull a load which nature never intended they should pull. . . . What right has the male to cramp the female? None but that of physical force, and as he stands on his self-erected pedestal, he rightly fears the results of education on the female. He scoffs at it, he essays with mighty hand to sweep it aside, for with it he recognizes the fall of his pedestal and he agonizes even while his lip curls. Oh you fat, self-satisfied males of the East, with your gluttonous bodies, press your heavy hands down, down on the heads of your females, or you will lose your glorious power and your immortal souls will be understood and valued at their true worth. . . . [Women have] the lighter touch, the more intuitive knowledge, the greater imagination, more poetry, more music, more art, more power of understanding human nature, more sympathy, more memory. And it is by memory that our lives exist for us. As we can only repent for the wrong we have done by remembering it, so forgetfulness becomes immoral. Our wills control our memories. . . .

Gertrude, traveling in her own memory and simultaneously on the Mediterranean, knows now that Mnemosyne is mother of the muses and, after Tunis, knows that the sea is the mother of life. The sea dominates several of the last pages of her *Travels* . . . It, too, is a woman,

> alive . . . vibrant with force, exultation and joy in its own beauty. . . . I became part of the passion of the sea. . . . The boats which she so indulgently allows to lie on her breast are as nothing to her. She shakes, reviles, cares not what may become of them. . . . She is the strongest, most beautiful of all, the Amazon of Nature. . . . Sometimes cruel man, thinking to glorify himself by subduing her, has taken a bit of her and forced her to quiet and lack of freedom.

The sea carries the party to Turkey where Gertrude recoils at the brutalization of Islamic culture. In Istanbul members of a sect of chanting, whirling dervishes beat and cut themselves into a state of bloody religious ecstasy. She wonders if these rites which appear horrible to her can in reality be "the true emblems of a beautiful religion," and decides that they are more like a recurring nightmare of hers in which "I travel everlastingly and in huge circles through space." The dark seething crowd threatens her.

> I saw them as living monsters about to tear me from my occidental surroundings. . . . A little white me alone among a sea of blackness. A great lump rose in my throat, a sob almost convulsed me, a long shiver passed through my body. . . . My God—what would they do

to me—I was in their power—and then someone spoke [probably Howard]: "It's all right, now we are through. You are pale. I don't wonder you were scared." [She has had enough for now of wild ecstasy. She] misses orthodox religion . . . wants it in its most sentimental form . . . pious hands to rock me to sleep . . . hopes of a future life to comfort my fears . . . the charm of Wordsworth, the daisies and buttercups of existence . . . the gayety that lurks in the voices of birds. . . .

Greece is welcome. At Olympia, once again she goes off by herself and spends an hour "dreaming among the statues in the calm of a little museum," thinking, "It is not good for man to live alone, but it is very good for woman to have many hours to herself. . . ." For the last time perhaps, she wonders if she has "the wherewithall to satisfy [her] craving appetite [for art and travel]." But this rationalization will no longer do. There is no problem about money. There never has been. The real problem continues to be her relationship to Harry: how to resolve her love for him, his frequent rejection of her, and their mutual lack of sympathy for each other's most profound interests.

After 220 closely written pages (not including the preliminary journals and loose insertions), *Travels in Foreign Countries and in the Mind* ends, as appropriately as her short story about a crumbling marriage, in mid-sentence. Gertrude, anticipating a visit to the Acropolis, writes: "It should be a quiet, serene day, and nature was good to us and gave us—" There is nothing more of the trip, though we know from the earlier journals that the party went on to other parts of Greece, Turkey, and Italy, as well as to two ports in Yugoslavia.

≈

While all this traveling in the mind is going on, Gertrude also corresponds a great deal. There are many letters she receives from Harry and others but only the unfinished draft, preserved in a journal, of one she writes to him (while he is on a trip in January):

Dearest—

In an unguarded moment you suggested that I write down all that I do while you are away, and I am just foolish enough to adopt your *careless* suggestion. It is an excuse to talk to you and let myself think of you, not to speak of the joy of talking of the person I love best in the world—*myself!* But, you silly baby, you refuse to believe all the "soft" things I find to say to you, and laugh at me for saying them, which is cruel to say the least and then besides hardly encouraging. Dear—already I miss you terribly, what will it be at the end of ten days! The children have just gone upstairs. I was in the nursery with them most of the afternoon and we all had a most beautiful time. My what a *good* day I have passed.

Church this morning and a sermon on Progress, also incidentally Foreign Missions and a jab at the people who "disapproved" of them after taking a "pleasure trip" through the East. It was a nasty one but —nothing could be *said*. I was late for church, so sat in the back pew and had to forego the pleasure of gazing at the back of J.B.'s head! [Another teasing reference to Jim Barnes.]

Then I lunched with the family which you will admit was a perfectly proper proceeding. Alfred and Elsie [his wife Ellen's nickname] were there, also Regi. It rained cats and dogs all the afternoon. I carefully gave the message "Not at home" and felt after this as if I ought to retire to my room to read the Bible. But instead I played with the children—and Mabel [Gerry] is coming to dinner!! Of course this kind of life makes me mad to have you.

What a hole town is on Sunday. It is so long since I have been here that I had forgotten. I wrote Helen Hay accepting for the wedding [to Harry's brother Payne]. Also I shall have to settle on a present without you.

Lena, Rollie, Lloyd Warren and Mr. Atterbury go to the opera with me tomorrow night. I can't say I take much interest in these proceedings.

During this period while Gertrude is writing *Travels*, just which proceedings interest her seems arbitrary. She doesn't attend an elaborate musicale at Grace's—Cornelius, like Harry, is away on business—at which Kubelik is violinist, Gerardy cellist, and Mademoiselle Marcella Sembrich prima donna, entertaining many Vanderbilts, Whitneys, and their friends, including Rollie, Bobby Sands, and Lispenard Stewart. However, at the end of the month Gertrude does go to a house party at Ne-Ha-Sa-Ne, the Webbs' huge camp adjoining the Whitneys' in the Adirondacks where many of the same people appear, though in the much more casual context of romping in the snow, coasting, and sleigh riding.

But by early February, Gertrude and Harry are together, and on the sixth they attend the Washington wedding of Payne to Helen Hay, the daughter of John Hay, not only the Secretary of State appointed by McKinley and continuing in that office now under Theodore Roosevelt, but poet, journalist, historian, biographer of Lincoln—a remarkable man, unremarked, or taken for granted, by Gertrude. Roosevelt and all of his Cabinet are present. Gertrude wears "white and silver brocade with a hat of purple primroses."

For a month or so, Gertrude and Howard Cushing have been in fairly constant correspondence. He writes now from Newport that he has not heard from her in at least two weeks and hopes that she is not sick.

Perhaps you are simply having a silent time, like me. . . . The somebody I wrote you about continues to interest me, but I think that is, briefly, on account of her looks—I don't know her well enough to see back of them. She certainly is enchanting looking—but that is not enough. There is no harm in having a little amusement by the wood-side, is there? I tell you that I am becoming a flirt, I think—no, not a flirt but an engager of life. I should like to have done with all depressions and misgivings—but I don't seem to be able to. The thought of what I might be flashes across me sometimes and what my life might be and the brightness and beauty of that makes me feel as if I were sitting in a dark cellar. . . .

In early March he writes on behalf of a young boy who has been working at the bathhouses at Bailey's Beach and asks if Gertrude will speak to Harry about a job for him in a surveyor's or engineer's office. In the same letter Howard refers to another young man, mentioned in previous correspondence, who has now "been examined by a lung specialist, but, poor thing, he is too far gone to be helped." As the words flow on, in handwriting that is small and neat, we get a more specific sense than in Gertrude's journals of the platonic sympathy which exists between them. Yet, sweet and considerate as Howard is, he can also be catty. After Gertrude and Harry go to Hickory Valley on a hunting party which includes the Newport-New York society figure Victor Sorchon, Howard writes, "I am so glad that you have enjoyed Tennessee—but the company, dear Gertrude, sounded to me rather chilling. However, fresh air is a great balance, isn't it, and I daresay that after a long day out of doors even Victor Sorchon would seem sympathetic—" Howard catches himself, comments, "That is spiteful," and then becomes tender again as he explains his sister Olivia's need for him since the recent death of her husband Andreas Andersen. Finally, he broaches her favorite subject, art:

I can't tell you what happiness I get out of work. It seems as if I could put the whole of myself into it in a way that I never could before, and these weeks of absolute monotony are the very thing I needed. I am looking forward with the greatest pleasure to my visit to you in May. It will be over four months since I shall have seen you. . . . A year ago today we were in Rome, weren't we? It seems to me that we were very undeveloped and unknowing people then—and I suppose we are now—but not quite so much so. . . . You never told me about your work this winter. Did you do anything? I often feel that you would enjoy the kind of life I am leading now—quite far from conventional demands, and with a definite object which makes all the days seem too short.

Give my love to Harry and Rollie.
Yours
H.G.C.

Before Howard's visit, he arranges to have Edmund C. Tarbell paint portraits of Whitney horses at $1,000 per picture, writing that Tarbell "would prefer to paint the horse being rubbed down or led in or out of the paddock, or in any characteristic way rather than the usual stereotyped lifeless way. You must make his acquaintance, for he is one of the nicest men I know and one of the most talented. I think it would be a good idea perhaps to have him come for a day to Roslyn [i.e., Westbury] when I am there in May, don't you?"

"Did you do anything?" In May, Gertrude shows Howard completed portions of *Travels*, probably reads passages of it aloud to him, along with the beginning of a novel, *As Seen Through a Glass Darkly*, written on Hickory Valley stationery. It is about Dora, a society woman, interested in art and literature, who is misunderstood by her husband and most of their social circle. She seeks understanding from various men—reminiscent of Howard, Rollie, and Jimmie—and yet despairs of ever finding anyone's complete understanding or her own complete artistic expression. The story is dark, the theme familiar, the work fragmentary and unsustained: an echo in words of recent sketches and small sculptures she also shows Howard, explaining why she has been unable thus far to do anything more substantial.

During Howard's visit much, perhaps too much from his viewpoint and Gertrude's, revolves around horses—Harry is playing a lot of polo at Meadow Brook and the racing season has begun—but there is time too for art. At dinner parties, along with Burdens, Webbs, and Mortons, there are Rollie, and a Signor Pipestrello, probably a musician or singer, and the pianist Josef Hofmann. And surely Howard has enough time alone with Gertrude to tell her about some of his recent commissions, including a prospective one at Biltmore, and to begin a portrait of her. It is a very loving and somewhat idealized painting. Gertrude, wearing a gauzy silk dress and the long rope of pearls given to her as a wedding gift by Oliver Payne, sits erect on a low-backed couch dreaming, with vulnerable eyes wide open. Her eyes—set wide apart under heavy eyebrows and upswept bouffant hair—are the focus of the painting. They seem to look inward as well as outward, toward the past as well as the future.

❦

Just after the racing season Gertrude becomes pregnant again. She and Harry leave Westbury for Newport. From there they make a brief trip to Sheepshead Bay for the Fourth of July weekend and then to Elm Court in Lenox for the wedding of Gertrude's cousin Lila Sloane to William Bradhurst Osgood Field. That wedding in the middle of 1902, and in the middle also of the difficult and decisive 1901–3 period of Gertrude's life, the period of *Travels in Foreign Countries and in the Mind*, is a turning point. The details of the wedding fade in old newspapers—the list of more than two hundred guests, including nearly every member of the Vanderbilt family; the 475 gifts, having an estimated value of $1,300,000, including a gold and silver tea set from Gertrude and Harry—but for years Gertrude will brood about what happened, what really happened beneath the details, before writing about it: first, two years later in "Plot for Story" and then, five years later, in her journal. In the story outline, the heroine's situation is like Dora's in *As Seen Through a Glass Darkly*:

A girl kept very much to herself, very imaginative and rather morbid . . . gets into the habit of leading another life inside of herself. . . . She lives in this life rather than in the real life about her because her surroundings are uncongenial. . . . She marries, quite happily, a man who cares a good deal for her but is the wrong kind of man. . . . Getting little sympathy from her husband on any subject and continually doing the things which she does not care about makes this habit [of fantasy] grow. . . . Gradually her imagination takes the form of making her life a story of love for another man. This man who has been in love with her one day tells her so and here her other life and her real life become blended for a while. It seems hardly a shock to her to enter into more or less culpable relations with him. However, she pulls up in time—at least before it is really too late but not before she has stored up a large share of unhappiness for herself. After all relations between them are broken off, she seems able to see more clearly what she has done and by very reason of her imagination begins to suffer intolerably. She thinks that her husband knows all and more than all. . . .

And more than all! That is the point—not the point of the story but the point to emphasize if we are to understand Gertrude's life during this period. The wife has not been technically unfaithful to her husband, nor has she really fallen in love with "another man" but rather with the "story of a love for another man." It is impossible not to see parallels between the wife's infatuation and Gertrude's for Jimmie Appleton. What doesn't appear thus far in the story is the husband's rejection of his wife or her suspicion of his infidelity, but now the wife begins to wonder why her husband does not blame her and concludes that there must be "another woman."

In the journal entry, written almost exactly five years after the Field-Sloane wedding, Gertrude returns to Elm Court, the Sloanes' country house in Lenox—and to "the other woman." She is the sister-in-law of a cousin of Gertrude's "so placed," as Gertrude says in "Plot for Story," that Gertrude "must openly break with her or see her often and intimately." Worse, she is not only of the same age and social background as Gertrude but strongly resembles her. Like Gertrude, she is tall and willowy and loves dancing. Unlike her, she is extroverted; she is a prize-winning horsewoman; and she is not pregnant (at a time when doctors restricted activities of pregnant women—in sex, travel, work, etcetera—much more and for much longer than today).

"The night after the wedding I cried almost all night and told Harry it was on account of Cornelius. The next day H[arry] was going to drive up to October Mountain. He said he wanted to see the place etc. I knew perfectly the reason. I will never forget that morning or the lunch that followed. I remember the Twomblys came and that I talked and laughed till I was almost mad. H[arry] came in late looking very badly. It was the hardest thing I had had in my life then, harder than Papa's death or Bill's, or C[ornelius]'s troubles. Barbara [the daughter with whom she is pregnant] had started then, which did not make it easier. . . ."

The rest of 1902 (and the early part of 1903, at least until Barbara's slightly premature birth) is mostly a nightmare for Gertrude. She returns to Newport but does not attend Grace's and Cornelius's Fête des Roses gala, with its midway side shows and full stage performance of the New York musical comedy *Wild Rose*. Nor does she often attend the races, in which horses from the Whitney stables are almost consistently triumphant. She is in no mood for play, and by now too distracted and uncomfortable for work. She is relieved in late September and October when Harry goes off on a five-week business trip with Daniel Guggenheim to purchase silver-, lead-, and copper-mining properties in the Western states and Mexico. However, a "desperate time" follows when Harry returns.

"What a winter! My health was very bad but it was as nothing compared to my mental health. . . . One very bad time was about Dec. when H[arry] went to Aiken for a week. He did not take Stewart [his valet, presumably because he wanted privacy with 'the other woman']. The time he was away dragged and my imagination was let loose. I got sicker and sicker, but if only my mind could have rested nothing would have mattered."

In addition to everything else troubling Gertrude at this time, Cornelius almost dies of typhoid fever, complicated by peritonitis. Day after day the newspapers report on his slow progress and each day his doctors send a telegram describing his condition to Gertrude's mother in Paris. There's a lot, too, in the papers about Gertrude's younger brother Regi. As early as the past June he has received unfortunate publicity when his diploma (along with those of "eleven other prominent [Yale] seniors") is withheld for not passing examinations. Now his name appears frequently in connection with District Attorney Jerome's gambling raids and Regi is alleged to have lost as much as $70,000 in a single night at Canfield's, an exclusive gambling house on 44th Street, adjoining Delmonico's. Harry's name also appears once as an habitué of Canfield's but, after an indignant letter to the *Times*, never again. Possibly exacerbated by these events and surely by her own emotional state, Gertrude's pregnancy becomes more and more difficult, pleasures of any kind more and more brief.

≈ *1903*

Howard spends New Year's weekend with Gertrude and Harry in Westbury and writes frequently afterward expressing concern about her depressed mood. On her birthday Jimmie Appleton sends a card with
flowers. On January 14, having been interested in Greenwich House Social
Settlement by her friend, its chairman, Meredith ("Bunny") Hare, and
elected a trustee in December, she attends her first board meeting, beginning a lifelong involvement, particularly with the sponsorship of art
classes. A few days later she has her old friend and favorite teacher at
Brearley, Ann Winsor (now Mrs. Allen), over for lunch. Just before their
reunion Ann writes, thanking her for opera tickets ("Do you keep a box
just for your friends' pleasure? What a weekly task that implies") and
commenting on Gertrude's pregnancy in an unintentionally ironic way:

> It is good to hear that there is to be another in your family. I grow
> so tired of seeing children alone or in couples. They do not make
> families at all. To my own thinking five is the least number that
> makes a real family. Where there are fewer, each individual is too
> prominent. But you have more than the *number* to consider. When I
> remember what you told me of the separation that a large house
> makes between children I realize your puzzles and wonder how you
> have decided to solve them. If one ever talked of half one thinks of
> talking about, how interesting conversation would be.

By February, Gertrude is increasingly confined, nauseated, and depressed. Now, or possibly in early March, believing she is going to die, she
scribbles in pencil a farewell letter to Harry, to be opened only in the
event of her death:

Dearest,
   One never knows what may happen in the way of an accident
when one is ill most of the time and, as I don't want to die without
you knowing a few things, I am writing this for you to read if anything unforeseen should happen to me. I suppose it is very selfish of
me to write it anyway, and that it would be far "nobler" (if such a
word can be used in this connection at all) for me to let you remain
in blissful ignorance of certain facts. However, not being "noble" but

only very weak and human, I have succumbed to the temptation of telling what in life I struggled madly to hide.

It seems so long since I have known that you did not care for me that I can hardly fix on a time when I began to realize it. After all what difference does the time make? Over and over again I would cheat myself into the belief that it had not all gone. I don't mean all affection, but all love. At any rate, to proceed with a story which you already know, I must say the realization that you cared for someone else was what in the end *made* me believe that as far as I was concerned all was over. See how quietly even clearly I have written that and yet for weeks the dim thought of it was such agony that I could not stand it. The dim thought receded and then approached again, a trifle nearer each time until a day came when face it squarely I must. And I did, and it is what makes it possible for me to live as I do today. No one will ever know the horrible agony of last spring and summer to me. Was I often peevish and irritable? Yes, I know I was, but something inside of me was dying. I was freezing and slowly, slowly getting a hold over myself. It is strange that the very thing which at first in connection with this thing gave me greatest pain, in the end was the only thing that made it possible for me to stand it. I refer to my flirtation with Jimmie. At first it seemed as if that might have been the cause of bringing the other about and then later it was the fact of having been through a flirtation which made me understand you might care really for me even while you amused yourself with someone else. I could see that from your standpoint you might have thought I did not care for you, simply because it amused me to have him around. That for a while helped me, but of course the difference of the two things was bound to show itself sooner or later even to me. Yours was not a flirtation. Once, no matter when, but there were lots of people round, something happened. It may have been a look only, it may have been a word, a tone—I lost all control of myself. I can write it quietly now (I am hardly crying) but when I think of the paroxysm I went into I shall never forget it. I had just enough control left to rush away and then when I was alone I fought my battle as I pray to God I may never have to fight another and when I met you again a little later I was even able to feel sorry for you. After that I went through a time of absolute darkness.

I don't want you to think that this is a long reproach to you. I know enough about caring to know that it cannot be controlled and now since you two have come to your understanding I only think it is hard lines on you both. But I am not a Christian really and though I have forgiven you (for what you can't help) I say frankly I often feel very bitterly towards you.

I am greedy for love and I don't get it, at least not where I can take it.

I have thought very often of an explanation but have always in the end rejected the idea as being of no use. Although the despair of not knowing positively has sometimes seemed one of the hardest things to bear. I have even tried, and put out feelers to see if you wanted to come to an understanding, but it always seemed to me the last thing you wanted. But now that I am ill and feel that I may not live, if there was one atom of doubt in my mind I would insist on an understanding, but there is not one and I have done my best not to nag you on this subject. I don't despair of your *ever* coming back to me. You have evidently both decided to do your best and after all what more can one ask. I know that if I had been something different it would not have happened and that your disappointment in me is perhaps largely accountable for it. If I could not hold you I had only myself to blame. Much as I have always cared for you I was able for a while to frivol with Jimmie. You have always known that that was only frivoling and that you always have been the only person I have cared for. Still, that could only bore you in your present state. But now—now when you read this and all the little things have been swept away and only the great truths remain you will be glad that I have said it even though you know it. I really think, my dear boy, that this is the best thing that could have happened. Could I have gone on without that for which I pine the most. I doubt it and been a good woman. I love love and I need it as we all do and perhaps I would have taken it even if I could not give it, rather than starve forever.

I know you must have suffered but after this blow is softened you will be happy and you are not so old. After all you did care for me a good deal and we were very happy.

For heaven's sake remember that Flora is horribly sensitive. Give her lots of love and bring her up to be strong and good. She has the possibilities of lots of unhappiness in her, poor little tot and she is closer to me today than anyone in the world. She will be moody and fanciful and inclined to think too much about things which will only make her unhappy, guard against these tendencies. Let her have lots of companionship. As for Sonny be good to him. He seemed at times really to like me. I think we would have been very close. How I loved him when he put his little hand up to pat my face. It seemed as if he really cared.

Good-bye dearest—remember I do not blame you. I believe that you could not help it. I only know that I had so much more love to give than you wanted that it used to choke me and that now I have confessed all and you can start fresh.

The letter is unsigned and remains sealed for the rest of Gertrude's life.

Barbara is "born 2 weeks too soon [March 21]. That was a bad time and it went on getting worse." Once again Howard writes:

I was so glad to get your note and to know that you could receive letters—I did not hear of your daughter's arrival until Wednesday, and then I did not write as my mother said you would probably not be allowed to read anything. I am so glad it is all over, and now when you are up you can take up your life again and perhaps some of the bothers [?] will have gone—at any rate you will be strong and more likely to disentangle things.

He goes on to discuss very frankly his own entanglements and ambivalent feelings about his friend, then returns to Gertrude:

Your picture has been invited to spend the summer in the Worcester Art Museum but I think that it has travelled about enough. It has also been invited to be photographed and put on sale—which I think is very impertinent. I of course refused. . . .

But probably at this moment nothing is further from her mind than Howard's portrait. It might almost be that of another woman, so miserable does Gertrude feel and so miserable does she think she looks.

Her youngest brother Regi is in the papers frequently again. Compared with him, Gertrude's other brothers, as well as Harry and his brother Payne, are conservative. Regi is the personification of a charming playboy and as such the focus of the press's attention. Even as an undergraduate at Yale, he had established himself as a gambler, a drinker, a poloplayer, a horse racer, and a ladies' man—not necessarily in that order. Now, precociously experienced and perhaps prematurely dissipated at twenty-three, he is about to marry Cathleen Gebhard Neilson who, like Alfred's wife, comes from one of the "new" wealthy Catholic families. In Newport, a few days before the wedding, he is out driving on Bellevue Avenue when three reporters, one with a camera, approach him. Before the picture can be taken Regi whips the photographer across the shoulders and spoils the exposure. With the crack of the whip we can almost hear the echo of his grandfather's "The [or My] public be damned!" However, no complaint is lodged against Regi. As the *Times* says, "He has been hounded by camera men lately and few who know of the unpleasant event today blame him."

The wedding itself is substantially a repetition of others. On April 13, the night before, Mrs. Vanderbilt gives a lavish dinner at The Breakers. The next day Mrs. Neilson has the wedding breakfast for two hundred guests at Arleigh, the Roth-Platt villa on Bellevue Avenue, rented for the occasion. Once again Gladys—now seventeen—is maid of honor. Once again Cornelius—aboard the recently purchased 233-foot yacht *North Star* and recovering from his illness—is absent. Once again wedding gifts receive great attention, including a diamond and emerald pin from Gertrude and Harry. But there's this difference: Harry is at the wedding. Gertrude is in no state, either physically or emotionally, to go. She will read about it —in the newspapers and in long you-were-missed letters from Gladys ("The presents were bully . . .") and from her mother.

Harry has hardly returned to New York when he is in the papers too— arrested for speeding in his automobile (eighteen miles per hour!) on Central Park West. He submits gracefully, complimenting Bicycle Policeman Kerrigan for doing his duty. At the West 68th Street Station he is asked his occupation and replies, "I don't know what name to give that."* In May the charge is dropped.

A portrait which no longer looks like her . . . a wedding which she cannot attend . . . Harry's arrest . . . What do these things mean to Gertrude? Is she supposed to be amused? And is yet another racing season supposed to amuse her too? And another summer in Newport? No, no, no. She has three children. She has a husband who she believes doesn't love her. She has played at flirtation. She has fantasized a trial separation. She feels committed to art but doesn't now have the energy or peace of mind to work much at it. Once again she begs to travel. Maybe that will save the marriage—and the children. The lessons of *Travels in Foreign Countries and in the Mind* are temporarily forgotten. Harry assembles a group. This time they will take along the two elder children, leaving Barbara behind with Mama. And they will visit Harry's father's Yorkshire Moor. And they will see Gertrude's uncle Willie and his daughter Consuelo. And Gertrude will do a lot of shopping—the children need clothes, she herself needs clothes. And Harry will have a chance to drive to his heart's content, as fast as he likes. It all sounds wonderful.

On August 14 the four of them and servants sail on the *Cedric* with two bachelors—Rollie Cottenet, again, and Yale Dolan—and one other couple, Nellie and Herman Duryea, co-owner of Harry's yacht and of several of his best race horses. Gertrude begins a new journal which is, at the outset, seldom more than a joyless itinerary. This is supplemented by the insertion of a single sheet of stationery, engraved "Holwick, Middleton In Teesdale, Darlington" (the "Yorkshire Moor") and headed "Tuesday Aug.":

> Our tenth day here and such weather! But I can see the charm of the life and I have enjoyed it all in spite of rain, cold, fog, wind, and the fact that I do not shoot. . . . The long day in the open air, the charm of the moor country, the long walks over pink heather, even the delicious hot lunches under a little tent, are full of enjoyment and possess an attraction very individual and lasting. Crouched in the corner of a butt, the rain pelting on my old aquascutum, dodging

* In later years Harry finds a name for it: "Capitalist," which he uses to answer various questionnaires and forms from alumni organizations, reference book publishers, etc.

Harry's gun—it does not sound pleasant but there is the excitement of the incoming birds, the lively view, and a certain something wholly charming which cannot be appreciated until it has been experienced.

This scrap from Holwick indicates how much Gertrude is still willing to put up with in order to be near Harry, to share experience with him, and perhaps ultimately to work out a complete reconciliation. The itinerary style is resumed in London and even in Paris, where Gertrude and Rollie precede the rest of the party. There she has dinner with Uncle Willie and Consuelo, and the fact is recorded, no more than that, no indication that she and Consuelo speak one word to each other, though they might have said a great deal about their respective marriages. Not until Aix-les-Bains is there a momentarily unqualified note of joy:

> At last! The land where one moves and breathes and has one's being. What a country . . . with its great and beautiful scenery, its charm, its polite and cheerful people. To come abroad has been the hope of my existence since I was here last and when it materialated [sic] my spirits rose 100% and all the world was "couleur de rose."

But within a few pages the joyous note dies:

> Harry was in an abominable frame of mind and jumped on everyone and generally was looking out for trouble. Of course when his pleasure in the trip was to have been automobiling it was hard luck to have that knocked in the head, still he might not have tried to spoil our fun. He did his best. Not for one second did he leave me alone. Finally I got horrible nerves. Even Hermie who usually agrees with everything he says and thinks everything he does right, left him and got so annoyed that he told me if he had not gone to bed they would have had a real scrap.
>
> After a great deal of talk Harry decided to take the train to Turin and let the rest of us go by auto over the Mt. Cenis. We all offered to go with him or to let him go in the machine but he would not. It was not gay to get up at six and go alone in the train, still I insist he need not have treated me as if I was responsible for the auto breaking. Much to his joy it rained the next day, but he went off and left us. We started 9:45, the roads very slippery and the rain pelting. Still it was a relief to get off and not to hear any complaints.

They go from Turin to Milan and then to Brescia and Bergamo, where Gertrude writes only: "Harry still unbearable."

By late fall Gertrude is thinking more positively. She writes Gladys: ". . . I am much excited over a studio which I have just taken in 40th St. [overlooking Bryant Park]. It used to be a stable but has been used as a studio for some time. I am going to fix it up a little and expect to get a great deal of satisfaction out of it." Soon she is sculpting on a larger scale again, has James Earle Fraser and another sculptor named Moretti in to criticize her work, and has preliminary discussions with the architect William Adams Delano leading to her first commission: five bas-relief panels for the new Lenox home being planned for her cousins Lila and William Field. As the year ends, the earnest resumption of work excites her far more than the ball for 600 which William C. Whitney gives in honor of Katherine Barney, yet another niece about to make her debut, though one who will become close to Gertrude and Harry in later years.

≈ *1904*

Friday, January 29, Gertrude's work—and, to an even greater extent, Harry's—is painfully interrupted. The previous night William C. Whitney, attending *Parsifal* at the Metropolitan, feels sick and leaves his box to rest in the Directors' Room. By Friday morning he knows he is sicker than he realized. Over the years he has had several "appendicitis attacks" and has refused an operation, but the present attack is acute. Dr. James recommends that Dr. Bull operate, which he does on Saturday. Gertrude, Harry, and Dorothy are in constant attendance. At first, despite serious inflammation, the operation seems to be a success. William has a strong constitution. Against his doctors' orders he talks for several hours on Sunday and Monday with his children. "Don't get angry, Nurse," he says, "I love my son and daughter. It does me good to chat with them." However, by late Monday peritonitis has developed and by Tuesday it is clear that a second operation must be performed. By now in addition to Gertrude, Harry, and Dorothy, William's sisters Susan Dimock and Lilly Barney are standing by and their brother Henry is on his way from Boston.

William is placed under ether, the second operation begins, and after half an hour his anxious family is told that he is dead. Though all of them have been aware of the seriousness of his condition, the shock is still terrible. No man of sixty-two had seemed more vital, more likely to fight off appendicitis and to go on living until a very old age. Of all the immediate family Harry is the most affected. William has been his closest friend, his most constant companion, his greatest teacher. The identification is so profound that he himself feels dead; for three days he cannot leave his room.

Meanwhile, the news travels to geographically more distant members of

William's family—to his other children, Payne in Thomasville, Georgia, and Pauline in Rome; to his stepdaughter Adelaide Randolph in Baltimore; to his aged mother Laurinda Collins Whitney, still in the old family house in Brookline, Massachusetts; to his former brother-in-law Oliver Payne in Cleveland. Of these, all except his mother, whose health is too feeble for travel, and Oliver Payne, who cannot forgive him even in death for remarrying, leave immediately for New York where all but Pauline will arrive in time for the funeral.

On Wednesday, when the first obituaries appear—on the front pages of newspapers not only in New York but throughout the world—crowds gather outside the Whitney mansion. Fifth Avenue and 68th Street are clogged with carriages and automobiles. Mourners representative of William's many activities—in law, politics, business, sports—come to pay their respects. Hundreds of telegrams arrive from both sides of the Atlantic. The state legislature adjourns. The state Supreme Court expresses its regrets and enters them into the Court's minutes. The Secretary of the Navy orders the flags on all ships, yards, and stations at half mast. Grover Cleveland, who will be a pallbearer at the funeral, says how "greatly shocked" he is. "Mr. Whitney had more calm, forceful efficiency than any man I ever knew. In work that interested him he actually seemed to court difficulties and to find pleasure and exhilaration in overcoming them. . . . I recall with more tender sentiment Mr. Whitney's devotion to his friends, his extreme consideration for all with whom he came into contact, his thoughtfulness for the ease and comfort of others and his ready impulse to help those who needed help."

Finally, on February 6, a cold windy Saturday, the cortege, preceded by six mounted policemen, leaves 68th Street and proceeds down Fifth Avenue to the Grace Protestant Episcopal Church at Eleventh Street. The pallbearers, besides Grover Cleveland, are Thomas F. Ryan, Elihu Root, Thomas Dolan, Grant B. Schley, P. A. B. Widener, H. McKown Twombly, Colonel William Jay, G. G. Haven, and Herbert H. Vreeland (representing J. P. Morgan, who cannot return in time from Montreal). The mourners are headed by Gertrude and Harry, Helen and Payne, Dorothy, and the Randolphs. The only empty pew in the church is William's own. There his children have placed a wreath of lilies "For Father." Bishop Doane of Albany recites a simple service after which William is taken by train to the "rural" Woodlawn Cemetery in the Bronx where he is buried next to his first wife Flora, dead now for more than ten years, and their daughter Olive, dead for over twenty.

We can only guess at the agonizing memories that go through Harry's mind during this past week, culminating in the cold burial at Woodlawn, and during the weeks to come culminating in the settlement of his father's estate. Every day the mail brings more letters of condolence, of which he saves more than a hundred addressed to him personally. These private communications, like the public expressions of grief, go typically beyond polite forms. Harry's friends and relatives and business associates seem all to have really loved William and to understand Harry's love for him. At random we read notes from Frank Polk, Craig Wadsworth, Phil Lydig, John Hay, August Belmont, Daniel Guggenheim, Chauncey Depew. . . . In every one there is a recognition of this *particular* father-son relationship, of what each meant to the other.

Week after week articles appear reviewing William C. Whitney's career, praising it, except, in some cases, for his last ten years when he had not fulfilled his promise; when, as even his old friend William G. Sumner says, he had "given up . . . his life to the pursuits which then occupied him exclusively"—the pursuits, principally "his horses or his houses" (to quote Henry Adams), which now almost exclusively occupy Harry, who must think at times that he is the continuation of his father's career rather than the beginning of his own.

In contrast, Gertrude is thinking about her new career. Before this difficult period and now during it, when she must spend much of her time encouraging and supporting Harry, she has been considering enrollment at the Art Students League. Founded the year of Gertrude's birth and by now the largest American art school, it is located just two blocks west of Gertrude's New York home, in a French Renaissance-style building between Broadway and Seventh Avenue on 57th Street, and offers the nearest thing to European academic training available in the United States. A month after Mr. Whitney's death Gertrude signs the attendance book, "Mrs. H. P. Whitney, 2 West 57," at about the same time as two other women of her generation who will, like Gertrude, distinguish themselves in commissioned sculpture—Anna Vaughn Hyatt (later Huntington) and Malvina Cornell Hoffman, both also from wealthy backgrounds, though not as wealthy as hers. Beyond registration, the League records are vague. It does not seem as if any of the three women spend more than a few months there, where Gertrude studies modeling with James Earle Fraser and the other two carving with Gutzon Borglum and where all three determine that they will soon need additional private instruction at ateliers in Europe.

≈

Though an appraisal of William C. Whitney's estate is not filed until late July, it is substantially settled by early June and amounts to about $23,000,000, mostly in Standard Oil, Consolidated Tobacco, and Guggenheim Exploration Company stock, and many parcels of real estate in New York and elsewhere. Half of the estate is left to Harry, the sole executor and the guardian of Dorothy, who is to receive at least $50,000 a year for her education and maintenance and three tenths of the estate in trust. In addition, there is an unusual provision giving an annuity of $10,000 to

Miss Beatrice Bend, as long as she remains unmarried and continues to chaperone Dorothy, who "has always shown a striking American individuality and penchant for doing her own thinking in her own way." Except for bequests of $250,000 each to William's stepchildren Adelaide and Bertie Randolph, the remainder of the estate—i.e., two tenths—is to be divided between Pauline and Payne, whom their father did not have the heart to leave out of his will, though hurt by them and though knowing they would be well cared for by Oliver Payne. On June 5 the *Times* describes Harry as "a new figure . . . in the financial world," controlling some $25,000,000 as trustee of the Whitney estate plus $10,000,000 of his wife's. He is "bronzed by his daily motor trips . . . of medium height and with a lithe sturdiness and healthful tan, acquired from living much in the open air." It is assumed he will continue the maintenance of the Whitney stables, but "according to a former business associate of the late William C. Whitney . . . the son has an abiding aversion to speculation, and never will be a commanding figure in the pit or on the floor of the Exchange, but will follow more in the footsteps of the Vanderbilts in husbanding their investments."

This would have gotten under Harry's skin, though he may have been amused by its appearance within the context of continuing newspaper stories about Regi's gambling. In March, District Attorney Jerome had commented: "If I could have put young Reginald Vanderbilt on the stand, there is no doubt that I could have convicted Canfield [who] I believe . . . would come into court and plead guilty rather than have a public disclosure made of all that occurred in his house on the night when a young man lost over $400,000." In June, Regi is still eluding the district attorney's process servers.

Through these months Harry is understandably difficult to live with, continuing to be despondent and in need of Gertrude's comfort. She writes in her journal that "new horrors began. The fights, the various wire pullings. The awful terrible desperate feeling of hopelessness that came over me. The force of circumstance!" For a time she feels that she is losing her identity, being sucked into Harry's, *and into Harry's father's*. Not only are they now living in *his* house in Westbury, with *his* daughter (when she is not traveling) as well as their own children, but there is talk of moving from *his* former house on 57th to the one on 68th, and there is constant talk about *his* horses, which Harry rents during the mourning period to Hermie Duryea. As if all this were not enough, Howard Cushing has recently married Ethel Cochrane, making the previously intimate relationship between him and Gertrude more difficult; Gertrude has just received word that her close friend Lena Morton has died (June 10) in Paris; and Dorothy is ill and must be cared for. It is a wonder that Gertrude can resume work on the panels for the Field house, but not that, on

June 27, she feels the need to start a new journal—one in which the entries will be longer and more confessional than those kept during her last trip.

Gertrude introduces a new theme: seeking situations in which her "advantages count . . . position . . . money . . . special gifts [i.e., talents]." Now, in addition to expressing herself in writing and in sculpture, she will, she says, express herself in patronage. In the first nineteen pages of the new journal this is the obsessive theme and after that—in this journal, in subsequent journals, and throughout her life—patronage will become for her a co-equal means of expressing creative energy. She tells herself:

> Take Harry into your confidence. There is no one who really will be more pleased to see what you want to do than he will. Because he is uninterested in your present life and aims does not mean that he will be in these. He has no real sympathy for your modeling. He may be right not to have—it is only developing a little talent and leaving your real power, which is your money and position, out of account. Why do what is fitting for Jane Smith when you are not Jane Smith? However, start your influence over Harry by getting him on your side and anxious and willing to help you. This road through life is the only one for you. Do not sink into a nonentity when the path for other things is open to you. And it is open. Go to your friends, to people who know you well and make them tell you what your good points are (everyone has some) so that you may make something of them. Why should you waste these talents anymore than your money and position which are also talents. Go and find out what they are. But first of all get Harry on your side. Talk to him about your aims, let it bring you closer together, let it fill the gaps in your life—it will lead you to happiness. The life you are leading now can never do that, never, never. Do not let this burst of enthusiasm pass. Fix it so that on it you may be carried on to do the actual work. Go to Adele, to Rollie, to Jimmie, to Howard, to Bunny [Meredith Hare], say to them, tell me I can do something. . . .

What she may be able to do—these ideas are still unformed—is help American art and at the same time her own career. She has vague thoughts about a school; a gallery; a museum; commissions for herself and others—public commissions, not dependent on family. She writes a letter to Bunny—"for he [as chairman of Greenwich House] surely will be the most useful of all"—and makes lists of other friends and of relatives to write or speak to. Each name is numbered, with later correspondingly numbered comments on "how they can be used for . . . advantage. . . . Mr. [Lloyd] Warren [a former suitor and now an architect] said you should use people, it is not wrong":

1. Harry: obvious.
2. Adele: to get a fairly good opinion of what you can do and of how people might be approached. Also help at approaching. . . .
3. J. [Burden]: business knowledge
4. Dorothy: Young now but that is the time to influence so that financially she would be interested
5. Gladys: Same as 4, also her sympathy and understanding would be of value.
6. Payne: good sound judgment. In the future financially, and a good partisan to have, could come in useful at times owing to influence over Harry.
7. Helen [Hay Whitney]: Name might help, also could boost along faint heart.
8. Helen B[arney]: Influences her father who is a patron of art.
9. Rollie: Sympathy . . .
10. Jimmie: a person to talk to who will always take an interest in all I do, then he has common sense and will do anything for me.
11. Howard: inspiring person, provided you are working on his lines. A great help, knows artistic people too and would work for me.
12. Bunny: could prod me and encourage me. Lots of common sense too and enough belief in my power to keep me going.
13. Lloyd: also would prod me, would be valuable as he knows people, has position, certain amount of money and energy, very useful.
14. Mabel [Gerry]: not much use except name.
15. Louise [Bristow]: sympathetic help.
16. Alfred: financial, name.
17. Elsie [again, the nickname of Alfred's wife Ellen]: might be able to work with her.
18. Regi: financial, name.
19. Cathleen [Regi's wife]: name.

Gertrude leaves seven more spaces, writes Jim Barnes's name and present address, then crosses them out, and proceeds to develop her general ideas:

To see artists and find out [their] wants would be a good start. . . . To found a Beaux Arts—with painting and modeling in connection. Tuition low. Scholarships. Exhibition rooms in connection. How much demand is there for Architecture in N.Y.? Lloyd could tell you. S[tanford] White. [Charles] McKim. Painting? J[ohn] Alexander [a fashionable portrait painter]. Modeling? [Daniel Chester] French. Raise money for building. $1,000,000 at 7% interest [she crosses out 7 and changes it to 5]. $50,000 for me to pay. Work government to give some. Alfred, Regi, Mrs. R. Goelet, Mr. Barney, Uncle Willie. Best teachers such as [she leaves a large space]. Lectures from prominent artists such as [again, a large space].

The space will stretch out into years as she struggles to balance the hardheaded manipulation of friends, relatives, and governmental agencies against the more tender demands of her commitment to art. The next day she dines with Rollie, who suggests that foreign instruction is necessary. "Get a good man (the best) to come over and run the school and paint his own pictures here. Those pictures would probably be bought by the people here, so that art in this country would receive that much impetus and gradually the atmosphere of N.Y. would be improved from the student point of view." Two days later she receives a reply to her letter to Meredith Hare: "a very nice answer . . . offering to see me *any* time, will arrange especially." Gertrude is "decidedly encouraged," she already has two friends in her camp, but she has "had no opportunity to talk to Harry on the subject, so that his attitude remains a closed book. . . . It strikes me that Helen Hastings [wife of the partner in the architectural firm of Carrère and Hastings, which had placed Gertrude's *Aspiration* in the Buffalo Exposition] knows artists well [and] that she will be of use. I shall ask her to lunch. [Finley] Peter Dunne [the humorous writer "Mr. Dooley," who had been a close friend and political ally of William C. Whitney] would have good ideas." The names—first those from her childhood, later those from the years of marriage (eight now!)—continue to come, the empty space to be filled, the dreams to multiply:

Then I think that the artists who influence things in this country should be gotten on my side. That might be hard. What would their idea be of having foreign instruction, would they not think it an imposition of their rights? But after all, on the ground that everyone who is any good in this country has studied abroad, and that we cannot send all these students abroad, and that the atmosphere which is so inspiring to art and which they must admit does not exist here, could in that way be brought over—these points might be used to advantage.

As encouraged as Gertrude has been, within a few more days she is blue and impatient:

My heart aches and aches and I feel today my inability to do the smallest things, let alone the big ones. In my own sphere, or in other words family, what can I do? Has Harry always refused to make any effort for me? I think so and yet I am not sure. The same feeling that used to make me take a book when I went out for a long time alone with him assails me now. I feel at times that I must set off a bomb under him or die. Bomb. I must try today to be outrageous. He will not go half way with me and I starve. The kids help, but—oh well, of course they do not really satisfy at all.

Now she writes the previously quoted passage about the deaths of Esther and Lena, as well as the loss by marriage of Howard and by awkwardness of Jimmie—those to whom she had once "talked out." She continues:

. . . I cry from sheer loneness, for Harry is bored by so much that comes my way, and who else is there? I feel as if my life was over and that the only thing I had now was an ambition—for I must have that. Of course there are the kids and I love them, but kids are kids and they do not fill the empty place.

Oh this dreadful ache! Is there no help for me. Try, little girl, try once more to be able to tell Harry, if not everything, at least most things. He does not want me to. He cares, you know he cares. Yes, I really think he does, but oh the difference. The aches. Courage, child, to take up again your life. I am so desperately tired. He is tired too, try to help him. I have, I have, I have done all the things that I thought would be good for him. I have madly tried to get closer to him, but I can't, I can't. I believe he holds me off on purpose.

Child, rest, you are weary, remember that he cares. Yes, perhaps (only perhaps?) still not as I want him to. My heart is bleeding for love and sympathy. Will I be able to go on forever without it? Child, rest, you are weary. Yes, I am weary and the night is dark, someday, perhaps, the light will come. I have let the best in me die too hard. I should have killed it off at once. I told Rollie that marriage was a game and I was right. I must not begin at this late hour to take it as anything else. It is a game and in games we keep on the alert and each move means something and if we make a misplay why we work to cover it up, and we laugh, but if we win we are pleased, but if we lose why then we are sorry but we do not cry. A game, yes a game. But I know all the time that to me it is no game. I am in deadly earnest. I love deeply. I cannot help myself. I passionately want a fitting return. With it I could be eternally happy, for love is my life. There is nothing else that really counts with me, that is the trouble. My ambition is forced, even my interest in close things, it is love from the beginning to the end—I choke it, I stifle it, but it comes out like a river that is dammed. The ache is there always now. If I could be satisfied once that he cared, that he really cared. Well, no matter, it is the middle of the day. The afternoon will be less hot and towards evening a calm will come. But of course it is not the calm I want, I hate it, it is the sun I want and a great deal of it, but it must shine on me.

After Fourth of July fireworks and a Punch and Judy show for the children—only a week since Gertrude has started writing about her dream of a "Beaux Arts"—she leaves Westbury for Newport, where Harry arrives for the weekend. They take the children on a picnic and have a splendid time. "Life did not seem all bitterness, indeed it seemed as if Harry cared for me and as if the kids were more attractive, sweet and good and beautiful than anyone else's kids, and I was happy." But still she does not mention her ambition to Harry, she "must wait for the psychological moment."

Now he leaves for Westbury, she follows with the children after a day but is so "dead beat" that she develops an earache and a headache. ". . . I will be lucky if I don't have a big breakdown. . . . My nerves are very bad indeed. . . . If only I could go off somewhere, somewhere where I could work and be alone for a little while, but my duty is right here and I must stick it out. And Lena, Lena, Lena I shall never see her again." Gertrude's mood continues to darken, she feels the need to "let off steam" (about ten years now since her book whose title incorporated that phrase):

My beloved Flora—she too is born to this heritage of agony. Her warm heart, her impulsiveness, and my little one, my poor little one who went through such torment with me before she was born. Sometimes I wish they had never existed, what right had I to bring them into a world where they with their natures cannot be happy. Yet I suppose if I could bring myself to the point where I could take them out and drown them the world would say I was mad. Mad! Why I would be acting with the greatest common sense.

I suppose too the world says of me I have everything to make me happy. What have I gained for what I have deliberately given away! I don't know, I think I have lost all things and gained nothing. I think that in the end I will do some perfectly mad thing and that then I will have given myself away and that the world will then know as I know myself that I am mad. I wonder if Harry suspects it, perhaps at times he thinks there is something queer with me.

With effort Gertrude goes to lunch at Mrs. Hastings', then returns to Newport with the children, "leaving Harry to wrestle with the temptation of town without a wife. His joy at being left was quite apparent, so thinly veiled that one could not call it veiled at all. Ten minutes after I arrived I could have killed myself, but the mists gradually dissipated to descend again in the evening."

Through July Gertrude keeps purposefully busy. She has time for everything except to tell Harry, during his weekend visits, about her project, her dream. She works in her studio. She enters into a more formal teaching arrangement with James Earle Fraser and hires a model. She has lunch sometimes with Adele. She visits Howard's studio to see his work (". . . improved wonderfully. I wonder if it is matrimony?"). She writes bits of fiction and another letter to Bunny Hare. She reads and makes notes on several books—a life of DaVinci, a study of French Impressionism, a survey of religions by Harold Fielding-Hall called *The Hearts of Men*. With this title in mind, she asks: "What is in a woman's heart? Oh what indeed! If I could transfer to paper my heart as it is, not as I think other people think it is or as I think it ought to be, there would be a book that would be a real book and a great book! For I suppose I am an average woman and it would be interesting as history if nothing else."

In mid-July, as Gertrude still waits for the psychological moment: "Harry seemed *really* glad to see me last night and said nice things about having missed me." And at the end of the month, when Harry spends a full week in Newport: "He was particularly nice. . . . We had one very agreeable evening when he said a lot of things which made me happy." But still the month slips by without Gertrude telling him about her project. As she tries to be cheerful on weekends we suppose too that she tells him less than her journal about her realization "that Lena was not properly taken care of, that it was a case of negligence, and that she might have been saved." And we are very sure that she does not share with Harry her response to a sad letter from Jimmie: ". . . He too is feeling his age [thirty-seven, eight years older than Gertrude] and the weight of his troubles. Well, at least he cares for me less than he did, that must be less of a trouble, but if it had not been for my insatiable love of admiration that might never have happened. Poor Jimmie, poor Jimmie it must be dreadful to care for a person so long—a married woman who can never, never look at you. He does care less I am thankful to say but is still I think in the state where he might easily care more again. I had no business to go on letting him see me. How the world has changed, how really old I am. I could no longer do things thoughtlessly, forgetful of all save the moment. And when the time comes, why then one realizes those things and pauses to think—when it is too late."

Gertrude wonders about her "power over men. . . . I fear that it is the lowest kind of power. It is not brain for of that I have very little, it is not beauty for of that I have none, only a pleasing appearance. . . . Howard said once I could have any man I wanted care for me. . . . But that was no doubt because Howard thought me . . . attractive. Mabel [Gerry] said, 'I never saw a man yet that you could not make crazy about you if you wanted to.' That is a *façon de parler*." And Gertrude concludes that she is "effective looking," no more than that, and that if she is going to impress people she must stop thinking and talking about herself and "begin to think of subjects far removed." Once again she makes a list: "Buddhism as compared to Christianity. The formation of rocks. The relation of the colors of the spectrum to Impressionism. Contentment as related to happiness. Roosevelt and the Negro."

On July 29 there will be opportunity to test these topics. After a seventh birthday party for Flora in the afternoon, Gertrude and Harry attend a large dinner party given by Elsie and Alfred at their home in Newport, followed by a dance for 120 guests at Cathleen's and Regi's Sandy Point Farm in nearby Portsmouth. And Gertrude is already thinking two weeks ahead to their departure for Europe when there will be still more opportunity with "a lot of people and different kinds of people." Gertrude makes another list—of clothes to take abroad. Since she is in mourning for William C. Whitney, there is no color—everything is black or white.

This trip Gertrude and Harry leave their children behind but take along Harry's sister Dorothy and her close friend May Tuckerman, along with Beatrice Bend and her mother (to chaperone the young ladies, as provided in William C. Whitney's will), the Burdens, Rollie,. and Lloyd Warren. In addition, aboard ship, to fill out a table of fourteen, there are two more couples, unidentified Smiths, and the Thompsons, from whom Harry leases Brookdale Farm, near Red Bank, New Jersey. Once again there is someone for everybody. During the entire trip, lasting about a month and a half, Gertrude makes only two short entries in her journal. The first is written at sea on August 14, two days after their departure:

". . . I frightened even myself just before sailing. . . . I am convinced [it was] mental rather than physical. I fell flat on the floor in my stateroom—a sort of faint I suppose and yet not an ordinary one at all. It is just as well I got away. Still I started with many misgivings which no doubt will soon return. Momentarily I feel more at rest, but I know how those things do come back.

"And my resolutions etc. Where have they gone? What have I accomplished? Alas. Make out now something to accomplish in Paris. Modern Sculpture, see all you can of it and secure all the photos of it possible."

Some two weeks later Gertrude writes in Paris: "Everything has gone quite smoothly and the last few days have been a great rest to me. Harry has been up at Holwick, the girls have been in London and I have been here, incidentally with Rollie. Most of the party come over on Thursday and I am not looking forward to it as much as I should. Paris is such a dangerous place. Fatally so for lots of reasons. Rollie took me to dine at Henri's tonight and we went to the Marigny [theater] afterwards. I did not enjoy it very much. Lloyd and Bertie [Hunt, Esther's brother and, like Lloyd, an architect] turned up and were rather surprised to see us."

Though these passages are brief, the first two emphasize patterns in Gertrude's life which are becoming increasingly clear: first, psychosomatic illnesses, physical manifestations of her depression which had previously been expressed more often through words rather than through her body; and second, a growing matter-of-factness in her acceptance of separation from Harry.

More details of this trip are available in a journal Dorothy keeps—one reminiscent of Gertrude's own earlier itinerary-oriented journals, and influenced, it would seem, by Gertrude's interest in art. September 2, the day after Harry and Dorothy and the rest of the party arrive at the Hotel Bristol in Paris, Harry and Gertrude organize an excursion to Versailles. A few days later they take Dorothy and her friend May to lunch at Voisin, after which the girls go with Gertrude to Callot's "where she is ordering all her winter clothes. The models there are lovely." And the next day the group, joined now by Mrs. Vanderbilt and Gladys, go to Chartres in three cars—a C.G.V., a Morse, and a Mercedes (Harry's favorite, in which he takes Dorothy, May, and Gladys). For over two weeks the party will be in and out of cars as Harry—seemingly in high spirits despite the usual automobile breakdowns—leads them through the Loire and then to Aix-les-Bains and other parts of the Savoie, and on to Geneva, Dijon, and back to Paris. By then the party has been reduced. Rollie has gone to Venice, Gladys and Mrs. Vanderbilt to Lucerne. At the Bristol, Dorothy writes, "our feelings were divided between the joy of being here again and the sadness at the thought of the long-talked-of automobile trip being over."

On September 21, Gertrude and Harry depart for the States, leaving Dorothy and May with Beatrice and Mrs. Bend. Eight days later Gertrude is in Westbury writing in her journal after "a jump," as she puts it, of more than a month. Her mind, she says "is naturally stagnant but also many years of allowing it to remain so have made it worse. Now it is entirely out of training and what it needs is daily exercise. An hour or so's serious reading on a useful if not very interesting (to you) subject." Then a surprise: "If Harry decides to run for Congress, work for all you are worth to understand and be well posted. Here is a plan. Get someone in N.Y. well up on city politics to give you a letter or two a week, to direct your reading, etc. Then work at it, keep at it, read only on that subject for a while, force people to talk to you on it. Show Harry at least that your interest is a real one." In a letter to Dorothy, written a week later, Gertrude says, "I got much excited about Harry's running for Congress. They [the Democrats who, since William Whitney, value the family name as standing for incorruptibility] wanted him to run in the 13th District which is Republican and which he thinks he could not possibly win in. He seriously considered it. Mr. [Elihu] Root was away but since he has come back he says [Harry] did right to refuse it. He thinks that Harry is right to begin a political career in Albany." On the front page of this same letter is a charming drawing of a child seated at the piano. Gertrude explains: "I found that Flora and Sonny had learnt to play the piano during my absence. Flora says, 'We need not take any more lessons now because we know how to play,' but Sonny answered her, 'Yes, we know how to play, but we must take lessons so as not to forget.' So you see their point[s] of view! I give them each a ten minute lesson a day and it is so good for my character, I feel sure. . . . They also learnt numerous songs during my absence which they sang (?) for me on my return. . . . The baby is the duckiest thing you ever saw."

Gertrude's frequent letters to Dorothy during this period are all cheerful and amusing in text and in illustration. Her journal remains more serious: "I made up my mind on the steamer to do 6 things this winter. 1—the children, to begin to interest their minds. 2—to get myself up on topics of the day. 3—to work at my Art Charity. 4—to work in some way for Mrs. S [Mary Kingsbury Simkhovitch, a prominent social economist, philanthropist, and patron of the arts]. 5—my modeling. 6—[following the dash, there is only a mysterious space]. Now the first move of all for any such winter is health. So as you are not quite well, first and foremost make an appointment to see Dr. James."

⇜

For both Gertrude and Harry the year ends in bursts of energy, expressed in very different kinds of activity. Harry is busy first with the acquisition of his father's stud. The sale is held at Madison Square Garden before a crowd of 10,000 on the nights of October 11 and 12, at which ninety-one head are sold for $463,650. The *Thoroughbred Record* describes the beginning of the auction:

> It was exactly 8:25 o'clock when Mr. William Easton, after making a few appropriate remarks introductory to the sale, ordered Hamburg to be brought into the sawdust ring at the Fourth Avenue end of the Garden. He looked in robust health, a magnificent specimen of horseflesh.
> "What will you give me, gentlemen?"
> There was a deathlike stillness for a moment, and the crowd looked in the direction of Harry Payne Whitney, who sat beside his racing partner, Herman B. Duryea. Mr. Whitney said, "$50,000."
> "$60,000," cried Milton Young.
> "$70,000," said Whitney.
> This was the last bid.

Harry buys one other stallion, Sandringham; the three highest-priced brood mares ($22,000, $16,000, and $15,000); and thirteen other mares, spending a total of $183,900 for eighteen head. Three days after the breeding stock sale, Harry is at Morris Park, bidding on fifteen race horses and nine yearlings, of which he buys four. Then he negotiates an extension of his father's lease on Brookdale Farm. There, particularly now, he will spend a lot of time, turning it into one of the most lavish thoroughbred farms in the country. Finally, at about this time we learn from Dorothy's journal, as reported by Cousin Jim Barney, "that Harry had fallen on his head out hunting and had consequently been rather queer for a day or two."

While Harry is busy with horses, Gertrude is still busy with lists, but now she is acting on them. She prepares:

The Winter's Campaign.

First—Work—but not more than 3 hours a day positively. [Among other pieces, she completes *Athlete*—a Rodinesque male nude (without a fig leaf), much more natural and expressive in its pose and modeling than *Aspiration* of three years earlier—which will be shown in the St. Louis Exposition.]

Second—Make and keep some men friends—3 intimate and 3 friendly. Perhaps Bunny and 2 others 1st class; Lloyd, Rollie, and J. Barnes 2nd class. Have the appearance of being rather gay. Have men lunch with you, drive with you, and go to concerts with you. Pick up a few more strays.

Third—Go to a great many concerts, lectures, exhibitions—to queer places of all kinds—generally keep yourself alive as far as interests go.

Fourth—Organize your charity and keep in touch with other charities.

Fifth—Cultivate a light touch in connection with Harry. Keep him amused and interested, also guessing a little.

As with the first "campaign," she is substantially successful in launching at least three of the other four. When Harry is away and even when he is home but not in the mood, she goes out independently, often to cultural events that don't interest him. Some of these allow her to meet new people or to re-establish contact with those whom she has known only slightly, such as the great Polish-American pianist Josef Hofmann, whom she met as a child prodigy when he played in her parents' home. Some, like Hofmann again, who is "very simple, very direct, like all great artists" mix easily with charity affairs. (For example, she pays him now to play at a benefit at the Waldorf for the Downtown Day Nursery.) But of all the campaigns perhaps the least certain is the one to keep Harry amused, interested, and guessing. In letters to Dorothy everything sounds happy. Gertrude and Harry are home listening to Caruso records on a player Dorothy has given them. They go to the Yale-Harvard football game. They go into New York to hear the returns of the election, which Roosevelt wins in a landslide, and then join the crowd walking up Broadway. They entertain Hofmann at Westbury. However, in Gertrude's journal, the happy moments, though more frequent than recently, are still mixed with many sad ones, and the affirmations mixed with many doubts.

I have become hard inside and that hardness is spreading so that now only a little softness covers it which is the inside—beware lest the outside also harden. That curse of manners which has come to hide all things is getting [to be] a menace to me.

It seems to me that things have become worse for me since I began to face them and to realize my position. Since I allowed myself the knowledge of my likes and dislikes. Now I have faced the fact that almost all the people I am thrown with I do not like and am not interested in. That most of the things I do are not congenial to me. For years I would not allow myself to think of this and then I got on—now I have come to a time when the foundations of my life seem to be giving way and all that I have built up is vanishing and to build again on the same old foundation seems impossible and the new foundations are so hard to obtain. This is what I see when I look right into my heart. I cannot succeed along the lines which I should succeed along in the position etc. I am placed in. I cannot be the sort of a person which my life demands me to be—so why not try and be my own self. That is something I have never tried to be. Say what you think for a change, be what you are for a change. Throw away the sham under which you have been masquerading and be what you want to be. Do you know what that is? Yes, to a certain extent, I don't know just what its development might be. You know then that it would lead away from Harry. I do. Yes, away in a certain way, but I am not sure that in the end you would not get nearer to him.

Now you are nothing, since you have not succeeded in being what he wanted you to be—he must see that. Would he not have more respect for you if you amounted to something even though it was not in a way which he admired? And then again he has his interests in life apart from you, why not have yours apart from him? But would not the following of such goals take you further in spirit from him and your home life every day? The immediate is what holds me now so that it is hard to see the ultimate. Now I need an outlet, an unbottling. I am stifled, I am suffocated—I have no outlet and through my own fault. I cannot speak. I have held my peace so long that to break it seems impossible and yet it tears at my heart, it convulses me. To talk—to talk—to talk until nothing remained. To empty out the overcrowded secret places of my brain. Now new matter accumulates and crowds, crowds until the pain of it is almost more than I can bear.

All the thoughts, the feelings, the agonies of past sorrows, going way back to my brother's marriage. Then my father's death, my own misunderstandings, Esther's death, my foolish flirtations, Harry's wanderings, Lena's death, all, all, all, still crowding my brain with their unutterable thoughts and added to each day by passing miseries.

As the year ends and as Gertrude approaches her thirtieth birthday, there are some consolations. The benefit for the Downtown Day Nursery has made $7,000, largely through her own efforts. She is spending Monday afternoons with Mary Morton (Lena's sister) at Greenwich House where they sponsor and instruct a sculpture class. And Gertrude's New York studio is being fitted more comfortably so that it will be "a place where I can be myself, see my friends, etc." She dreams now of writing a book under a *nom de plume* that will be "good enough to be published" and of making "a decent statue." But even these dreams, both of which will eventually come true, are presently centered on Harry:

". . . These things will elevate me in the eyes of H.P.W. That is my chief reason for wanting to do them—of course the other reasons are obvious. The charity I have made a good start with. It is more or less easy and the performance was enough of a succes for me to feel that even if I did nothing more big this winter I would have showed Harry that if I wanted to take hold of a thing I could."

As much as Gertrude cares for Gladys, there is not a word in the journal about her sister's coming-out party. The journal is now for other things. However, Harry writes to his sister about the event:

Dear Dorothy,

Gladys had her coming out dance last night & it seemed to bring out how you are all grown up. I went over [to Mrs. Vanderbilt's] before anyone came to see things. Gladys was perfectly self-possessed, as you wd. be & could not be rattled. She looked sort of nice & young, but as I told Gertrude (& I am not sure she thoroughly sympathized, though agreeing), we will make that look sick next year [i.e., at Dorothy's own coming out]. Sit up straight.

This is just a line to catch a boat & open communication.

I have missed you a great deal. Not having you & Beatrice in Papa's house has made Westbury pretty blue. That is why I have not written.

Harry

Christmas afternoon Harry visits his father's grave, as he will every Christmas, except for one year abroad, the rest of his life. There he stands before the severe slab of polished gray granite marking the family plot, first acquired for little Olive (January 22, 1878–June 5, 1883), used again ten years later for Harry's mother, then three years later for Pauline's first child, Flora Payne Paget (November 6, 1896–November 7, 1896!), and now finally for his father. The great granite plinth, about forty feet high, supports nothing—nothing but the stark fact of death.

≈ 1905

Gertrude is now, and will remain for several years, in a sort of marital purgatory somewhere between the hell of Harry's rejection and the heaven of his physical attraction. Here, her own art and her art patronage (among other "good works") compensate for dreams, lost and still being lost, of marital bliss. She has come to accept Harry's "wanderings" with the hope that deeper than these is his love for her and their children. And Harry himself accepts her "foolish flirtations," providing they are discreet and with men he considers socially acceptable. Allowing for the conventions of the time, she has a great deal of freedom to work and socialize as she wants in her private studios and in her homes. This is not the trial separation about which Gertrude has fantasied but rather a trial compartmentalization of interests.

Until summer—with interruptions for house parties in Westbury and Aiken and Newport—Gertrude maintains an energetic schedule, getting her own work done (a bust, a life-size figure, and three small figures, including *Pan* and *Boy with Parrot*, both in the expressive style of the previous year's *Athlete*), while at the same time entertaining many of Harry's friends, attending their sporting events, and entering into the spirit of such country play, organized by Harry, as ice hockey matches for the children, grass fights, and "sardines," an elaborate variation of hide-and-seek.

This is the first year in which Harry races horses under his own colors. His earnings are just over $170,000, a larger sum than his father ever won in a year. Harry is also playing more and even better polo than before and is one of only six players in the country rated at eight goals or better (three are rated at nine). He wins the men's singles championship at the Racquet and Tennis Club. And, finally, his family's social events, particularly the marriage of his cousin Helen Barney to Archibald Stevens Alexander, recently elected to the New Jersey Assembly—as well as those of Gertrude's family, mostly now parties for Gladys—are as frequent as ever.

As summer approaches, Gertrude begins to think about a trip:

. . . it would be a good thing for Harry too. Helen is away now [her father John Hay is ill and will die July 1] and if I went Harry and Payne could combine and have a wonderful time. . . . I am tired and Harry is too. . . . I get steadily worse. Yesterday an awful headache in the afternoon and chills and fever, so I had to send for the doctor. . . .

MONDAY, JUNE 12: Am quite well again, but have had to be very quiet all the week. I am going to town today in regard to an offer [to do a commission, possibly a pair of male and female caryatids for the Hotel Belmont, then being planned] I have had from Whitney Warren [Lloyd Warren's brother also an architect, and best known for his design of Grand Central Station]. I hope I am going to be able to accept it, but it all depends on details which I have not yet heard. . . . What I want to ask Whitney: Where figures are going? If I am to do two of them and if I am to do them under Lalière [presumably a sculptor or an architect in the office of Warren and Wetmore] or alone? How much time I will have to do them? How useful the sketches will be to me? Will it be practical to do them at Newport? I want to do them if I possibly can as it will be good practice for me and also it starts me in a practical work (decoration) and, puts me out of the class of amateur and this in itself will be a great thing for me.

TUESDAY, JUNE 20: I saw Whitney that Monday and he took me to see the models and Lalière, also took Lalière to see my work. I liked the sketches fairly well and on Wednesday let Mr. Warren know definitely that I would accept. Lalière is to go to Newport and the work will be done there.

In preparation for the commission she goes to New York again, this time to see Hendrik Andersen, who is there on a visit:

. . . I had a delightful time, spent all day wandering about at the [Metropolitan] museum, etc., lunched with Rollie at Sherry's. Andersen was very attractive and sympathetic. We talked about work and art, etc., etc. and I enjoyed it all. He has much but not all by any means. His work interests me but I do not like the last group as much as the bronze group which he did some five years ago. But I admire him because he is a man of one idea and that kind always accomplishes much. He did not say anything nice about my figure [which she is working on in New York] except that he liked the pose. In fact he said a great deal of it was "bum." He was right, it is awful. Each time I see it I hate it more. The pose *is* fine, but the execution, well it's beneath contempt.

In Westbury during the last week or so of June, Gertrude strengthens herself by taking walks of four to six miles a day. Then she makes a last trip to New York to finish her figure there, and to make final arrangements with Lalière about the commission as well as to discuss it with

James Earle Fraser, whose studio she visits. "His drawings are splendid, also some of his bas-reliefs." Before leaving for Newport she can write: "How much happier I am than a year ago. . . . It makes me ill just to look back and read those dreadful pages in which I had laid bare so much of my very soul." However, in Newport, though she doesn't permit herself to be unhappy, she exhausts herself again.

Worked all day and in the evenings on sketches. Harry was away those weeks [at various races, including the Brighton Handicap where, after his horse Artful wins, the *Herald* describes him as "the happiest man ever seen at a race course"] which gave me lots of time to work hard. All plans changed and we sail August 8th. . . . Had one of my bad fits Monday night [July 24] . . . and in consequence an awful head all day Tuesday.

[The following Sunday is another] horrid day, rain and no fun, no work, no nothing. Soon I will be off now—and all the horrid feeling of settled-downdom over. My depression tonight is awful and I had such a horrid time last night and I ought to have had a nice time. I get worse and worse as time goes on. I am almost impossible now. I can only feel real joy that H[arry] is off to Saratoga tonight, that I am not going, and that for a week again I need do nothing. Life is hateful. I almost think I am sick. I feel so nervous and overwrought. Some Resolutions or even my friends will speak to me no longer. *Never* talk about your modeling. Change the subject no matter how awkwardly you are obliged to do so. Cultivate a frivolous view of life. Always say what you don't mean. Never be serious. Never talk on any one subject more than 2 minutes. Never talk about automobiles, golf, your children, your summer plans, your travels. Never allow yourself to be led on to talk seriously about yourself.

Originally they plan to go abroad without the children. However, on the night of August 9, when Gertrude and Harry say good-by to Flora and Sonny, they decide suddenly that they can't bear to leave them behind—it will be hard enough leaving Barbara—so they stay up that night packing and all four board the *Baltic* the next day, bound for England. After two weeks there they go on to Paris to meet Dorothy, who has been abroad for a year and must now be outfitted for her coming out in New York in the fall. Harry waits for his sister at the station and takes her to the Bristol where Gertrude, Adele, and Bunny Hare welcome her. After a night's rest the outfitting begins in earnest, as described by Dorothy in her journal:

Gertrude and Mr. Hare walked around Leopold's with me where I had my hair washed. After lunch the real work began—Harry, Gertrude, B.B. [Beatrice Bend], and I all sallied forth together, first to Paquin, then Worth, Doucet next and lastly Callot. At the former place we ordered a long grey suit, at Worth 4 ball dresses, one dinner dress at Doucet, and Callot we return to on Monday morning. We dined with Mr. Lew Thompson at the Ritz.

Mr. Thompson

Gertrude	Adele
Mr. Preston	Harry
D.W.	
Mr. Hare	Beatrice

It was a very nice party and the dinner was delicious and the music delightful.

This entry of Dorothy's is typical and, once again, reminiscent of Gertrude's earlier journals. It is almost as if Dorothy is keeping her journal *for* Gertrude (and for us) since Gertrude no longer considers such details as seating arrangements interesting. Dorothy is still young enough to find everything interesting: the seating arrangement in the Bollée on an automobile trip to Fontainebleau, fittings, the second visit to Callot, fittings, visits to furriers, fittings, Massenet's opera *Manon*, fittings, side trips to cathedrals including Mont. St. Michel, fittings, Versailles, fittings. . . . Finally, on September 17, the fittings are completed and they leave Paris for London. There they are met by Pauline, who takes them to Claridge's where they stay for a few days before boarding the *Kaiser Wilhelm II* for New York.

For Gertrude this trip has seemingly been no more than a rest and "a change." From August 25 (two weeks after their departure) until October 7 (ten days after their return to Westbury) her journal, as such, is abandoned. Then, before abandoning it again (for almost six months this next time, except for "fictional" and essayistic sketches), she writes three times in less than two weeks, emphasizing how little has really changed:

OCTOBER 7: More plans being laid, more parties being schemed, more plots thickening, but alas how much doing? Dear me, the same old cry. At least there is Dorothy now as an excuse. . . . Everything centers round her and to make her happy is my one and only cry. But incidentally as she must be taken around I am looking for something for myself. That is to go out with. No one to play with is ghastly, and so I must find me a few playthings. I must make the most of my opportunities. This is the way I size it up. I am not at all a society person, or a social person. I am stupid in a crowd. I am dull and uninteresting. My good point is that I have a certain small amount of charm. This must be judiciously used. Alone with people I do best. So alone with them I must be. I must make them think I like them very much. That is my only power. I am supposed to be very indifferent, so if I wildly seem to care it will appear to be real. I must pick out the most likely people and work on them, after that more opportunities will come. But remember this is but one side—the real life is the struggle for an object—try again on the Art School. Bob Chanler [an artist] will be here, he will help. Lloyd [Warren] will help. Work on it. For heaven's sake do something. Time is passing, you are 30 years old! Oh God and what have I done in my life. Nothing, nothing, and most of it is over.

October 11, Gertrude enters what amounts to a short essay on herself as a "misfit . . . quite frankly square [in a world that is] quite certainly round," and concludes that "it is better to be a real thing in the wrong place than a bad imitation." The next week she writes at greater length about ways of dealing with the house parties Harry loves in that "round world," so that she can be herself. The solution, once again, is the addition of men in the arts and architecture who will interest her and be helpful to her career. One new name, Charles Dana Draper, a Harvard-educated stockbroker, four years younger than Gertrude, is not in the arts but close to them as the grandson of Charles A. Dana, founder of the New York *Sun*; brother of the well-known monologist Ruth Draper; and uncle of the later equally well known dancer Paul Draper. At first, Charles is an escort of Dorothy's but later more frequently of Gertrude herself.

Though Westbury is now almost a continuous house party, perhaps the most interesting social event at this time takes place overseas: the separation of Gertrude's cousin Consuelo from the Duke of Marlborough. In two long, unwittingly ironic letters from Paris in late October and early November, Gertrude's mother describes the situation:

It is very sad about Consuelo, is it not? Anne [Vanderbilt, Consuelo's stepmother] told me that they were to be separated but did not explain specifically whether there is to be a divorce, but as you will probably see Anne you will hear all about it. She made no charge against M. in talking to me except to say he was impossible and that he had insulted C. in every possible way and that for two years there had been trouble. Of course the English will point to the example of her Mother and Father [i.e., to their divorce] which is unfortunate as that does give M. a leg to stand on, but they certainly cannot put anything to C's charge, altho' I hear the Churchills are furious and are going to be as unpleasant as possible. She will live in her London house, but altho' they hope she may have the children they are not sure. It's excessively sad and, as C. will be always an object of observation under any circumstances, the outlook is unpleasant.

. . . Her Father [William K. Vanderbilt] will not listen to there being any divorce; queer is it not after his own experience! I heard that separation papers have been signed and that each one is to have the children 6 months at a time. Believing as many do that M. wishes a divorce perhaps this is not true. He makes charges of course implicating 3, some say 6, but the real reason seems to be that she is physically repulsive to him and that he cannot bear to be near her. What her charges are I don't know. I heard the final break came when she said about two weeks ago she was going to Paris to get her winter things. Go and stay, he said. She came and saw her Father who went immediately to London and arranged matters. So of course this gives a chance to say that M. wants the separation, that W.K. offered untold sums to stop it. I am repeating gossip but strange to say I have not a word to say about her charges except in that one time I wrote to C. asking her if I could do anything for her and if she would come to me here for a few days. She answers that Jeannie Tiffany is stopping with her, etc. but as Aunt Tiffany has already been twice divorced, herself, it seems a slender support for poor C. How like a man to get out of the way. Why could not W.K. have stayed in London for at least a few days after the publicity? He got well out of the way *before* the papers got the story!

⮐ *1906*

The house parties in Westbury continue until just before January 29, when Gertrude and Harry give a large coming-out ball in New York for Dorothy, postponed because of a death in Mrs. Vanderbilt's family. It does not, as Harry has promised, make Gladys' coming-out party at the end of 1904 "look sick," but it is attended not only by all branches of the Whitney and Vanderbilt families (including Grace and Cornelius, Jr., as well as Mrs. Cornelius, Sr.) but by virtually all branches of American "society" as defined, we may assume, by Harry. His friends from the world of horse racing and polo are there, Gertrude's newer friends from the periphery of the art (and architecture) world are not. The most lustrous guest is Alice Roosevelt, accompanied by her fiancé Representative Nicholas Longworth, who like so many of the other guests arrive after hearing Caruso sing *Faust* at the opera.

In the entrance hall of 2 West 57th Street are tall palms and tropical plants placed against a background of tapestries hung from the stairway. The only cut flowers there are American Beauty roses which overflow into the drawing room, filled like a conservatory with these and pink carnations and complementary plants, almost all in highly polished silver vases. (The floral decorations are provided by The Rosary, a comparatively modest business owned by Rollie Cottenet, but for many years *the* florist to society.) In the drawing room Gertrude stands tall and erect beside her younger, shorter, but equally elegant sister-in-law. Probably Dorothy is wearing one of her new ball gowns from Worth and no doubt Gertrude is wearing something just as stylish, possibly a gown from Doucet or Callot, bought in the course of their shopping together. Neither outfit is described in the columns of newspaper copy devoted to the ball because the society reporters don't see them but only the gowns visible at the opera such as Alice Roosevelt's of pale rose-pink satin, Grace's of sapphire-blue velvet, and Gladys' of cream-white chiffon satin.

The white and gold French-paneled ballroom shimmers in the light of electric chandeliers hung with feathery ferns and asparagus vines. At the west end of the room the orchestra, led by Nathan Franko, is screened off by palms and pink roses. During the first part of the evening there is general dancing. Soon after midnight a supper, catered by Sherry's, is served on small tables in the dining room. Then the cotillion begins, led by Worthington Whitehouse with Dorothy. Among the favors—silver picture frames, matchboxes, face-powder cases, brocaded bags for opera glasses, boutonnières, etc.—are some that are more unusual: American Indian headdresses and fur hats for the men, tomahawks and Red Riding Hood hats and capes for the women. These are used in two cotillion figures on the two respective themes. Finally there is a figure in which the dancers carry animal-shaped balloons. The ball is conceded to be a great and very original success.

Shortly after it Harry is again being mentioned by Tammany as a possible political candidate—this time to succeed "Big Tim" Sullivan as congressman from the Eighth Congressional District, the Bowery. As the *Times* says, this "would be a distinct innovation in politics." However, Harry is believed to be "especially popular" and "has been making frequent appearances on the East Side." It would appear that if Harry wants the nomination he can have it and that if he accepts he will win, but the story dies. Possibly Harry, like his father, does not want to run for elective office. Possibly he does not want to leave the area where his horse-racing, polo, and financial interests are centered. Possibly, too, Gertrude is reluctant to uproot her family and her studios. There are many possibilities, none mentioned in Gertrude's journal, which she resumes in the early spring, a brand-new maroon leather, gilt-edged book which she intends to be more particularly "a record of Artistic Possibilities. Thoughts relating to Art, subjects for statues, composition, symbols, all manner of substance which affects my Artistic life."

The book is not really separate but, like previous journals, a chapter in the big book, the ongoing story of her life. Gertrude writes in it only from April 2 to 10, before putting it aside for a year and a half. Yet in those first twenty pages, written in between the busy events of nine days, she presents an ever broadening interest in the arts and introduces us to one of her new art world friends who will become increasingly close to her, as well as to a male model who will pose for some of her best sculptures of this period and a later period in Paris. The friend is the painter Robert Winthrop Chanler, whom she has met during the past year through her own efforts as outlined in her lists of useful people. A descendant of John Winthrop, Peter Stuyvesant, Robert Livingston, the Hudson River Astors, and the Marions of South Carolina, he seems to have inherited the most individualistic and unconventional strains of these distinguished families along with a considerable fortune which, at the age of thirty-three, he has substantially spent on women, travel, art, extravagant entertainment, and expensive gestures such as running for the unlikely office of sheriff of Dutchess County, to which he has been elected after campaign costs of $20,000. "Sheriff Bob," as he is called, is huge—about six and a half feet tall, with broad shoulders, a solid neck, a large head, strong handsome features, great curls of pale blond hair—and an appetite for life to match his physique. His marriage to Julia Chamberlain in 1893 has probably been doomed from the start—he cannot be satisfied by one woman any more than by one of anything—and he is presently separated from his wife and two daughters, who are in Paris. After a two-hour early evening visit from him on April 2, Gertrude writes:

. . . how fine he is in his way. Put aside the fact of his being a fraud and a flirt, and he is inspiring. To hear him talk about art, to hear his ideas, to see the great truths coming from him is worthwhile. The fact that he mixes it all up with admiring remarks and such like perhaps only adds to the force of it. Frankly I like admiration and from that kind of a person it means something, for the moment of course only. He says live—live—get all you can out of life and he wishes the best of all things. "I would like to see you go to the Devil" were his words and instead of being shocked or reproving him I merely smile and I suppose my Puritan ancestors would turn in their graves were they to hear our conversations. Ah there you have it, the devil, is that what I mean when I crave experiences? To a certain extent, yes, but not entirely, of that I feel sure. I am sure that he is a genius and to know such a man and to hear him talk freely and truly about himself that is an experience, and one worth having—I can always keep him where I want him too, because 1st he is not really carried away and 2d because he does not affect me. If he were not to a certain point in sympathy with me, he would not give me so much. Vampire. Oh what does that matter. Take what you can, you need not think men cannot take care of themselves. He sails in a week, during that time do all you can, look your best, appeal to him in all ways and listen, listen with a thousand ears to what he says. Store away what you can. Take the treasures and make them part of yourself. He is a real person, he is a natural human being, study, probe, squeeze if possible. He will never feel it. He is too big. Words and personality drop from him simply as so much dust or air, he does not miss it. There is plenty of both to be had. He is a kind of Walt Whitman. He and Howard and I could have wonderful times. I could talk to him with my soul laid bare, because being a natural person, he brings out the natural in others.

Tomorrow I shall go to the studio. I shall go early and lunch there and then Mac [the model, Edgar McAdams] will come and his beautiful bare body will be more beautiful than ever and I will look at him and be glad that I am alive and that my heart beats now quickly, now slowly, and there will be symmetry of lines that will call to my soul and those dormant things in my mind will awake and I will long with a terrible pain to express them. I will look at the blue vase and feel something of its message and I will look at the perfect human form and I will be mystified and my soul will cry out in anguish because it cannot express what it feels.

APRIL 4th.

To see Whistler etchings and lithographs with B[ob] C[hanler] is a treat. He has a feeling for a line, a spot, a bit of color which is wonderful. Mr. K. [possibly Otto Kahn] told him that the dome in the distance [was] the Tomb of Napoleon. "What do I care about that," he cried angrily, "does it matter to me *what* it is—It is a spot." We went to the Art Exhibition and to see his giraffes [four of them eating oranges from white birch trees!]. The latter was a real sensation. It is great. I mean it seems to me to be really very great. He says it is and he loves it. We went to see the big studio [147 East Nineteenth Street] he has taken. He has a faculty for getting the best, which I admire. . . .

Yesterday afternoon and this afternoon I worked. . . . Mac was beautiful and took the poses I wanted as if he felt them. The hours flew and it seemed as if in absence I had gained a certain facility. I seemed better able to express what I wanted. The Pasteur group is what I worked on. After this week I shall put it away and start another with entirely a different idea, or at least arrangement. I must put this out of my mind entirely. But for the present it absorbs me. The figures of Death and Disease daily grow—in possibilities at least. I see in them poses which not only satisfy the eye momentarily but which might express a beauty and a strength not to speak of an individuality all their own. I have added to the group a crouched figure intended to represent Ignorance. The original idea being to make something more interesting at the back and then the notion that Pasteur had so much Ignorance and Superstition in his life to overcome, that no group would be complete that did not have some sign of this. It is a nice pose I have chosen but as to whether it expresses just the idea or not I am not at all sure. After all how can one express Ignorance, that is a staggerer. What is ignorance? Lack of knowledge. How express a lack of anything? . . .

APRIL 5th.

The Hindu dancing of Ruth St. Denis suggests many things. One might find there the inspiration for a great work. The mystery of the Orient and the sensuous Eastern dancing, the long lithe lines of grace, the strange contortions of the perfect body, the fleeting smile, unfathomable, the action of the bare waist, the suggestion of the long lines of the back just discernible, the grace of the long arms, the weird power of the long hands, their motions, their strength, their subtleness. Ah me—if I could express what it all means to me—the East—then indeed I would be able to do something really great. But it is so hard to catch hold of, to put into any tangible form. To feel it is easy, to make others feel it is well nigh impossible. I should like to lie in a semi-darkened room for a long time, listening to weird music and then when the mind was properly arranged and attuned, I should like to see her dance once more. After that the man I love must come to me and we must love each other madly and as do those closest to nature. Then I could go out and conquer the world and leave on its crest the impress of my footstep. The technical difficulties of my group bother me very much. The amateurish look which is difficult to escape. . . .

APRIL 9th, SUNDAY.

[After returning to New York from a small house-party weekend in Westbury with the children, Rollie Cottenet, Charles Draper, Frank Polk, Mabel Gerry, Mr. and Mrs. L. S. Thompson, and possibly Dorothy.]

After a day spent mostly in the open air and with healthy influences I feel totally wrong, restless, unsatisfied and as if I had missed something. I found the other day the poems of Oscar Wilde and they answered a chord long since grown dull. I learned some of the verses and they linger in my mind playing havoc with my imagination.

The ugly auto trip to Roslyn [Westbury] was beautified by— [Wilde's] "To drift with every passion, till my soul"—etc.—"passionate pain" and "deadlier delight"—lived in my mind like lights of another world, the world in which I really belong. Then the children and I wandered in the fields and their companionship and love encircled me and hid the ideals and hopes of that other world. . . . Why not take advantage of this time and spend it entirely in the studio, working and trying to put into form the too real thoughts of my restless mind. The longing after—the groping for—the mad reaching for, all the heartfelt aches, the tired mind, the heartburns, the closing of heated lids, the open mouth and the white smooth body. I will take off my clothes and will exercise my long body till I am so tired that my head no longer reels. I will think of health and of good things and will shut out the bad and glorious thoughts that kill me. Then sleep will come and in the morning all will have passed and my conventional self will have come back. With one last mad cry I demand why shall the conventional come back, why must I live like what I am not, and I beat my head against the cage and I weep and I grind my ugly teeth together, for I know that I am not bigger than circumstances and that I am not big enough to put the world aside and that it is my doom only to *see* the possibilities and never realize them.

The next day Gertrude is still thinking about Wilde's poetry. She transcribes thirty-two lines of it, directing herself to "Look back often and read these poems." One beginning "Nay, let us walk from fire unto fire," ends "Have we not lips to kiss with, hearts to love, and eyes to see!" Gertrude answers, "Ah, indeed have we not."

As she commits herself more and more deeply to art—to her own and to that of others as well as to romantic dreams about Art and Artists—Harry commits himself just as deeply to horse racing and polo. When one of his three-year-old colts, Burgomaster, wins the Belmont Stakes ($25,000) and Harry receives the champagne-filled silver cup, it represents a degree of achievement and recognition in his field far beyond anything Gertrude has experienced in hers. And this same year he has four other stakes winners. In horse racing there *are* winners. First place is a clear-cut and final statement. In art, one goes on asking, like Gertrude, "Has any artist ever felt that he has said all he had to say?"

In polo Harry's involvement is even more direct—he is not only backing the horse, he is riding it himself—playing the game as aggressively and successfully as anyone of his time, wearing out a fresh pony in each period. During a scrimmage in a match on June 9 at the Meadow Brook field, he swings his mallet so hard that he blinds one eye of an opponent, Robert J. Collier, sending him stunned to Nassau Hospital. The incident is covered on the first page of the *Times:* "Mr. Collier's eye was torn from its socket. . . ."

Yes, sometimes happily, sometimes not, Harry is recognized. When, if ever, Gertrude may wonder, is a creation like Rodin's new sculpture *The*

Thinker a front-page story? Is the answer never, even for him? And if so, surely never for her? It is difficult to admit that, except for the artist himself or herself, what happens in the studio lacks drama, but there it is: the world prefers stories of sporting events or of any kind of compressed action, like that two weeks later when Harry Thaw kills Stanford White.

≈

At their very different paces, Harry's polo matches and horse racing and Gertrude's sculpting and study continue. The New York/Westbury season ends, there is a brief visit to Aiken, the Newport season begins, and soon once again it is time for Europe. They sail July 26 on the *Kaiserin Auguste Victoria*. Beginning August 1 in Paris, before starting another journal, Gertrude keeps *My Motor Log Book/A Handy Record*, conscientiously filling in the printed blanks (at least at the beginning—the book covers every summer from now through 1912 and becomes, even this summer, progressively more deficient) from one city or town to the next, with departure and arrival times, distances covered, number of stops, time of run, weather and road conditions and, when applicable, a listing of guests and "incidents of run" (brief comments on restaurants, hotels, and sights—usually "good" or "very good," "nice" or "very nice"; sometimes "picturesque" or "fine" or "excellent"; infrequently "poor" or "bad").

On the first run—from Paris to Nancy (310 kilometers)—Rollie Cottenet is once again with them and they go "40 miles in one hour." The next stop, after lunch in Sarrebourg and drinks in Strasbourg, is Baden-Baden where Mama and Gladys are staying. Adele and J. Burden join them in Neuhausen. After trips to Heidelberg and Metz they all return to Paris. About the middle of the month Harry and J. go to London and on to Holwick while Gertrude and Adele take an apartment together at the small but fashionable Vendome. Later in the month Gertrude and Adele make many excursions—to Fontainebleau, Chantilly, Rouen, Chartres, Pierrefonds, Reims, Beauvais, Poissy. . . . The itinerary is strenuous. Place names begin to blur.

September 7, Gertrude is again aboard the *Kaiserin Auguste Victoria* (it is not clear whether or not Harry is with her), writing to Gladys:

> The bridge table does not attract me, the deck looks deserted & the rugs gone and generally the air of getting off tomorrow early, so I have taken to the writing room & will bore you again.
>
> I cannot believe that my holiday is over for I look at it in that light. Of course I do have lots of other good times during the year but somehow the time of going abroad is the best. It is different and the days seem long, which is nice, and all the rest of the year seems the same length as the few weeks abroad. And if you did not do it, think how short the years would be & how much too fast time would pass.

I really did some nice sight seeing this year and saw quite a lot of perfectly new things, which I enjoy, for new impressions are so necessary and you never know but that out of them may come inspiration for all sorts of new art ideas. I try to remember all I have seen and just how I felt when I saw things. I tried to train my memory too—to remember details and to be able to express what I saw and felt. That is so hard. For I believe that one kind of expression helps another. What drool you will say.

I gave myself two presents in Paris—one a diamond comb for my back hair (mine was lost) and the other one of three narrow diamond collars, worn on a black velvet. It is quite pretty & very useful with all the low dresses. I got 2 suits at Druillet's, two dresses, a tea gown & a waist at Carné, 1 velvet dress at Worth. Otherwise everything at Callot. There is a jump for you.

From Gertrude's return until the end of the year, she records house parties in Westbury. The names are familiar now and pretty well balanced between Gertrude's and Harry's relatives and particular friends: Dorothy, Gladys, Mabel Gerry, Regi and Cathleen, Alfred and Ellen, Rollie, Bunny, Charles, Lloyd, Frank, Worthie. . . . Even Jim Barnes is invited twice and appears once. Nevertheless, Gertrude is lonely. In October she starts a new journal. Again she intends for it to be something separate from the main journal, a place now "to pour out my inmost soul." And again it is really a chapter—a very small one this time, only three entries—of the big book. October 25 the theme is stated or, more accurately, restated:

. . . We can never really approach one another. Forever we strive to get closer and forever we cannot. . . . Everyone must have felt the longing to lay all bare, to be absolutely understood, to understand someone else, to know to the bottom. Think if one could express that feeling. It would be a work of Art, for it is essentially universal and it has not been expressed so far as I know, and feeling it as I do, if I have the technical ability I will be able to express it. It is for that I work.

OCTOBER 27th.

A horrid fit of depression almost drove me mad last night, but today I feel better. The morning in bed settled my jangled nerves and I can now think and speak without weeping. I had a dreadful longing after the very thing I described two days ago last evening, and I made a feeble effort to get closer but I was immediately thrown back onto myself and, with the realization of how alone I was, I subsided into the corner of my bed. This morning Mabel and I talked. . . . Harry has gone to a football game. . . . I never was meant for the gay world alas! . . . I feel like a debutante reviewing her subjects, only they seem of less importance. A. stands for Art, aims, alphabet and angles, B. for bats, bottles, beer and bohemia, C. for cats, cans, can-cans, caramels, corks and cabbages, D. for dunces, dukes, damns, drabs, darkies, dances, dinners and doors, E. for eggs, elephants, esoteric something and enigmas, F. for Fourth of July, foam, filth, fans, fancies, follies, force etc., etc. If I could only remember till dinner time my conversation would be scintillating.

On this note the little book ends, but almost as if to belie or balance the forced lightness, Gertrude inserts a rough sketch entitled *l'éternelle séparation,* standing figures of a nude male and female, entwined but also clearly separated. The year itself ends also about as it began—with a house party that includes Rollie Cottenet and Charles Draper, and with a ball in New York, this one a block from their own house, at the home of Mr. and Mrs. Charles B. Alexander, where once again Worthington Whitehouse leads the cotillion in this era of light-footed waltzers.

⇜ 1709

The pace quickens, becomes hectic—a shuttling again between dinners, dances, operas, plays, ballets, and concerts in the city and weekend house parties in Westbury. In Gertrude's Line-A-Day, the events are that summary, that generic. Rarely does she name an actress (Nazimova once) or an opera (Richard Strauss's *Salome,* based on the Oscar Wilde play, twice —a rehearsal and the first American performance). In contrast the dinner parties are *only* names with Harry's frequently missing because he is in Aiken or elsewhere in the South. Gertrude's rhythm of work is badly broken, her studios hardly mentioned.

February 24, Harry and the children leave for Aiken, with Dorothy, Helen, and Payne, their cousin Katherine Barney, her fiancé Courtlandt Barnes, and two other bachelors. Gertrude waits in New York for the arrival from abroad of Mama and Gladys, takes them to the opera the next night, and a few days later boards the train to Aiken, with Adele Burden, Lloyd Warren, and Rollie Cottenet. March is a revolving house party. Two days after Gertrude's arrival Harry, Payne, Katherine, Courtlandt, and one of the bachelors leave. Five days later Harry and Payne return with Jimmie Appleton, John Ellis Postlethwaite, and William Stackpole, a stockbroker friend of Harry's, five years younger than he, who attended Harvard and who becomes now an increasingly frequent visitor to the Whitney homes. The next day J. Burden arrives from Cuba. Three days later Rollie and Lloyd leave. A week later Gladys and her friend Lorie Sheffield arrive. The next day is Barbara's fourth birthday and there are "mild celebrations," after which Helen and Payne go off to Thomasville, and finally toward the end of the month Gladys leaves, and then the rest of the party. The busy (and, here, far from complete!) schedule of arrivals and departures is one aspect of Aiken, an aspect which must have been burdensome to Gertrude as hostess. In photographs we see the schedule within the schedule, the costume changes for sports and parties—Gertrude and the other women (even "Eleo" Sears, a great athlete of the period) looking more formal than the men, Harry typically in riding clothes and Payne dressed for tennis.

But what we don't see here or in the Line-A-Day is the deflection of leftover energy, which might have gone into her own sculpture, going now into serious consideration of all sorts of art problems. For this we turn to a large scrapbook which Gertrude begins early in the year, in the midst of all those Westbury and Aiken house parties. The book starts with a list, in Gertrude's handwriting, of an art exhibition she is organizing at the Colony Club—a very exclusive "social, artistic, mental, and physical" club for women, founded in 1903 by J. Pierpont Morgan's daughter Anne, Mrs. J. Borden Harriman, and about forty charter members including Gertrude, now opening in a new Georgian building at 30th Street and Madison Avenue, designed just before his death by Stanford White and containing murals by Robert Chanler and a fountain by Gertrude.

Two thirds of the exhibition is what we might expect: first, a collection of miniatures done by academicians, mostly portraits of club members and their families, including children and other relatives of Gertrude herself; second, two display cases of antique lace, originally belonging to Marie Antoinette, Cardinal Hohenlohe, Empress Marie Louise, et cetera, and now the property of club members. However, the final third of the exhibition—contemporary American paintings—is a surprise. There are three works each by Arthur B. Davies, Ernest Lawson, and Jerome Myers—all comparatively unrecognized, all working with local subject matter in styles somewhere between Romantic Realism and Impressionism, and all at odds with the National Academy of Design. In addition there are one to three works each by fourteen men and one woman (Bridget Guinness) ranging from a middle ground including Blendon Campbell—a friend of James Earle Fraser, who undoubtedly advises Gertrude on some of the selections—to such established reputations as Sargent and Whistler.

The exhibition opens April 9 and, because it is private, receives little attention except from the artists involved. Gertrude buys two paintings by Lawson, who writes to thank her, to clarify which two ("Jas. Fraser . . .

was in doubt"), and "to express . . . appreciation of the exhibition. . . . Such things give a good deal of incentive to younger men." Arthur B. Davies enlarges upon this more general theme:

Mr. Fraser has spoken to me of your desire to insist on a more vital movement in those American artistic qualities as yet not sufficiently perceived elsewhere. There is so much to commend the variety of interest and attraction about your present Art Exhibition. Your beautiful new club house is itself a true revival of supreme interest and to those who are endowed with a faculty of expressing themselves with an inherent distinction in action, manners and art, your opportunity is unique. It would be to awaken a love for this happy ultimate, and a justification for our great uniqueness in commercial life. Believe me I hope you may be a turning point in this movement, a means of attainment for an art of style and true beauty.

Beyond these letters, word is going around among the artists, especially those opposed to the Academy, that in Gertrude they have a friend, a very rich friend, willing to introduce their work to others as rich as herself. She is already in correspondence, too, with Daniel Chester French, chairman of a National Sculpture Society committee seeking adequate exhibition space. However, her present scrapbook best presents the story of her growing concern for American art and artists. It is the collaged equivalent of her earlier journals. With no commentary now, she pastes in clipping after clipping about the formation of the Academy jury and its rejection of thirty-three artists, including Davies, Lawson, and Myers, as well as Robert Henri, perhaps the most respected and influential of the new wave of American realists. She pointedly places items regarding the sale of Renoir's *La Famille Charpentier* to the Metropolitan Museum—$18,480 at auction—in juxtaposition to accounts of other auctions at which a major Inness goes for $1,700 and a Ryder for $1,225. A similar (though less justifiable) contrast exists in a newspaper account of the Carnegie International awards where first prize goes to Gaston La Touche's academic *The Bath* and second prize to Thomas Eakins' powerful, realistic *Portrait of Professor Leslie Miller*. There are dozens of articles about other exhibitions, auctions, prizes, art institutions and their acquisitions; and through them all runs the theme, implicit if not explicit, of the neglect or inadequate appreciation of the non-academic artist, Americans mostly but also foreigners; visual artists mostly but also composers, particularly Richard Strauss, whose *Salome* is being attacked in Paris as immoral. (Once again Gertrude transcribes long passages of Wilde's poetry.) In page after page of clippings, lists, and transcriptions Gertrude's message is clear: her concern about the aesthetic and economic freedom of the artist, the exhibition of his or her work, and its ultimate recognition by purchase (or prize). The painting portion of the Colony Club show is the existential counterpart of the new scrapbook and previous journals.

In April, while the show is being installed and exhibited, there are only three insignificant entries in the Line-A-Day. Not until July 6, when Gertrude resumes her journal, is there an explanation. Then she writes: "A long, long jump [from October 19, 1905]! . . . I think it is enough to say that all my agony was not imagined, that none of it was, that it was all worse than I thought. Think of my never having positively found out till this spring . . . about the 15th of April."

What she has positively found out, what she recapitulates, is the five-year-old story of Harry and "the other woman." But what is different, what is "worse," now, so many years later, is that Gertrude has been told by a friend (identified only as "Mrs. L.") that the affair continues and is not only more lasting but more serious than Gertrude has ever believed:

. . . there has always been one thought that has sustained me . . . that I really did understand and that, though it was all fearful, yet it did not mean the one thing that would have made everything impossible. I felt (it is strange) that he cared for me most really. . . . Strangely clear it all seemed, and therefore, and therefore alone, I was able to be as I was. Perhaps the way I was was all wrong, but after he knew how I felt, and he did, for at the time I could not hide it, then if I was able to be as I was, why was it not better? It seemed so to me. I acted as I would be acted by and because I knew that he was almost as unhappy as I was. Now comes the working out of it all. Details were almost harder after the first few weeks than at first when the strain was so great that it was work every minute to keep from giving in and behaving dreadfully. Now at times I shiver to think what I might have done just at first. But I have hold of myself now and do not so often lie awake half the night thinking—thinking of all the things that were happening to other people while certain things were happening to me. There have been days when I feared most of all that the time would come when I would not care, when it would all not matter to me and when everything in my heart would be cold and dead. It has not come yet and I am fighting against that as I never fought for anything before. And yet at first it was oh just not to be able to feel, oh for moments when I could forget. I would get thinking of a certain time, a certain event when he had done a certain thing, looked a certain way and my mind would insist upon the full explanation of that act or look, the logical conclusion. Then—well then—but what is the use of details? I believe (strangely perhaps) that Mrs. L. meant kindly by me. I am glad that she said what she did. It is funny, I have never yet been sorry for that. I told her politely that she had an evil mind which was equivalent to saying, "I am a fool, I don't believe you," but it is better to have her think that, than to think the truth.

Gertrude is sick at heart and will during the remainder of this year develop many physical ailments in response to her misery. Most of May is spent in bed. On the eighth she drives out to Westbury with Gladys. That night they dine and dance at Belmont Park with Harry and Mr. Belmont himself and a group of their own house guests, including Rollie Cottenet, Charles Draper, and William Stackpole. Gertrude has "great fun," but the next day misses the opening at Belmont, as she is in "bed with horrid cold." There she remains for four days until they return to New York to see her mother and sister off to Paris. The following weekend Gertrude takes Howard and Ethel Cushing to the races and then to Westbury for the night. Immediately after their departure, she has arranged to be operated on in her house for hemorrhoids—"a family failing," as Mama calls it in a letter from Paris—and Gertrude is in bed again until the end of the month.

June is blank in the Line-A-Day but on the tenth Gertrude writes Gladys, "I have not been able to work at all lately. . . . I am about well again now but find I cannot do very much without getting tired, so I am going to take care of myself for the next month so as to be able to enjoy abroad. . . ." She looks forward to seeing her sister and mother in Carlsbad and to meeting the Hungarian Count László Széchényi to whom Gladys will soon be engaged.

After a "Cheerful 4th. Many firecrackers, etc." Gertrude, with William Stackpole, takes the children to Newport for the summer. Her journal entry of July 6 continues:

> Now everything in me is concentrated on going away, on getting out of it all, on leaving behind the scenes that are so full of evil suggestions. At first I wanted to go alone, to hide my head somewhere and weep until my tears were dry. Then perhaps I could lighten the weight on my chest. But I have hardly cried at all and now I do not want to go alone, I want to go with people who will distract and interest me. I want to forget my world in another world. I want to see beautiful things. I want to meet people who know nothing about me and, if I do not interest them for the moment, who will not speak to me. I want to have foolish adventures and laugh at things and people and be taken far, far out of my own life. Can this happen? I have always believed that the things happened to people for which they had prepared themselves. Looking for adventures one usually finds them. But for adventures one must be charming looking and talking etc. and so I must spruce up. When I appear on the steamer Tuesday I positively must look very smart and very attractive. Unfortunately I cannot change my face but I can do a lot as far as getting myself up

well goes. My corsets can be a little tighter, my belt a little neater, my gloves, shoes and collar immaculate, my veil well put on, and my carriage better than usual. I am going to make a special effort to look well all the time I am away this year. I feel that I have gotten very sloppy and I need freshening up, especially as I get uglier every day.

July 7, Gertrude returns to New York on the night boat with William Stackpole. She has a strenuous day in the city, spending the morning at the studio, the afternoon at a polo match in Rockaway, and the evening at the Burdens'. She and Harry board the *Kaiser Wilhelm II* at 3 A.M. and the ship sails later in the morning. Because there is only the brief reference to visiting the studio and because it is unlikely that she would have tried to work in the midst of such a busy day of departure, it is probable that the visit was not to her Bryant Park studio but to a new one, found by the painter Blendon Campbell, which she has just bought at 19 MacDougal Alley, off MacDougal Street, between Eighth Street and Washington Square North, in Greenwich Village. From letters received by Gertrude during the summer, we know that work is being done there which she must have ordered; and from comments by Campbell and the events preceding her departure, we understand the twofold appeal of being further removed from her midtown social life and closer to the bohemian ferment and "adventures" of the Village, as well as to James Earle Fraser, Andrew O'Connor, and other sculptors in the Alley. Nevertheless, there is no mention at this time of 19 MacDougal Alley, and she does not return to her journal until the end of the crossing:

It seems dangerous to carry this book about and I intended leaving it in the safe in N.Y. but forgot. So I might as well write in it till I get someplace where I can put it away. . . . I must say I was pleased to see my little sprucing up apparently did some good, for Monday I found myself very much noticed and on this trip I think I have attracted attention. But alas Friday night I was ill and by Saturday my face was enormously swelled and my entire body as well as face covered with red blotches. The blotches had been coming on for two days. The itch is something fearful and the first 2 days and nights were dreadful. It is better now but still hurts and the swelling has only gone down a little. I fear it will spoil my short time in Paris now. It is certainly a most unpleasant experience. Perhaps a punishment for thinking too much about my appearance. At any rate it cannot take from me the joy I shall experience when I go to the Louvre and the Luxembourg, and I can go there heavily veiled. . . .

Except for a few notes on German art and a brief entry written August 5 in Munich ("2 delightful trips [Nuremberg and Rothenburg] but no time as yet to write about them"), this journal is abandoned for a year.

Even the Line-A-Day is substantially abandoned. In it, after Carlsbad where Gertrude and Harry leave Mrs. Vanderbilt and Gladys, there is only a partial itinerary (supplemented by the *Motor Log*) of tours through France with Adele, while Harry is in Holwick, "bored," as he writes, "with everything & everybody."

Just before returning to New York a great deal of mail catches up with Gertrude. There's a long letter on The Brook club stationery from William Stackpole to "Dear Mrs. Whitney," reporting that he has been in Newport and visited the children. "We played 'Duck on the Rock' (if you know what this is) & croquet. I don't think [the children] have ever been better. Flora tells me you are sailing for home the 20th. What is your steamer & what day do you arrive? I am enclosing one or two pictures which I think you will like. The one of Flora was taken on her birthday & is quite good." After admitting "confidentially" that he has tried unsuccessfully to interest her brother Alfred in going into horse racing with him, after thanking her for her postcards, and after passing on news that Frank Polk is engaged to Miss Elizabeth Sturgis Potter, of Philadelphia, he ends, "I hope that Harry is feeling well & that you will surely be home about the 27th. With regards to all & hopes that you are enjoying everything, I am yours/Wm Stackpole." The letter is at once intimate and formal—careful. The same can be said about one from Jimmie Appleton. Though it begins a little more daringly—"Dear Lady"—he, too, thanks her for her cards, gives her news of horses (a show in Mineola), and ends, "Welcome to you all. It will be good to have you back. /Yrs JWA."

Two other letters of a different sort are typical of many Gertrude will receive throughout her life—those from beneficiary to patron. One is from her model Edgar McAdams, who has become increasingly interested in art and is using her studio (probably the one at Bryant Park) to sketch in during her absence. "I am *so* glad you enthuse," he writes. "I can only say that it is a very great pleasure to know one who lives, or tries to live, every moment of their life. And as for any criticism of your letters, I consider it a great compliment that you should feel that I will understand. . . . And Paris—how I would love to be there. It seems I have heard of no other place so much in the last few years." The second letter is from Arthur Lee, a more advanced art student, formerly at the League with Gertrude but brought to her attention by Rollie and now already in Paris due to their generosity. He writes to thank her again for that opportunity and for "the good gift you sent me on my birthday. . . . I am safe in Utopia for another two years. . . ."

⪡

Gertrude and Harry return from Europe at the end of September. By the first of October they are already at the races, joining Helen and Payne in their box, from which they watch Harry's filly Stamina win the Produce. Harry is by now recognized as an expert on horses. The New York *Herald* quotes him as he inspects another winner: "My what a grand fellow he is! Since I last saw him he has finished and improved! What a beautiful horse he is. And he is a race horse too!" The paper is also interested in what Gertrude is wearing: a "princess costume of plum colored cloth combined with black velvet; large white hat lined with black velvet and topped with coque plumes."

Yes, at the races Gertrude is beautifully dressed and presumably beautifully composed. However, that very evening she opens the *Artistic Possibilities* journal she had begun in the spring of 1906 and, directly after the quotations from Oscar Wilde's poetry, makes this entry:

> One year and a half has passed and the same feelings and emotions rack my poor body and mind. Now perhaps they are in more control and also in more serviceable form. At least I feel as if I could sometimes open a drawer and take something out on a given subject. It would be of no value except that it was the formed thought of someone who had been steeped in chaos, but it would be genuine and real. I have had two summers of travel, and a year of real work. The first year in which I have accomplished anything. I have very little to show for it, but the time has come positively where not a month must pass without my having something to show, I must create now. The language, faltering it is true, is known a little, so that I can express myself. I am old, if I do not start to speak now I never will. This is to be my winter. I have enough started to tide over the times when inspiration will not come, and the spring must not arrive till I have something done which I can show. Besides the two sketches which I must finish I must bring forth many ideas in the form of rough sketches. At least 2 a month. They must cover many subjects, many thoughts foreign to my nature (that gives breadth) and also those deep things which I know to be true because I have lain in the dust and acquired them. They are bits of me now to be pulled away with strong unkind hands.

For seven weeks Gertrude is extraordinarily busy, even for her. In Long Island she resumes a schedule of work, horse races, and other social events (including a dinner party for Consuelo at the Mackays' and an afternoon call from her). In New York she goes again to operas, plays, and concerts (this time specifically naming only one, a concert by Fritz Kreisler), and supervises the final work to be done in her MacDougal Alley studio.

On November 17 she writes again in *Artistic Possibilities*, by which time she has ". . . moved into the new studio which abounds in suggestion and inspiration. The ceiling is high and one's ideas soar upward. I felt at once that I must do something large in it. Here one would never putter over little things. The light comes down direct from the sky in all its glory and illumines the human form. Great vistas of possibility open out before one. Life is lived in such a place and eras in one's existence marked." Gertrude is right. Nineteen MacDougal Alley does mark an era in her life. Initially it is a small marker—a twenty-five-foot-wide former carriage house, with two floors, each about twenty feet high—but it will be her final New York studio and grow eventually into the Whitney Museum of American Art.

Malvina Hoffman, who is working in the MacDougal Alley studio of Alexander Phimister Proctor, describes Gertrude's studio as enthusiastically, if not as romantically, as Gertrude herself:

> In sharp contrast [to the more ordinary MacDougal Alley studios of Proctor, Fraser, and the painter Edward Deming] was the perfect order of Gertrude Whitney's splendid place on the north side of the alley, with high, well-lighted studios and fully equipped workrooms. The array of modeling tools and glistening saws and chisels that hung over the workbenches, turntables that really turned, stands that did not wobble—the whole atmosphere of the place excited me and filled me with awe. Mrs. Whitney herself, tall, thin, and fragile in appearance, worked tirelessly but was never too busy to help young sculptors; her generosity was well known to the profession.

Gertrude's *Artistic Possibilities* entry continues with copious quotations from John Addington Symonds' *Essays Speculative and Suggestive* (1890). His aestheticism—like Wilde's and like J. K. Huysmans' (whose recent obituary she has clipped and saved)—appeals to her and she thinks now about getting back to her *Science* bas-relief of Pasteur. Symonds might almost be whispering to her as she writes:

> . . . I begin to see lines, the noble pose begins to fill my mind. A man erect and full of sentiment stands in the back of my brain. His carriage is indicative of that power in him. The folds of his apron fall in Greek lines showing the feeling of his body. It is all feeling. . . . That figure begins to rise before me—master the large symbolic figures above it. As a composition it must be fine, for it must be conceived from the inside out (as Mr. Fraser says). One line follows another, I feel it forming in my brain even while no pose exactly indicates it. It will be *the* group. I shall stay in bed tomorrow and work it out, for just now I know that Pasteur has the inspiration of a lifetime.

During the next month, in both Westbury and New York the most frequent entry in Gertrude's Line-A-Day is the single word "Worked." However, on Sunday, December 15, in Westbury, she writes, "Horrid day," then turns to *Artistic Possibilities* where, in a long entry, it becomes apparent that the horridness is not connected with her work. That seems to be going encouragingly well:

And I went to the Studio one day and drew [the Pasteur figure] on a piece of plasteline. It only took a moment, for it was all formed in my mind. I left it standing there and Mr. Fraser happened to come in. He said, "That is fine, it is great, cast it just as it is!" Of course [Pasteur] was only suggested in the roughest possible way but it just did have the feeling. I sent Mac's [McAdams'] head to the exhibition in 57 St. and it was accepted. So it is there on exhibition now and gives me a distinct feeling. I have never cared about exhibiting or wanted to and had any feeling of pride about it, but I see now that as long as I have gone into the thing seriously I must do so. I must finish up something. Have something to show people and be sending about to different exhibitions. For instance it will help me with the Pasteur group, that is in the minds of the women connected with that, if I have had success in a worldly way. I will finish the man on the rock and send it to Baltimore.

Nor is the horridness directly connected with a letter she now transcribes, written to yet another art student she has helped get to Paris (identified only as M. but probably McAdams). She asks M. about Arthur Lee and his ménage:

. . . I think you know how I feel about these things . . . in his case (that is, having *one* friend) it is very apt to interfere with his work and make him lose some of his ambition. But I realize our human side and I think that the fact of giving in to certain feelings makes us the sooner get rid of them and then we have more energy and ambition for our real work. . . . Everyone who has lived a little while knows how far away passion is from *oneself* at times and it means no more than being hungry or thirsty. Only be careful.

She catches herself, tells M., "if you are hungry and thirsty, eat and drink," recognizes that she is "delivering a lecture." A paragraph following the transcribed letter more directly explains the "horrid day": "We had a discussion last night as to whether people produced more if they were unhappy than happy and also if they were more sympathetic. Certainly in theory if one is happy one should have more to give that is worth giving and exuberance and energy to put into work. . . . I have an impulse, I will follow it."

The following day Gertrude goes to New York and works all day—possibly on a piece called *Paganism* (a very different theme from her lecture to M.), possibly on *Man on a Rock*, later called *Wherefore* (a despairing *Thinker* with head bowed in his lap). In either case, her sculpture, though intensely expressive, is still evolving and still very much under the influence of Rodin. However, considering the strain and distraction of shuttling between Long Island and New York, quickened now by the holiday season, the year ends with a very positive entry in *Artistic Possibilities*:

"I suddenly feel that I have power and I know that I am going to use it. I suddenly know that I am and that no one can change that. I have suffered and I have received much, but God be praised I have given more, and perhaps because of that and perhaps because of something I know nothing of now I am a person. In the past I have been praised in a certain way but have never been able to understand what it was that people felt in me, but now suddenly I know and I am going to use it to the limit."

Also at the end of the year, Gertrude receives a fifteen-page letter from Hendrik Andersen in Rome. Even at that distance, perhaps because of it and because they write openly to each other about their professional problems, he understands her situation:

> I realize how difficult it must be for you to find time to write, for I find it hard having not one third of the demands upon my time that you surely must have. . . . I am very glad indeed that you have taken a large studio in New York and nothing will please me more than to realize that you will have a chance to carry out a number of things before spring. I often wish that I could be in New York so that I could look in upon you and help you if possible with advice, or in any way. I remember how fast you worked and how much you advanced . . . when you studied with me in New York and Newport . . . my hopes of your continued progress and success is an absolute certainty. . . . So many can but so few will make an effort to do more than the commonplace, and to most the mere fact of living well is in itself all absorbing and without limit.

Andersen tells Gertrude that he has had to stop work for six weeks because his "nerves got in a very bad way," then describes at length a fountain group of Night, Day, Morning, and Evening on which he is again working, expecting to finish in about a year. "It was very good indeed of you to be willing to let my statues rest in your garden 'undressed,' not that I begrudge having work once done hidden in storage, but I begrudge still more spending a cent on hiding it, when so many cents are needed to carry on what I am doing." The subject of money, the need for it, has been broached. In the next long section of Andersen's letter cents will pile up into dollars as he explains that the fountain on which he has been working in plaster for eight years should—*must*—now be cast in bronze if it is to endure. The central group of four will cost $20,000, two horses will cost $12,000, related smaller figures (on the horses and elsewhere—an unspecified number) will cost $1,500 each. Andersen dreads to beg or ask help, but . . .

No doubt all of this can be read as the heart of the letter, its point; and no doubt Gertrude reads it that way. Increasingly, over the last few years, she has asked to be accepted as an artist, especially by other artists, and she has tried at the same time to accept herself as a very rich woman. The dual role is difficult, the balance delicate. Having made the lists she has made and having already asked those on it for favors for herself and others, she knows how humiliating charity can be for the recipient, how condescending for the benefactor. And she knows that it is as easy for the rich as for the poor to feel exploited. At this time, when requests for help are much less frequent than later in her career, her best defense against the paranoia of the rich is to avoid such schematic characterizations and to review each appeal individually. Within the context of this particular letter, the broader one of her continuing relationship to Andersen, and the still broader one of that to other artists, it seems probable that she sends Andersen a check, improbable that it approaches the $40,000 or so for which he is hoping.

The last five pages of his letter are devoted to Henry James, who visits Rome in July when Andersen does a bust of him; to Edith Wharton, whose work Andersen finds superficial; to Maxim Gorky, whose book on America "seems as if he saw it all from a balloon. James saw it all at close range. . . ."

⇜ *1908*

As during the past several years, New Year's Day is spent in Westbury. There, Gertrude, Harry, the children and their friends, and Gladys and her fiancé Count László Széchényi, are joined by Adele, Bunny Hare, and Bob Potter. All have fun around the Christmas tree and are entertained by a Punch and Judy show and magic tricks. A week later, after a night of opera and theater, Harry goes south with Lew Thompson. The next day, her birthday, Gertrude writes pointedly, ". . . the children gave me flowers & two other people remembered." Neither is Harry.

While he is away Gertrude attends several parties for Gladys, László, and his family, who have begun to arrive from Hungary for the wedding scheduled for January 27. In the same weeks she gets a considerable amount of work done, including the final touches on a fountain figure of Pan for an ornamental pool designed in collaboration with the architect Grosvenor Atterbury and the muralist Hugo Ballin. This project is submitted to the Architectural League of New York, *hors concours*, since Atterbury is one of the judges. Nevertheless, it wins first prize with the stipulation that the $100 in prize money for each of the collaborators be withheld.

Gladys' wedding in the 57th Street home of Mrs. Cornelius Vanderbilt, Sr., is as grand as other Vanderbilt weddings but, in several respects, different from them. First, the guest list of about 400 contains, beside the expected names, dozens of members of the Austro-Hungarian nobility, of whom many of the men, including the groom, are dressed in hussars' uniforms. Second, the couple is married in a Catholic ceremony by Monsignor Lavelle of St. Patrick's Cathedral, and Pope Pius X sends a cable. Third, perhaps most important from the family's viewpoint and that of an inquisitive public, Grace, with Cornelius, Jr., is received by his mother. More than that, to emphasize publicly a reconciliation that has taken place toward the end of the previous year, Alfred, as nominal head of the family, permits his older brother to give away the bride, who is attended by her cousin Ruth Twombly and her close friend, Gertrude's sister-in-law Dorothy Whitney. Gertrude's daughter Flora, now ten and a half, is the flower girl. Fourth, as soon as the ceremony is over, Cornelius and Harry board a special train to Philadelphia where they will be ushers at Frank Polk's wedding, just as he was at each of theirs almost twelve years earlier.

After Gladys' wedding, the social pace continues—some of the Széchényis remain in New York—accelerated now by a flurry of cultural activities, including many operas, a musicale at Helen's and Payne's where Lena Cavalieri sings and Fritz Kreisler plays, another art exhibition which Gertrude helps to organize and install at the Colony Club and, most important historically, the exhibition of The Eight at the Macbeth Galleries from which, in addition to the Lawsons bought the previous spring, she now buys his *Floating Ice*, Henri's *Laughing Child*, Luks's *Woman with Goose*, and Shinn's *Girl in Blue*, writing a check on February 2, the day before the opening, for $2,225. What this means to The Eight is evident in John Sloan's diary: "All the sales (7) . . . were to three buyers. Mrs. Harry Payne Whitney, the rich sculptress—at least she has a fine studio for the purpose—bought four." Also evident is Sloan's condescension, perhaps aggravated by her not having bought anything of his at this time. Years later (in 1949) his tune changes, his tone mellows. Then he writes that "Mrs. Whitney . . . had the audacity to buy four pictures from that show of 'ugly . . . black . . . illustrations' which are now considered charming examples of the American realist school. At that time, to buy such unfashionable pictures was almost as revolutionary as painting them. Certainly, to one group of financially unrecognized artists the gesture of appreciation was a stimulus."

Not until February 10 does Gertrude return to her own work:

> . . . I have practically done no work since Jan. 20th. I got to the Studio at 1:15 and I sent Thrasher [a studio assistant] out to buy some plasteline etc. The bell rang at about quarter to two and I went down to open the door. A big good looking man was there. He said, "I am a

model." He did not look like one. I said, "Who sent you?" He said, "An artist down there." "Mr. Fraser?" I asked. "Yes." I said, "Come up and show me your figure." So he did and I liked his looks. So I said if he would leave me his address I would let him know in a few weeks when I wanted him. He dressed again and wrote his address on a piece of paper for me. Then he said: "Would you mind if I stayed and watched you work a few minutes?" I said, "No, of course not." And he stayed till I stopped work at five-thirty. He talked and he turned out to be from Tennessee and has travelled almost all over the world. I have engaged him for working beginning the 24th and am now looking forward for that time to come.

Ten days later Gertrude makes her final entry in *Artistic Possibilities*. It is as affirmative as what she had written at the end of the previous year:

. . . probably because I have passed through such a time of stagnation, I have now come to a time of feeling and thinking. Every faculty again seems alive. I want things, I am going to get them, and I am aware of what is passing about me. I am gloriously alive. But with it I feel the power of suffering. I know that I have it in me and I know too that if it once got the best of me something dreadful would happen. . . .

Appropriately, the book does not end with words but with six ideas for bas-reliefs on a house—small sketches of Ambition, Happiness, Work, Struggle, Peace, and Plenty, perhaps related to the reliefs she has done for the Fields—and then with a *carte postale* of Rodin's *Le Penseur*.

≈

Gertrude is now working so hard that she doesn't go to Aiken with Harry when he leaves March 18. Rather, she spends time in her studio almost every day as well as some evenings when she does not go to the opera or theater or to have dinner with her mother who, with Gladys married, is now alone. During the spring Gertrude gives the children several treats, sometimes riding with them during weekends in the country and once taking them to see Buffalo Bill's Wild West Show where they ride in a stagecoach during his fight with the Indians. . . . Soon, once again, it is opening day at Belmont (May 13). Gertrude attends that with Harry and watches him in a polo match the same day. Then she gets back to work, which is facilitated by Harry's leaving a few days later for tarpon fishing in Florida. From late May until mid-June she works mostly on a relief which is unidentified but which may have been a commission from the architect William Adams Delano. In any case, he visits her studio at this time to see the work, as does James Fraser to criticize it. The next month less work is done, principally a bust, possibly of Devereux Milburn, a Meadow

Brook teammate of Harry's, and the Long Island season ends with a house party July 11 and 12, described in a letter from Charles Draper to Dorothy Whitney, who is in Europe:

. . . The party gathered from polo at Rockaway, sat down to dine at about nine-thirty, you can imagine the guests, the usual Arthur Burdens, some Brooks', the polo players, Hatch, Bunny, Miss Nicholas & Miss Sheldon, R. L. Bacon [the son of the American ambassador to France], I. Black people sang & played for us during the banquet and later we danced and went in swimming in the tank. Mrs. Arthur [Burden] performed some steps and Milburn went through one or two feats of horsemanship for the entertainment of the guests, he appeared on a pony in the hall about 12 o'clock arrayed in one of those lovely silk gowns and made quite a sensation. [Harry, ever since his honeymoon in Japan, has frequently worn kimonos around the house and has had extra ones available for his friends.] On Sunday all hands were very quiet. I had a look at your new greenhouses which are coming on nicely and then went over to comment on Mrs. Harry's bas relief things. They are really very fine and I am enthusiastic about them, it had never struck me somehow that she could do anything like these. The architect is very well pleased and the old man with the house is getting something very fine in decorations.

After that party Gertrude delivers the children to Newport, spends a day swimming with them, and then returns to New York to sail with Harry on the *Kaiserin Auguste Victoria*. They arrive at Plymouth Thursday, July 23, take the train to London, and spend the weekend at the Ritz. In two days Gertrude visits the Franco-British Exhibition and the National Gallery and sees both Maud Allen and Isadora Duncan dance. On Saturday Harry leaves London to play polo and the next day Gertrude leaves for Paris. In addition to his interest in polo, Harry has decided, partly because of the beginning of repressive legislation in New York, to "invade" English horse racing and will by September have shipped over twenty-four of his best horses, including sixteen yearlings.

In Paris, at the peak of the tourist season, many of Gertrude's friends await her. She is hardly there before she is lunching with Rollie, Consuelo, and Whitney Warren. That first night she dines with Warren at the Madrid. Within another day she has been in touch with Arthur Lee and Edgar McAdams and takes them both to lunch. So, by the second night, when Harry arrives from London, she is already very much in touch with both her worlds—the wealthy aristocrats and the aspiring artists. Everything she and Harry do during the next few days, before he leaves again, moves between these worlds—a night at the Moulin Rouge, an afternoon at the Louvre, Feydeau's hit farce *Occupe-toi d'Amélie*, the best restaurants, a drive through the château country. . . . One can feel Gertrude expanding in Paris. There is hardly enough room in her Line-A-Day to contain events. And yet, accustomed as she has become to a schedule of work and to some form of daily self-expression, the Line-A-Day will not do. August 1, after Harry leaves again, she turns to her "real" journal, the one she has not written in since the previous August, the one dedicated to no specific theme but herself:

One year! And probably the most eventful of my life. Not a word written, and that is because one does not write when one is cheerful, and when one's life is crowded to overflowing with rather exciting incidents one has no time or desire to chronicle them. Last year abroad meant a good deal to me in one way. I met people and got in with them and enjoyed myself. . . . Back in N.Y. I was able to make a pretty serious change in regard to someone and though at first I found it hard, I very soon was much happier on account of it. Later I met someone else whom I liked very much but in entirely the wrong way. I am glad I have had this because I don't think I could have it again and although I had it before I did not learn the lesson, but I think I have now. This sounds complicated and so it was, but as I look at it now it seems to me to have been a natural almost necessary development, and that without it I could not either have understood life or have ever been happy again in it. . . . I have worked really hard the last two years and I have accomplished something. My technique is still very bad, but it is better than it was and my mind is full of ideas. I have not led a very good life in any way, but my art has become better, my home is happier and I have more to give my friends. . . . I was brought up to have control above all things and so I stifled and subdued myself always. Then came my happiness and a little loosening of the control, a little of the joy of giving and taking. Then my agony and the return of the control. Now I certainly have taken off the brakes. Am I coasting for a fall? Some of my friends have told me so. Charles [Draper] among others, and naughty boy he gave me a little shove down.

If I were asked to explain H.'s attitude towards me and life now, I would say that he is semi-grateful for my way of taking last year's revelations, and fond of me—a little more than he was—and semi-repentant. It's useless for me to say that I have not changed in my feelings towards him, but I think on the whole it is for the best. I am able to think of the right thing to do now, I am not entangled in my affections and probably that is mostly the reason that I am happier. I understand him better, in fact a little too well. But he has so much that is fine and attractive and his brains that have wasted and gone to seed are such a charm—unfortunately oh horribly, desperately, unfortunately—I *know* that he fooled me. Suspicion therefore came in and I have it all so ready in my mind, the suspicion that is the curse of sensitive people. But I have done many things not to make me sensitive and I am almost hard now in some ways.

I love my work because it has made me happy and given me confidence in myself, and because it stretches into the future offering me always happiness. It is not dependent on humanity, it is something that I have made for myself and that I possess and cannot lose for it is part of myself. There is no question that I have also cultivated a love of excitement. I have played with love. I like admiration and I get it. The children are growing up, there is only a little while, and we were given so many feelings and possibilities. Shall we die without trying all? I am weak, weaker than I ever knew or imagined, but I have lived in this year and I am not sorry. I cannot even be sorry for the wrong things I have done.

Why not face the fact that the passionate love between two people married a long time dies, and try and make a friendship in place of it that can live? Because I cannot face friendship, or I do not want it from a person from whom I have had other things and to whom I have given all. Don't look around everywhere in life except in your own home. Consider that first and after you have done your best for that, then you are free to look around. But when I looked in my own home I saw only agony and I could not bear it, so I ran away quickly and on the road I found things that I liked and that made me forget and I picked them up and played with them. So that's the way I see it now. I wanted all the good and conservative things of home life, no one who knows could say differently, but probably through my own fault I could not get them, then I lay down and it seemed as if the sorrows of the world piled themselves upon me. I struggled, ineffectually at first and finally battered and torn I rose again to face life. And now I don't want good and conservative things in life. Well, it's all to an end, but what end? It seems as if the conclusions that I have arrived at after such struggles were only the very beginning of understanding. I am a child and I am desperately old.

Though this confessional entry is not explicit, it is obvious that Gertrude has had at least two meaningful affairs during the past year, affairs that have gone beyond her earlier "flirtations," though how much beyond is not, and never will be, obvious. Not only has she loosened her conditioned stifling and subduing control but she has learned to use that control to protect herself. She is, as she says, both "a child . . . and desperately old"—capable now of satisfying her appetite for experience while at the same time sufficiently experienced to do so with discretion. Her life is no longer restricted to "naughty" (read "charming") boys from her own circle, like Charles Draper and Jimmie Appleton; her circle is—and has been—enlarging. August 3, two nights after the last entry, she describes taking three of her newer friends, all artists whom she has been helping, to Chartres in her car—the sculptor Arthur Lee; Barry Faulkner, a painter whose work she has shown at the Colony Club and who has just won a Prix de Rome; and Morgan Russell, who has posed for her frequently— then a sculptor (who had studied with James Earle Fraser and who later often referred to himself as a "sculptor manqué") but ultimately most important as the founder of a school of color abstraction called Synchromism.

. . . It was a heavenly day, not a cloud but fresh, we all enjoyed it I think talking no end of rot about art and life and generally having a perfectly cheerful time. The cathedral I love, and it made me feel all sorts of big and real things which of course lead to nothing. There is a very early Puvis in the Musée and Faulkner liked it very much but Russell thought the colors bad, this plunged us deeper than ever in futile talk. Arthur asked me if I had any principles and I said two— one was to act and tell the truth, and the other not to miss anything in life. Of course that led to everyone wanting to tell what they thought of principles without listening to what anyone else said. Arthur was going to teach me the maxixe, but he got so terribly sunburned yesterday bathing that it hurt too much. I fear we talked about the Almighty very intimately, and they babbled about pancake colors and spotty complementary colors and line, till of necessity I had to tell them there was no such thing as line in painting. They said only the Impressionists believed that and I found myself fighting a mighty battle. My golly how keen they all were. It was bully, each had his weakness and it was fun to work for a rise—I thought in the cathedral today a comforting thought. I have realized lately that I change very quickly about caring for people and it has made me feel very very badly, for it seemed to be a sign of shallowness. We change in the artists we admire, in the art we worship, in these things and we consider it a matter of growth and development. Why not the same with people? If they do not keep pace with us, why is it not development and the fact that we are not satisfied with what they have to give? I am beginning to understand more of companionship and intellectual oneness and to think that it is the only thing that really counts. Perhaps because a person I know has made me feel that I could be a companion and friend. Other people to whom I have been close have always made me feel that I could not, that I had nothing in that respect to give, and that shut me up more and more.

August 5, more new friends appear in the journal:

And I shall say when I write to him: "And one night I started intending just to have a quiet little dinner with McAdams and talk a combination of business and art. And we went to a restaurant called

[Lavenue's] and came out into the cafe afterwards to have a smoke and coffee and a funny little fellow with a great big dog [a Great Dane] was sitting in the corner with a lot of artist friends and pretty soon Mac introduced him and his name was [Jo] Davidson. I did not find out that whole night that he knew you and we made a night of it, but the next night I met him again and he said something about you and he saw right away that I knew you. It was strange that I should have happened to have your book of poems with me [a collection of Musset]. I had been to the Luxembourg that afternoon and sat out in the gardens afterwards and read. I said, 'He gave me this book,' that was perhaps foolish to say, but—well I said it. We talked about you a little and he drew a picture of you which he tore out of his sketch book and gave to me. I said, 'Do you ever write to him?' He said he did but you never answered. I said, 'When you write him tell him you met me and we had an amusing night at Montmartre.'

"Did he—I wonder?

"I like him. I went to see his work and he has done some good things, I think."

Jo Davidson, twenty-five at this time, is a prototype of the hungry, ambitious young American artist in Paris because he can get better training there than in the States and live better on less while learning. Born in extreme poverty on New York's Lower East Side, the son of Russian-Jewish immigrants, he, like Gertrude herself and so many of the artists she knows, has studied briefly at the Art Students League. Except for that, their interest in sculpture, and their mutual friend, they would seem to have little in common. Even physically—he is short and stocky, dark and black-bearded—the contrast is startling. And yet Gertrude responds to his energy and ambition, recognizes that a man who has supported himself by selling burned-wood portraits may, as he hopes, become a successful, perhaps the most successful, portrait sculptor of his generation.

Davidson's friend, the man to whom Gertrude is writing or thinking about writing, is John Gregory, a London-born neoclassical sculptor, four years younger than Gertrude, with features as ruggedly, if not classically, handsome as those in his sculptures. Although she does not say where they have met it was most likely also at the Art Students League or possibly, a few years later, when he was working and living in Hermon A. MacNeil's studio in College Point, Long Island, before continuing his studies in Paris and Rome. In either case, it is clear, within the context of the journal and the surviving drafts of letters, one of which is addressed to him as "Dear Vagabond," that their relationship has not been intimate until the past year when he has been in New York, before leaving to spend the summer in Plainfield, New Hampshire.

Friends of Gertrude's remember a story from that year which shows a playful side of her character seldom expressed in her journals. She made a bet with Gregory that she could walk out of a theater without being recognized by him. He lost as he watched Gertrude, veiled and bent over like a little old lady, hobble out on someone's arm.

But now, on August 6, the last day before Harry's return, Gertrude thinks again about John Gregory and continues the "letter" to him:

. . . Mon bien cher cher—how I want to write you again as I did, to pour out to you the tenderness and feeling that is in my heart and the myriad thoughts that are in my brain. And I myself said no—Myself I laid down the law, I had the nerve in the very moment of my weakness to say no, this is the end. Think of it, wasn't it wonderful. What made me do it? How many times I have asked myself that question. Was it because instinctively I understood you, or was it really strength and because I feared your power. What does it matter now except that I tied my hands and that my very soul can ache and ache and you do not offer a word of sympathy. No, not sympathy, that I do not want but understanding. And yet to be honest this is only the second time since I came away that I have *really longed* to be in touch with you. Oh I have wanted to see you and to go and do things here in Paris with you, but so have I with other people. But tonight is different. Perhaps it was Davidson did it. He brought you up like I don't know what before me and I like him, I am sure, because he likes you. In the back of my mind I know that you will not stop loving me yet awhile, and I know also that I will see you again and in the same way that I saw you before, even that I will show you this scrawl. And I was glad Davidson liked me and could talk and talk to me and sing and recite poems in every language, for what could be further than he and me unless it was the spirit of you unconsciously that brought us together. Oh mon cher, it is all strange, and I only have to wait a little while because we will meet again and we will both understand. But the real reason that I said no in N.Y. was because I did not want the responsibility to myself or to you of this, but nature knows differently and there you are. But surely if we do meet again and we are unchanged I will do one thing. Of that I promise myself, although it is selfish, I will do it for surely surely no good can come to either of us if I do not do it. I will tell you truly about myself. How many men and how serious. Then if your caring can last, why I will be honest and only with that can happiness come. One man who loved me—I told him that I did not love him and he said, "For God's sake lie to me. I know it is not true but let me forget and say just once to me 'I love you.'" That is not like you just as he is not like you, but he never forgave me I think, because I could not tell the lie for him. Perhaps it was selfish, but I would not desecrate those words for him. Would I ever have been able to forget it? They have just started playing Boheme downstairs. It is a fine clear night and I am alone. Good-bye and goodnight and when I remember that I know what I know then I say au revoir.

When Harry returns, he and Gertrude make a ten-day trip to Hungary to visit Gladys and László and, later, Mama. Harry dismisses the country in a letter to Dorothy as "an awful place," and Gertrude seems equally dismissive in her Line-A-Day filled with such brief comments as "bad trip . . . little car . . . rain . . . lake fishing." However, one such entry, "Gypsies," does mean something to her as explained in another drafted letter to John Gregory:

They tell me I must not say "très excitant" here, but in English I think it is perfectly proper. But really there was one thing I did do which was "très excitant" and that was my Hungarian brother-in-law had the best Gypsies come all the way from Pest to play for us one night up in the country. They played from 8 till 2 with scarcely a stop and I have never known what music was before. That is, emotional music. I was mad, crazy, intoxicated, anything you want. I would have done anything, gone anywhere. They played for us four people as if to an audience of the greatest account and our emotion as necessarily led them on just as they excited & stirred us. I shall never forget it, nor can anyone who has never heard them imagine what it means. How you would have loved it. I wish you could have been there. . . .

Gertrude and Harry have just one day together in Paris before he leaves again for London. They pack a lot into it—lunch at Voisin with Rollie, dinner at the Ritz with him and Lloyd and Whitney Warren, a "stupid play" which they leave early. After Harry leaves the next morning, Gertrude spends the afternoon with Whitney Warren and the evening with him, Lloyd, and Adele. The next day (August 19) Gertrude writes:

It is rather wonderful to be told perfectly frankly what a person thinks of you especially if the person has been drinking a little and it is very disagreeable and is probably the truth. I came home after it anyway with lots of ideas and a great many thoughts such as: Why take the ideas of life from the very high anymore than from the very low? And what a fool I am after making a real impression spoiling it by two words and the idea that it would be fun to write a treatise about society as we think we are and as others think us. And so on, but all much on the same lines, for after all it was on those lines that I became excited and I was. I felt as if I had been slapped in the face for a minute and then I rose smiling. Really, I did, and I consider that a good deal. For it's funny that lately I have felt that I was going through this all as something that was necessary for the future. For instance I was full of all this coming home and was to have dined with Adele, found message saying no, could write and preserve it! I will express myself in writing as well as sculpture before I die. I *must*, for I have something to say and people *must* listen. This idea has become a certainty in my mind.

Possibly the "person" here is Whitney Warren, with whom she has spent most of the previous day; or possibly Harry, with whom she was the day before. (Her busy schedule could easily have kept her away from her journal for a day.) Either way, for two weeks while she and Adele motor through southern France and Spain, Gertrude discontinues the large journal and turns to a small black notebook in which she records their itinerary; makes many rough sketches in ink, mostly of dancing and running figures; and scribbles in pencil thoughts or, more accurately, afterthoughts connected with the large journal but scattered here and there throughout the smaller book. Again, there is no way of knowing for sure whom she is writing about. Sometimes we guess Whitney Warren, sometimes John Gregory, sometimes Harry himself:

He has been an experience and I have been one to him. Well it will be easier for him to get over me thinking me a horror as he does or at least if he does not nothing matters for then he has behaved this way from a motive which I hate. I did nothing horrible and only an evil mind could think it so. Last time he insulted me I was willing to think he was carried away and had a certain right on his side, but this time I can see no excuse and the more I think of it the more I think I am right in supposing that he wanted an excuse to break with me. I did not say a word in self-defense, he called me a horrible name and I said, "What does it mean?" and he called me another horrible name and I never said one word. I just sat looking into space not understanding why he should say it and then the thought came to me there is nothing to be said if he thinks it that is the end there is no explanation and if he says it and does not mean it why that is the end too, and so I never said a word and I heard the doors close after him as he went away. The last thing he said was "I suppose I can be free" and I did say "yes" very low. I will never speak to him again till he apologizes—never—he insulted me and until he has taken it back I will not speak to him.

One thing that can never be taken from me is the knowledge that I was able once in my life to recognize a real soul. It came to me disguised and offering no allurements, but beneath the surface I beheld the real and I made it my own. Later I suffered for it but never regretted it.

The kind of person that I hate most of all is one that is unresponsive to the fine points of life, one who, fed on beef and beer, staggers through existence with the pious belief that he is doing his duty because he never breaks a commandment. He is the apotheosis of all that is revolting.

On September 2, the day before Harry is due to rejoin her in Paris, Gertrude returns to the previous large journal:

Why will some people never admit that they have had a good time? Why worry myself about things that I have sworn to myself to worry no longer over? If one has accepted the fact that people have a certain kind of a disposition which one does not like well, why make oneself unhappy about it? But for heaven's sake understand it. It has been a good while now that I have faced the fact that certain people cannot be counted on for what they say, will never do anything that is any trouble, or give up anything that they want. There is only one kind of pleasure that I can get from them and though that is not of the highest it is a bond and I will try and preserve it. Everything goes well till one expects something from the person, but if one for a minute forgets and expects something, then one can weep or gnash one's teeth or anything else. I feel strangely tonight. All the wild and ungovernable in me is aroused. I wish I were a gypsy and could take to the open road. If it is true about Willie, [either her uncle William K. Vanderbilt or his son of the same name] I understand it. It is awful, it is terrible, it is low, but the call of the blood, the desire for life and not the narrow path, but the open road. The voices of the night call, the way is open, but I will never go, at least I pray to God I will never go. Sometimes it comes over me like I know not what horrible force and I want to be free, completely, absolutely free. The only man who ever could have held me would have been the man who had my confidence and alas I have never given that. Oh the dreams of the beautiful unknown, the path of thorns that one would travel so willingly. I don't feel tonight that I will ever meet G[regory] again and I don't even want to. Life is only intolerably sad tonight with no love and no hope. Probably H[arry] feels that way often, for I cannot give him much and he is human too and must want it, and he gets no doubt the consolation from others just as I do, only it is not the real thing anymore than what I get is, but one cannot starve entirely and so stale bread is better than none. And we might both of us have had the big thing, the real thing, the understanding, but we never will together and all the ink is shiny on the page and I will never have but second best. I feel and feel tonight and I am glad, for often I feel nothing only think and think till my mind is like a cavern and I seem lost in it. My kids, my dears. I need a god more than anyone and I have none. Not even Love is my god for I know that does not last. I have braced lately, now I will not allow myself to get into an unhealthy state again. Try and do something for someone. Do it right away. What is it?

Gertrude and Harry spend several days in Paris, shopping, and dining most frequently again at Voisin and the Ritz. Adele and Rollie are often with them and Harry's sister Pauline arrives from Deauville. Finally they go off alone by car for a day at Le Mans where they watch Wright fly (once for five minutes, once for six and a half), two days at Reims, and then four days in Rennes, Quimper, Dinard, and Cherbourg where Harry considers buying brood mares. It is time to return home.

Aboard the *America*, Gertrude writes: "The trip is over and I'm going back to my normal life. I had a thought this morning for some work. 'Les Aveugles,' a group of three people walking, eyes closed, groping. It could be great. Also a column broken, around which are seated and semi-reclining figures. Sculpturesque. I can see it."

Gertrude and Harry go directly from the ship to Westbury where the children are. A few days are devoted to them—there are rides and picnics —but quickly Harry returns to his work and Gertrude to hers. For Harry there are horses to be shipped to England, others to be bought here, and a business trip to visit his mining interests in the West. John Hays Hammond, a senior executive of the Guggenheim Exploration Company, describes in his autobiography a trip at about this time to the Silver Lake mine in Colorado on which three of the Guggenheim brothers and Harry accompany him. The mine is up about 13,000 feet. From it the ore is brought down in buckets on an aerial cable. Because of a heavy snowstorm the horse trail is buried and, against company rules, Hammond decides to get to the mine in a bucket. Harry wants to go with him but Hammond will not take the responsibility. Much to Hammond's surprise when he gets to the top, there is Harry poking his head out of another bucket approaching the landing stage. Hammond writes:

He followed me into the mine and all day scrambled nimbly up and down ladders and over piles of rock. His athletic prowess stood him in good stead. In the evening we went back to the mill in two buckets as we had come. I have never seen anyone make friends more quickly with the miners, prospectors, and other old-timers than Harry Whitney. He had a personal magnetism and a disarming friendliness that made him popular in the West as well as in the East. "You could beat even Teddy [Roosevelt] if you would go into politics," I used to tell him. Harry also had his father's good judgment and generosity. In many later years of business dealings with him, there was never an enterprise in which we were associated wherein Whitney did not only urge my receiving the profits due by definite agreement, but also an additional sum to which he thought I was entitled.

Gertrude goes back and forth between her Long Island and New York studios and is again spending some time at the Colony Club where she is on the Art and Literature Committee. Not until the end of October does she return to her journal (before once again abandoning it—for more than two years):

It has certainly been a horrid blow and what makes the situation more serious is that the other man is waiting . . . if I fall, I give up the remains of his friendship. Well, that is the case and I had better face it. I love to amuse myself and I think always that I can stop just when I want. I can't. I have not the balance, the control. I let myself go for a second and there the whole thing has gone. Oh my god what am I going to do? The other man does not attract me, but I have let him make desperate love to me. As much love as you can make conversationally. He is going to do everything he can to get me and he is not the kind to stop at trifles. Now I face it. Let him go on? Yes, because he does not tempt me but only amuses me. But won't the day come when the excitement, the sensation will tempt me and then where will I be? It does amuse me to have someone in the stage he is in now—but—well all the buts in the world will not stop you and you know it. Of course I can stop whenever I want. The same old story and another friend gone.

⇐ *1909*

The new year is pretty much Harry's. During most of it, the plans that he and Gertrude make for themselves and the children center on his horses and, more specifically, on the Meadow Brook polo team of which he is captain. As 1908 marked Harry's substantial entry into British horse racing, 1909 marks it into British polo.

He and his teammates—Devereux Milburn and the brothers (J.) Montgomery and Lawrence Waterbury, with Louis E. Stoddard as reserve—are determined to bring back the America Challenge Cup, in England since 1886 and not challenged since 1902. For years Harry has bought fine English and Irish ponies so that the Meadow Brook team is one of the best mounted in the world. As recently as this past summer he has scouted the British teams twice at Rugby where he finds the polo crowd "too cheap and professional," by which he means that too many are military types, cavalry men, without the wealth, education, and social position of his own team. Any other "professionalism" (i.e., within the game itself) would have appealed to him. No one at this time does more than Harry to change the game "professionally." It is he who insists that ponies be in condition to go at top speed throughout a match, by putting in fresh ponies for each period and by insisting on a better grass field surface. And it is he who shifts the emphasis of the game from defense to offense, particularly by using the back man for long passes and goal attempts.

That back man is Dev Milburn and since 1906, when he joined the Meadow Brook Club, Harry and the Waterbury brothers have known that he is the recruit they need in order to "invade" England successfully. Dev, a powerfully built man, is by now the strongest hitter the game has had. He has been playing in the New York area since the age of fourteen, then with the team at Oxford University where he got his B.A., and then with the Myopia Club in Cambridge, Massachusetts, while getting his law degree at Harvard before returning to New York to join his late father's distinguished law firm, Carter, Ledyard & Milburn. Besides being a very experienced player—especially for a man still in his twenties, nine years younger than Harry—he is innovative and has developed a near-side backhand, instead of making his pony cross over in the traditional manner.

In addition to Harry's and Dev's specific innovations and the Waterburys' fine steady play, the Big Four, as Harry's team comes to be known, has a general style of play that is an improvement over the British. Like other contemporary American teams, the Big Four is aggressive. It meets the ball whenever possible and hits under the ponies' necks rather than using backhanders. In short the Big Four, with all of its regulars rated ten goals, is surely a threat to British domination of the sport.

Harry has an enormous amount of work to do—the logistics of housing five men, and in some cases their families, as well as forty or more ponies and their trainers in England, much of which is his personal responsibility as captain and, in effect, manager of the team.

While Harry is busy with his plans, Gertrude's year gets off to a bad start. Since just after Christmas, Sonny and Flora have had measles. By New Year's Day in Westbury, Barbara has caught them too, and Gertrude has a cold. On January 4 she writes in her Line-A-Day that she is "In bed with tonsillitis" and five days later, on her thirty-fourth birthday, that "4 people remember it this year," but at least she is over her illness and goes with James Earle Fraser to *Pelléas et Mélisande.* Except for a few dinner parties, there are no more daily lines until May, when Gertrude, the children, and the Waterbury brothers board the *Mauretania* to join Harry in England. There, near Windsor, he has rented Oakley Court, on beautifully kept grounds overlooking the Thames. Harry has a special train meet his family and the Waterburys at Liverpool and take them to Windsor.

The Big Four, with Stoddard playing regularly before Milburn's arrival, has an uneven record—dutifully recorded by Gertrude—but even though some preliminary matches are lost, it is already recognized that Milburn will make a big difference and that the American team is better mounted than the British. There is the general complaint that the American millionaire has bought all the good British ponies, the cry "You cannot play polo on foot!" and finally a successful appeal for the loan from British players and clubs of ponies for the big matches, the best of three, at Hurlingham. The third match is unnecessary. The Big Four wins decisively, 9–5 June 23, 8–2 July 5. Through these two months of polo and many horse-racing and coaching events in which Harry is also involved, he, Gertrude, and the children receive and are received by the King and Queen and other members of the British aristocracy, especially the Pagets, Consuelo, and the Hurlingham team's Lord Wodehouse (surely not part of the cheap, professional polo crowd). It is a period during which Gertrude and Harry are particularly close to each other and also to the children. They all do a lot of boating on the Thames and Gertrude is constantly encouraging during the polo matches. In addition to more general support, she sets up a system of "nurses" for each player and is herself "Chief Nurse," as Harry testifies in engraved letters, below the gilded image of a polo player, on a silver pillbox.

Between matches Gertrude makes several short trips to Paris and sees some of her artist friends—among them, McAdams, Lee, O'Connor, and Davidson—and she receives letters from John Gregory, which, though addressed to "Dear Lady," assert a continuing and increasing desire to be independent of her largesse and a refusal to be "toadying."

Jimmie Appleton is still writing his "Dear Lady" letters too. In one, on July 24, he says that he will not be able to sail in mid-August as he expected. ". . . It was a great disappointment, especially after hearing from you about a possibility of a trip with the Duchess [Adele] and Rollie. . . . What have you been doing since the great polo victories? Did you start right off on a spree or are you still being very, very good? . . . Every time I think of that Duchess, Rollie & Queen trip I kick myself & cuss my luck."

There is no *Travels in Foreign Countries and in the Mind* with which to answer Jimmie's questions in detail. But now there is really no need for such a book. In 1902, Gertrude was much more desperately seeking her identity, particularly in art; and attempting to define her situation, particularly in marriage. By now she has come to accept, however reluctantly, the independence of Harry's interests in business and sports (so often combined) and in other women, just as she accepts the independence of her own career in sculpture and of her "flirtations" with other men. No, this trip is not a sustained spiritual journey; it is more simply a vacation, a well-earned change, however restless, from her own work and from Harry's polo and horse-racing conquests.

After the polo matches, the Whitneys and the J. Burdens move, for the end of the racing season, from Oakley Court to a house in Newmarket and rent hotel accommodations for their children and the "Mademoiselles" at Dinard on the Brittany coast. Before settling the children there for most of the rest of the summer, Gertrude takes them on day's outings to the Louvre and St. Germain and, with her mother, to Versailles. As soon as the children leave, Gertrude makes a quick round of studios—Edgar McAdams', where she has worked a little this summer, and those of the sculptors Arthur Lee and Michael Brenner and the sculptor become painter Morgan Russell. With that fast tour behind her, she starts on the more leisurely one with Adele and Rollie to Venice, via Milan, while Harry goes to Carlsbad with Bunny Hare and Phil Lydig.

In Venice, the Queen and the Duchess, escorted by Rollie, see and resee all the sights, moving from one to the next by foot or gondola and breaking their ardent tourism with swims at the Lido, drinks there and at cafés on the Piazza San Marco, meals in elegant restaurants, and an occasional visit to an artist's studio or to a friend's yacht anchored in the harbor. After two weeks Adele leaves and Rollie and Gertrude make a trip to Padua. Then Gertrude leaves him and goes on alone to Verona and Milan before returning on August 9 to Paris where an important letter awaits her from John Barrett, director of the International Bureau of American Republics, asking her to do a fountain sculpture for the Pan-American Building in Washington, D.C. As she sits alone in her room at the Hotel Brighton on the Rue de Rivoli, we can almost see her eyes brighten, her lips stretch into a smile, before she telegraphs her acceptance. Ideas for the fountain, "which will not be simply another Pan," are already forming in her mind as she goes out to meet Adele Burden, Helen Whitney, and Charles Draper, the perennial bachelor who has just been with Helen in Trouville, in much the same role as Rollie's with Gertrude in Italy.

While waiting for Harry to arrive from Carlsbad, Gertrude writes a little portrait of Helen Hay Whitney:

When I first met her she was in the heyday [pun?] of her youth, a rather gypsy-looking girl with enticing brown curls on the nape of her neck, a slim figure, vivacious, and a ready gift for writing poetry inherited from a brilliant father. She was the college belle, men & boys flocked around her. At the age of twenty-two [1898] a book of her verses was published and attracted considerable comment on its own merits [and in 1907, *Gypsy Verses*, dedicated "To G.V.W. because she is my friend."] . . . She made a love match. She had had every advantage both from a worldly standpoint & an intellectual one. Her husband in the same strata of life was full of charm, clever, a first-class sportsman. . . . There was only one dissimilarity in their tastes. He did not like intellectual people and she did not like sports. He was proud of her poetical ability and she of his prowess in sports. Had she not married she would have drifted into literary company. . . . She had (as I see it now) two failings which wrecked her life. 1st, an inferiority complex greatly exaggerated by reason of her jealous love for her husband & not being appreciated among his friends—and [2nd], her fear of leaving him at times to indulge in her own desires. It was a fatal mistake. . . .

Gertrude goes on to describe Helen now as a "misfit . . . playing a part & playing it continuously, with no relaxation. . . ." Payne, Gertrude says, is "tied to" a different woman from the one he married. "Everything in her bore witness to her frustration. . . . She grew very fat. . . ." In this sketch Gertrude's identification with Helen is obvious, her projection perhaps less so, for in later years, after Payne dies at an early age, it is not to poetry that Helen returns but to Payne's sporting life; as head of the Greentree Stable, she will become "first lady of the American turf." Once again Gertrude is telling herself that she must follow her career, must be true to her own being, in mind, spirit, and body. She has an increasingly intense fear of becoming fat, as symbolic of abandoning not only the body but the dreams of one's youth. More and more she exercises, dances, and takes long walks.

☙

When Harry arrives in his Renault, he and Gertrude leave an hour or so later for Dinard. For two days there, they and the children do a lot of swimming in the very cold water and make plans to have Flora join Gertrude on an automobile trip from Paris to Switzerland and northern Italy and for Sonny to join his father for shooting at Holwick. Then Gertrude and Harry get in the car again, assuring the older children that they will see them in a few days, giving little Barbara a more lasting hug, and off they go, via Rouen, to Calais where Harry gets the boat to England while Gertrude returns to Paris, stopping on the way to see churches and cathedrals in Lille, Amiens, and Beauvais.

After Flora and Mademoiselle join Gertrude, she fits her daughter into as many of her own plans as possible. Before and after their trip, besides the usual rounds of shops and restaurants (often with Helen), Arthur Lee visits Gertrude and Flora at the hotel and they in turn visit Jo Davidson at his studio. Gertrude and Flora are clearly having fun together, and Harry writes from Holwick: "Today at last it did not rain much and we had a pretty good shoot, 227 brace in a high wind. Sonny was out with us and had a fine time."

The family reunites in Paris, then goes to London where they spend most of their time with Pauline and Almeric. From The Deepdene, the Pagets' home in Dorking, Gertrude writes:

Dear Mr. Davidson,

I am so sorry I could not come back and see you as I wanted to have a talk about several things.

I am going to send you a check at the risk of your thinking me presumptuous, partly because if you do come to America I want you to try Flora again and partly because some time I want the torso of the woman that you have done. Will you take it like that?

I hope you come to America. It's good to go and look around there once in a while just for the interest, come and look at me! too. Anyway, whatever you decide, thank you for the good times you have given me and for your kindness.

Au revoir

G. Whitney

This is one of many examples of Gertrude's responsiveness to other artists. Unfortunately few documents survive. In the early years of Gertrude's career they were not, typically, saved (Davidson's are an exception) and in the later years they were, again typically, destroyed, probably at Gertrude's request.* A different kind of example exists in a reply to Gertrude, written at about the same time, by the dancer Ruth St. Denis:

Dear Mrs. Whitney,

Your letter took my breath away! but in this breathless condition I will try and explain that I don't take pupils in a regular way as such—but quite informally I enjoy helping anyone who is really serious in their love of expression by movement.

On Sunday next we go to Scotland for two weeks—but expect to return at the end of that trip—and if you are still in town and would like to have me help you a few times—to arrange some dances I would do so with pleasure—you should try to think out one or two dances—or impressions that appeal to you most—get a collection of good music and some reels etc. and then I would come and help you to get order out of dreams!—that's the way I do.

Yours Sincerely

Ruth St. Denis

If this method!! appeals to you—will you send me a line in about three weeks time—here and then we could see if there would be time for both of us to work a little.

Alas, there is no time now for dancing. Gertrude and her family are about to return home on the *Lusitania*, and she is anxious, perhaps more

* In 1949 John Sloan wrote (in *Juliana Force and American Art*): "No one will ever know the extent of the private benefactions Mrs. Whitney performed. . . . The records have been destroyed, probably at Mrs. Whitney's request. But of my own knowledge I know of innumerable artists whose studio rent was paid, or pictures purchased just at the right time to keep the wolf from the door, or hospital expenses covered, or a trip to Europe made possible."

so than any of them, to get to New York. She wants to begin work on the new commission and her impatience, despite many friends aboard ship, probably accounts for her entering, for the first time in years, the ship's daily run in her Line-A-Day. Almost as soon as they arrive, Gertrude goes to her studio to confer with John Barrett and with Albert Kelsey of the architectural firm of Kelsey and Cret, about the terms of the commission. They settle on $1,000 for a full-size (eight-foot-high) plaster cast and arrange to meet in Washington the following week to examine the fountain site. "They got me cheap," Gertrude writes later in a story about this commission. Preliminary work—research and progressive studies—is substantial. The fountain has two superimposed basins, supported by a column on which there are three figures in relief, each representing a period in Mexican civilization—the Mayan, the Aztec, and the Zapotecan. The fountain is decorated with hieroglyphs of these periods, and from the lower basin eight feathered serpents' heads spout water. Since Gertrude has never been in Mexico, she must have visited many museums and libraries, studying Mexican objects, photographs, and texts.

At the same time—through the fall, spent mostly in Westbury—Gertrude continues to sponsor art classes at Greenwich House and for many weeks shares her studio assistant (formerly one of Rodin's) Edward Minazzoli with Herbert Haseltine, an accomplished sculptor, specializing in horses whom Harry has commissioned to do the Big Four. Haseltine fits well into the Whitney household. Born in Rome in 1877 of American parentage (his father William Stanley Haseltine was a well-known landscape painter and a National Academician), he came to America in 1893 for further schooling, ultimately attending Harvard until junior year. He is an artist whose talent and social acceptability (he is also a cousin of Malvina Hoffman) Gertrude and Harry can both appreciate, and they do so to such an extent that it interferes with his work. He writes years later to Flora:

> . . . finding that I would never get seriously to work if I continued to sit up late, I confided to your mother the unheard of plan to cut out dinner and have supper with you children and Mademoiselle instead, which of course I thoroughly enjoyed. Everything I needed for my work, your mother saw that I got it: the studio arranged at the end of the barn, the wooden horses for the recalcitrant riders to pose on. Eddy Minazzoli put at my disposal to assist. I shall never forget the day she and I plotted to have plaster casts made of the heads of the four players. Your father first, and how he laughed at the discomfort of the others as one after the other they had to go through the ordeal and how Larry, unable to stand it any longer and go through it, pulled off the unset plaster from his face to breathe for fresh air.

1909 ends with a blizzard. Beginning on Christmas Day, just after the arrival in Westbury of Mama and Regi and Cathleen, Gertrude notes

"Snowing hard" and by December 31 "Roads still impossible." But real as this snow is, it is no more so than the blizzard of things which awaits Gertrude and Harry in New York. James Henry ("Silent") Smith, the Wall Street financier who has purchased William C. Whitney's house at 871 Fifth Avenue, has died and the executors of his estate have prepared a sumptuous illustrated catalogue of "The Palatial Mansion and its Exceedingly Rare and Costly Artistic Furnishings and Embellishments." The four-story, approximately 54-room building (55 feet on Fifth Avenue, 200 feet on 68th Street, completely redone by Stanford White for Whitney a dozen years before) is to be auctioned Tuesday, January 18, and the unattached contents (914 catalogue items of art, furniture, and furnishings, not including linens, silverware, china, or other "ordinary" household equipment) during the remainder of that Tuesday, the following four days, and two evenings. The house is furnished with Renaissance and Baroque furniture, most of it French and much of it tapestried; dozens of oriental rugs and pieces of pottery; French and Flemish tapestries; exotic screens; sculptures by minor Italians and by Saint-Gaudens; and hundreds of paintings, of which many are anonymous or "School of" but many too are by Van Dyck, Cranach, Murillo, Lawrence, Gainsborough and, among the Americans, John La Farge and Harry W. Watrous. Most of what is at 871 once belonged to William C. Whitney. Harry, again identifying profoundly with his father, does not want to see the collection broken up. He decides to preclude the auction by making an offer for everything—the building ($1,600,000) and its contents (about $400,000, subject to adjustment by appraisal). We don't know Gertrude's reaction to the purchase, but it is probably not as affirmative as that of Harry's sister Dorothy, who hears about it in Ceylon and is overjoyed that this home she has loved will be back in the family as a monument to the spirit of William C. Whitney. No, surely now Gertrude is more involved with her existing studios and with the hope for a permanent one in Paris than with any desire for a larger, more lavish New York home. Eight seventy-one—as much as the Big Four—is Harry's. Gertrude's Line-A-Day comments on it during the next few weeks are indeed terse.

≈ *1910*

JANUARY 3: To town. Negotiations for house at 871 Fifth Ave.

JANUARY 4: Harry left for South [presumably Aiken]. Settled about house. Dined at H. Cushing's studio.

JANUARY 22: Dev dined. Last night in old house.

JANUARY 23: Moved. Lunched Adele's. Musicale Birdie's [Mrs. William K. Vanderbilt, Jr.'s]. 20 for dinner 871.

The dining room is, of course, one which Gertrude and Harry have known well from the days when William C. Whitney was in residence. Gertrude never described it then and she doesn't now. Yet it is a perfect introduction to the opulence of the house, though this 36-by-33-foot room has only about a third the area and ceiling height of the grand ballroom, adjoining it, through a conservatory, to the east. Here is its description in the Smith catalogue:

The Dining Room is on the right of the Main Hall and overlooks 68th Street, from which it is lighted by a bay window, with a single window on each side. The three interior walls are entirely covered, from baseboard to ceiling, with old Italian paintings. Toned with age, these paintings constitute a unique decoration for a New York interior, and the room easily ranks among the most notable in this very notable mansion. The paintings are on canvas, applied to the walls, and include innumerable figures wearing the costumes of many nations.

The entrance doorway from the Main Hall is provided with a monumental frame, gilded in every part and known as the Golden Doorway. Two Corinthian columns with decorated drums stand on plain square bases. The entablature has a frieze of scrolls and arabesques, and on the summit is the lion of St. Mark.

The ceiling was brought from a palace in Genoa. It is of the coffered type, with forty-two panels, seven one way and six the other. The squares have a black ground, with an arabesque decoration in monochrome and a central rosette. The separating beams have a similar decoration on a blue ground, with gilt rosettes at the crossings. The whole is surrounded with an outer border of arabesques on a blue ground. The oak floor has a border of mottled red marble.

The mantel, in the centre of the north wall, is one of the most interesting in the Mansion. It is a beautiful antique of Fiesole stone. The hollow curve of the facing has a small diaper of fleur-de-lis, and slender columns on decorated bases support consoles that carry the overmantel. The latter is very delicately carved, with small pilasters and panels and a frieze with groups and arabesques. The large central panel above contains a representation of a fight on a bridge and includes a number of figures in high relief. On each side is an arched niche with a single figure in the round. Similar niches on the sides are without figures. Over all is a plain slab applied directly to the wall, on which are three shields. All of this beautiful structure was once picked out with gold, much of which is still visible. The fireback is iron, with a fleur-de-lis diaper, and a central panel showing two cupids upholding a shield.

In this baronial space, Gertrude's and Harry's twenty guests sit at an eleven-foot-square carved mahogany table, each on an Italian Renaissance chair upholstered with ruby-red velvet cut in a design of leafy scrolls on a golden silk background. At least as recorded, the move has been easy, strikingly casual, even allowing that the details would have been handled by existing and new staff.

Once at 871, Gertrude returns immediately to work on the Aztec Fountain, as she has come to call it. During the next two months or so, though going to the opera and dinner parties as usual, she spends sometimes as much as twelve hours a day at her studios. In the Westbury one, she now keeps a large snake to study for the fountain's stylized spouts, and she is in frequent correspondence with John Gregory and Herbert Haseltine (who has just left for Europe)—both of whom are very supportive in their letters. Gregory is generous with anthropological and aesthetic advice:

I believe that your idea of the development of the Aztecs through the Red men to the future is based on error. I read parts of half a dozen books today and could find nothing to bear out your argument. [He cites sources in detail.] By placing your woman figure in front you create two equal positions for the other figures and I think there is good psychological reason for this arrangement. You thus have a pyramid with the really important idea at the top, as it were. [He sketches a diagram.] I consider the woman as positive while the others are negative—she is the voice crying in the wilderness. She personifies the triumph or possibilities of civilization over unenlightenment.

Herbert Haseltine's letters—first from aboard ship, then from Paris—are generous too but in a more personal and playful way, less specifically professional:

Where are you this instant (6 in the afternoon)? In the studio of course, working natürlich. . . . How is Burnett [Gertrude's butler]? . . . Paris may be all right but MacDougal Alley for me—"Oh yes"— "Oh no"—"You can't go upstairs"—"There's never been such work done in the Alley before" [Hazy is quoting Burnett] etc.—That's what I want to hear, and no matter how carefully I listen I never hear these words spoken on the Bullyvards. . . . How is the fountain? What are your plans—No artist makes plans so you haven't got any—Yess. . . . When are you coming abroad? I almost bought a wrought iron well for you, also a very amusing chandelier—I thought . . . might be a foundation for your studio in Paris. Studio in Paris. Studio in Paris.

Studio in Paris. S.I.P. *Sip.* When you sip your cocktails it will remind you of the idea.

Gertrude needs no reminder. As she completes her formal Aztec Fountain and works on such smaller, more private, though still Rodinesque pieces as *Paganisme Immortel* and two separate but related figures of *Boy with Pipes* (Pan-like) and *The Dancer* or *Dancing Girl* (Gertrude-like), she is very aware that moving from midtown to MacDougal Alley has not released her from New York's social pressures. By mid-February a dinner party of hers has increased to thirty guests—the Philip Lydigs, the Moses Taylors, the Frank Polks, August Belmont, W. K. Vanderbilt, Jr., Lady Paget (visiting the States), the Victor Sorchons, the Osgood Fields . . . and at least one fashionable society artist, Prince Troubetskoy, who does a portrait of Gertrude at about this time—and by the end of the month another has grown to a hundred. Then, in addition to many of those at the previous, comparatively large party (and in addition, also, to a troupe of Russian dancers, including Pavlova and Mordkin), Gertrude and Harry have more relatives (e.g., Cornelius and Grace; Alfred, who has divorced Ellen French and is with his future wife, Mrs. Margaret McKim; Regi and Cathleen; Harol Stirling Vanderbilt; Adele and J.; Ruth Twombly; Helen and Payne), old friends (e.g., the Cushings, the Whitney Warrens, Lloyd Warren, Jim Barnes, Charlotte Barnes, Rollie Cottenet, Charles Draper, Lispenard Stewart, William Stackpole, Bobby Sands, Eleo Sears, Worthie Whitehouse, Bunny Hare), and new friends, mostly Gertrude's (e.g., Ruth and Dorothy Draper, Bob Chanler, James Fraser, Mrs. Stanford White, Edward Knoblock, Norman Hapgood). It is a familiar catalogue, except for the decorator Dorothy Draper (married to Charles's brother), the playwright Knoblock, and the editor and writer Hapgood—nevertheless a lot of people to deal with, more than Gertrude knows in Paris.

Two days after this big supper party, Gertrude receives word that her "marble group"—*Paganisme Immortel,* which Eddy Minazzoli has been reproducing in stone from her plaster—has been accepted by the Academy. And at about the same time, in this year (like the previous one, without journals) Gertrude receives what amounts to a postscript to her correspondence with Ruth St. Denis, now back from England—another letter in which the salutation must have something to do with the way Gertrude presents herself:

Dear Lady!
I often go to tea at Nautine's. It's delightfully odorous and the tea good. Would you & your sister-in-law [Helen Whitney] like to come one afternoon next week? (This week is pretty "full up.") I've always wanted to hear what you wanted to do.
Monday or Tuesday would do me—come and fetch me at the theatre—or meet up in the little balcony.

We don't know whether Gertrude sees Ruth St. Denis on this occasion. We do know, though, that she attends a great number of social and cultural events (often a combination of the two) during this very busy period. In March there's a dinner party followed by bridge; the next night one from which she goes to *Electra* with Charles Draper; the next night *Salome* followed by a weekend in Westbury; when she returns, a lecture by the artist-architect Paul Chalfin and then dinner at the Delanos'; the next night dinner at the Fields'. Not until March 11 does she get to the Academy to see *Paganisme Immortel,* and not for another week of more operas and more dinner parties can she make the Line-A-Day entry: "Worked. Dined home with Harry." One wants to add an exclamation mark—the simple event is that rare.

By late March Gertrude has completed the fountain, and on those days when she is at the studio—rarer now—William Stackpole visits often. "Stack came for a little while. . . . P. C. [either Paul Chalfin or Phil Carroll, a brilliant lawyer descended from the aristocratic Maryland Carrolls— both of whom she's seeing frequently] and Stack." But mostly she's thinking about Paris and about S.I.P., that Studio in Paris. She continues to correspond with Herbert Haseltine about it and, though no other letters survive, it is likely that she has such friends, colleagues, and protégés there as Davidson, O'Connor, McAdams, Lee, and Russell—to whom at this time she sends a generous check—all out scouting for a suitable place.

Gertrude is also now planning a real (and really elaborate) studio in Westbury to replace the improvisatory old blacksmith shop. She goes over her requirements with her friend the architect William Adams Delano, whose well-connected firm, Delano and Aldrich—the designer of the Colony among other clubs—has been the subject of a spoofing advertisement in the program of the recent Beaux Arts Ball:

DELANO AND BALRICH

We have four rejected designs for an Art Gallery
for sale below manufacturer's cost.
These are equally desirable
for Mausoleums or Car Barns.

Bill spends a day with Gertrude in Westbury to study the site—in the woods about a quarter mile from the main house—and discussions continue until she and Harry are ready to leave for Paris.

In those weeks before leaving, Gertrude attends the first no-jury, no-award exhibition (April 1–29) of the Independent Artists, so long discussed and nurtured by Henri, Sloan, Myers, Davies, and others of their group. She is pleased to see her *Study of a Head* exhibited along with work by Gutzon Borglum, her teacher James Fraser, and only four other sculptors. (The show, in rented galleries at 35th Street and Fifth Avenue, contains primarily paintings [260] and drawings [145], with works by virtually all the American Realists.)

Also before leaving for Paris, she attends a meeting of women sculptors and two meetings concerning a small competitive exhibition of work by young artists for which she offers cash prizes (one ultimately won by John Gregory). And she visits the department store owner Benjamin Altman at his home at 626 Fifth Avenue to see his superb art collection (left on his death in 1913 to the Metropolitan Museum) and perhaps to discuss with him his interest in fostering American painting through the National Academy of Design. In the same week she goes to three of the four auctions of paintings owned by the late Charles T. Yerkes, a financier and traction magnate who acquired as much art as Altman, though not of the same consistently high quality. (Yerkes made one remark almost as notorious as William H. Vanderbilt's "The public be damned." When asked by Chicago reporters why there weren't enough streetcars, he replied, "It is the straphangers that pay the dividends." After his death in 1905 he was re-"immortalized" in Dreiser's novels *The Financier* and *The Titan.*) Gertrude buys four paintings: a large Guardi for $20,000, two small ones for $1,250 each, and a Bartoli for $3,200. On the Saturday she and Harry are to leave for Paris she takes in one more art exhibition before meeting him aboard ship. It is no surprise that in the first letters Flora and Sonny write to Paris both refer to her having "almost missed the boat."

Finally, Gertrude has her first studio in Paris—at 72 Boulevard Flandrin, a handsome *maison bourgeoise* which still stands on the corner of the boulevard in the Sixteenth Arrondissement (the Porte Dauphine *quartier*) and still contains several ateliers. It is a solid-looking seven-story building, protected by an ornamental iron entrance. In an autobiographical sketch, probably written the following year when Gertrude meets Rodin, she describes her apartment as consisting of "a fine big studio on the corner, a tiny dining room opening out on my small hall, and beyond a large bedroom and bath. Housekeeping was simple, my menage consisting of a cook [Eugénie] and a maid [Marie]. Five minutes with Eugénie in the morning left me free to work uninterrupted all day." A painting by the British artist James Pryde, done probably in 1912, gives some sense of the scale and furnishings (not yet in place). Gertrude is on a chaise (*très*) longue, as Marie makes up a canopied, crested bed at least twice her height. In *The Death Bed*, another more famous painting by Pryde, done probably a little later, Gertrude's bed is the focus of the painting, totally dominating two mysterious figures, and there are vague framed pictures on the wall, a high-backed Renaissance sedan chair, and what looks like a cluster of feathers hiding a light. Finally, in a short story of Gertrude's, she refers to a Louis XV table in the dining room on which there is always a glass bowl filled with flowers and Chinese lacquered panels in the background. All of this suggests a rather regal, though eclectic and improvised, studio/pied-à-terre, which is a far cry from the much more personal studio Gertrude is presently building in Westbury and the one which she will eventually buy in Paris.

As to the trip itself, Gertrude and Harry seem to spend most of their time separated by the Channel, though they return together in time for Fourth of July "fireworks and dancing" at Westbury and spend the next two days sailing to and from Newport on Wilson Marshall's famous racing schooner *Atlantic* with Cynthia and Arthur Burden, Mary and Charles Rumsey, Charles Draper, Dev and Monty. Soon afterward Gertrude has a "minor operation," perhaps the reason for returning from Europe. The children are at the Whitney camp in the Adirondacks and it is probable that she joins them there to recuperate, while Harry returns to England. She now writes what seems at first to be an imaginary exchange of love letters, both sides of the correspondence in her hand:

> She received in the mountains on July 31st the first letter from him since the Paris one:
>
> Dearest, I have each day in my thoughts written you a letter—a letter lost in the daily turmoil that has surrounded me—and in the uncontrollable avalanche of emotion, retrospect, longing and every other inexpressible thing which is the response to your image in my soul . . . in full accord with tradition in our lives I am writing at four in the morning of a hot restless night. . . .

As if indeed from an avalanche, on and on the words tumble for four more pages. Then:

> I have always told you that this has been graven deeper in our lives than you would realize—that you were fighting against it, only to learn that life without love is nothing—and now I'll say more—that life that fights again love that exists is an attempted inversion of natural law. . . . I want to see you before you sail. Let the woods talk to you, dearest, oh that I could as my thoughts and longings do.

With much more restraint "the woman" (i.e., Gertrude) replies:

> I was counting on a last view of you. . . . I fear I shall be far up north as I have promised to stop a few days at Bar Harbor . . . and then it will be another month before I see you again—c'est très triste tout ça.

Gertrude leaves for Paris, with Flora, Sonny, and Barbie, who will stay with Mademoiselle at the Hotel Castiglione. Aboard ship she opens a package of letters, one for all except the terminal days of the crossing. Again the letters are in Gertrude's hand, again it would seem they could be fiction:

Letters written to the steamer to Her. For Sunday Nov. 6th 1910.
My dearest:

When you start to read this I hope that you will have had a good
night's rest and feel very much refreshed. The ship will be rolling
along & you will probably have gotten about ⅓ through that dullest
of all days, a Sunday at sea. What time is it now, about 11 o'clock, &
have you finished a rather good breakfast in bed? Do you want to
know what I am doing, well, I am in church. You see I have an old-
fashioned notion that when one is in trouble, or dejected if you go to
church, it seems as if the service was meant to comfort you & you get
consolation there. And I am sad & lonely. The sunshine has gone out
for a little while & though I know it will come back, yet it does look a
little dreary just now. I miss you so, my darling, I would give the
world just to see you for one minute. . . .

Now the words roll on like waves. "For Monday" more of the same.
"For Tuesday" a sonnet beginning "When in the loneliness you leave
behind . . ." after which he asks: "Do you like it as well as when we read
it that night in front of the fire at W—[probably Westbury] just one
week ago tonight? Do you care for me as you did then? I do not want you
to long for me so that you are miserably unhappy & yet I want to think you
are caring for me so much that nothing else in the world makes any
difference. . . ." "For Wednesday" a sermon: "Let us consider ourselves
favored mortals to be blessed with such a love as ours. Let us believe that
whether we are together or apart we will be better for it, lead better lives
for it, cherish it, and hold it sacred as long as we both may live." "For
Thursday"—but by now Gertrude has stopped transcribing. The letter is
on Racquet and Tennis Club stationery:

Dearest:—

Just think of it, tomorrow you will be actually in France. You will
see Harry again & before you know you will be in your dear Paris, seeing lots of old friends and getting in touch with the artistic atmosphere you love so well.

I hope it all amuses you and makes you happy and makes you able
to do such great work as I feel sure you can do.

A trip around the country will be a rest for you & when you get
back to Paris I hope that everything will be comfortable there.

Will you forgive a few last words of advice from one who loves you
more than anything else, & cares more about your future success and
happiness than he does about anything else.

I think I can put it in a few words. *Just be true to what is best in
you.* You don't have to do anything more than that. Remember that
you are a wonderful person, that you have a role that is above the
common herd and you must not do anything which is not in keeping

with that role. I mean you are a big person and be big in everything. Don't fool around with the things that are not worthwhile in life. Don't let little people or foolish affairs have any part in your life. Don't let them count with you, and afford them opportunities of intercourse which make them intimates so that their thoughts may affect yours. You seem so much above all that to me that I do not think it can influence you. I know that you are going to give all these things their proper place in your life. That's the idea it seems to me! Not to keep them out of your life exactly but *keep them in their proper place.* Remember they are unimportant and don't ever let them affect your real life, your real self.

Last of all, my darling, remember there is one person who is always with you in his thoughts, who loves you, oh so dearly. Whose dearest wish it is to bring out what is best in you, because if you can express that to the world you will have done something great, whether you express it in your art or in your life.

Remember that every little thing you do is vital to me. Everything that you do that is unworthy of you makes for my unhappiness and every good action, everything well done makes me proud & happy.

Do not ever make the mistake of thinking anything you do does not matter. It matters more than you picture even in your vivid imagination—matters to your character, matters to your children, and matters to me.

Don't think this is a lecture, little girl. It's just my great love for you that makes me so earnest—perhaps so tiresome? And if it all bores you don't try to think of what I have said, just forget everything else and imagine that I am telling you what is first, last, and eternal "I love you." "I love you." "I love you."

W.S.

W.S. is William Stackpole, once Harry's young friend but presently, of course, much closer to Gertrude. Now fragments "From Her Imaginary History" fall into place as drafts of an ongoing letter written to him aboard ship, beginning Sunday, November 6:

Oh dear, it *was* a comfort to find your letter for me this morning. I took it out of my locked bag last night and with the fortitude of a Spartan put it under my pillow—unopened. Except that I was dying of sleep I could never have borne having it there unread. . . . I slept 13 hrs! Without one conscious moment. I sat with my electric lights [therapeutic] for 25 hot minutes and then a pine needle bath & massage made me ready for—well anything. I imagined you saying the things in your letter and a little of the thrill you give me took possession of my body and my arms ached for you. I arranged your pictures in the locket. . . .

MONDAY.

The sky is made of grey wool and so I write you, even were it blue satin I should do the same. . . .

TUESDAY.

My dearest, today I have your sonnet and it seems to me even more beautiful than when you read it to me in front of the fire that night a million years ago. And your letter makes me happy, it has so much tenderness in it, and seems to want the things I have to give always. Oh dear you have brought into my foolish life something very big. I am going to make myself a better bigger person for you. Now as I look back on the last month I see how you absorbed me, not so much at first, but gradually more and more, till I only lived with you & all else were blank spaces and waiting moments. . . .

WEDNESDAY.

Your letter this morning was as serious as mine yesterday, but five times as nice. A tiny glass of chartreuse and a great many too many chocolate caramels put me to sleep for 12 hrs. This will be a day, I fancy, with no tremors to disturb its serenity. Mrs. Hastings' brother-in-law who turns out to be a friend of Jimmie's will talk to me for a few hours and I will finish a very interesting book about [illegible]. I will think of a certain person to whom I sent a careful Marconi (by the way, is it "Billstack" or just what?) and my thoughts about him will be delightful and understandable and almost comfortable. . . . When my light was out last night I was in the studio with you again & it was one of the first nights we spent together and a great emotion held me and as you leaned towards me it seemed as if something in me would break from emotion. And you put your arms around me & took me to be entirely yours & a tremor ran through me. . . .

I have invented two new groups [of sculpture] in my head, and I want to get them into form. One is the idea of the 2 women—the animal creature created to reproduce the race, the happy savage before she has been cruelly educated by civilization; with her, is the struggling horrible example of woman today, developed enough to be dissatisfied with herself as a savage & with not enough brains or education to be able to find her fitting position. . . . My other idea is man holding by the hand a little boy, they are both walking forward, and in the eyes & face & body of the man you feel that he has given up ideals but he still walks on. . . .

THURSDAY.

Your dear "sentimental letters" as you call them. They give me such joy. Can I always make you happy? If I could only put my arms around your neck now & pull your lips down to meet mine. You would believe then what I tell you, but across the ocean a thousand years away will you feel my sincerity and devotion. You *must*. Listen —I kiss your lips—now do you?

The fog horn blew all night and it's gloomy & tedious again today. Jimmie's friend talked to me all the evening and is planning to remain longer in Paris. How foolish. As if I cared what he did. It's just the effect of a most boresome journey. It got on my nerves yesterday: "Why doesn't something happen?" . . . I did not know just at first that my love was going to be like this, so big & serious. I confess I thought I was going to keep it merely as a not too big part of my life, but that was in the past before I knew, now I want to give you all I have & I want all you have got & I know that is a lot.

It's Friday, thank God. It's just before dinner & soon J.'s friend will arrive with the cocktails, ice etc. I can't believe that I shall be in Paris soon. . . . Dearest, I have worried about you today, about things that I have never mentioned to you before, about your giving up some of your youth to me. It suddenly did not seem right. I am 34 [actually thirty-five, almost thirty-six] my life is led, I have no business to take even a slice of your youth [thirty-three] from you. . . . Listen. Let's agree to be perfectly free for these 2 months. I want you to play, to try other distractions, loves if you will & not to feel in any way bound to me. Then if at the end of the time we feel as we do now we can come to each other with open arms. . . .

Even cut into fragmentary examples, there is some chance of being misled by the disproportionate amorous emphasis of "Her Imaginary History." Though now it is obvious that Gertrude has gone beyond flirtation —and infatuation too—love is not what she is going *toward*. Her objective in having a Paris studio, as in having one in New York, is to be able to work in peace and in a supportive environment where she is taken seriously and appreciated for her own sake. The studio is the place where, the means whereby, Gertrude believes she can earn love through her work; it is only subordinately a place, an end, for love itself. Moreover, as journal material, amorous fantasy is more interesting, because more specific, than artistic fantasy. A lover, like William Stackpole, exists. An idea for a sculpture project, like those "two new groups" and many others to come, is vague until executed. And as for writing about the studio routine itself, that is deadly.

❧

Harry, who has just arrived from England, is waiting in his car at Cherbourg to take Gertrude and the children to the Hotel Castiglione. However, Gertrude must quickly have looked up Jo Davidson. On the back of the last fragment (for now) of "Her Imaginary History" she begins a note to John Gregory, written on ship's stationery, with a caricature of herself in a large plumed hat being leered at by Davidson as a horned and bearded devil. The note says:

> Back in Paris and fascinated once more by the fascinating place. Wicked old devil how he laughs at us and leads us on. I was glad to hear about the dear little frog girl. . . .

The "frog girl" is a reference to an elaborate Arabian Nights-like tale, written by Gregory and probably just transmitted by Davidson. It concerns a worshiper of the "Batrachian nymph" (i.e., Gertrude) who holds the secret of life (i.e, love). Gregory then moves from his ancient verbal parable to substantially the same visual one. His sketch, to which Gertrude has replied, shows a nymph on a cliff bending down to kiss a young man standing below her on a projecting twig, under which he writes:

> It is called *Illusions* . . . the heart-interest is the question, "How long will it hold him?" not "How did he get there?" . . . I came across a quotation the other day, "L'amour fait passer le temps" and I have changed it into "Le temps fait passer l'amour." . . . I am working away steadily and quite uninterestedly. Are you having a great time? I suppose so. Oh! Paris!

Between November 13 and December 2, Gertrude and Harry and possibly the children—by now the *Motor Log* lists only major departures and arrivals—travel to Bourges, Lyon, Avignon, Toulouse, Pau, Biarritz, Bourgos, Madrid (with a side trip to Toledo), and back to Paris. There, for the first time in more than two years, she feels the need to keep a journal, as such, and for twelve and a half francs buys one bound in black leather with a heavy lock on it. She begins:

DEC. 5th—MONDAY. PARIS.

Yesterday Harry and the children went to England and I was left alone here. I walked out into the streets and I held my head up and it seemed no effort to move and every corner hid a possibility and each beautiful thing was an inspiration. The studio was in a terrible state with no hope of getting in even the working part for a few days. I got two letters from America and another this morning [from William Stackpole]. They made me feel as no letters have since I used to get them from J. [probably John Gregory] and over the whole world I got a thrill and felt faint with wanting. I spent the afternoon with H. [Herbert Haseltine], went drifting about and went to the Luxembourg, in the evening he insisted I should go out and dine (an exception) and it was rather nice. We had a good dinner, I had a drink when I came in, a cocktail, and we had champagne for dinner. I was a little excited, not really, and coming home he suddenly grabbed me and kissed my lips. It is terrible, but I loved it, and felt it through and through. He said, "Are you glad to see me again?" and I felt quite faint. That was all. I got hold of myself in a second and I don't think he knew how affected I was.

Today I was out of the hotel before nine and walked a lot after doing what I could at the studio. It is rather hopeless and I shall not get in the living part till after Xmas.

R[amsey] T[urnbull, the friend of Jimmie Appleton's whom Gertrude has met aboard ship; like Jimmie, very involved with the breeding of beagles] came to see me this afternoon and was rather nice. He either likes me or wants me to think he does, I am not quite sure which. I like him because of his admiration and there is something attractive about him too. Shall I encourage him for fun? He will not really feel badly and there is not much in the way of fun now.

I am really longing to get to work and feel nervous and restless. Am riding early tomorrow, so will put my light out. It is 10.

11 o'clock—My mind gets thinking, thinking and I can't sleep. About nothing of importance or worthwhile, still just thinking. My china, how the pictures will look on the gray walls? When S[tackpole] comes, the hour he will get here and how I will meet him? Shall we spend our first evening in the studio or how? Will the red damask I bought in Madrid look well on the piano? Shall I pay my calls tomorrow or wait till my motor arrives? When I go to England will I have to stay more than 2 days? Shall I get R.T. to take me to the opera? What music would I feel like hearing? What does it mean, the fact that I liked H[aseltine] to kiss me and that still I believe I am in love with someone else? Would I like anyone I liked and who was attractive to kiss me? Shall I come back here and dress right after my ride? Shall I read or draw only in spare moments? I will write S. perhaps that will calm me.

TUESDAY DEC. 6th

I slept very badly. Too much coffee perhaps, anyway did not want to get up at 7:30. Took a ride in the Bois, very muddy, but nice. Went to the studio where I got a letter and a cable. "Thanks for cable miss you always much love." After dressing I wandered again stopping in antique shops & enjoying it.

I had an idea—about the only good one I guess all day. Suppose the sight and understanding of beautiful things made you more beautiful. It might perfectly be true. What made me think of it was very simple and personal. I was going along in a very simple and not exaggerated suit and no one was paying any attention to me. I saw a few things I liked and suddenly I noticed that people in the street were looking at me etc. etc. That idea would make a good short story. I added to my letter to S. and sent it off tonight. There will be a few days now when I don't hear. The studio is painted but not dry. I drew a little today. Feel restless again tonight. Shall draw and then to bed.

WEDNESDAY DEC. 7th

Not such a busy day. Started at 10:15 went to 72 [Boulevard Flandrin] and met Hazy, etc. Got letter from S. Chose a lovely stuff for my walls. Decided some important questions. Etc. etc. A good many dull things and a few pleasant ones. Went out to dinner with H., quite nice. Yes, rather nicer than usual I think.

It is wonderful to look ahead to *nothing* unpleasant. No dinners, no bores, nothing but work and the things I want. Painting in studio itself will be finished tomorrow—that means my things can be unpacked the next day. Shades put up Saturday, work start Sunday. Hurrah! Drew a little today, tried to be freer if less correct. It's 10:30, must put the light out.

THURSDAY DEC. 8th

This has been a strenuous physical day starting with massage at 8:30. Ride at 11 and roller skating for 1½ hrs. The Luxembourg was thrown in and of course a visit to the studio. I wish dreadfully that I could start working. Shall console myself by thinking of subjects for groups. Take the simplest and most frequently experienced feelings, for instance. Love, hate, friendship, passion, faithfulness, suffering, joy, mental torture, conscience pains, jealousy, envy, longing, desire, cunning, self-sacrifice, hope, morbidness, etc. These are all things that everyone understands. Take them as subjects for a series of works. I have done despair, passion and paganism, also longing in the moth [perhaps abbreviation of *mother*]. I had a good idea for joy, in the mother walking forward holding the child high up in her arms, the 2 laughing at each other. I think I will work that, it was good. Pleasure might make a good one.

Then there could be more subtle ideas expressed, probably by more than one figure—to this series could belong such subjects as my favorite idea of the separateness of humans in spite of all physical and even intellectual nearness. The two women—the old and the new and the fall of the child, the sufferer between them, the satiety of the body in contrast to the eternal unsatisfaction of the mind. The big wanting of little things, the roads that lead to the unknown, the mystery of the future, the touch of genius, the big stagnation of riches, the wall that separates kings from the world, the "common touch." That's from a poem of Kipling's that begins "If you can keep your head when all about you, Are losing theirs and blaming it on you."

It's a bully poem and holds a world of philosophy. There would be an unlimited number of these, and the more subtle the more to the point.

Then there could be just beauty—a simple standing figure of a man, so beautiful and so beautifully modeled (!) that it need have no other meaning.

Then a series of monumental works. Large groups for public places. The industries, fountains, endless subjects for fountains there are and very attractive I think. Dancing fawns and laughing kids, or caryatid. My old pose of a man holding something on his shoulder was good as a pose, the seated woman, legs crossed and stiff position of the arms holding a basin over his head or with arm like this [rough sketch of figure]. Monuments to dead people. A sarcophagus, I want to do for myself. The shape of the old ones and in the reliefs to represent my life symbolically. For instance, up to the present time (and I can go no farther) the biggest items have been in my life—love and struggle. Struggle for the things I wanted and against the influences of stagnation etc. around me. So I should take these 2 splendid subjects for the long sides of the box. At the ends I should let "youth" meaning children be at one end and "pleasure" at the other. These subjects could all be made into something fine but the difficulties of a long composition of that kind are various and many. I think in feeling and execution it should be very modern. I lived today and from that standpoint I should like it to represent me. . . .

During the next several days, as the decoration of the studio is being completed, Gertrude makes many more notes and sketches for future projects, answers a letter from Stackpole, visits the Louvre and, with Ramsey Turnbull, has dinner at Laperouse and goes to *Madame Butterfly*. Finally, on Tuesday, December 13, she is able to begin sculpting. ". . . It was splendid. All day I felt that life was really beginning for me. . . . I am going to do *nothing* but what helps my work. I am mad about it. Nothing else in life counts. . . ."

But Gertrude's exhilaration is short-lived. The following day she writes:

Worked all day, lunched at Hazy's. His sister and [Le Marquis Emanuele de] Rosales [an Italian sculptor with a studio in London whose bronzes are highly finished and often inlaid] were there. Oh! so few days before I must go to England, see all those very nice but far distant people. I got two letters tonight from them and it made me hate the idea more than ever. I can think of no possible reason not to go, but I can cut it very short. Arrive afternoon of 23d leave 27th morning and I can spend all my time with the kids. I feel entirely out of humor for those people. I know what will happen, I will get an awful fit of the blues and drink all the time to get over it, be a wreck when I get back. However this is one of the hardships that must be faced. Think of what you are going to do. Friday I leave. Eight days still. How much can I do in that time? Think. Don't worry your head over what a lot of foolish idiots are doing. I don't but I don't want to have to be there to see them. In my mind they are thoroughly on my nerves. Courage. How selfish I am and I must be if I want to accomplish anything. Will I ever be any good. Probably not really. Is it all worth it—shall I give up my life of intrigue? That question has strangely enough become ever present in my mind.

Over the holidays Gertrude puts aside the new journal, but in her Line-A-Day we see that she follows exactly her plan to cut the visit to England very short. This may not be only because those waiting for her, excepting the children, are distant or foolish. Among them are "the other woman," Gertrude's cousin by marriage. "She" is "in house"—i.e., Little Dalby Hall in Melton Mowbray, Leicester—Gertrude writes tersely on arrival, along with Helen and Archie Alexander, Maude and Larry and Monte Waterbury, and Cynthia and Arthur Burden. The following day Mary [Harriman] and Charles Cary ("Pad") Rumsey arrive. That may be some relief as Pad is an accomplished sculptor, though one, like Hazy, who does primarily horses and mounted polo players rather than the "big themes" which interest Gertrude. However, she notes a reaction neither to the Rumseys' arrival nor to the few other events which are recorded in the Line-A-Day. The Christmas tree, church on Christmas Sunday, a walk with the children, the hunt, the return to Paris, *Louise* at the Opéra Comique on New Year's Eve—all appear in a sort of shorthand that will not be expanded until . . .

≈ *1911*

New Year's Night Jan 1st.

Such a long time since I wrote and I am already at a point when it is hard to write the truth, at any rate there is my visit to England which was almost entirely excruciating agony. And all day going over I got myself in the mood, read, and thought of Harry and the kids and as soon as I arrived I felt the antagonism of H. who came to meet me at the station. His eye wandered etc. and at once he began to tell me all the hunting details. Of course I felt a million miles away and the feeling grew. Flora and Sonny sat up to see me and I was able to plead fatigue pretty soon and go to bed. I was tired for I missed connections and did not arrive till almost ten. Then I confess everything seemed to die inside of me, I felt as if life were passing away amid my full consciousness and in greatest agony. First I said to myself I must hold on, then I was afraid that if I held on I would not be able to later and I said now take off the brakes—but to cry was impossible, I have a dim idea that I was in front of the sofa on the floor biting pillows. I tried to analyze my feelings so as to be able to comfort myself, it was hard. Of course first and foremost was the idea that the step I had taken [i.e., establishing a studio in Paris] might have built an everlasting wall. Then the terrible reaction from the peace and quiet and happiness of the life I had had. Then the boredom of what should not bore, then the feeling that these people did not want me, and the fear that I had let others interests and people go unquestioned in Harry's life (not questioned in words). In other words the sacrifice that I had made might be so much too big. My nerves you can imagine were in an awful state and something happened I am sorry to say that night that has never happened (except if we were having an open quarrel) before. I let him see that I did not want him. I tried harder than I have tried for a long time to do anything to hide it, but I could not. Then a little later I made a most terrible effort and he took me although he knew that I could not feel it, I showed him that I wanted him to. It was a terrible night and I scarcely slept. Everything broke and I cried and cried and in the morning could hardly get control of myself. That day I arranged Xmas tree and presents etc. and the evening was not so bad. The next day Xmas, we were very busy. I went to church with Helen Alexander and for a walk with Flora in the afternoon. Harry never asked me to do anything with him or came and talked to me. I don't think we ever spoke to each other except in bed.

Monday night I made a terrible effort (not that I was not making enough all the time) and I said how sorry I was to be going and how I felt that I had been terribly out of it (he said he did not think so and that he thought I would like it if I stayed and I said I could not give up now the thing I had attempted to do). We had a rather nice talk but through it all I felt most horribly far away and wondered if he did too. Probably not at all the way I felt. When you are leading that sort of a life you bother your head very little about feelings and shades of emotion. The trouble is my life exaggerates them.

The kids were dear and most satisfactory. I left Tuesday morning and for various uninteresting reasons only caught the night train to Paris. It was not as bad as I thought, but cold. I slept after leaving Calais till we arrived in Paris. Took a bath, breakfast and dashed full of enthusiasm to the studio. I started a head of [Adolphe] Ramon [an assistant and model] days before leaving and was crazy to go on with it. Eddy [Minazzoli] was still away on his vacation. Some progress in the studio.

I worked hard and with real joy Wednesday, Thursday too, but something went mad in my [illegible] in the afternoon and I did something that let R[amon] see I was interested. He behaved most beautifully, but said a great many things that might much better have remained unsaid. That he had always cared, etc. etc. I had asked him to go to the opera with me that night and I thought it best (anyway it amused me) to go. We dined and had a nice evening. He really behaved perfectly. We went for a little drive afterwards and he sang to me. (The next day Eddy was back.) I had several chances to say little things and I did and we laughed a little over me, which was the footing I wanted it to be on. But he said my "caprice" would quickly pass, that he knew I had never even noticed how he felt etc. He said something about the impossibility of such a situation and when I wanted to speak he showed his control of the situation and himself by saying "Let's go back to work." He really was rather extraordinary for it is certainly easy to see one effect I have on him.

Yesterday all was serene, but I was not satisfied with that. I made a situation again today. Two days ago when we talked there was one thing he mentioned very frankly. He said, "You would not want that." And my answer was quick you can imagine. The devil got into me this afternoon and I led him on. Again I can only say that he behaved like the gentleman he is. Then we talked again quite frankly and finally we came to a pretty good understanding. It remains to be seen how good a working plan it is.

I have known since Wednesday that S. is probably not coming and I think that had something to do with it. It is lonely—but never was I so lonely as when I was in England.

Here Gertrude stops this journal (she will not begin another for fourteen months) and locks it, with seven eighths of the pages left blank, silent and mysterious. However, there is another fragment—this one called "Her Imaginary Life"—in which she theorizes about a relationship very much like hers with Stackpole: "One picks up the scraps of other people's lives and swings for a while in their orbits irrespective of one's own. This has often struck me as being the explanation for one's seemingly extraordinary behavior, at times as if one felt one must for the moment answer to the other person's wants, be the piece in the puzzle for which they are searching. . . ." Gertrude is, of course, discounting "her" wants but, having done so, "the piece of the puzzle" fits as neatly in place as if there were no puzzle, as if there were simply a lonely man and a lonely woman.

"I stepped thus strangely enough into someone's life (at least to me this has been the only explanation I have ever felt adequate to the occasion).

The man was intelligent, what is commonly called good looking & therefore totally uninteresting to me. He was heavy and since he had a sorrow —the girl with whom he was in love died—I came along and not caring in the least but being bored at the moment, gave him a line of talk that took him off his feet. He wanted to see me all the time, I stirred his imagination & took him out of himself."

"Her" defensive phrases are transparent—"totally uninteresting to me . . . not caring in the least . . . wanted to see me all the time"—and they lead, by another leap of rationalization, to "R." (almost surely Ramon). They go to the opera, they eat, they go for a drive afterward and he sings, but in "her imaginary life" the evening is more explicit. On the drive to a *cabinet particulier* he sighs and she asks, "What is the matter? Are you sick?" "Sick with excitement," he replies. In the private dining room, when dinner is about half over R.

leaned over to me and suddenly pressed his lips to mine. His arms held me for a moment & I seemed to melt against him. His eyes were aflame when I looked at him again. His Southern blood was roused. I stood up a moment and his eyes took in the lines of my figure, I raised my arms & smiled a little at him, he threw his head back & his arms stretched for me. I kneeled on the little bench beside him & I drew his head close to me. I passed my hand over his eyes, he closed them, trembling. I put my face close to his face, gently, quiveringly, lovingly and then stung to sudden passion I found his lips with my burning ones. When we left the place it was with only one thought, one desire, we were both possessed of it. I did not make the pretext of refreshing, I simply said, "Are you sure we won't either of us be sorry?" "Sorry! I?" he cried. "And you?" he asked, holding me tight. And so he paid the bill and the little-rather-sympathetic-and-distinctly-worn-waiter looked at us reflectively and for a moment I felt cool and wondered what he was thinking of us, and then R. got up from the table and I saw that he was handsome & strong and I remembered that he loved me, and it seemed as if a fever were burning in me, but my hands were cold. Once in the street I said, "Let's walk a little," and the crisp air brought me back to clearer thought, but it did not cool my desire and I felt his like a torch at my side. I thought of the practical side of such things and hated it.

They get a taxi, R. sings to her again, and they go to a small hotel where a maid leads them upstairs.

How I hated the beastly surroundings, the details. The maid in the meanwhile had turned on the light, and she was about to arrange the bed. "You can leave it, I will arrange it," said R. hastily and I was grateful to him. [The maid leaves. R.] very deliberately went to the door & locked it. It seemed to me my life was suspended as he came towards me. Every pulse in me beat. He pushed my head back, he looked in my face as if he wanted to absorb me, & then he kissed me, our lips drawn irresistibly together, drawn by the great physical attraction of the sexes, provoked and played upon for days, & finally finding its fulfillment.

Whether romantic fiction or not, we suppose that these last words are nearer to the truth than any one-sided need on the part of Stackpole, "R," or anyone else. And we wonder if Gertrude, despite her romanticism, isn't a little too worldly and sophisticated for the rather moralistic Stackpole. She is older and more experienced than he, but beyond this, beyond and deeper, is her relationship to Harry and the children. The bond to Harry in particular is, however strained, still strong, and it forces an ambivalence on all her outside relationships, a compulsive pattern of attraction and rejection, selfishness and guilt.

&

Except for another brief visit to Dalby Hall in mid-February, Gertrude continues, through early March, to work hard in her new Paris studio, mostly on a bust of Ramon, which she calls *Head of Spanish Peasant*. The piece is more realistic, more carefully modeled and smoothly finished than her previous work and it also penetrates more deeply into the model's character. Beneath a bandanna, Ramon is very much there—strong, sensuous, and direct. In short, the bust represents a considerable advance in Gertrude's technique, and she submits it to the Spring Salon.

During these months Gertrude is, as always now, moving back and forth between her two, often overlapping, worlds of art and society. She frequently sees Hazy, who is about to marry a Miss Madeleine Keith, and Adele, who has been in England and joins Gertrude in Paris. However, her most important new contact is Rodin, whom she meets through the Duchesse de Choiseul, a daughter of the American international lawyer Frederic R. Coudert. The duke, a compulsive gambler and an authentic but impoverished descendant of Louis XV's Finance Minister, accepts his wife's love affairs, providing they are profitable. The one with Rodin (for two years now) has been that. Over seventy and the greatest living sculptor, his work is in demand and the duchess is in absolute control of it— Mistress of the Master, his "Muse," as she calls herself. She stops visitors by saying, "No use disturbing him since I am here. I handle everything. I am Rodin!" Wearing heavy make-up, jewelry, and feathers, she dances the *bourrée* or does a strip tease to the music of a phonograph. The poet Rilke, who had earlier been Rodin's secretary, comments, "Every day adds something more grotesque and ludicrous to his old age." And yet it is easy to understand the rapport between the duchess and the "Queen." The Duchesse de Choiseul has acted out, continues to act out, some of Gertrude's most extravagant fantasies, has progressed from "pupil" to "Mad-

ame" to "Muse" and "little bacchante." On the other hand Gertrude *is*
the duchess' fantasy: money. They barely meet and discuss Gertrude's
own work and her interest in Rodin's when the duchess invites Gertrude
back to Rodin's atelier, the Hôtel Biron. There Gertrude buys a marble
sculpture of a man and woman making love (much more explicitly than
in his famous *The Kiss*) and, as Gertrude says in her short unfinished
sketch celebrating her contact with Rodin, "the cher Maitre had himself
spoken to me about my work and expressed the flattering desire to come
to my studio." The prospect is "pleasant though terrifying, fearful and
thrilling." Rodin is more than a successful Hendrik Andersen, he is a god.
Gertrude is in awe of him as "the old Renaissance coming back in a new
form . . . directly the pupil of Donatello." Neither Rodin's first visit nor
subsequent ones are described, but in several letters to "Dear Duchess"
and in one to "Cher Maitre" himself, it is clear that he has been generous,
encouraging, and helpful with criticism of Gertrude's *Spanish Peasant*
(then in plaster) and a caryatid. He also leaves two terra cotta figures, improvised for Gertrude, illustrating principles of planar and axial organization which he feels characterize, respectively, Greek sculpture and that
of Michelangelo. These small figures, alive with the imprint of the
Master's fingers, will remain among Gertrude's most prized possessions.

After the completion of *Spanish Peasant* and before Gertrude returns to
New York, Ramon goes on vacation to visit his family in Alicante. From
there he sends a letter beginning: "I am writing chiefly to congratulate
you; Eddie [Minazzoli] wrote to me that the bust was accepted in the
Salon. Good for 'Her.'" About when this letter is received Gertrude is giving a dinner party at the Ritz for Hazy and Madeleine Keith to which
Adele, Rosales, Gladys, and László are invited. Two days later the same
group, plus Knoblock, attends a wedding dinner at the Café de Paris.

Before leaving France, Gertrude thanks Rodin for his counsel and for
explanations "which will be precious to my work" and sends him cuff
links. He wires *bon voyage* greetings and thanks her for her gift.

Gertrude, Harry, and the children return home on the *Lusitania* before
she can see *Spanish Peasant* installed at the Salon. However, Gladys writes
that it "looked perfectly splendid. It is tremendously advantageous in the
bronze, and looks better than almost anything there [ranging from three
pieces by Rodin to two by Rosales, one by O'Connor, and one by Haseltine, a study for *The Big Four*]. This is absolutely true & I wish you could
see for yourself. When are you coming back to finish the figure?" Gladys
is evidently asking about the caryatid, and Gertrude probably knows already that she won't get back to Paris until late summer. Until then there
is just too much to do—some of it revolving around Harry, who will this
year spread his horse-racing activities back to the States and, as captain of
the American team, defend the America Challenge Cup; much of it revolving around Gertrude herself and the completion of her new Long Island studio.

Possibly for the first time and possibly with the intention of publication (though, if so, undoubtedly under a pseudonym), Gertrude has a manuscript of hers typed. (To complete the possibilities, the typing may well have been done by Juliana Rieser, social secretary to Helen Whitney and now recommended to Gertrude, in whose life she will play an increasingly important role.) The untitled manuscript is a first-person narrative of a woman who has just returned to New York after some five months in Paris, "spent in living, in loving, in feeling, even in being," the last phrase crossed out and changed to "in joyously being." She is "distinctly annoyed by the streets, by the impassiveness of the buildings, the vehicles, and especially the people. They spoke of winter, of coldness, of mental and moral frugalities." In New York there is no hint of spring. She has her chauffeur drive her "over the great iron bridge with its massive solidity, its air of belonging to the everlasting hideosities of life," to the country. Sitting in rugs and furs and with the "latest, tightest French skirt clinging to . . . rebellious legs," she feels a "malaise in the atmosphere" and is "more impressed than ever by the lack of spring."

. . . I got out of the motor and sent my man away so as to walk the last mile and a half to the house. [She comes to the rough road which leads to the new studio. She sinks into "the slimy, late spring mud," she climbs the little hill and "sings herself," remembering the spirit of Walt Whitman.] Studio! . . . this spot, secret and hidden, in an enchanted wood.

The workmen had gone and left the place solitary. The building could be seen clearly through the thin winter branches . . . unfinished but beautiful enough to need no apologies; the hole that is to be the garden, deep in dirt, not a vestige of trimmings, no green, no adjective to put before the noun itself. A little tremble came into my knees. . . .

For a long time she continues to study the unfinished but already impressive studio, contrasting its classical proportions, its symmetry, its posed placement on what will be a reflective pool and formal gardens, all this elegance of the European Renaissance, with the "hideosities" and "agonies," as she has called them, of America. Paris, she feels, has helped her to see through all this, helped to satisfy her "starving for beauty and for significance." Even unfinished, her studio is already a reminder of Paris, of French history and culture.

From the silent empty studio she walks through the wet woods to the rambling main house. There everything is dry, warm, comfortable, cozy, but also noisy, even suffocating. A Victor Talking Machine is playing music, the children are playing games, two foursomes of adults are playing bridge ("one at high stakes with men only"). There is talk of a tennis match the following morning, of the superiority of English over American

fox hounds, of polo. At dinner her partner, who thinks of her as "ARTIS-
TIC" (her emphatic capitalization), attempts to discuss "the harm Rodin
has done to art." She infinitely prefers the hounds and polo. After dinner
she becomes "as always . . . more conscious of the upholstered furniture."
A guest (possibly based on Rollie) recognizes her state of mind and plays
the piano for her—first, some Puccini and Debussy; then an aria from
Charpentier's romantic opera *Louise* (which Gertrude has heard as
recently as New Year's Eve, identifying, then as now, with its suppressed
heroine and its Paris setting, in which the city represents poetry, freedom,
bohemia). In Gertrude's story "she" gets up when he starts to play from
Louise and says:

> "No!"
> "Let me, please," he answered very gently, and he looked me
> straight in the eyes. "Don't think you mustn't—that you have not the
> right to live; if you want it, it's yours," his voice broke off.
> "I just can't stand it," I explained, "it's not my superiority, oh no."
> "It's just your—?"
> "Selfish difference."

The cord breaks, the notes trail, his hands fall off the keys. He looks at
her, his sensitive face raised, and his hands return to the keyboard—to
Louise—and he plays "the answer": *Tout être a le droit d'être libre, tout
coeur a le devoir d'aimer.* . . .
This 22-page story is a finger exercise, so transparently autobiographical
that it can be read as yet another piece of Gertrude's journal. However,
during approximately this same period, while less actively sculpting, she
writes a 98-page story called "White Voices," which is more ambitious not
only in length but in the fictional shaping of her experience. With
"White Voices" there is no doubt about Gertrude's desire for publication.
She receives several letters on this subject from Juliana Rieser, who is by
now acting not only as secretary but as encouraging critic and, in effect, as
literary agent. The script itself is neatly typed, affixed to a binder in which
the pseudonym "Phyllis Lane" appears on the title page, along with "August 1911," which must be the date of the final corrected copy, as Miss
Rieser refers in an earlier letter to having submitted the story under the
name "Metcalfe" and having been asked what sort of man he was.
The heroine of "White Voices" is familiar: "a kind of princess" with "a
tiny spark of real independence." Her husband is away fishing for tarpon.
She is "tired of Fifth Avenue, of the rich man's theater, of 'Italian gardens'
and, above all and fatally, of my own personality." She has an Idea which
becomes a Plan: to pose nude but masked for a sculptor who will not be
told her identity or that of her protector, who will pay for the piece. However, she must find a Trustworthy Person to execute the details of the
Plan. She runs into him on Sixth Avenue, a gentleman painter—a type

not unlike Howard Cushing—who has been her introduction to bohemia. They discuss the plan in a tearoom at Macy's where the painter is concerned about the risks to her—sexual and economic. She might be attacked, she might be blackmailed. The details are worked out, and then Trustworthy Person introduces her as "Miss Smith" to Mr. Burns, a sculptor reminiscent of John Gregory.

As the modeling sessions progress, Miss Smith reveals more and more of herself. She has traveled widely, remembers Tunis, her "first consciousness of the East," and elsewhere often uses language from *Travels in Foreign Countries and in the Mind*. Inevitably, Burns is as fascinated by these revelations as by her very white, lithe body with beautiful hands and feet. With increased intimacy comes increased expectation but, as almost always in Gertrude's stories (as in her life), this is expressed by Miss Smith's withdrawal, if not quite outright rejection. Burns, feeling that she is laughing at him or amusing herself at his expense, destroys the sculpture. She begs him to restore it, which he does while declaring his love for her. She says only that he must come very soon and see her and her husband, and he replies, "Goodbye forever—elusive, lovely, impossible—goodbye, Dream Girl."

Juliana Rieser submits "White Voices" to *Harper's* magazine and receives some encouragement from an editor there but ultimately the story is rejected. Then she tries the *Century, Scribner's, Everybody's, Atlantic Monthly*. There are more rejections, each conveyed to Gertrude in the most sensitive and protective way. Finally, Miss Rieser gives it to Miss B. M. Walker, a reviewer for *Bookseller's* magazine, who replies:

My dear Miss Rieser:

I read the manuscript yesterday and enjoyed its workmanship as I have no other for many a long day. You say that you did not write it, so it would be impolite of me to doubt you, but there is so much of you in it!—your suggestions, allusive and subtle dialogue, artistic appreciation and original viewpoint of life etc. show you.

Strictly speaking it is not a story. It is an episode, an incident—sketchy, impressionistic, clever. There are some exquisite bits of writing in it, and a clever handling of a dangerous, erotic incident, which deceives the reader.

Artistically the story is delightful; analytically it stretches the credulity and is inconsistent—although there are jaded society women of whom it is doubtless true. The concealing of the heroine's name is a clever bit of artistic work and the method of bringing her back to a true estimate of the values of life and the power of her environment —and the introduction of her friend in the studio as a means of making her realise the danger of her situation—is especially praiseworthy.

The theme of the story is commonplace—social discontent of the moneyed matron, but the treatment of it is delicate, original and fascinating. The author can rest assured that she can write. The story is worth publishing, but it is too allusive to readily find a magazine. The reading public wants a story with a beginning, a middle and an end. They hate to think. Personally, I hate the directly obvious, consequently this story, which gains its point by suggestiveness, especially appeals to me. . . .

Except for Miss Walker and Miss Rieser, there is little affirmative response to the story and, within Gertrude's circle of friends, considerable personal concern about the readily identifiable heroine. One of her admirers, the lawyer Phil Carroll, is particularly distressed by the risk of exposure, here as in her sculpture:

. . . It seems too much like you, and what is worse, too much like you in material setting. It is impossible to differentiate you from it. . . . I object to the baring of certain intensely intimate impulses, strivings and emotions to the hopeless public gaze. Remember that these same impulses and emotions which in a warm and living princess are so entrancing in their play and interplay cannot well bear, except under the touch of the highest art, to be fixed upon the printed page. As a sublimely graceful movement in a dance may enthrall and captivate all who see the dancer, and yet when caught upon an instantaneous film be perpetuated only as a grotesque gyration, so an emotion which would be adored as it flitted illusively down the stream of life, may come to quite another meaning when shown in the inevitable exaggeration of a book, or frozen in the outline of a statue.

While "White Voices" circulates—until Gertrude herself abandons it, as yet another fragment of her life, among her burgeoning papers—she exhibits a sculpture at Richmond Hill House on MacDougal Street (presented along with paintings by such more established artists as Charles W. Hawthorne and William Glackens); she receives (in addition to Gladys' early letter about *Spanish Peasant*) several encouraging ones now from Hazy, Rosales, and Mama ("so delighted at the improvement in your work & think it so far ahead of anything else you have done"); and she watches the basic structure of her Westbury studio near completion. Yet the exhibition, the encouraging words from Paris, even the emergence of the large new studio are all modest and personal accomplishments compared with Harry's public triumphs in polo. Not only does Gertrude attend the matches at which his Big Four successfully defend the America Challenge Cup but she is hostess again and again at lunch and dinner parties for as many as forty polo enthusiasts—almost always Dev, Larry, and Monte but frequently too Adele and J., Helen and Payne, Louis Stoddard, Bill Stackpole, Phil Carroll, Charles Draper, Rollie Cottenet. And not only are there the official matches but dozens of pickup matches, some with the British players at the Morgans' and the Phippses' and the Hitchcocks'. Polo dominates this spring. There is barely time for tennis, swimming, sailing, and fishing or for brief excursions to Coney Island, Rockaway, and Long Beach or for an occasional evening of bridge or casino. There is barely time for conversation, except about polo and, late in June, the news from Kiel, Germany, that one of Harry's yachts, the *Bibelot* (owned jointly with R. W. Emmons), has won three of five international races for the Emperor William Cup.

By then Gertrude is suffering from a rash (possibly poison ivy, as she tells Flora, possibly nerves), and by July she is recuperating at the Whitney camp in the Adirondacks. Gertrude has been there briefly before, but on this longer stay (eighteen days) we are given for the first time—in correspondence and in her Line-A-Day—a sense of its size, beauty, and privacy. To get there Gertrude, Harry, the children, and their new tutor, Mr. Shattuck, just graduated from Yale, and Mademoiselle take a night train to Racquette Lake, then a boat up the lake to a carry, where Adele Burden and her children meet them and continue on Big Forked Lake to Camp Deerlands on Little Forked Lake, one of many separate rustic but comfortable camps built on promontories throughout the property of about 100,000 acres of lakes among mountains, all inaccessible except by water or by foot. The virgin forests are full of game, the clear cold lakes and streams full of fish. Gertrude recovers quickly. In an Adirondack guide boat (a cross between an elegantly detailed wooden canoe and a rowboat with overlapping oars so that they must be used hand over hand) she rows frequently to and from the camp at which the Burdens are staying. She also takes long walks which stretch out, day by day, into mountain hikes of as much as twelve miles. And she swims and fishes. After a few days Harry and his guest Monte Waterbury, who has arrived the day after the Whitneys leave for New York, and Gertrude and Adele take their children on an overnight camping trip to Moose Pond. There they have "great fun" fishing and cooking their catches over open fires. They return late to Deerlands and get a good night's sleep. The next day Harry arrives for the weekend with another guest, William Stackpole. Gertrude notes only that she "did not feel well."

The Whitneys, the Burdens, and "Stack" spend much of the weekend fishing. Then Harry leaves again for New York, this time with the Burdens.

MONDAY. Stack & I fished. Rained afternoon. Slept in tent, delicious.

TUESDAY. Flora, Barbara, Mlle, Stack & myself went to Moose Pond to spend the night. Very hot day.

WEDNESDAY. At Moose Pond. Bathed, fished, came back late.

THURSDAY. Stack & I took sandwiches & long walk. 10 miles. Got back in rain storm.

FRIDAY. Harry arrived this morning. Walked, fished afternoon.

SATURDAY. Same as usual.

SUNDAY. Left with H. & Stack on the night train for N.Y.

The children remain at Camp Deerlands. The story, if it can be called that, of this last week in the Adirondacks is ossicular. It needs fleshing out. Does Stack still love Gertrude? Does she love him? Do they love each other? . . . There are only clues—particularly his attentiveness to Flora who, like her mother, is now keeping at least two journals (a diary and a Record of Plays Seen, which also includes operas, minstrel shows, circuses, et cetera). "Mr. Stackpole" frequently takes her and "Mama" and sometimes the other children to theater. He also often plays casino with Flora and sometimes a game in which a word is chosen and each participant must write a story about it on a tiny piece of paper. Tuesday evening, August 1, as Mademoiselle puts Barbie to sleep at Moose Pond, the word is "rival." The next morning the word is "liberty," and Flora has "great fun [making] Mama guess something. It was that I didn't see why Mr. Stackpole, Mr. Milburn, Mr. Waterbury and all the men she knows well don't call her by her first name. She asked the funniest questions and I know Mama and Mr. Stackpole didn't think I understood them but you bet I did. Mr. Stackpole does call her by first name when nobody's around." Flora sees that there is something "different" about her mother's relationship to Stackpole but, at fourteen, there is no realization of how she herself is being used by them for protection in a situation where Harry suspects nothing and treats his rival with complete trust, almost as a member of the family.

Gertrude's correspondence of this period with other people refers, understandably enough, to other things. Except in one letter to Flora, Stackpole is never mentioned. And even deep in the Adirondacks—as once high in the Lenox hills—other worlds intrude. As always there's the family. On Gertrude's side, her sister Gladys is sick, having her second baby, but even so writes mostly about Gertrude's "troubles. Your poisoning [the rash]. Sonny's mumps & his failure to pass the Groton exams." (Sonny does pass them later.) There is no mention now either, as there has been earlier in the year, of their brother Alfred's "troubles": widely publicized litigation with Dr. McKim, preceding a substantial settlement so that he can marry Mrs. McKim. On Harry's side, he must screen his sister Dorothy's suitor Willard Straight, a brilliant and cultivated "outsider" who has worked his way through Cornell University (not quite an acceptable school) and then distinguished himself in finance, representing the Morgan-Rockefeller interests (very acceptable) as well as those of the United States Government, in the Orient. There is no question about Straight's ability—he is, at thirty-one, not only the former American consul general at Mukden, Manchuria, but the present Peking representative of a prestigious American banking consortium, headed by J. P. Morgan, for Far Eastern economic development. There is doubt about his background—besides coming from humble origins, he has always lived "on salary" and E. H. Harriman has refused to let him marry his daughter Mary who, like Dorothy, met him on a trip to the East. However, Harry accepts the objective qualifications of this handsome ambitious self-made man whom his sister obviously adores, even accepts their desire to be married at a September wedding in Geneva—a location selected less because of Pauline's poor health (the public reason) than because of Dorothy's and Willard's strongly mutual wish to have a small private wedding rather than a New York "circus." The formal announcement of their engagement is made July 20 by Harry.

As to Gertrude's other worlds which touch her comparative isolation in the Adirondacks, John Gregory writes four letters, all once again addressed "Dear Lady" and all once again asserting his independence. In the first, he wishes Gertrude luck with "White Voices" but teases her about "living and enjoying the simple life." In the others he considers a loan from her but not without expressing his great pride and his reluctance to be indebted to her:

> If I humiliate myself I become insincere and if I blame you then you'll hate me. . . . Probably no one has ventured to find fault with you and I know I have done so often, but I plead that it was always because the situation impelled me to.

Ramon reports twice on construction progress in Westbury:

> In the studio proper, all the things to lock up the windows have been put in. The panel for Mr. Thompson's fountain has been finished. . . . The work outside goes on as usual. In the garden few plants have been replaced by new ones. It looks about the same. The groined ceiling at the entrance of the building has been finished, and the grass is being put down off the entrance. The place begins to take a much nicer tournure. . . . Eddy [Minazzoli] worrying comme d'habitude.

Howard Cushing writes:

> Will you be very good and let me know, before you sail, when you expect to come back. I shall be ready to start my decorations any time after. . . . [Gertrude has commissioned him to do murals in the stair well.]

And finally—among regular correspondents of this period, such as Jimmie, Bunny, Adele, James Fraser, and Paul Chalfin (also commissioned to do mosaics in the Westbury studio)—Hazy reports on Gertrude's studio in Paris and on other matters there:

Tomorrow I go to see Madeleine (yours) [the maid] to settle up month's expenses, wages, etc. I went to see Rodo [an influential member of the Société Nationale des Beaux Arts] and chose a horrible green group—he admired your bust at the Salon and said that you have a very excellent chance of becoming a sociétaire next year—if you send something more important than a bust—so again let me impress [on] you not to waste any time—when do you come? Remember also to let Rosales know so that he can arrange to do that head of you. . . . I think Madeleine (mine) and I will go to Switzerland somewhere for September if not before as it is getting terribly hot.

Gertrude and Harry spend only three days in New York and Westbury, then return to the Adirondacks for a final week before leaving for Europe. However, even during this brief absence, Flora writes a long letter saying in many ways how much she misses her mother. Gertrude replies from the Colony Club:

Dearest Flora,

We got down to town yesterday morning without any excitements. It was pretty hot and seemed horrid after the woods. I did a lot of shopping and Papa & I went down to the country in the afternoon.

Mr. Stackpole telephoned that he is sailing tomorrow, he is coming to see me this afternoon to say good-bye. It is nice and fresh today and I imagine it must be perfect in the mountains. I got you a white felt hat I think will [look] splendid and not get used up as quickly as a straw one. . . .

The garden of my studio has come on wonderfully and really begins to look like a garden. I did not see any of the dogs, but everything else looked much as usual. Mr. Monte Waterbury came for dinner.

Now I am in town again to finish my shopping and see about some things in the studio in town.

Give my love to Sonny & Barbara and remember me to Mlle. and Mr. Shattuck.

I send you hugs and [am] dying to get back.

Love
Mama

At Camp Deerlands there are two more letters from John Gregory to "Dear Lady." In the first he can barely contain his rage and hurt pride within seven closely written pages. Three short paragraphs from the heart of the letters—and the heart of the man—adequately convey his emotions:

Perhaps you may be at fault. Your whole life you have imposed your will on everyone but your equals. . . .

You ask everything from me—do you offer anything?—I don't want it, but you are speaking of reason and being natural. You offer me the sincere contact of one third of your life, for which you have told me there are three worlds in which you dwell, in exchange for my completeness—I think that an imposition.

Do you think I'm flattered to escort you to Bohemia?

His next communication is short and apparently final:

It is just one week since I got your letter and my rage increases.

I have written you every day and torn up the letters. I am in despair. This is the last and I enclose yesterday's [evidently lost or destroyed by Gertrude]. I quit. That's all. Over three years you have kidded me and now I see the whole business. I can not and will not continue. . . .

I'll have no more commerce with you. I have only one life to live and I'll live it my way.

I enclose clipping concerning someone who also called me poseur [possibly Jo Davidson, which Gregory would have considered the pot calling the kettle black].

You're a weakling and I want no more of you.

Gertrude and Harry have one more hectic day, split between New York and Westbury, before boarding the *Olympic* for Europe. On ship, as Gertrude writes Flora, she takes a Turkish bath and a swim each day and reads "till my head is in a muddle: 4 novels and one serious book in . . . hardly 4 days." At Southampton, Harry and most of his and Gertrude's friends leave the ship and Gertrude goes on to Cherbourg and from there to Paris where she has a week to herself, in the studio and in the art world. As to her other worlds, she writes to Mama and the children, shops, and sees Lloyd Warren. When Harry arrives, he and she go immediately to the Hotel National in Geneva for Dorothy's marriage. It is indeed a simple wedding compared with those, so long ago, of the principal guests: Gertrude and Harry themselves, Pauline and Almeric, Helen and Payne. A civil ceremony precedes the brief religious service, followed by a breakfast for about twenty. For the first time in this generation a Whitney wedding doesn't appear on the front pages. As Dorothy wanted, having been exposed to so much family publicity (starting, for her, most profoundly and painfully with the coverage of her father's death), the wedding is reported quietly, on inside pages, and without intimate details.

Gertrude and Harry take the night train to Paris, have lunch the next day at Prunier's and dinner at the Café Madrid. It is evidently a perfect day. Soon after returning to Holwick for shooting and making arrangements to have hunters sent to Dalby Hall and ponies shipped to Westbury, he writes, "Dearest, Paris was very nice, wasn't it?" The words are eloquent in their understatement.

Now alone again in Paris—as magical for Gertrude as for Murger and Charpentier and with the advantage, as compared with their heroines, of touring bohemia rather than being trapped there—she again spends most of her time in the studio, working so seriously that when her mother arrives after the birth of Gladys' second baby (named Alice for her), Mama writes, "I will not interfere with your work & so will only go to your apt. at hours convenient to you. I know how short your time is & how annoying it is to be interrupted."

At the end of September Gertrude joins Harry in London. They have a good day there too and spend their last night, before sailing, with Hazy and Edward Knoblock, seeing the latter's exotic play *Kismet*. Knoblock is riding high. Not only is *Kismet* a great hit but he had just finished collaborating with Arnold Bennett on *Milestones*, which will be produced the following year. It is likely that Gertrude first meets Bennett at this time, though Harry may well have met him previously through ownership of the *Metropolitan* magazine, one of the comparatively smaller properties inherited from his father. In any case, Bennett is planning a promotional trip to the United States in October and November and, despite an exhausting schedule, arranges to spend a few days with Gertrude and Harry. There is no record of those days in either Bennett's journal or Gertrude's, but we can imagine his relief in escaping from the literary lion hunters to the quiet and privacy of the Long Island estate, and we can also imagine his surprise at seeing the nearly completed palatial studio emerging from the near-English countryside. Gladys writes in late November: "I am much impressed by your having Arnold Bennett to stay. Is he as delightful as his books?" We too wish we knew.

At the end of the month, during what will be a period of quiet until the end of the year itself, Gertrude opens the volume of her journal which was finished October 30, 1908, rereads it, and adds two more sad sentences: "Three years have gone. Book put away and so many things to say that perhaps it did not seem worthwhile even trying to say them." However, she has, of course, said some of these things in her intermediate journals of 1910 and 1911; in her fiction; in her sculpture; and in her life itself. During this three-year period she has grown a great deal. She has adjusted to an independent, but still loving, marital relationship. Her children, particularly Flora, are old enough now to have relationships with, based on friendship as well as maternalism. At thirty-six, she has established herself as a serious young sculptor. And, more quietly, she has established herself also as a patron of the arts. Indeed the year ends with checks, ranging from $100 to $1,500, going out to many artists, including John Gregory (!) and Arthur Lee, and to at least one institution, the National Academy of Design (!). However, this soon, the idea of the (1913) Armory Show is already incubating at the Madison Gallery, part of the Coventry Studios, a decorators' establishment run by Clara S. Davidge and partially backed by Gertrude. There, Mrs. Davidge and her protégé Henry Fitch

Taylor, a landscape painter and the director of the gallery, discuss the problems of getting recognition for non-academic art with three of their more progressive young artists: Jerome Myers, Walt Kuhn, and Elmer MacRae. For obvious reasons Gertrude is brought into these discussions early.

⇜ *1912*

By the beginning of the year Gertrude and Harry and the children, except for Sonny, who is at Groton, have returned to Europe where they have a new living arrangement, or at least a variation on those of the past two winters. Harry is again at Little Dalby Hall, but he now has Barbara, not quite nine, with him. He writes enthusiastically to Gertrude that "Barbie rides every day & looks awfully well & is very sweet." Harry himself is doing a lot of hunting, even in the snow, and has, as usual, a home full of friends and relatives.

"Today Arthur [Burden] & Jimmie [Appleton] went beagling & I got all the rest off to Leicester to buy furniture etc. So have got an afternoon to myself. Before lunch I went to see the crippled horses—Henry broke one down for good yesterday & I had quite a fall on Gretton & he is out of business for at least two weeks. In the bad going he missed his feet over some rails and fell. We slid about 8 feet, I with one leg under him. I am very stiff today but glad he did not turn (instead of sliding) & break me in two. Helen [Whitney] was right behind & said she was scared to death 'cause it looked quite bad."

Gertrude runs different risks—both aesthetic and social—in her Paris studio. Flora, fourteen and a half, is established with her governess, Miss Givenwilson, and a maid in a nearby apartment belonging to a Mrs. Cameron. There, frequently Gertrude has lunch with her daughter and sometimes dinner, when she brings along one or more of her artist friends, before all of them go on to the opera, the ballet, or theater. Often, too, Gertrude and Flora shop together. In late February, when Flora joins her father and sister at Little Dalby Hall, Gertrude writes to her almost immediately: "I miss you awfully and do wish you were still here. Paris is just about the same, only now I hardly ever go out as I work even more than ever. . . . I went to try on my clothes and liked them very much. . . . How do you like my new paper?" The paper is engraved with a rose in red, green, and black above Gertrude's initials on a hand-laid lavender border

—one of eighteen boxes of similar stationery (five for Flora, engraved with her name), purchased at Saintyves, Papetrie de Luxe, 350 Rue Saint-Honoré. That costs 585 francs, 10 centimes, about $120 (1912 dollars!) The clothes are, of course, still more expensive. Among Gertrude's early March bills are four totaling 16,800 francs from Paul Poiret ("the Sultan of Fashion," who served his apprenticeship with two of Gertrude's previously favorite couturiers, Jacques Doucet and the House of Worth, but who, in the décor of his own salon as well as in the clothes presented there, evokes an Arabian Nights atmosphere of brilliantly colored, sometimes shimmeringly metallic Turkish trousers, kimono blouses, turbans and high aigrets, tassels, embroidered floral and avian decorations, Persian brocades—in short, a world of exotic fantasy very close to Gertrude's). There are also bills from lesser couturiers—two from Poiret's brother-in-law André Groult, totaling 1,268 francs; one from Gabrielle for 336 francs; and another from the fan maker Fauçon for 180 francs. As in 1907, when suddenly Gertrude bought so much jewelry, we wonder again if Gertrude is indulging in economic therapy, if beneath the seeming resolution of so many of her problems there is an underlying emotional agitation. Only one journal survives from this year. It is small and thick, bound in black leather, with the usual silver clasp. In it Gertrude makes but one entry, in pencil, covering seven pages, and dated precisely:

FRIDAY FEBRUARY 29th
When something comes to one out of a clear sky, a beautiful thing that one has no right to expect, a thing of meaning which one has done nothing to deserve—when this happens—no matter what the result may be, one sings a song of praise. It has happened to me. And the reason that I put this great value on what I have been given is because I want and need it. It's the breath of my life. It's happiness. It's the lost complement of myself that I have found. I will tell it all as clearly and truthfully as I can, though it's hard now not to see it all colored by last night.

Of course I knew he was interested in me, found me sympathetic, but that's all I thought. I liked him right away, his apparent sincerity, his great talent, his tastes and loves which he scarcely needed to express, I knew so well. The beginning of one of our sentences always suggested the end to the other. I wrote him a note in all innocence to ask if I could go and see his work. And he told me to come a certain morning. I liked him right away and we talked and he showed me his work which is big and strong and full of meaning, like himself. I asked him if he would come and give me some advice about my statue and he arranged to come on a certain day. I can't tell it all—I remember that I felt he had something big to give me and that I calmly told someone I was going to try and make him fall in love with me. Then I forgot about it. He came a few times only, but we always talked a lot and he stayed late. He seldom sat down and he sometimes walked about while talking. He encouraged me about my work even while he made me feel its horrible weakness. I let my mind think of him as caring for me sometimes and it always thrilled me, but he seemed never to feel anything but great interest, perhaps admiration. How many times did he come? I think four in all counting yesterday. Twice he lunched with me.

Yesterday he came about eleven. I worked while he helped me to see things till 12:30. We lunched. He said he loved to do what he was doing because I understood and was so enthusiastic. He was a little different, a little more intimate, but still that was all. I had told him before of Rosales doing my figure and late in the afternoon after [Adolphe] Ramon had gone I told him that I had been to pose a few days before [i.e., for Rosales, who did several sculptures of her]. He asked me about it and I showed him the photographs. He was struck—serious, intent. He said they were among the most beautiful things he had ever seen. I felt then his great and real admiration at least for my physique. We watched the sun set and then I went and sat on my sofa. It was almost dark in the studio. He stood close by and talked. Once I longed, I remember, to put my hand out and pull him down by me. I noticed that he looked at me strangely. Finally he leaned against the side of the sofa, I moved to make room for him. It was so dark by then that we could only very dimly see the outlines of each other. Then a fearfully strong feeling came over me to lean against him, and while he talked the feeling came over me "it will come—we will care, it *must* be." And it seemed as if I was a leaf on the water or a tiny atom in a universe of force. I got up after a while, it was so dark and so wonderful just sitting, then I got frightened. He said, "Heavens it is seven o'clock," and we were both amazed. "I think I will go on the boulevards," he said. "Take me" slipped from me. I saw he wanted me to come, but still we stood and talked a little. Then he said, "Aren't you coming?" So I went with him, childishly, enthusiastically, I am afraid. It really seemed like a great experience. I wore my black velvet dress, I thought he would like it. I dressed in such a hurry I forgot to tie my shoe strings, he tied them for me. We started like two kids on a holiday! He took me to a place in a passage off the boulevard, done Moorish style, which seemed to me like a divine place. The only personal nice things he had told me were that he thought me very intelligent and beautiful. It was an evening never to forget. He made me feel that of all the things in the world that one might do, being with me like that was the best.

Separate from the barely used journal is a cycle of "Letters from the Searcher to the Dream Man," fourteen pages written in Gertrude's hand and dated between March 17 and 19, but without a year. However, it is clear that these "letters" are written just after Gertrude returns from Paris to Westbury. Whether "real" or not, whether sent or not, they are directly and sequentially related to the truncated journal:

. . . Two men that think they love me came yesterday to see me. One overcome with passion for my body (I could see it in his eyes) the other controlling it because he knew I did not want it, and there were enough letters and telephone messages to satisfy my inexhaustible vanity. I see the old life crowding back. Would I dine, would I lunch, would I do the forty things that bore me. . . .

My boy comes home [from Groton] Tuesday, so for ten days I shall not work very hard at my own work. I shall try and wipe out my absence from the family bible. One of my friends, while I was away, has gotten very religious [probably Stackpole]. He always was inclined that way. I see signs of being reformed! Are you afraid for me? He reads the bible, even quotes from it and no one used to be gayer or more given to Broadway delights. He is fearfully unselfish and would cut his arm off for me but I feel unable to cope with such a strange phase.

I am in my big Stanford White bed with its painted Renaissance ceiling and its twisted golden columns. It's huge and low and divinely comfortable, but it is Renaissance and you would despise it, I expect. If it were stiff and little and Gothic how you would go into ecstasies over it! Mysterious Gothic! Tall, long, folded-armed ladies of Chartres how often I think of them. Do you? And I feel a cold wind blowing and I see a procession of boys in capes go by and I know that it all was in a former existence. How untrue to say that we do not remember our former lives. I remember thousands of mine in dim moments when the world stops to let me think.

I was lazy this morning. I shall not be lazy much longer. I shall remember each day words that the Dream Man spoke. He told me I was at my prime; that now, now was the time, that the best was there to be uttered, but—it needed time, concentration. He believed in me and so I will always know that if I fail it is because I did not have the courage, for it is there we are cowards—if we do not push the crowds aside to get it said. . . . Now I shall go back into the studio again and dream of what is to be. . . .

The little upstairs hall is a thing unknown in the history of the world. The black and white checkered marble floor sets off Howard's impossibly romantic ladies ["Persian" murals in the stair well, including a portrait of Gertrude]. The colors are Eastern if you will but it is all modern and strange and links the old and the new, just as all beautiful things are linked, Chinese and Gothic and—life. I adore the touch of things, don't you? I want lovely things to be perfect to the touch, I want the things I touch with joy to be perfect to my imagination. I want so much. And you alone have even for the eighth of a second given it all to me. . . .

You are real now. You are the only thing that counts and I love you as one does when all the padding is out. I hate this life of pretense and ridiculous ideas. Dear love, I want to run to you, to leave the absurdity of the world. If I had no children I would give up all things. I would take my life into my own hands. Oh that blue room, do you remember, Dream Man, how I loved you then. Do you remember how you told me one afternoon in the studio how I must never forget that you loved me for good and all. I have been able to cry tonight, as I have perhaps never cried before.

I only love my little warm children and the life you mean, I don't even know if it is you. Now I shall try and stop crying and I shall put out the lights and go to sleep. Good night, Dream Man, I love you always.

Who is Gertrude's present "Dream Man"? We know that he is a sculptor whose career has progressed further than hers and whose work and criticism she respects, and that he lives in Paris but is probably an American who has had some previous contact with her and her social milieu. Among Gertrude's many acquaintances in Paris there is only one who seems to satisfy the basic criteria as well as the details of mutual chronology. He is Andrew O'Connor, Jr., born in Worcester, Massachussetts, just half a year before Gertrude but, as the son of a sculptor, committed to art in his teens and an assistant to John Singer Sargent by the age of twenty. We remember now that Gertrude met him at the turn of the century (soon after her father's death) when, through the efforts of Daniel Chester French, O'Connor received the commission to do the Vanderbilt memorial doors at St. Bartholomew's Church. At that time, it seems likely, O'Connor would have seen Gertrude's early efforts at sculpture and, along with others, may well have played the role of informal critic and teacher. However, soon after completing this commission he settled in Paris with his wife Jessie, who in these early years was almost exclusively his model, and began raising a family (four sons), exhibiting (from 1906 on) at the Annual Salons, and accepting (from the same year on) many of the commissions that French and Saint-Gaudens, who also admired his work, didn't have time for. Though Gertrude lost touch with him during these years, she would have been completely aware of his progress and would have admired his professional single-mindedness. The strong character of the man is evident not only in his work (much of it carved directly in marble) but in his rugged, stocky physique. In photographs he presents an image something like Napoleon's or the young Picasso's, with mouth set and forelock falling over dark determined eye.

The sculptures O'Connor would have seen (and perhaps helped Gertrude with) in 1912 include a nude figure of a standing male athlete with one hand gripping the back of his head in a gesture of contorted *Despair* (the final title of the piece); a related *Portrait Head of an Athlete*; another *Head of Young Man*; and finally, her then most ambitious piece, a fountain commissioned for the New Arlington Hotel in Washington, D.C., of three male figures (slightly larger than life) supporting a basin of leaves, grapes, and fish about eleven feet in diameter. The symbolism is neither so original nor so coherent as that of her "Aztec" fountain, but the sculpture itself (carved and enlarged, as always, by assistants, from her studies*) is considerably freer than her previous work.

During the spring Harry is breeding thoroughbreds both in the States and in England, where his stable has one of its greatest seasons, winning thirty major races, and he is playing a great deal of polo although there is no international match this year. Gertrude—along with four other women sculptors, the best known of whom is Anna Hyatt—shows five early bronzes at Frank Purdy's Gorham Art Gallery, associated with and located in the tony Fifth Avenue jewelry and silver store. She is also sponsoring and participating in an art class given by Bernard Karfiol in New York. But most of her time she spends in Westbury. There she works in her old studio while still waiting for the new one, which she visits frequently, to be completed; and she writes a considerable amount of fiction under the guidance of Maurice Newton, a graduate of Harvard for whom "few other things are more fun than writing." He commutes between his university club and East Hampton, seeing Gertrude in Westbury or at her Mac-Dougal Alley studio as she wishes, at a charge for criticism of $50 per month. It is a busy period leading, in July, to the need for a rest in the Adirondacks. There she receives a progress report on her studio from Arthur Lee:

Dear Lady,
    Cottenet invited me out to dine and while we enjoyed the good food he told me that you had all the sculpture to do for a five million dollar hotel in Washington. So he said we may make a good guess that she does not want to do all that herself. Being affluent, as rich in gold as Michel Angelo was in genius, the only end of this work that would interest you would be where your spirit could play untram-

---

* For a bronze sculpture, the following stages were typical: (1) first clay model, called "sketch model"; (2) second clay model, called "study model"; (3) study model enlarged to full size, usually by assistants, under supervision of artist; (4) plaster cast, also fabricated by assistant under supervision of artist; (5) bronze cast and patination by foundry, usually under supervision of assistant and, at final stage, of artist. For a stone sculpture, the first four stages were the same. Then a cast would be made, and the stone carver (assuming that, like Gertrude, the artist was primarily a modeler) would take the cast and point it up on the stone in the size wanted. Obviously the assistants were, at the least, extremely capable artisans, if not creative artists; and carvers, in particular, often exercised considerable imagination in translating a concept from one medium and/or scale to another, dependent on the number of points used.

meled. Now I so interpreted Rawlins that this meant there might be work for me. He said go down to Roslyn [i.e., Westbury] and find out, anyway you ought to see my garden down there etc. etc. I explained that I had already asked you for something and told him that I had written you that he had said you had said that you would pay for the bronze. He stoutly denied this and would not stand sponsor so I smiled and told him I would go down to Roslyn the next day and exonerate him. So I took my nerve with me and arrived at Roslyn studio a little before twelve.

O what a god-like place or shall I say goddess? The studio as splendid as a temple and the garden O glorious! I was glad I had come. Ramon was hospitality itself and a true Spaniard, showed me thru the temple of art. Cushing's decorations look well and Chanler's give one the feeling of a Jules Verne novel.

As soon as I saw the strangely dull blue pool I ran back to the enchanted house and stript and I dove in. Ramon and I raced and reveled in the water and I marveled at the magic of this wonderful place in the woods. Chanler came and waiting for him to undress I danced around your lawn like a faun in a fine frenzy and frightened your queer grey blue silk colored birds who fled awkwardly out of my way. Then Chanler came with his huge bulk and heaved himself plump into the middle of the pool sending a splash all around the place and cajoled his fine bulldog in with a swooping reach of his left arm. Oh how I enjoyed that swim. Only wish you had been there to see us. I dove and Chanler splashed until we had our fill. . . .

No wonder Arthur Lee finds the studio "splendid as a temple." The space—approximately 60 feet long by 40 wide by 20 high—is as generously and beautifully proportioned as that of any studio anywhere. Of the major areas in the building, the studio itself is the only bare and purely functional one. The entrance vestibule is about to be decorated by Paul Chalfin, who will soon set black, white, and brown stones in a classical pattern on the floor and, toward the end of the year, place a mosaic of glazed tile on the groined ceiling. Howard Cushing's lush, near-tropical mural begins in the downstairs hall, extends like a processional up the curving stair, and culminates on the wall facing the upstairs landing with the portrait of Gertrude. She is standing daintily but regally, dressed in a plumed cloche, black and white tunic, orange harem pants, and upturned brocade slippers. (The splendid tunic, designed by Bakst, is already known. Gertrude has worn it at a costume party given by her and Harry at the beginning of this year, and it will be still better known a year hence, by which time Rosales will have completed a sculpture of her in it, John Singer Sargent will have drawn her in it, and Baron de Meyer, the most fashionable of fashion photographers, will have done a series of portraits of her in it, one of which will appear in *Vogue*.) Robert Chanler's murals are equally exotic: the walls of Gertrude's bedroom present medieval court and battle scenes done in black and white in deep perspective; her bathroom with a sunken marble tub is turned into the "Jules Verne" nacreous grotto full of fish and marine life. Other than storage space, an assistant's shop and apartment, and a small kitchen, there are only two other spaces, a sitting room to the right of the entrance and a gallery of her own work to the left. The former will not be decorated until 1914–18, when Maxfield Parrish will do a series of high wall panels on an Arthurian theme. Meanwhile, Gertrude is thinking about the garden, being landscaped by Rollie. In addition to placing various pieces of her own sculpture (different ones over the years), she has commissioned John Gregory to do two standing figures and, as Arthur Lee has mentioned, exotic birds move freely everywhere.

☙

July 24, Gertrude, Harry, Sonny, and Loup, the German shepherd Gertrude has become increasingly fond of, board the *Mauritania*, leaving Flora and Barbara with their grandmother at The Breakers. Gertrude keeps no chronological journal or Line-A-Day during this trip and her Motor Log is incomplete. But between departure and return (in mid-September) she writes twenty letters to "Dearest Flora," intended to amuse her daughter and very different in tone from her journal. There are reports from aboard ship where Loup sleeps under her bed and Sonny plays cards with a man Gertrude calls "the gambler" and from London where Pauline and Almeric, Adele and J., Helen and Payne all welcome her before the last four and Sonny go to Scotland, and Gertrude goes to Paris. There she works on the Arlington fountain until a trip with Harry to Venice, where they join Rollie Cottenet and make a side trip to Padua so that Gertrude can once again see Donatello's great equestrian statue of Gattamelata outside the Basilica del Sant'Antonio and Giotto's frescoes in the Cappella degli Scrovegni. A few days after their return to Paris, Gertrude writes, "I have been married sixteen years today—that is a long time! Poor old me."

Gertrude's fond devotion to Flora is sufficiently apparent. However, between the lines there is more than a suggestion of Gertrude's guilt at having left Flora behind. And, whether there too between the lines or there by omission, we suspect Gertrude's serenity during these trips with Harry. The letters are, after all, to a daughter just turned fifteen, for whom, as for Gertrude herself except in her private writing, one of the highest virtues is not to complain. So we search beyond the immediate correspondence, wondering, for example, if during this trip she has again seen the "Dream Man"—or a "Dream Man."

Once again we find a transcribed cycle of love letters—almost forty pages, beginning:

On Sept. 1912 she wrote him from Paris, dated Sat. Evening: "You have just left, dearest, and it does seem hard to have you go. It seems wrong too when I so desperately need you—in every sense of the word, and not only want but need you—just as I said last night. . . . There are still struggles for us to go through, you may be sure of that —for I know myself and I am beginning to know you too well not to see that our natures will clash many times before they find their final adjustment. . . ."

Through seven long paragraphs her passion mounts, ending:

"And then when the night has really come I feel the body of you against my poor little quivering soul, and then the body of me against the soul of you."

When Gertrude returns home the correspondence continues. She writes "after an engagement made and broken for another reason":

"I am simply broken-hearted, dear about today. A message came this morning from my mother saying she was to be in town only for a day and to meet her. . . . I will make *no* engagements tomorrow and will meet you V. Hotel 12:15 if *you* can."

A week or so later:

"You say I never write you dearest! That is not the reason I am writing now—but I so seldom have the time and am able to be alone and undisturbed. My getting in the house is the signal for so many people to pounce on me. Anyway, now, dear, I am tucked away in my bed and Harry is dressing for a man's dinner. (We might have had this evening.) So I can talk to you undisturbed. Do you know that the way you treat me often seems unjustifiable and strange? Do you ever put yourself in my position and ask yourself how you would like it if I suspicioned and questioned you all the time. . . . My thoughts of you are as jealous as yours of me, but—somehow I have taken you simply and I shall go on doing it till I *must* stop. I want to make you happy and if I do not succeed then it would be better for me to disappear from your life. I know that I must have been hard to deal with these last days for I have been very nervous and at times really suffering—and you have been good and kind and gentle to me. You hurt me beyond words this afternoon but then perhaps you had a right to think I should see no one but you. These superficial things are of so little importance but they just can't be left out anymore than one's bath or food or exercise. I wanted to send you just a long affectionate letter tonight—but my head aches so and I feel so rotten that I will just send this off hoping that you will know that it carries you a great great deal of love. . . ."

The man is obviously more jealous and demanding than Gertrude, less accepting of her life apart from him than she is of his apart from her—if indeed, as (seemingly) a young leisure-class bachelor, he has anything like her familial, social, and professional obligations. November 20 she writes:

"I waked up! Finally—I am afraid I drank too much! I am sorry because it could not have been very pleasant. Anyway—I know I waked—and found myself alone! Horrible experience! You had gone —I remembered nothing, except that once you had been here and that now you were not. Sorry—very—but it is fatal to drink champagne for lunch. I will soon start for the country and I hope recover my senses. I wish I could sleep forever. As that seems impossible I will say good-bye. Have a nice dinner and think of me *kindly*—(if possible).

Yrs foolishly.G."

Their relationship becomes increasingly difficult. "After a supper party" (as she notes before the transcription) it reaches toward a climax:

"My dear, child, I think you had been drinking last night, otherwise I cannot make myself believe that you would have said the things to me which you did. But I know that you mean them and so I am glad that they were said. And I came to the only real conclusion for us now. If you feel that way about me it is only possible for us to say good-bye. It hurts in every way and my heart is torn, but I have tried over and over to make you happy and I am unsuccessful. In Paris it was not like this—it might not be again, but here I cannot see my way to any other solution. I refuse to give up the pleasure I get from my friends and seeing them in my own way. I am not the person you need in your life. I care for you just as always, but my selfishness makes it impossible for me to give up certain things which you want me to. I tried it and could not, so you had better let me pursue my horrible course alone. It will never be the course I was pursuing before we met, for you have changed me in more ways than you know. I cannot help being glad that I have known you as I have because it has brought something real and big and fine in my life, and even the unhappiness cannot outweight the rest. I am not parting in anger and I hope there is no anger in your heart for me. All my best wishes and hopes go with you and please, if you can, keep me as a friend in your life. I love you and I would not be surprised if I always did. But you make me desperately furious at times and this horrible up and down cannot go on. When you get the rest you so much need, I am sure that you will see me in a little different light. Not that I am trying to whitewash myself. My interest and love will be with you on your trips (now and your trip through life). I have understood you better than you thought and I love you far more than you can see now. Will you please destroy my letters and send me back the bronze [presumably of

herself, as in the story "White Voices"]. I had written you a long letter—shall I send it?—it only says the truth, for once—and that you
did not see. My love unchanged and not quite as unworthy as you
think. I will send it. I would like to see you again but not today."

Before resuming what Gertrude calls "extracts," she interjects: "Winter
letters not of much importance, only as showing general continuance of
things." It is clear already, and will be more so during the remainder of
this correspondence, that the moment's "Dream Man" cannot be Andrew
O'Connor. As the extracts continue into 1913 it becomes increasingly
probable that the mystery man is again William Stackpole. (In the Social
Register it is noted that he sails for Europe in early August and returns in
September.) However, this part of Gertrude's life, like so many others from
this particular year, some mentioned, some not—e.g., the death of Archie
Alexander; the commissions being completed on the Westbury studio; the
beginning of a long separation, ultimately ending in divorce, between Regi
and Cathleen; the marriage of Juliana Rieser to a fashionable Manhattan
dentist named Willard Burdette Force; presently vague thoughts, expressed in correspondence with John Gregory, about a club which will be
a "free gathering" of artists—all must for the moment be left fragmentary.

One other fragment of 1912, having much greater public significance, is
not mentioned anywhere among Gertrude's papers at the time of its oc-
currence (April 15) but frequently from the end of 1912 through 1915:
the sinking of the *Titanic*. Though Gertrude has no relatives or very close
friends among the more than 1,500 passengers and crew drowned in this
worst of all maritime disasters, many of those lost (e.g., Colonel John
Jacob Astor, Benjamin Guggenheim, F. M. Warren, the great bibliophile
George Dunton Widener, the noted horseman Clarence Moore, and the
painter Francis Davis Millet) and saved (e.g., Mrs. E. D. Appleton, the
family of William E. Carter, the French sculptor Paul Chevré, Miss E. M.
Eustis, the publisher Henry Sleeper Harper, Mrs. Warren, Mrs. Widener
and her son) are from Gertrude's immediate world. No doubt she feels
the tragedy personally and, more broadly, like so many, feels its social implications too—the loss of optimistic faith in technology (the ship was
supposed to be "unsinkable"); the chivalrous, gentlemanly, even sacrificial
behavior of some ship's officers and many of the men traveling first class,
combined with discrimination (resulting in grossly disproportionate loss of
life) against second class and steerage. In many ways the sinking of the *Titanic* represents microcosmically the end of a value and class system which
will be macrocosmically destroyed during World War I.

Soon after the *Titanic* disaster Natalie Hammond (wife of John Hays
Hammond, the mining engineer who had been very profitably associated
with Harry's father and Harry himself as well as, among others, Cecil
Rhodes and the Guggenheims) organizes a committee of women to
memorialize those who lost their lives, particularly the men who sacrificed

theirs for women and children. By November Mrs. Hammond is in correspondence with Gertrude, seeking help (which Gertrude gives) in connection with a theater benefit and hinting that the committee's ultimate goal, a monument in Washington, D.C., "may suggest something to you in your work."

⇌

⇌ *1913*

Gertrude and William Stackpole intend to have a rendezvous early in the new year, just before she and her family (except for Sonny, who is still at Groton) leave for Europe. However, Stackpole's

illness prevented his leaving the house for several days and 2 nights before she sailed. She was going to a party. It had been arranged that she was to get away for a little while and meet him—but he was too ill. Written Jan. 3d: "Dearest Child, How I wish I could be near you and take care of you and make you better. It is hard not to be able to. I promise you, no matter what happens tonight, that I will not go to the studio. Sleep well and peacefully. Remember that someone loves you, wants you, needs you, is thinking loving thoughts of you, dear kid. It is hard to have to be away from you, but to want to be near you so much is wonderful too and in the end you will know how much all of this means. I will not call you up on the telephone for fear of waking you."

From the steamer on January 9, her thirty-eighth birthday, she writes:

. . . You will hear that I have thought about you a great deal! I worried too about your health, but I felt that you were much happier and that helped some. It was a great relief to get your marconigram.

It's been rough but I have not minded it. I made believe to be tired so as to avoid the crowd, bridge, useless talk. Not very friendly of me, was it! But I wanted to read and think. I did both—a lot. I have dreamed many dreams about Paris. Dear Child, I hope we have got things fixed now. I have been through many unhappy hours just as you have. I trust and pray they are over.

I shall probably land late Saturday and spend an endless night getting to Paris. But the joy of getting there! And the excitement of really starting work again! The free life, the answering to no one for your hours and occupations. I must be very selfish for I do love it. I just like to wander about too, never knowing where I am going to end up. I often do it all alone. Don't laugh, that is the truth.

I hope you did not take the H. thing too seriously [within the context of these letters, not Harry]. I know all about him and it is not his personality that I was considering. That I believe to be very unattractive although he is undoubtedly clever. I shall wait developments and not be the first to make the move.

As for the artist and the casts, I shall do nothing about that till you come. My friend who is on the steamer wants to come over to Paris just about the time you would be there. I have talked a great deal about being busy. Everything else will take care of itself. I gave no encouragement to the fairy tale man, so I think he will go to Bermuda. So you see, dear, I have been cleaning house again and this time I hope more thoroughly.

Gertrude writes at length again the following day:

Dearest, it will seem a long time before you come and I know I will often be sad and depressed. Somehow I don't feel very courageous tonight, but just as if I would like someone to put their arms about me and be very gentle to me. I wish I were not so perverse about things—I love my independence and in the next breath I long to be protected! Surely women are idiotic beings!

I have just finished a whole lot of letters thanking nice people for sundry flowers etc. One impassioned suitor (mind you a man whose handwriting I did not even know) sent me a fresh bunch of orchids for every day. That was going some! I am glad beyond words to get away from that life, that chasing and continual sparring as you call it. To get to a land where all is simple and direct and I can take the cartridges out of my revolver and not be scared I am going to get fired at. You know that feeling. How I am going to work! As I never have before. I am going to try and put all the unhappy things in my life out of sight and for these two months be happy, giving myself up to happiness entirely without dread or fear of the future and as something to which I have a right. For one has got the right, hasn't one, to hold on to the joys? There are so extraordinarily few of them floating round. That sounds like a gloom talking and I guess I have not much courage, for this going off by myself, though brought about entirely by myself, always brings home to me the sad necessity that made it so, and that's my failure in life, and one does not think of failures cheerfully!!

Again, Harry is at Little Dalby Hall with Barbara and many guests; Gertrude at 72 Boulevard Flandrin, though working on the fountain much of the time at a larger studio at 57 Rue Chardon Lagache; and Flora at a nearby apartment where once again, between tutorial sessions, she often has lunch with her mother. Gertrude writes to Stackpole almost immediately. Even the transcribed extracts are long but, though Gertrude describes these as "uninteresting, dealing with trifles," they give a better sense than her journal (which will soon be resumed) of her work routine and that joyous opening up which always accompanies her returns to Paris. We can almost hear *Louise* being played in the background:

> Dearest dear, It has been a heavenly day! Not the weather, that was beastly, but I woke up cheerful, excited to get to work and with the happiest feelings inside of me you can imagine. . . . There is a chance that I can finish the old fountain for the Salon and perhaps that is why I am so happy. I flew at it and had a fine day's work, six good hours (it was dark at four). . . . It makes me feel marvelously to be at the real work again!! I wanted to take a walk but it was raining in torrents so I came home, had my massage and here I am now writing to you. Oh dearest! In this very room we had our long talks last summer. You lectured me on unthinkable dangers which all materialized. We sat on the big table, dangled our legs and talked ourselves blue in the face. It's all the same and if you could have had my delightful feeling, even at 6:30 of a dark winter's morning, when I got here, you would realize how much this place and life mean to me. Eddy [Minazzoli] had my fires going, flowers everywhere and something hot to eat, so the trials of an all night journey without a sleeping car were forgotten. My blue bed was like celestial sky come to earth and it was not till two that afternoon that Marie woke me up. The sun was shining and all the world just waiting for someone to be crazy about it. . . .
>
> This morning already came H.'s note. Funny. I am sure I don't know how he discovered my presence for I was not announced in the paper, anyway my presentiment was right. It is an invitation to dine Feb. 1st. Ye gods! . . . Tomorrow I shall be called at seven (it is dark at seven) and it won't be easy to get up—but I am now all for the Salon! Am entirely alone, no prospect of any fun till you come, absolutely nothing and as happy as anyone could be. Do you understand it? I accept it and am grateful. . . .
>
> TUESDAY.
>
> It seemed like the middle of the night at seven this morning and it was barely daylight when I left the apartment at quarter to eight. I have made arrangements for the *mouler* to cast the basin of the fountain Thursday, so you see I am losing no time. . . .

My dearest, I cannot help but be happy, the work goes and you are coming!

Gertrude is putting most of her energy into her work and her letters to Stackpole. Her journal, between letters, echoes but does not amplify her sense of euphoria: "To be in a continual state of happiness is absurd. . . . I am working like a dog and thinking of nothing else. Family and responsibilities have disappeared into the vague and my soul soars in the realm of modeling."

The next letter is dated January 20, a week after the previous one:

Everyday the work has been from 8 in the morning till 4 . . . with the exception of one afternoon. . . . O'C had a bust bought . . . last year, and a man called S. (who is the principal buyer of works of art for the government) was to take O'C. to the Luxembourg to see Benedite (the director) about placing it. O'C. very kindly asked if he could bring me. . . . S. really seemed interested in my work and goes so far as to talk of buying something of mine for the Luxembourg! This is all in the air and a *profound secret*. But I have heard through someone else that he thinks me really good and "une femme charmante." . . . At times I believe I suffer as much as you do from lack of me. The last few days it has been especially bad. I get a sort of mental and physical ache. . . . Didn't I make love to you enough in my little letters left at home for you? How insatiable you are! I always say that, don't I? and it is true, but I like you to be insatiable. I often forget your big appetite and starve you. . . .

WED.

Today they brought me, to the studio about 11:30 your two telegrams. Oh dearest. To think of you really being off! . . .

THURS. JAN. 23d.

Last night was very enjoyable. Salome always gives me a thrill. Dearest, when I got in last evening I got your Marconi. It is all very thrilling. Somehow until you were actually on the ocean I could not believe you were coming. . . . Did I tell you that after regretting H.'s invitation, he wrote and asked when he could come and see me. After that I had to appoint a day. His visit bored me, he politely sent a large bunch of red roses the day after his call. As he has been at Nancy ever since, I have not seen him.

The second figure goes much more rapidly and easily than the first. I am in the swing of working now and enjoy it intensely. . . .

Come just as soon as you possibly can. I send this off scribbled as it is and disconnected. It takes you heaps of love and kisses and desires for you.

Gertrude follows this with three letters to London where Stackpole is waiting to cross to Paris. Though these letters are filled with loving sentiments, their effect is to stall him. Sunday:

> . . . the work has told on me and I am afraid you will find me looking poorly. It has not been more than 6 or 7 hours a day but I have not let up at all and finishing things is a strain on one's nerves. The second figure must be finished tomorrow night. Tuesday I shall start the last one. . . . [Monday:] . . . I am simply longing for you and it is hard to work today with my mind continually on you. But the statue must be finished. . . . You must be good and try not to absorb me too much, for when one's mind is entirely wrapped up in someone, one does not have anything left to put into one's work. . . . [Finally, the following Sunday:] Can you come earlier this afternoon? Something has turned up. O'C. wants me to dine with him tonight to meet some important personage and I suppose I ought to do it. I am disgusted and disappointed, but I believe it to be the right thing to do. I can arrive at 4 so we can have till 6— And the statue is finished!!!! Think of it. It somehow got itself done. And I shall make a few sketches tomorrow, but can lunch out with you as well as dine —so we really gain more than we lose tonight—In a great hurry.

We can imagine Stackpole's wounded pride and jealousy mounting to rage. It is doubtful that he could accept the four-to-six rendezvous suggested by Gertrude, except to try to persuade her to keep their evening engagement. If he tried, he was unsuccessful. We learn from Gertrude's journal that he spent those late Sunday afternoon hours arranging for detectives to follow her. In the journal, she describes the end of that Sunday night at a *cabinet particulier*:

> Two men in a taxi . . . were waiting outside, they had sent the driver in to find out the gentleman's name. None given of course. Here was a nice mess! I got very quiet and collected. I do when I am really frightened. There was no other entrance, there was no use in waiting all night. I immediately thought of the other man. He would be just the sort of person to do a fool thing like that. So we left and I was taken home. It was obvious they must have known me. I did not sleep very much and the first thing I did the next morning was to write an angry letter. I carefully did not mention the circumstances so that I would know at once from his answer if he was the person.

The letter:

> I am sorry you did it—just as I am broken hearted myself at having told a lie. That does not seem to help matters though. Perhaps it is better that this should have happened. It came to me in the long

hours of the night that we had eventually to separate, for you see I just can't live up to it and I just won't be treated that way. I refuse absolutely to put up with such treatment, though I recognize that you are provoked to it. You have a right to think hideous things of me, the truth (that I lied to you) being scarcely less hideous. Lies are not pretty, but I cannot keep them out of our lives. I have tried over and over again. Our relation does not seem to be strong enough for that. I will not be placed in such a humiliating position, whether I deserve it or not, and I will not give up the life I choose to live. That sounds bald and cruel, but we must get down to the truth of the matter. Don't imagine that I am only thinking of myself, no, on the contrary, it is because of my love for you that I have taken this resolution. I should have come to it sooner, after repeated experiences in N.Y. I cannot make you happy, let me go, it is far better that way. How you could have taken someone to spy on me is something I cannot conceive of. Strangely enough I believe that you *know* I did a foolish thing and not a *bad* one last night. However that has nothing to do with the result. I should like you to *know* that to be the truth because of your belief in human nature. My dear, we are not suited. I cannot be honest with you. Everything in me sinks—I made a mistake—I thought I could change—it is not fair to you to put you to such tests. So, dearest—in tears and sorrow I accept what I now feel to be the only solution. Believe that I love you, in my way, but it is not the way to make you happy. . . . Don't let's debase our love by accepting a second best. I gave the big, unselfish love once in my life and I guess it is not there to give again. . . .

Stackpole does not deny what he has done but maintains that it has been for her good. Gertrude replies that she sees "no other solution" but to break off their relationship.

I will do again what I have done before, and you will be miserable and I will be too. Each time we rub a little more of the glamour and sacredness off our love. I won't do it. I won't lead that life. I am going to try to be good, but it will be alone. This is final.

Stackpole writes that she is cruel. Again she replies:

I don't want to be cruel, and I don't think that it is possible for me, behaving as I believe to be right, to be anything than what you will consider cruel, unless you will look at it from my standpoint. Two people care about each other—one of them does something which is wrong and a violation of all they hold sacred; the other does a dirty trick, an act which no gentleman would permit himself no matter what the circumstances. That happened in N.Y. I should have known enough then to put an end to something which was impossible. I did not. The thing takes place again after promises and explanations—all futile. I tell you it is final.

If you want to see me and talk to me I will do it, but there will be no other conclusion reached. This is true. On the other hand I consider it extremely dangerous to meet you. The other man in the case has every reason to want to know your identity. He is a dangerous man and if only for his own interest he wants to discover. I do not think he would sink to the depths of having me watched, but he might. If you want to put me any more in his hands than I already am, all you have to do is insist. I cannot forgive you for your behaviour any more than you should me for mine—I tell you absolutely the thing must end *now*. If you want to make things a trifle easier for me you will go away, you will tell me that *all* my letters will be burned as soon as possible and you will leave Paris. There is no hope of anything else between us. I cannot put it too strongly, no matter if I see you or if I don't this will be my final decision.

Please be kind and make things a little easier for me. Nothing will make me think of you with more kindness than the conduct which I suggest. Good-bye, I would prefer to have you *not* call me up in the morning.

Gertrude has, of course, touched a nerve—she has accused Stackpole of not being a gentleman. His reply runs more than five long pages, all meticulously transcribed by Gertrude, though edited here:

There is no man worthy of the name of gentleman who will permit his honor to be sullied without defending it. Nor will he fail to protect the woman he loves by every means at his command, even from herself. Your quick and cruel condemnation of me which you could not make with any sense or purpose of justice knowing me as you do, remembering any or all of the thousand things that have occurred in the past that have shown in me attributes of the gentleman: your determination from the first that you would not see or talk to me all show but too clearly your purpose throughout. I do not for one moment attempt to excuse my conduct. I am not ashamed of it in the least and would do it again as calmly as I would police my house from a burglar. . . . Do you know any man, really, who unless he were grovelling at your feet and incapacitated for anything else than parroting your views who would not firmly but kindly put a stop to it? All that you object to in the step I took is a mere trifle as compared to what you were doing to yourself and to me. . . . No! I am proud and glad I did it—not glad though that it was carried to the point where his suspicion was aroused, though what difference that can make considering where he took you with your consent and his obvious opinion of you, I fail to see! Still, since you chose to look at it your way, I will too. The peculiar part of this whole thing is that I have been compelled to stoop in order to finally show you the value to yourself of running straight and the danger that surely awaited you in the end if you did not. . . . If I have been the means of waking you up to a higher standard of living and of self respect, even at the cost and terrible sacrifice inflicted upon myself, it shall not have been in vain. Your attitude is not womanly—not fine: but rather that of a spoiled child who has committed the cardinal sin of having been found out. . . . I'd like to believe that there really is some human feeling in you behind the heartless cruelty you have heaped upon me and behind the deadly insult you have given me in that last note of yours. I can only take it and suffer the more realizing how careless you are of the harm you do. Of course I am going away, have stayed on only to struggle for what seemed the good and right to the end. I shall not go to——again. My only trips were to get my things left behind, overlooked on the first trip—slippers under the bed and so on. As for the letters, I shall think! They are preciously dear to me—the only thing I have in a wrecked life that I can hold lovingly in my hands—and they are safe—safer with me than you are with yourself. Whether about them I shall emulate your example and think only of myself I cannot say. Someday I will let you know, if you care to know.

When I contemplate what I was when I met you and before that—perfect health, high aspirations, efficiency beyond all my needs—a great belief in the fundamental beauty and goodness of life—a career that was firmly in my hands for great accomplishment—a courage equal to my responsibilities and a beautiful love in my heart to give you: and I now gaze upon myself, broken, wretched, utterly miserable, insulted, deserted and wronged, life but a grey desert of ashes endless before me, crushed and stunned before it all, I find nothing left but courage and graven in my heart and image in my soul a wonderment at this miracle of evil. And all I asked of you was fidelity and truth since you gave me love.

There, for the time being, the correspondence stops. Stackpole returns to New York, Gertrude to her journal. February 9: "I have been in Paris four weeks today. From the heights I have been in the depths, and now I am pretty well established in a sort of equilibrium which I hope to be able to uphold. It has been a time strangely uneventful and then, of a sudden, fearfully, I may say horribly eventful. This book is no history of outside events of my life, it is to deal with those inner thoughts of 'my vie artistic,' but as all important facts bear a direct result on one's thoughts so these incidents influenced all my feelings and sensibilities of the past week."

Gertrude describes her routine during the first three weeks: a call at seven, a bath, breakfast, work from eight till noon, lunch, work from one-thirty until dark, "varying from four to five. Ramon then made me a cup of tisane which I drank with pleasure for by that time I was very tired." She records the time spent on each figure: nine days on the first, with a day out to modify the basin and an afternoon to visit the Luxembourg with O'Connor and Sequin, the "S." (in her letter to Stackpole) who buys art for the government; six days on "the second gentleman"; a day and a half on the third, substantially completed the previous summer. The remaining days are spent with the caster, Merli; with O'Connor, to whom she has loaned a room in the large temporary studio and from whom she receives assistance and advice (particularly, to "get big planes correct, to consider no details" but to "make of it something simple and big"); and with herself for two days between the completion of the second and third figure, when she "pranced about Paris like a child playing hooky and shopped and enjoyed life." Then (she is still writing soon after Stackpole's departure):

All this week I have worked at Boulevard Flandrin on three sketches. Not so fearfully hard. Took one afternoon to go with O'Connor to his studio at Clamart where I saw again some of his very beautiful work, for there is nobody whose things I admire more. He is going to do a group for my studio [at Westbury] and I was anxious to see the sketch. It is a fine and original idea and if he carries it out it should be the greatest piece of modern sculpture. One afternoon I took Flora to the Luxembourg and gave her a little lecture on art. Then we stopped at Haseltine's studio, saw his huge horse which he is doing for the Salon. He asked us to lunch the following day.

In the meanwhile I have left the telling of my unpleasant experience to the last.

It is easy to imagine that my joy in finishing the fountain had to be celebrated and I accepted an invitation to dine alone with a gentleman. He says since that he mentioned the fact that it was to be in a cabinet particulier. That is unimportant because I probably would not have objected anyway, but I did not understand him if he spoke of it before. He was to come for me at 7:30, which he did in a taxi.

Now it so happened that another man whom I knew in Paris and whom I had seen a few times asked me the same evening to dine and, having first accepted, I made up an excuse and got out of dinner with him. So—we sallied forth, very cheerfully, work is over, here's for a good time. I did not like the man, in fact had been warned that he was a dangerous and selfish person, but he was good looking, fairly amusing and had been paying me very marked attention. He was new, and the moment was propitious to do something a little startling and entertaining. I had been submerged, I can call it no less, in my work and truly I had not been thinking of the evening or its consequences at all. Delicious dinner and some pretty broad things said. At any rate I cannot imagine how I came to do it, but I let him take me to some address (don't know where) with no idea of anything but sitting around smoking and talking. Of course he was angry when he found me obdurate and some pretty hard things were said. We must have been there about an hour (it seemed much longer) but I was afraid of parting with him any more harshly than was necessary. As we got to the door, the concierge spoke to him. Two men in a taxi had followed us and were waiting outside. . . .

We know the rest of Gertrude's journal account; we know the correspondence immediately preceding and following the event itself, but we don't know the whole story, the true story. Surely, Stackpole cannot be honestly described as a "man whom I knew in Paris and whom I had seen a few times." Nor, knowing Gertrude, is it likely that she would have quite so casually stood up a lover who has crossed the Atlantic to see her. More probably—for even when Gertrude lies there is an impulse toward the truth—she has done what she originally wrote to Stackpole: gone "to meet some important personage" because she believes she "ought to do it." She has stalled Stackpole, too, because she felt she ought to finish the fountain. By now only one kind of important person could have made her behave in this way: someone who could help her career. One possibility is Andrew O'Connor himself, but probably he is known to Stackpole and is being used, as in Gertrude's note, only as a decoy. A better possibility is Sequin. He can help Gertrude's career—and probably already has.

❧

Before Gertrude leaves Paris at the beginning of May, the design of her fountain for the New Arlington Hotel will be reproduced in various sizes and materials. One marble version, the same size as the Arlington's, is intended for the Spring Salon. A smaller reproduction in bronze will be placed in the garden of her Long Island studio. In response to a $3,000 commission from Carrère and Hastings (confirmed by Thomas Hastings in late January and reconfirmed by the sculptor Alexander Stirling Calder in early March), another cast will be submitted, along with an ornamental frieze, to the 1915 Panama-Pacific International Exposition. And, finally, still another version will go to Knoedler's art gallery for an exhibition the following March of the National Association of Women Painters and Sculptors. Gertrude is busy with all this by mid-February when Flora goes to visit Harry at Little Dalby Hall. She writes her daughter: "I worked till three yesterday & today, took a walk, went to the Louvre and to the marble cutters. The figures are advancing very quickly now. There are nine men working on them."

At the same time or soon after, Gertrude is working on three new figures, *Bacchante, Boy with Pipes,* and *Chinoise.* Of these *Chinoise* is the most interesting, both in itself and in terms of Gertrude's development. In it she has moved from the "classicism" of the fountain and the lingering influence of Rodin (still evident in *Bacchante* and *Boy with Pipes*) to a highly stylized mixture of art nouveau "modernism" and "orientalism." A Buddha-like figure of a woman in a flowing robe stands on a lotus blossom with one hand raised, index finger touching thumb, and the other lowered, with fingers in the same position. Her eyes are shut. Her expression is serene. She is a self-portrait of Gertrude, a dream of herself in a state transcending commissions, careerism, the transient details of life.

We don't know just what has led Gertrude to this particular mystical image. Her travels, her visits to museums, her reading, her suffering, perhaps most of all, must each have contributed. Among the many extreme contradictions in her personality, for many years now—surely since her honeymoon—has been the conflict between Western materialistic activism and Eastern contemplative quietude. In her search for a meaning to life, a resolution to its conflicts and her own, she may well have read the work of Emile Coué (1857–1926), the French therapist, at Nancy since 1910, who has been treating patients by autosuggestion. In any case, she begins now to keep yet another small notebook which she fills with sketches for the *Titanic* Memorial (cruciform right from the start) and with thoughts, grouped on separate pages, that seem to combine Couéism, mysticism, and bits of autobiography:

Health-Harmony.
I have health.
My body is in perfect health.
My head, my arms, my legs, *all* of me is healthy.
My heart is healthy.

I substitute Harmony and Health.
I am in harmony therefore I possess health.
I am harmony because I am one with the beauty of the universe.
No discord exists in me.
My soul is harmony.
Harmony is being at rest.
I will not have discord.
I will not hear discordant voices.
I will not tremble because of a jarring note.
There are no jarring notes.
All is harmony.
My soul is at peace.

Beautiful health.
I have health.
The cells of my body are beautiful, are healthy.
There is no flaw in my health.
I my soul and my body *are* health.
My brain is clear.

I am vital.
My heart beats normally.
My heart does not thump.
My heart is steady.

I am not miserable.
I am not unhappy.
My heart is well.
My life is worthwhile.
My children love me.

Two Ideals.
Two Personalities.
Two Protests.
Two Desires.
Two Divergent Aims.
Two Different Outlooks on Life.
Why not two?
Divergent and different affections are not necessarily inharmonious.
My interest in books does not interfere with my absorption in dancing.
Divergent and different affections are not necessarily inharmonious.
Love for my husband does not hurt love for my children.

One Life

I desire a full perfect and independent life.
I desire to work out my thoughts and my intense emotional and imaginative life.
I desire to use to its utmost every faculty in me.
I desire the joy which comes from creation.
I want the things which help to keep alive my imagination.
I want stimulus from the outside and the inside so that my desire for creation may be satisfied.
I know that if I do not use all my possibilities life has no charms.
I will have more expression, more love and more power.

Another Life

I am given great affection.
I cannot express what I feel.
I do not care about the occupations of the people who surround me.
I envy their ease, happiness and dislike their superficiality.
I feel myself inferior to them in cleverness.
I hate their point of view of life.
In the atmosphere of this life I shrink from showing my real self.
I am not stimulated by this life. I feel as if a weight held me to the earth.

I think of harmony.

I think of music.
A chord is beautiful.
Life is beautiful.
The universe is harmonious.
In the depths of the soul are unbelievable beauties.

I, as part of the universe, partake of its beauty.
The things which I see around me are perfect.
I have a body which is perfect.

I am strong.
Others feel my strength.
My heart works normally.
My heart is normal.
It beats but I am not conscious of it.
It beats with the world and is therefore normal & beautiful.

≈

However much she is involved with her work, however much she is attracted to a more contemplative life than that to which she was born, Gertrude is still far from becoming a recluse. How far is indicated in Edward Knoblock's autobiography. There he describes an "Oriental feast" given during this winter by him and his friend the sculptor Emanuele de Rosales for "an American lady who had always been most hospitable when I stopped in New York" and for another man. Discreetly, Knoblock never mentions either Gertrude's name or that of Herbert Haseltine, who has by now been married for two years:

. . . Rosales and I worked at the preparations of it for a whole week. *Kismet* has just finished its run in Paris, and Guitry very kindly gave me carte blanche to borrow any of the costumes and properties I wished to use. We turned the dining-room into an Eastern tent. In one corner of it we spread a rug and piled up cushions. A low table served for the food. It was covered with 7 different coloured table cloths, one on top of the other. The place was lit with gaily coloured candles.

I had not said a word to the other two guests. The only condition I made was that they must come in Eastern costume. The lady, I knew, had a beautiful one designed for her especially by Bakst. She wore it. We three men were also dressed in flowing robes with turbans wound about our heads. We met in my sitting-room in which nothing had been altered. At the appointed time a huge negro from the French colonies, whom I had hired for the occasion, appeared through the dining-room doors, salaamed and announced solemnly:

"Diner est servi."

This was the first surprise. The next was that we all had to creep into the tent. Here a fantastic meal was served. After each course the little table was cleared, and a tablecloth removed revealing another of a different colour and design. Rose leaves were scattered over the guests at intervals by the solemn negro.

For the kous-kous (a Tunisian sort of mutton ragoût with rice) we produced large mother-of-pearl spoons. The last course was a triumph of invention. Pistache ices in a glass cup rose from plates piled high with rubies and pearls of the very finest Bon Marché imitation. At the end of the meal I clapped my hands and, as if by magic, five Indian musicians appeared. I had discovered them wandering about the Boulevard St. Michel. They had come from India to give recitations. Their leading spirit was a singer called Ramaswami, who proved to be an admirable artist and fell in with the mood of the evening, telling us many charming tales of Indian folklore related to music and song. I had also thought of a photographer who appeared at a wave of the hand and took flashlights of us all. But the climax of the evening was reached when our fair guest of honor, filled with sudden "Arabian" fire, sprang up, and grasping a huge tambourine, improvised an exotic dance of delightful posturings to which the musicians played an inspired accompaniment, while we three pashas, sprawling on cushions, clapped our hands in rhythm to the music.

At last the feast was over. The rose-leaves lay withered on the floor. The candles had guttered. The final thing I remember was going to the window and seeing a huge full moon in a cloudless sky looking down on the silent gardens of the Palais Royal below. . . .

Knoblock's recollections are confirmed by a photograph of the oriental feast. There Gertrude sits, elegantly erect in her Persian tunic, jeweled headband, and pearls, smoking with the three men sprawled around her. This is one of the few unretouched photographs of her from this period. Granted the harshness of the magnesium flash and the closed eyes in response to it, we have at least a very candid image. Without benefit of fashion photography, Gertrude is clearly stylish, even avant-garde. Short hair, headband, cigarette, costume (which did not, like the men's, have to be borrowed) all anticipate more general, public acceptance of such things. She has, with work, exercise (particularly, long walks), and massage, retained her trim, elegant figure. Her face, too, has remained lean. If anything, the cheeks are now somewhat more hollow, the nose a little more pronounced, the mouth slightly coarsened. Though she has never been a conventional beauty, she has become more than ever what the French call *une jolie-laide*.

≈

At about the time Knoblock is transforming his dining room into an Eastern tent Kuhn, Myers, and MacRae, now led by the better-established and -connected Arthur B. Davies, are transforming the Armory of the New

York National Guard's 69th Regiment, at Lexington Avenue and 26th Street, into eight octagonal galleries for the exhibition (February 17–March 15) of some 1,600 paintings, sculptures, drawings, and prints—the largest presentation of modern art until now. Volumes have been written on the Armory Show and its influence on the history of American art. For our purposes it is enough to describe it generally, with particular emphasis only on its relationship to Gertrude.

The dream of an exhibition of the more progressive tendencies in American art has grown and changed enormously since the discussions two years earlier at the Madison Gallery. These have led to the formation of the Association of American Painters and Sculptors with Alden Weir, president; Gutzon Borglum, vice-president. However, it soon becomes clear that Weir is neither politically strong enough nor aesthetically open enough to arrange for a major exhibition at a suitable location. When he retires as president, Kuhn and/or Myers and MacRae approach Davies, who reluctantly accepts the job—on his own terms. He is not only established as one of The Eight but as the protégé of the perceptive art dealer William Macbeth and the collector Benjamin Altman, who have given him a studio in New York and a trip to Europe. Davies' culture and outlook are broad. He understands the history of modern art—its evolution from the past as well as the most radical experiments of the present. At fifty-one, his mature vision shapes the show; and what he lacks in energy is made up by younger men, particularly Kuhn—thirty-three now, in 1913—acting as secretary of the association.

It is a measure of Davies' exceptional integrity that, once he becomes president, the association is no longer dominated by his own group (i.e., Henri and other members of The Eight). Instead he insists on showing them within a context of the most daring European art and European-influenced American art. The former means, in brief, presenting the roots of modernism in the work of the classicist Ingres, the romanticist Delacroix, the realist Courbet, through the Impressionists to the Fauves and Cubists. The latter means presenting the work of such Americans as Alfred Maurer, John Marin, Marsden Hartley, Arthur B. Carles, Arthur Dove, Max Weber, and Abraham Walkowitz—all shown at the 291 (Fifth Avenue) Gallery of the great photographer Alfred Stieglitz prior to the Armory Show, of which he is an honorary vice-president.

All of these Americans—whose styles derive, broadly speaking, from Fauvist expressionism and Cubist formalism—represent tendencies for which Gertrude has as little sympathy (measured mainly by her purchases) as for the great School of Paris artists who influenced them, particularly Matisse and Picasso. No, Gertrude is basically committed to the American realists. Though in this her taste is ahead of the academically oriented general public, it is still far behind Stieglitz's and will continue to be as he adds Georgia O'Keeffe, Charles Demuth, Stanton Macdonald-Wright, Elie Nadelman, Gaston Lachaise, and others to "his group." Having said this, it must also be said that, despite her personal preferences and comparative provincialism, Gertrude never backs away from supporting what has become an International (rather than National) Exhibition of Modern Art. She gives $1,000 for decorations, as does her sister-in-law Dorothy Straight, the two together contributing about twenty per cent of the initial budget.

Like so many others (about 100,000 attend the show in New York, another 150,000 or more in Chicago and Boston), Gertrude may laugh at Marcel Duchamp's *Nude Descending a Staircase* and at the Cubist paintings of François (later Francis) Picabia and the reductive sculpture of Brancusi, but she cheers the inclusion of the American artists she believes in—The Eight, the younger Realists, such sculptors as Jo Davidson, James Earle Fraser, Charles C. Rumsey, and Mahonri Young, as well as the fantasist Bob Chanler, whose nine decorative screens filled mostly with exotic birds and plants painted in seductive, shimmering, iridescent colors attract more attention, for very different reasons, than any other works except those of Duchamp and Picabia. Finally, it is possible—especially given the size and unevenness of this historic show—that, had Gertrude not been classified as a patron, she would have been included as an artist, but frequently wealthy artists pay twice for their patronage, and sometimes wealthy women artists pay a third time as they are subjected to male condescension.

≈

In early March, Harry delivers Barbie to Paris, where she stays in the apartment with Flora, and he boards the *Bremen* for New York. In the two months before Gertrude returns with the girls, she completes the small sculptures on which she is working, enters the *El Dorado Fountain* in the Spring Salon where it receives honorable mention and good reviews, makes considerable progress on the *Titanic* Memorial, and takes Flora on a short trip to Madrid for the bullfights.

Yet, busy as Gertrude still is, Harry is even busier. As team captain he is, first of all, concerned with the many details surrounding the Big Four's second defense of the America Challenge Cup. Although the match is not scheduled until June, practice begins April 1 in Lakewood, New Jersey. Already a grandstand for 40,000 spectators is being built at the Meadow Brook Club on Long Island, and newspapers are describing the forthcoming match as "the most expensive game ever arranged in the history of modern sport." This year, unlike 1909 and 1911, Harry and his teammates know that the British will arrive well mounted. Led by contributions from the Duke of Westminster, they have raised about $500,000 for the purchase, grooming, and shipping of the finest English, Irish, Egyptian, and Indian ponies. Led by Harry, the Americans have spent about the same amount, mostly on the grandstand.

Concurrent with Harry's polo activities are those in horse racing. Belmont Park will reopen in May and for that Harry arranges to have two of his best horses, Iron Mask and Whisk Broom II, shipped from England to the States. On Decoration Day, when the track reopens, the horses are in peak condition. Gertrude, who has by then returned with the girls, goes to the track with Harry. About 10,000 fans are milling outside the gate because there are no ticket sellers, and Pinkerton men are pulling people off the fences. Harry, as an officer of the Racing Association, orders the Pinkerton men to open the gates, guaranteeing payment for the large crowd. Then he and Gertrude go to their box and watch Whisk Broom II win the Metropolitan.

This spring belongs to Harry. Whisk Broom II goes on to take the Brooklyn and the Suburban handicaps. Iron Mask wins the Toboggan. Pennant, who has been racing in the States, wins the Futurity and is Harry's biggest money earner in this year when his stable is the biggest American money winner. When Harry's name is not in the papers for winning a race, it is there for winning a polo match. When not there for either of these reasons, it is mentioned in connection with his new sloop *Barbara* which Robert Emmons II races to several victories while Harry is playing polo. Harry's name even appears twice for automobile violations—once for racing three friends to the polo field in Hewlett, Long Island (his chauffeur is fined ten dollars for driving at thirty-two miles per hour), and once for injuring a pedestrian at Madison Avenue and 85th Street (it is not clear whether Harry or his chauffeur was driving). Finally, in a very hard-fought match (4½ to 4¼), the Big Four successfully defend the cup, and Harry commissions Hazy to sculpt his favorite pony, Ralla.

Immediately after all this Gladys writes from Great Tangley Manor, Guildford, about forty minutes outside of London, where she and László have settled, partly because of heavy financial reverses suffered by him and other Hungarian nobles. Even her letter is mostly about Harry and how unfairly the Big Four have been treated by the British press. ("The papers here had been so ridiculously confident that you really thought we hadn't a chance.") She asks about an injury to Monte's finger. She quotes a telegram from Pauline: "WERE YOU REALLY AFRAID OF BEING BEATEN?" But finally, unlike most of Gertrude's relatives and friends during these weeks, she writes about the fountain: "I think it was rotten they didn't give you a medal at the Salon, and everyone else thinks so too. Edith & Uncle George [Vanderbilt] were so enthusiastic about the fountain and said, as everyone does, that it is by far the best thing there. . . . The only thing is to understand their way of doing things, and that is the only excuse. What foreigner got the medal?"

Yes, most attention is on Harry and the prizes surely go to him. When Gertrude again exhibits several small works, with other women sculptors, at the Gorham Gallery, the event is reported in *American Art News*—and then perfunctorily. Another event—almost public by Gertrude's standards

at this time, though private by Harry's—is the completion of the Westbury studio. We can imagine it being viewed by friends and relatives as a
very beautiful, expensive toy—as significant in itself as the work produced
in it. To Gertrude's friends from the Village it must have been awesome.
In his *Artist in Manhattan,* the painter Jerome Myers recalls an opening
party:

> I can hardly visualize, let alone describe, the many shifting scenes of
> our entertainment; sunken pools and gorgeous white peacocks as line
> decorations into the garden; in their swinging cages brilliant macaws
> nodding their beaks at George Luks—Robert Chanler showing us his
> exotic sea pictures, blue-green visions in a marine bathroom, and Mrs.
> Whitney displaying her studio, the only place on earth in which she
> could find solitude.

This opening party is evidently not the only one. Relatives of Gertrude's still remember another to which Bob Chanler sent two kangaroos
—a gift which so infuriated Harry that, after much shouting on his part,
Gertrude had to get rid of them. This is a detail Myers would not have
missed. On the other hand, his concluding statement is too generalized, if
not altogether presumptuous. Gertrude has been able to "find solitude,"
to the extent she wants it, in Greenwich Village and in Paris. Indeed
there is considerable evidence already (and more later) that MacDougal
Alley and Boulevard Flandrin are more congenial to her than Westbury
and at least as exotic as Westbury is to Myers. Even now Gertrude is
negotiating, through Thomas J. Regan at Harry's office, for the leasehold
at 8 West Eighth Street, a twenty-five-foot-wide, three-story brownstone
backing up to the yard of 19 MacDougal Alley. Though there is nothing in
Gertrude's journal about her intended use of the additional building, letters and drawings from her friend the architect Grosvenor Atterbury make
it clear that she plans two large exhibition rooms on the ground floor, an
office at the front of the second floor and a private room connecting with
19 MacDougal at the back, and a studio on the third floor. Gertrude's
hope of having a gallery in which American artists can congregate and
show their work is progressing now from the dreaming to the planning
stage. The alteration on which Atterbury is working will become the
Whitney Studio, the first major step toward the Whitney Museum of
American Art; and the second-floor office will soon be occupied by Juliana
Rieser Force, ultimately the first director of that museum. By August, Atterbury has estimated structural costs at about $7,000 and has filed plans
with the Building Department. By the middle of the month open questions have been resolved and Gertrude departs for Europe with Harry,
Flora, and Sonny, leaving Barbara in Newport. The summer arrangements
are typical—Harry and Sonny will go to Holwick, Flora to the Paris apartment, and Gertrude to 72 Boulevard Flandrin.

A letter from Natalie Hammond indicates that Gertrude has proceeded with her scaled studies for the *Titanic* Memorial and is about to send them to Washington. There are two long letters (and a separate explanation of "Synchromism") from the now non-figurative painter Morgan Russell, thanking Gertrude for her help over the past years—a monthly stipend beginning about 1906, which will continue through 1915. "You have made it possible for me to arrive at a personal vision," he writes, and offers her in gratitude a choice of any or all of his canvases, including a large one dedicated to her, *Synchromie en bleu-violacé,* on the Genesis theme "Let there be light." Again, if only now in a few letters, there is enough evidence that her continuing activity as artist and patron is, or should be, satisfying. However, these increasingly public aspects of her life still do not compensate sufficiently for the lingering pain of her relationship with Harry. December 4, after her return to New York, she starts a new journal:

A gray depressing, aching day. Everything aches, the furniture groans, all the shadows are ink and there are no light spots. Last night it seemed as if I had come to the end of my strength. I simply could not stand the feeling of the house. It had been a day so full of painful things, culminating in a splash of agony that seemed beyond control. The three men who were dining with me went out, and I fled myself. Fled, in a tea gown and a heavy coat which could not keep my teeth from chattering, into a taxi that rattled and bumped its uneven way down Fifth Ave. The Alley was as peaceful as my soul was disturbed and when the key turned in my own little door, the snap in my mechanism answered—a little later I lighted the fire and sat in front of it for an hour and a half's communion with myself. They are not so pleasant these hours alone, but my distress was added to by a terrible consciousness of G[ladys]'s physical suffering [in delivering her third daughter, also Gladys]. I begged an all understanding God to let me help bear it. (My backache today may be something, but the poor child is still in agony.) But I gained a little of what I had come for— self-control and when I left my tears were all shed (for the time) and the horrible pain in my heart was bearable.

It's another day and another awakening to pain. G. still suffers horribly. I pray to have some of it. Physical pain is a horrible thing. It affects everything. Mental pain seems more concentrated.

Loneliness is like the pain of an aching tooth. It gnaws and gradually drives one crazy. . . .

Gertrude's loneliness is even more painfully apparent in a letter to Harry written the same day on 871 Fifth Avenue stationery:

It seems very obvious that we are drifting further and further apart and that the chances of our coming together are growing remote. I

say this for several reasons—there is no inclination on your part to
have explanations which might lead to understanding. Also our mutual indifference to the pursuits and pleasures of the other is leading
us constantly to have less even to talk of and forms no bond on which
we might rely to bridge our difficult moments.

Of course for a very long time we have done absolutely nothing together because we wanted to. You perhaps do not realize this. We eat
together, as rarely as possible and from habit. We *never* go out
together—perhaps because I can't do the things you want to do, perhaps because you don't want to do those I can. However this is only
to show you how completely our lives are separated, not to blame you
or myself. Everyone of your pleasures (I don't think I exaggerate
when I say this, just think it over) is disconnected from me. Most of
mine from you. You are dependent on me for nothing. Our occupations are separate, our pleasures are not the same, all the things I
think essential you look down on, I look down on you because you
have thrown away most all the things I admired you for. I don't trust
you, you talk to your friends of the things I don't want talked of. You
are a hypocrite, which I don't admire. Now there are a lot of things
that balance these thoughts of mine in your own mind. I do this &
that. I am this and that. . . . [Gertrude's elipsis.]

I think that just so long as we will not face the situation we will go
on being miserable. I know I am unhappy and I guess you are, pretty
often.

If we had an understanding we could perhaps face things as they
are and build up something new and possible for a happier future.

There is one very important phase of it all that I have not yet
spoken of: that is, women in your life and men in mine. I suppose
that is the hardest thing of all to be honest about or to understand.
You have several times behaved pretty rottenly, but I think, at least
you have not been terribly open about these matters, so that they
were very much discussed. But you are now behaving differently. I object to this. There is no use, I suppose, my objecting to your caring
for someone else, it would simply be ludicrous, but I do object to several things which I will state. I have never been seen around all the
time with *one* person. I have never been talked about with *one* person. And another thing, I object to ——'s going abroad [to visit
Harry] *without* [her husband]. It would make people talk a lot and
I object on that ground. You have let me have a great deal of liberty,
a studio, living alone in Paris, but no one has even insinuated that I
used my studio for anything but to work in it. Even in Paris where it
would have taken so little to give one a bad name I have not been
maligned. All this probably seems unimportant to you. I don't blame
you for the things you don't give me and that I want because it must

be my own fault not to inspire them, but just the same it's hard not to get these simple things that everyone craves and almost has a right to. I don't take them from other people because, well, I often wonder just why. But if you loved someone else entirely and were giving that other person *all* the things I want, you wouldn't be mean enough not to let *me live*, would you? Would you have the courage to tell me and let me try and find a little happiness, before it's too late?

I suppose all this is very badly expressed, it's hard to put these sort of sentiments into words. I have been really desperately unhappy, it's not a mood or a passing idea and if you will let yourself face the truth I think you will realize the truth of what I say. It makes me sick, all this superficial sort of game, and I am not going to throw the rest of my life away. I am going to face things and understand as much as I can, and then build on a solid foundation for I am tired of the sand that crumbles and will not hold my poor little house.

Gertrude neither addresses nor signs the letter. She seals it, puts her initials and the date on the envelope, and hides it. There can be little doubt that, early in the year, when she wrote Stackpole "I gave the big, unselfish love once in my life and I guess it is not there to give again" she was thinking of Harry. Though a relationship like that with Stackpole is "serious," it is also largely the product of loneliness, hurt, and desperation, expressed as much in fantasy as in bed. Gertrude breaks her heart—and ours too—in trying to reach Harry, like others earlier in her life, with unmailed letters. We scream at her once again to put an address on the envelope—a stamp, if necessary. We shout futile warnings, across the distance of decades, that otherwise these autocommunications can reach only the dead-letter office.

The next day she writes in her new journal:

It goes on being bad, but [Gladys] had a better night. I saw her for a moment today. Yesterday when I went there and found her still suffering and looked for a moment at her pale face and closed eyes it took my little remaining self-control. I wept like a baby. I tried to rest later so as to be more able to be normal with L[ázló] and H[arry] at dinner and it seemed to go all right. Today is like the horrible day after—with somehow no hope for a brighter future.

Some people are afraid of everything. Men fear marriage and women and run. I am afraid of the shadow in strange places and of the thoughts that stir me to weird actions. I long for the entirely normal. I want to work hard and escape thinking. My back still aches and I want to sleep till total oblivion holds me. I am tired—weary—dead—discouraged. I despise human nature. I hate people and myself. I want to be alone with work. The world is revolting. The loves are sordid and the hates are inhuman. It must always be—"not to be."

The little frills of convention can no longer cover the filth of reality. My emotions are nothing—but the world is beyond improvement. I shall help to push it down. I shall help with my body to drag it a little lower, and with my soul I shall laugh at ideals. When life assumes this attitude it's time to look to heaven for help—!

Shall write no more for the present. Shall try and make someone happy.

The Revelation.

Short Story—

Point—how through a portrait man sees the woman he loves as old woman and can of course no longer love her.

1. Artist loves woman.
2. Gets great artist to paint her.
3. Sees portrait (in which everything is exaggerated).
4. Disillusionment.

That is a really great plot. Don't let *anything* dissuade you from writing it.

I am convinced of a few things. You (G.W.) are a great personality. You *must* use it. It may be rotten, but it is strong. Take it, play with it, use it, lovingly and exquisitely play on the strings of it. Play havoc with all other forces. Admit no master. Get away with the things other people struggle alone to look at. Be calm. Put over everything in loving, give up nothing in anything else. Love till you can no longer—take everything and be triumphant. Genius is the knowledge of one's strength. You have it. Give your love but never your power. Accept the little music[?] of the gods, give the huge joy of fools. When life is over and worms destroy, remember that the most foolish saying of *your* (my) little soul will exist and in the face of the *Titanic* Memorial will be seen the love, the agony, the joy of my soul. I love what I have written now, for it is the truth.

≈ *1914*

After a holiday weekend in Westbury, Gertrude and Harry begin the new year at 871 Fifth Avenue with one of the now comparatively rare large dinner parties of their now comparatively short New York social season. Thirty-eight relatives and friends attend, including the Payne

Whitneys, Mabel Gerry, Ruth Twombly, László Széchényi, the Howard Cushings, the lawyer Phil Carroll, the decorator Alice Nicholas, and Alfonso de Navarro, the heir to his father's construction fortune and now a top executive of the Portland Cement Company. The list, in Gertrude's Dinner Party Book, goes on, indicating many mates, like Gladys, indisposed by illness, or others traveling out of town alone. The regrets are at least as interesting as the acceptances: Charles Draper; his sister Ruth; Frank Crowinshield, whom Gertrude has known, first as a young publisher, since at least 1894, and subsequently as assistant editor of William C. Whitney's *Metropolitan* magazine, and now as editor of the new, chic, adventurous *Vanity Fair*; Alice Longworth; the Charles Dana Gibsons; the Arthur Burdens; and the Willard Straights, who early this year found the *New Republic*. . . . However, although Gertrude records all these names and many more in her book one wonders if at this time she could have concentrated on a large party. Any day now she expects to hear who has won the competition for the *Titanic* Memorial commission. Between January 2, the night of the party, and January 6, when the Whitneys sail again to Europe, she writes a note to Mrs. Hammond:

> I should like to see you before going. I want to show you the large sample of Belgian marble as you can judge of its beauty so much better than by the small piece which I sent you. Has any decision been reached by the Committee in Washington? I don't want to ask indiscreet questions but I am anxious to plan my winter's work and I am holding all my other orders over so as to be able to finish the *Titanic* Memorial in case I should be honored by receiving the commission.

On the day she sails she receives official word from Mrs. Hammond that her design has been accepted with the understanding that the memorial will be completed within a year and a half at a cost not exceeding $43,000. The next day, when she is at sea, the announcement is made to the press, and that evening and the following day it is in all the papers. Again, we find a letter transcribed in Gertrude's hand, which we can only suppose is from Stackpole, despite the "finality" of the previous year's correspondence:

> Dearest, this came today on the front page of the American. I saw it in the subway first. Someone next to me was reading it. I got a copy. Hundreds of people seemed to be reading it in the crowd. Somehow the picture caught me. I saw you through the tawdry print. "My God," I almost cried out, "I know her. She's wonderful, the most wonderful person in the world. But she's gone away, you fools, didn't you know that she'd gone away?" And then the loneliness came again and I carried the copy around all day and talked to people about business and things and thought of you and thought of you

and hoped that someone would speak of you and went and dined abominably and came home—and found your letter.

Dearest, today has been despair. You remember how we have often said that things must change sometime, that nothing could keep on the same. It seemed easy to say that when I could feel you near me and thought that I had touched the zenith of the joy of being with you. I little knew the depths to which I could descend upon your going and into which I am still going down. Surely there must be some corresponding height to which we will someday come, for the pendulum must swing both ways. It will be millions of miles up, dear, and it is hundreds of years away but it is coming surely, surely coming —There! I feel better about it, for I have a creed of faith to fall back on. . . .

This letter is not, of course, in the large, posterity-oriented scrapbook which Gertrude begins now: congratulatory messages, newspaper clippings, commemorative poems and collages, memorabilia of all kinds pertaining mostly to the *Titanic* Memorial but also to other work by her of this period. There are letters from relatives, friends, acquaintances, strangers, all enthusiastic about her being selected to do the monument, so closely is she identified with the world that sank in 1912 and with the sort of woman for whom husbands sacrificed their lives, so perfectly does her cruciform image of a nude youth (Ramon has posed for his body) express the spirit of self-sacrifice which will become still more meaningful this year with the beginning of the World War. A particularly touching letter comes from Nathan Straus, whose brother Isidor, his partner in the ownership of Macy's, went down on the *Titanic* accompanied by Isidor's wife, who wouldn't leave him:

Dear Mrs. Whitney:

I want to congratulate you most cordially on the acceptance of your design for the Titanic Memorial and to tell you how much I appreciate the deep feeling that you have expressed in the face and in the tense lines of the figure.

As you know that disaster came very close to me in the numbering of my brother Isidor and his wife among the victims, and it is gratifying to me to know that their deaths will be so tenderly commemorated in the remarkably sympathetic figure that you have been inspired to design.

In the widespread arms of your noble embodiment of grief I like to see an expression of the feeling that helped mightily to sustain me under the crushing burden of my personal loss. As I then wrote—

"In the Titanic tragedy all creeds were at least united in the brotherhood of death.

"If one could only hope for a brotherhood of life!

"Why wait for death to teach us the lesson of human fraternity?"

Very sincerely yours,

Nathan Straus

&

In Paris Gertrude works hard on the memorial, refining her earlier studies, experimenting with the effect of changes in scale and in types of marble, completing a separate large head of the figure. In addition to seeing Flora almost daily, Gertrude sees a great deal of the sculptors Haseltine, Rosales, and O'Connor. Of these she is most involved with Andrew O'Connor and now writes twenty-one pages about their relationship, concluding:

> . . . I found something in you which I had never possessed, and I longed to have it. So after a while I held out my arms and it came. You gave me so much, far, far more than I ever could reward. You gave me part of yourself. You talked to me. You told me about what you were going to do. You talked in another dimension. I staggered. I tried to understand. You put ideas into me which I had never imagined. You pictured an art which had never existed. You said that the last word had been said in certain kinds of expression. No one can hope to give the purity of form better than the Greeks. Why attempt that? You said if I would work hard you would make me the greatest woman sculptor. . . .

&

Gertrude's rhythm of work is interrupted early in February by Flora's having an attack of appendicitis with complications serious enough to bring Harry and Barbie from Dalby Hall to Paris. While waiting for the operation to be scheduled at the American Hospital, Harry and Gertrude go to their favorite restaurants, La Rue, Café de Paris, and Voisin. As soon as Flora has substantially recovered, Harry returns to England with Barbie; and Jimmie Appleton, who has been at Dalby Hall, visits Gertrude. Jimmie, like Flora, is recovering: a few weeks before, while hunting, he has hit his knee on a post. Now he recuperates, lunching first at Gertrude's studio, then dining out with her, and later taking her to theater and the Grand Guignol. Jimmie, a bachelor his entire life, is still very devoted to Gertrude, but she has relegated him to a circle of admirers. Indications of lingering infatuation are on his side, not on hers. Indeed her capacity for infatuation has, just now, a new focus. During her remaining weeks in Paris she is bowled over by the cosmopolitan charm of one of the most romantic characters she has ever met: Conte Francesco Mario de

Guardabassi, a forty-seven-year-old native of Perugia, equally talented as an opera singer and a portraitist of society women.

During this year, perhaps crucial to her because of her approaching fortieth birthday, Gertrude has many portraits done by many artists—a large sculpture by O'Connor, a small one in silver by Rosales, another in bronze by Paul Troubetskoy, a crayon drawing by Sargent, a lithograph of her dancing with a macaw by Troy Kinney—but none means as much to her as a pastel by Guardabassi. Looking at the work itself, a rather vague and romantically ethereal sketch on a 22-by-27-inch sheet of paper, it does not appear to have taken many sittings—perhaps just enough for Guardabassi to "pose" for Gertrude as she poses for him. We can imagine this tall, powerful, virile man, pausing for a moment to stroke his black mustache as he tells Gertrude about his days as a protégé of Madame Melba. We imagine him, too, strutting about his vaulted studio (near the Faubourg St. Germain) which he has transformed into a medieval Italian workshop filled with period benches, wardrobes, and chests as well as a grand piano at which perhaps he again interrupts his work to play and sing an aria from *La Bohème*. Whatever the actual number of sittings, they lead (according to Gertrude's Line-A-Day) four times to tea, once to a walk, six times to dinner, once to opera, twice to theater. Guardabassi is very much a part of Gertrude's life by late March when she, Harry, and Barbie return to New York, leaving Flora behind with Miss Givenwilson to continue her studies while recuperating, and returning just too late for the funeral of George Washington Vanderbilt, who has died suddenly from heart strain after an appendicitis operation.

Aboard the *Olympic*, Gertrude writes Guardabassi a long letter in two parts:

Mon Cher,

The trip seems like Eternity. I wonder what you are doing, thinking, feeling. But seriously, Paris seems like a dream, an unreality. The rush, the many experiences and emotions all crowded into such a short time. My thrills and agonies over my work, and the many ups and downs of feeling in my personal life. You can understand all of this, I know, if you let your mind rest for a moment on the complexity of emotion that I necessarily went through during the last month. Never in my life have I been so deeply stirred. For truly my statue was brought forth in deep anguish and although there were moments of real joy these were only moments. In other ways I was very happy and so between pleasure and suffering it seems now as I look back as if I were an instrument played on by hands stronger than human. Mon cher! Did I make you the least little bit happy?

The Latins are different from us. Do you feel the dreadful lack in me that I feel in others? That fear, that holding back? God, I hope not. For my part I feel so close to you. Your interest I feel and your wanting all my thoughts I feel too, and the little somethings that make for joy or grief, and I love it. There is a warmth to it, a something human and loving in it that thrills me to the bottom of my soul. I have thought so much of your talents—your beautiful voice that simply must be used, your painting, of your life and the marvelous gifts you have been given.

We all have to do tiresome things, be nice to people etc. etc. but make that part of your life as small as you can. Go straight for the big recognition you should have and don't waste time. Keep your eye on that. I want to see you succeed and be at the top of your profession as you should be.

Believe me, if my little power can do anything for you, you will have all. My ways are deep and I cover my tracks with discretion, but none the less when I want something it often happens (no one knows why). Be especially careful in mentioning me. I am surrounded by people who could and would like to overthrow me, because I am successful. I do not say these things because I do not trust you, that you know, for had I not trusted you my actions would have been very different, but because so far I have had liberty and I am placed so that a few whispers could take it from me. And I treasure it. . . .

This letter has become long and serious. Next time I write I will laugh with you, now dear I can only pour out a little of what is in my heart. Please don't feel me far away from you. Remember me as I do you, that is all I ask—and I will be happy. Write often.

The old boat goes throbbing on. I have been on her since the beginning of time. Have read a beautiful book [a novel, not specified, by Dostoevsky in French translation] and have slept. All those last hours in Paris are a nightmare. Up to when I left you Tuesday night I was happy. Somehow I felt like a kid while you were making the casts and also when we were so dirty and rushed back to eat. How thirsty we were and how good the cocktail tasted, do you remember. And then, after I washed a little, we ate together in my dining room. I feel suddenly as if I must come back to you as if I must see you as if it were wrong for me to leave so. After that all was black. I knew all of a sudden I was very tired and then came the horrible disappointment of sleeping and then waking, the lights in my face, the chill of the morning—too late. . . .

At the pier the Whitneys are met by Gertrude's mother, accompanied by William Stackpole. This would have been easy for him to arrange with unsuspecting Mama, in a spirit of helpfulness to his old friends. There is no indication of Gertrude's reaction either in her Line-A-Day or in the letters she writes to Flora immediately after arrival—just the fact that Stackpole is there. Perhaps by now he *is* just a fact. Harry goes to his office.

Gertrude and Barbie go to Mama's for lunch, where Gladys' three daughters are staying while she is on a trip. After lunch Gertrude and Barbie go to see the fountain at Knoedler's before meeting Harry to drive to Westbury. From there Gertrude writes Flora:

> . . . still some snow left . . . and it looked very brown and unspringlike. The [indoor] tennis court is finished and extremely attractive. My studio looked bleak, the ivy being still done up in brown canvas, but I have two new statues enlarged and plenty to do without considering the landscape! Sonny got in from [Groton] this morning. I went to meet him at the station. His pink face (except for dirt!) was all smiles. The first thing he said was: "Why did you leave Foufi [Flora]?"

After a day of playing tennis on the new court, Gertrude writes again:

> To-day when I got to town I went right to see Auntie [Gladys] who arrived yesterday. She loved her trip and brought me a parrot! She sails on the 7th and says she will stop a day or two in Paris to see you, although she had intended to go straight from London to Pest. I would give anything to be back in Paris. Except for Sonny it is simply beastly here and I long for the other side of the ocean. Auntie does not want to go back at all! It's always that way. Don't you think if all goes well that it would be better for you to stay over a little longer. If you stay till the end of May there is quite a good chance of my coming over for a few weeks and bringing you home. The Lusitania sails April 21st and I have my eye on her. It would be great fun.

Once again, beneath the comparatively calm surface of her letters to Flora, there are deep currents of agitation rising. Despite work and social activity in Westbury, she feels alone. Surely Stackpole no longer means to her what he once did; and O'Connor and Guardabassi are in Paris. In late March and in April, as Gertrude works on both the *Titanic* Memorial and the *El Dorado* frieze (a high-relief running about 75 feet and containing 41 life-size figures), long, impassioned letters begin to arrive from Guardabassi:

> Mio dolco e caro amore! I did not realize really what had happened until I got your telegram from the boat yesterday and then I felt as if part of me had been torn from me and I was longing to get it back.
>
> My thoughts have been with you every minute since I saw you last, haven't you felt them? I am sure you have; you showed in your telegram which made me happy and miserable at the same time and wanting to take next boat and come to you! Even the weather is in sympathy with my broken heart and in keeping with my dark moods. I have been all day long looking at your started picture in which I suppose only myself sees thousands of things and makes me think of

thousands more! By the way, you were just the sweet thoughtful, delicate, darling self to suggest what your secretary wrote me this morning about the picture and I thank you with all my heart: but I *cannot* accept what you so generously are offering me. When you come back and we finish it and you *like it* we may talk about it: but I would so much like to keep it myself. You can help me with other people as I need to work and working I am much happier and will make time seem shorter for your return. I wish I could write better English to express all my thoughts of love and admiration for you: but you are so sensitive and you must read between the lines and if you fail to understand my writing you look the little picture; that will always speak to you, the wonderful words, t'amo tanto and I want you—to come back! Do write me often, it will be the only consolation for me to know that you think of me.

Tuo

Gertrude does write often, usually in French. In the midst of loving phrases she reminds Tuo: "Je voulais être libre. . . . Je voulais la passion sans l'amour. Ce n'est pas bien joli ça, mais c'est bien plus confortable." The game is familiar to Tuo. He responds with increasing passion, urging her to come to Paris, while at the same time asking favors:

I worked on your picture so to be still with you and I am going to send you a photo of it—I think you will like it! I wanted Mrs. A[lmeric] P[aget] to see it even unfinished: but she has not been able to go out for several days on account of her health. She was awfully nice to me and I liked her immensely: she spoke of having her children done and possibly one of her with the younger girl. I hope she will not change her mind. I should love so to do it if she has not the time now, I could go to England. Do suggest it to her, as if I can't arrange anything with the Boston Opera here I should love to go to London and do some work and it would be a splendid opportunity to do Mrs. P.'s children to start with. I am crazy to hear from you about so many things but principally that you think of me some time and that you wish you were back here pour retrouver notre petit coin d'art et d'amour!

A few days later he invites Flora and Miss Givenwilson, by now Gertrude's personal secretary in Paris as well as Flora's governess there, to see the portrait.

They really liked the picture so much and Miss G. said that she would insist with Mrs. A.P. to come and see it, so that she would decide to have the picture of her children done. So I expect now to hear from her every day. Your dear little girl is so charming and looks the picture of health. She liked the studio so much and took great fancy for Didi [his dog] who amused her immensely with his little tricks. I

was so happy to see her who is part of you and has so many characteristics of you & vivacity and exuberance of life.

He responds to the first part of her shipboard letter:

You are not an Anglo Saxon you are above everything an artist and
artists have no nationality. One big flame burns in them all alike—
there is only one art one love one passion and these three marvelous
chords are harmoniously vibrating in your divine body regardless of
blood or nationality. You impersonate the cherished dream of
woman of my life, the realization of which came so suddenly as you
made me feel that really I had never loved before. . . . I must deserve your love. You want me to be a great singer: I shall do all in my
power again to become one especially if your dear helping hand
is going to play an important part in it as to be given to me a fair
chance. Mr. K. [the banker and patron of the arts Otto Kahn] is the
one to insist that I shall sing at some of the performances to be given
at the T[héâtre] des Champs E[lysées] this spring when all the directors will be here. If you could talk to him directly will be more to the
point.

We don't know whether Gertrude speaks to Otto Kahn, only that if she
does it is no help. In May, Tuo writes that "The Opera Boston here is not
much of success and the intrigue that has been going on has disgusted me
more than ever for the theatrical life." But she helps him with other intro-
ductions and his letters continue to be full of kisses, baisers, bacios. Except
for a few drafts, Gertrude's letters have been destroyed, presumably at her
own request. (Tuo writes, "Trust me always with your letters I shall destroy.") However, from Tuo's side of the correspondence, we sense a slight
slackening of her interest and of her need for him as an outlet for her
lonely romanticism. Had Gertrude really wanted to return to Paris, she
would have. If she needed excuses, there are Flora's confirmation in April
(attended only by Aunt Pauline and Uncle Almeric of the family) and her
daughter's return in late May. She "explains" to Flora:

I had wanted, of course! to get back to Paris (if only to bring you
safely home) but it does not seem possible to arrange and after all I
guess I am more needed here. Papa's arm is better and he goes to
Lakewood, although he cannot play any polo yet. I am trying to get
on with my San Francisco work [the El Dorado frieze], but it does
not go very rapidly. Am going to Washington soon to investigate the
ground [i.e., the site] for the Titanic.

Though Harry will continue to play some friendly polo, he will never
again play in the more competitive and dangerous international matches.
He is already past forty, Gertrude fast approaching that critical age. Her
next few letters to Flora are all, in part, concerned with her body, still

beautiful, but aging, especially when compared with the body of Diana Watts, an English dancer and mystical physical therapist, presently giving lectures and demonstrations in New York, whom Gertrude has met through their mutual friend Ruth St. Denis. "I am going swimming with Mrs. Watts in the Colony Club pool this week. . . . It will be fun—if only to see her, for she really has the most lovely figure I have ever beheld."

Soon after, Diana Watts writes Gertrude:

I would love nothing more than to answer *all* your questions, show you everything I can—*give* you everything I know—for you are one of the vital things of America & your strength of purpose & will to work have opened a door that is closed to most. . . . I will tell you & show you all I can that you may be able to keep your own splendid little body in perfect condition—in many ways it is very wonderful now—I see that—but it might be much more so—

So much for Diana Watts's and Gertrude's own body. As to Ruth St. Denis', Gertrude writes to Andrew O'Connor that she

came to dance one day & suggested I make a statuette of her. She was beautiful against a dark red curtain with few clothes and her strange gestures, but alas! she has grown older and heavier. C'est la vie, hélas. I wish I were a man because then when I get despairing I could go out and get drunk. How horrid of me to talk that way. It is revolting, but none the less true. These ups and downs are fearful. I have to hang on to myself like mad. This is an outburst, such as I never make to anyone—forgive it, I am sure you understand the struggles.

"The struggles" now have little to do with the statuette of Ruth St. Denis, much more to do with life itself and, as to a specific sculpture, with the *Titanic* Memorial. As she writes O'Connor:

A few days now and my memorial will be done! (That is till I see it 12 ft. high.) It meets with the approval of the few who have seen it here, which instead of inspiring me with delight has left me sunk in unexplainable depression. I hope you like it—and that is all I care. I have tried to keep it simple and young (everyone wants ten dreary years added to his life). I can't do it—poor darling he gave up so much more being a kid! The details I have left—to be put in if necessary afterwards. I have gone through every emotion while doing it— moments of such despair and agony as to be absurd & then exhilarations that could not be accounted for. Mr. [Henry] Bacon [the architect, formerly of McKim, Mead & White and later most famous for his design of the Lincoln Memorial] came to see it last week. What a nice person he is. We spoke of you. I shall see him again soon. . . . I have wanted so to make this miserable statue beautiful and to express a simple big truth and it is terrible to see it so puny. The drapery will probably need simplifying when it is enlarged.

Gertrude writes (and receives) so many letters this year that for the moment she has apparently neither need nor time for her journal. Yet her neglect of it, combined with the strain of completing the *Titanic* Memorial and not completing the seemingly endless series of figures for the *El Dorado* frieze, may well explain an attack of colitis, first described in several letters to Flora and then more generally in what seems to be a draft of a letter to Tuo:

Thank the Lord I am at last in the country! Still an invalid (d— it) in the sense that I am stuffed with soft slimy foods and a trained nurse puts beastly hot things on my stomach that make me feel like a hot water bottle myself. I have forgotten how to speak, and talk by making gestures, and as for thinking, nothing beyond fear and hunger affect me. I have no black rings under my eyes and my complexion is simply brilliant—for I never do a single thing I shouldn't. Now I am allowed to come to the studio every day and out in the garden and loaf and nod my head in the sun like the parrots themselves. Every day a different young man can come down and lunch with me and I loll in a chaise longue with my nicest summer muslins and fancy slippers for what else on earth have I to think of. Indolence is surely the best thing in the world, it makes one feel like a Roman Emperor and a houri all in one. The garden is a mass of color. I have added three more birds to my family and they and the Japanese azaleas' deep red tend to make the garden rapturous. Excuse exaggerated terms but I feel exaggerated. No plasteline mars the beauty of my recently manicured perfumed body. My spotless white lingerie gown is set off by a ravishing "garden hat" of corn color. I find my mind has adapted itself to this changed life. My ideas of art are as light, frothy enough to approach the degenerate. Life is a purple garden in which the bubbles of the soul rise like tiny buds to beautify the earth!! Don't expect it to mean anything. Sense is a horrible thing, only the hopelessly dull know facts and are accurate.

I should like you to see the garden now—all the parrots and the fountain and the big Italian jars. It wouldn't matter if you saw me or Loup. He is sitting by me now and sends his regards to Diddy. Very formal. "Diddy would go in at the very end of the procession if it was a grand dinner," Loup says and therefore he cannot associate with him. Loup is a snob of the worst sort. He is sometimes horrid to me because I have no title and I work.

The man who came to lunch today is an architect. He has lived mostly abroad and is very fond of the ladies but a bit wary. Tomorrow's man is mad and a decorator or a mad decorator, both are equally true. I will die of exhaustion after he has gone and all the gruel in the world won't resuscitate me. So the day after I will have someone who would like to have an affair with me—that always brings me to life—and after that someone I want to have an affair with and after that—I am perfectly nutty and if I don't stop I may never be able to, for I think I have been wound up like an 8-day clock.

It's six o'clock on the village clock and exactly my bedtime so adio.

While recuperating Gertrude is also in correspondence with Andrew O'Connor. He is very sympathetic about her illness and, connected with it, about various frustrations she has had with the *Titanic* Memorial Committee: the age of the sacrificial figure (her desire for a youth has prevailed), the degree of nudity (the committee's desire that the crotch be covered by drapery has prevailed). He himself is planning a garden figure for her in Westbury and wants it to be of her. She responds:

> I have been thinking a lot about the garden proposition and I am very thrilled at the idea. You meant me to pose for it—didn't you? I like that too as an idea but I fear it, for to do it and be recognized would be cheap and absurd and I don't choose to be either one or the other. But—to pose for you I will and would love it. For you to put me to the music you want where there is no connection with me! I am only too willing to do that, and my body will make itself as beautiful as it can to inspire you and come up to your conception. Let's think of that. You putting me into that tender spot at the end of the garden—but at the same time making a second figure which will answer the requirements for the time being—putting that in my place— till the curious eye is satisfied and then substituting myself. Am I exaggerating? Perhaps. The figure that Rosales did of me I have had to put away—no one saw it without *knowing*. Perhaps that is the reason I fear. I do not wish you to sculpt me for the world to admire and my pride to be satisfied. I want you to do it so that your ideal through me may give to the world a work of art such as no man has yet produced!

At the same time, probably through Harry's office, Gertrude is arranging for the purchase of O'Connor's studio at 51 Rue Boileau (later renumbered 49), as he plans to return to the States.

Even while suffering from extreme physical discomfort, Gertrude thinks a great deal about commissions—past, present, and future. However much more feebly, she continues to fight the losing battle against Mrs. Hammond's committee for the revised design of the *Titanic* Memorial. And she has her assistants—particularly, from now until the end of her life, Salvatore Bilotti, a well-trained Italian stone carver—working on the mechanical enlargement of her figures for the Panama-Pacific Exposition frieze. And she considers a commission to do a twice-life-size statue in marble of the recently deceased diva Lillian Nordica (as Isolde). . . . Yes, alas, commissions are the one way she, like most other sculptors of the period, can get work out into the world and receive public recognition, "success" on something like Vanderbilt/Whitney terms. Yet as we look at Gertrude's major monuments (to date as well as to come), we are disappointed by their impersonality. We miss what exists typically in the sketches and studies for these works (and, also typically, in the best of her journals and letters)—intimacy, immediacy, tenderness of touch—qualities lacking in almost all large-scale public sculpture which, by definition, cannot be intimate and which, generally, demands the surrender of the artist's own hands to those of artisans. Too often Gertrude betrays her intimate talent in the pursuit of public commissions. And yet the pursuit goes on. We are reminded already, and will be again and again, of Henry James's description of the nineteenth-century American sculptor William Wetmore Story, who "worked bravely on, from year to year, meeting as he could the conditions, often, inevitably, the reverse of inspiring, involved in the appeals reaching him for monuments to American worthies—making, that is, the best of the dire ordeal of the sculptor fighting for his idea, fighting for his life, or for that of his work, with an insensible, an impenetrable, a fatal committee." Yes, this is at least part of Gertrude's pursuit too in what James calls ironically the "long marmorean adventure."

Gertrude's own commissions are not the only ones preoccupying her. After a two-year delay while completing "acres" of murals for the Curtis Publishing Company for whom he is the outstanding illustrator, Maxfield Parrish is ready with the first two of four panels, each about six by nineteen feet, for the sitting room of the Westbury studio. The paintings are what has been agreed upon—in Parrish's words, "on the North wall [not yet ready] a fete [of] youths and girls [who] will have sauntered off onto the other walls. . . . As a companion tone to the rich brown of the wood work . . . a band of rich beautiful evening blue; those to be the two big notes of the room. I feel sure you will agree with me that outside of Niagara Falls there is nothing more beautiful in all nature than figures against a sky of r.b.e. blue. . . ." Like his art, Parrish's humor is light; life's is a bit heavier. Nothing works. The panels are off by a few inches. The light in the room is inadequate. T. R. Fullalove, Parrish's beautifully named installer, will struggle for four more years, cutting and patching these panels and installing the remaining two, one of which, the crucial north wall, will be so out of scale that Parrish will question his abilities as a mural painter and offer to return $4,000 of his fee (refused by Gertrude). But, returning to 1914, yet another commission *of* hers, rather than *to* her, goes smoothly: a five- by six-foot pewter low relief of Flora and Sonny in profile on ponies sculpted by James Earle Fraser for "about $25,000," according to the New York *Times*. We cannot help but make the comparison between the two commissions. Clearly Gertrude values sculpture much more

344

highly than painting. Even if the *Times* is inaccurate—it does misspell Fraser's name and refer to Sonny as Harry Payne Whitney, Jr., rather than Cornelius Vanderbilt Whitney—we suspect that Gertrude would only have exaggerated Fraser's fee as a gesture of professional solidarity.

ⵤ

July 28, Austria declares war on Serbia. Germany, citing Russian mobilization, declares war on Russia. . . . Though the World War has in effect begun, its vast implications are still generally invisible and surely so to most Americans, including Gertrude and Harry. Early in the year he has bought from Gertrude's uncle Frederick the *Warrior*, a 282-foot twin-screw steamer. On July 29 Harry, with his brother Payne, begins what he calls in the ship's log a "Neuritis Cruise. . . . 270 miles in 20½ hours. Sea very rough to the Cape—screw came out for first time in history of yacht."

Soon after Harry returns Gertrude goes to the Adirondacks for further recuperation as well as the usual peaceful revitalization. But there she is pursued by letters. Guardabassi has had an attack of phlebitis in his left foot. He is suffering as she is but wishes mostly that she would write more often: ". . . your letters more rare, seems they are adjusting themselves to the cruel reality of facts, and you don't seem to miss mine if I don't write as often! C'est la vie et c'est naturelle! But I do miss you just the same and I am counting the days when I will see you again and hold you in my arms in a long long kiss!" Though Gertrude writes to Guardabassi less frequently and less passionately than heretofore, he amuses her as a safe distant infatuation. Stackpole, who continues to write, is a different, more threatening case, a relationship which must finally be broken off. Gertrude drafts a letter:

> It is one of those glaring semi-gray days which you can't quite call hazy. We are up on Little Tupper Lake camping in a log house. Everyone has gone off fishing, I stayed behind. I have re-read your letter and I have thought over all you say and have said. Thought over all our relations of the past and then analyzed my feelings of the present and gone further still imagining various futures that might exist for us. Truly it is hard for me to imagine our coming together again. I have listened to your arguments—among my letters that you gave me back was a copy of the letter (the last letter) sent to me by you in Paris. I was able to read it coldly now, dispassionately, and under all my actions I saw clearly that thing which at the time caused me to act unconsciously perhaps but rightly and firmly, that fundamental difference of opinion as well as the certainty that my love was not big enough to make me change my mode of life. But, dear, out of it all has come to me a very deep and real lesson. You have changed, unhappiness in various forms has come to you and you are re-constructing your life, building on solid foundations, for after the

earthquake one knows the places fit to build on and out of it will come more happiness and satisfaction. Yes, and I am re-constructing too. Perhaps you have not seen me enough lately to see how I have changed. I don't want the playthings anymore. I got down to solid rock with you and only real things count now. I have decided to control my life. I can no longer enjoy the blowing about of my surface-soul with every wind of circumstance.

There follows a startlingly revealing passage, crossed out in its entirety and with a specific line through the (now) italicized words:

It was a phase, perhaps I had to go through it, anyway it is over and I have laid out for myself a course of action which I will roughly indicate to you—not to raise any discussion, merely because as my friend I know you will be interested and I think it will simplify matters for me to tell you at once . . . on my return I have decided if possible to have another child. This means a great change in my life, my work etc. I should like to have it next summer. It will be a hard life (till then) for me to look forward to, but for many reasons I believe it to be the only thing for me to do. If I ever want another it is the time to do it, and as *a punishment or* a reminder to me of how different my life is to be, nothing could be better.

Another child? Is she that lonely? Does she need to be punished that much? Reminded that often? Or is she now, in the absence of Guardabassi and with the abandonment of Stackpole, perhaps moving closer to Harry? The answers are not immediately forthcoming. Gertrude concludes:

You say in your letter as you have many times before that I am trying to fight our love. I am not. I am only trying to fight following that easy physical impulse which necessarily exists when people care for each other and which would lead us only to more unhappiness.

One thing I want to say. If the love we have for each other is such as you describe, a little time will not efface it nor need we fear circumstances which momentarily keep us apart.

So much for Stackpole. Perhaps now, perhaps sooner after Paris, Gertrude also writes a "letter" to Harry which, as is so often the case, changes into a letter to herself:

After this long time, dearest, I am going back to you and there is no joy in me, only depression. I shall be very happy to see you again, I care for you as much as ever, but dear, going back means so many things I hate. It will pass and after a while my spirits will come back, but now it is as if the world was on my shoulders. That may be the real reason and it may not. Perhaps it is because I behaved badly while I was away. I will try at least to be honest with you.

I went back for a little time to a man who has loved me for three years and besides that I became infatuated with another man and I let him make the most desperate love to me. I loved you all the time but I was excited and unnatural and it did not seem to me to be very bad.

Here, on a new page, the "letter" to him breaks and the one to herself begins:

To be a little interesting for his benefit—
Stories—
Ideas—
Books—
And make him talk—
Something light and impersonal to start with.

How sad that at this late date, almost eighteen years after marriage, Gertrude must make topical lists for Harry as if he were a new suitor. How sad—and how unrealistic in relation to him as well as to her. But maybe after making the list she herself recognizes that there are no simple, easy solutions or resolutions. For several more pages she vacillates between more complex, more difficult alternatives—none satisfactory:

Tiresome accuracy of some people. Having had plenty of time to think have come to the wise determination of getting as much fun and making up as much as possible for lost time. Silence alone with oneself makes one realize the beauty of insincerity. Aunt Lulu's story of the gardenias. Mlle. de Maupin's complications. The angel's position in regard to the hero.

Quick change to something very proper after this. The tiresomeness of people who always do careless things and can't once at least be thoughtful.

A delicious ideal life in which everyone was on their own with desperate affairs, continually changing, on hand. The desire to love a great many people in order to forget tiresome things. . . .

The brutal idea of a perfectly respectable woman throwing her daughter at the head of an ill rich man and the fact that everyone respects and looks up to her as respectable and superior. The salamander. Life in the West and its horrible effect on man. Theoretically fine but in reality terrible. The necessity of getting away from self—the terrible burden of self—exercise as an antidote to thought. Women lovers. The desire for the ideal which is at the back of it. The horrible desire to be understood which spoils all amusement. The deadening influence of love. The interest that comes for the new. Taking away individuality—levelling process. Why can't we lie decently anymore, or could we ever? Teaching children to lie. Development of our latent powers of evil. If each person found out if there were more good or more harm in them and then developed that, we would be stronger more useful people. Spoiledness—willingness to do things for other people—concentration.

Is the feeling of crossness and general disagreeableness which I constantly have now due to the fact that I do things not considered perfect or to the fact that things are all rotten and so many things continually make me unhappy that I have the feeling of necessity?

Finally, on a separate sheet, there is an "Interlude," as Gertrude titles it —another solution or resolution, directed first to Stackpole, then to Harry:

Break—It's the only thing to do. I hate breaks, they are contrary to my nature. I prefer to drift into a different relation. Make him see that you have been seeing other people and that your interests are beginning to go in other directions. But that is heartless to a person who cares and it is much better to say—I have not changed, only it seems to me best; and this I will do today. Why? Because it must come some time and anticlimax is awful. Now be—nicer to H., you have been horrid long enough. You have made him think pretty seriously that probably you are bored and perhaps you like someone else. That is good, now be very nice for a while. Life is revolting anyway and the sooner you can get yourself into condition not to feel stings—the better. There are only stings and no amount of little pleasures and satisfactions can cover the pain. So harden yourself. That seems to be something that will not happen—the hardening.

≈

August 3, Germans enter Belgium. August 4, British declare war. . . . But the war is still not taken quite seriously. August 8, Rollie Cottenet and Phil Carroll send a telegram to Gertrude and Harry, together now in the Adirondacks: "CONSIDERABLE DISTURBANCE IN EUROPE WE THINK WARRIOR WELL EQUIPPED SHOULD SAIL PROMPTLY TO ALLEVIATE SUFFERING OF UNFORTUNATE INCLUDING THE UNDERSIGNED." However, by late August there is no more joking. Now Rollie writes seriously to Gertrude: "I wish Harry *would* send the *Warrior* to Europe and let me go on her. It could do an awful lot of good in *many many* ways." And Phil is about to enlist in the French air force. And Gertrude herself is in correspondence with the former ambassador to France, Robert Bacon, who is already abroad setting up the American Ambulance (later the American Field Service) while his wife remains behind to raise funds. Gertrude and Harry contribute generously (perhaps initially as much as $250,000) to the establishment of a field hospital, and from late August on, as Gertrude becomes increasingly involved with war relief activities, it is clear that her commitment to France (coupled with Harry's to England) will not be satisfied by

TOP: *Vanderbilt homestead, New Dorp, Staten Island.*
S. C. BURDEN REPHOTOGRAPH.
BOTTOM: *Portrait of Commodore Cornelius Vanderbilt, painted from life in 1837 by Henry Inman.*

THE DAILY GRAPHIC

AN ILLUSTRATED EVENING NEWSPAPER.

39 & 41 PARK PLACE.

VOL. XIX. | All the News Four Editions Daily. | NEW YORK, THURSDAY, MARCH 20, 1879. TWELVE PAGES. | $12 Per Year in Advance. Single Copies, Five Cents. | NO. 1868

William H. Vanderbilt, as caricatured in the Daily Graphic, *March 20, 1879, one of many such caricatures of him and his father appearing on the front page of this publication throughout the 1870s.* GEOFFREY CLEMENTS.

TOP LEFT: *Alice Gwynne Vanderbilt as "Electric Light" and* TOP RIGHT: *Cornelius Vanderbilt as Louis XVI at Mrs. William K. Vanderbilt's ball, March 26, 1883.* MORA/ GEOFFREY CLEMENTS REPHOTOGRAPH.
LEFT: *Gertrude "As a Rose" at 1883 ball.*
BILTMORE HOUSE & GARDENS,
ASHEVILLE, N.C.

TOP: *1 West 57th Street,
seen from 58th and Fifth.*
BYRON COLLECTION,
MUSEUM OF THE CITY OF
NEW YORK. LEFT: *Entrance
to 1 West 57th Street,
showing portrait of the
Commodore to the left and
Saint-Gaudens fireplace in
background.* S. C. BURDEN
REPHOTOGRAPH.

The Breakers, designed by Richard Morris Hunt and completed in 1895. S. C. BURDEN
REPHOTOGRAPH.

TOP: *Gertrude at the age of seven, relief by Augustus Saint-Gaudens.* DE W. C. WARD/ S. C. BURDEN REPHOTOGRAPH. LEFT: *Gertrude, c. 1885.* MORA/ S. C. BURDEN REPHOTOGRAPH.

TOP: *Gertrude's brothers (l. to r.): Cornelius III,
Reginald Claypoole, William Henry II,
and Alfred Gwynne, c. 1888.* S. C.
BURDEN REPHOTOGRAPH. BOTTOM:
Gertrude with Gladys, c. 1891. FRANK H.
CHILD/S. C. BURDEN REPHOTOGRAPH.

August 17th

"How do you do,"
the people say down at the beach,
"Is the water cold to-day?" and
they shake hands "à la 400" and
then sit down and begin talking.
Suddenly one of your friends goes
by in her bathing suit and you
immediately discuss ~~them~~ her.
The littlest children of all play in
the sand, the little children fight,
and the children flirt. Such a
very young atmosphere down there
that I should think a married
person would feel quite out of place.
It's a very undressed atmosphere too,
by the way, extremely so, but no one
seems to care as I suppose it is all
right. The fellows and the girls
stand around and talk in their
bathing suits or sit in the sand

Page of Gertrude's My Letting-Off-Steam Book, *August 17, 1893.* GEOFFREY CLEMENTS.

TOP: *Gertrude, c. 1893.* DAVIS & SANFORD/S. C. BURDEN REPHOTO-
GRAPH. BOTTOM: *Esther Hunt, October 1894.* E. F. COOPER/
S. C. BURDEN REPHOTOGRAPH.

William Collins Whitney as a young attorney and his wife Flora Payne Whitney. W. KURTZ/ S. C. BURDEN REPHOTOGRAPH.

TOP: *Vanderbilt mausoleum, built by William H. Vanderbilt and designed by Richard Morris Hunt, Moravian Cemetery, New Dorp, Staten Island.* FIONA IRVING.
BOTTOM: *Whitney family monument, Woodlawn Cemetery, N.Y.* FIONA IRVING.

Harry Payne Whitney with his sister Pauline, c. 1892. AIMÉ DUPONT/S. C. BURDEN
REPHOTOGRAPH.

Cornelius Vanderbilt's private train, the first in Palm Beach, March 14, 1896, in front of the Hotel Royal Poinciana, where Harry proposed to Gertrude. The party (l. to r.): Philip M. Lydig, Helen Morton, Gladys Vanderbilt, Amy Townsend, Captain A. T. Rose, Mrs. Cornelius Vanderbilt, Edith Bishop, Mabel Gerry, Thomas Cushing, Edward Livingston, Dudley Winthrop (hidden), Craig Wadsworth, Gertrude Vanderbilt, Lispenard Stewart, Harry P. Whitney, Sybil Sherman, Cornelius Vanderbilt. BERT AND RICHARD MORGAN/S.C. BURDEN REPHOTOGRAPH.

William C. Whitney's house, Old Westbury, designed by McKim, Mead & White, which became Gertrude's and Harry's favorite country home. RICHARD GACHOT PRINT

Gertrude and Harry in Japan on honeymoon, 1896. S. C. BURDEN REPHOTOGRAPH.

Three generations—Alice, Gertrude, and Flora—1897. ALMAN & CO./S. C. BURDEN
REPHOTOGRAPH.

Adele Sloane Burden and Gertrude at Niagara Falls, 1897. GEOFFREY CLEMENTS RE-PHOTOGRAPH.

TOP: *William C. Whitney's ball, January 4, 1901, "New York's first cotillion of the new century."* HARPER'S WEEKLY/S. C. BURDEN REPHOTOGRAPH. BOTTOM *(l. to r.): Payne, Helen, Harry, and Gertrude Whitney, c. 1902.* S. C. BURDEN REPHOTOGRAPH.

Harry Payne Whitney in costume, North Africa, 1901. S. C. BURDEN REPHOTOGRAPH.

Mrs. Harry Payne Whitney *by Howard Cushing, oil painting, 1902.*
COLLECTION OF WHITNEY MUSEUM OF AMERICAN ART.

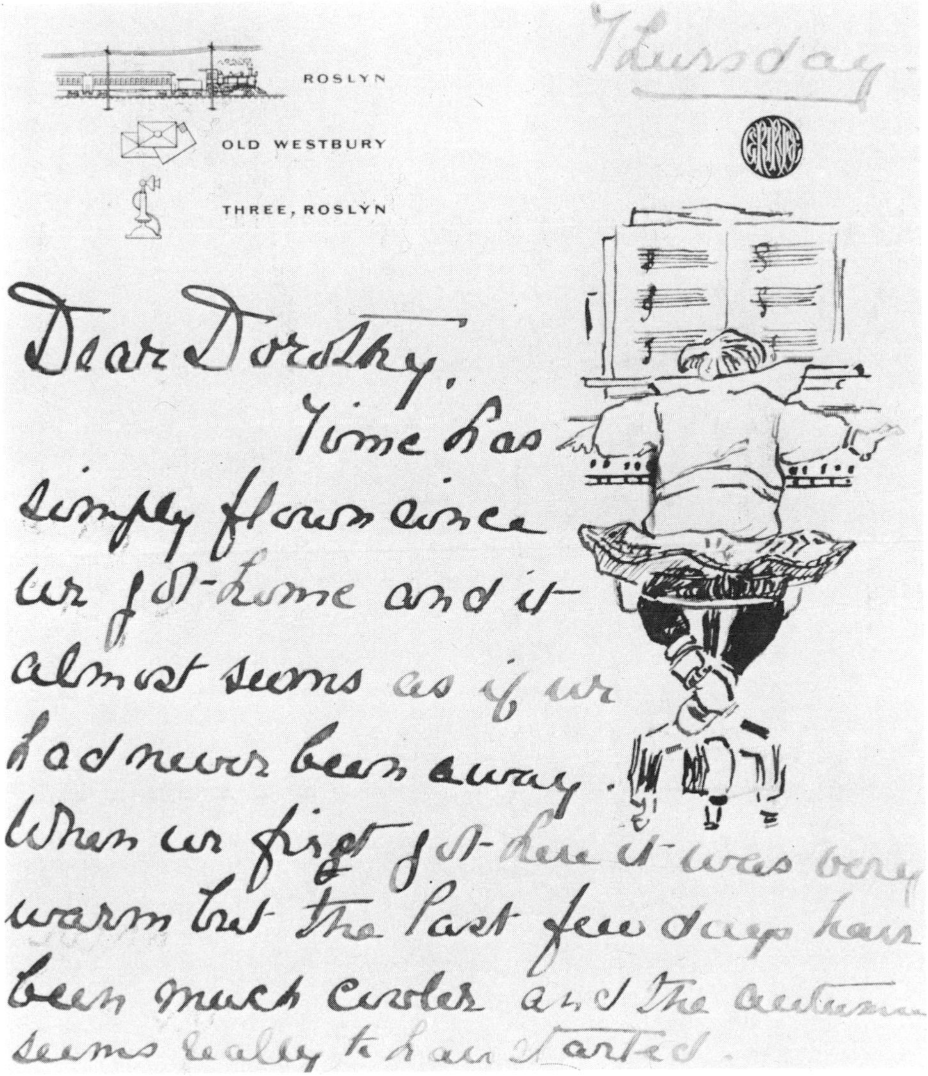

ROSLYN

OLD WESTBURY

THREE, ROSLYN

Dear Dorothy,

Time has simply flown since we got home and it almost seems as if we had never been away. When we first got here it was very warm but the past few days have been much cooler and the autumn seems really to have started.

Letter of Gertrude's to her young sister-in-law Dorothy Whitney, October 7, 1904. **GEOFFREY CLEMENTS.**

Gertrude and Harry at their Newport home, about 1905, during brief period when Harry wore a mustache.

Flora and Sonny Whitney at the wedding of Helen Barney and Archibald Alexander, April 8, 1905. HISTED/S. C. BURDEN REPHOTOGRAPH.

Joye Cottage, Aiken, S.C., 1907. BACK ROW: *Gertrude, Adele Burden, Beatrice Bend, and W. Douglas Burden.* MIDDLE ROW: *Charles Draper, Dorothy Whitney, Barbara Whitney, Helen Hay Whitney, Payne holding his son John Hay ("Jock") Whitney, C. V. ("Sonny") Whitney, and unidentified couple.* BOTTOM ROW: *Flora Whitney, James A. Burden III, Harry, Joan Whitney, Shiela Burden, James A. Burden, Jr., and Meredith ("Bunny") Hare.* S. C. BURDEN REPHOTOGRAPH.

Jo Davidson at work, c. 1909. S. C. BURDEN REPHOTOGRAPH.

Gertrude, c. 1909. BRADLEY/S. C. BURDEN REPHOTOGRAPH.

Dalby Hall, Melton Mowbray, winter 1910–11. BACK ROW (*l. to r.*): *Archibald Alexander, J. Montgomery Waterbury, Arthur Burden, Henry Bull, James Appleton.* FRONT ROW: *Phyllis Langhorne Brooks, Helen Barney Alexander, Cynthia Carey Burden, Flora Whitney, Shiela Burden, Harry P. Whitney, and Barbara Whitney.*
S. C. BURDEN REPHOTOGRAPH.

Gertrude dressed for a party, possibly a Beaux Arts Ball, c. 1910. E. F. FOLEY/S. C.
BURDEN REPHOTOGRAPH.

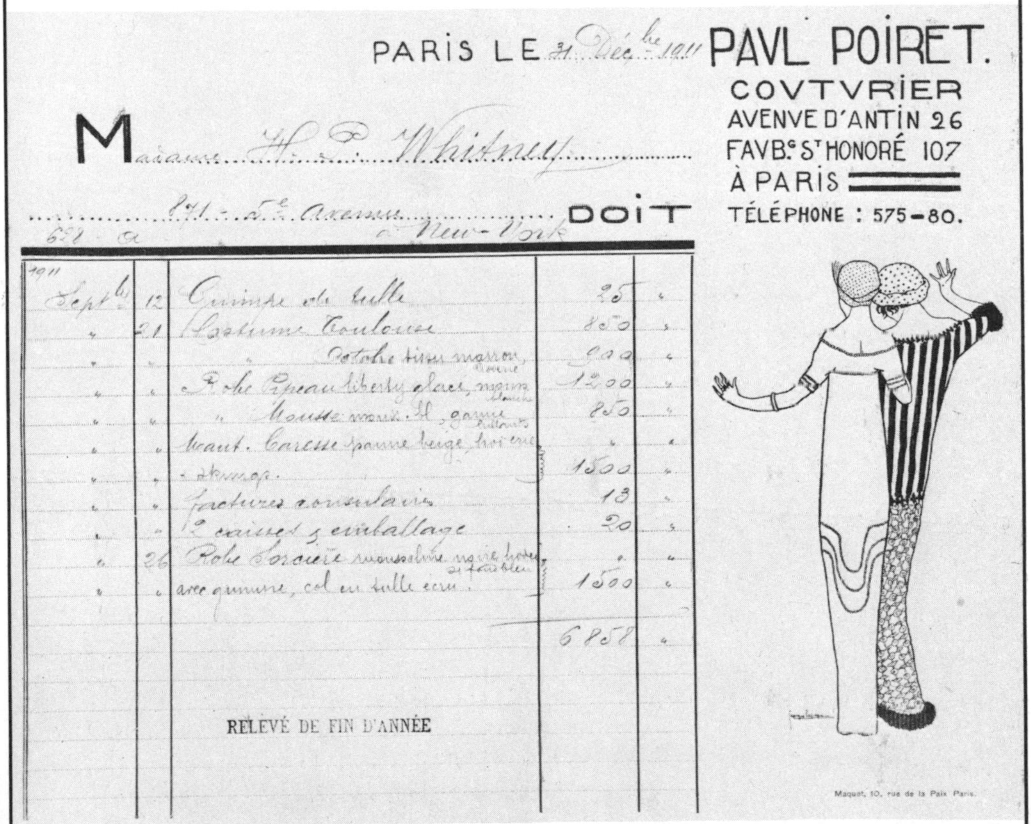

PARIS LE 31 Décembre 1911

M adame H. P. Whitney

171 5th Avenue New-York

DOIT

PAVL POIRET.
COVTVRIER
AVENVE D'ANTIN 26
FAVB.s St HONORÉ 107
À PARIS
TÉLÉPHONE : 575-80.

RELEVÉ DE FIN D'ANNÉE

Maquet, 10, rue de la Paix Paris.

Typical bill from Paul Poiret to Mme. H. P. Whitney, dated December 31, 1911. s. c.
BURDEN REPHOTOGRAPH.

TOP: *Gertrude at Westbury studio with Loup.* S. C. BURDEN REPHOTOGRAPH. BOTTOM: *Westbury studio, designed by William Adams Delano, substantially completed 1912.* S. C. BURDEN REPHOTOGRAPH.

Oriental feast, Paris, winter 1913. Gertrude with Arthur Knoblock, Emanuele de Rosales, and Herbert Haseltine. S. C. BURDEN REPHOTOGRAPH.

Gertrude working on one of the figures for Arlington Fountain, 1913. S. C. BURDEN
REPHOTOGRAPH.

Gertrude, Flora, and Barbara at polo match, c. 1913. S. C. BURDEN REPHOTOGRAPH.

Gertrude in Bakst costume, c. 1913. BARON DE MEYER/S. C. BURDEN REPHOTOGRAPH.

Titanic *Memorial*, 1913–16, being enlarged in granite. Note "points" on smaller figure in plaster. S. C. BURDEN REPHOTOGRAPH.

Gertrude with Loup in Paris, c. 1914. BOISSONNAS & TAPONIER/S. C. BURDEN REPHOTOGRAPH.

Gertrude in tableau at the Clarence Mackays', October 17, 1914. BAUMANN/S. C. BURDEN REPHOTOGRAPH.

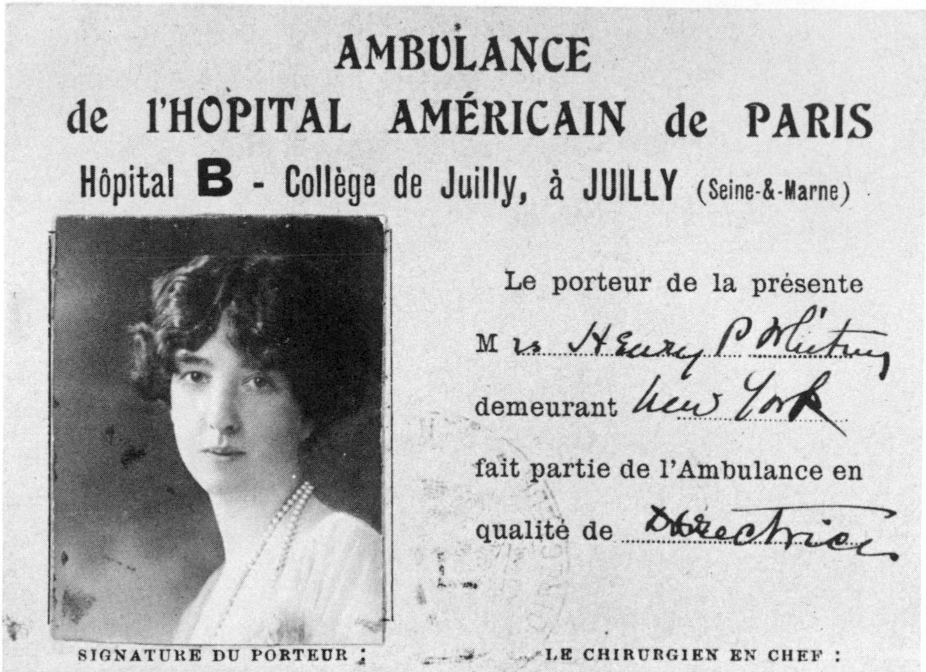

AMBULANCE
de l'HOPITAL AMÉRICAIN de PARIS
Hôpital **B** - Collège de Juilly, à JUILLY (Seine-&-Marne)

Le porteur de la présente
Mrs Henry P Whitney
demeurant New York
fait partie de l'Ambulance en
qualité de Directrice

SIGNATURE DU PORTEUR : G. V. Whitney.

LE CHIRURGIEN EN CHEF : Walton Martin

Le Medecin Inspecteur
Directeur du Service de Santé
de la 5e Région.
D. Pales

Gertrude's identification as "directrice de l'ambulance" at Hospital B, Juilly, signed by Dr. Walton Martin, 1914. S. C. BURDEN.

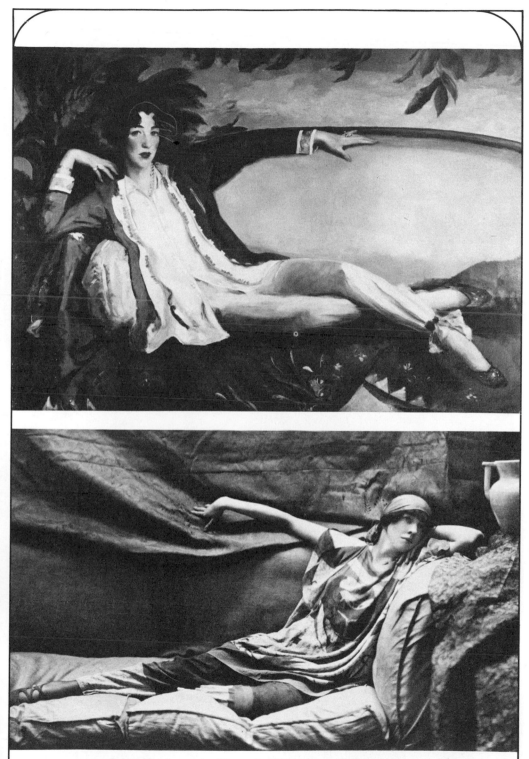

TOP: *Robert Henri portrait of Gertrude, 1916*. PETER A. JULEY & SON.
BOTTOM: *Gertrude, c. 1916*. JEAN DE STRELECKI/S. C. BURDEN REPHOTOGRAPH.

Two portraits of Gertrude, c. 1916.
BARON DE MEYER/S. C. BURDEN
REPHOTOGRAPH.

Gertrude with Despair *1912, photographed March 1917.* JEAN DE STRELECKI/
S. C. BURDEN REPHOTOGRAPH.

Gertrude in a tableau, c. 1917. S. C. BURDEN REPHOTOGRAPH.

Gertrude with friend in car displaying poster for Alley Festa, 1917. S. C. BURDEN
REPHOTOGRAPH.

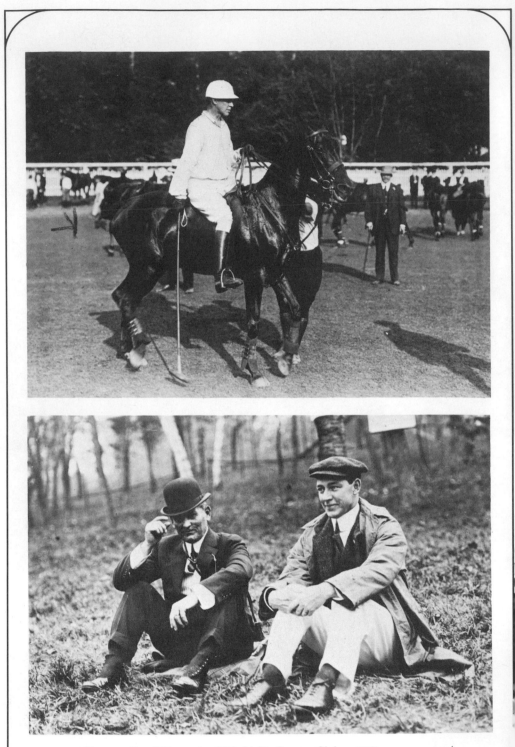

TOP: *Harry on Royal Diamond at Philadelphia Country Club, c. 1917.* EDWIN LEVICK/
S. C. BURDEN REPHOTOGRAPH. BOTTOM: *Harry with his trainer Jimmy Rowe, c. 1908.*
PAUL THOMPSON/S. C. BURDEN REPHOTOGRAPH.

Gertrude at benefit for French Milk Fund, December 28, 1918. INTERNATIONAL NEWS
PHOTOS.

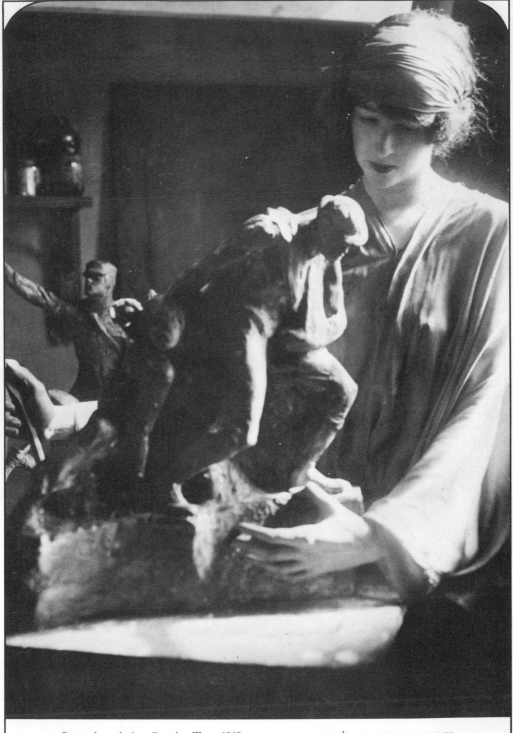

Gertrude sculpting On the Top, *1919*. JEAN DE STRELECKI/S. C. BURDEN REPHOTO-GRAPH.

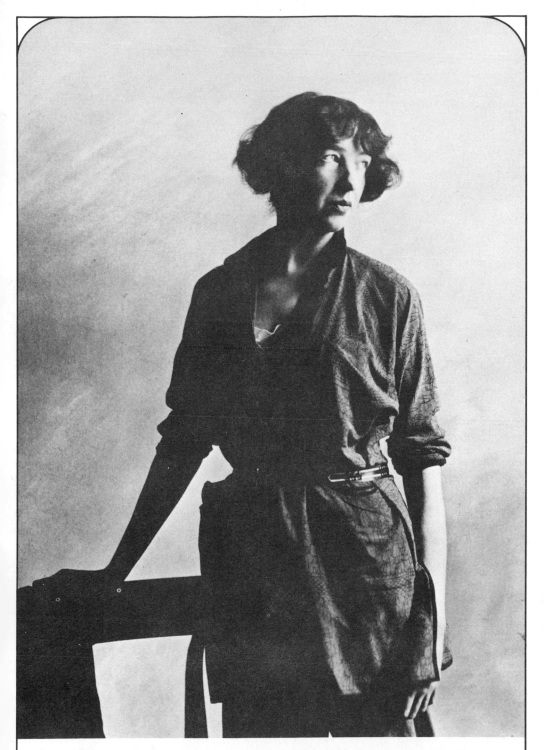

Gertrude at about the time she exhibited World War I sculpture at the Whitney Studio.
JEAN DE STRELECKI/S. C. BURDEN REPHOTOGRAPH.

Wedding of Flora Whitney and Roderick Tower, April 19, 1920. FRONT ROW *(l. to r.):*
Cornelia, Alice, and Gladys Széchényi; Beatrice and Whitney Straight. BACK ROW:
Geoffrey Tower, Flora, Roderick, and Barbara Whitney.

TOP: The Social Graces, *dry point by Peggy Bacon, 1935, showing a party in Juliana Force's apartment above the Whitney Museum.* COLLECTION: WHITNEY MUSEUM OF AMERICAN ART. RAINFORD. BOTTOM: The Whitney Studio Club, *dry point by Peggy Bacon, done in the twenties, showing Stuart Davis (in front of turbaned woman) among other regulars.* COLLECTION: WHITNEY MUSEUM OF AMERICAN ART. GEOFFREY CLEMENTS.

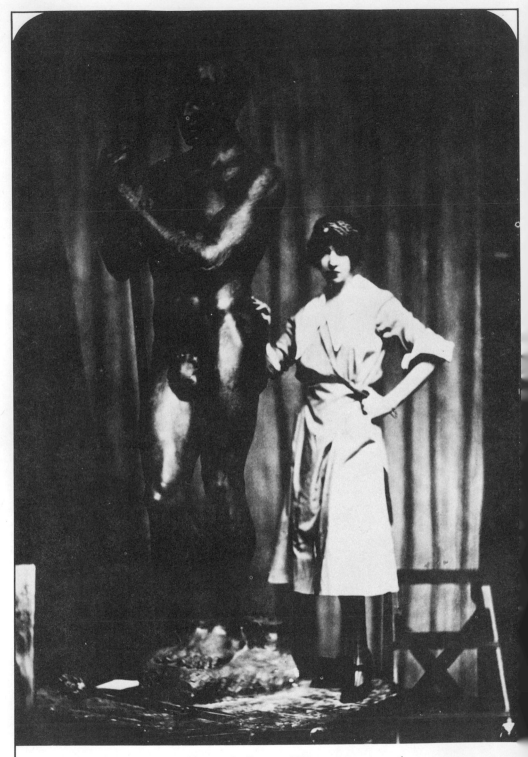

Shepherd, *memorial to Herman B. Duryea, 1921.* NICKÓLAS MURAY/S. C. BURDEN
REPHOTOGRAPH.

Charles Draper and Gertrude (veiled) at the Newport Casino. INTERNATIONAL NEWS
PHOTOS/S. C. BURDEN REPHOTOGRAPH.

TOP: *Gertrude in front of her 19 MacDougal Alley studio with model for Buffalo Bill monument, completed in 1924.* INTERNATIONAL NEWS PHOTOS/S. C. BURDEN RE-PHOTOGRAPH. BOTTOM: *Dedication of Buffalo Bill monument, July 4, 1924.* STURM.

Harry and Gertrude at wedding of their daughter Barbara to Barklie McKee Henry, June 25, 1924. Mrs. Cornelius Vanderbilt and Mrs. Devereaux Milburn in background behind Harry. FOTOGRAMS NEWS PHOTO SERVICE.

TOP: *St. Nazaire monument in plaster behind Gertrude's Paris studio.* S. C. BURDEN REPHOTOGRAPH. BOTTOM: *Section of St. Nazaire monument being cast in Paris foundry.* J. ROSEMAN/S. C. BURDEN REPHOTOGRAPH.

Flora and Gertrude en route to St. Nazaire Memorial dedication, June 5, 1926.
BAIN NEWS SERVICE/S. C. BURDEN REPHOTOGRAPH.

Water color done and captioned by Guy Pene du Bois. GEOFFREY CLEMENTS.

Opera Box, *1926, by Guy Pene du Bois, showing Gertrude.* GEOFFREY CLEMENTS.

Gertrude and Harry at Belmont, June 6, 1928. PICTORIAL PRESS PHOTOS/S. C. BURDEN REPHOTOGRAPH.

RIGHT: *Columbus monument, 1926–29, Huelva, Spain.* L. ROISIN. BELOW: *Gertrude inside base of Columbus monument with her sculptures of King Ferdinand and Queen Isabella.* VIDAL/S. C. BURDEN REPHOTOGRAPH.

Gertrude with her eldest grandchild Pamela Tower. FOTOGRAMS NEWS PHOTO SERVICE.

TOP: *Exterior of Whitney Museum of American Art.* BOTTOM: *Portrait of Juliana Force, first director of the Whitney Museum, in her apartment above museum.* CECIL BEATON.

Portrait of Gertrude taken just before museum's opening, November 17, 1931.
EDWARD STEICHEN.

RIGHT: *"Little Gloria" with her mother Gloria Morgan Vanderbilt, c. 1932.* HAL PHYFE/S. C. BURDEN REPHOTOGRAPH. BELOW: *Gertrude with her niece Gloria at about the age of fifteen.* MORGAN PHOTO SERVICE/S. C. BURDEN REPHOTOGRAPH.

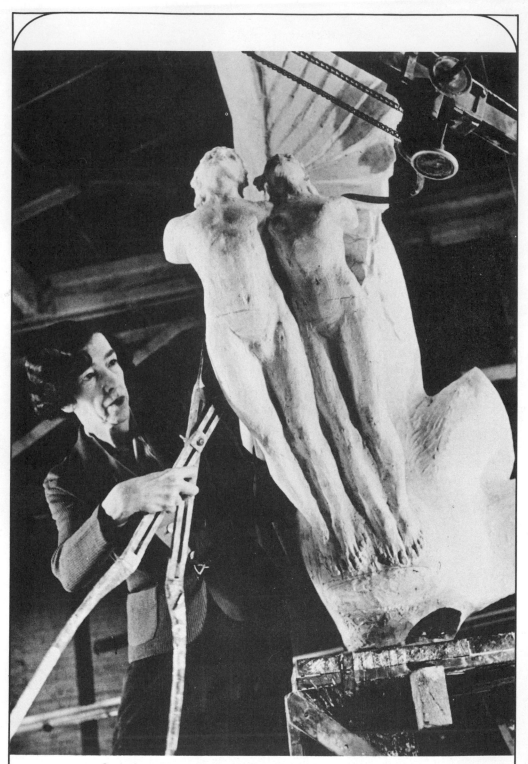

Gertrude working on Spirit of Flight *for 1939 New York World's Fair.*
WALT SANDERS/S. C. BURDEN REPHOTOGRAPH.

the donation of money only. Like Bob Bacon, like Phil Carroll, like her own aunt, the second Mrs. William K. Vanderbilt, who with Bacon is running the American Hospital, Gertrude wants to go to France. Her motivation is mixed—some part romantic, even crusading; some part restless and confused; but all, especially in the light of her future contribution, serious. Later (Paris, November 16) she will write:

It began back in August, when I was up in the [Adirondacks] woods. It was in a canoe one night that I first realized that the world was fighting. It grew in me like some disease. . . . It drove me mad. It yelled to be noticed. The first actual form that I can remember it took was one still afternoon on the *Warrior* sailing up to Newport. I expressed it awkwardly enough and in no coherent form to Rollie who was sitting on deck with me. Finding no encouragement from Harry, it left me at times only to return a greater need, a more insistent cry. It never took the form of nursing or mufflers or masseuse. Luckily for me it did not have to, but whatever the expression, I knew that if I ever expected to have peace I must listen to it. There came a moment of entire indifference, but through it I was only possessed by one dread—the dread that the difficulties might have killed the desire.

First and foremost I wanted to be over there. I wanted to stand beside my friends. I do not know many French people, but the working people I love and I adore the gold that France has lavished on me. For every joy she has given me I want to repay her; for the outstretched arms of her gay countryside I want to thank her with my sympathy; for her laugh as I meet her, her tenderness and beauty—I must give her of my heart. And this war! It is the uprooting of all that has gone before. It is convulsion, madness, and greatness. Every element that human nature is capable of will rise to the surface; unheard of feats of courage will come out of it; despicable acts will be perpetrated; genius will triumph; traits unborn will be born; and I want to be a part of it, an infinitesimal speck to be sure, but still a speck in the great colossal upheaval. How to do it was the question. Was I insane, or merely looking for excitement, as I was told so many times? "Send a cheque, send anything, only don't do a thing yourself." That was the echo of the feeling that surrounded me. Cheques could not still my desire, but I controlled myself, and to make sure that it was no idle whim or longing for adventure, I waited. But while I waited I watched.

In September, Flora leaves for Foxcroft, an exclusive new Middleburg, Virginia, boarding school with an emphasis on riding, where she will be in the first graduating class; Sonny returns to Groton; and only Barbara, now eleven, complicates Gertrude's plan to go to France. The child is already desperately unhappy because of the announced departure of her nurse Lizzie. Gertrude, with the help of Miss Givenwilson, does what she can, by arranging parties for Barbie in the studio where she hopes that her younger daughter will be "distracted by the birds," and by telling herself (and Flora, in a letter) that "Luckily children forget quickly." By mid-October Barbie seems happier and Gertrude is able to finish the last high-relief figures for the *El Dorado* frieze. In one of her frequent letters to Flora she writes: "I have to keep myself very occupied or I get so lonely I don't know what to do."

The month is indeed packed with activity. She participates in a Nassau Hospital benefit at the home of Clarence H. Mackay where in flowing veils she dances with nine macaws—some hers, some borrowed—in an oriental tableau. She helps to organize a Committee of Mercy "Fashion Fete" at the Ritz-Carlton and makes a statement to the press: "It will be very interesting to see just what the designers here can do independently of Paris. They cannot hope to become great original designers all at once. Such ability comes slowly, especially when you have been in the habit of copying. Nevertheless, many people have felt that the French designers have not entirely understood the peculiar vigorous beauty of the American woman, and it is possible that New York dressmakers may be able to suit her even better than the French." She has thirty-two guests for tea at the studio to meet the great Russian ballerina Anna Pavlova. With Juliana Force, she begins to plan shows at the new Whitney Studio on Eighth Street, mostly now for the benefit of war relief. (There will be two in December, one a "50-50" exhibition and sale from which half of any proceeds go to the artists—George Bellows, Arthur B. Davies, Cecilia Beaux, Robert W. Chanler, Howard Cushing, et cetera—and the other half to the American Hospital in Paris.) And in the midst of all this Gertrude is arranging her passage to France. Letters to Flora summarize the progress. Late October:

> . . . Roughly this is the plan. I send an organization complete in itself of say 8 doctors, 25 nurses, 20 ambulances. There goes with them everything necessary for their maintenance—assistants, chauffeurs, medical supplies, instruments, stretchers, blankets, linen, underclothes for soldiers, certain foods. In fact it is an organization in itself, self-supporting, and this organization *under* the supervision of the American Hospital will be put nearer the fighting than Paris is. So the soldiers will not have to be taken so far to be cared for. There are a great many people in France doing just this today—but they need more. The next step is to get a house over there and fit it out for use. . . . Already [Robert Bacon] has spoken to the doctors and it will be merely a question of picking and choosing as there are many doctors as well as nurses who want to go. We expect to get a good many volunteers which means the money we would have to pay them allows us to take care of more soldiers.

Besides this I have a big lot of underclothes, sweaters, blankets for children & soldiers which is going on a French boat tomorrow and will be in Paris by the time I am there.

It is all so interesting and absorbing that I feel excited beyond words. Papa gets back tomorrow and he *will* be surprised, but I feel sure that he will also be sympathetic.

[October 30:] . . . At first Papa was awfully opposed to my going, but when I promised that I would be back by Xmas and explained all the plan, naturally he felt differently about it. So that now he is perfectly willing to have me go and we have talked over many details together. All day yesterday was one of intense excitement. Getting the Packard with tires etc. into the boat sailing for Havre tomorrow, a chauffeur, a maid, besides all the doctors, nurses, ambulances and supplies. Passport! Very important. Oh dearest! It will be interesting and if I find I am of no use over there, I shall come right back, and in any case I shall be back for the holidays. And what a joy it will be after the hard work to hug you all again. You must write very often, for lots of times I shall be very lonely and always wanting to know just how you are and *all* details of your life. Mr. Regan is here now with the papers. Mr. Bacon comes in a few minutes. Ten ambulance motors go tomorrow and in no time we will have a splendid organization. Good-bye, darling. I had a long talk with Cousin Adele last night & she encouraged me a lot.

Passport! Very important! Suddenly, as Gertrude nears forty, she lies about her birth date, changes it from 1875 to 1877, and it will remain 1877 on official documents for the rest of her life. The photograph attached to the passport is retouched and handsome. Her hair is short and parted in the middle; her wide-set eyes are emphasized with mascara, her mouth with rouge. The famous Payne pearls hang from her neck in a double rope. The description follows:

Stature 5 Feet 8 Inches
Forehead *medium*
Eyes *green*
Nose *straight*
Mouth *medium*
Chin *small*
Hair *brown*
Complexion *fair*
Face *long*

On November 4, after writing affectionate farewells to Flora and Sonny and arranging for Barbara and Miss Givenwilson to visit Flora at Foxcroft,

Gertrude sails on the *Lusitania,* accompanied by Robert Bacon; four surgeons, including an old family friend, Walton Martin of St. Luke's, who will be in charge of the field organization; fifteen trained nurses; and six hospital interns. Against Gertrude's wishes, the newspapers report all this in detail—and more:

> The project is being financed solely by Mrs. Whitney [who is] ready to put a large share of her fortune into this work. . . . Her mother, Mrs. Vanderbilt, arrived in New York from Newport last night to bid her goodbye. . . . [Mrs. Whitney] was encouraged by the example of her sister, Countess Széchényi . . . who has gone to the aid of the wounded in Austria.

The arrival of Gertrude and her entourage in London and then in Paris, as well as subsequent trips during the war years, are also covered by the press. However, the day of arrival in London (where she stays at the Ritz while Dr. Martin and his staff are at the Grand) Gertrude begins a new journal, one that means a great deal to her as she writes and rewrites and has portions typed for possible publication. In its various metamorphoses, it contains the facts of newspaper or public reality and those of personal reality as well.

> London, November 10:
> I did get a thrill at 3:15 today—a funny deep down thrill. Passing through the country between Liverpool and London gave one no feeling of excitement nor any feeling that the country was at war; but a second after the train had stopped, myriads of signs printed boldly on taxicabs served to give me the first shock of realization—enlist NOW, join kitchener's army!
> England *is* fighting then! It is true that she wants more recruits and wants them badly. Lord Kitchener's cry for men and still more men is no idle newspaper phrase. Winston Churchill may talk of "business carried on as usual" but it is the end of his sentence that has significance—"during the alteration of the map"! . . .
> My rooms at the Ritz were ready for me, fires burning and everything looking cheerful after the fog and dreariness outside. It was warm, so I opened my window. In less than a minute the waiter knocked at the door. He came in hurriedly, pulled the curtain tight, and vanished after giving me a reproachful look. "Splendid night for Zeppelins," I thought. "It would be bad luck, after getting as far as this, to be blown up without seeing a d— thing."
> Paris, November 15:
> I came on this journey fully prepared for any emergency. I travel with a belt full of gold, which causes me great pain every time I attempt to move; with a passport in a bag which I carry uncomfortably & awkwardly under my dress; with a beautiful model [Ramon] armed

to the teeth and pale with fear; with a large box of chocolate in case
there is no food in the country; with medicines for every known and
unknown disease; with a vaccination mark on my arm and typhoid
germs inside me; with pyjamas in case of necessity; with warm underclothes and also with stockings that are *not* openwork; with a thermos
bottle and a Kodak! . . .

[In London] we determined to move over our large party . . . via
Folkestone and Dieppe. Bob [Bacon] left me in order to dine with Sir
Edward Grey, and Almeric Paget appeared to take me to see Pauline.
Pauline was excited and sympathetic about the hospital and Almeric
wanted to help by occupying the most important position in the or-
ganization and spending—well—perhaps two or three days a week in
France!

It seems some people are so scared of aeroplanes that they have
spread nets over their houses. However, if a bomb falls on your net
and bounces off into the house of someone else, you are responsible!

They told me the number of dead and wounded among the English has been appalling. Whole families have been wiped out and the
French are considered to have put too much of a burden on the English troops. Kitchener himself has just been to France to arrange for
them to have a rest. They have been for days in the trenches without
taking off their clothes, and part of the time they were on half rations
besides. Pauline cried as she told me of their sufferings. . . .

We looked like a very respectable Cook's touring party when we
left Victoria. . . . I arrived at the station laden with Mother Sills [a
seasickness remedy] and flowers provided by the Pagets. It was blowing a gale, and I tried to distribute the sea-sick medicine among the
nurses, but most of them were haughty or would not take enough,
and of course they suffered greatly afterwards. I shall never forget our
two small cabins on the tiny boat in which we travelled from Folkestone to Dieppe! No horrors at the front can equal those six hours.
We are now ready for anything! It rained and the wind blew, the
windows leaked, and everyone [who] could not lie on the sofa lay on
the floor disgracefully oblivious of decency. Each had a bowl and, as
the sea grew rougher, the bowls upset and their contents added to the
water which came rushing in through the leaking windows, soaked
the poor women who lay moaning on the floor. Nobody cared. A hat
was ruthlessly sacrificed in the disaster. I had no sensation but one of
amusement, for one had to have that or one would have died of
agony and disgust. Mr. Bacon escorted (I can use no better word)
each sufferer who succumbed into one or other of the cabins, handed
her a bowl, and sympathetically retired.

We must have presented a disreputable appearance when we arrived at Dieppe, and the drunken Consul who was supposed to look

after our party was undoubtedly entirely justified in his familiar treatment of us all.

Whether the Mother Sills went to my head, or what happened, I do not know, but that night I had a strange hallucination. When I went to take my bath, I saw distinctly the outline of a man's body against the glass window over the washstand in my bathroom. I thought he was interested in seeing me take my bath, nothing more, but I decided not to gratify his curiosity. When I got back to my room, I distinctly heard in the adjoining room a strange noise. It was like some machine clicking. By standing close to the door which joined the apartments, I noticed a vile smell coming through the keyhole and a more distinct click-click, click-click. It seemed to me a little strange, although I was prepared for anything by this time, but it made me uncomfortable for I could not imagine what it was all about. It was now after midnight. The strange smell, which I fancied was growing stronger, and the noise of the machine persisted. Someone must be spying on me! I went to the window to open it as I always do before going to bed—it refused to be opened! Pull as I would, the blamed thing refused to budge! Then I had a feeling, an instinct, I was perfectly calmly and unalterably sure that the creature in the next room wanted to suffocate me. The moment I thought of this idea, it explained everything. I was now not in the least frightened. I did not know why he wanted to kill me, nor did I care, but I determined it would be idiotic of me to allow him to succeed. So I set to work with great precaution to pull the sheets and blankets off my bed into the sitting-room. Then returning, I silently put out the lights in my room and closed the door noiselessly. Once in the sitting-room I took a deep breath, opened the window, locked the door and fell immediately into a profound sleep on the chaise longue.

In Paris Gertrude is still, at first, waiting and watching. She has hours in which to remember the past and record it in her journal, while other hours are full of meetings—some official, with Ambassador Myron Herrick, ex-Ambassador Robert Bacon, Dr. Walton Martin, and various French doctors; some social, with Whitney Warren and Philip Carroll's brother Charles and his wife. Everything—past, present, and future—focuses now on the war; everyone she sees (or at least, reports seeing) is in Paris to help the war effort. There is hardly a word about art *per se* in this long journal, but between its lines is the implication that the survival of France *means* the survival of art, the survival of civilization itself. She writes, "Whitney [Warren] . . . was different. And I suddenly felt that these people [he and the Carrolls and others who had arrived in Paris before Gertrude] had been living in what I had only been imagining."

After a few days Ambassador Herrick puts a limousine at her disposal. She, Robert Bacon, and Walton Martin visit "the American Ambulance" at Neuilly-sur-Seine on the northwest outskirts of Paris. There a Dr. Du Bouchet meets them "with his charming faint smile. . . . He held my hand for a moment as he made his little speech. . . . My statue that he had seen last year—*Self-Sacrifice*—(fancy his remembering!) *that* was sacrifice, and now the sacrifice of life existed here in France, and I was erecting my *second* monument to sacrifice which would be lasting. I cannot put it as he did nor give the impression of his charm as he said it, but he is certainly a dangerously clever man. . . . The hospital is immense, and oh! so white and complete and efficient looking."

The inspection of the hospital and subsequent discussions go on for a long time—about six pages in Gertrude's journal—but the long and the short of it is Dr. Du Bouchet's announcement that the French government has offered Gertrude's unit to the Belgian government, which has accepted it!

"Belgium?" Gertrude asks.

Yes, Dr. Du Bouchet explains, the Belgians are in need of hospitals. There have been atrocities. . . . Gertrude listens politely but unresponsively. Belgium!

"I was staggered. However, my self-control endured the test and I kept saying to myself: 'Of course I must be mad, for they cannot be.' At any rate it was dashing—this first news—to be sent to a place now occupied by the Germans!"

After the meeting, Robert Bacon, Walton Martin, and Charlie Carroll go to Dunkirk for three days to meet with Belgian officials and to do some scouting behind the British lines. Gertrude spends Saturday, Sunday, and Monday at the hospital in Neuilly, "talking to department heads, seeing dressings, chatting with nurses and patients, serving tea (!) and generally trying to get to know people and be taken for granted."

The men return tired and disappointed. There are more meetings, more discussions, all leading to the desirability of setting up a hospital in France —*anywhere on the French soil* Gertrude loves. A day passes and Bacon appears at Neuilly, where he finds her working in a ward.

"Can you be ready to leave in two hours?"

Gertrude's heart jumps. She nods assent even before being told that they're going to inspect a possible hospital site north of Paris, *in France.*

Emilie, her maid, packs a bag for Gertrude while she changes into her warmest clothing, eating a bite between each garment.

" 'Madame will see—fighting?'

" 'Qui sait? Je vais dans le Nord, Emilie, that is all I can tell you. I expect to be away one night, but if I don't get back there is no need to worry.'

" 'Madame will have her gaiters?'

"Yes, and her sweaters, and her furcoat, and her woolies—woolies of all kinds, for an open motor is no joke in such weather."

As Gertrude and Robert Bacon, accompanied by three military chauffeurs, drive north and then east—through St. Denis, Beaumont,

Beauvais, and Poix—Gertrude sees "the first indications of war": trenches, some completed, some under construction, some "looking like ordinary golf bunkers"; barbed wire; bridges blown up to prevent the Germans from crossing; convoys moving toward the front; nests of *mitrailleuses* (machine guns); a line of Paris busses, advertisements and destinations painted out with gray paint ("so vividly did they recall the Champs Elysées that one looked instinctively for chestnut trees and taxicabs").

Everywhere Gertrude's party is stopped by sentries and eyed with suspicion, especially Gertrude herself. At Abbeville, in the British sector, hotels are full, having been commandeered. Again overcoming intense suspicion, the group gets rooms over a bar. There, while the men go to see the local general—Gertrude's presence would not be "considered professional"—she remains in her room. "I do not feel in the least strange, only very happy and rather exhilarated."

The next morning, while the men complete their business, Gertrude wanders through the town, stopping at the cathedral, where she makes an offering to the poor. She is sure of one thing: that, despite British urging, "Abbeville was not the place I had dreamed of in which to establish my hospital."

They look further. Finally, in Juilly, close to Compiègne, on the Oise, about a hundred kilometers north-northeast of Paris, they are offered the Collège de Juilly in the French sector. This boys' school—founded in the seventeenth century; rich in history (the great writer Montesquieu is its most famous alumnus); dignified and solid in architecture; situated in a beautiful park—is the answer to Gertrude's dreams. In her mind, she begins almost immediately transforming dormitories and classrooms into wards and operating rooms. "It must have some faults. Well, it did, if no heat and no plumbing can be called faults." As with her sculptures and the Whitney Studio and so much in Gertrude's life, the dream of a hospital is willed into being—this dream much more quickly than others, because of wartime priority, energy, and spirit. By January, heating and plumbing will be installed, medical equipment and beds placed (150 initially, 225 later and until a few months after the armistice), ambulances garaged.

But meanwhile, as Gertrude and Bacon return to Paris, there is a lot to be done. She barely has time to record her initial impressions of Juilly: ". . . the whole place is romantic, the long alleys of big green-trunked trees, the lake, the pigeon tower, the statue of St. Genevieve [who started the college to express her thanks for a spring which burst from the ground there when she was thirsty], the stream that stagnates close by, it all has a charm, a dignity and peace that once felt is hard to forget." Now she is working regularly again at Neuilly, mostly "over the boxes of warm things sent from America." Monday night she goes to a dinner at the Tucks' in honor of the Herricks, who will be leaving in a week. (Herrick has been appointed by President Taft in 1912 to replace Robert Bacon as ambassador and, the following year, has been requested by Woodrow Wilson to stay until now, when he is replaced by William G. Sharp.) Tuesday night she dines with Mr. and Mrs. Charles Carroll and his brother Phil, who will drive an ambulance for Gertrude's unit until he can join the air force. Wednesday there's a dinner meeting with Robert Bacon, Walton Martin, and the architect Carroll Greenough, to resolve Juilly alteration plans. Dr. Du Bouchet, Dr. Gros, and Charlie Carroll join them after dinner. All hope that the hospital can be ready in a month. Thanksgiving Thursday, Gertrude seated next to the American painter Walter Gay, has lunch at the embassy with Myron Herrick, who says: "agreeable things . . . that the A Ambulance was splendid etc. . . . but that my unit [B] had given it a chance to branch out as it undoubtedly was doing through the example of this unit and that the work of Americans would become an important factor in establishing international feelings of confidence and sympathy."

That afternoon Gertrude meets again with Walton Martin, as well as Phil Carroll and Tommy Slidell, another old friend and fashionable bachelor of the period (Princeton '05) who has come to France to volunteer his services. Friday is described in two sentences: "[It] was a black day. I had a *crise de nerfs* in the evening and cried most of the night." Saturday is worse. Phil Carroll arrives early in the morning to discuss hospital matters and Gertrude's "equilibrium was about established by the time [she] arrived at Neuilly." However, just as she gets there, she finds a new patient dying of gangrene in the ward to which she reports. He is only twenty-one. His mother, his father, and a priest stand beside him. The parents have two more sons at the front, one they have not heard from in months. The nurses look tired. Some have been crying. Gertrude leaves this scene and goes to sit down next to a patient she knows: "the little man with the bad leg, the broken arm, and the bayonet wound. Then I looked at the faces of the wounded . . . read in each the question "Will I be next?" and I thought to myself, never a word of complaint, never a murmur against the powers that break suddenly."

About a week after Gertrude returns from Juilly, she chides herself: "I wish I were not so far behind in my writing. I must try and catch up." As always, for her, life (including the dream) must be recorded before it can materialize and become "real." She remembers, for example, a visit with Bob Bacon and Dr. Gros to a *pâtisserie* in Poix where "they ate pastry and brioches, macaroons and chocolates, and we all laughed, heaven knows why, while Mr. Bacon called loudly for absinthe. I shall remember the little shop longer than the convoys we passed . . . one gets to the point where a certain kind of impression can no longer have its effect. . . . I want the little loves and hates of a small life, the tiny interests of a fireside. I want to knit and look on at life . . ."

The next day, Monday, December 1:

Last night, when I was about as far down as one can get without real cause, an announcement was made to me which brought me out of the depths. There were a lot of reasons for going north again. The Belgian officials must be interviewed about postes sanitaires, General O'Donnell was to be talked to on the subject of the . . . automobiles. General Castleman seen—did he want a unit of cars? and very incidentally I might fill a car with warm things for the Belgians. That's where I came in. "I should love to go." I was afraid to show how pleased I was, for I had worked hard for just this.

Everything seemed to change in a few moments. It was absurd to be unhappy and I dried my tears and forgot the weight of the world. And we arranged a great many things that needed no arranging.

And the next morning set off, three cars, three drivers, three men and myself. Phil said beneath his breath: "It was wonderful of you to arrange this for me." We packed Dr. Gros' car and the Packard full of warm clothes.

I found time to go to the station and say good-bye to Herrick, but at last we were off. The excitement was not quite the same as on the first trip, although now we were going to a far more interesting zone.

At Echouen we were stopped several times. It is one of the big forts of the Camp Retrencher of Paris and played a big role in the war of 1870.

We had never traveled so fast before and the faster we went the faster Champoiseau [the military chauffeur who had first driven Gertrude to Juilly] wanted to go. He ate up the roads with the little Schneider, one long stretch after another vanished almost as soon as it appeared.

Stretching over the fields were what looked at first like gigantic serpents but on closer inspection proved to be trenches. Fields of barbed wire entanglements had been constructed and I wondered if the wires were connected with electric current as I had heard many were.

About 20 k. from Paris the road suddenly changed its color and a moment later I realized that the ridiculous red and blue uniforms of the French soldiers were indeed a conspicuous mark. The road was full of them, as far as the eye could see, blue and red, red and blue, once in a while a red cross broke the monotony. They were going the same way we were—their outfits were new, the sun shone on the polished metal dishes which hung outside their knapsacks. They were of all ages but the glow of health and good cheer was on them and certainly to the casual observer they seemed fit and efficient. To be sure their packs looked very heavy, but their boots and clothes appeared good and their horses well fed and cared for.

We passed a lot of them, mostly infantry, field guns too, ambulances, trucks covered with gray canvases, more guns, cavalry, the sunlight glinting on their swords, infantry again—all going north, all, I imagined, with dreams of conquest in their hearts. I thought how differently German regiments would look—how their gray uniforms would blend with the landscape while the red and blue blazed itself against the meadows, the road, the villages, and shrieked its presence to the enemy. I pictured too the solemn faces of the Germans, the look of determination, the cropped heads, and I looked once more at the smiling faces of my French friends, the gleam of mischief and the joie de vivre in their bright eyes. Pretty soon they will be at the business of killing, and many, many of the little Frenchies will find their way back—to a hospital or a grave, but with the smile still on their faces.

Here the first draft of Gertrude's war journal breaks off. However, we know from letters, sent and unsent, that she—probably escorted by Phil Carroll—spends the ten days or so after her second trip to the front, and before returning to her family for the holidays, partly at Neuilly, partly in Switzerland where her sister Gladys is working for the Red Cross. The next trip—December 15—is to London where, two days later, with her sister-in-law Dorothy Straight, she boards the *Lusitania* for New York.

The seven-day crossing is extremely rough: Captain Dow says the ship is "under water" part of the time, and Charles Schwab—president of Bethlehem Steel, in England to negotiate war contracts—says that he is sick *all* of the time and that the crossing is "the most distressful" of the fifty-two he has made to Europe. But once again Gertrude proves she is a good sailor. She spends much of the time writing (and rewriting):

DECEMBER 17th. At Sea.
It comes over me that now on my way back to America I should size up my impressions in two ways. The real way, the big understanding and realization of what I have seen and lived and again the —presentation (a big word for a little thing) of it which I want to make on my return. I have not thought much of that side of life so far. I have lived in my art and in a little circle . . . struggling not at all for the opinion of people and oblivious to [their] estimation. It is unimportant what . . . effect . . . this experience has had on me, but I happen to have been in a place which is the center of the interest of the world at present and therefore (through no personal reasons) people will be interested and even (should I wish it) pay attention to me. Therefore it becomes of interest to me to present my little tiny point of view right and clearly and without prejudices.

. . . I now want to take a place which up to the present I have ignored. I wish to have a certain power, and to have that power I must be someone, not only through my private or artistic life, but through the influence which by reason of my position I can exert.

There are two sides to the presentation of my idea: the big war side, the universal interests and forces which have been called into action through the great war, and the smaller but none the less strong point of dealing with the sick. On this subject I should know something. I should have a general broad idea of the work that is being done and a specific personal knowledge of that part of it which I have seen. As to this there can be no doubt. Something between the two there is also, the effect which this side of it made on the big subject, the international importance of the sympathy as expressed by one nation to another.

As I look back and try to size up the particular effect the experience abroad has had on me, I feel one thing very strongly—a bigger interest, a deeper desire to enter into this vast troubled sea, a longing far more real than ever before to be part of so big and disastrous a horror. My enthusiasm has in no way flagged, my desire to *do*, myself, has not diminished. In me still burns the flame of action or want to participate. I want to see it through. I want to get deeper into it. I have so far only skimmed the surface of the great depths.

The thought that perhaps strikes one most of all is the ease with which one becomes used to sights and experiences which one would have supposed would go on striking surprise or horror into one. In a few days one no longer looks at continual streams of Red Cross ambulances, soldiers on their way to the front are always of interest but they do not seem unusual, dressings of horrible wounds are sad but it seems as if one had seen them forever. "Ravitaillement" [provisioning] one looks at as at taxicabs and so on. The same way that the thought of danger becomes nil. Darkened London waiting for its bombs, the searchlights of Paris hunting for aeroplanes, the battleships accompanying steamers suggestive of dangers, but the dangers themselves certainly never for a moment gave me a qualm or a tremor. No, it was in a deeper reason I had to look for my excitement, something which started when I was far away from the actual field of danger, something which had been growing in me since in the Adirondacks I first had the realization of war. The nearer I got to the seat of it all the greater became that inner excitement, but I almost became calmer, as I on the outside got nearer, for like a great deep down feeling, the deeper it is the harder it is to express, the more hidden in the intricacies of oneself. . . . All of this is feeling and as such all right from my own standpoint. Now how about the facts of it from the same standpoint. Well, I know there is a necessity for people like myself over there. The development of the friendliness of America and France etc. today is needed. A few people cannot perhaps make it, but everyone can help in a small way. The fact of Mr. Bacon's going over and staying over through the dark days was deeply appreciated and loved by those people. They are up against it, they have their backs up against the wall, everyone who goes to them with sympathy is acceptable. The jealousy, which one hears spoken of, is only I believe among the small not among the big and as such must be considered. The question of red tape too, so much criticised, is right. Countries at war cannot have anyone and everyone rushing in to mess up things. . . .

For twenty pages—many little more than lists of places, distances between them, generals and doctors in charge of them—Gertrude recapitulates her travels during the past month and a half. She criticizes those who wanted to go to the front "out of pure love of excitement and a desire to have a front row seat in a show," but a few pages later writes, "I had hoped an aeroplane raid was going to be made—no such luck." Though she again expresses resentment at being left out of male military conferences, when she finally participates in one at Fruges, she says:

> . . . I was a good deal thrilled at actually being in the Headquarters of the English army, the place in which Lord Roberts died a few weeks before "within sound of the guns." What a splendid death, to be sure, with his Indian troops around him, too, he could not have been so very miserable to die at 82 like that!

Balancing Gertrude's romanticism and her profound commitment to the Allied cause is complicated. She ends this part of the *Lusitania* journal or re-journal:

> My thoughts tonight have all been about home and the general situation there. My attitude about coming away and so on. It is hard, but I think I must have a great deal of patience. I know that when H. realizes that I have made up my mind to come back [i.e., to France] he will try and say a great many disagreeable things and ridicule the idea of my being of any use. If this experience has done nothing else for me I hope it will have softened me towards certain unhappy aspects of my life. But it has done something else too. It has made me see more clearly the line of usefulness in life and cast behind me more ruthlessly those people who will acknowledge no duties or responsibilities. God, grant me the clear vision. Do not lose your temper about anything, but do not be trodden underfoot.

Now, in mid-voyage, Gertrude drafts and redrafts, corrects and recorrects—first in pencil, then in ink, then pencil again, then ink again—a long, initially mysterious, obviously hesitant letter:

Dear Dearest-Person-in-the-World,
    The last three days have been a century. I have been alone and have had to look into myself and find an answer to my questionings. I did not realize how I would feel when there was no possibility of seeing you for days and weeks. I did not know the horrid empty feeling I

would have—a physical sensation—as if I had not eaten in days, and then too the despair that swamped me. I said I won't stand it, and the realization that I just must stand it came to me. I am glad you said to me that you knew I cared, glad that you told me you felt my love, for somehow that has made these days easier for me to go through, I don't know why. I don't know anything. I only know it's for good and all, that I love you and that no matter what happens, no matter even if you get tired of me I must go on loving you. Somehow one knows. I look back on all the heavenly things you said to me, the divine experiences we had together and I try to be happy, but I am going further away from you every second and I only know that I am miserable.

I have played at love as you know but now it is different and I am afraid when I think of how you can hurt me—for once before in my life I really loved and I suffered as I never hope to suffer again. So be good to me dear for you can hurt me beyond all things because—I love you. . . .

Your two letters came to the steamer. I am so glad the mission was successful. I had a feeling in Switzerland that I would not see you again. . . . My time with Gladys was like an oasis and when I got back to Paris I was all right to tackle the last few days of work. Mr. B[acon] had decided not to go back to America but insisted on taking me to London. . . .

I did let him kiss me as you know but it's very different from other things and I am sorry now I did it as it only made him unhappy— while I meant to make him a little less miserable. I will cable you when I sail for there is an excuse for that even if it should be opened. I hope to get away the 8th if there is a steamer. . . .

"Dearest-Person-in-the-World" is almost certainly Phil Carroll. Of the other men Gertrude has seen frequently during this period, Myron Herrick has already returned to the States; Robert Bacon is probably the man she let kiss her; and Dr. Walton Martin, though a friend, has, it would seem from subsequent correspondence, maintained professional distance. (Another name which comes to mind, though really from another time— so completely and quickly has the war changed everything—is Guardabassi. However, as we will later discover, he has enlisted as an officer in the Italian army.)

⇜

While Gertrude has been gone the press has devoted considerable space to the establishment of the Juilly hospital as well as to her war relief activities at home, particularly those arranged before her departure at the Whitney Studio. But now, as anticipated aboard ship, she is to the public more than a famous society figure, more than a sculptor of talent—she has been *there*, at the front; the world cares about *that*. As soon as Gertrude disembarks from the *Lusitania*, she makes a statement to the press: "I have come home for the Christmas holidays and expect to return after the New Year."

≈ *1915*

The Christmas holidays must have been difficult for Gertrude, her joy at seeing the children tempered by a bad cold of Sonny's which he still has when he returns to Groton, and anxiety on the part of Barbara (not yet twelve) at Gertrude's announced intention to return to France. And, no doubt, hovering above all this are Harry's objections to Gertrude's plans. We can imagine the echo of his rational arguments (alluded to in her journal, if not specifically quoted as his words): "Send a check, send anything, only don't do a thing *yourself*." Yes, probably her money, her support, her help are needed more than she *herself*, though her presence, like that of other socially prominent persons, has great positive propaganda value. Yes, she recognizes that her children need her. Yes . . . but . . . but . . . Harry hasn't seen what she has seen, hasn't felt what she has felt . . . and continues to feel. . . . It is impossible to express. Perhaps it is not rational. Perhaps, as with the first trip, she cannot expect his support. Perhaps, again, she can expect only a shift from opposition to resignation.

A "strain"—as she calls it in a note to Bob Bacon, written soon after her return—continues. She is torn between New York and Juilly, living in New York physically, in Juilly emotionally. For many hours she works with Miss Givenwilson—previously the perfect governess and now the perfect secretary—on the public "presentation" of the private war experience, thought and written about aboard ship. It becomes now a cool, factual, historical account of the establishment of the hospital at Juilly, with none of the personality or emotionality of the journal, and a plea for "sympathy, expressed in a practical way . . . forging a link which will serve to bind [France and the United States] ever closer." When ready for the press (in both English and French), Miss Givenwilson's typing fills four legal-size pages. The article is quoted from in many newspapers and run in its entirety, along with a picture of Gertrude, in the January 6 *Times*.

During the past two weeks Gertrude has also been working with Irene

Givenwilson, as well as James Earle Fraser and Juliana Force, on the arrangements for a prize competition at the Whitney Studio from January 16 through 24 in painting, sculpture, and architecture for the benefit of the Fraternité des Artistes, a relief fund for the families of French artists affected by the war. The jury consists of artist and architect friends—Fraser himself, Paul Chalfin, Howard Cushing, William Adams Delano, Grant La Farge, Paul Manship, and Alden Weir. The subject for the sculpture competition is one close to Gertrude's heart: "The Struggle." Another benefit for the Fraternité des Artistes is planned for early February—an exhibition of modern art, both American and foreign, from the A. E. Gallatin collection, then particularly rich in works by Whistler. With these arrangements made, Gertrude sails for Europe on January 9. It is her fortieth birthday, though, as noted, her passport states that she is thirty-eight.

Aboard ship Gertrude writes yet another brief history of her involvement with the war effort, ending, "Perhaps I was mad to want to be there, mad even to want to help. Send a check—that's the best way, I was told. But checks could not still my desire." The rest of Gertrude's war journal is filled mostly with notes on military, hospital, and diplomatic staffs and their procedures, schedules, and qualifications. There are only two dated entries. The first is brief and mysterious:

> JAN. 24th. Amiens.
> Actually here again, Howard Cushing and I, this time by ourselves!

Well, of course, Howard may have judged the competition at the Whitney Studio and then joined Gertrude in France but, more likely, last-minute arrangements were made for him to escort her—probably with his wife. In a letter that Charles Draper writes to Gertrude this same week, he wonders "what the Cushing family have found to do in Paris, France." A few days later Howard disappears from Gertrude's journal. By then she is at Juilly:

> JANUARY 31st.
> Our wounded have come. Last night at exactly nine o'clock three ambulances and Dr. Martin's car with himself, Dr. Vogel and Dr. James arrived, and a few minutes later six "blessés" [wounded] were lying on stretchers on the floor of the receiving rooms. . . .

Though, in letters written during January, Harry continues to wish that Gertrude were home, he expresses the wish gently:

> I hope you are coming back soon & of course to do it cheerfully, the hospital will have to be running smoothly. . . . [I have been] very nervous, did not get better, & got more and more worried about myself. Spent practically every night alone in the country, could not sleep at all & got worse & worse. I finally took trional a couple of

nights & got sleep, but did not feel any healthier. . . . Come home soon. Don't go to Pest [to visit Gladys]. This is gloomy, but it is the way it [perhaps the drug, perhaps Gertrude's absence] works.

In the next letter from Harry, also written in late January, he has a cold and is again in Westbury, "very lonely and gloomy." Barbie has arrived for the weekend and he hopes that the following week, if he is feeling better, they will visit Flora at Foxcroft.

It is not difficult to imagine the guilt and longing Gertrude must have felt when she received these letters. Perhaps there are tears, perhaps stomach tension, as she reads them in a ward or dormitory of the hospital. Now, even among the wounded, even remembering how anxious she was to return, she is probably tempted to go home and comfort Harry. Probably, too, the frequent letters and newspaper clippings sent by Miss Given-wilson make Gertrude sometimes long for home:

> I don't know whether to be glad or sorry that you are sailing for home on the 13th—for such is the news Mr. Whitney gave us last night. Of course as far as having you here is concerned, we leap with very joy at the thought. But somehow I feel that you yourself would have more inner satisfaction by remaining over longer & actually seeing the fructification of your wonderful work, & that is indeed due to you, the giver of so much. . . .
>
> The [Benefit] Exhibition has closed its doors, & from the point of view of numbers it was a great success, there having been nearly 800 during the nine days. But owing to the small entrance fee, I had only $142.00 to hand over to Mr. Lloyd Warren. Quite a number of people came three & four times & expressed the opinion that it was one of the most interesting of New York's Art Exhibitions, & very many asked if you intended to hold it every year.
>
> Mr. Whitney has had a bad cold for the last few days, & is going down South to get rid of it. . . .
>
> It will interest you to hear that Mr. Henry Price the needy English sculptor (about whom a lady wrote to you to interest you on his behalf) won third prize in "The Struggle." The winners of all the first prizes in sculpture were poor men.
>
> . . . Mr. Whitney has just left to go South. He is still rather hoarse, so the trip will probably do him a lot of good. He tells me you are probably sailing later on account of delays in the installation at Juilly. I think you are quite right. . . .

By mid-February the hospital is functioning well, serving both war casualties and, while there are extra beds, civilian emergencies. February 13, while on a brief trip to Paris for supplies, Gertrude writes to Flora from the Ritz that she is "busy and happy . . . interested in each case." Yet we have the sense that her mission is completed, that she can no longer justify remaining abroad, and we suspect that she has promised Harry she will return at this point when her presence is no longer really required.

Surely the *Times* is inaccurate when a month later—March 15—it reports that Gertrude has returned in response to a message from Harry stating that Flora is ill at their home in Westbury. Harry writes to Flora at Foxcroft the very day of Gertrude's arrival:

> Mamma is not in yet but is due this afternoon.
>
> We are going to [Westbury] because Barbie has a cold & slight fever. It is too bad as she has been so well.
>
> I did not write Miss C. [Charlotte Noland, head of Foxcroft] about your coming because I want to arrange plans when Mamma gets here. We will either get you here or come to Washington & I want also to get a California trip arranged.
>
> About the hunting—I don't like taking foolish risks & you know when hounds go hard you would be tempted to get away from Miss C. or any other that does not know much about hunting. It would be different with a good horse. I hope the riding does not hurt you.
>
> Are you sorry you joined Miss C.'s foolish fraternity?
>
> > Love,
> > Papa

One reason to go to California is that on February 20 the Panama-Pacific International Exposition has opened in San Francisco with Gertrude's forty-one-figure *El Dorado* frieze and gates and the previously completed three-figure fountain installed. As during the period just prior to her last return to the States, Gertrude's name has appeared frequently in the papers—first because of the exhibitions at the Whitney Studio, then because of the exposition, where the fountain has already won a Medal of Award. However—in an exposition filled with excessively symbolic "palaces and courts of the universe" and decorated, equally excessively, with symbolic sculpture by forty-five artists such as Fraser (*The End of the Trail*), French (*The Genius of Creation*), A. Stirling Calder (*The Nations of the Occident*), Manship (*The Joy of Living*), and Charles Rumsey (*Pizarro*), all dealing with large themes—it is the symbolism of Gertrude's ambitious frieze and gates, more than the fountain, which provokes questions, commentary, and analysis. Forgotten critics such as Juliet James and Eugen Neuhaus write entire books explaining the exposition, and Froma Eunice Wait Colburn, author of *Yermah, the Dorado*, writes a long article in which she attempts, in Gertrude's absence, to speak for her, perhaps based on an earlier interview:

> It is like [Gertrude Whitney]. I cannot but think that a prescient feeling over this terrible situation in Europe governed her. . . . It does not follow the old legend in that the divine figure of the being

that lived in the sun, the consoler of mankind, is not revealed. Sad humanity is barred out. We are left with the impression that human suffering and human tears must be eternally vain. . . . The men, you must remember, who made up this Spanish expedition, were generally released convicts induced to take this chance for dreams of gold. It was the interpretation of the Spanish conquerors who turned the ancient legend of Dorado into the legend of the land of gold, the legend of the fountain of youth to inspire their lagging soldiery.

On and on Mrs. Colburn interprets Gertrude's symbolism. No doubt the central figures of a man and a woman with arms outstretched are barring the gates of El Dorado to the running, stumbling, struggling, supplicating masses of humanity on either side. However, the theme, appropriate to California, was commissioned and then developed by Gertrude prior to any awareness of the "terrible situation in Europe." From Gertrude's journals we know, as Mrs. Colburn couldn't, what aspects of hell Gertrude has found in her hereditary El Dorado. Indeed, the consolation and revelation, which Mrs. Colburn seeks in vain among these academic nude figures, are nakedly expressed only in the journals, letters, et cetera—that is, once again, in Gertrude's small private visions rather than in monumental public ones, fabricated mostly by other hands.

Though Gertrude cannot say this and would surely have disagreed with such an estimation of work into which she has put so much time, she is nevertheless straightforward in replying to the questions of correspondents and interviewers about *El Dorado*. In indirect quotation, the *Times* says:

> . . . she would like to have it explained that the legend of El Dorado was the subject assigned. . . . The legend induced many explorers to lead expeditions in search of treasure, but nobody found El Dorado. . . . The gold was taken to symbolize all the material and spiritual advantages for which human beings yearn—quickly acquired wealth, extraordinary power, the well-beloved. The seekers, represented in the side-reliefs, have had a glimpse of El Dorado, the Gilded One. Each in his own way, has seen, and is pursuing; those nearest the door enthusiastically, for they seem to have almost reached their goal. El Dorado, however has just disappeared through the gateway.

≈

The family does not get to California until the fall. Now, in the spring, Gertrude is too busy to make the trip. The past continues to intrude. Not only are there letters to write and interviews to give about *El Dorado*, leading to inquiries about possible future commissions; but more correspondence and interviews, more explaining and re-explaining about Juilly, much of it prompted (in late March) by the visit there of French President Poincaré and American Ambassador Sharp, both very favorably impressed by Gertrude's hospital. Another aspect of the past moving into the present is the preparation of a contract with a stone-cutting firm for the fabrication of the *Titanic* Memorial. As to the present itself, there's the family to deal with; exhibitions at the Whitney Studio, including several more for war relief and a new series of competitions sponsored by Friends of the Young Artists; and, finally, Gertrude's desire to get back to making sculpture, particularly now of many subjects that have come out of her recent experience, such as nurses, soldiers, pilots, and trench warfare.

It is difficult for Gertrude to get started. When she arrives in Westbury, Barbie has the grippe, swollen glands, and a high fever. After a few days Dr. James recommends that they move to town where he can watch her more closely. Then Sonny arrives from Groton and Gertrude takes him to *Androcles and the Lion*. Another theater party is planned for Flora's arrival from Foxcroft. Barbara is hardly recovered before Adele's father, Gertrude's uncle William Sloane, dies in Aiken, and plans are being made for a funeral in New York. The days creep on, her sculpture waits.

Gertrude's impatience is evident in a note to Frank Crowninshield at *Vanity Fair*, over Miss Givenwilson's signature as secretary:

> Mrs. Whitney has asked me to write and answer your letter of the 10th. In spite of what you say she is altogether too busy to think of posing for sketches or such-like frivolities! Also she really thinks too many sketches and pictures of her have appeared lately and the public will be growing very tired of always seeing her in every paper and periodical.

This is a comparatively minor distraction. On May 7 there is a major one: a German submarine sinks the *Lusitania* off the coast of Ireland. Among the missing, ultimately the dead—1,198 out of 1,959—is Gertrude's younger brother Alfred, age thirty-eight. Gertrude wires her brother-in-law Almeric Paget in London:

> CAN OBTAIN NO NEWS ALFRED. HAVE INSTRUCTED WEBB-WARE ALFRED'S SECRETARY AND ALSO A REPRESENTATIVE OF AMERICAN EXPRESS COMPANY MAKE EVERY POSSIBLE INVESTIGATION WHICH NOW DOING. MOTHER HAS INSTRUCTED BOTH REPORT YOU AND HOPES YOU CAN ASSUME FULL DIRECTION AFFAIRS AS ANXIOUS OBTAIN ABSOLUTE INFORMATION AND BE CERTAIN ALL POSSIBLE STEPS PROPERLY TAKEN WHATEVER THE OUTCOME.

The painful waiting for news is described in a series of letters, written from Sunday morning on, to Flora at Foxcroft:

> Yesterday was a dreadful day. All day we waited hoping for news of Alfred, but none came, and although I am trying to keep up hope it seems almost hopeless now. . . . My poor mother and Margaret [Alfred's second wife]. I was at 57 Street all day except when I went

down to see Margaret. She moved up in the afternoon to Grandma's. She has a great friend, a Miss McCormick, who came with her so is as comfortable as possible.

Friday from one o'clock on there were extras every few hours. No one could believe that there was any danger to the passengers. The Cunard line gave out word that all on board were saved. I went to [Westbury] late (we had a lot of people for the races, but Papa was in Louisville, he gets back this afternoon) feeling worried of course but not extremely so.

Yesterday there were many conflicting rumors but in spite of all our efforts we could get no definite word. Everything was being done from London too but no news was to be had. That makes it look almost hopeless. There is just a chance that he may have been injured and therefore not identified, or that he may have been picked up by a fishing boat and landed in some little place on the Irish coast. He could not swim and there does not seem much hope.

Tommy Slidell was on board & was saved. John Hammond's brother was saved, his wife has not been heard from. What a vile thing to do. It seems inconceivable that any country can be so brutal. Sinking the ship, yes, that is war, but why didn't they give the non-combatants time to get off. Of course it may be days before we hear anything definite and we may never know what happened.

I am glad you are better dearest, your letter worried me Friday.

Let me know how you are. If I possibly can I will come on to Washington Saturday but I may not be able to.

Love & kisses dearest

Sunday afternoon Gertrude writes again:

Mr. Slidell has cabled that he and Mr. Stone were together in the smoking room when the boat was struck. They got life preservers and ran on deck. Stone went to one side, he to the other. He never saw Stone again. He saw Alfred, who had a life preserver—then he saw him take it off and give it to an old woman. The boat went down almost at once after. Alfred rushed off as if to get another life preserver —Slidell never saw him again.

I am still trying to hope but really it looks hopeless.

It is just the sort of thing Alfred would do, and if he died that way, perhaps it makes it a little easier for the people who care for him.

Two days later:

We have still no definite news, only stories told on all sides of Alfred's coolness and bravery. A Miss Loney who was saved as well as Mr. Slidell saw him give his life preserver to a woman and now today there is a Miss Lines who saw him helping children into boats. On all sides come these stories, so that if he gave his life one must at least try and remember that it was a splendid death. I feel too that if the loss of the Lusitania brought this country to a realization of its responsibilities and roused our apathetic citizens to action, it would be some consolation for the loss of life. . . .

Another two days:

Thank you darling for your telegram. You were quite right to send one to Grandma. Of course until we positively know that Alfred is dead we try to keep up hope and Margaret will not admit that there is no hope. We all say we have hope but down in my heart I cannot believe it. . . .

Alfred's death has a profound effect on Gertrude's life. Again the past intrudes. For weeks Gertrude broods, filling a scrapbook with clippings and letters about Alfred from all over the world; remembering their relationship as children, closer than to her other siblings, and regretting that she has seen comparatively little of him in recent years. Condolence notes, mostly addressed to Mrs. Vanderbilt, but many to Gertrude herself, remind her of the past, the painful, the dead: her sister Alice, who died just before her own birth; her eldest brother Bill, dead now for twenty-three years; the troubles surrounding Cornelius' marriage to Grace; Papa's first stroke and his death a few years later; Esther; Lena Morton; Uncle George . . . The list goes on as she mourns with Mama, another constant reminder of the past, and as she completes final arrangements for the fabrication of the *Titanic* Memorial, loaded now with more personal significance than ever before. (The press, also, frequently cites parallels between the sinking of the two ships and the heroic behavior of their passengers, Alfred having been by far the most prominent aboard the *Lusitania* and the one whose name appears in headlines.)

During this period of mourning Harry is loving and supportive. Early in the century it is not uncommon, after a death in the family (usually, the immediate family), for a horse owner's colors to disappear from the turf for a year or even more; but Harry makes this gesture for Gertrude more than for Alfred who, though a horseman, has been involved mostly with coaching. As Harry looks forward to his greatest season in racing, he leases his entire stable to L. S. Thompson, the owner of Brookdale Farm, just after Regret wins the Kentucky Derby—the first filly to do so—and the "Thompson Stable" leads all owners in earnings ($104,106).

In late June, Mrs. Vanderbilt, still very depressed by Alfred's death, comes from Newport to stay with Gertrude and Harry in Long Island for a week, just before Flora, Sonny, Barbara, and Miss Givenwilson leave for the Adirondacks and Gertrude and Harry for the Lathrop "cottage" which they lease in Saratoga. Thus a complicated, commutational summer is planned in which the entire family will reunite occasionally in the Adirondacks while Harry spends the racing season in Saratoga and Gertrude goes to New York for the second Friends of the Young Artists exhibition and to Newport for the Art Association's annual (since 1912) exhibition in which her sculptures of Barbara and of a caryatid will be shown along with works by other local artists including her former teacher Hendrik Andersen. But much of this changes by the end of July. Then, on black-bordered stationery, she writes from Westbury to Flora at Camp Deerlands:

It is an awful bother to have the operation for appendicitis, but Dr. [Walton] Martin [who has just returned from Juilly] was so convinced that it was the best thing to have that I finally gave in. They seemed to think that it would be hard on everybody for me to let it go over, that every time I had a pain in my "tummy" the whole family would worry & Dr. Martin felt sure that sooner or later I would have a real attack. I am going to ask him to make a very small cut & also not to take it out if *it* is not very ill! Don't you think this is a good idea? Dr. Martin came down this afternoon & we chose Sonny's room for me to be operated in & my room with the porch in which to recover. Two nurses have arrived & three doctors appear in the morning. Charles [Draper] is here to cheer me up & I have been swimming so you see all goes well & I am only depressed not to see you all for two weeks. Tell Sonny I kiss his unshaven face & Barbie's pink cheeks & you too dearest—on the nose! Give everyone my love & I will write as soon as they let me put a pen to paper. I would like all you girls to sleep *in* the camp while I am away. You & Alice [Davison] can take my room and Eleanor next Barbie (if she can stay over) *ask her.* Then the boys can have the tents.

The rest of this letter and another of equal length, written to Flora the same day, deal mainly with sleeping arrangements. The second ends:

. . . You take my place at table and make everyone behave. Be very careful with the boys. You are older now and you must not be the least immodest or familiar. They will like you all the better for it. Don't ever let them touch you even jokingly. I know you know them all so well they seem like Sonny, but you are grown up now and you must have more reserve. This is not intended to be a lecture, but only to remind you of your extreme old age [eighteen]!!

The newspapers are full of Gertrude's appendectomy, blaming it on the strain of Juilly and Alfred's death. Also, they report that Mrs. Vanderbilt has left Newport to be with her daughter and that Harry, who was to have played polo with the Meadow Brook team at Narrangansett Pier, has been prevented from doing so by his wife's illness. Not until August 9—nine days after the operation, by which time the papers have stated that Gertrude is "recovering rapidly"—does she write again to Flora:

I have been feeling perfectly well until yesterday morning. Had sat up & was to have had my feet down yesterday & walked today, but yesterday morning I waked up with a pain in my groin. As yet my leg has not swelled & we are hoping that the ice bags will cure the old thing before it gets bad. It is just the way my phlebitis began before and certainly it looks suspicious. But my fever is very slight & I am using mind cure as well as ice bags to make it go away! Anyway, leaving here Wednesday night, as we had decided, is out of the question, Dr. Martin says, and we are hoping for Friday. It is pretty maddening as I have made such a good recovery and was feeling really well. . . .

Gertrude recuperates in the Adirondacks where she reads many books, some topical, like *Behind the Veil of the Russian Court* by Count Paul Vassili and *Diary of a French Army Chaplain* by Abbé Félix Klein; some eternal like Strindberg's *The Confession of a Fool* and perhaps other books by this master analyst of marital combat. (She has ordered *The Confession* and "any other Strindberg" from Brentano's.) At the same time, with Miss Givenwilson, she plans the third Friends of the Young Artists competition for mid-September, and one on the theme of "The Immigrant in America" for mid-November. However, on September 9 she is still not well enough to go with Harry, Flora, and Barbara to Philadelphia for the launching of yet another yacht. This one, the *Whileaway*, costs about $250,000, is 175 feet long, with a draft of only thirteen feet, specially designed for shallow waters. As the *Times* says, "Mr. Whitney is very fond of . . . exploring any gulf, bay, or river mouth that looks interesting."

⇜

Partly because of the stringencies of recuperation, complicated now by phlebitis, partly because of the continuing special demands of Juilly, the *Titanic* Memorial, and the Whitney Studio as well as the usual demands of family and social life, Gertrude is for the present understandably unable to establish a studio schedule conducive to the sustained creation of new work. Excepting some sketches on war themes and a fountain, never completed, for a room Robert Chanler is decorating in the new home of the Colony Club, Gertrude does only one finished sculpture, a separate *Titanic* head, exhibited at the Gorham Gallery in November. The rest is bits and pieces from the various threads of her life, a flux of phenomena, news items:

ITEM: September 24, William Stackpole marries Florence H. Williams.

ITEM: September 29, Harry buys hydroplane. According to the New York *Times*, "Mrs. Whitney, who has recently recovered from an operation, is an interested spectator and will fly with her husband when he receives his license."

ITEM: October 1, Guardabassi writes a long letter enclosing photographs of himself in uniform. Regarding her appendicitis, he writes, "Fortunately enough you are of marvelous constitution and have great recuperative power. . . . You belong to Europe; to the warmer climate especially; your big heart is with us; because your genius is a Latin one, you belong to the rare natures who can conquer heaven but are satisfied to live in hell, if necessary. . . ."

ITEM: Later in October, Gertrude flies with Harry.

ITEM: November 13, Harry is elected to the Board of Directors of the Wright Aeroplane Company.

ITEM: November 15, "The Immigrant in America" opens at the Whitney Studio. Like many of the exhibitions there during this period, the aesthetic standards are low (typically illustrative and/or propagandistic), the cause worthy (to encourage the naturalization of the estimated 13,000,000 foreign-born residents of the country, many of whom have taken no step toward citizenship). The first prize for sculpture ($500) is won by Beneamino Bufano. His work is typically crude in conception and execution: a cluttered group of men carrying tools, mothers carrying children, a child carrying a cross. More sensational, though not a prize winner, is a hand modeled in blackened plaster, squeezing a black heart, from which tainted golden coins drip. When Theodore Roosevelt visits the exhibition, with characteristic honesty he pronounces the hand "morbid," admitting that he dislikes the grotesque and that he has the taste of a bull moose.

ITEM: November 16, Gertrude, the children, Harry's cousin Helen Barney Alexander (widowed since 1912) and Frederick Watriss (whom she will marry early in 1917) all board Harry's private car, the *Wanderer*, to make the cross-country train trip to the Panama-Pacific Exposition in San Francisco.

ITEM: November 24, President Poincaré announces that the Foreign Office gold medal has been bestowed upon Mrs. Harry Payne Whitney for her work at Juilly, upon Mrs. William K. Vanderbilt for her work in the American Ambulance, and upon Mrs. Robert Woods Bliss, wife of the Secretary of the American Embassy in Paris, for organizing the care of orphans. The medals have been dispatched to the United States for presentation by Ambassador Jusserand.

ITEM: November 25, Countess Széchényi has converted her palace on Andrassy Street in Budapest into an orphanage for 300 children. When the Countess appears, the children surround her, calling her "Mother Gladys."

ITEM: December 6, the Whitneys, Helen, and Frederick return from California, after a side trip on muleback to Grand Canyon.

ITEM: Later in December, Harry arranges for the purchase of a 297-acre farm for brood mares on the Paris Pike, about five miles north of Lexington, Kentucky.

ITEM: December 15, Gertrude has an appointment with Robert Henri —whose painting she has known (and purchased) since at least as far back as 1908—to discuss the details, including costume, for a portrait.

ITEM: December 17, Gertrude has Madame August Strindberg to tea at MacDougal Alley.

Bits and pieces from a life, flowing on toward . . .

≈ *1916*

Gertrude is one of those people who seems to have more time the busier she is—time for everything: family, friends, institutions, the creation of sculpture, and the written record of these activities. But all this presupposes her usual great healthy flow of energy, and this has not yet returned. Instead, she continues to mark time in a sporadic, punctuated, indeed "itemized" rhythm that lacks the continuous melody of the long journals and the major sculptural themes and commissions. In her correspondence, particularly with Gladys, there are references to an unspecified "illness," presumably the lingering phlebitis, and in one letter she says that Harry has "won out" in overruling her projected return to France this summer, where her new studio, formerly O'Connor's, has been improved and made ready for her by Eddy Minazzoli.

Perhaps the most important argument in persuading Gertrude not to return is that Flora will be nineteen in the summer. At the beginning of the year Gertrude and Harry are already planning her coming out in Newport, and as early as March, Gertrude authorizes William Adams Delano to start construction of a ballroom annex to the Newport house, even though he is in receipt of only the roughest estimates (about $30,000), so that it will be ready for parties in the summer. This year, the year also of Gertrude's and Harry's twentieth anniversary, they will do more entertaining than since the first decade of their marriage.

Meanwhile, the year begins with Gertrude completing the arrangements, including a fee of $2,500, to have her portrait done by Henri, until the Armory Show probably the most influential of the American Realists who would later be dubbed the Ash Can School. However, no label could be more inappropriate to the present enterprise. Gertrude chooses bright colors for her outfit, a loose aquamarine blouse and royal blue jacket with red frogs and yellow lining; darker aqua silk pants gathered at the ankle (all possibly from, surely reminiscent of, Poiret), above embroidered slippers, exposing high insteps. Yet even the elegance of the costume is nothing compared with her pose. Gertrude literally drapes herself from the cushion at one end of a couch to her feet at the other end. Her slim arms and long exquisite hands follow the curve of the couch's back. She is all flowing silk, except for the emerald intensity of her widespread eyes, the stony strength of her nose and mouth, the glint of jewelry (four rings, a bracelet, and pearls). Henri has been criticized for superficiality and facilely seductive brushwork, but here everything works. No other portrait of Gertrude so completely unifies the surface and substance of her personality, the contradictory aspects of soft romantic tenderness and tough puritanical resilience. The life-size portrait is too stylized to be "lifelike," but it is alive.

The year begins, too, with continuing activity at the Whitney Studio. No matter what details Gertrude is relieved of at home by Miss Givenwilson and at the Studio by Mrs. Force, it is important to recognize (more than has been done by many art historians) that Gertrude is, in effect, *the director* of the exhibition program of the Studio, even by now an incipient museum. Nothing is done there which is not connected with her interests, her life.

The first show of the new year is typical: "Modern Paintings by American and Foreign Artists." The precedence of *American* in the exhibition's title is typical, and so is the prominence of American paintings themselves, many from Gertrude's own collection—works by Henri, Bellows, Lawson, Luks, Davies, Parrish, La Farge and, very prominent, a moody portrait of Flora (almost anticipatory of Balthus) by Gertrude's old friend Howard Cushing.

John Sloan, another of the American realists whose work Gertrude has known since at least 1908, though she has not as yet bought any of his work, is not included in the exhibition because of an incorrectly addressed invitation. When the letter finally reaches him, he replies by asking Gertrude to consider giving him a one-man show. "The dealers in the city are not inclined to show more than one or two of my pictures at any one time —most of them not at all—and I feel that a collection shown together would be, at least, an artistic success, and might attract considerable public notice." Gertrude knows that Sloan has had to support himself by freelance illustrations and, beginning this year, by teaching at the Art Students League. She replies immediately that she will be delighted to exhibit his work and invites him to meet with her at the Studio to discuss the details. They meet, agree on a selection of work and on a time for the exhibition, which is squeezed between January 26 and February 6 of the now busy schedule. The show is well received and widely reviewed. As Sloan writes to Gertrude in the spring: ". . . due to the prestige which my exhibition at 8 W. 8 established . . . I have passed through the most successful winter of my career. . . . Mr. Kraushaar is to handle my etchings and paintings as well—his attention was quite surely attracted to my work by my 'Whitney Show.'"

For almost twenty years Gertrude has been buying art, commissioning it, sponsoring it, exhibiting it, sending checks to artists here and abroad. For about ten years she has been working seriously and hard at sculpture, often under difficult conditions, as we know but as her contemporaries did not. Yet she, like Sloan, has never had a solo exhibition. Perhaps now, in a period of comparative fatigue and ill-health, she recognizes that she owes herself the same patronage she has extended to others, that charity begins at home. Even now as she plans her first one-woman show (then still called "one-man"), she is commissioning a sundial by Paul Manship and a small plaster sketch of herself by Jo Davidson and is in the midst of correspondence with C. S. Pietro about yet another competition for Friends of Young Artists. But finally, bravely—given the prejudices against women artists, American artists, rich artists—Gertrude plans her show.

The simple, four-page catalogue lists twenty-five works. Ten of them are commissions or related thereto, starting with the 1905 plaster casts of bas-reliefs for the Osgood Field house in Lenox, and moving forward in time to a reduction in bronze of the Aztec Fountain, a photograph of the *El Dorado* frieze, the first and second sketch and final model for the *Titanic Memorial* and the separate study for its *Head*. The other fifteen works include *Paganisme Immortel* (1907), *Head of Spanish Peasant* (1911), *Wherefore* (1910), and *Chinoise* (1913). Altogether, though not a full retrospective, it is a well-selected sampling of her work.

Newspapermen and magazine writers are fascinated by the show, some because of Gertrude's position in society, some because of the work itself, particularly that related to the much-publicized *Titanic* Memorial. The review in the New York *Tribune* by Royal Cortissoz, a conservative, indeed anti-modernist, critic, is the longest and most prestigious of the many articles which appear:

> Mrs. H. P. Whitney's studio, which has been the scene of so many public exhibitions that it seems a gallery rather than a private workshop, is now for the first time given up to a display of her own work. It conveys an interesting impression of the ideas and aptitudes which she has developed as a sculptor, and in one heroic statue, which dominates the collection of some twenty-odd pieces, she makes an appeal that is doubly reinforced by the poignant nature of the subject . . . the Titanic Memorial. . . . The first model is histrionic, the second partakes of the same error, but is a little stronger. The final composi-

tion has the monumental simplicity which belongs to the conception. . . .

. . . it is in her treatment of the figure that she most clearly reveals her traits as a sculptor, in the full length nude of an athletic type, in the Arlington Hotel Fountain, and in smaller productions like the "Sketch for Monument to a Sculptor."

We do not know under whom she has studied, and it is to be counted to her credit that her works offer no evidence on that point. One group, the "Paganism Immortel," suggests that she has been attracted by Rodin's subtle modelling, but if she emulated it in that marble she has not persisted in the path then followed. It would have proved a doubtful course. The nuance in modelling is not at present to be reckoned among her resources. Her strength lies altogether in a straight-forward handling of realistic forms; she aims at the truth and gets it. She gets it, too, in a certain fulness and force. The best quality in these sculptures is the energy they suggest in the sculptor. Style, beauty, the charm of a fresh and original talent, have yet to appear. The promise of them, if discernible anywhere, lies in the vitality of her ideas and the honesty of her workmanship.

In late February, soon after the opening of Gertrude's exhibition, she, Harry, Flora, Helen Alexander and Frederick Watriss, family friend Alice Winthrop, Jimmie Appleton, Lew Thompson, and Henry Bull, a neighbor in Aiken who is president of the National Steeplechase and Hunt Association, all leave New York on the *Whileaway* for about a month's trip to Florida and Cuba. Life aboard ship is luxurious and relaxed, though not as informal as might be expected. Even while lounging on cushioned wicker deck chairs and railing banquettes, the women typically wear hats and long dresses or elegant slacks and the men almost always wear shirts and ties, usually with jackets. Gertrude is hardly ever without a veil, Harry hardly ever without a Panama hat and jacket, even when fishing, or harpooning shark, barracuda, and ray, or, from an auxiliary boat, shooting alligator in the Everglades. These specific images are from family photographs, but more generally we can imagine the days drifting by, floating from meal to meal and drink to drink, from one kind of fishing to the next and one card game to the next. . . . A brief stay at the Royal Poinciana Hotel, where Gertrude and Harry were engaged, is, after twenty years, both a sentimental journey and a reminder of youth, higher hopes, healthier bodies.

After the trip, the social pace quickens. In late March and early April, Gertrude is hostess for at least five war relief benefits, and from April 12 on, when the Russian Ballet opens at the Metropolitan Opera, she attends every Nijinsky performance that she can, has some social contact with him and his wife through Otto Kahn, Rollie Cottenet, and Josef Hofmann, and wants always from now until the end of her life (even after Nijinsky is institutionalized) to do a sculpture of him from life—a wish that never materializes beyond pencil sketches.

⤳

In mid-May Harry resumes racing under his own colors, then returns to Florida for fishing. From there he writes: ". . . The bother is the crowd, over fifty boats fishing in the pass. It is a lovely sight with the full moon & lanterns on each boat & tarpon jumping. But it is much too crowded. However, it is a healthy life & the weather is wonderful. I hope you are not overdoing & have time to miss me a lot." But, as always, Gertrude is overdoing. Howard Cushing has died suddenly in late April, and she is already arranging for a memorial exhibition of his work at Knoedler. As with other causes, she is no longer timid about using her influence and power: "Mr. Cushing had so many rich and influential friends in this city, and they would welcome an opportunity to visit your galleries. . . ." Roland Knoedler replies in the affirmative. Gertrude is also in correspondence with Maud Howe Elliott of the Newport Art Association where she has joined the Committee on Jury and Award for the Annual Exhibition. In the course of that correspondence Mrs. Elliott echoes Gertrude's feelings when she refers to Howard as "one of the real forces for 'Art' in our country. He was an exquisite man."

After several letters, Mrs. Elliott suggests that Gertrude should have an exhibition in Newport "from the double aspect of a sculptor and a collector. . . ." She offers dates just before and just after the Annual, which will run from July 11 to 25. "The time should be left to your convenience. It has seemed to me that you might prefer the earlier date, on account of the entertainments for a young debutante that make August at Newport rather a breathless time." Flora is, of course, the debutante Mrs. Elliott has in mind, and Mrs. Elliott has surely some realization of the extent of the entertainments already being planned and of the demands in time and energy they will make upon Gertrude, who shifts the exhibition to dates later and later in the summer until it is finally set for August 28 to September 15. Meanwhile, as with the shows at the Whitney Studio, it is Gertrude—not Miss Givenwilson, not Mrs. Force—who scribbles twenty-nine pages of notes and installation sketches for the forthcoming exhibition of her own work and of that which she has collected. Both groups overlap what has recently been shown on Eighth Street, but beyond this there are many alternatives: dozens of small pieces by Gertrude, never mentioned in this text; and dozens of works by other artists that have somehow crept quietly over the past two decades into her homes and studios—purchases, commissions, gifts from artists appreciative of her support.

Gertrude is also in correspondence with Henry McBride, the art critic for the New York *Sun*, concerning the possibility of enacting a law (still being explored today) under which artists would share in some small way —he suggests two per cent—if the resale price of their work increases during their lifetime. . . . And she is supervising negotiations, handled by Thomas Regan of Harry's office, for the purchase of 10 West Eighth Street. . . . And she visits Washington, D.C., to see the new site on the Potomac for the *Titanic* Memorial (the final site until moved in 1966 for the Kennedy Center) and Quincy, Massachusetts, to inspect the almost completed sculpture. . . . And there is a Sculptors' Day at the Allies' Bazaar in Grand Central Palace where Gertrude is in charge of the Authors' and Artists' Booth, aided by other women artists including Anna Hyatt, Malvina Hoffmann, and Laura Gardin Fraser (James Earle Fraser's wife). . . . And at Gertrude's Long Island studio there is a huge party (Miss Givenwilson lists 431 names), an extrapolation of the party in March at 871 Fifth Avenue, but with a few more friends and relatives to balance partially, only partially, two hundred and fifty or so representatives of the art world, an inclusive group of painters, sculptors, illustrators, publishers, architects, dealers, collectors, and patrons. . . . And two and a half weeks later, just before leaving New York for Newport, Gertrude has three hundred guests at a luncheon and reception in the studio for Republican presidential candidate Justice Charles Evans Hughes. (She is on the Executive Committee of the Women's National Committee of the Hughes Alliance, mainly because of Hughes's support of women's suffrage, of the Allied cause, and of Rooseveltian "preparedness." Harry, although a lifelong Democrat, now for reasons probably having as much to do with Gertrude's commitments as with Democratic economic and labor policies, donates $30,000 to the Republican National Committee.)

And . . . and . . . and . . . again the conjunctions are too numerous to list, again Gertrude is overdoing. As the Newport season begins she sends Miss Givenwilson to France to resolve various problems at the Juilly hospital and to see to final details in connection with the sale of the former studio and Eddy Minazzoli's refurbishment of the new one. Miss Givenwilson writes from France: "Your presence for even 2 or 3 weeks could soothe all the frictions and also make real that which is rapidly becoming a myth—namely that you are the supporter and founder of Juilly." As Miss Givenwilson knows, Gertrude has in this year alone contributed 1,080,000 francs ($186,840) to the hospital, where now there is squabbling about the addition of seventy or eighty beds.

≈

For Flora's coming out on August 4, Gertrude and Harry have long since invited almost five hundred guests to a supper dance in their new ballroom on Bellevue Avenue and The Cliffs. The list, slightly longer than that for Gertrude's studio party in June, runs twenty-one columns in the

Invitations book, almost two full columns in the *Times*. But for this event there are no artists. About half the guests are relatives and close friends of Gertrude's and Harry's, about half Flora's contemporaries, again mostly the children and nieces and nephews of the older generation. And again the names are familiar—for example, Appleton, Astor, Auchincloss, Barney, Belmont, Biddle, Bull, Burden, Carroll, Drexel, Duke, Fish, Gerry, Goelet, Hammond, Harriman, Havemeyer, Hitchcock, Jay, Ledyard, Lorillard, Mills, Morgan, Phipps, Roosevelt, Sorchan, Stevens, Vanderbilt, Warren, Waterbury, Whitehouse, Whitney, Widener, Winthrop. . . . Little has changed since the parties of Gertrude's and Harry's own youth. Some names are missing because of overseas military, medical, or war relief service (e.g., the Straights, the Széchényis, the Pagets). Some new names fill old offices (e.g., the Russian ambassador Bakmeteff, the Spanish ambassador Riano) and some not new (e.g., Rhode Island Governor R. Livingston Beeckman, Rear Admiral French E. Chadwick, New York Governor Charles S. Whitman, Admiral Cameron McRae Winslow). The *Times* is not exaggerating when it reports that the dance "brought together the entire Summer Colony."

The dance itself is preceded by many dinner parties. Gertrude and Harry are guests of Mr. and Mrs. William Payne Thompson while Flora is guest of honor at a dinner given by Mr. and Mrs. T. Suffern Tailer at Honeysuckle Lodge, to which all the debutantes of the season are invited. After dinner Gertrude, wearing black with jet trimming, and Flora, wearing white with silver trimming, complement each other beautifully as they stand together, both tall and slim, to receive guests at the new ballroom, which gives them the colorful background their cleverly contrived costumes lack. The ballroom—completed in less than four months by working nights and weekends—is bright blue and yellow, decorated with flowers, mostly roses, all brilliantly lit, as is the adjoining court, between it and the old wing of the house, where a fountain and bright dewy tents shimmer in the moonlight. The smell of the sea mixes with that of flowers, perfumes, colognes, cigarettes and dark Havana cigars. Cultivated voices, laughter, the popping of champagne corks, the clink of ice mix with the sound of music as couples dance alternately to Conrad's Orchestra and the Hawaiian Band. At midnight supper is served at dozens of small tables in the tents and in the house. The evening is perfect. Flora's introduction to society is perfect. As she dances gracefully with her dinner partner Quentin Roosevelt—a stocky, solid young man built like his father —the war seems very far away.

Many guests attribute the elegance of the party and of the new ballroom to Gertrude. Among hundreds of thank-you notes, Helen Alexander's says this most directly: "Flora's party was such fun and you must be awfully proud of the house—I felt it more yours than Delano's—you really seemed to be enjoying Newport more than Harry—which is a joke—don't you think so?" Another bread-and-butter letter is from Quentin Roosevelt, who has "committed the cardinal sin of staying in Newport for more than three days." His letter includes a catalogue of minor as well as major events:

a confused, kaleidoscopic impression, from which no single day stands out, of Cousin Courty and Cousin Catherine [Barnes], mice, dances, Packards-without-doors, "Papa's crew," dinners, Ethel Harriman's imitations, Mr. Draper's Pady Friends, the Whileaway, Mr. Whitney on Phil Carroll's gold tournament, Flora in the Scripps [her automobile], and the ocean drive—all accompanied by a pleasant, subdued tinkle, as of ice against the sides of a cocktail shaker.

The parties continue. August 6, Gertrude and Harry have twenty-six for dinner at eight-thirty, half their friends, half Flora's; August 7, thirty-six guests, the same pattern; August 13, about seventy, the same pattern; August 20, about forty, the same pattern. August 25 the pattern changes: they have only sixteen, all old friends of theirs, though not particularly close ones. Without the date there would be no clue that this is their twentieth anniversary, it is simply another night. In August alone, on only six occasions Gertrude and Harry have entertained almost seven hundred guests. This does not include dinner parties of less than sixteen (the minimum recorded in the Invitations book), or spontaneous luncheons at home or at their clubs or aboard the *Whileaway*. Nor, in terms of energy spent, does it take into account the nights when they are entertained, seeing an average of, say, fifty people a night, another twelve hundred or so, mostly the same people—the Four Hundred, stretched by now to maybe Five Hundred.

By August 28, when Gertrude's show opens at the Art Association, she and Harry must have been exhausted. The association's Annual Report describes the exhibition as

. . . unique in several respects. She utilized the whole of the lower story, the hall, staircase and landing, and the grounds as well. The exhibition was of twofold character, showing Mrs. Whitney as an artist by the full and interesting exhibit of her own sculpture, and as a collector by a large number of paintings from her private collection by artists of distinction, both American and European. The building looked its very best. The large model of the Titanic Memorial was placed upon the landing of the stairway, where it was extremely effective. On the lawn were placed two fountains [the Arlington, reduced in bronze; the Aztec, cast in plaster]—one, a bronze group, was playing during the exhibition. It is to be hoped that some day the Association may possess such a fountain, as after it was removed there was a distinct sense of loss. All the expenses of this unique and beautiful exhibition were borne by Mrs. Whitney.

As here, and in the papers, and in her own life, there is too much confusion between Gertrude-as-artist and Gertrude-as-patron. (She never does give the association a cast of the fountain.) But since this selection of her own work virtually duplicates what she has shown in New York, it is now worth taking a quick look at the list of forty-two items from her collection.

Unlike other collections of the time, two thirds of the works are by American artists, including three each by John La Farge and Ernest Lawson, two by George Bellows, Robert Chanler, Howard Cushing, Robert Henri (the portrait of Gertrude is shown now along with *The Laughing Child*), and James Whistler, and single examples by Cecilia Beaux, Arthur Davies, Frederick Frieseke, Charles Hawthorne, George Luks, Maxfield Parrish, Howard Pyle, and Edmund Tarbell. The inclusion of Beaux—one woman among twenty-eight American artists—is reinforced by the inclusion of England's Beatrice How among the fourteen foreign artists, making a total of two out of forty-two. Both sets of statistics are a beginning: ultimately no collector of her time will buy and show more American art or more work by women than Gertrude.

The day after the opening Gertrude, Harry, the children, and their summer doctor Harold Santee leave Newport for the quiet informality of the Adirondacks. There Gertrude swims in Little Forked Lake, washing away memories of the past hectic month, as Harry, who has just bought a motion picture camera, photographs her splashing around, finally relaxed. The rest of the family, the Four Hundred, and Newport itself at first intrude only in written communications. Immediately, there's a telegram from Dorothy and Willard Straight announcing the birth of Michael Straight. A few days later Mabel Gerry writes from Newport: "Oh! my dear, I heard *such* a lovely tale about your exhibition here. A prim person walked from statue to statue till, finding the nude figure of a man, he turned to his companion and remarked, 'Of *course* Harry must have posed for *that!!*' Don't you love it?" And Mrs. Elliott writes twice: "The exhibition is thronged constantly and is the chief point of interest in Newport. How important it is considered by art lovers, I think, is proved by my having received a letter from Mrs. Gardner of Boston [the great collector, advised by Berenson] saying she will come down on Saturday and spend Sunday here in order to see the exhibition, and, as she has been very ill and spares herself when possible, I think this is a real compliment." The balance of the letter explains expenses for the exhibition (about $1,200) and, months before the Annual Report, expresses the wish that "somebody give the Art Association the beautiful bronze fountain. . . . Some of our members should club together & get it for us!" In the next letter, too, Mrs. Elliott wishes that "some intelligent member or members" would present the fountain "as a permanent memorial of one

of the most interesting artistic experiences that life has brought me."
Then: "I hope that our Treasurer sent you her check for $450, for the
beautiful bronze Caryatid, which was sold for the price scheduled, $500.
You will remember that our rules oblige us to retain 10% on all sales, so
that we had, even in the case of one who has so greatly benefited the Association, to follow our rule." (It is a rule which Gertrude herself will follow
at the Whitney Studio and its successor institutions.)

Many letters, stretching from now until late in the year, concern the *Titanic* Memorial. Mrs. Hammond is disappointed because congressional approval of the site has been delayed and wonders, "Is there any influence
you can bring to bear?" The quarry is disappointed because it has not received payment and continues to store the monument at its own risk and
inconvenience. The stone carvers are disappointed because they cannot
complete their contract, including the base, until the site is approved.
Similarly, the packers and shippers are disappointed because they are
standing by awaiting instructions as to whether the piece will go by rail or
ship, again depending on the exact site. And, of course, Gertrude is the
most disappointed of all as she deals with one unpleasant letter after another, refusing to be put in the middle, and yet, for her own sake and that
of the contractors, doing what she can—including another brief trip to
Quincy—to straighten out some of the problems and put this nagging
commission behind her.

～

Since the summer Gertrude has been in correspondence with Dr.
Elizabeth Severn, a "psychologist and metaphysician," offering spiritual
guidance toward increased concentration, accomplishment, and fulfillment. We can only guess that some friend of Gertrude's, sympa-
thizing with her hectic social situation in Newport, has recommended Dr.
Severn as "good" the way friends in the past have suggested "good" for-
tunetellers and destiny decipherers, occultists of all kinds, readers of stars,
cards, numbers, tea leaves, crystal balls, cranial bumps, handwriting,
dreams. Dr. Severn reads "character." Most of what she has written to
Gertrude is general and platitudinous—e.g., "There are two supremest
powers in nature: the human emotion and the human will, the one purely
power of creation, the other of execution. In order to create something im-
mortal in art our emotions have to be intensified by the will." But now, as
Gertrude lingers in the Adirondacks after Harry has left, Dr. Severn seems
to be directing her "lessons" (as she calls them) at least partially toward
the bureaucratic snarl impeding the final placement of the *Titanic* monument, which she mentions specifically: "Six months or a year are not long
days for a true love to wait and use the time in pouring it out the more
dynamically in our art. You are so deeply philosophic, so susceptible, so
full of mystic and romantic vision, with an open mind to the unknown

beyondness that it is just such a deep pain that tunes in your heart the most delicate chords for esthetic creations" and partially toward the relief of yearning for a distant lover: "If you were not an artist, had no other ambition or call than what life gives us in the social joys, it would be a different thing. But fortunately you have a genius as perhaps only one or two women have in one century, so it would be a crime to humanity to ignore that and not pour the emotions that cannot find an immediate outlet in love into art."

In the Adirondacks there is no outlet for Gertrude's art. She can admire the local craftsmanship in rustic cabins and furniture and in elegantly and practically designed guide boats, but for her own work she needs a fully equipped and staffed studio. Perhaps she sketches a little. There are undated notebooks in which the subject matter seems to come from this time and to anticipate war monuments on which she will soon be working. Perhaps she writes a little. There is the rough draft of at least one story, probably written now. In it Gertrude describes a two-day camping trip to Moose Pond with Flora, Sonny, two guides, Dr. Santee, and Gertrude's dog Loup. The pond, four miles away, is "profusely inhabited by loons, gulls and deer." The scene is idyllic. New York and Newport no longer exist. There is hardly any sound but that of bird calls, the gentle creak of oars in locks, the swish of fishing line.

≈

When Gertrude returns to Westbury in October, Miss Givenwilson greets her with folders of accumulated letters, clippings, brochures, announcements, solicitations, bills. Many of these Miss Givenwilson has been able to take care of in what's called "a routine way," though her exquisitely protective replies belie any sense of the "routine." Other items require Gertrude's attention. In addition to dozens concerning Juilly, the new studio in Paris, the financial support of artists, exhibitions at the Whitney Studio, exhibitions of Gertrude's own work, possible commissions and purchases, the unending details concerning the *Titanic* Memorial, there is another request from Frank Crowninshield of *Vanity Fair.* The reply again illustrates both Gertrude's ambivalent attitude toward publicity and privacy (as complex as that toward art patronage and production) and Miss Givenwilson's style in the role of secretary (as opposed to that in the more personal letters we have seen):

Dear Mr. Crowninshield,

I have been able to find a moment to ask Mrs. Whitney if she will let you have her photograph for your "Hall of Fame," but she is very unwilling to do so. She has two objections, first that she has already appeared in that afore-mentioned "Hall of Fame," & second, that being the mother of a debutante daughter, she is going to have all the trouble in the world in keeping out of the illustrated papers & magazines. And so she is going to give blunt refusals to every request, so please forgive this first blunt refusal.

Yours sincerely
s/Irene Givenwilson
(Secretary)

During the fall it is Harry, more than Gertrude, who receives publicity, most of it unwelcome. In early October he is forced to resign as a director of the National Bank of Commerce, due to the Clayton Act forbidding interlocking directorates. Later in the month his $30,000 gift to the Republican National Committee heads the widely publicized list of individual contributors. Two days later he is in the papers again. Now, as the principal stockholder of *Metropolitan* magazine, Harry, among others, is being sued for breach of contract by Sergius Michaelow Trufanoff (known as "Iliadov, the Mad Monk"), who has written "revelations" concerning Rasputin and Russian court life which the magazine refuses to print. (By the end of the year, when Rasputin is assassinated and the case drags on toward settlement, Trufanoff's allegations may no longer seem so far-fetched.) But the most unwelcome news, the most painful, reaches Harry on November 22 and the papers the next day. His sister Pauline—only forty-two, two years younger than Harry himself—has died in Esher, Surrey, after three weeks of illness and a lifetime of poor health. The papers all trace the Whitney family history as well as that of the Pagets, recounting Almeric's adventures as a young man in the real estate business in Minnesota, his success, his marriage to Pauline, their return to England where he became high sheriff of Surrey and, since 1910, an M.P. Pauline's life is seen through his. Only their children—Olive and Dorothy (named for her sisters, the first of whom had died at six)—seem equally to represent Pauline and her husband.

Gertrude has been looking forward to hearing the Indian poet and mystic Rabindranath Tagore on November 22. Instead she spends the evening with Harry, sharing memories of Pauline and of their childhood together, when Harry was the somewhat distant and romantic older brother of a close friend. The next day Gertrude and Miss Givenwilson begin cancelling social engagements planned for Flora—two large dinners and one huge dance to which 277 married couples, 178 single women, and 311 single men have been invited, including at least one new name, that of Cole Porter. And for the rest of the season (through April 1917), the Whitney box at the opera is given to friends, relatives, and such artists as the Frasers, Paul Manship, and John Gregory. The year's enormous social activity comes to an end, except for Flora's dancing class on Wednesday afternoons.

During the mourning period Harry is sicker and more depressed than he has been since his father's death. His reclusiveness at this time, plus Gertrude's own avoidance of large social functions, permit her gradually to resume a regular studio schedule, working mostly in Westbury where her principal assistant—formerly with Saint-Gaudens, and with Gertrude since sometime between his death (1907) and the start of her work on the *El Dorado* frieze (c. 1914)—has the perfect punning name Ardisson (Gaeton Ardisson, in full). Besides suddenly having the time again in which to work, she is encouraged to do so by several purchases of her work, the most important being A. E. Gallatin's of the *Head of Spanish Peasant*. Like Leo and Gertrude Stein, the Cone sisters, John Quinn, and Walter Arensberg, Gallatin is one of the great collectors of contemporary avantgarde art, almost entirely of the School of Paris. Gertrude's inclusion in this collection, so different from her own, is very meaningful to her. In response to a note from Gallatin inquiring about the number of casts (three), she has Miss Givenwilson write that "Mrs. Whitney . . . is proud and pleased that you should have added the Spanish Peasant's Head to your collection." There are other encouragements too: Following the success of the *El Dorado* frieze, the San Francisco Art Association Palace of Fine Arts offers her a retrospective. In Philadelphia, the Plastic Club includes her *Titanic Head* in an exhibition of "50 Women Sculptors of America." In New York, Gertrude is made an associate member of the National Sculpture Society. And there, too, about forty young women from Hunter College meet with her at her studio, and another group of students from Greenwich House, of which Gertrude is by now vicepresident, meets at the studio to discuss the decoration and facilities of their new building. Also, the shows at the Whitney Studio continue, including those of the Friends of the Young Artists, who now want Gertrude's approval of an exhibition of designs "for the wall (18 by 22 feet) of the dining room of a country house." Approval is suddenly seeping through Gertrude's life—approval both granted and received by her.

Besides helping young people, she is as always (often secretly) helping more mature artists. She encourages Jo Davidson by commissioning him to do a polychrome terra-cotta bust of her while he is working on the monumental uncommissioned *L'Appel aux Armes*, which she will later arrange to have shown at the Newport Art Association. Through Davidson she meets the French composer Edgar Varèse, who is living in New York and has just broken his foot. She sends him to her friend Dr. Walton Martin for consultation and then pays that bill as well as those of the specialists to whom Varèse is referred. Soon after this she responds to an appeal from Mrs. Ralph Pulitzer for $1,000 so that, on Palm Sunday evening at the Hippodrome, Varèse will be able to conduct the first performance in America of Berlioz' *Requiem*. At the same time she is arranging for a three-part exhibition at the Whitney Studio called "To Whom Shall I Go for My Portrait?" Part One (December 4 to 18) includes works by Troubetskoy, Luks, Henri, Bellows, Davidson, Fraser, and French as well as by Cecilia Beaux, Mary Foote, Frances Grimes, Lucile Blum, Eugenie

Shonnard, and Gertrude herself (shown anonymously). Again, and increasingly, one recognizes Gertrude's emphasis on American art and on art by women—unique emphases at this time.

The catalogue of Gertrude's patronage could continue. There are dozens of check stubs, thank-you notes, fragments of correspondence—all indicating her generosity to artists who can't sell their work or pay their medical bills or rent or whatever. One appeal, arriving at the year's end from Ruth St. Denis on tour, must remain fragmentary:

> I am taking the liberty of telling you about Margaret Severn as a Dancer. She and her mother visited our school at Denishawn and I consider her one of the most remarkable young dancers I have ever seen. She has technique and a unique personality and if she keeps on at the rate that she has been going these last few years she will make a very wonderful artist. I believe that Dr. Severn knows you in her medical capacity, as it were, but I don't know that she has ever spoken of the daughter's dancing. You are such a good patron of us artists that I feel emboldened to send you these few lines about Margaret. If ever you were giving an affair where a breath of something altogether delightful and unique was wanted, I can heartily recommend Margaret Severn's dances.
>
> May we hope to see you when we arrive in New York in March? Are the parrots all well?

Though we don't know what, if anything, Gertrude does about Margaret Severn, we do know that, after this year, there are no more "lessons" from the young dancer's mother.

⪻ *1917*

In January and February the second and third exhibitions of "To Whom Shall I Go for My Portrait?" are held at the Whitney Studio. The second includes several important American artists missed in the first—Sloan, Davies, Shinn, Sargent—as well as Rosales' *Persian Dancer*, the portrait of Gertrude cast in silver, and John Butler Yeats's *George Moore*. In addition there are many loans to the show directly from Gertrude's family, such as portraits of Joan and Jock Whitney and their mother Helen Hay Whitney by Ernest Haskell and of Jock and his pony by Herbert Haseltine. And finally there are eighteen photographs by Alfred Stieglitz, Jean de Strelecki, Clarence H. White, Arnold Genthe, and Baron de Meyer, one of whose portraits is of Gertrude. Though Stieglitz himself has been showing photographs as works of art in his galleries since 1905, Gertrude's doing so within a more popular, less specialized, and certainly less self-serving context is adventurous. There is nothing of equivalent historical importance in the third exhibition, though it does include a typical period portrait by Guy Pène du Bois, who will later do Gertrude seated in her opera box, and A. Stirling Calder's portrait of his son "Sandy" (Alexander), whose "mobiles" will later become more famous than any works by his father.

While Gertrude is showing all these portraits—119 in the three exhibitions—she is working on several of her own: a charming small one of Flora seated in an enveloping armchair; another of Jo Davidson standing; another of Col. X, the subject of which remains as mysterious as the title; and still another of Captain Guardabassi, done from memory and from photographs he continues to send from Italy. At the request of Almeric Paget and his daughters, Gertrude is considering, perhaps even sketching, a memorial statue of Pauline, and she is definitely continuing now to do sketches on war themes. In short, she is again very much at work, on a very regular basis.

~

In addition to exhibitions sponsored by the Friends of the Young Artists, there have been three competitions in 1915 sponsored by the same group—the first, at the Reinhardt Galleries, on the theme of "'War' by Young Sculptors," the second and third, at the Whitney Studio, on "Labor" and on "'The Mausoleum' by Young Architects." For these competitions Gertrude has been the single largest contributor of prize money ($250 for each) and, when available, a member of the jury. Now, in early 1917, as she and C. S. Pietro plan the fourth competition—"Decoration for the Lobby of a Theater"—Gertrude writes to him suggesting that they dispense with awards and instead have the donors of awards select and purchase the work they like best.

Though Gertrude herself is responsible for this new policy (immediately, that of the Whitney Studio too and, later, through its various metamorphoses, of the Whitney Museum of American Art), she has undoubtedly been influenced by statements of William Glackens, who the previous year founded and became the first president of the Society of Independent Artists. As John I. H. Baur writes in *Revolution and Tradition in Modern American Art*, "'No jury—no prizes' was at the heart of the Independent movement, whose goal was to establish an annual exhibition in which any artist, modern or academic, professional or amateur, could have his work hung by paying a small entrance fee. The idea had been born in Paris with the founding of the Société des Artistes Indépendants in 1884. . . ." However, although born that long ago in Paris, the idea is new in New York, and no one does more than Gertrude to encourage its proliferation there and ultimately outward to the provinces. In addition, during many years, beginning now, of huge annual exhibitions of the Independents, the membership (or entry) fees seldom equal costs and the resulting deficits are largely covered by Gertrude, a director of the society for fifteen years.

As with Gertrude's private charitable contributions, it is impossible to list all of the public organizations to which she gives time and money. The time varies from gestures that take minutes, such as permitting her name to be used or dictating short letters, to commitments that take hours, weeks, months, years of hard work and long policy-making meetings. The money varies from hundreds (typically the smallest measurement) to thousands of dollars. The spectrum of these activities at the beginning of 1917 is typical. Besides her work with the Whitney Studio, the Friends of the Young Artists, and the Society of Independent Artists, she is still in close touch with Juilly and is contributing more than $15,000 a month to its support. In January she guarantees $5,000 toward a projected exhibition of Meštrović's sculpture at the Baumgarten Galleries; forms a committee to plan and execute a memorial to Howard Cushing; and, for the Stage Society, does the third-act set—appropriately and fancifully, the tower studio of a wife and husband, both artists—for Arturo Giovanitti's war drama *As It Was in the Beginning*. In February she meets with Charles Dana Gibson regarding an exhibition of sculpture by five artists in the circular basins of the Boston Public Garden; writes to Elihu Root asking him to discuss "art in industry" with Lloyd Warren, now chairman of the Beaux Arts Institute of Design; serves on a jury considering commissions for the Plainfield, New Jersey, Municipal Building; dressed as a nun, attends a "medieval pageant" with Lloyd Warren, sponsored by the Architectural League; gives $5,000 to the Art Alliance of America and an unknown amount to a group of New York Dadaists, including Marcel Duchamp, toward the publication of *The Blind Man*, intended to celebrate the inauguration of the Independents but ultimately, because of their rejection of his "ready-made" *Fountain* (a urinal signed "R. Mutt"), celebrating Duchamp himself. By March, Gertrude is understandably weary. She joins Harry down south, boarding the train to Palm Beach and flying with Henry Bull from there to Miami where the *Whileaway* waits to take them, by inland water route and the Savannah River, close to Aiken and a reunion with Sonny during his Easter vacation.

               ≈

When Gertrude returns to New York it is difficult to think about art. Everyone's mind is on the war. April 2, President Wilson addresses Congress with his famous speech beginning, "The world must be made safe for democracy." April 4 to 6 the Senate and the House pass a resolution recognizing a state of war with Germany. April 16 the United States declares war.

From now until the end of the war most of Gertrude's art, as well as her art patronage, will subserve the war effort. A tribute to Maréchal Joffre is planned at the Metropolitan Opera House for the second week in May. Gertrude is on both the ticket and the program committees. On the latter she and Rollie Cottenet, among others, arrange "Tableaux of Nations Assembled in Homage to the New Democracy." She joins Mrs. Philip Lydig's Committee for the French Theater and another committee, the Central Depot and Kitchen, in Hicksville, Long Island, led by Cynthia and Adele Burden "to collect, preserve and store, for future use, all farm and garden products." With the Friends of the Young Artists, she plans a war poster competition (an exception to the new rule, excused by both the worthiness of the cause and the nature of the medium). And finally—finally, only for the moment—Gertrude and other artists in or near Mac-Dougal Alley (French, Fraser, Davidson, Chalfin, et cetera) join together in planning an Alley Festa for four days in June on behalf of the Red Cross and Allied War Relief. Under the supervision of Lloyd Warren they decorate and illuminate the Alley and their studios so that the entire place becomes a sort of bazaar of boutiques, booths, bars, restaurants, gambling, and other entertainments. The Alley Festa is very successful. With expenses of less than $8,000 it grosses about $70,000 and with no expense sells $540,000 in Liberty Bonds—all as audited, free of charge, by James Marwick of Marwick, Mitchell & Peat.

Harry is also involved with the war effort. On June 7, during the week of the Alley Festa, a fleet of airplanes (perhaps his among them—the news item is ambiguous) circles City Hall, dropping Liberty Loan leaflets. There is no ambiguity about his subscription to the loan—$1,000,000—and two weeks later he contributes $100,000 to the Red Cross War Fund. In addition, along with his brother Payne, his close friend Colonel Lew Thompson, and George F. Baker, Jr., the son of the chairman of the First National City Bank, he is one of the four largest individual contributors ($25,000 each—J. P. Morgan & Co. contributes another $100,000) to the First Yale Unit, an aviation training program to which, for the duration of the war, he lends the *Whileaway* for errands and patrol duty when the seaplanes are in the air. There are jokes at the time about "roughing it at Huntington [Long Island]," and there is some justification for criticizing this and other similar pilot-training programs for being patrician, snobbish, university- and particularly Ivy League-oriented, alumni-sponsored, et cetera. However, despite this criticism, it must also be said that the young men attracted to these programs are more often than not well qualified as officer candidates: they have not only the patriotic fervor of those protecting the status quo but ethnic ties, particularly to England, and the advantages of education and athletic training. The spirit of the first American fighter pilots is quite comparable with Gertrude's own mixture of romanticism and commitment to the Allied cause. An analogous situation is that of Gertrude's brother Cornelius who, too old to fly, distinguishes himself as colonel in command of the 102nd Engineers (Spartanburg, South Carolina) and, soon after going overseas in May 1918, takes part in the defense of the Poperinghe Line and rises to the rank of brigadier general. As to Harry, although items concerning his generosity appear sometimes in the papers when he feels his gifts will encourage those of others, we don't know what else he is doing privately and to what extent he is contributing to Gertrude's gifts, some from commingled funds. Judging by letterheads of many organizations, it seems to be a convention of the time that the wives of rich men, rather than the men themselves, serve on committees; and surely Harry is anything but a committee man.

Though Gertrude and Harry are in the fortunate position of giving gifts more often than receiving them, they do receive one now. On June 27, Harry's uncle Oliver Payne dies and, as threatened at the time of William C. Whitney's second marriage, has almost cut Harry out of his will. However, wanting posthumously to express his affection for his once favorite among the Whitney children, he leaves Harry a very fine painting, often admired by his nephew—Turner's *Juliet and Her Nurse* (Venice, 1836). Appraised at $75,000, it is a gesture which Harry appreciates even within the context of a fortune left to Payne, having about a thousand times that evaluation.

≈

During the summer in Newport, while Miss Givenwilson works on the arrangements for a retrospective exhibition of Gertrude's sculpture to travel to the Toledo Museum of Art and seven other Midwestern institutions, Gertrude works on two exhibitions of paintings and sculpture by other artists at the Newport Art Association, and then on its Annual, where she shows a nine-foot cast of Davidson's *L'Appel aux Armes*, since retitled *France Aroused*, and, under the auspices of the French Heroes Lafayette Memorial Fund, intended, at twice the scale, to be shipped to France to commemorate the turning of the tide of battle at the Marne.

The Annual opens August 6, the third anniversary of the battle. In the afternoon sun, the large shrouded statue looms above Gertrude, Mrs. Maud Howe Elliott, Governor Beeckman, and Mr. Harrison S. Morris, president of the association. Seated opposite them on the lawn are more than two hundred members of the association and their guests—the Hamilton Fish Websters, the Craig Biddles, Rev. and Mrs. William Safford Jones, Mrs. William Payne Thompson, Mrs. Ralph Pulitzer, Mrs. Eugene S. Reynal, Mrs. John R. Drexel, et cetera—and, standing in straight ranks, two hundred apprentice seamen from Fort Adams. Perspired smiles flash across the lawn, fans flutter, the Fort Adams band plays a march, Mr. Morris makes "appropriate remarks," Mrs. Elliott gives "a brief address" and introduces the principal speaker, Governor Beeckman. Though not a word of his speech (or anyone else's) is recorded in the newspapers, we can imagine its patriotic content, the applause which follows, and the music. Then Gertrude pulls the strings which unveil the statue, and everyone stands to sing "The Star-Spangled Banner." What they all see— described in exactly the same words in each of the local papers, based on Davidson's statement in a press release—is "a woman of heroic size, her face expressing absolute mastery of her enemies yet showing the woe of past events, her hands clasped high above her head and her muscular limbs representing peasant strength."

Or, at least, that is what they are supposed to see. In his autobiography *Between Sittings,* Davidson quotes from letters after the unveiling: "It is not art: it is a wild deformity. It is not the 'Spirit of France'; it represents one of the shrieking sisterhood—an awkward, lank-limbed Valkyrie. . . ." And: "I cannot understand how anybody can so insult the French people as to offer them, as a representative of their graceful, beautiful, noble, brave, determined, unflinching spirit, the hideous, screeching, straddling maniac. . . ." Davidson finishes this chapter of his life by stating, "I did not receive one penny from the funds that had been collected . . . and I was more in debt than ever."

Patronage is a complicated business.

❧

While Gertrude is busy in Newport, Harry makes at least two trips. The first, in late July, is to Kedgwick, New Brunswick, with the girls, the Watrisses, and Bill Thompson. Harry writes:

> Dearest,
> It has been a long trip so far but will soon be over. I think the kids love it all. . . . Flora casts well & is having a fine time & looks 100% better. Barbie can't cast at all. The guide has to do it for her & then she lands the fish. Bill Thompson is the life of the party. It would have been a morgue without him. I got poisoned the day we got here (Sat. evening) & it lasted bad for two days but to-day I think it is over. Barbie got some too but it only lasted a day. Then Flora got a headache & started a cold, nobody knows how, & I dosed her. You have to have a doctor & medicine chest to travel with these girls. We will arrive (D.V.) at N.Y. Monday morning. I will send the girls to Roslyn [i.e., Westbury, where Miss Givenwilson is] & come down in the afternoon or if you come to town will send the girls & self wherever you say. Have Stewart tell me at train.
>
> Love
> H.

The second trip is to Saratoga for the races.

But now, for a bit, Harry's mobility, like Gertrude's, will be somewhat hampered by the departure in September of Miss Givenwilson to join the fighting in France. She has wanted for a long time to go and does so now at last with Gertrude's complete encouragement, despite obvious inconvenience, perhaps acting once again as her surrogate and possibly even as Harry's and, as it turns out, as Flora's too. Miss Givenwilson—typewriter, as always, in hand—goes off not knowing what she will be called upon to do and wanting only to be useful. While working briefly as Mrs. William K. Vanderbilt's secretary in the Canteen Service, she visits Juilly and reports to Gertrude on its progress ("Mrs. Vanderbilt told me to tell you that Juilly had not yet been taken over by the American Red Cross, & would probably not be so for some time yet, especially as everything is going on so well. All at the hospital hope it will always remain your foundation & under your control, & it is still being run in that way, as there was a surplus at the bank of about 1,000,000 francs in July"), its present needs (including, at the end of a long list, "One hundred more comfort bags such as you sent before, & which have roused the greatest enthusiasm . . . they are being used as the model for comfort bags being made in Paris now. . . . I know Flora & Barbara will be pleased to hear this"), and the love and appreciation of nurses still there from Gertrude's time and of patients whose letters, poems, photographs, beads, and other souvenirs Miss Givenwilson forwards.

In October, Miss Givenwilson is assigned to the Aviation School of the American Expeditionary Forces, where she is surprised by "so many friends in the camp"—that is, friends she has made through the Whitney family, notably Gertrude's close friend Phil Carroll and Flora's fiancé Quentin Roosevelt, to whom she became engaged, without public announcement, before he went overseas. At the Aviation School, Miss Givenwilson is organizing a cafeteria and an airfield service so the men can get hot drinks between flights. She ends her first long letter: "Quentin is my right hand here, & it is lucky for me to have him here. Much love from your devoted I. Givenwilson."

Just as Irene Givenwilson—it becomes increasingly difficult to think of her impersonally as Miss Givenwilson—represents the spirit and courage and competence of many women who join the A.E.F. early on, so Phil Carroll and Quentin Roosevelt represent these qualities among the first American war pilots. Quentin's letters to Flora are really a separate, though related, story. Phil's to Gertrude—even if only in a few extracts from many letters—belong here. October 29:

. . . I am meeting more and more Americans in Paris. August Belmont turned up today. They are all engaged in what we call the *guerre de luxe* and are a disgrace. Why they let them come here no one knows and having let them come, why are they not sent home? They eat food, take up space, and accomplish nothing. Wish they would let you come and keep away all the rest. . . . I saw Quentin today and gave him your message; he will go to England for a while I think in charge of some men who are to take a course there. He is well and doing all right.

December 2:

This is the anniversary of my starting for Dunkirk 3 years ago, do you remember? . . . I don't believe I shall ever approach the excitement I felt then. . . . Your last letter seemed to be pretty sure that you were not coming over. Have felt very blue since it came.

Gertrude has evidently been considering the idea of returning to Paris, if Sonny, now at Yale, goes there for his military training. In subsequent letters Phil advises that he train in the States.

While Gertrude corresponds with Irene Givenwilson, Phil Carroll, and many others overseas and continues her war work at home, Harry remains comparatively detached from the war. In the fall he makes two trips to the Greenwood Plantation in Thomasville, Georgia, to shoot quail, wild turkey, and duck. With no self-consciousness, he reports, "This place seems entirely remote from all worldly activities & interests," and quotes Lew Thompson's black boatman, asking, "Boss, what became of the war? Is it still going on?"

During the second trip, around Thanksgiving, Harry has all three children with him. For a man of forty-five, he is feeling old, sick, and depressed, but the feeling of oldness, even at this age, is understandable in a man who *has been* one of the great competitive athletes of his time; the sickness, a liver condition, is chronic; and the depression has been aggravated by Pauline's death the previous year and his own intimations of mortality. ". . . I wish you had come with us. I suppose by now you are quite dead, but the work must be almost finished. I hope so as I need cheering up when I get back. Getting older & older every minute & a crowd of kids doesn't make you feel younger."

Gertrude's work, to which Harry refers, is the Hero Land Allied Bazaar, opening on four floors of Grand Central Palace for sixteen days from November 24 on, except for Sundays. The official fund-raising literature for "the greatest spectacle the world has ever known, HERO LAND or Over the Top with Uncle Sam and His Allies," describes army, navy, and police drills; sparring contests; vaudeville performances; historical pageants; operatic recitals; parades; public choruses; a British armored tank and gun crew of eight taking a German machine gun nest; simulated trench warfare; three motion pictures; a reproduction of Bowling Green when New York was New Amsterdam; the Red Cross Tea Garden "under the able direction of . . . younger members of the Junior League"; "a soda water fountain, presided over by well known women in our social life" (including Flora); an old English theater connected with a restaurant and chop house; the season's debutantes (again, including Flora) in costume, in booths and concessions. . . . The simple Alley Festa has exploded into a multimedia spectacle which, to use the word coined this year by Apollinaire, can best be described as "surreal." Gertrude, serving with Paul Chalfin on William Adams Delano's Decorations Committee, is given a paragraph to herself—well, not quite to herself:

> Ancient Bagdad in New York will be reproduced at Hero Land with a good measure of sincerity and faithfulness. Mrs. Harry Payne Whitney has made a striking series of color sketches for the scenery and costuming of this part of the entertainment. Bagdad was, as is well known, the residence of the famous Haroun al Raschid, who was such a dominating personage in the Arabian Nights, and the fantastic note in Bagdad has given Mrs. Whitney a chance to reveal to us many romantic and colorful scenes: Eastern gardens, oriental wells, dream castles, beautiful dancing girls, and a picturesque, open air and life-like market place. Bagdad, as it will be shown, is under British occupation. The Indian Government has sent many marvelous uniforms of Indian soldiers, which will be worn by British Tommies who have come here especially to assist at Hero Land.

Yet, whether the paragraph is given fully or shared with Haroun al Raschid, the Indian government, and British Tommies, Gertrude probably receives more public attention than anyone else involved with the Hero Land Bazaar—certainly more than her sister-in-law Helen Hay Whitney, chairman of the ticket committee, more even than Marion Davies, peripherally *of* the American Godmothers League, who is always mentioned and usually pictured in the Hearst publications.

Gertrude deserves the attention she gets. Her Bagdad is one of the most popular attractions at the bazaar and perhaps the most personal. *Vogue* describes the opening night:

> Probably the most picturesque feature of the bazaar was the Streets of Bagdad, arranged by Mrs. Harry Payne Whitney. One had access to them by a built-in staircase, draped in black and white and flanked by two extremely decorative but highly irate parrots, who made no secret of their distaste for the entire affair. On either side of the staircase, niches illuminated by stained glass windows served as resting places for gracefully posed Orientals and for brilliant peacocks and other gorgeously plumaged living birds. Then at the top, one came upon the Rajah's well, where in a setting of orange trees gracefully betrousered and impressively bejewelled Oriental maidens served one with a delicious drink in a long-stemmed glass.

Birds, the Orient (Tunis?), trousers, Poiret, long-stemmed glasses, the recent Alley Festa . . . images from Gertrude's life flash by, making us ask again if personal commissions like this and such decorative environments as she has created in her homes and studios and for tableaux and plays, as well as the intimate sculpture she makes solely for her own pleasure, would not be more satisfying than waiting forever to test the ultimate endurance of bronze or stone monuments, while more transiently testing her own endurance against that of commissioning committees. But by now we know the answers to these questions. The romantic in Gertrude may delight in the sensuous and transient, but the Puritan in her will always insist on what's socially useful and permanent as bronze.

❦

Though, as Harry has supposed, Gertrude is "quite dead" from her work on the bazaar, she immediately joins yet another committee—all women, this time; all, as always, familiar names: Belmont, Jay, Hitchcock, Atherton, Delano, Gibson, Hastings, Pulitzer, Rumsey, Vanderbilt—to arrange a war-charity exhibition entitled "Allies of Sculpture" on the Ritz-Carlton's roof garden. The show is comparatively small and conservative, with one exception—a group of four polychromed plaster figures by the Polish-born, Paris-trained Elie Nadelman. Of these, one in particular, *La Femme Assise*, is a highly stylized and very witty portrait of a seated hostess with the great weight and curves of her posterior balanced delicately on a two-legged, wrought-iron chair. Her feet are placed almost together; her hands are folded demurely in her lap; her expression is vacant; her high, pale blue coiffure is adorned with a wrought-iron bow, echoing the ornamental curves of the chair. Two and a half feet high, she is, in short (even the size has been chosen for comic effect), a doll-like caricature of the elegance and stiffness, the politeness and blankness, of hostesses Gertrude and her co-committee women have seen all their lives, most recently on the lawn of the Newport Art Association. The piece, immediately retitled *The Hostess* by newspapermen, steals the show, but three women on the committee—Mrs. Perry Belmont, (Alva, formerly Mrs. William K. Vanderbilt), Mrs. William Jay, and Mrs. Ripley Hitchcock—first remove it, then relegate it and the other Nadelmans to a remote corner of the exhibition, viewing his work with too much seriousness as, simultaneously, they attack it for lacking seriousness and therefore the high purpose of art. Gertrude defends Nadelman, and soon his pieces are back in the center of the show. But a week later *The Hostess* is found mysteriously smashed, whether by a committee woman or cleaning woman we will never know.

And thus the social events of the year end, except for a small New Year's Eve party in Westbury, which Dorothy Straight attends and describes to Willard, overseas:

. . . only four men were there not in uniform—and it was quite a scene—many young aviators from Mineola and hydro-fliers from, I don't know where—and of course dozens of officers from Upton. [Three aviators from the First Yale Unit are actually living with the

Whitney family while they complete their training.] When midnight struck and we all formed in a big circle and sang Auld Lang Syne, one tried not to think of what the new year would bring forth to the majority of the people in that room! I think it best to have no imagination these days. . . .

⇜ *1918*

As if the war weren't brutal enough—and, with the introduction of poison gas, becoming increasingly so—this is the year of the influenza epidemic which kills some 20,000,000 people throughout the world, 584,000 of them in the United States. Flora and Barbara contract comparatively mild cases of the flu, and Gertrude takes Flora to White Sulphur Springs. Barbara, after recovering, returns to Foxcroft. Harry returns to Thomasville with a heavy cold, seemingly not the flu, and there the weather is miserably chilly and wet and his cold gets worse. And Sonny, almost nineteen, having enlisted in the Signal Corps in the fall of 1917 and gone on to Ground School at Princeton, now begins air force training at Fort Worth, Texas.

While Gertrude is away, Robert Chanler works in her MacDougal Alley studio, decorating it in a style as exotic as and even more unifiedly personal than that of the rooms done by him in Westbury. He has installed a large screen and seven stained-glass windows filled with submarine flora and fauna—patches of iridescent red, yellow, and green against a predominantly blue background. All of this is familiar, though nonetheless impressive, Chanler iconography. What's new, startling, and unique is the decorative design of the mantelpiece and chimney. A huge fire, in molded plaster, painted mostly bright red and gold, blazes from the floor, twenty feet up the chimney, and across the ceiling where the sculptural forms flatten into low relief. Half hidden among the flames are nymphs, birds, fish, reptiles, dragons, gargoyles, a fantastic world of real and imagined animals. On January 19, Chanler writes his "Dear Patronne" that the work is finished, "the mantel is fine, simple, and will not bother you." Though what's "simple" for Robert Chanler is not so for most people, in Gertrude's case he is right. She is more than a "patronne," she is a friend who shares his enthusiasm for the exotic environment and the theatrical style of life. Chanler ends his letter:

. . . I know no one who is gay except you, & I do not see you enough. I miss you & am at the same time glad you are away. You worried me so & made me jealous. When you come back I suppose I'll have my worries doublefold. You are a terrible woman. My heart began to grow & get younger & then you shut your door & I—then I suffered. . . . Goodbye.

> God bless you.
> Robert

⤐

Since Irene Givenwilson's departure for France, Constance Starke has replaced her as Gertrude's private secretary. By the turn of the year Miss Starke is handling routine correspondence (Gertrude's private correspondence *is* private and always handwritten by herself); appointments; bills; domestic and studio payrolls; solicitations; charitable contributions; invitations, acceptances, and refusals; transportation arrangements; occasional bridge debts; tickets for the opera, ballet, theater, and lectures. . . . However, Juliana Force has increasingly assumed responsibility for the details of art exhibitions—particularly at the Whitney Studio, including those of the Friends of the Young Artists. Though Mrs. Force has had neither art training nor art education before coming to Gertrude as a secretary, she is learning fast, and it is obvious, from her correspondence as well as contemporary accounts, that she feels sympathetic toward artists and enjoys socializing with them. She loves her job, her "boss" (as she calls Gertrude), and the art world in general. As she begins now to play a more and more important role in Gertrude's life, it is time to take a closer look at her.

Born in Doylestown, Pennsylvania, December 23, 1876, one of eleven children of Juliana (Schmutz)* and Maximilian Rieser, both German by birth, she is now forty-one, almost exactly two years younger than Gertrude. Except for chronological and astrological proximity (Capricorn, with its emphasis on ambition, time, order, precision, et cetera), Juliana's background is very different from Gertrude's. Her father is poor—first a hatter, then a grocer. The children, all boys except for Juliana and two sisters, must support themselves early—and respectably. In Hoboken, to which the family has moved, she is recognized by her high school principal as an exceptional student and with his help is sent—ultimately for a year and a half—to Northfield (Massachusetts) Seminary for Young Ladies, founded by the evangelist Dwight L. Moody to provide "opportunity education." From there she returns to Hoboken, teaches composition and stenography at a local secretarial school, and in about 1908 opens her own business as a public stenographer in Manhattan—a daring move at this early date, especially for the daughter of proud, Germanically correct

---

* In addition, Juliana Schmutz had twins by her previous husband, Julius Kuster, who died young, and then three more sets of twins by Maximilian Rieser, including Juliana and Maximilian Rieser, named for their parents. No wonder that this confusingly prolific genealogy is stated inaccurately even in standard reference books.

parents. It is in this capacity—perhaps more specifically as a social secretary—that she works for Helen Hay Whitney and then for Gertrude, and that she marries Dr. Willard Force, who seems by now, after six years of marriage, to occupy a small and rather vague part of her life. Physically, too, she is a contrast to Gertrude. Short, with auburn hair and bright green eyes, she has the look of a sprightly Pennsylvania Dutch housewife. And yet, despite outward appearances, she shares Gertrude's ambitiousness (probably, in both cases, emphasized by competition with many brothers), she enjoys the social status given by her position (in her own mind, far beyond that of a dentist's wife), and she relates the artist's specific struggle to the more general struggle she has known in her own life. Though Juliana Force is not well qualified to perform what is becoming a curatorial job, she makes up for this by her quick intelligence and her ability to act as a buffer for Gertrude in dealing with many beseeching artists. When necessary, Mrs. Force can say no, or she can be outgoing, particularly in large, time-consuming, art-world groups. She complements and protects Gertrude's own vitality.

While Gertrude is still away, Mrs. Force writes a nine-page progress report on "Eight West Eighth Street" stationery, very different in tone from Irene Givenwilson's letters dealing with similar subject matter. Mrs. Force is gossipy, humorous, and surprisingly familiar. She encloses, for Gertrude's consideration, a photograph of a painting of a dancer by Luis Mora. "It costs 1500 & I'm paralyzed with fear that you won't have money left to come home." She transmits attendance figures ("700 people only") for the first American exhibition of Andrew O'Connor's sculpture (at the Jacques Seligmann Galleries under the auspices of the Whitney Studio and for the benefit of a Red Cross affiliate run by Edith Wharton) and asks if she should not send Seligmann "a check for 250 and a note for you explaining that the very cold & cruel winter had a lot to do with the bad showing?" She reports that the critic Royal Cortissoz has visited the Studio to preview an exhibition of "Indigenous Painting" which will open when Gertrude returns, to be followed by "Indigenous Sculpture." Cortissoz

had a lot of fun with the Indigents [sic] & wished you God-speed! He is terribly nice & boyish—on warm days; otherwise rheumatism. . . . The Russian dancer [someone Gertrude is supporting] says she knows nothing of business & that she dwells among the stars, but she has called up twice for her check and if I can spell her name, don't you think I'd better send it? Mr. [Gifford] Beal [another artist supported by Gertrude] took me to lunch today & we buried Mr. Henri. It is great fun to joke with an engineer-painter. I didn't mean to but we ate 5 dollars of your check to him. . . . We are still having Spring [i.e., a brief warm spell] & everybody looks nice here. It gives me courage to send my love to you down there.

In February, when Gertrude returns to New York, as always she faces more mail. A long, sad letter from Hendrik Andersen in Rome is entirely about the recent death there of his sister-in-law, Howard Cushing's sister, Olivia Andersen. A warm, cordial note from Edith Wharton in Paris thanks Gertrude for "giving the gate money" of the O'Connor exhibition to the Red Cross, then mentions Olivia: "I know you must have felt very much poor Olivia Andersen's death. It would have been a great blow to Howard, for those two seemed always so much more alike than the other members of the family." A very enthusiastic letter from the Toledo Museum describes the installation of Gertrude's traveling retrospective and the fine reception it has received there and in the cities where it has previously been seen. Finally, a brief but forceful note from Mama, in regard to Sonny's air corps training, will suffice to indicate, if only barely, the wide spectrum of mail which greets Gertrude: "I know these are not easy days for any parents nor do the decisions rest entirely with them. But it does seem so terrible to think of the dreadful consequences to all the flower of our youth who are in no way fitted for the awful odds against them. Nothing can justify letting them go if you have enough influence over them to keep them here for another year—every six months you can gain for them to get strength & experience ought to be claimed by their parents for them. This is the way I feel & I know I am right." Mama encloses a newspaper clipping about "German spies" (or, more accurately, three men with Germanic names) who have alledgedly substituted lead for steel in the wing braces of fighter planes being manufactured by Curtiss.

The idea of the "Indigenous Art" exhibitions is close to Gertrude's heart for reasons of both fun and philosophy. First, twenty painters have been invited to choose by lot from an array of different-sized, blank canvases that hang, already framed, on the walls of the Whitney Studio. Each artist is then to do the best picture he can, as quickly as possible, thus creating a truly indigenous work—that is, indigenous to the Whitney Studio. We can see why this idea appeals to Gertrude, who does so much of her most personal work under conditions that are impromptu, rushed, and pressured. We can also see why some artists such as Henri and Bellows refuse to take part.

In the center of the Studio a table is loaded with paints and brushes and, beside them, bottles of whiskey and boxes of cigars and cigarettes—all the creative tools. The artists have several days in which to produce. Stuart Davis, then only twenty-three and one of the youngest artists in the show, goes right to work on a fragmented Gloucester landscape, typical of his paintings of this period. Robert Chanler brings with him an assistant who uses a spray gun while Chanler pushes the paint around. George Luks paints a little and drinks a lot, itching more and more with each drink to get at the canvases of other artists. At lunchtime, when Walter Goldbeck leaves, Luks studies Goldbeck's almost finished portrait; yells, "My God, look at that thing!" and goes to work on it. Some of the other artists partially save the painting, but now Leon Kroll feels the show is anti-art and drops out. That leaves one large blank canvas. As Guy Pène du Bois recalls in his autobiography, *Artists Say the Silliest Things:*

> We all worked on it, compiling the signature from the first letters of our names. The resulting signature was Russian [actually Kudo du Slmodach Bey-Oglhi from the first two letters of Kuhn, Dougherty, Du Bois, Sloan, Mora, Davis, Chanler, Beal, Young, Glackens, and Higgins], and the painting, to any casual observer, exceedingly modern. The gentleman critic on the *Herald* celebrated a new though somewhat confusing genius in his columns.

After "Indigenous Painters," the Whitney Studio is devoted for two weeks to an exhibition of "Chinese Modernists," organized by the Librarian of the Royal Asiatic Society. Then the "Indigenous Sculptors," including Gertrude, take over. Again the artists are supplied with working materials as well as liquor and tobacco. Again there is a good deal of fun. Paul Manship makes a Fallen Angel with wings too large for flight. Jo Davidson does a humorous bust of Paul Dougherty, who had exhibited with the "Indigenous Painters." More straightforward pieces are done by James E. Fraser, Laura Gardin Fraser, Eli Nadelman, Mahonri Young, E. McCartan, Hunt Diederich, and Gertrude herself, whose untitled work is probably one of the many studies of nurses and soldiers she is working on at this time. However, the most amusing piece in this exhibition is a collaborative work, a slender figure of a woman on a pedestal, with a host of admirers at her feet attempting to storm her position. The base of the pedestal bears the inscription: "Erected in admiration of the woman and sculptress who can cage twenty sculptors without bloodshed resulting therefrom."

≈

As the war drags on, Harry and Gertrude, like her mother, become increasingly concerned about the possibility of Sonny being sent prematurely overseas. They feel that by establishing ties with his commanding officers they may be able to assure the extension of his training, perhaps in Mineola. Harry had hoped to visit Sonny at Fort Worth in March but now, swamped by work on the liquidation of the *Metropolitan* magazine as well as other business matters and faced with penalties on about $2,000,000 in taxes, he persuades Gertrude to do the necessary ambassadorial job. In mid-March, just before the opening of the "Indigenous Sculpture" exhibition, she and Flora go to Fort Worth. There they rent a rather cramped brick bungalow. Though many of the officers and trainees are wealthy and well connected—for example, Roderick Tower, who knows Gertrude and Flora from Wednesday afternoon dancing class in

New York—the social life, like the bungalow, is drab. Among the many letters Gertrude receives from Harry, Constance Starke, Juliana Force, Irene Givenwilson, Natalie Hammond (and others, regarding still unresolved problems in connection with the *Titanic* Memorial), Phil Carroll, John Gregory, Frank Crowninshield, Blendon Campbell, Charles Draper, Frederic Soldwedel, Jo Davidson, and Robert Chanler is the beginning of a reply to Chanler: "Dear Bob, Life in Texas is not very gay. In spite of the fact that I know a lot of officers, that—" Though a tiny, truncated fragment from what, judging by the numbers of letters saved, must have been a voluminous correspondence, it tells the Fort Worth story. The only wonder is that Gertrude and Flora remain there until about the end of April. During the month Harry writes encouragingly about Gertrude's activities, gloomily about his own:

> Every hour a telegram from you was late or did not come at all I felt sure [Sonny] had been hurt or at least had done some foolish thing without leave. I know you have helped him a great great deal & I know you will always look back on it as the best winter's work you have ever done. . . . I have not had a cocktail since you left, only one scotch at lunch & one at dinner & nothing but work worry & gloom. [And later in the month:] . . . if you stay a week longer than you mean to & cultivate Sonny's officers, especially Reinhart (even if you don't like him much), you will be rounding out the winter's work. I am having no fun, never see anybody & am trying to get through things so as to get down there. . . . Everything here of course is blue & I am very deep blue. I will be put in a bug house soon.

But, working nights and weekends, Harry completes his business at the office in time to avoid tax penalties. At the same time, possibly with advantages to Sonny in mind, Harry enlists in the army and is commissioned a major for "special service," connected with the air force, as he is by now a director of the Wright-Martin Aircraft Corporation in which he has invested heavily. Late in April he joins Gertrude, Flora, and Sonny at Fort Worth. That brief visit is a blank as stark as the local landscape with its rigid rows of barracks. When they return to New York in early May, Harry is in frequent communication with Theodore Roosevelt about Sonny's progress in training (he has just received his commission), Quentin's progress in combat, and the air force in general.

Gertrude returns to her own work and to a new patronal activity, about which for some time she, Juliana Force, and their artist friends have been thinking and, more recently, corresponding. It is the Whitney Studio Club, an outgrowth of the Whitney Studio and the Friends of Young Artists, combining the exhibitive and encouraging aspects of these with recreational amenities. "I have often asked artists and students where they went when they were not working, what they did in the evenings and what library they used. The answers opened up a vista of dreariness which appalled me, revealing a terrible lack in our city's capacities."

The Club, which will open in June, is situated in a brownstone at 147 West Fourth Street, one of several buildings owned by Gertrude in proximity to her Eighth Street and MacDougal Alley properties—all, except those she herself uses, offering reasonably priced studio and apartment space to artists. This particular building is occupied, above the English basement and first floor, by the artists Blendon Campbell on the second floor and Salvatore Bilotti on the third, and their families. As discussed before Gertrude's departure, Juliana Force has laid out, with Mrs. Campbell's help, a billiard room in the front of the "basement," an art library in the rear, and a squash court in the back yard (because Campbell and Du Bois, though almost no other artists, play the game). On the "ground floor" (up a few steps), there are two exhibition galleries and a small office. All the furniture—made at the nearby Greenwich House, of which Gertrude is still a director—is brightly colored. So, too, are the walls (except in the galleries) and the "modern" curtains of sapphire satin lined with chartreuse silk and bound with scarlet cord. All this interior decorating is done by Gertrude's friend Dorothy Draper.

Much about the Whitney Studio Club is as eccentric as the squash court (e.g., the Club even owns a ouija board). However, Gertrude's eccentricities, strongly reinforced by those of Juliana, lead logically, if meanderingly, after one more step (the consolidated Whitney Studio Galleries), to the Whitney Museum of American Art—at once the most humanly supportive and most humanly fallible of American art institutions. But now Juliana Force, who has been Gertrude's buffer in many of the activities of the Whitney Studio, becomes the official director of the Club, of which the only requirement for admission is talent and the recommendation of a member. The five-dollar annual dues are treated as casually as everything else having to do with businesslike procedures. For example, there is no accurate record—and presumably there never was one—of the membership. It must be pieced together from Gertrude's autobiographical writings and statements, as well as those of such other artists as Xavier J. Barile, Louis Bouché, Blendon Campbell, Jo Davidson, Stuart Davis, Guy Pène du Bois, and Katherine Schmidt—all charter members who refer to other charter members, of whom the more prominent are Peggy Bacon, Gifford Beal, Alexander Brook, Robert Chanler, Glenn O. Coleman, John Flanagan, William J. Glackens, Samuel Halpert, George O. ("Pop") Hart, Edward Hopper, Rockwell Kent, Leon Kroll, Yasuo Kuniyoshi, Robert Laurent, Reginald Marsh, Kenneth Hayes Miller, Henry E. Schnakenberg, and Dorothy Varian. Within a few years the Club's membership will grow from less than thirty to more than four hundred, including most of the prominent painters, sculptors, printmakers, illustrators, and cartoonists living in New York and a few writers who paint, most notably John Dos Passos. As the membership grows so will the exhibition program, supplementing and complementing what is being done concurrently at the Whitney Studio. Though the Club's initial show in June—work by the charter members—might have appeared at the Studio, subsequent exhibitions will move further afield, such as "Art by Children of the Greenwich House School" and "Photographs of American Indians by E. L. Curtis."

As Gertrude looks forward to the Club's first show and backward to the first public activities at the Whitney Studio, she has the right to feel proud of having established the two show places most hospitable to American art. As so often at moments like this, she turns to her journals, trying to find not only the order in events but in the development of her own personality. She rereads her 1913 journal, beginning with "A gray depressing, aching day," finding hope then mainly in the existence of the studies for her *Titanic* Memorial (still not erected in 1918), and ending with the words "I love what I have written now, for it is the truth." She dates the page following December 5, 1913:

> Tuesday, May 14th 1918. . . . 4½ years! Was it *I* myself who wrote those strange lines—what was the agony of my soul just then which so suffered? And how I tried to encourage myself by thinking that I belonged to the elite. Was that the only way? All mediocre people feel themselves geniuses! I don't even remember passing through that horrible phase. Let us hope it is over. Then I was old. Now I am young. I hate words and only care for deeds. A silent world, one in which things happened perpetually but were never spoken of. Onward and forward. (Again words) what can I *do*?

Perhaps she will write an autobiography. The next three pages contain notes for some such project—all tightly organized:

Activities of Past 4 years:
I Historical. Get good history of the war—about 2 *vol.*—individual books—
II Political. Back numbers of some weekly. Books.
III Social. Talk to people of different classes about changes.
a. economic b. financial c. character.
IV Artistic. Exhibitions. Magazines. War work.
V Personal. News of Friends.

We are accustomed to Gertrude's tendency to overcompartmentalize a life in which all compartments overlap. More surprising now is the order of priorities, the placement of the historical, political, and social aspects of her life above the artistic and personal. This order is an expression of her mind and is substantially contrary to the direction in which her heart has led and is leading her. The war—she believes correctly, as indicated in letters of this period—is nearing its end. Though a profound experience for her and one to which she will refer in her writing and sculpture for the rest of her life, it has not been so much a matter of history in the large sense as of personal history including her love of France, "the male world of action," and so forth. Similarly, politics in the large sense has played only a small part in her life, typically subordinate to her interest in art, to getting her own work and that of so many other artists out of the studio and into the larger world. In this process she has now met "people of different classes," mostly artists, and entered their social worlds from which she was protected in her earlier years. (a.) She knows these artists' economic situations. (b.) She responds to their financial problems. (c.) She understands their eccentricities of character.

Enough on the historical, political, and social. It is to protect herself from these pressures that Gertrude has delegated so much responsibility to Juliana Force and has chosen to devote more of her own time to the artistic and personal. She continues to work mostly on war sculpture and to correspond mostly with artists.

News of Friends: Jo Davidson is in Scranton, with one of those "little lamps" on his head, looking for subject matter in the coal mines. Edgar Varèse is in New York. Having conducted Berlioz' *Requiem,* he now wants Gertrude to join the Executive Committee of his New Symphony Orchestra (devoted to "futurist," meaning "contemporary," music). She joins. Phil Carroll is in France: "I want so much to see you that any substitute for seeing you will do." In short, he wants a photograph: "the one I once had for a little time, taken with a veil and pearls. You must remember—you made me give it back." She sends another print. Bob Chanler, whom she has helped through a financial crisis (though he will eventually receive a large inheritance) thanks her "for all and for what is to come and for many many things" and advises her that "the absinthe is to arrive on Tuesday." Captain Guardabassi writes on behalf of the Italy America Society, of which he is a trustee. On the third anniversary of Italy's entrance into the war, Caruso and Scotti, among others, will sing at the Metropolitan Opera House. Yes, Gertrude will be a "patroness." Yes, she will take a box. Yes, she will run a benefit auction at 871 Fifth Avenue. Yes, Flora will be a "flower and program girl."

News of Family: June 1, William K. Vanderbilt succeeds A. H. Smith as president of the New York Central Railroad. June 12, Margaret Vanderbilt, Alfred's widow, marries Raymond T. Baker, in a simple wedding three years and one month after the sinking of the *Lusitania.* Relentlessly time moves on. July 14, Flora's fiancé Quentin Roosevelt is shot down and killed about ten miles inside the German lines in the Château-Thierry sector. Theodore Roosevelt, whose four sons have all been in action, two of them wounded, is crushed by Quentin's death, but before making a public statement arranges to break the news gently to Flora. With that done, he makes a statement, very different in feeling, to the press: "Quentin's mother and I are very glad that he got to the front and had a chance to render some service to his country and to show the stuff there was in him before his fate befell him." Flora need make no public statement. Temporary physical changes are eloquent. For a time her eyes look sunken and haunted, and she loses weight.

The summer is, to use one of Harry's favorite words, *gloomy.* The Whitneys spend the usual amount of time in Long Island, less than usual in Newport, and more than usual in the Adirondacks. In Westbury and Newport, Gertrude sculpts in her studios. In the Adirondacks she writes some stories and refreshes her spirits. During late September and early October (this year and the next two years) Harry goes hunting and fishing in Montana with Buck Wells and other friends of his who give him the nickname "Moody." Sonny is now an accomplished flight instructor—and more than that. He is one of a few pilots selected to do stunt flying, all over the country, to promote the sale of war bonds. But mostly the Whitney family, like everyone else, waits for the war to end, watching first one, then another, of the Central Powers surrender: September 30—Bulgaria; October 30—Turkey; November 4—Austria; 11 A.M. November 11—"cease fire."

Of course it doesn't end just like that, on the minute. The suffering of soldiers and civilians continues and there are the postwar casualties of overexertion as directly related to the war as bullet wounds. On December 1, Dorothy's husband Willard Straight, who has been on active duty in France, dies of pneumonia. On January 6, 1919, Theodore Roosevelt, who had been considered too old for combat duty but had given so much of his energy to the fight for "preparedness," dies in his exhausted sleep. And, looking forward just a few more months, Gertrude's friend Robert Bacon returns home from Paris in March, physically ruined, and dies within another two months.

Nor do the victory celebrations end immediately. Perhaps the most elaborate is the Free Milk for France Fund's Carnaval de Victoire and Masque de Triomphe at the Ritz-Carlton. The hotel's entire ground floor and first sublevel—Japanese gardens, grand ballroom, lobbies, lounges—are canopied with blue material festooned with crystal tassels and chandeliers, suggesting the night sky. French officers mingle with members of New York, Boston, Philadelphia, and Washington society. The crowd, moving from area to area, is entertained by a Neapolitan Quintet, Egyptian and Japanese dancing, Yvette Guilbert's songs . . . and yet, despite all the entertainment and activity, Gertrude steals the show. There is hardly a newspaper which does not mention and/or illustrate the "elaborateness" and "uniqueness" of her costume. *Vogue* says, "It was purely imaginative, taking its inspiration from no period nor country, and was made of white satin with a stiff short skirt patterned in fanciful designs and a high eccentric head-dress." But that doesn't begin to suggest what can be seen even in crude black and white photographs: the sparkling crown reaching at least a foot above her head like a pair of serpents or Viking horns; the jewels strung from ear to ear tightly beneath her chin and then loosely onto her bosom; the stylized, unspecific animals appliquéed to the satin bodice; pendant sleeves of shimmering lace; the abstract, geometric design of the tunic; the satin leggings. All this is, indeed, "imaginative," a product of Gertrude's fantasy of East and West that goes beyond anything she has ever done in sculpture, not only the drab war themes on which she has been working recently, but even the immediately prewar *Chinoise.*

≈ *1919*

Gertrude is thinking about returning to Paris. Soon after the armistice Jo Davidson has returned there, with the help of a loan from her, to do busts of the Allied leaders. She envies him. Eddy Minazzoli has her new studio ready. Guardabassi implores her: "La vie sans toi est insupportable." If she won't come to Paris, he will come to New York. "Be patient my precious one," he writes, "you may be certain that the minute I am free I shall sail. Life is too unbearable for me without you, nothing interests me any longer, I have nothing in my mind but *you, you, you.*"

Yet almost two years will pass before she sails. Harry, the children, war memorial commissions will all detain her. For the time being her travels are again "in the mind," a mixture of wartime crossings and peacetime fantasies, expressed sporadically in rushed, autobiographical fiction. Gertrude has too little time for serious writing, none for rewriting. And she hardly has time for more than appearances at the public exhibitions at the Whitney Studio, at the Whitney Studio Club, at commercial galleries where she sponsors artists in whom she is particularly interested, and at less frequent private exhibitions organized by her at the Colony and Cosmopolitan clubs. Through Juliana Force, Gertrude buys works from almost every show she is involved with, but this is largely a matter of signing checks which go out regularly along with those for dozens of other causes, both private and public, ranging from the most intimate crises in the lives of unknown artists to the national and international disasters in the day's headlines.

Most of Gertrude's energy is presently devoted to war pieces with such titles as *Refugees, Honorably Discharged, Orders, Spirit of the Red Cross*

Nurse, Château-Thierry, The 102nd Engineers, and *Private in the 15th.* She is also working on two of the relief panels for Thomas Hastings' Victory Arch, to be erected at Madison Square.* Some of this subject matter comes out of her direct experience, recorded in sketches; some out of newspaper photographs. Some will remain small and intimate; some, in addition to the Victory Arch panels, will be developed into war monuments. And it is that possibility, as much as her family, which seems to hold her in the States. Surely she is tempted by reports from Jo Davidson in Paris who, like her, seeks not only a spiritual home for himself but a secular home for his work. As he completes a bust of Foch and is about to begin Joffre, Clemenceau, and Pershing, he writes:

> Really, Gertrude, you must come over. I cannot tell you what this place is like now with everything going on, it is no doubt the center of the whole world and great things are happening all the time, you can almost see history being made before you, and you see it in great gobs, like some great big sketch for a huge monument. The monument of the future, and how different it hopes to be from the past! and how much more wonderful! I cannot explain it to you. One must be here and get it first hand. Everybody talks and has something to say, and they say it crudely but surely straight from the shoulder. They are like so many impressionists trying to express themselves quickly and certainly and they all expect something and don't know what. Gee, I wish I could write, or sculpt, or something to tell you what I see and feel. Doing all these busts is really a thrilling experience. . . .

Though it will still be more than a year before Gertrude goes to Paris, she begins now, whether consciously or unconsciously, directly or indirectly, to plan that trip by planning a so-called "Overseas Exhibition" of American art (from Eakins to the present) to go there and to other cultural capitals of Europe. She heads a committee made up in part of the presidents or directors of major American museums, the presidents of the National Academy and the Sculpture Society, and John Singer Sargent, Andrew O'Connor, and Thomas Hastings. "The Committee wishes, in order that every possible dignity shall surround what [it believes] to be an undertaking of very great importance to the United States, that the Government take this proposal under its patronage and help the Committee with its advice and general direction." Perhaps the government gives some advice, perhaps the committee does, but predictably it is Gertrude who gives the project its "general direction," and it is she who will ultimately—

* The arch, like so much temporary public art, was done in staff (a mixture of plaster and fiber, resembling stucco) with the hope, in this case never realized, that by public subscription it would be redone in marble and bronze. However, Gertrude, unlike less wealthy artists, took the precaution of having her staff panels cast in bronze as well, and they survive in the garden outside her Westbury studio.

in 1920, at the Venice Biennale and, in 1921, at the Grafton Galleries in London and at the Galeries Georges Petit in Paris—organize it and pay for it. Even now she is discussing possible loans with Juliana Force, corresponding with Eddy Minazzoli about exhibition space in Paris, and having Miss Starke survey the Pittsburgh area for fine American paintings.

Early in July, just before leaving for Newport, Gertrude writes to Gladys in Hungary, summarizing news of herself and the family:

> . . . You will find naturally some change in my kids. Sonny is about Harry's height, has been rowing on the Freshman crew [at Yale to which he has returned], so you see is very strong, and has the same fatal blue eyes that are continually getting him in messes. He is in the Reserve Aviation as First Lieutenant. Flora, twenty one, think of it, lost her fiancé in the war (it was not announced) has developed tremendously. Can you see Flora a perfectly good secretary? She knows short hand, type writing and acted for a while as secretary to Mrs. McCormick, head of the Woman's National Republican Committee. Besides she loves dancing and all normal things. Barbara is preparing for college. I don't know if she will go but she wants to take her exams. She goes back to Foxcroft for two years.
>
> As for Harry and myself we are, I am afraid, getting old. Unfortunately, I don't feel so and still have a perfectly good time in life! . . .
>
> I had a beautiful scheme all worked up in regard to a big art exhibition to take place at the Luxembourg next winter which I had to go to Paris to arrange. That was my excuse for a passport. . . . I could sail early in September, do my business in Paris and then join you, it would be too wonderful, I would simply love it and at that time it would fit in with the family's plans. If I could get a passport for Flora as my secretary I might bring her along. And then we could all come back together! . . .
>
> We had great excitement over the big dirigible which flew across the ocean and landed at Mineola the other day. She is perfectly beautiful to look at, like a big silver tarpon. . . .
>
> Did you hear that my friend Bob Bacon died a month ago? It was a great shock, he was one of the best friends I had. His son has asked me to do his bust, and though I love doing it, it is very difficult and depressing. . . .

At about the same time Gertrude writes to Herbert Haseltine in Paris:

> Your letter made me feel like old times, and old times were fun, weren't they? Always merry and bright, I see you are. What a horrible time it has all been! My God let's hope it is over. So you are doing over your place! And working again! I hear about you now and then from people over there, Delano and Jo Davidson and such like, and I

gathered you had not changed, in spite of your advancing years. I am up to my ears in work and it's fine. I could not do a stroke while the War was on. Tommy Hastings was a brick and gave me the two most important panels on the Victory Arch to do. Very short time to do them and great fun. Now I have my place full of work, two fountains (orders) for out West; a monument, a bust, and I am finishing up fourteen sketches (don't faint) of war things which I did in connection with the Arch this winter. Am planning for an exhibition myself in the autumn. I may come over in September although I don't really want to go to Paris now from all I hear. Flora is old [twenty-two this month] Sonny is aged [twenty] and Barbara is grown up [sixteen]. It's disgusting. *I* am still as bad, as dashing and as reckless as ever. Goodbye. I was all cheered at hearing from you again.

Sometime between writing these letters and settling in Newport for the season, Gertrude decides to send Flora to Paris with Dorothy Straight, hoping that Dorothy, in mourning for Willard, and Flora, less officially but no less feelingly mourning for Quentin, will cheer each other up. The trip is a success. From the Ritz, Flora reports on a visit, with Rollie Cottenet, to Gertrude's new Rue Boileau studio—a stucco-finished three-story corner house, connecting, past a private garden, with a separate building containing the studio, main living room, and concierge's apartment above. Gertrude's bedroom and the living and dining rooms are furnished substantially with the large-scale pieces she had at the Boulevard Flandrin apartment, including the piano, which Rollie begins playing immediately.

He was so thrilled to find a good one again. But he insisted it ought to be tuned as it would go to wrack and ruin unless it were done, so we told Eddy to have it tuned right off & then we all said we hoped you wouldn't mind. The big room was very dirty but it's most attractive—all the bronzes are about; the Rosales things standing out especially—they really looked too lovely . . . the familiar streets, the reckless taxis, the Paris smells—everything went to give one a tremendous thrill & I have not gotten over it by a long shot. It's very curious to see the people in the streets. The women in black clothes with heavy crêpe veils and skirts literally just below their knees—it looks too ludicrous & gives you the funniest sensation.

[Aunty Dorothy and I] have been trying to get our dress making over so that all the rest of the time could be better occupied. Have been to Chanel, Jenny & Callot—the last as usual having much the prettiest things. Haven't been to Poiret yet except in the evening. He has arranged a place where you go & dance out of doors—it's delightfully done & very amusing. Mrs. Harriman, Gen. Haines, Lloyd Warren & an Italian called Bosio & I went the other night. The Italian is a cousin of Margaret Lawrence's, most attractive & dances beautifully. We are all doing the same thing again on Friday.

The Paris Herald reported that you were here so you've been inundated with mail—all advertisements so I have opened them. Have seen Mr. Haseltine twice. He was here to tea today. Seems just the same & was most amusing. . . .

This is the first evening we've been peaceful & it's rather nice. The Americans here somehow leave a bad taste in your mouth—most of them, that is. I wish you could see the clothes! They are getting shorter & shorter & as for the evening dresses—there is nothing to them at all—literally nothing above the waist in the back & cut entirely out under the arms—it's too awful.

Well, good night. I do wish so that you were here—everyone does & have all asked if there isn't a chance you will come. I hope Newport has been amusing. . . .

Within a week Flora reports again. She has been seeing a lot of Bosio, who is

most delightful and companionable. . . . He & Mr. Cottenet & another Italian & Aunty & I had such a good time yesterday lunching across the Seine & pottering around after. . . . Have twice been to Jo Davidson's studio—his busts are wonderful I think, but Mr. Cottenet says that to him they are just like photographs. . . . Went one day to tea at Mr. Haseltine's place—it's going to be too lovely when completed. [The rest of the letter is mostly about clothes she has ordered for herself and for Gertrude.] There is one [for Gertrude] that I have absolutely no doubts about. It's a teagown at Poiret—gold with black fur.

Gertrude, in Newport, having arranged for one-man shows of Andrew O'Connor's sculpture and Guy Pène du Bois's paintings, must now, even more than usual, have part of her heart in Paris. And surely another large part is in New York, to which she commutes continually to work on her war sculptures. She is there, at 8 West Eighth Street, when she receives this letter from Harry, written on 871 Fifth Avenue stationery, in a large hasty scrawl, immediately after returning from Westbury:

Dearest,

I am nearly crazy. I have not slept a wink all night.

By the worst piece of luck in the world—I would give ten million dollars if it had not happened—I ran across your Stackpole letters last night in the country.

You are the only person I have ever really loved. The only person that means more to me than anyone else, man or woman.

I believed in you & trusted you because you are true & big.

I told [Harry] Sinclair on Sunday that Monday was our 23rd anniversary & that we each loved each other better than anything else in the world.

Now the bottom is knocked out of life. It's all lies. Are you all a lie? Are you all false? Is nothing real? I love you too much to let today go by, because I think it is your body & not your heart that did it all.

I have got to know how many men—of course I know Jimmy kissed you on the Sheelah—but I don't want names—I want *you*.

Harry

It is a painful letter, a particularly painful anniversary letter. We wonder, of course, why Gertrude left the Stackpole correspondence where it could be found. (We guess she may have had it spread out on her desk while considering its incorporation in a work of "fiction.") We wonder why Harry read it. (But if it was spread out, Harry had little choice. Stackpole's handwriting is bold and clear. All Harry would need to have seen was one "Dearest Gertrude" and a few more words.) We wonder how Gertrude replied to Harry. We can imagine white lies, reassurances, a reconciliation. We can also imagine—and this may answer some of the questions—the need, conscious or not, to provoke the long-postponed honest and open talk in which both Gertrude and Harry face the separation and loneliness of much of their married life while at the same time acknowledging (as Harry has done in his letter) the profundity of their love which transcends separate interests and relationships. These are imaginings, but there can be no doubt of Gertrude's and Harry's loyalty to one another in moments of need, moments of pain or sickness. This is such a moment. Although we don't know exactly how the reconciliation is achieved or if perhaps it leads to the acceptance of greater freedom for both parties, we do know that by early October, when Harry is again hunting in Montana, their relationship is sufficiently relaxed for him to close a letter: "I wish I were home. Feel lonely and depressed. Even with such a bad wife, home is pretty good. Love, Harry."

Home is pretty good, but still Gertrude and Harry are seldom there together. He remains in Montana. She, after making final arrangements (including newspaper and magazine interviews) for an exhibition of her recent work at the Whitney Studio in November, takes Flora and Sonny to the Adirondacks. From there, a week or so later, she writes to Harry:

Dearest, I don't know if you will get this letter as you don't seem to have been getting mine, but I have many things to tell you and so will take a chance. To begin with something has happened about Flora which you won't like—I don't. It's Rod [Roderick Tower]. They informed me the other afternoon that they were engaged. It made it rather hard, his being there too. I was rather flippant about it and said "she's a changeable child" and such things—also "I don't believe you know your own minds." But that didn't go very well. Then I said of course nothing could be decided till you came back. Rod was very sweet, I must say, and said of course he knew that and that he wanted to wire or write or something. This all happened Thursday afternoon, and since I have been trying in subtle (?) ways to influence Flora. Talking about the difficulty of knowing one's mind, & about her own disposition about life & other things that count. I don't really think she is very much in love, but I may be wrong. I think the thing for us to do is to prevent its being announced, then she may change her mind. I have nothing against Rod, I think he is a rather sweet person at bottom. Flora tells me he has a lot of determination and very decided ideas about things. I have worked Flora up to interest in courses at Columbia and she has started one course already. I don't see that there is anything to do except give her time & hope she will get over it. Knowing Flora I think there is a very good chance that she will.

I haven't heard from Sonny since he left [here], but I guess he is all right. He was still very weak last Monday. [He had had Vincent's angina, with a high fever.].

Love, dearest, & for heaven's sake come home soon. I can't handle all these family matters alone.

G.

Or: home is pretty good, but it takes two to make a home. Before leaving for the Adirondacks, Gertrude has arranged Barbara's schedule at Foxcroft. Now she is in correspondence with Thomas Regan of Harry's office about getting a tutor for Sonny. And she continues to be concerned about Flora, remembering how little she herself knew her own mind when she got married and perhaps dwelling on this theme as her brother Regi now divorces Cathleen after sixteen years of marriage, the last seven separated.

In a letter from Jimmie Appleton, just as he's about to leave for the beagle trials, he says that he hears from Helen Whitney that Gertrude is considering "3 weeks disappearance from the world that knows you." But we wonder if even that would permit her to do all she wants to do or if indeed she doesn't need the stimulation, even the abrasion, of family and social life to do all she *is* doing. This, in the Adirondacks, means a lot of hiking, boating, and writing, including now, besides correspondence, sketches and outlines for the expansion of previous attempts at autobiographical fiction. However, the authentic texture of Gertrude's life is once again better expressed in her correspondence (as heretofore in her journals and sculpture sketches) than in what she intends as more public art.

Besides letters to her family and to Jimmie Appleton, there are many others to old friends such as Charles Draper and Phil Carroll—loving letters, if not necessarily love letters, full of the fresh air of the Adirondacks, of animal sounds, of open space, but full also of the recognition that this is only part of her life, that the other parts, the other "choices" to which she will return, are real too and not mutually exclusive. There is professional correspondence with Juliana Force about Gertrude's forthcoming show; with John Gregory about the supervision of the final stages of a war monument; with Jo Davidson about Paris art gossip; with the newly formed Society of American Painters, Sculptors, and Gravers about accepting membership and exhibiting with them in November; with the journalist Alleyne Ireland (formerly secretary to Joseph Pulitzer) about their respective literary projects. . . . The days become shorter, the nights colder. New York waits. As Alleyne Ireland writes, "There's nothing like getting good and fit in the Fall, it gives you a fine springboard from which to leap at the gaieties of Winter."

Gertrude needs a surplus of energy. On November 3 the first annual exhibition of the Painters, Sculptors, and Gravers opens at Gimpel & Wildenstein on Fifth Avenue. Here, though showing work she is sure of —studies of the much-admired *Head of Titanic Memorial*—she is the only woman among the fifty-two members of the society, a strong list of contemporary American artists including Bellows, Chanler, Du Bois, Flanagan, Fraser, Glackens, Hassam, Henri, Kent, Lachaise, Luks, Manship, Nadelman, O'Connor, Prendergast, and Sloan. No doubt she feels the challenge of this context. The next day her own exhibition, called "Impressions of the War," opens at the Whitney Studio. For it she has selected twenty-four pieces—the seven named earlier in this chapter, a panel of the Victory Arch, and such others as *At His Post, His Last Charge, Gassed, Blinded, On the Top, His Bunkie,* and *The Aviator* (for which Sonny posed). All of these pieces are free sketches, small in scale, large in emotion, expressing an intensity which is often lost when later inflated into monuments. As Guy Pène du Bois says in the catalogue foreword (placed opposite a tender, moody De Strelecki photograph of Gertrude in her studio working at *On the Top*):

> These Impressions of War are not presented as complete statements, each smoothed and rounded, each rhetorically correct. Mrs. Whitney caught them out of a war-ridden air. They are neither the statements of a war correspondent nor of a soldier. They have nothing of that naive conscientiousness which asks that the craftsman push his work beyond the point of his vision. In supply of such fact they are nebulous as their inspiration. That could, over here, very well have combined documentary frailty and spiritual might. How many Mohammedans have seen Mohammed? But Mrs. Whitney saw War through the medium of hospitals and with not over-distant glimpses of the front, for five months—enough time to absorb a tremendous amount of data—in the winter and spring of 1914-15. The memory of that epoch must always have been in the back of her head. It was constantly revived over here. She came to her studio from a war canteen, a war bazaar, a war lecture or a war committee. Armed with enough

callousness, she might have managed a Venus or an Adonis in that perfection of line and form and surface which seems, somehow, to spell peace. Instead she threw masses of clay together in the shapes of men, men who were not merely men but men at war, men enveloped in the chaos of a mad dream, given their character by it and their reality and their unreality.

Du Bois's foreword—unquestionably approved by Gertrude—is aesthetically defensive. Her own interviews, which appear now, hashed and rehashed in dozens of newspapers and magazines, are sociologically defensive. The most typical is an anonymous full-page piece in the Sunday New York *Times* magazine: "POOR LITTLE RICH GIRL AND HER ART: Mrs. Harry Payne Whitney's Struggles to Be Taken Seriously as a Sculptor Without Having Starved in a Garret." The title and subtitle set the tone. The writer dismisses the myth of "the poor struggling artist" without understanding that wealth doesn't obviate the necessity for struggle. Then Gertrude in her own words recounts the personal history we know, the prejudices she, as a rich woman, has had to face:

When I first started the sculpture work, my friends took the attitude of . . . watching one of their number performing a difficult parlor trick. It half amused them, half interested them, but few . . . took the thing seriously. However, one is always amusing to one's friends. That is one of the rights of friendship. They neither could nor would understand why anybody who didn't have to work, who didn't have to spend a number of hours over a mess of clay, should do so of her own volition. . . . It was not especially easy to work with this spirit constantly being expressed. Not only did I have to learn how to make my fingers more facile, but I had to fight, fight all the time, to break down the walls of half-sympathetic and half-scornful criticism based on no other concept than the one that it wasn't done by people in my position.

A few years passed and several of my things began to attract some notice. . . . Then a decided change came over those who had previously been inclined to laugh at the work. They were somewhat impressed by the favorable opinion of the recognized artists. And here let me say that the artists themselves were always kind and helpful and encouraging in their attitude. But no sooner had I succeeded in breaking down a portion of the wall of the prejudice of my friends than I found another, a much mightier one, staring me in the face. The public at large refused to believe that I was doing anything serious. The people I met were all very nice about it. Very. In the manner that a fond parent pats a wayward child on the head. . . .

People would look at me, then at [a sculpture], then make the bland assertion that they could not understand how a woman my size could build up a statue of that height. Mind you, I am not feeling sorry for myself. Not a bit. I am simply telling you this to give you some idea of the type of criticism.

Gertrude contrasts the situation of the artist in America, particularly the woman artist, with that in France. There, she says,

The attitude is a receptive one. "Show us what you can do." The surroundings in which you live make no difference to them either way. You are neither scorned for poverty nor condemned for wealth. As a matter of fact, the last is highly desirable. It helps so many others to get along in the camaraderie that makes student life in Paris so happy.

One of the strongest prejudices against which a woman in my position has to fight is working in a studio. . . . It is all right for a poor struggling artist to seek out a place of seclusion where he can have his north light. It is conceded to be necessary to him. He can't work without it. But let a woman who does not have to work for her livelihood take a studio to do the work in which she is most intensely interested and she is greeted by a chorus of horror-stricken voices, a knowing lifting of the eyebrows, or a twist of the mouth that is equally expressive. And much more condemnatory. Again I say, I am not complaining at the treatment that I received; I have no cause to complain; I should not, perhaps, be doing the work that I am doing today if it were not for the battle I had to fight to show that I was not merely amusing myself.

I understand perfectly the attitude that people take. I understand perfectly that in a good many instances they are justified in taking that attitude. The renting of studios has become fashionable among a number of young women who desire to be what they call in their most expressive moments "free." They are free as far as doing any work is concerned. A good many of them furnish their studios beautifully. Therein, perhaps, lies their contribution to art. They spend half an hour daily messing up a palette of paints or a lump of clay, and therein, I say, lies their injustice to art. Therein, too, lies the injustice to those who are honest in their desire to devote themselves to their work. Conclusions are based on experience with a number of instances. It is natural that the few should be condemned for what the majority have apparently proved to be a truism.

To go on, however, about this matter of breaking down the wall of public prejudice. Time and again I discovered that where a group of laymen had to decide between two people a question of assigning a commission to an artist, the woman of wealth lost out. And for no other reason than because she was a woman of wealth. This, in spite of the popular belief that wealth can go a long way in gaining fame and position. It may in other fields of work, but where painting or sculpture is concerned, people sternly demand the traditions of a youth of poverty.

After the Titanic Memorial at Washington went up and my work on the two panels on the arch at Madison Square was noticed by men standing high in the opinions of the people, there came a definite change. It is the type of change that always follows public recognition. Those who formerly had been inclined to discount the work I was doing were now ready to assure me that they had always been convinced of my abilities. That, by the way, was more than I had always been convinced of. It was the kindness of the men and women who were doing things in the work of art that helped me through the dark ages.

However, I am not sorry for the experience. There is this to be said about a popular attitude of the kind against which I was pitted—it places you with your back against the wall and brings out all the fighting qualities in you. Flagging interest is continually urged on into action by the thought that you are expected to make a failure of things. Doing the unexpected always has its power of charm.

Gertrude's presentation of herself is strong. If some of her statements, like Du Bois's, are exaggeratedly defensive, we can at least understand the need to protect herself and her work. She is dealing professionally with the media as it exists in 1919. Her words are chosen carefully, as are the De Strelecki photographs in the catalogue and newspapers and magazines. The eight-page catalogue itself is carefully printed in sepia on heavy cream-colored stock. And the exhibition is spaciously installed, with the larger pieces placed in the court outside the studio against a background of evergreens. Nothing is left to chance.

The show receives far more press coverage than, for example, the at least equally important first annual of the American Painters, Sculptors, and Gravers. The attendance is large—so large that the exhibition is extended from two weeks to almost four—and finally totals 6,871. And the reactions, public and private, are almost uniformly sympathetic to both the work and the persona of Poor Little Rich Girl. The most negative criticism appears in the Brooklyn *Eagle*, but even here we feel the writer bending backward to understand something mysterious, ambivalent, perhaps inscrutable about Gertrude as an American Goddess (for, indeed, the Poor Little Rich Girl is one such deity):

> In the sculpture of Mrs. Whitney is revealed the personality of the woman. It is rare that sculpture is so autobiographical, so temperamental . . . the work of Mrs. Whitney is [not] structurally sound. The form within is not sufficiently felt. But we should all be willing to grant to art which is essentially emotional a license which we would not give to more architectural work. Mrs. Whitney's art reveals an impulsive, generous nature, enthusiastic, impatient. . . . Nowhere

else in sculpture do I find our [American] character so well expressed. The faults are the faults common to us all. The qualities are our qualities. There is an American harshness as of steel and in Mrs. Whitney's sculpture it is apparent. There is also a tenderness which, were it not combined with this hardness, one would almost call sentimentality. It is admirably expressed in *Home Again* in which we are brought face to face with the drama of the return of a wounded soldier to the one whom he loves. A broad idealism, a love of humanity, a generous carelessness, these are the predominant characteristics of Mrs. Whitney's sculpture. They are the characteristics of America.

Forgetting the aesthetic judgments, there is something right about such phrases as "tenderness . . . combined with . . . hardness" and "a broad idealism" and "a generous carelessness." There is something right about the popularity of this show. In a few years Scott Fitzgerald will write about the "vast carelessness" of the rich in his visionary novel *The Great Gatsby*, but meanwhile, on the verge of the twenties, Gertrude has helped to enhance the image of being at once rich and American, an artist and a woman.

≋

Being on exhibition is a very different sort of work from making what is exhibited, but it is work nevertheless. As Gertrude's name and picture appear frequently in publications, old friends are reminded of her existence. There are congratulatory letters—some catching up on years of lost contact—which must be acknowledged. There are new commission possibilities and, in Charles Dana Gibson's case, the revival of former interest in placing sculpture in the Boston Public Garden. There are more than the usual number of requests for help, even a pathetic letter from her former model and helper Ramon, whom she has not seen in more than two years, asking for old clothes for his wife. And it seems, too, that there are more than the usual number of invitations, including two to receptions for the Prince of Wales, one a large dinner at the Waldorf-Astoria "on behalf of the former War Council and their associates of the American Red Cross," the other a more intimate lunch at H. R. Winthrop's where Gertrude is seated to the right of the prince (Harry prefers not to attend).

Gertrude is looking forward to a comparatively quiet holiday season after her show comes down on November 24. But that very day Sonny, driving down from Yale with two friends in his Stutz runabout, hits a horse and wagon. One friend is killed and Sonny is seriously injured. However, he recovers quickly enough so that Harry can go on a shooting trip to Virginia in early December and Gertrude can plan a dinner dance for Barbara and her friends the day after Christmas. From Foxcroft, Barbara writes:

It's perfectly great that you're going to chaperon and I hoped you would, only I was afraid you would be so bored. . . . It certainly is great about Sonny [his recovery] & do give him my love & tell that I expect him to come to dinner on the 26th and also the dance, for I am scared of having a rotten time. Also if he would ask about three of his friends, for most of the girls will be 17.

Barbara's party is evidently small. The next night, for the benefit of postwar Belgian relief, there is a big social event, probably the biggest of this season—the world premiere of Maeterlinck's *L'Oiseau Bleu* at the Metropolitan Opera House, followed by the Blue Bird Ball at the Waldorf-Astoria. As always there has been a committee, and as so often Gertrude has served on it. This one, headed by her cousin Mrs. William K. Vanderbilt, Jr., has not occupied much of Gertrude's time. Virginia ("Birdie") Vanderbilt has run the Blue Bird Campaign for Happiness. She has had a small recital at her Fifth Avenue mansion where the composer of the opera, Albert Wolff, accompanied the soprano Mademoiselle Delannois. She has solicited the purchase of boxes at the opera. Henry Russell, another committee member, has persuaded Maeterlinck to leave the seclusion of his villa on the Riviera and to attend the premier. However, there are last-minute touches that suggest Gertrude's theatrical sense of public relations. When Maeterlinck lands in New York on Christmas Eve, Fifth Avenue from Washington Square up is decorated with blue birds and large blue "Welcome to Maeterlinck" banners, and shops are draped with blue. Maeterlinck cannot have been unaware of the Vanderbilt contribution to his welcome. As Russell records, the poet expresses amazement at the simplicity and beauty of Grand Central Station, saying, "People who are capable of such colossal achievements will, in time, develop the more intimate arts." Maeterlinck might have been speaking directly, if subtly, to Gertrude, as indeed he might have been too in the text of *L'Oiseau Bleu*, with its thematic statement that the bluebird of happiness is in one's own heart.

⪦ *1920*

As the American twenties begin—Prohibition will become effective this January 16, one year after ratification by Congress—we can see Gertrude and Harry as both historical contributors to a new life style and living relics of a past one. Their world has been democratized. Now "everybody" will be relatively rich. "Everybody" will own cars and cameras and country homes. "Everybody" will drink cocktails and play bridge. "Everybody" will wear comfortable, stylish clothes. "Everybody" will go abroad.

The most popular athletes will not be polo players and yachtsmen and the owners of racing stables. Babe Ruth, Red Grange, Jack Dempsey, even Bobby Jones and Big Bill Tilden (both born into comparatively rich families) will not belong to "society" but to "everybody." The most glamorous figures will no longer be found on society pages but on motion picture screens. The big wedding of 1920 will be that of Douglas Fairbanks (né Ulman) and Mary Pickford ("America's Sweetheart").

Though Edith Wharton's *The Age of Innocence* will be published in 1920 and receive a Pulitzer Prize the following year, the characters in the novel are, like Gertrude and Harry (who might too be in it), at once historical, perhaps even antiquarian, and yet still alive. It will remain for the next generation's writers—those like Millay, Fitzgerald, and Hemingway—born in the nineties, to be young enough to live the twenties and present them in their work, however much haunted by the past. It is no more an accident that Hemingway will toward the end of the decade take the names of both his heroine and hero in *A Farewell to Arms* from Barklie Henry, the first husband of Barbara Whitney, than that she and Flora and Sonny will all be divorced. These Whitney children, too, are part of the twenties in a completely present way that their parents can't be.

But we are getting ahead of our story. The point is that Gertrude and Harry—just forty-five and almost forty-eight, respectively—are for the first time placed clearly, if uncomfortably, between the anachronistic and the vanguard.

❧

Gertrude's year begins, almost typically now, with Harry away, this time on a business trip to Chicago. He wires, "SPLENDID MEETING HERE HARD WORK ALL DAY AND LATE NIGHTS COULD NOT FINISH SO WILL NOT BE HOME UNTIL WEDNESDAY HOPE PARTY WAS FINE LOVE HARRY." We know nothing about this particular party, but we do know that Gertrude has, as always, renewed her subscription to the opera. In Harry's absence, facing the prospect of further absences, she makes a "List of Men for Opera." There are forty-two names. About half are very old friends such as Jimmie Appleton, Charles Draper, Lispenard Stewart, Worthington Whitehouse, and Lloyd Warren. The other half are newer friends, mostly from the world of arts and letters: the sculptors John Gregory, Andrew O'Connor, and Paul Manship; the painters Gifford Beal, Childe Hassam, Guy Pène du Bois, and (surprise!) Mario Guardabassi; the critics Royal Cortissoz and Forbes Watson (presently the editor of *Arts and Decoration*, whom Gertrude will, from 1923 on, back financially as editor of *The Arts*, the leading progressive American art magazine of the twenties); the writers Alleyne Ireland and Lord Dunsany (whom she has met at the same time as Maeterlinck—an awkward meeting for the two writers, who had not read each other's work and had nothing to say to one another).

At about the same time Gertrude is making another, partially overlapping list of men who have figured in her life and through whom, like so many of her fictional heroines, she can tell her own story. The chapter titles of this playful, abortive autobiography are:

1. [Edgar] McA[dams] "His Victory" [protégé and model during Gertrude's early years as a sculptor]
2. Hirsch "The Nude—A Study" [possibly the painter Stefan Hirsch, who may also have modeled for Gertrude]
3. [John] Gregory "Moment Musical"
4. [Herbert] Haseltine
5. [William] Stackpole "A Capable Man"
6. [James] Appleton "Love me little, love me long"
7. [C. H.] Duell [a lawyer and politician whom Gertrude knew in 1912 and who had just died] "Her Mistake"
8. [Frank W. "Pinky"] Andrews [one of Gertrude's New York and Newport suitors, 1894–96]
9. Rumboldt "Paris Night—Hugo" [possibly one "H" of Gertrude's 1913 Story of the *cabinet particulier*]
10. [Adolphe] Ramon "Recollections & Reminiscenses of Spain"
11. [Andrew] O'Connor "The Irish as I have Known Them"
12. [Lloyd] Warren
13. [Robert] Bacon
14. [Robert] Chanler
15. [Philip] Carroll "Arms & The Man"
16. [Charles] Draper "The Struggle"
17. [Ivan] Narodny "Russian Interpretations" ["secretary extraordinary" to Robert Chanler, whose work he wrote about]
18. [Alleyne] Ireland "Scotch Folkore"
19. Wilson "An Interlude" [?]
20. [Jo] Davidson
21. [Mario] Guardabassi "The Moeurs d'Italie"
22. [Thomas] Ridgway [a Bar Harbor friend of the Vanderbilts]

Like Gertrude herself, the list is mysterious and defies definitiveness. Not only does it include men about whom we know little or nothing, but it excludes others, such as Mo Taylor, Jim Barnes, and Howard Cushing, who we know meant a great deal to Gertrude, surely more than some of those whose names appear. And Harry's name, like Harry himself at this moment, is most conspicuously absent. Yet we feel once again that his is the obligatory chapter, that he himself, in elusive bits and pieces, contains aspects of almost all the other men.

Harry returns for Gertrude's birthday and a series of the sort of parties he prefers to avoid. For example, a few days after his arrival they are invited by Mrs. Junius Spencer Morgan, the wife of J. P. Morgan's grandson, to a ten o'clock dance at the Colony Club. For the same time, the same night, Gertrude receives the following invitation:

My dear Mrs. Whitney,

When I asked my very beautiful visitor, Carolyn Cowles, whom she most wanted to meet while here, she said you. Tho' not a sculptor herself she is most interested in the subject and for years, it seems, has been enthusiastic over your work! On Wednesday evening, Jan 14th at 10 o'clock I am having a few authors, artists, and "just socialists" in to a "stunt" party. Mrs. Douglas Robinson, Blanche Wagstaff, R. U. Johnson and several authors are to read something of their own: Montgomery Flagg and several other equally interesting "sketchers" will draw—and so forth. It would give Miss Cowles more pleasure than you can possibly realize if you would come in for a little while. As we are to be rather a late "cabaret" I hope you can arrange it.

Very Cordially Yours,
Helen S. Woodruff

Gertrude accepts both invitations, saying she and Harry will arrive late in the evening at Mrs. Woodruff's. The next night, the same story—a dinner at the home of Ogden Mills and then a dance for Emily Hammond given by Mrs. W. D. Sloane. It is not surprising that after another few days Harry departs for the South.

While he is gone Gertrude is busy as ever. There are the nights at the opera. There is dinner one evening "in the back room of the St. Regis" with Alfonso de Navarro, who has theater tickets for the popular murder mystery *The Acquittal*. There is the annual dinner of the Poetry Society of America. There is a meeting with Lloyd Warren at which Gertrude agrees to be a patroness for a fancy dress ball in March.

These scattered clues hint at Gertrude's social schedule. At the same time she is in constant touch with Juliana Force about the Whitney Studio Club. In January there has been the important first exhibition of paintings by Edward Hopper, along with drawings and etchings by Kenneth Hayes Miller. In February, Curtis' superb photographs of American Indians will be shown; in March, drawings by Italian masters; in May, work by girls of the Greenwich House School. The schedule is so full that in the same month, for an exhibition of Russian posters, Gertrude offers the Whitney Studio, which has not been open since the exhibition of her own work there in November. Russian posters! In the postwar period of the "Red Scare"! In May 1920—only two weeks after the indictment of Sacco and Vanzetti! The show is as much a testimonial to Gertrude's unassailable position (she is by now a sustaining member of the Republican National Committee) as to her openness to all kinds of artistic expression.

But mainly now and through the rest of the year—indeed, through most of the rest of the decade—Gertrude is thinking about monuments, making them, and writing about them. Because of their metamorphoses from sketches (many shown in her 1919 exhibition), it is difficult to assign exact dates to the sculpture of this period. For example, she seems already to be enlarging and modifying *Bunkies* for the Washington Heights Memorial on Riverside Drive in New York City and *Doughboy* for a 4th Division Memorial, ultimately abandoned.

In February an "Open Competition of Ideas for New York City's Permanent [War] Memorial" is exhibited at City Hall. There are sixty-five proposals for arches, buildings, bridges, soldiers' and sailors' clubs, auditoriums, a war museum, an aquarium, a sunken garden, a pier, a "Great Bronze Book in a Classic Belvedere with a Pipe Organ behind the perforated Stylobate," et cetera. Gertrude responds by writing an impassioned article on "The 'Useless' Memorial," published in the April *Arts and Decoration*, edited by Guy Pène du Bois. It begins:

> The man who invented the idea of tacking on to a memorial a club house, stadium, water gate, bridge or lodging house was indeed a man of wicked proclivities. Perhaps he was innocent of ulterior motives, which brands him a plebeian, but perhaps he was insidious or corrupt, or a builder, a contractor, a philanthropist, an architect or a politician. . . .
>
> Art doesn't enter into our lives, that is the trouble. It has nothing to do with what we think, feel, and the way we act in everyday existence. Art is much the same as religion to the majority; something to approach once a week or when our friends die, with bated breath and best clothes.
>
> There is nothing serious about art.
>
> The joy of living, which is testified to by Walt Whitman in his work, would help to make people realize this if we could find it expressed in all the art of our country. . . .

She quotes from Whitman. She quotes from Wilde. The entire article is a sustained argument on behalf of both life for life's sake and art for art's sake. (The principal illustration of a good "useless" memorial is her old favorite, Saint-Gaudens' statue of Admiral Farragut, mounted on a pedestal by Stanford White, in Madison Square.) And yet, while disparaging utilitarian memorials—a plea really for greater artistic freedom—it seems never to have occurred to Gertrude that, just as applying sculpture to buildings can be restrictive, so too can applying intimate sculptural ideas to monuments. In an editorial, the New York *Times* summarizes Gertrude's article, treating it respectfully and adding one more strong argument to those against utilitarian monuments ("that in every instance they exemplify a diversion of funds from the object for which they originally were collected"). At the same time the newspaper criticizes Gertrude's display of "irritation" and "anger" about a subject which can be argued either way.

Though as many useful as useless memorials will still be built (and, in both categories, a far greater number of ugly than beautiful ones), the response to the article does encourage Gertrude—and Du Bois, Forbes Watson, and others at *Arts and Decoration*—to publish five more articles by her between June and November. The first of this series, called in its entirety "The End of America's Apprenticeship in Art," is accompanied by an editorial note which indicates that the series was substantially completed, or at least roughed out, prior to June: "In [the series] will be shown the progress which American art has made since its imitative beginnings and by facts, not theories, that the time for the nation's recognition of its own art as an independent manifestation is at hand."

In addition, a private journal of this period, *Notes on Art*, contains most of the ideas and much of the text that will appear in the articles. One passage, about midway through the journal, establishes her main theme and contains the strengths and weaknesses of all that follows:

> Do not forget Rodin, Dubois, Manet, Monet, Meunier, Baudelaire, Anatole France [space is left for more names]. Do not detract from what they have done. They too, many of them, were seers, or were great followers, but when someone says Rodin to you, say Saint-Gaudens to him. If he confronts you with Manet, mention Sargent or Whistler, when he speaks of Baudelaire or Anatole France do not let Poe or Bret Harte be forgotten.
>
> We struggle along towards that little hill from which we can get a better view of the high mountain. The Himalayas are grand, Fujiyama is superb, Mont Blanc of surpassing loveliness, but what about the Rockies? Must we think nothing of them because they are American? Are they so close to us that they look small?

Gertrude's writing, sculpting, and patronage—all interrelated—continue despite a social schedule which becomes heaviest in April, with the marriage of Flora to Roderick Tower, followed ten days later by the marriage of Rachel Littleton to Cornelius Vanderbilt, Jr.

Flora's wedding—4 P.M., Monday, April 19, at St. Bartholomew's—is like old times. A large crowd gathers early on Park Avenue, outside the church, to get a glimpse of the wedding party. Gertrude and Harry arrive in a chauffeured limousine with Flora; Sonny, an usher; and Barbara, maid of honor. Another limousine delivers Gertrude's sister Gladys (the Countess Széchényi) and her three eldest daughters, Cornelia, Alice, and Gladys, all flower girls in white organdy. Another delivers Dorothy Whitney Straight and her daughter Beatrice, another flower girl in white; and her son Whitney, the page. The crowd gasps at the men in top hats and tails; the women and girls in above-ankle-length dresses and feathered or beribboned Victorian bonnets; Whitney Straight in a "Gainsborough costume" of white satin trousers and open flowing white silk shirt. The procession of limousines is steady now, filled with Vanderbilts, Whitneys, Sloanes, Webbs, Twomblys, Shepards, Pagets, Barneys, Watrisses, Barneses, Schieffelins, Harrimans, Iselins, Morgans, Belmonts, Pulitzers, Fabbris, Hammonds, Fields. . . . The crowd gawks at these members of the Whitney and Vanderbilt families and their friends, most of them recognizable from the society pages. The groom's family is less recognizable, though hardly anonymous. Charlemagne Tower of Philadelphia has been United States ambassador to Russia and to Germany. His son Roderick, graduated from Harvard in 1915 and later a captain in the air corps, has spent much of his time in New York City where he is presently a member of the Stock Exchange and of the Harvard, Knickerbocker, and Racquet clubs. He is a handsome, rugged, gregarious young man who seems to complement perfectly Flora's much more delicate and soulful beauty and rather playful personality.

Gertrude has not designed the match, but she has designed the decorations for the wedding and supervised the costuming of the bridal party. Inside St. Bartholomew's, along the nave, eleven-foot-high standards of Easter lilies are arranged in wide fans. Behind the altar a box tree with a beehive-shaped top is half covered with more lilies. Pink rambler roses cover the sides of the chancel.

The bridal procession is led by Sonny and seventeen other ushers, followed by Flora's five small cousins, the girls carrying pink rosebuds set in ferns, Whitney Straight carrying a white lily set among white roses, and Barbara in light emerald-green chiffon with a matching hat, whose brim is covered with leaves. Finally, Flora comes down the aisle holding Harry's arm. Though he has gained weight over the years he is still youthful-looking and handsome, his profile sharp, his walk athletic. Flora wears a scarf veil of old rose point lace, arranged across her coiffure of short curls with the edge brought down to her forehead. A cluster of full-blown white roses on her right shoulder holds the veil. The short satin bridal gown has an overdress of white silk net and lace embroidered with crystal. The train is lined with chiffon and bordered with a narrow Grecian design, also embroidered in crystal. Flora's only jewelry is a diamond plaque suspended from a thin chain. She carries a gold-bound prayer book. She shimmers in the soft light of St. Bartholomew's.

The ceremony is followed by a reception at 871 Fifth Avenue. The ballroom is decorated with a screen of white flowers. There Gertrude stands at the head of the receiving line, wearing a dress of oyster white with a Russian blouse of henna and black gauze, embroidered in gold and black, and a black hat covered with henna chiffon and flat henna ostrich feathers. When necessary she introduces Flora and Roderick to the guests, who then proceed through the Marble Room—which has been turned into a rose bower with flowers and foliage falling from the ceiling to the floor—to the dining room where pre-Prohibition champagne and other refreshments are served while the ballroom is arranged for dancing.

On Wednesday, following the wedding, Gertrude writes to Flora, who has just spent a few days aboard the *Whileaway* with Rod, before leaving for the West Coast and then their honeymoon in Hawaii and Japan:

> I was awfully glad you called me up yesterday morning. I must say it gave me a shock though when they said "Mrs. Tower" and I wasn't quite sure that it wouldn't be Rod's Mother. You sounded fine too and the lovely warm day must have been beautiful on the water. Today is not so good, anyway you had a grand start.
>
> A good many people stayed and danced after you had gone on Monday & a few stayed very late (about 8). Sonny was extremely genial but perfectly respectable! He left about 8.30 to return (as he said) immediately to New Haven. Then Papa and I beat it to the country. Barbara had gone to bed perfectly exhausted but very happy. We wondered if you were already at Glen Cove and Papa suggested that we pay you a visit!!
>
> I can't realize that you are married. Of course I am going to miss you terribly, not only miss seeing you but just knowing you are in the house and planning things and all the rest of it, but then of course that couldn't go on always and I feel that you are going to be very very happy and that you are going to make the nicest possible home for yourself.
>
> I stayed here all day yesterday and planned fixing up the piazza & making a covered over place to sit on the terrace which will be nice when it is warm.
>
> You are going to have the time of your lives! It must be a great feeling to start off with three months ahead of drifting and going about & doing just what you like. . . .
>
> Will you order me from the Chinese place (was it Gump's?) in San Francisco three (different colored) suits (like I had before, they are like pajamas) and tell them to send the bill with them to me, N.Y. . . .
>
> Everyone thought you had never looked better. Compliments as to arrangements and wedding generally were gratefully received by Mother. It seems so funny not to have anything to do! Papa doesn't talk of going away till the end of May, and I know he would be

lonely if I sailed now. I expect we will move down here as soon as the weather is settled & I will work in the studio here.

Tell Rod his behaviour was excellent! His mother & I had a few nice words together. She is so sweet I am sure I should be very fond of her if I could see something of her.

Best love my own dearest child and all good wishes

Mama

Try to get a little fatter!

Papa sends his best to you both.

The Vanderbilt-Littleton wedding is even larger than the Tower-Whitney wedding; more than 3,000 attend, breaking all records at St. Thomas' and forcing some guests to stand in the vestibules and aisles. However, though Cornelius, Jr.'s mother, Grace, has long since established herself as the "first hostess" of New York City, Gertrude and Harry, despite their comparative reclusiveness (especially his), retain a special magical place in the hearts of those still as interested in "society" as in Hollywood. The crowd on Fifth Avenue is no larger than that on Park ten days before, and the two weddings, both fully covered in the newspapers and fashion magazines, receive equal space.

❧

This year in horse racing is Harry's best to date. With $270,075 total prize money he leads the list of owners. He would have in 1915 too, but then, after Alfred's death aboard the *Lusitania,* his horses were running for Thompson. And he would have done even better this year, except that his five fine three-year-olds are no match for the great Man o' War, though one of them, appropriately named Upset, has beaten Man o' War at Saratoga the previous year, the only loss in his twenty-one races, five of which set world records. Gertrude joins Harry at some of the important races, including the Dwyer Stakes where another of Harry's three-year-olds, John P. Grier, loses to Man o' War, who "broke Grier's heart at the eighth-pole." However, Gertrude and Harry are never together for long— briefly in Westbury, briefly in the Adirondacks, briefly in Newport where the Howard G. Cushing Memorial Gallery, resembling an elegant miniature of Gertrude's Westbury studio, finally opens.

In late July they, along with the rest of the world, receive the news that William K. Vanderbilt has died in Paris "after a lingering illness [probably, like Gertrude's father, a series of strokes] which became acute on April 15 last, while he was attending the races at Auteuil." At his bedside are his second wife, his only daughter Consuelo, and his two sons, William K., Jr., and Harold. The *Times* goes on to quote William K., Sr.:

My life was never destined to be quite happy. It was laid out along lines which I could not foresee, almost from earliest childhood. It has left me with nothing to hope for, with nothing definite to seek or strive for. Inherited wealth is a real handicap to happiness. It is as certain death to ambition as cocaine is to morality. If a man makes money, no matter how much, he finds a certain happiness in its possession, for in the desire to increase his business, he has a constant use for it. But the man who inherits it has none of this. The first satisfaction, and the greatest, that of building the foundation of a fortune, is denied him. He must labor, if he does labor, simply to add to an over-sufficiency.

The funeral is held at the American Church on the Avenue de l'Alma and the body returned home to be buried on Staten Island.

Soon thereafter Harry goes west once again for hunting and fishing and Gertrude, for the first time since the war, prepares for her long-delayed trip to Europe. Before their departure, Flora tells them that she and Rod have decided to settle on the West Coast. Her parents respond typically. Harry writes from New York:

Dear Flora,
Here is a check book. Sign the cards & mail to the office.
You don't necessarily have to spend the money but there it is.
Wire at once your address when you get to San Francisco.
Too bad the weather did not stay lovely, but I don't suppose it mattered.
Much love & happiness,

Papa.

Gertrude writes from aboard the *Aquitania:*

Dearest Flora,
You will be starting tomorrow on something new and I think something wonderful. It is great to have a chance of beginning, so to speak, at the beginning with someone in life & you can do so much yourself towards making that life, and of course it is that feeling which brings the greatest happiness. If Rod had gone on with his business in N.Y. many things would have been different of course. One thing which is one of the frequent causes of trouble for people— money—would have been different, as Rod would have been supporting you. That would have been for you both much nicer. It is what is expected of a man and naturally no man wants to feel he is being supported by his wife's family. But in the end this way will be so much better that it is certainly worth the difference. But you want to be economical and careful so that Rod will feel you are helping him & that above all what he does & makes *counts*. It will be a great incentive to him and it is of course what he expected to do and would have done had he not changed his business. I see in him a lot of ambition and go, an independent spirit and a desire to get ahead. I see also some of the Porcellian easy going traits [i.e., of Rod's club at Har-

vard] which need in the beginning some pushing. Do you? But the desire to forge ahead is strongly there. It was in his aviation work. I think too he is ready to take trouble about things & people, & he makes friends easily as you do. That is a great asset in a new life. One has to make more effort (as in Fort Worth) than living among people one has always known.

All this sounds prosy but I have been thinking about you both a lot. Destroy it but don't forget it—it may have some sense.

This is a grand boat but the people are awful. They look like 3d class English dealers in antiques & business men of the dullest type.

I am going to swim this afternoon (I couldn't before).

Have been picked up by strange looking people. I picked up a man I thought was a Spaniard (for no other reason) and found he was a South American! Another man I thought not so bad was a dealer in lace! One little man who trailed me about for a couple of days turned out to be a friend of Sonny's! One man walked up and down in front of me till I was nearly dizzy—with a copy of Arts & Decoration under his arm!

She is the finest boat I have ever been on. All the officers & even the stewards are plastered with decorations. The 1st steward, who is devoted to me, is so covered with lace & medals you might think him the captain. We make stupendous runs—534 [knots] yesterday. The two first days were warm & lovely. It is cooler now & overcast but smooth. We'll land early Monday morning.

Read Blood & Sand, Ibanez. It is marvelous. The last Snaith [?] book is good but too long.

Much love dearest to you both.

(Tear up this letter)

Mama

Like everyone, Gertrude makes trips for various reasons. Often she has traveled to get someplace where she can settle down and work more peacefully. But now, having worked hard at many things, she wants a month of change, cultural stimulation, replenishment, privacy. She intends to stop only briefly in her beloved Paris and then to see parts of southwest Spain she has not previously visited. Once again she feels the call of the East, the Moorish East.

During this trip she will keep her last major journal, *Spain 1920*, though there will be smaller journals set in Egypt and Spain at the end of the decade.

PARIS, SEPTEMBER 28TH TUESDAY.

It is the same, it has not changed—physically anyway. Arriving, coming out into the street, the smell of it, the thrill of it—for it came, the thrill which I had not expected.

My rooms [at the Ritz] are on the Place Vendome, high up, and the moon looked in on me when I threw the windows open. Oh Paris! I felt the cry of Louise. "Everyone has the right to be free—." And today all day the sun has shone as if especially for me; considering it all it was as if the accumulation of my many visits here were giving me joy. Its responsiveness, its beauty reached me through every pore. With one sweep rut was removed from my life. I lived again.

Sept. 30th. Thursday. Paris.

. . . I went to see Jo Davidson and we had a grand talk. He showed me his Doughboy for the cemetery at Suresnes. It is handled in a simpler way than his other things and promises to be good. We sat on the sidewalk of L—— and reminisced. It seemed as though everyone who passed had assumed some especially interesting character for my benefit. No doubt it was the loveliness of Paris and the warmth of atmosphere and sympathy of surroundings that did it.

Jo was nice. His intercourse with celebrities has improved him. He had many anecdotes and impressions to tell.

These three days in Paris have made me feel that certain things which I considered of big importance before are less than of no importance at all. The smile of Paris is in my heart.

October 5th Tuesday. Madrid.

Coming to Spain was after all strangely unexciting. I have looked forward for ages to coming, this trip was taken for the purpose, and when I left for Spain and driving here now has been on an unemotional level. . . .

I already knew the northern country of Spain, having twice motored to Madrid. It is as fine as I remembered it, strangely weird and black. Until Burgos one passes through the foothills of the Pyrenees, now through some arid plain, then over a gray rocky peak with no sign of vegetation or habitation. It was a day of sunlight with lumbering clouds, clouds that fitted the wildness of the scenery, making one feel that here was the proper place for tragedy and struggle.

October 8th Friday. Cordova.

I arrived in Madrid Monday night at eleven (about), my train being a couple of hours late.

I spend most of Tuesday at the Prado.

Lunching at the Ritz alone I had plenty of opportunity to watch the people who are mostly Spanish.

The men, if one were to judge them typical, are not handsome.

A little, rather crooked man, well dressed and of evil expression evidently thought himself a winner. He ogled the women. Sitting with him was a man—one wondered what chance had led them together—dignified, old, a true El Greco. His hooked nose, the long emaciated face, the fire of fanaticism in his eyes.

A big man who occupied the table of honor and to whom all bowed in respect interested me. His harsh voice and guttural sounding words reached a radius of tables about him. His movements were harsh too, he had the face of an actor, he appeared false but one felt power, self-confidence. Such a man would make use of the weaknesses of others.

Late I took a walk and found the crowds rather disconcerting. The men stare, follow and often speak to one. I suppose my clothes are conspicuous. I felt very alone. It was ridiculous to want someone to look after me but I did. I regretted having come alone, I wished I had told someone, anyone to meet me. I looked into the faces of the passers-by and they seemed to be either antagonistic or too friendly. If a really nice looking man had spoken to me I think I should have answered—but they all had such hideous shoes!

Then I got interested again, what was the force behind this crowd? What strength in the houses, the street, what power in the slow moving figures? Was it a huge conspiracy leading to a definite end?

Then it seemed that thoughts do not depend on time or country for there swept over me the memory of my own problems, pushing into the background the Puerta del Sol.

It seemed that there were two of me. One figure the sensible middle aged woman with a family, with ties of the most ordinary and pleasurable kind. A family whom she loved, longed to make happy; a person well dressed, normal, healthy. But someone else was in the background, a restless person, a lonely, selfish weak person with violent desires and wild dreams of impossible things.

OCTOBER 9TH SAT. CORDOVA.

Here, with the odor of oranges about one, all evil moods are forgotten. The torments that come, the moods when one seems caught and dragged down into sorrow could have no place in such surroundings. It was the beginning—I was going to be able to forget all morbid thoughts or complications during my stay—I would cling to the easy life, to the beauty, the freedom—it would be given to me. My isolation flung me suddenly into this life. The heavy weight—where was it?

The first impression I had of the mosque will remain in the house of my life like the beautiful tapestry on the wall, unforgettable. . . .

OCTOBER 10TH. SEVILLE.

Yesterday afternoon my Arab friend (for so I chose to call him) took me for a drive in the country. The smug-faced guide of the hotel gave us a scornful look as we started.

Two horses whom one felt would soon end their existence in the bull ring were hitched to an open victoria and were to take me to the house of a doctor—someone who possessed a garden. Clouds had gathered and though the sun was bright there was a chill in the air.

Through olive groves, past fig trees and cactus we struggled, over a road white with dust and dangerous with holes. I saw much life on the way and finally arrived at the top of a hill from which could be had a very lovely view of the surrounding country and of Cordova. The last part of the trip is accomplished on foot through the garden which extends to the very top of a mountain.

The garden was a mass of flowers, cypress trees, pomegranates, magnolias. I amused myself making believe that it was mine for three months and that I was to live there and work from Spanish models. The Arab would be my servant, he would bring me other Arabs, gypsies of dark beauty. After the day's work was over (I would work out of doors) I could bathe in the little pool in the garden. A gypsy would bring me my dinner on the terrace below the pool where I could look at the faraway hills and afterwards they would dance and sing for me. Sometimes I would invite a few friends to stay, but we would pay little attention to each other. Sometimes I would love desperately someone (just because it fit the pictures). We would love under the pomegranate tree, with the fruit hanging down over us, then we would love under the stars and the scent of oranges would be in the air, while gypsies sang in the distance. My love would be Pan, arrived from the woods, and he would go away and not bother me afterwards. The dream vanished, I swung from unreality back to reality, and yet was it real, this place of dreams?

"Beautiful, sympathetic," murmured the young Arab. He too had been dreaming.

The only form of amusement at night in Cordova was the cinema! There were also dancers there and I decided to go. The show was bad, not Spanish, and I found myself very conspicuous. Also the proximity to my neighbors gave me cause for serious alarm. My ankles and neck began to give signs of immediate contamination! I left after a short time. . . .

I was able to better enjoy the cathedral itself this morning. When I went in I heard music. A service was going on and the figures in black, in gorgeous robes, the boys with incense, all the appurtenances of the Catholic Church were present. The elaborately carved choir stalls, the gorgeous architecture of the choir are things which priests and pomp look well against. Peering through the arches I could see the great columns of the mosque. The fine though florid pulpit with an ivory bull in agony supporting the carved top was typical. A spot of purple light came down through a window bringing into highlight a piece of exquisite carving on one of the columns. (It seemed strange that my necessity had led me just here.) The voices rose in the shrill abrupt way of choir voices, then the chanting of a priest, mechanical, bored but charged no doubt with emotion to the believer. And a peal from the organ, as though to blazen out the truth. They formed themselves into a procession now, led by priests carrying various gold and silver ornaments. They all moved with a slow rhythmic motion away from the choir out into the mosque. I thought they would leave the church and I followed to see them till the end. But I now perceived that there were lights in the Mihrab, which they were slowly approaching, great high candlesticks placed on either side of what appeared at a distance to be a bier covered with black velvet. The candlesticks were of black and gold and huge candles burned in them. The black of them and of the black velvet stood out clear against the carvings, the tiles, the mosaics. I felt as if something in my throat had closed up. The procession advancing towards the Mihrab spread incense about them. The gold of the priests robes, the red of their mantles, the white of their surplices shone in turn as some shaft of light from a high window touched it in passing. The organ stopped playing and the voice of the Head Priest took up the chant. Faintly it descended, gently it insinuated itself into one's soul then rose, almost harsh to suggest future punishment. In spite of oneself, in spite of the consciousness of melodrama and of false glamor my heart beat fast.

I felt expectation, something was going to happen. The dramatic voice of the priest continued, now sustained by other voices—then the tinkle of bells, then more incense. There passed to me through the mosque, in the incense, a cloud of excitement. I could not move, I melted, I was fiery all in one. All was now silent. A decrepit old man entirely clothed in white and gold crept to the black bier, with raised arm he began to intone, no doubt it was a prayer, to me it seemed a curse, so sinister had the scene now become. He was not a man, he was a spirit. Time had stopped. In a maze I saw them move away, the procession re-forming itself, returning from the barbaric setting to its own rightful setting of tall arches and carved choir stalls. A poorly dressed man with a lot of jangling keys came into the Mihrab. He was in a hurry, he tumbled over himself so anxious was he to extinguish the candles, to set the candlesticks back against the wall, to remove the black velvet from the empty table which it covered! He slammed the iron gate which led to the Mihrab, he locked it quickly and shuffled away his mind evidently fixed on other things. A few minutes later I met the priests dispersing. Some were big and handsome, one followed me; he had a sensual and beautiful face. He would have spoken to me except that just then two elderly priests appeared from behind a pillar deep in conversation. They might have been plotting, and if they plotted it was of evil. The priest with the beautiful, sensual face gave me a lingering look and moved on. I smiled at him as I walked away.

OCTOBER 11TH SUNDAY AND SEVILLE.

At a station between Cordova and Seville a man got into my compartment. He was neither tall nor short, he was Spanish and looked like a gentleman. I was pleased for I wanted to talk to someone. It developed that he spoke very little French and no English although he could read a little English. In spite of these difficulties I was able to get quite some information from him. I wanted to see a bull fight. I had missed a good one which was to have taken place in Madrid on Thursday but was postponed on account of the bad weather. Would there be one in Seville on Sunday? Yes, probably, he would find out. After a thorough search of his paper he could discover no mention of it.

He seemed surprised at my disappointment and was evidently unable to understand the explanation I made. He did not like bull fights. It was possible there would be a novillada, a fight with young beginners and young bulls and no horses, but it would not be much good, I gathered.

I told him that I was an artist and that I wanted to see some really characteristic dances, also some young painters' studios. He told me he painted a little himself, "an amateur," that he collected pictures. I questioned him about a number of the men whom I had read about. He gave me the names and addresses of others. He was interested when he found that I knew Archer Huntington [the adopted son of the railroad magnate]. I wished his French was better for there were distinct gaps in our conversation. I had given him my name and address in Seville before the train arrived at our destination, and he said he would let me know all about the bull fight and whether it was worth going to. His name is Santos.

Seville looked gay, the sun was out, the streets crowded. I wandered to the Calle Sierpes (serpent) to see life. No carriages can pass in the street, it is packed at all hours with people, rich young men staring at the women, poor people with plenty of time, heaven only knows why, toreadors with their following of admirers, women in black with shawls and without. Balconies overhang the street. Below are stores, cafes, clubs, above barred windows with now and then a smiling face behind the bars. Patios are visible through the open doorways. And children, many children with pinched faces, pale and oval, with sad eyes. Most of the people look poor, rather rough like the type of men in Velasquez pictures or like El Grecos. Some too have the strong hard faces of a Zurbaran. They are, many of them, clean shaven, wear short tight black coats, light trousers and the hats of which I spoke before. Their features are apt to be large and severe, they seldom smile and there is a melancholy look in their eyes that haunt. Character the Spaniard of Seville has in looks, and sometimes he is very handsome.

Most of the famous bull fighters have come from Seville. These are looked up to and worshiped by the populace.

This morning I received a very polite note from Santos. Its mixture of French and Spanish made it difficult for me to decipher. The concierge helped me out. The bull fight was a [novillada] and would not be of any interest. Would I give him the pleasure of taking me to see some dancing at the ——— that evening. It might be good, it might be bad, but it was the most characteristic in Seville. He would call for me at 10:30. I felt mildly interested and—accepted. . . .

OCTOBER 12TH MONDAY SEVILLE.

Santos came and we went to the ——— ———. We occupied a box in the gallery above the hall. The floor was crowded with men in black clothes seated at tables and drinking abstemiously. In the boxes girls in Spanish shawls circulated. They were mostly fat and not attractive. I think I was the only foreigner present and consequently conspicuous. We drank jerez out of tiny glasses while waiting for the curtain to go up.

When the curtain went up I saw a hideous background of badly painted French design, a glare of light. A poor band began to play. But—the music was Spanish and suddenly appeared a woman of prepossessing appearance whose semi-Spanish costume appealed to me.

I liked the way she moved and she was young. The movement of her body was swaying, she had fine, strong arms, her body was too big, her ankles thick, but—she exhibited skill and gave me suddenly a glimpse into Spain.

Santos seemed to consider conversation unnecessary and I was glad. I caught his eyes on me many times during the evening as if surprised at my enjoyment of anything so uninteresting.

A little play was going on in the box next. A very pretty girl talking to a man completely enamored of her. After a while she disappeared to re-appear on the stage. She was very pretty but she could not dance. He applauded and I seconded him. No one else took any interest. Santos smiled. When the girl came back to her seat she and the young man bowed and smiled at me. We all had a drink together.

Other girls danced, some sang. Some had real character and fire. Once I was carried away by a thin girl with real abandon.

Santos approved my taste. We were strange companions in a strange land. He no longer spoke at all, but looked at me out of melancholy eyes. The fat Spanish girls hovered over him, he said things to them I could not understand and they laughed, but he remained serious. I tried to make conversation but he remained in silence.

"Now," he said, "they will dance the flamenco."

The curtain rose. All the fat women who had been hovering over Santos and the boxes were seated in a semi-circle on the stage. At one end sat a very thin man in very tight clothes. The music was very Eastern, it moved with rhythm. I would have liked to dance myself. Santos understood. He gave me a sympathetic look.

A woman with very long arms, a big waist and a small pink shawl tightly drawn over her bosom got up from her seat and stepped to the center of the tiny stage. She moved very little, her arms crept along her body, her head turned from side to side. It was all mechanical and rather clever. I was left cold. After a few superficial moments she sat down. The music continued and each in turn did her dance. Often they were encouraged by the others, by shouts and cries, by strange sounding tones. Had they been young and beautiful the effect would have been very different. At the end the man danced. He was really good.

All this somehow made me sad. Longing came over me. How idiotic, I said, to feel like this.

Santos was speaking: "Now we will go to ———."

I don't know where we were to go. I felt mildly crazy and wanted to go home to bed.

"Thank you a thousand times, monsieur, but I regret I must now go back to the hotel."

A particularly fat lady in a shawl had approached my companion. He evidently said no to whatever it may have been she suggested. And we left the hall.

All of which was very interesting. As we strolled back to the hotel I ventured to express my pleasure. "Being alone I could not have gone to the ———."

"We do not understand Americans—how is it you are alone?"

"Nor we, Spaniards—" I interrupted.

"Will you come back to my country?"

"I hope so. You see I have Spanish ancestors," I told him.

He looked at me out of his gloomy eyes. "Ah, now I understand!" And with that we parted.

OCTOBER 14TH WEDNESDAY, GRANADA

. . . The hotel is almost empty. It is an unsympathetic hotel but the view is fine. It stands well over the town on the same hill as the Alhambra only on the opposite side. During the night I heard the cry of what seemed to be Arabs calling the hours. A little moon, very little, lights, hills and Moorish roofs.

As I sit here looking out I think of the full life, not wasted, maybe misspent but not wasted. It is of the life of a friend of mine that I think. She had done most things—travelled to many lands, danced and played, taken risks with men, palled with unknown people, made a reputation in her line, loved without restraint, tried various forms of excitement and heaven knows what else—I thought just then she was right—perhaps even I envied her.

A fleeting golden haze out of doors, the scent of oranges, the lethargy of the moon which spread its aura, a feeling of jerez dripping down into my being, formed a heaven. Then it all stopped, no sound came from outside, from inside. Foolishly I thought: "Sensation is over, over." The room was cold. Slowly I drank in the night and the sensations it brought. Was this the gamut? I watched the moon. A call went up, a human call but one which my soul answered: independence. Tomorrow, I would be the slave of tomorrow.

I seemed to see a vision and a voice that came from far off. It said: "You are tasting the cup, you are drinking the wine."

Gertrude continues her tour of the Alhambra, writes about its history, then in great detail about a bullfight in Seville, then about Cordova. What she is seeing and what she is remembering fuse. In her final journal entry—headed "October 16th. Late in the afternoon at Cordova"—it is not always clear where she is. As she says, she is "haunted" by Granada, wondering, "Would my castle in Spain be only a castle in Spain?" Despite being in Cordova, she writes, "Now [the Alhambra] was real, I could touch the column (I did so lovingly), the mountains were within my reach, surely they belonged just a little to me." She remembers the tombs of Ferdinand and Isabella in the cathedral of Granada. And she remembers an English artist she has met at the Alhambra:

He is cockney but paints very well, with a broad sweep and a good sense of decoration. He loves a gypsy and stays on and on (five years now) in Granada, unable to leave. She and the place and his dreams hold him. "I will come," I told him, "I feel it. I love it," and I waved over the valley. "There is no gypsy for me, but there is something just as strong, perhaps even just the same—it's after all the desire for life." I bought one of his pictures and he gave me another. We parted happy.

And, finally, she remembers the trip from Granada back to Cordova. The journal ends:

. . . I was tired from the bad road and weary from my multitude of emotions. In the cafe on the corner I sat and drank, oh horrible dissipation, 2 portos and ate 2 rum cakes! The girls and men all remembered me in the little cafe through which I had passed a week before and smiled me a gracious welcome. I was enamored of Cordova and found time to visit the mosque once again.

Tonight I leave for Madrid and my heart is very heavy.

Spain is over—my holiday almost at an end.

The holiday is almost at an end but Spain is not "over." It, like North Africa, will echo in Gertrude's mind through the rest of her life and will, at the end of this decade, lead to her largest commission.

⇐ *1921*

During the rest of the twenties, except for the end of the decade, the years of Gertrude's life will seem to grow shorter—partly because of less documentation, particularly journals; partly because of more time spent in her studios both here and abroad. She is as busy as ever but her energy is increasingly more focused on work, steady work, mostly war monuments. "The studio drama" itself is not dramatic. She is working in a fairly free, realistic style and will move only slowly, under the influence of Cubism and Art Deco, toward more simplified stylization. Even more undramatic, indeed tedious, is the need frequently to meet and correspond with memorial committees. War heroes (often generals or colonels), bureaucrats (often fine arts or planning commissioners), fund raisers, and of course architects—but with more justification—all have opinions about prospective monuments and force aesthetic, budgetary, and "moral" compromises. As with the *Titanic* Memorial, for which, only now, Gertrude receives final payment, money is always, and nudity sometimes, an issue; and though Gertrude could easily resolve economic problems, she is professionally insistent on being paid adequately for her work. In addition, there are dozens of smaller matters that these committees get into—the prominence of military insignia, the hierarchical grouping of combat teams, and so forth—smaller, but necessitating hours of time-consuming changes.

During this decade Gertrude will also be writing a great deal, mostly fiction, mostly with a view toward publication, and mostly, like her public monuments, lacking the intimate authenticity of her more private work. In drafts of short stories, novels, and plays, some worked and reworked, some unfinished or fragmentary, there is a proliferation of Gertrude-like heroines. Little of this material can be dated specifically and what can adds almost nothing to the image we already have of a woman torn between East and West, idealism and materialism, meditation and industry, private work and public activity, family and profession, and the dozens of other dichotomies with which we are familiar.

But now, early in 1921, Gertrude is occupied with a different kind of writing. The following letter to General Summerall, written at the suggestion of Theodore Roosevelt, Jr., is typical:

Dear General,

I have been looking forward to your visit for a long time. Having worked for and thought so much of your Division you can imagine perhaps the help you gave me by talking so frankly yesterday of your ideas and ideals. You made me feel a part of you all in spirit and I am starting with the greatest enthusiasm to work on the design along the lines suggested by you.

I want to say something about the caisson. I was so concentrated yesterday on trying to find out your point of view of what the monument should be that I did not want to interrupt you to suggest my ideas of the symbolism of the caisson. It seems to me that the thought you so well expressed about awards and medals, a thought all the men had, applies also to the caisson in this sense: it typified the honorable and dreamed of funeral of heroes—not merely death but glorious death, victory to the living, love & honor to the dead, which I think to be fitting for the dead of the First Division, just as the medals are for the living.

The recent burials in Paris and London of an Unknown Soldier were the outpourings of the nation's feelings towards their dead heroes and were typified by a coffin on a caisson as the principal feature of a much thought-out effort to show their pride and also their love for their dead. An ordinary grave would be nothing but a gloomy sadness, which I agree with you would not express the spirit of your Division but the glorious hero on the caisson does. It has always seemed to me that a monument should suggest somewhere in its composition heroic death as well as heroic accomplishment and triumph.

I am looking forward to seeing you soon.

Very sincerely,
Gertrude V. Whitney

Happy New Year!

Gertrude does not ultimately receive the 1st Division Memorial commission. However, through a much vaster correspondence with Colonel Hersey—this one conducted mostly through Juliana Force, whom Hersey calls "Mrs. Whitney's executive officer"—Gertrude does receive the commission to do a memorial for the 4th Division at the National Cemetery in Arlington, Virginia. But "receive" is not finally the right word. The receipt is more like a promise with many strings attached, then a broken promise with many broken strings, then a tangled curse. Though this is an extreme case—the correspondence will continue until 1930 and end then with litigation and the abandonment of the project—it is revealing to outline the preliminary steps, all taken in 1921, in order to understand the frustrating and enervating outcome:

1. In early January, Gertrude visits Arlington to inspect the site with Colonel Hersey; Charles Moore, chairman of the Commission of Fine Arts; and Thomas Hastings, the architect. Hersey explains that the War Department has approved the site, subject to design approval by the Fine Arts Commission. Also, he requires the design for the fund-raising campaign.

2. In early February, Hersey expresses confidence that he can raise $100,000 from former members of the 4th Division and requests estimates from the sculptor and the architect to assure him that their fees and total construction expenses will not exceed that amount.

3. In late February satisfactory budgets are transmitted.

4. In early March, Hastings' plans are completed along with his renderings showing *Doughboy* in proper scale, raised on a pedestal within the sunken stone terrace of the Arlington site, and Gertrude's clay model of the monument is being photographed.

5. March 16, Colonel Hersey writes to Colonel Canfield, also of the 4th Division:

> . . . In general terms, it is purposed not to erect an enormous monument piercing the sky, but to dig out this hillock, making it into an amphitheatre with a green at the bottom, sloping sides and terraced approaches. At the bottom of this amphitheatre in the center of a circular green, stands the heroic figure of the ideal man of the 4th Division, not depicted with the fierce fighting face so commonly set forth, but a composite of what America sent to the war, a man like yourself, Bach, Markle, Lloyd-Smith, and others we can think of; the strong, virile face of the officer and man combined, a fully equipped soldier, eager, alert, but withal showing that refinement and unselfishness combined with bull-dog tenacity that has been so characteristic of the 4th Division.
>
> I think that her first attempt can be improved upon, but it is wonderful even now. She has more of the side view at present than the eager, forward, "let's go" soldier which I think the more desirable. I have not made this criticism to Mrs. Whitney yet because my idea is not necessarily the correct one. Perhaps, many would prefer her own conception as it is now expressed.
>
> I expect to go down to New York next Saturday to the West Point dinner and wonder if you could meet me, perhaps, and see Mr. Hastings, Mrs. Whitney, if she is in town, and give me your own criticisms of what is being attempted. I believe that the strength of the 4th Di-

vision man touched up with the genius of a great sculptress with its setting looked after by an architect whose fame puts his ability beyond question and set in Arlington on a site that I believe the best, is going to make a combination that nothing can surpass as a world-war memorial. . . .

6. April 8, Colonel Canfield is authorized "to engage Mrs. Whitney as sculptress."

7. September 28, a formal agreement is executed and a $500 down payment made to Gertrude.

All of these details take time. Though we lack the equivalent documentation for the Washington Heights War Memorial (at Broadway and 168th Street), on which Gertrude is simultaneously working, it is not difficult to extrapolate.

While devoting so much energy to obtaining commissions, Gertrude's social life is curtailed but not abandoned. One of the busier stretches is in February when Clare Sheridan, an English sculptor and writer (best known for her *Mayfair to Moscow*), is visiting New York. Like Gertrude, she is highborn (a Jerome, related to the Churchills), energetic, and bohemiaphilic. Unlike Gertrude, her politics are far to the left—she has done busts of Lenin and Trotsky. The two women have fun at a large dinner given by Frank Crowninshield at the Coffee House club, followed by charades. Within a few more days they attend luncheon parties given by the editor of *Town and Country*, at which Jo Davidson and Mario Guardabassi are among the guests, and at Mrs. Cornelius Vanderbilt, Jr.'s Fifth Avenue home, where the crowd is less lively. A week later Gertrude gives her own luncheon party at the MacDougal Alley studio; like the other events, it is described by Clare Sheridan in *My American Diary*:

> . . . I sat next to Mr. Bob Chanler, whom I hadn't met before. He has the head of a great French savant, and a voice like the roar of a bull. He was once [1910–12] married to [the Metropolitan Opera prima donna] Cavalieri! On my other side, Mr. Childe Hassam, the painter; opposite Mr. —— and Jo Davidson. There were lots of people I didn't know, and among them I met a Sheridan cousin called Pittman. Good looking and nice, I was glad to claim him. Paul Manship came in afterwards, he and I and Davidson and Bob Chanler, unable to bear the noise or the absence of air, at the end of lunch went upstairs to the studio and danced to the gramophone. Mr. Chanler, rather mad, and attractive accordingly, kissed me in a moment of expansion! That is very American. They may kiss in public!
>
> After lunch Ruth Draper did some imitations. It is pure genius.
>
> It was difficult to drag oneself away from such an attractive party. I like Mrs. Whitney and her breakaway from the conventions. She

seems to achieve the real bohemian spirit. I remember John Noble telling me about her years ago—she is the fairy godmother of struggling artists.

Jo Davidson and Paul Manship came down to my exhibition. . . . It was nice of them to come, sculptors are not as nice to each other in England as those here have been to me. There seems to be a different spirit here. I had a hectic time, wanting to talk to all my friends who turned up.

I came home in time to dress and Jo Davidson called for me and took me to the Opera House. We had not time to dine. It was the first time I had been to the opera since Moscow. The house was a full one and very enthusiastic. The stalls seemed to consist mostly of alien music-lovers, and for the most part not evening dressed. It was very democratic and harmonious. I liked it.

Afterwards, Hugo fetched us and we went to Guardabassi's flat for supper. He made the macaroni himself and I helped him. He sings and he paints, and he seems to be a useful person to have about the house!

We were a noisy crew, and there were repeated requests from below that we should make less noise! Which seemed to me curious for a studio flat. An American party is always noisy. I can't make out why one should be unable to hear oneself speak. I think it is that they talk in a key higher than we do. They have a great sense of camaraderie, and when they get together to have a "good time" it is bewildering. I wonder what they think of us? I should think they find us deadly.

In addition to working on and for commissions—one way of getting work out into the world—Gertrude spends much of March preparing for spring exhibitions in Paris and London—another way. March 26 she sails for France with about twenty of her pieces (another half dozen or so are in her Paris studio) and with Juliana Force, who will stay at the Crillon attending to many details while Gertrude is at the studio.

"Details" is a relative term. Gertrude's life *is* details—perhaps even more, both quantitatively and qualitatively, than most lives: quantitatively because of the number and complex interweaving of her interests, qualitatively because of her own acceptance of their significance. She has already made lists of the work which will be in the show, ranging from such early pieces as *Wherefore, Spanish Peasant,* and *Chinoise* to sketches or full-size casts of her most recent commissions. She has selected photographic illustrations for the catalogue. She has read the catalogue introduction by Léonce Bénédite, a sympathetic blurb by the curator of the Luxembourg Museum, and thus a representative of *l'art officiel,* who, at least partially encouraged by Gertrude herself, devotes too much space to the "poor little rich girl" theme and a perhaps more appropriate amount to Gertrude's war work in France. He errs and oversimplifies even more than American journalists as, for example, when he says that she "discarded the insipid restlessness of society life and devoted herself entirely, in her modest studio, to the laborious career of a sculptor." Now, with Georges Petit, the director of the gallery in which the exhibition will be held, Gertrude reviews all this, studies the gallery space, makes dozens of installation sketches, goes over catalogue mailing lists, invitations to the *vernissage*, local and foreign press releases. . . . No, these are not details, they are Gertrude's life.

The exhibition is well received, if with considerable emphasis on Gertrude's position in society and on her past and continuing devotion to France. Among many congratulatory letters, two are particularly meaningful. Gertrude's early protégé Morgan Russell writes that this is "the first time that a work inspired by the War made me feel a lyrical emotion—you have expressed one of the rare sympathetic aspects of the gigantic butchery—fresh and without false sentimentality." Jacques Seligmann, the senior member of the French branch of the banking family, is able to express his appreciation more materially: "You probably do not care very much for the opinion of anybody, but I want to compliment you and to express my thanks for the chance which you have given to us in Paris to see your marvellous things. I can assure you that your exhibition is a revelation . . . and I only want to write you that I am one of your real and sincere admirers; I have not the pleasure to know you, but nevertheless, I want to write it to you.

"My idea is to offer your No. 7, what you call the 'Cariatide,' to the Metropolitan Museum in New York. I went to your exhibition very early yesterday morning, and there was nobody to tell me the price; I hope that it is not above 3,000 Frs. If it is possible to get this beautiful and marvellous bronze at such a low price, I would offer it to the Museum. I have given so many things to the Metropolitan Museum of New York this year that I really cannot afford, being myself in business, to give more, especially as modern things are not at all in my line. But I think that this No. 7 is such a marvel that it ought really not to leave America, and I should be delighted if you can afford to let me have it for that price."

Gertrude, through Petit, accepts Seligmann's terms, and the piece is presented to the Metropolitan after its exhibition in London. At about the same time Petit sells a *Titanic Memorial Head* to the Luxembourg.

In London, at Thomas McLean's Gallery (under the direction of the larger Leicester Galleries), Gertrude has many of the same details to face as in Paris. The show and catalogue are slightly smaller (twenty-two pieces instead of twenty-seven, sixteen pages instead of twenty-four), Bénédite's introduction is translated, but the biggest change is in the presentation of Gertrude herself. Having always used the professional name Gertrude

Whitney or Gertrude V. Whitney, now for the first and only time a catalogue is titled:

SCULPTURE BY

GERTRUDE WHITNEY

(MRS. HARRY PAYNE WHITNEY)

If Gertrude is remembered in France as a war heroine—and indeed she has been—Harry is remembered in England for his polo playing, horse racing, fox hunting, and shooting. One newspaper or magazine article after another reminds the British public that he was managing captain of the Meadow Brook Big Four which won in 1909, 1911, and 1913. Others refer to Gertrude's being a first cousin of Consuelo, who is just now, in May, finally divorcing the Duke of Marlborough in preparation for her marriage to Louis Jacques Balsan, a retired lieutenant colonel in the French army. And still others connect Gertrude with the American "Overseas Exhibition" in Venice the previous year, in London earlier this spring, and scheduled to travel to Paris this summer before being seen in New York in the late fall.

Too much, if not all, of this attention is external to Gertrude's work, and even the dozen or so British publications which deal more directly with the work do so mostly at the level of singling out favorite pieces (the *Titanic* Memorial is particularly popular). As with Gertrude's commissions, we wonder about the exhibitions of her work, asking if they are worth the price she pays in energy and anxiety, concluding that her continuing need to get her work seen and have attention paid to it—to her—must compensate for everything.

In late May, when Gertrude returns to New York, perhaps it occurs to her again that the goals and prizes are more clear-cut in horse racing than in art. Harry is having another great season. His stable earns $241,680, second only to that of the Rancocas Stable of his friend, the oil tycoon and sportsman Harry Sinclair (later to be involved in the Teapot Dome scandal). Indeed, Harry's stable would most likely have been first, except for the death of its largest money earner, Broomspun, who, after winning the Preakness, breaks down in the Carlton Stakes and has to be destroyed.

Gertrude spends about three months working hard on commissions in her MacDougal Alley and Westbury studios. Harry is pretty much on the racing circuit. Flora is in Los Angeles, expecting her first child about the end of November. Sonny is on a trip to Alaska with Douglas Burden. Barbara, home from Foxcroft, has become a good rider and spends as much time with Harry as with Gertrude. The summer rushes by as, for Gertrude, only a summer of work can. In August she decides to return to Paris for a few weeks of fun and shopping. Many of the clothes she buys now, for herself and for her daughters, are from the recently opened shop of Jo Davidson's wife Yvonne.

The rest of the year is broken into bits of time. There is a month in New York during which the Whitney Studio shows the "Overseas Exhibition" from which Gertrude selects seven contemporary American paintings (including Kent's *Bones of Ships,* Sloan's *The Haymarket,* and Du Bois's *Doll and Monster*) to give to representative museums across the country. In the same month she shows pieces of her own at the exhibition of the National Association of Women Painters and Sculptors and at the annual of the New Society of Artists. Another month is spent on a trip to Los Angeles to be with Flora when she gives birth to Pamela Tower. The San Francisco *Examiner* headlines the story:

> MRS. WHITNEY NOW A GRANDMOTHER
>
> BABY GIRL WILL INHERIT MILLIONS

⤳ *1922*

According to society columnists, not since before the war have New York debutantes had so active a season as this one. Surely there has been no season so dominated by Vanderbilts and Whitneys—three great-great-granddaughters of Commodore Vanderbilt: Barbara Whitney, Adele Sloane Hammond, and Shiela Burden; two granddaughters of William C. Whitney: Barbara, again, and Helen and Payne Whitney's daughter Joan. Barbara's cousins have made their debuts at the end of 1921. Barbara, who will be nineteen in March, makes hers January 4.

It is a mammoth affair. Some eight hundred guests are invited to dance at 871 Fifth Avenue in the same oak-paneled ballroom, embellished with gold ornaments and hung with Gobelin tapestries, where William C. Whitney introduced to society his nieces Katherine and Helen Barney (now Mrs. Courtlandt Barnes and Mrs. Frederick Watriss) and where, after his death, Gertrude and Harry (within the softer ambiance of Gertrude's floral decorations) received the guests at Flora's and Rod's wedding. The room is steeped in history. The family names on the guest list have changed little over the years. Indeed, for many here tonight who, like Gertrude and Harry themselves, remember those other events, surrounded by intervening marriages and divorces and births and deaths, the past must be a single moment, one great, self-canceling and ultimately neutral flow of time. Hosts and guests alike *are* time.

This evening Barbara has been the guest of honor at a dinner party in the Park Avenue home of the Sheridan Nortons, whose daughter Marie will marry Sonny the following year. It is one of many such parties scattered throughout the best residential sections of the city. And now, after dinner, Barbara takes her place beside Gertrude to receive at the end of the corridor leading to the ballroom. As on several occasions—mostly, in the past, with Flora—Gertrude's gown contrasts strongly with her daughter's. Gertrude wears ruby-red velvet which beautifully sets off the Payne pearls. Barbara, shorter and plumper, is more simply dressed in white satin and chiffon. Together they stand like a tableau of Innocence and Experience. There is no question that they *and Harry*—still so attractive; still, for this crowd, a sports hero comparable with the great younger athletes who have emerged from humbler backgrounds—are the center of attention. However, two other couples, one from each side of the family, provoke considerable exotic interest: the Count and Countess Széchényi (László has recently been appointed the first minister to the United States under the new Hungarian regime) and the Honorable Charles and Mrs. Winn (she is the daughter of Pauline Whitney Paget and he the second son of Baron St. Oswald).

So much for the past/present that haunts this room. Among the debutantes of the season, there is the present/future too: Ellin Mackay, daughter of the communications magnate Clarence Hungerford Mackay, a friend and Long Island neighbor of the Whitneys. Except for her social standing, Ellin, like so many in the ballroom, is anonymous, but in four years she will shock almost everyone here, especially her own family, by marrying the author of several of the most popular songs being played now by the orchestra (such "standards" as *Alexander's Ragtime Band, Everybody's Doin' It, A Pretty Girl Is Like a Melody*): Irving Berlin, born Israel Baline! in Russia!

The parties for Barbara, her cousins, and her friends have just begun. A few nights later Gertrude and Harry give a dinner at 871 Fifth, preceding a dance at the Burdens' for Shiela. Also, Gertrude is on the permanent committee of the Junior Assembly, a series of three debutante dances strung out until early February.

But of course not all the dinners and dances are for Barbara. Later in February there is the Ball of the Fine Arts at the Astor—an event which Gertrude particularly likes because "the list" is loose, a mixture of high society and bohemia. She brings Alice Roosevelt Longworth as her guest. Bob Chanler, dressed as Pierrot, an enormous Pierrot, tends the "old-fashioned bar"—i.e., one, like all bars during Prohibition, at which no liquor is supposed to be served. However, Chanler, like almost every man at the ball, surely like every popular man there, has several hip flasks—he has room for them in his voluminous silk pants—and the party is far from "dry."

A more sedate affair, with which Gertrude is directly and less playfully involved, occurs at the end of the month: a gala concert at Carnegie Hall, where five conductors, including Leopold Stokowski, will lead three symphony orchestras for the benefit of the American Academy in Rome, now for the first time raising funds for fellowships in music (in addition to those in architecture, painting, and sculpture which have existed since Charles F. McKim founded the Academy in 1894). As so often, Gertrude is on the committee and for this occasion has been commissioned to do a medallion of the musician, conductor, and composer Walter Damrosch, for whom one of the new fellowships will be named. The medallion, executed quickly, is a minor work, a simple realistic relief of Damrosch in profile—one of Gertrude's few commissions of this period unrelated to the war.

Another in this category is much more important. Early in January, W. R. Coe, a Long Island acquaintance of Gertrude's—and, like her, a good friend of Bob Chanler's (from whom Coe, again like Gertrude, has commissioned murals)—writes to her about her possible interest in doing a memorial equestrian statue of "Buffalo Bill" Cody in Cody, Wyoming. Coe encloses a recent letter from Caroline Lockhart—a writer living in Cody, where he himself has a splendid vacation home—in which she recommends "Mrs. Harry Payne Whitney" for the job and reminds Coe that the "$5,000 appropriated by the State [soon after Cody's death in 1917] for some such purpose" should be used now: "if we do not get busy we will lose it." Coe, in his covering letter, tells Gertrude that he feels she "would be a very desirable artist for the work," and asks her how she feels about it and what reply he should make to Caroline Lockhart. We don't have Gertrude's response, but it must have been enthusiastic. By February 26, the birthday of Buffalo Bill, Mrs. Mary Jester Allen, his niece, announces to the press that Gertrude has received the commission and that she was "the only woman sculptor with whom the Colonel was acquainted." Although Gertrude has seen at least one Buffalo Bill Wild West Show (with the children in 1908), Mrs. Allen's statement smacks of the same sort of exaggeration indulged in by "Ned Buntline" (E. Z. C. Judson), who dubbed Colonel William F. Cody Buffalo Bill and turned him into a popular hero in a series of sensational dime novels and in two plays starring Cody.

No, Gertrude's interest in Cody is not and was never personal. What does interest her about this commission is its uniquely American character. She immediately recognizes the popular, heroic, even mythic power of Buffalo Bill and from the start thinks in terms of a work that will express his energy in a dynamic pose. As always for a major commission she reads up on her subject—not only Buntline's works and Cody's own autobiography but general histories of the West. She studies equestrian statues and action photographs of Buffalo Bill and other cowboys. She plans to import a Western horse and rider and have more photographs taken. For two and a half years she works on this memorial while devoting herself simultaneously to her other commissions and to her many family, social, professional, and patronal obligations. Not since the *Titanic* Memorial has she given so much time to a single work, and not since it has she received so much publicity. By completion of *Buffalo Bill*, hundreds of clippings will fill four fat albums.

Meanwhile, in early April, Gertrude has finished work on the Washington Heights War Memorial and in the middle of the month goes to France and Spain for a six weeks' holiday, allowing just enough days to return in time for the unveiling of the memorial. Everyone in the family but Harry seems to know and accept her being gone until late May. On the fifth he writes:

Dearest,

I feel like a gloom. Somehow or other I got it in my head that you would be back by now, though the children seemed surprised at the idea. That is why this is my first letter. I thought you wd. be back.

Anyhow—I caught cold at White Sulphur & haven't finished with it yet. Have been living alone in the country & have read till I'm sick of all books.

Have had several seances with your son which is not pleasant. Have not been cross or disagreeable with him. But he has only one idea in his mind. Marriage in the early fall & love feasts between us & the Norton family.

Barbie is sweet & has had parties of girls in the country. "Toodles" [Murray], "Sheelah" [Burden], etc.

[Harry] Sinclair left two weeks ago for Mexico & then his little boy, 10 years, getting over measles, got mastoid in both ears & had to be operated on. Mrs. S. is run down & nervous & not too well. So I have been consulting with doctors & quieting nervous woman.

Then Sinclair got back by special trains day before yesterday & developed temperature, had his own ears pierced & seems pretty sick.

Then Harry Davison is to be operated on again tomorrow in the country. I think it is the end. [He dies the next day. Gertrude will sculpt an eagle for his gravestone.]

Then April 28 was my 50th—terrible.

Flora & Mr. [Endicott] Peabody [the founder and headmaster of Groton School] & Payne remembered it.

All those glooms. It's been raining hard all day. It is beastly.

When you get back you must pay more & nicer attention to your poor old husband. The dogwood is just out in great quantities & you might get a country habit.

Why not do your next thing in the country studio?

I don't feel cheerful so I won't write more, dearest. Life seems lonely.

> Love
> Harry

But a few days later Harry writes again:

Dearest,

Harry Davison's funeral—It made me feel very gloomy. A lot of old men, keeping themselves going a little while longer. Then lunched at the Links Golf Club with John D. Ryan & his grown up son, & watched John go out to play that beastly game of golf so as to keep alive. He complains that his son won't take enough advice & get enough benefit from the father's knowledge & experience. Sic.

Then played polo & then came to this house [871 Fifth Avenue] so as to get away from my room in the country.

Well, dearest, you will be home soon now thank heaven.

There does not seem to be anything to write about.

Barbie rides horses & is full of health & life. Flora sent her some new cunning kodaks of the baby.

> Much love
> Harry

While waiting for Gertrude's return, Harry's gloom persists even as he distracts himself by building an elaborate shooting box, called Forshala, in Thomasville, Georgia. In addition to his chronic colds, his equally chronic sense of aging, his depression at the death of Davison, and the physical collapse of Sinclair and his family—both *Harrys* with whom he identifies —Harry himself is very concerned about Sonny. Hence the bitterness and irony of his comments on his son, echoed in those on young Ryan. On the surface, as with Flora two years before, there is the usual parental doubt about a child being ready for marriage, knowing his mind, et cetera, but beneath the surface there is a scandal brewing which will not become public until summer, though Harry and Gertrude have inklings of it now and have had for some time.

In brief—unlike the many long, lurid newspaper stories which will appear—Sonny has had an affair with a dancer named Evan Fontaine who is about to sue him for $1,000,000—paternity and breach of promise. As the facts emerge, there is no certainty that the child is Sonny's; there is certainty that "Miss" Fontaine was married to Sterling Adair at the time Sonny "proposed," that she obtained an illegal annulment by committing perjury concerning her husband's consent to it, and that her mother committed perjury by stating that Evan had lived with her husband for three hours, when actually they lived together for a year. A letter from Evan to Sterling is found, asking him to help her by stating they haven't lived together. Sonny's lawyer characterizes Evan's action as a "blackmail plot," timed to embarrass him with Marie Norton. After some six months of suits and countersuits and tabloid stories about Gertrude's opposition to the love affair, Flora's acting as the courier of love letters, a plot to murder Adair, and another to kidnap the baby, Evan's case is finally thrown out of court.

All this will appear in upsetting headlines soon after Gertrude returns on the *France*. But now she herself receives much smaller stories, set in much smaller type, about the unveiling of her Washington Heights War Memorial—a soldier, sailor, and marine in a rather stiff and contorted composition of mutual aid, which stands about seventeen feet high, from the bottom of the white marble layer-cake base to the tip of the soldier's bayonet fixed to the rifle strapped to his back. Though the memorial is intended as a lofty tribute to servicemen from the Washington Heights area, the dedication ceremony is an occasion for politics and patriotism at the level of local wards, churches, temples, and veterans' organizations.

May 30 is a warm spring day. Gertrude wears a black silk bonnet with a short veil and an eagle-shaped diamond pin on the crown and a coat in matching black silk with a bright lining. Over her arm she carries a fur stole. Elegant white gloves extend far up into the full-cut sleeves of her coat. She is surrounded by a priest, a rabbi, a minister, politicians in frock coats, and veterans in uniforms which no longer fit properly. She faces a much-decorated corporal who has had part of his face shot off and raises one gloved hand as she places the other on the flag and is sworn an honorary member of the American Legion. She is, as she will write later, "hot, embarrassed and upset."

There are other hot, though more pleasant, days this spring. Sonny, in his senior year at Yale, is again on the J.V. crew, and Gertrude and Harry, with Marie Norton, board the *Whileaway* to see the races. June 7 (the day of John Gregory's marriage to Katherine Rensselaer Crosby), Gertrude is one of seven (including Judge Benjamin Cardozo and the Rev. Endicott Peabody) to receive an honorary degree from New York University (hers is Master of Arts)—the first of several such degrees she will receive.

During the remaining half of the year Gertrude works in Long Island and New York on *Buffalo Bill* and other sculpture commissions. And, as usual, she does some writing, both fiction and non-fiction, including her first (perhaps only) paid literary commission, an article called "Fear—the Destroyer" for the *Ladies' Home Journal*, which pays her $500 for it this November and publishes it in the following February. As in her pieces for *Arts and Decoration*, she is both committed and chauvinistic, as she emphasizes the need to buy and support American art rather than "stagger on with that scared taste which makes us choose the hat we don't want, the house someone else thought should be ours."

⇜ *1923*

Commissions—the work on those already won, the competition for those sought, the endless correspondence and committee meetings—these are what continue to dominate Gertrude's professional life and penetrate too often into what time remains in her private life. Commissions—and exhibitions, also increasingly dominated by commissions.

Gertrude begins the new year with a retrospective exhibition—this one at Wildenstein—carefully, as always, prepared for in the closing months of the old year. There are forty-nine pieces shown, stretching back in time to *American Athlete* and one of the *Four Seasons* panels done for the Field house in Lenox, both completed in 1904, and moving forward to the Washington Heights Memorial and the most recent study for *Buffalo Bill*. Thus, even in selecting her earliest work, Gertrude chooses to emphasize commissions. And her pricing further emphasizes this emphasis. Small early works like *American Athlete* or more recent war sketches *not intended as monuments* are priced typically at $500. Casts of monuments are, even allowing for the difference in size, priced disproportionately higher. Of those for sale, the Aztec and Arlington fountains are each $8,000.

This retrospective, particularly because it comes so soon after all the publicity concerning the *Buffalo Bill* commission, receives more attention from both the press and the general public than any previous exhibition of Gertrude's. The opening, late the afternoon of January 4, by invitation only, is attended by dozens of Gertrude's relatives and friends, including artists, architects, decorators, and museum officials. The press treats it as "an event as important socially as artistically" (*Doings of Society* by "Debutante"). This theme is expanded by Lida Rose McCabe of *Town Topics* in "Bringing the Artist to Society—Incidentally, Art to the Public," an article covering several recent openings. McCabe discovers in what she calls "the Vanderbilt-Crowninshield Committee . . . the germ of society's art gesture"—in other words, a chic powerful art establishment which includes, besides Frank Crowninshield and Gertrude herself, Mrs. Cornelius Vanderbilt, Mrs. W. K. Vanderbilt II, Robert Chanler, Rawlins L. Cottenet, Miss Mary Cass Canfield, Mrs. William A. Delano, Miss Elsie de Wolfe, Thomas B. Hastings, Otto H. Kahn, Clarence H. Mackay, Condé Nast, Mrs. Cole Porter, John Singer Sargent, and Leopold Stokowski. McCabe continues:

Mrs. Whitney was two years assembling her work. The card to the private view . . . was in her own name. Despite her employment of two secretaries [including Juliana Force], they went out through the same bureau that distributed . . . private view invitations and to practically the same list [i.e., the art establishment]. Every afternoon of the three-week free exhibition that followed the private view she was at the gallery to meet visitors. How the public loves to see in the flesh a creator of beauty! Ten thousand strong it came to this *tour de force*. That so frail a physique could have achieved so much, and in spite of the handicap of large wealth and strenuous social obligation, is a marvel.

For the January *International Studio*, Guy Pène du Bois writes yet another "poor little rich girl" piece in which he says that between Gertrude "and any real recognition there has been a wall of money." The *Times* seeks "virility" in Gertrude's work and finds it in "Buffalo Bill's figure bending from its prancing steed" but not in the war sculpture which "shows a certain feminine tenderness and remoteness from the actual sensation of the fighter." Then, like so many other journalists, this anonymous one lists the guests at the opening. And, finally, Helen Appleton Read of the Brooklyn *Daily Eagle* interviews Gertrude, reporting that

. . . Mrs. Whitney spends all day and every day working in her 8th St. studio. She never accepts a social engagement in the daytime. Mrs. Force, her charming secretary, guards her against the calls which are constantly being made upon her time, which allows her the absolute seclusion necessary to her work. It is Mrs. Force who managed Mrs. Whitney's own exhibition abroad, as well as the selected group of American artists. The 8th St. house, so familiar to the public because of its jade green doors and window casements, is entirely given over to Mrs. Whitney, the sculptress. On the first floor are the exhibition rooms, in the back Mrs. Whitney's studio, upstairs Mrs. Force's office and the little pink taffeta-hung boudoir where Mrs. Whitney gives her infrequent interviews—at this particular time too frequent. All the newspapers and magazines are trying to get interviews, and Mrs. Whitney frankly admits that she hates an interview. Mrs. Whitney does not find it necessary to be untidy and unattractive in her working clothes. She wore a bright pink cotton dress, with white collar and cuffs, and had a purplish silk bandana tied around her head. The grey and pink boudoir with the gay Frieseke pictures on the wall, made a charming background. . . .

In all of these viewpoints, however partial and fragmentary, there is, as we now know, some truth, some fiction, and even some myth. But the show is an event. About ten thousand people do come to see it. And Gertrude does find pleasure in that public fact—whether more or less than in laudatory private communications from such artists as John Sloan, Bob Chanler, Howard Chandler Christy, and Blendon Campbell we cannot say.

During the last week of January, the last week of the show, Gertrude receives a letter from Irene Givenwilson, now with the Red Cross in Washington, as curator of their museum. She advises Gertrude formally that the organization proposes to erect a memorial outside its national headquarters to Jane A. Delano, founder of the American Red Cross, and members of the Nursing Service who died during the war. "The Committee feels that it would prefer a woman to undertake the commission and they have asked me to ascertain from you whether it would be possible for you to stop off in Washington on your return from the south and consult with the Chairman of the Committee on the subject and if possible to submit a sketch and probable cost of such a memorial." In handwriting, under the typed body of the letter, she adds: "This is the official communication! It would be wonderful if you could undertake it. I have just come from the Committee meeting where I've been telling them about all your work & advising them to visit the Wildenstein Galleries."

This is an auspicious beginning. The subject is tremendously appealing to Gertrude. She has a friend in court. For once being a woman sculptor seems to be an advantage. Yet, as with the 4th Division Memorial, committee meetings, revised studies, correspondence, and political infighting will drag out for years. In summary, Gertrude accepts what she considers a commission, goes to Washington, and in April submits a model of a central bronze figure of Jane A. Delano, surrounded by four stone reliefs with a connecting stone bench. Gertrude believes that her proposed memorial has been well received, but Irene Givenwilson advises her confidentially: "There is one member who is anxious to have the commission given to Paul Manship. This is Miss Minnigerode, sister of the director of the Corcoran Art Gallery. He is an ardent admirer of Paul Manship and had a very extensive exhibit of his works here two years ago." That is the first hurdle. It takes almost a year for the committee to persuade Miss Minnigerode and to draw a $50,000 contract. It takes another two years to try to overcome the opposition of Charles Moore of the Fine Arts Commission, who had also opposed the 4th Division Memorial. Now he sabotages the project before a congressional committee which must authorize any monument on government property. The Nursing Committee suggests changing the location from the street to the Red Cross's private garden. Moore disapproves the erection "of so elaborate an architectural setting wherever the Memorial might be placed"—and finds the Red Cross site suitable only for a single figure.

Thus time and energy will flow on. By 1926, Irene Givenwilson will be Irene Kilner. By 1927, Lucy Minnigerode will be apologizing to Gertrude for "the delay and seeming negligence and tangle." And not until 1933 will the design be approved for a single figure by Dr. R. Tait McKenzie, best known for his anatomical studies of athletes at the University of Pennsylvania where he has been professor of physical education for twenty-six years.

Again we can only exclaim, commissions! And again we are ahead of our story, which cannot be focused entirely on present moments. Just as Gertrude's new and old abortive commissions overlap and even reverse, so do other aspects of her life. For example, now, as "Fear—the Destroyer" is published, so is the first number of *The Arts* under Gertrude's sponsorship and with Forbes Watson as the new editor. There is no mistaking Watson's collaboration, or at least mutual sympathy, with Gertrude in his first editorial: "*The Arts* is not afraid to enjoy American work just because it is American. It does not intend to wave the flag, but quite frankly it does intend to stand with the American artist against timidity and snobbery." But now, even as Gertrude finds (hires) another voice in support of her own—and both in support of American art—much of the January issue of *The Arts* is devoted to articles by and about Albert C. Barnes, whose aesthetic and collection are far more universal and anti-historical, far less "democratic" and "socially oriented" (in the narrower sense), than Gertrude's. Similarly, although the Whitney Studio has last shown the "Overseas Exhibition" of American paintings, it is now planning a May exhibition of "Recent Paintings by Picasso," together with "Negro Sculpture" (both organized by Marius de Zayas, the brilliant caricaturist, collector, writer, et cetera, who has done similar shows for Stieglitz), while at the Whitney Studio Club there are exhibitions in January of paintings by Adelaide Lawson and John Dos Passos and sculpture by Reuben Nakian, who begins now (and until 1928) to receive an allowance from Gertrude of $250 per month, plus $100 for rent.

We cannot follow all the exhibitions, all the checks to artists. It is enough to say that Gertrude's patronage of other artists, like the work on her own commissions, moves forward and backward in time and to and from Europe, always again overlapping and interweaving. This is true also of the family and social strands of her life. Sonny—like, so many years before, his namesake, Gertrude's brother Cornelius—is abroad spending most of his time with Marie Norton (his Grace Wilson). He writes from the English Club in Pau, Basses Pyrénées, early in the year, determined to marry Marie, preferably in France to "avoid all publicity" of which he has "had quite enough lately" (meaning the Evan Fontaine case). He reports that Marie has become a good hunter and that, never having been over a jump in her life, she is now taking everything in sight. Mrs. Norton will soon arrive in Paris. Won't they, too, come for the wedding? Gertrude, Sonny knows, loves France (which, of course, is not the issue). Harry would love the hunting and golf and tennis (same comment). Letters and cables cross the Atlantic until finally Gertrude and Harry acquiesce.

February 20 they sail aboard the Cunarder *Berengaria* with Barbara—Flora cannot come because of her second pregnancy as well as the recent death of her father-in-law—simply announcing to the press that they will attend the wedding of their son to Marie Norton on March 5. Soon after their arrival Gertrude presents a cast of *The Spirit of the Red Cross* (not to be confused with the Delano Memorial) to the War Museum in the Invalides. The papers say, "the face of young Cornelius Vanderbilt Whitney will be immortalized" as the aviator in the group.

The wedding is simple and small—a civil marriage in the City Hall of the First Arrondissement, witnessed by Gertrude and Harry, Mrs. Norton, and Marie's two unmarried sisters; followed by a religious ceremony at the Church of the Holy Trinity (Marie has converted from Catholicism to Episcopalianism) and a wedding breakfast at the Hotel Brighton. Newspaper writers and photographers and motion picture cameramen are forced to wait outside until the ceremonies are over.

Sonny's wedding in Paris precludes Gertrude's and Harry's attendance, the next day in New York, at a marriage which will, within a decade, affect Gertrude's life even more profoundly than the wedding of her own son. On March 6, Gertrude's youngest brother Regi, now forty-two and divorced from Cathleen Neilson for three years, marries Gloria Morgan, 17, one of the glamorous and precocious identical twin daughters of a professional American diplomat and a Chilean mother. It is another small private wedding, another at which the bride and groom elude reporters and cameramen.

❦

Harry leaves for home as quickly as possible. He has not hunted or golfed or played tennis and he has not enjoyed the Paris winter. As Charles Draper writes Gertrude, "Harry got in . . . and beat it for White Sulphur."

Sonny and Marie are in Rome, where they have run into Hendrik Andersen and listened to his troubles. Andersen writes at length about the meeting to Gertrude in Paris. Sonny doesn't mention it in his letters. He has troubles of his own. Although the breach of promise and paternity suits against him have been dismissed, the perjury case against Evan Fontaine and her mother is now being prosecuted—and publicized. Sonny wants to keep traveling for at least five months, and for a year if necessary, until the publicity has died down and he can return quietly to New York.

Flora, six months pregnant by now, is in Aiken with her daughter Pam and with Shiela Burden and her friend Toodles Murray.

Juliana Force is beset by problems at the Whitney Studio Club, which has outgrown its quarters on Fourth Street and is about to move to 10 West Eighth Street, a larger house adjacent to the Whitney Studio. In addition, there seems to be some technical or casting problem with a forefoot of Buffalo Bill's horse.

And Barbara, still with Gertrude, is talking about wanting to become engaged this coming summer to Barklie Henry, the young banker and sportsman whose name will figure in Hemingway's *A Farewell to Arms*.

Gertrude has a lot to think about, in late March, on the return voyage home.

In New York she meets frequently with Juliana Force. They inspect the near-final study for the Buffalo Bill Memorial, with particular attention to the troublesome forefoot, and make arrangements to have Smokey, the horse from the ranch formerly owned by Buffalo Bill, shipped to New York for final modeling. They tour the new club's expanded facilities—better exhibition and social space, a large room for evening sketch classes for which models will be provided, a good administrative office where the painter Alexander Brook will soon be installed as Mrs. Force's assistant. They visit the Whitney Studio, just being freshly painted for De Zayas' Picasso/African show, which Mrs. Force thinks will be a great success. They discuss having him do at least five more special shows of European and American art during the coming year—another Picasso exhibition; Rousseau; Maillol; American and French Prints; and the so-called Durand-Ruel group, seven American artists (Charles Demuth, Walt Kuhn, H. E. Schnakenberg, Charles Sheeler, Eugene Speicher, Allan Tucker, and Nan Watson) who will be shown at Galeries Durand-Ruel in Paris at the end of this year before being shown at the Studio.

As so often, Gertrude seems to be thriving on all this activity. Her neighbor Daniel Chester French writes to his daughter:

> Mrs. Whitney called me up the other day and asked me to come in and see her statue of Cody. She herself was more striking than the statue, in a gown of orange and dark blue flowered stripes, brilliant beyond reason. With her dark hair and white skin and crimson lips, she was by far the brightest thing on the landscape and very attractive as usual. Her statue is better than I had been led to believe. It has a good deal of spirit and gives the picturesqueness of the subject.

As Juliana Force predicts, the Picasso show is a success—with the art community, if not with the general public. Forbes Watson is ecstatic. In *The Arts*, he describes the show as "what a number of artists have called the most beautiful exhibition of the year and certainly one of the most perfectly arranged exhibitions ever held in New York." More objective critics agree. For example, Henry McBride of the New York *Herald* writes that the paintings "lend an air of great distinction to the rooms, and in turn the rooms, which have recently been done over in pearly tones, set forth Picasso as seldom before."

While Mrs. Force occupies herself more and more completely with the heavy exhibition schedule at both the Studio and the Club, as well as with some of the details concerning Gertrude's commissions, Gertrude herself is sculpting almost full time and almost always in her MacDougal Alley studio. She is with Flora in Westbury when her daughter's second child, a boy baptized Whitney Tower, is born June 30. Otherwise, she is at work in July when Barbara's engagement to Barklie Henry is announced. She is at work in August when, following President Harding's "sudden death," the Teapot Dome scandal receives increasing publicity and it becomes obvious that Harry may be implicated because of investments he has made in his friend Harry Sinclair's oil companies. She is at work in October when Flora christens the $8,000,000 navy fuel ship S.S. *Whitney* (named for William C. Whitney) by breaking a bottle of sweet cider over its prow —in the new, champagneless tradition of Prohibition christenings.

On and on now, through almost everything, Gertrude works. It is a relief (for us, as probably for her) that she and Harry attend the wedding, November 2, of her dead brother Alfred's son, William H. Vanderbilt III, to Emily O'Neill Davies. And the year ends with another kind of relief: the equestrian statue of Colonel William F. Cody a/k/a Buffalo Bill has been completed and officially accepted by the committee representing the state of Wyoming.

⪦ *1924*

January 3 Harry is in Washington, testifying before the Senate Public Lands Committee on his part in funding Harry F. Sinclair's favorable lease (allegedly obtained through bribery and without competitive bidding) of U. S. Navy oil reserve fields in Teapot Dome, near Casper, Wyoming. He sits beside his attorney, Frank Longfellow Crocker, a descendant of the poet, born in Portland, Maine, in 1876, educated at Bowdoin College and Harvard University Law School, and in private practice until 1923 when he became associated exclusively with Harry as his principal legal and business adviser. Frank, like Harry, is handsome and powerfully built, and the two together exude the self-assurance of prominent clubmen as, in a deep and even voice, Harry states that in October of 1922 he purchased 50,000 shares of Sinclair Oil Company and 50,000 of Mammoth Oil Company, the Sinclair subsidiary which holds the Teapot Dome operating lease, giving "adequate security in exchange"—i.e., 8,000 shares of Standard Oil of New Jersey, 2,000 Standard Oil of New York, and 6,000 Reynolds Tobacco. In November of the same year a second block of 50,000 shares of Mammoth cost him $4,025,000 cash, and a third block of 55,000 was obtained in exchange for 23,000 shares of Reynolds. The committee thanks Harry for his co-operation but requests that he be available for further testimony. On February 18 he is subpoenaed to reappear the following week. Then he repeats his previous testimony and agrees to furnish books and records of his transactions. This takes only fifteen minutes and he is never called again.

The committee is not really looking for the sources of corruption, which probably lead to the late President Harding himself. Nor is it looking for a more general corruption within the capitalist system itself, which is booming and would therefore be a politically unpopular target. No, the committee will be satisfied to invalidate the leases and to punish Secretary of the Interior Albert B. Fall, who accepted the bribes, and those who actually gave them to him. Fall, Sinclair, and Edward L. Doheny (another major oil entrepreneur who had leased another naval oil reserve, in Elk Hills, California) are all eventually indicted. Fall is convicted for accepting bribes but neither Sinclair nor Doheny is convicted for giving any. In 1928, Sinclair is finally acquitted of the charge of conspiracy to defraud the government but the next year is found guilty of contempt of court for having jurors in the 1928 trial followed and of contempt of Congress for refusing to co-operate with a Senate investigating committee. Though Sinclair goes to jail for a term of six months, he remains president of Sinclair Oil until his retirement in 1949.

Teapot Dome is one of the two major political scandals of the twenties, the other being the Sacco-Vanzetti case, in many ways its reverse image. Though Teapot Dome is not surely a major event in Gertrude's life, it does come closer to home than, for example, Sacco and Vanzetti. It is at the least a cloud which hangs over her life and Harry's through the rest of this decade. To some extent, because it has been a blow to both Harry's pride and his investment portfolio, it will drive him to his most daring and successful mining speculation—the development of the huge Flin Flon tract (midway north in Manitoba, almost on the Saskatchewan border) into the Hudson Bay Mining and Smelting Company, the large Canadian producer of precious and industrial metals. And to some extent, Teapot Dome may drive Gertrude even deeper into her commissioned work. That is the context in which she prefers to see the Whitney name publicized, and she will have her wish many times this year.

Between Harry's appearances in Washington, he escapes to the new Forshala Plantation in Thomasville. From there he writes to Gertrude:

Dearest,

I am very disappointed you did not get down here. It would have cheered me up & I feel damn gloomy.

Nothing but health health health. [Liver] Spots are always getting a little better, but I wish they would hurry up as I am sick of this &

want to get out. Clarence McCormick is very nice & stays on. Andy Sage comes to-morrow & I think we will leave in about a week.

Old Corey is at Lew's & they are a nuisance. Keep dropping in & boring us.

I'm delighted about B.B. [Buffalo Bill]. O'Connor's opinion must have given you a real thrill.

I suppose I will go to Aiken about Feb. 20 or 22 & haven't got people yet. No energy to do it. I must send some wires but sort of don't care. Think I will get Sonny & Marie. Would like to see them.

Have you any plans? Better come to Aiken a little.

> Love,
> Harry

Gertrude has no time for Aiken. During the next several months she will take on at least three more commissions—a sculpture for the Mount Hope Community Mausoleum; a monument in Washington, D.C., to the Daughters of the American Revolution; and, most important, a memorial in St. Nazaire, France, where the American Expeditionary Forces landed June 26, 1917. All of these will receive considerable publicity but none so much as the Buffalo Bill Memorial, already popular in comparatively small preliminary versions. But now, early in the year when the final version is cast at the Brooklyn Bronze Works—a twelve-foot-high, thirteen-foot-long, three-ton statue; the largest ever made by a woman—there are announcements by the Buffalo Bill American Association of its plans for a sunset ("end of the trail") unveiling on July 4 in Cody, where Buffalo Bill's fourteen-year-old granddaughter will pull the string; and of Gertrude's own plan to exhibit the plaster original at the Grand Palais in the Paris Spring Salon. Colonel William F. ("Buffalo Bill") Cody! His cute granddaughter, posed almost always on a horse! Sunset! The Fourth of July! Gertrude Vanderbilt Whitney! Great-granddaughter of Commodore Vanderbilt! Wife of sportsman Harry Payne Whitney, whose stable will this season again earn almost a quarter of a million dollars in winnings (second among owners), plus almost half a million in breeding (first)! Cody! New York! Paris! These, through the end of July, will be the attractive ingredients for a stampede of journalists writing about Buffalo Bill and Gertrude, their families, their friends, their travels, their exploits, their careers.

At the end of March, while Gertrude is already hard at work on the new commissions, Juliana Force goes to Cody as her surrogate to inspect the foundation for the monument's fifteen-foot-high, almost two-hundred-foot-wide natural stone plinth and to seek local financial support in addresses to the Cody Club and the Women's Club. Mrs. Force admires the site, rising above the Shoshone River and facing the eastern entrance to Yellowstone Park with its snow-capped mountains, and speaks charmingly of the West, which she has never before visited. She also does an excellent job of explaining the background details of the commission and of the life behind it—Gertrude's struggle to succeed as a sculptor, even though a rich American woman. Her words are almost interchangeable with those spoken by Gertrude herself a few nights later at a national fund-raising dinner led by General John J. Pershing at New York's Biltmore Hotel, where it is announced that the entire project, plinth and all, will cost $250,000.

At the Paris Salon, Gertrude's *Buffalo Bill* receives *une médaille de Bronze*, the highest "award of honor" that can be given to a foreign artist. In May there is a Park Avenue street fair for the benefit of five major New York charities, and Gertrude donates a small replica of *Buffalo Bill* and one of the *Titanic Head*, until this time her most popular sculpture but now second most popular. On June 7 the press is invited to the Brooklyn foundry for a private viewing of the huge new finished bronze. Standing at about the height of *Buffalo Bill*'s stirruped left foot, Gertrude is flanked by Albert Ross, the architect who designed the plinth, and Ricardo Bertelli, who cast the statue. This image appears in newspapers all over the country, usually with a small insert of Jane Cody Garlow on horseback. Interest in the sculpture is so great now that several Fifth Avenue stores beg to exhibit the piece before it is shipped west. Gertrude confers with Ross and Bertelli. The size and weight of the monument are too great for any of the display windows. Mayor Hylan is contacted. He calls the park commissioner, F. D. Gallatin. Hurried arrangements are made to install the sculpture beside the Central Park Mall for one week beginning June 11. That day, on some sketch sheets for the St. Nazaire Memorial, Gertrude writes an account of her feelings:

I got a terrible kick out of my drive through the Park this morning. I didn't really think the B.B. had arrived but there he was looking the size of a house, covered with rags, surrounded by horses in a newly painted grey truck [trailer]. The vicissitudes of B.B. would fill a book —dull, except for its human side, or maybe inhuman. Anyway he has halted on this trip west for a few days in a fine spot & under unprecedented circumstances . . . where thousands of people every day can't help—no matter how much they want to—can't help but see him. He is still covered with dirty old clothes so I don't know how he will look, but if he does not look well it will be my own fault & not because of his setting. My own psychology interests me. At the unveiling of the 168th St. Monument I was too hot, embarrassed & upset to get any kick. Probably I won't today but the feeling I got just at the idea gave me more pleasure than the pleasure I have ever had from one of my works. When something is done, it is done & my interest flies to the next thing. There were so many moments during the last year when it vaguely entered my head that no one wanted my statue

(I admit it never worried me very much). People seemed to think I should be feeling badly & I suppose their reaction had a little effect on me—but it was a very little effect. My interest in the conception of the whole never for a moment waned & the effort which I had to put into it kept me far too busy to worry about details as to what someone might be thinking.

By the late afternoon when Gertrude returns to the Park the statue—still on its trailer which is obscured now by leafy branches—has, after some bickering between Commissioner Gallatin and Juliana Force, been placed properly, facing the setting sun. Gertrude hears him say, "Don't let's take the edge off Mrs. Whitney's pleasure."

Soon Mayor Hylan arrives with a delegation of Campfire Girls in American Indian costume and Boy Scouts in uniform. A juvenile band from the Hebrew Boys' Home plays the national anthem. Dr. George F. Kunz, president of the American Historic and Scenic Preservation Society (also vice-president of Tiffany and Company); Robert D. Dripps, secretary of the American Buffalo Bill Association; and Judge Elbert H. Gary, president of U. S. Steel, each say a few words, mostly about Buffalo Bill's "pioneer spirit," which they compare with that of Columbus, Shakespeare, and Beethoven, all represented in nearby statues.

This time we don't know if Gertrude is embarrassed. There are no clues in what she writes, on some more sketch sheets, the next day:

> The most important thing which came out of it all was that maybe? perhaps? possibly? certain people will be interested enough to give a replica of the statue to Central Park & to London.
>
> I wonder if I am, or am getting, conceited? I hope the weather clears up so that I can go & listen incog. to the remarks made by the passersby—that will get me over it, if I am which I often suspect myself of being. If conceit means admiring what you do, I am. If it means thinking your work superior to good work, I am not. I happen to like my conceptions, I couldn't do them if I didn't. The fact that they always fall short of my ideals is painful. . . . I suffer because I know they could be so much finer, but I enjoy because the child has been born & is my own.

Until now Gertrude has planned to go to Cody for the final unveiling and related festivities (a stampede, a rodeo). However the Central Park experience and the distracting events leading up to it, last-minute arrangements for Barbara's marriage to Barklie Henry, and the need to visit St. Nazaire before proceeding further with that monument, all make her reconsider. Despite the pace at which she has been working, she feels she has fallen behind and decides finally not to go to Cody but to leave for France a few days after the wedding. Meanwhile *Buffalo Bill's* westward journey continues to be news. The covered statue, carefully braced on a low-sided New York Central flatcar, attracts crowds in Albany, Buffalo, Erie, Cleveland, Evansville, Chicago—all commemorated by clippings from a service to which Gertrude subscribes. In Chicago the car is being switched to the Burlington and Quincy railroad on June 25, Barbara's wedding day.

The wedding list—at least, the Whitney side's family and friends—is one with which we are familiar. Flora Tower is the bride's matron of honor. Three cousins of the bride are among her attendants: Helen and Payne Whitney's daughter Joan, who will, a week and a half later, marry Charles Shipman Payson (with Barbara, then, as an attendant); Adele and J. Burden's daughter Shiela; and Regi and Cathleen Vanderbilt's daughter Mrs. Harry C. Cushing III, whose young stepmother Gloria Morgan Vanderbilt—younger, indeed, than Mrs. Cushing herself—has earlier in the year given birth to a girl recently christened Gloria Laura Vanderbilt. Complicated as these family relationships are, we emphasize only that Gertrude, already twice a grandmother, is now deeply moved by the marriage of her youngest child. That is her present emotional involvement—a sense of completion of a part of her life. On this June day—with the completion, too, of *Buffalo Bill* very much in her mind—it would be almost impossible for her to imagine the divorces which face Barbara and her other children and even more impossible to imagine how profoundly and painfully entwined her life will become with that of her new young sister-in-law Gloria Vanderbilt and her baby.

But now Gertrude's mind is on the wedding—the first (again, something she doesn't know) of many in Westbury. She delights in the yellow and blue arched floral arrangements she has supervised in Trinity church and the related ones in the gardens of her home. She delights in the groom, who has distinguished himself both in his studies and on the varsity crew at Harvard and who, like herself, has artistic yearnings, particularly literary—he is writing a novel (never published) and verse. She delights in the simple plans Barbie and Barklie (known as "Buz") have made for their brief honeymoon—a trip to Provincetown, Massachusetts, aboard the *Whileaway*, returning in time for Joan Whitney's wedding. She delights in a long intimate letter Buz sends right after the wedding, saying to "Dear Mamma—for I shall call you that now" that he has "never enjoyed two days more in my life, and the groom is supposed to have a rotten time. I do believe you worked harder to make it a success than you did on the *Buffalo Bill*, and I know how much that means."

❦

Gertrude sails June 28 aboard the White Star liner *Majestic*, carrying the largest number of first-class passengers (884) ever taken in or out of New York on one voyage. Reporters roam the pier and the cabin deck, interviewing the monumental personalities of the day. The theatrical producer Lee Shubert is in search of new European plays. Another producer, Morris Gest, will attempt to hire the deposed king of Greece to play the Knight when *The Miracle* reopens in August. The lawyer Max Steuer has just recently been consulted, at a fee rumored to have been $1,000 per hour, by the attorneys defending Leopold and Loeb in the Bobby Franks murder case. Murray Hulbert, president of the Board of Aldermen and an intimate of Governor Al Smith, who he is confident will get the Democratic nomination for the presidency and beat Coolidge, is a member of the American Olympic Committee; he is on his way to the games in Paris, after which he will consult with former Premier Georges Clemenceau and the new Premier, Edouard Herriot, on urban transportation. Lord Kenyon, pro-chancellor of the University of Wales, has attended Kenyon College's centennial celebration in Ohio and, while in New York, has studied the eleven-year-old Rockefeller Foundation, which he finds "interesting." Dr. Sikitsu Tanadote, a member of the Imperial Academy of Japan, has been in Washington trying to reform the restrictive U.S. immigration laws. . . . The list goes on, a very different sort from those of the prewar era when reporters, representing the public, were more interested in inherited wealth—and blood. Now they are interested in people who *do*, rather than inherit, things. No one boarding the *Majestic* receives more attention than Gertrude.

Aboard ship Gertrude gets into her usual routine of a very light breakfast; massage, bath; walking vigorously around the deck; a simple lunch; reading, writing, and sketching in a shaded deck chair or in her cabin; cocktails and dinner, most often at the captain's table. In her letters and sketches it is evident that she is still thinking a great deal about the completed *Buffalo Bill* and *The Daughters of the American Revolution* (in progress), even as she looks forward to resolving the final details of the scale and siting of the St. Nazaire Memorial. On the last day of the voyage she sends a telegram to Governor Ross of Wyoming:

REGRET INFINITELY THAT I AM UNABLE TO BE WITH YOU ALL TODAY. PLEASE CONVEY TO ALL MEMBERS OF THE ASSOCIATION MY BEST WISHES AND REGARDS. WOULD LIKE TO EXPRESS AGAIN MY APPRECIATION OF YOUR SYMPATHETIC AND UNFAILING INTEREST AND UNDERSTANDING DURING THE PAST TWO YEARS AND ALSO TELL YOU HOW DEEPLY I HAVE APPRECIATED THE HONOR PAID ME IN HAVING BEEN CHOSEN TO MAKE YOUR STATUE TO OUR GREAT AMERICAN PIONEER BUFFALO BILL.

In France she receives several congratulatory telegrams in reply, of which perhaps the most touching is from Jane Cody Garlow: JUST UNVEILED YOUR WONDERFUL STATUE OF MY BELOVED GRANDFATHER. BEST WISHES.

A few days later Gertrude learns that the road leading to the Buffalo Bill Memorial has been renamed Gertrude Vanderbilt Whitney Drive. But by then she is in St. Nazaire, entirely absorbed by the possibility of several magnificent sites along its rocky Brittany coast.

Gertrude has learned from the problems she has had, and continues to have, with other commissions. The day before leaving New York she has hurriedly entered into a contract with the St. Nazaire Association, protecting herself against the kind of situation she faces with the American Red Cross—i.e., consideration of another sculptor's work (Manship's) during the long period of fund raising and obtaining legislative approvals.

Attached to the "agreement to agree" is a rendering by Albert Ross of Electus D. Litchfield and Rogers, the same architect who designed *Buffalo Bill's* plinth. It shows a helmeted American soldier with arms outstretched, holding in his right hand, beneath the crosspiece, a large anachronistic sword. He stands on the back of an American eagle, with wings spread, perched on top of a columnar base which grows naturalistically from an outcropping of coastal rocks. In scale, the bronze soldier stands about fifteen feet tall, the bronze eagle spreads his wings about thirty-eight feet wide, and the stone base rises about seventy feet high. In symbolism—equally monumental—the rendering reads as three cruciform emblems of sacrifice: soldier, sword, and eagle.

Gertrude meets with the mayor of St. Nazaire and the administrator of bridges and highways. They show her various available sites past the dock and shipbuilding areas of the congested port. She selects a particularly dominant and rugged promontory. Already, in her mind, she can see the monument, surrounded by water at high tide, embracing the harbor; she soars with the image, knowing that the verticality of her conception and Ross's will be as right here as was the horizontality of the Buffalo Bill Memorial in Cody. Ross has already estimated that the cost of the base will not exceed $14,000—or possibly less in France. Roynon Cholmeley-Jones, chairman of the St. Nazaire Association, has assured her he will raise $100,000 by subscription. Even allowing for the cost of fund raising, and for Ross's fee (presumably modest—say, ten per cent of $14,000) and her own (whatever that may turn out to be), and for site preparation and other contingencies, there should still be more than enough money left for casting the huge bronze. In Gertrude's mind, so optimistic now, the monument is already erected, shimmering in the summer sunlight. The harbor, the world looks beautiful, more and more beautiful.

Later in July Harry writes from Westbury to Gertrude in Paris that Barbie is pregnant, that it "probably happened the first week," that she "seems contented and rather pleased," and that "Buz is splendid. Has much sympathy and understanding." Harry continues:

> Baby coming middle of March—I think will upset all his spring term work and think for their future good—Barbie's health—not only in those months, but maybe forever and also the baby's health—they had better seriously consider coming home Jan. 1.
>
> We should have come back from Japan at once [a reference to Ger-

trude's early pregnancy on their own honeymoon]. If they stay over, they *should take* a small house in London probably. . . .

I went to Newport to get Gladys & kids—also to talk house to your Mother. [Mrs. Vanderbilt is about to move from 1 West 57th Street, farther up Fifth Avenue, to a smaller mansion, the home of the late George Gould at 1 East 67th.]

Regi has been upsetting her & Anderson was ready to quit.

Gladys agreed that as the sentimental feeling was no more we should still go ahead as before planned. Regi was drunk & apparently is most of the time—Gladys wanted me to take him to task but that is impossible. Gloria is no good. . . .

Gertrude cannot have been in Paris for long. (Rollie Cottenet and Forbes Watson, both of whom she would have wanted to see, write letters expressing regrets at missing her there.) Probably she stays just long enough to shop for clothes and to make arrangements for another retrospective exhibition. This one, to be held at Durand-Ruel in December, will be about half the size of the previous year's show at Wildenstein but will, like it, emphasize commissioned work and, unlike it, have the protection—almost mandatory in Paris—of an elaborate introduction. Camille Mauclair, the writer—once a distinguished disciple of Mallarmé but now forced to do some commissioned work—begins by quoting the late great Rodin on Gertrude:

> "I see many foreign artists who come to show me their sketches and ask my advice. Among them are women and sometimes fashionable women, whom I distrust. They think they are making sculpture to amuse themselves and astonish their friends but they have not got the moral courage necessay to truly liberate themselves from the prejudices of their milieu. There is one of them, however, who is an exception. Aristocratic and very rich, she works with the sincerity and fervor of a poor artist whose ideals are the only luxury. She despises snobbishness. She has renounced everything for our so hard yet so beautiful profession. She is an American called Gertrude Whitney. She has the gift. I think she'll go very far. Remember her name and try to follow her exhibitions."

Mauclair goes on to place Gertrude in the tradition of "the very lively school of American sculpture of which the great Augustus Saint-Gaudens was the initiator," followed by her teachers James Fraser and Andrew O'Connor. The right names are dropped (note: not Hendrik Andersen's), the most monumental accomplishments are recited.

≈

When Gertrude returns in August, she goes right to work on the St. Nazaire Memorial and other commissions. As usual now, Juliana Force helps her with much of the correspondence and details, while at the same time running a very active program at the Whitney Studio Club. Since early in the year Mrs. Force, with the assistance of Alexander Brook, has administered a series of exhibitions "selected by individual artists [all members of the Whitney Studio Club] with a free hand to choose the work that most appealed to them, with the single proviso that no artist could contribute his own work to his own exhibition." Important shows have included "Early American [Folk] Art," selected by Henry Schnakenberg, who shares this then unfashionable interest with Mrs. Force; "Picasso, Duchamp, de Zayas, and Braque," selected by Charles Sheeler; "Portraits and Religious Works," selected by Yasuo Kuniyoshi. But Mrs. Force is most involved with the first exhibition of work by Reginald Marsh (scheduled for November) and is also expanding the Club's activities to include traveling shows.

Flora and Rod are now in Westbury. Barbie and Buz have settled in Oxford where he intends to continue his studies. Marie is expecting a baby in December; she and Sonny are temporarily in San Francisco, where he is working, particularly on the development of Flin Flon, in Harry's Metals Exploration Company, while waiting still for the completion of the perjury phase of the Evan Fontaine case.

Not until Christmas do Gertrude and Harry have most of their family with them for a big dinner in New York—Flora and Rod, Marie and Sonny, Regi and Gloria, Cathleen and Harry (Cushing). Four days later Marie has a seven-and-a-half-pound boy, Harry Payne Whitney II. Gertrude, less than two weeks from her fiftieth birthday, is now three times a grandmother and is looking forward to news from England of Barbie's pregnancy.

⪻ *1925*

As last year, Gertrude will try to devote most of her time to commissions, but now she will be increasingly distracted by all kinds of family problems. In late February, at her Eighth Street studio, she has just privately shown the final model for her St. Nazaire Memorial—modified only in such details as the eagle's slightly lessened wing span and the more pronounced cruciformity of the sword hilt—when she leaves for Europe with the announced purpose of arranging for the casting of the bronze. However, since the turn of the year she has been planning to be with Barbie during the last month of what has been a difficult pregnancy. As early as

January 3, Mabel Gerry, then in London, has found "a suitable house, properly staffed"—which is an understatement. Chandos House, built by Robert Adam in the early 1770s on Queen Anne Street in Marylebone, is a Georgian masterpiece, justly famous for its fine projecting porch and covered entry and its magnificent staircase with wrought-iron banisters. As to staff, Mabel has arranged for two footmen, "the odd man," one kitchenmaid, four housemaids, "a good cook," a scullery maid, and an "absolutely honest butler" who "will get a boy on buttons."

Gertrude's crossing is stormy, her stay in London—with only brief visits to Paris—even stormier. Barbie's complications—about each of which Gertrude writes in detail to Harry—are depressing enough, but in addition there are hints that Flora's and Rod's marriage is not going well and, on top of this, the more sudden news, just three days before Barbie delivers her baby, that Harry has taken a terrible fall while playing polo in Aiken. According to the *Times*, "his mount tripped and, after falling, rolled on the rider. . . . The accident was caused when the mallet swung between the horse's forelegs and threw him." Harry writes to Gertrude—from his bed, in a rather shaky hand—just four days after the fall and one after hearing that Barbie has given birth to a girl who will be named Gertrude Whitney Henry:

Dearest

I have had a horrid Aiken & this fall has made it real good.

I overdid the first three days—polo, tennis & squash—& think I knocked something out. Anyway I spent most of the next week in bed, felt sick & not hungry & heart felt thumpy.

Then I began to get around & decided to play polo the day Dev got here, & got a bad fall. Did not come to for five minutes or more. Dev thought I was dead & the Doctor who was only a few feet away said he expected me to be crushed in—collarbone & quite a concussion— don't remember anything, even how I got home & what I said to people in house or to Dr's when they were fixing me up.

So had bad headache for several days—mind not always clear—& no food or hunger for 3 days—funny how it acts on stomach nerves.

Today had coffee & couple of spoonfuls cereal & am glad to wait till night. Long night.

Dr's say I can go home in day or two—just in time to miss Flora. . . .

So glad to hear last night late about Barbie & am waiting for more news & a little worried. Much love to her & to you. I wish you were here.

Do not see anybody except perhaps Dev every other day for five minutes. . . . But head cleared up yesterday afternoon.

More love,
Harry

Within the context of more details concerning Barbie's delivery—twenty-two hours, by forceps—Gertrude replies:

> . . . What bad luck to break a collar bone. I know it is very painful & prevents you doing the things you want to. I hope it is the left side anyway. [It was.] . . . I hope darling you are getting on well. Of course I wish I could be with you, but then you don't think much of me as a nurse.

Good nurse or not, it is clear now in a flurry of letters and cablegrams between Gertrude and Harry that she would have returned, had it not been for Barbie's continuing illness and Flora's mounting marital problems. Gertrude spends countless hours comforting Barbie and trying to reason with Flora who, like Rod, wants a divorce but cannot agree on any of its terms, especially those having to do with custody of the children. Gertrude meets with Flora's London lawyer. Harry, even in his weakened condition and suffering from constant headaches, meets with her New York lawyer.

Besides their daughters' problems, there are Sonny's. Immediately after Harry's polo accident he comes east to be with his father. However, within a few days of his arrival he is served papers by representatives of Evan Fontaine and her mother, initiating yet another suit, this one evidently arranged through a corrupt Westchester judge. Harry must go through more painful meetings with lawyers before, at their suggestion, Sonny returns to the West Coast. As Harry writes to Gertrude, "Even Sonny said that you and I were not getting much from our children but trouble & worry. I wish I were with you or you here & the troubles lumped together. . . . It's all a horrible spring."

This season is so horrible, so completely dominated by emotional and physical pain, that Harry barely mentions the wedding of his sister Dorothy Straight to Leonard Knight Elmhirst. What pleasure her second marriage might have given him is probably neutralized by present events, though it is unlikely that, under any circumstances, Harry would have taken his new brother-in-law to his bosom. Dorothy, widowed since 1918, has devoted most of her time to her children and to liberal politics, including her continuing support of the *New Republic*. Through her late husband's philanthropic interest in several programs at Cornell University, she has met Elmhirst, who is working his way through the agriculture school by teaching English. Seven years her junior, he is at least as idealistic as she and still rebelling against the feudal values of his father, a landed Yorkshire clergyman. He has earned his bachelor's and master's degrees at Trinity College in Cambridge; spent the war years in Mesopotamia and India (where he has been attracted to the anti-imperialist teachings of the poet Rabindranath Tagore), and returned to Bengal, after studies at Cornell, to initiate education and rural development courses for the agriculture school of Tagore's International University. Gertrude's devoted friend Charles Draper—who, during this period, visits Harry frequently and then reports to her in long, gossipy, sympathetic letters—describes Elmhirst as "quite a nice crank." That may well be what Harry thought too. Whatever his distracted and headache-ridden thoughts on April 3, the date of the very small wedding in Westbury, at Dorothy's home near his own (Harry is not well enough to attend the ceremony but is visited immediately afterward by the bride and groom), the marriage will turn out to be by far one of the happiest in his family and will within a few years produce one of the most remarkable and successful contemporary experiments in rural redevelopment and education—the progressive school and cultural center at Dartington Hall in England.

Again, time itself rushes forward, but for Gertrude, as for Harry, it drags. Even in a rather summary letter, written in Paris—Gertrude's beloved Paris!—to Mrs. Force sometime in early April, we have that sense:

Everything has been dreary here . . . so as I had no cheerful news I didn't write. Poor Barbie had a bad time all around . . . gave Buz and me many anxious times. I got in a specialist, of course, & both he & her regular doctor agreed that absolute rest was necessary for two months at least. Then F[lora] & R[od] arrive on the scene with a more acute situation than ever before. I straighten that out to the satisfaction of both, R. goes back, & F. within two weeks changes her mind!

F. & children are living at my studio here, so I haven't got a quiet spot in sight. But I try to buck myself up with the thought that at least I have been able to be of some help. This altruistic point of view does not somehow bring the comfort to me which in principle it ought! At any rate I got away at last from London for a few days & could rinse my mind with practical work on the St. N. The enlargement will be ready Sept. 1st, so I shall return then. In order that the work can be finished on the fatal day, my casts have to go to the bronze foundry Sept. 15th. Of course incidentally I have worried about Untermyer. [She has received a commission from Samuel Untermyer, the great liberal lawyer and philanthropist, to do three pairs of bronze gates and related figures for a shrine at Woodlawn Cemetery in memory of his wife.] Six weeks loss of time in America on the doors is pretty serious & two months & a half to do them in looks pretty short. Well, it just can't be helped—so that's that.

I never was in love with England & now I hope & pray I shall never have to go back there after I sail.

. . . Met three of Duse's & Duse's daughter's friends. [The great Italian actress Eleonora Duse died the previous year, and Gertrude is hoping to receive a memorial commission.] . . . I have met a few people I like but they are cosmopolitan, just happened to be born in the British Isles. . . .

When Gertrude returns from Paris to London, Barbara's health is no better, and Gertrude, like Harry, begins to get headaches. Everything is going wrong. She cannot extend the lease at Chandos House beyond April 30 but finally finds another house. May 1 She writes Harry.

Dearest,

This is moving day. Mrs. Russell, my present landlady (who has been filthy) moved out at 12 & we had to do all arranging from then until 5 when Barbie leaves Chandos House. I had to make quite a lot of changes but anyway her rooms look very cheerful & gay. The outlook is on Regents Park facing South. I am waiting for her now. She is being moved in a chair which will be put into a sort of ambulance. . . . Baby is here already. This is a general plan of the house. [Gertrude sketches a professional-looking plan.] Over Barbie's room I get a room, Marie [Gertrude's maid] next on the front. Buz or Flora in room over nurse's. One bath on that floor. Nothing over Barbie's room. On the ground floor billiard room and dining room. One flight up big very nice living room, the whole of front, & smaller back sitting room.

May 3d. Barbie arrived in good shape. . . . She had a good night's sleep, likes her room very much. I had it looking quite gay with flowers and bright cushions. One bed (for the day) in the bay window where she has a lovely view of the park. . . . Buz arrived yesterday late & has spent practically all day today with her. . . .

Wednesday I am going to Paris for three days to see about work & also to get a little change. Flora is coming to stay in the house so that someone will be here. . . . When I come back I am hoping & praying that [Barbie] will be able to move a little & then as Buz is not returning till the end of the month I shall probably be of some use myself. Of course we are not out of the woods, still I can't help feeling encouraged.

I have been to a few nice dinners, several times to the play & today motored up in the Cambridge direction.

It gets warm for a few hours only, rains part of every day and is generally vile.

Much love dearest. I hope you continue to improve. The new house & grounds must be looking wonderfully. I never thought I should be so homesick for America!

G.

"The new house" could be either of two being built at this time on the Westbury property: one for themselves, one for Flora—probably the former. Though Harry and Gertrude had begun planning them early the previous year, within the context of more serious concerns, Harry writes no more about them now than he did about Dorothy's marriage. But again Charles Draper reports:

> . . . the house looks fine inside & out but your hands will be full putting the finishing touches on a whole lot of things; nearly every unfinished spot I asked about was awaiting your return & decision about colors, kinds of furniture, etc. The architect has a way of planting maple furniture (it all looks to me as if it belonged in the cook's room) about the house and H.P.W. is fed up on it, you will have to send it all away and suggest something else. . . . Tell Flora & Rod that they are getting the swellest road I have seen in a long time. Their house is getting hidden in the trees. I did not go up—

Except for the last short trip to Paris, and one to Duse's grave, in Asolo, Italy, Gertrude remains until the end of May in London. There, besides going frequently to theater, she attempts once again to write a play of her own. Like earlier fragments of fiction, this play is unfinished and untitled —indeed, most of the characters in it are unnamed—however, it represents much work (forty-four pages of notes and dialogue) and an ambitious concept. The theme, as outlined, concerns a "Hero" (one of the characters never identified by name but only in this way) who, though successful in the eyes of society—rich, attractive, and powerful—considers himself a failed mediocrity and is on the verge of suicide. Hero complains to God that he has "never had a chance," mainly because his mother was "a foolish, vain woman" and his father gave him "everything from the time [he] was a small boy." God offers Hero three more lives—i.e., three more sets of parents, representing the aristocracy (which is very nearly his station in real life, anyway), the middle class, and the poor. In each life his selfishness—first accompanied by pride, second by dissatisfaction, and third by ambition—leads to the loss of his beloved and to violent death. In each, Hero's dying words are: "I never had a chance."

Though the incomplete play is a murky mixture of expressionism and drawing-room comedy, it is clear as to Gertrude's continuing ambivalence about Harry and her present pessimism about life and love in general.

After three and a half mostly miserable months abroad, Gertrude arrives in New York on June 5. She is just too late to see the Tenth Annual Exhibition of the Whitney Studio Club, the largest yet—356 works by approximately half that number of artists—so large that Mrs. Force has had to install it in the Anderson Galleries at Park Avenue and 59th Street. Gertrude can only satisfy her interest by looking at the catalogue. Most of the names, each typically represented by two works, are familiar by now: . . . Beal . . . Benton . . . Brook . . . Campbell . . . Chanler . . . Davis . . . Dos Passos . . . Flanagan . . . Glackens . . . Gropper . . . Hopper

. . . Kuniyoshi . . . Lescaze (the architect, recently arrived from Switzerland) . . . Marsh . . . Nakian . . . Schnakenberg . . . Sheeler . . . Sloan . . . Soyer . . . Spencer . . . There are no real surprises for Gertrude—one for us. Near the end of the list, just before Gertrude's *Study for St Nazaire Memorial,* we find two sculptures, *Study from Life* and *Crysis* (sic), by Flora Tower.

≈

The summer is hectic. There is the decorating to be done at Westbury (Gertrude commissions Max Kuehne to design her bedroom furniture on which he paints fanciful animals and flowers); the commissioned work to get caught up on; and new commissions to go after, of which the most important is the Providence (Rhode Island) War Memorial. This opportunity is brought to Gertrude's attention by Miss Katherine Minahan, who has been trying to interest influential people in placing a duplicate of the St. Nazaire Memorial in New York Harbor and wants now to act as Gertrude's agent in processing the Providence commission through various jurisdictional committees. Their arrangement is loose. There is no written contract but, rather, a vague verbal understanding that Gertrude will pay Miss Minahan for her time and reimburse her for expenses.

As so often in the past, the situation looks encouraging: Miss Minahan seems to know her way around, and Providence has, soon after the war, appropriated $300,000 for a memorial, delayed mostly by disagreement as to the proper site and the "right" artist. Now several sites have received preliminary approval, and Gertrude is as "right," as famous as any commission sculptor in the country. The more she is briefed by Miss Minahan, particularly as to the city's desire for trophy and record rooms within the monument, the more Gertrude believes that the solution should be basically architectural, with perhaps a symbolic sculpture of "Providence" at or within the base. What she has in mind is a huge, fortresslike tower, similar to some she has seen in Europe but unlike anything in America, with the possible exception of the Pilgrim monument in Provincetown. She meets with Albert Ross to discuss feasibility and approximate cost, and then on July 7 goes to Providence with Juliana Force and Katherine Minahan to inspect the sites and, the next morning, to make her first presentation to Mayor Gainer and other city officials.

The meeting goes well. Gertrude, without even preliminary sketches, talks about her concept in pretty much the terms of her 1920 essay on "The 'Useless' Memorial," explaining once again that a memorial should be just that and nothing else, though pointing out that she does intend to provide rooms in the base. She stresses the need for centrality and proper scale, comparing the proposed tower with the Nelson monument in Trafalgar Square, the Arc de Triomphe in Paris, and the Bunker Hill monument in the middle of Boston Common. To give Providence something of such distinction will require a very large monument, probably not less than 250 feet tall.

After the meeting, which lasts about an hour, the mayor announces to the press that he has been impressed by Mrs. Whitney's presentation, that a committee will review it during the next several weeks, and that "In justice to Mrs. Whitney, we could not disclose the nature or character of her proposed design, since to do so might involve the infringement of her idea by another."

Initially, the stories and editorials in the Providence papers are sympathetic. Encouraged by these and the favorable reaction of his committee, the mayor authorizes Gertrude to proceed with detailed plans and a model. Working closely with Albert Ross, she spends a considerable part of the summer designing a tower—finally octagonal in shape—topped by an open-arched "Temple of Sacrifice" intended to contain a beacon visible for thirty miles. As the studies advance, the height is fixed at 270 feet, the width of the octagonal base at 70. In an attempt to keep cost down, the memorial is to be constructed of brick and terra cotta on a steel frame. To relieve the heaviness of these materials and give them life, particularly at night, each face of the tower is to be lighted by exterior torches (in addition to the beacon at the top). As this gigantic illuminated pedestal soars on paper—higher and higher, in sketch after sketch—so does its cost. Ross now estimates $500,000.

The Providence War Memorial is at this point—i.e., almost ready for translation into a scaled model and presentation to Mayor Gainer's committee—when, September 4, Gertrude's youngest brother Regi dies at Sandy Point Farm in Portsmouth, Rhode Island, following two violent hemorrhages. The newspapers there and all over the world say he dies "suddenly," but it is difficult to accept this word within the context of his obituaries, which reconstruct the life of a gambling, womanizing, heavy-drinking, hard-riding playboy, with emphasis on the Canfield case and his most recent marriage to Gloria Morgan. No, there is an inevitability about his dying young (at forty-five), dying fast—if not "suddenly"—as he had lived. Besides, in addition to the warnings inherent in his life itself, there have been more specifically medical warnings, and his mother is with him when he dies.

For Gertrude, Regi's death is the final crushing event in a year of crushing events. He is the third brother she has lost. Of four, only Cornelius survives; and of seven children, only he and she and Gladys. These are painful statistics, memories, ghosts, which fill Gertrude's mind as Harry arranges for Regi's entombment in the Vanderbilt mausoleum at New Dorp: the private train, the limousines, the chartered ferry—all a hauntingly familiar pattern.

With the gloomy arrangements made for the return trip, Gertrude and Harry take the train and a car to Portsmouth. Probably on the way they talk a lot about their children. Barbie's letters have been increasingly cheerful. Little Gertrude, or "Gerta" as she and Buz call the baby, is healthy, and it is evident that Barbie's own health is improving. In a recent letter to Gertrude she has said about what Sonny said to Harry earlier in the year: ". . . you are such a wonderful person & what a hard time you've had with us three!" But Sonny's troubles with Evan Fontaine are about over and, in addition to his work on Flin Flon, he has just joined the Colonial Air Transport board of directors, following another interest of Harry's. And Flora is in La Bourboule, in the Auvergne Province of France, quietly getting her divorce, happy in that decision, and concerned only "to know that Papa is improving so slowly." So there are a few bright spots, if only glimmers of optimism, in the general gloom.

In Portsmouth the world becomes dark again. Regi's widow, Gloria, has returned with her mother from New York the day before Gertrude and Harry arrive. The friction between the twenty-year-old widow and Gertrude's mother, now eighty, is already apparent. The dowager Mrs. Vanderbilt is in charge. She has made the arrangements for the funeral at St. Mary's Episcopal Church, near Regi's home. She has dictated who shall sit in each of the private compartments on the train to New York—she in one; Gloria in another; and Regi's daughter Cathleen, who will arrive the next day from California where she has been traveling with the Mackays, in the last. Gloria is no match for the weight of Mama's years, authority, and money.

When Cathleen arrives there is more friction. In her autobiography,* Gloria tries to spare her stepdaughter the pain of seeing Regi, whose face has been distorted by the hemorrhaging, and says, "You can't go in there." Cathleen thinks Gloria is refusing to let her see her own father. She screams, "How dare you!" and leaves the house.

"With that leaving," Gloria writes, "the first link in the heavy Vanderbilt chain snapped in two." But, of course, that is an oversimplification. If other links have not already snapped, the chain is at least a rusty tangle of mutual resentments and frustrations. Only Harry—a Whitney "who could put his hands on five million in cash at an hour's notice"—is treated sympathetically in this section of Gloria's book "for his tenderness of heart and his fineness of character and his splendid face" and for giving her "his check for $12,000 for mine and [Little] Gloria's immediate personal expenses."

* Here we are quoting from Gloria Morgan Vanderbilt's first autobiography, *Without Prejudice* (E. P. Dutton, 1936). In 1958, *Double Exposure, A Twin Autobiography*, by Mrs. Vanderbilt and her twin sister Thelma Lady Furness was published by David McKay Company. For our purposes, there is no need for detailed comparison between the two texts. Enough to say that there are inconsistencies in fact and tone. The earlier book is closer to the events surrounding Regi's death and the subsequent Gloria Vanderbilt custody case, and therefore more emotionally transparent. The later book is cooler in tone, more carefully written—indeed, at times, like a legal brief.

During the trip to New York and for some time thereafter, Gloria sends Little Gloria and her nurse to The Breakers, which pleases her mother-in-law. However, in New York there is still more friction. There, the limousines are waiting to take the Vanderbilt party onto the ferry and over to New Dorp. Gloria wants her mother-in-law to join her in the first car. Mrs. Vanderbilt refuses: the widow always drives alone in the first car. Gloria suffers through the ritual, thinking "how bitterly [Regi] had contested every step of his thumb-ruled existence—every moment of that restricted and charted life of his—and how he tried but could escape none of it—for here he lay now with the Vanderbilt dead." Again there are oversimplifications, but they indicate a mounting anger directed toward the Vanderbilts and an emotional conflict between trying to please and attack the family, a conflict both aggravated and curbed by her economic dependence.

Even this soon after Regi's death, Gloria knows that, by Vanderbilt standards, she has been left comparatively little money—$500,000 outright and dower rights in the houses and stables. Since she is still a minor, even this is tied up in trust. The rest, about $5,000,000 (after the payment of Regi's large debts, including, for example, an unpaid butcher's bill of $14,000), is divided equally between Cathleen, who is twenty-one, and Little Gloria, who is one. "From this moment," Gloria writes, "I was never to make a move that entailed the expenditure of money in which I could act as a free agent."

Later in the month, as Gertrude stays on at The Breakers with her mother and Little Gloria, there is talk of a memorial sculpture of Regi. Whether because that would be too painful for Gertrude or because she wants to resume work on the commissions she has already started, she highly recommends Jo Davidson for the job. Again, Gloria makes an effort to please. She writes Gertrude that she is "glad to hear that Mrs. Vanderbilt is well and that Little Gloria has taken a place in your hearts." She "cannot think of anyone who would be more advisable than Jo Davidson to make the bust of Regi." She will gather photographs and send them to Jo. She thanks Gertrude "for all [her] sweetness."

Again, Gloria is trying to please, but as the saga continues into the fall and into many seasons to come, there is the other side too—lawyers; the liquidation of Regi's properties on which she realizes another $130,000 ($45,000 for Sandy Point farm, bought by Regi's neighbor Moses Taylor, Gertrude's suitor of long ago); the successful application to the New York Surrogate's Court for $4,000 a month to support and maintain Little Gloria; and, perhaps most shocking to the Vanderbilts, the decisions to rebaptize Little Gloria as a Catholic and to live abroad, closer to her own relatives, several of whom are in England and France.

It is a saga which will move, relentlessly through the years, closer and closer to Gertrude. But now she plunges back into her work, particularly the Providence War Memorial. In mid-November she and Albert Ross revisit Providence and study the best site that has been offered, presently occupied by the Central Fire Station. A month later they, Juliana Force, and Katherine Minahan are prepared to make a full presentation to Mayor Gainer's committee.

Where at the last meeting Gertrude had relied on only a few penciled notes to convey the spirit of what she wanted to do, now she has a prepared speech with extra copies for the press; a scale model of the tower with photographs of it; prints of Ross's rendering, in relation to existing buildings; site plans; and a detailed budget ($478,500). Gertrude presents the background of her interest in the commission, explains why she and Ross have decided on the particular site, scale, and type of monument. "I believe first and foremost a war memorial should epitomize the spirit of the war . . . should never be mistaken for a bank, a church spire, a club or a hotel. . . ."

As in July, the mayor and his committee are impressed by Gertrude's charm, sincerity, and style. As then, they recognize that the war has meant a great deal to her; that she is, in a sense, "a veteran"; that she (and they) will receive much more publicity than they would using a less well known sculptor (or architect). And now they are additionally impressed by the thoroughness of the presentation and her willingness to guarantee personally that the memorial will be completed for not more than $500,000. That guaranty, too, they realize, has a very different meaning from one given by the usual sculptor.

The committee votes for Gertrude's design, subject to the City Council appropriating an additional $200,000 and approving the relocation of the fire station. The next day, December 16, the newspapers in Providence and elsewhere are full of stories and pictures of the new memorial. Two days later the Providence Post of the American Legion endorses the design. It takes two more days for the local chapter of the American Institute of Architects to voice its objections. The group dislikes everything about Gertrude's memorial—its location, its "alien style," its alien (i.e., non-local) designers, its magnitude, its cost. They offer, without fees to themselves or expense to the city, to submit a design by January 28 that will come within the original $300,000 appropriation and be simpler, more dignified, more *useful*. Mayor Gainer, various councilmen, and the Legion again support Gertrude's design. Other politicians and architects support the local A.I.A. There are angry editorials and letters in the local papers supporting both sides of the controversy. However, since Providence has waited since the war to proceed with the memorial to its dead, there are no convincing arguments against waiting one more month to see what the A.I.A. comes up with.

There the matter stands—completely unresolved—at the end of the year. At the same time, complications in connection with the St. Nazaire Memorial are mounting. During the summer Andrew O'Connor, in Paris, has sent two cables to Gertrude, the first simply advising her that this memorial must be approved by the American Battle Monuments Commission (General John J. Pershing, Chairman), and the second stating that such approval is certain. However, in early September, at the time of Regi's death, Gertrude receives word from Washington that the nine-man Fine Arts Commission (headed by Charles Moore, who has given her trouble in the past, but also including Gertrude's old friend William Adams Delano) recommends that the War Memorial Commission, under its jurisdiction, rather than the American Battle Monuments Commission approve *St. Nazaire*. It is a dizzying and frustrating bureaucratic tangle, which leads in October to senatorial recommendations for design changes.

Working with Juliana Force, it takes Gertrude almost four weeks to compose a letter of eight typed pages to General Pershing, summarizing the previous correspondence, including previous American and French approvals, and advising him that the Fine Arts Commission has now

> suggested several changes in my design which, had they been made at an earlier stage of the work, I might have considered. If these changes were made now (even admitting that I would consent to such a proposition) there would be no possibility of erecting the memorial on schedule. The members of the St. Nazaire Committee are unwilling to extend the time of the unveiling, both because of their completed arrangements and consequent publicity, and also because of the time and expense involved in another year's work. . . . I very much want your opinion in the matter and will appreciate whatever help you may give me in straightening out this misunderstanding.

The letter is effective. On behalf of General Pershing, General Hersey contacts Senator Reed and, though the Fine Arts Commission will not budge in approving the design, it is willing to permit erection because of the advanced stage of the project. At the end of the year plans for an elaborate unveiling ceremony in St. Nazaire in June are moving forward at the same time as all progress halts on Gertrude's Providence War Memorial.

⇒ *1926*

January 9—two days after attending the large wedding of Consuelo Vanderbilt II (the daughter of Mr. and Mrs. William K. Vanderbilt II) to Earl E. T. Smith of the uncommon Newport Smiths—Gertrude and her mother sail for Europe aboard the *Leviathan*.

The Roman IIs above indicate the passage of time. So does the date. Gertrude is fifty-one.

The six and a half weeks' trip is planned partly as a birthday treat; partly as a way of comforting Mama, who has been extremely depressed since Regi's death, the resulting problems with Gloria, and her own recent move from the 57th Street mansion; partly so that Gertrude can supervise the final details of casting the St. Nazaire Memorial as well as resolve some open matters concerning its unveiling and attendant publicity; and partly just to get some sun and rest on the Italian Riviera. Harry, Flora (now divorced), and Neily (now Gertrude's only surviving brother, Mama's only surviving son) all come to see them off in a heavy snow-storm. Again, Gertrude is one of the passengers most prominently noticed in the press, but one couple receives more attention than she or anyone else: Ellin Mackay and Irving Berlin have just been married and are starting their honeymoon.

Despite the inauspicious weather, the crossing to Cherbourg is "marvelous for any time of year . . . the service and food excellent," as we know from a Line-A-Day which Gertrude begins aboard ship. Except for spending time with Mama, Gertrude does pretty much as always: she takes Turkish baths and massages, walks, reads, writes. A black-bordered letter to Gladys gives a better sense than the rather stark Line-A-Day of the voyage and the first few days in Paris:

> Dearest Gladys,
> You would be very pleased if you could see Mama today. Just as you said, she became a different person after two days. She takes the greatest interest in everything. On the boat the luxury, ease, comfort of it all amazed her. She liked seeing the people, she speculated as to who and what they were, was disappointed that I did not have the occasion to present Mr. Berlin! and we had such a nice time talking about books etc. Of course we often don't agree but that makes it all the more interesting. She did not seem to mind the trip from Cherbourg and we were lucky to land at 10 A.M. & arrive in Paris before 9. We have lunched together, Rumpelmayer, Colombian Hotel every day, have done some shopping [at Yvonne Davidson's, among other places] but I have been out for dinner every night but one. As she goes to bed at 9:30, I don't think she cares. I want to get this letter off tomorrow so goodbye & love,
>
> G.

The dinners and the parts of the day when Gertrude is not with Mama are spent mostly with sculptors, particularly Andrew O'Connor, who has been overseeing the casting in sections of the huge St. Nazaire sculpture and goes with her to the foundry; and, less frequently, Jo Davidson and Herbert Haseltine. After nine days Gertrude and Mama take the train to

Bordighera, where they stay at the Hotel Cap Ampeglio, enjoying its spectacular view of the Mediterranean coast. As Gertrude tells Gladys in another letter, Mama "seems quite happy sitting about in the sun, walking in the town, & motoring short distances." They take Italian lessons together and try to read the Italian papers "with more or less success," and "never talk about family troubles or household difficulties but about books, traveling, and abstract subjects."

Gertrude makes one short trip alone to Alassio, where the Davidsons are staying with the famous journalist and social reformer—less neutrally, the "muckraker"—Lincoln Steffens and his new young wife and infant son, in a villa high on a hill overlooking the town and the Ligurian Sea. In her Line-A-Day, Gertrude records that she dined with them and comments, "Delightful people, delightful spot." In his *Autobiography*, Steffens says a little more: "Mrs. Harry Payne Whitney, the sculptress, drove over from Bordighera to dinner, full of humorous complaint that artists and writers were all snobs who held her off as a rich woman instead of taking her in as an artist."

When Gertrude and Mama return to Paris, Gertrude again spends a lot of time with O'Connor, but even more now with various ambassadors in the American, French, and Italian embassies—particularly with Myron Herrick, the American ambassador to France, and with various Salon officials. Although the details of these meetings are not spelled out, it is clear that they all have to do with the unveiling of *St. Nazaire* and the exhibition of its plaster model at the Spring Salon. Gertrude complains tersely that one official "was too tight to talk business."

The trip home is rougher than the one coming over. Gertrude again records Turkish baths, massages, walks, and now many cocktails, but the most cryptic entry is "Lost Providence wireless." That could only have contained bad news. While Gertrude has been away, Providence newspaper clippings have been carefully mounted for her in yet another scrapbook. A few of their headlines pretty well tell the story:

LATEST DESIGN FOR MEMORIAL

Local Architects Offer Ornamental and Useful Plan

VETERANS DISCUSS MEMORIAL DESIGNS

TWO WAR MEMORIAL REPORTS PLANNED

MEMORIAL BOARD WAS "HYPNOTIZED"

COUNCIL ABANDONS ALL PRESENT WAR MEMORIAL PLANS

February 25, the day after her arrival and reunion with Harry, she writes, "Studio. Have been asked to go in competition for a monument in Union Sq. Accepted." For the next three months "Studio" and "Worked" will be the two most frequent entries in her book—and increasingly after

Harry and Flora leave for Aiken on March 2. Interspersed with work are frequent luncheons or dinners with Mama, with Barbie and Buz, with Flora after she returns from Aiken in mid-March, and with such old friends as Phil Carroll, Charles Draper, Jimmie Appleton, the Delanos, and Alice Nicholas, who is helping Gertrude complete the decoration of the new Long Island house. Many of these family and social events are combined with an afternoon at the Metropolitan Museum or an art gallery, and frequently in the evening she goes to theater or the opera. One day in April—atypical but indicative of Gertrude's love for the theater—she "Couldn't work. Went to matinée *The Great God Brown*. Dined with F[lora]. Saw *Artists and Models*. Too much Al Jolson."

During Gertrude's trip Juliana Force has been very sick with bronchial pneumonia, but now she is recovering and Gertrude sees her often when at the MacDougal Alley studio. The exhibition program at the Club is as active as ever, and Mrs. Force is particularly proud of the good reception one of the new traveling shows—sixty paintings by thirteen artists, including Preston Dickinson, Du Bois, Hopper, Sheeler, and Spencer—is receiving at the Boston Arts Club. By March 7, Mrs. Force is well enough to join Gertrude at the opening of the eleventh Whitney Studio Club Annual—again so large that it must be shown at the Anderson Galleries—and then at 871 Fifth Avenue where Gertrude has "about thirty-five" unspecified guests, mostly artists, for cocktails.

As Mrs. Force usually entertains the artists in her apartment above the Whitney Studio, this is a rare occasion, remembered in some detail by Katherine Schmidt and Louis Bouché among others. Both tell the same story about Niles Spencer feeling somewhat overwhelmed by 871 and spotting a man wearing a Vandyke who looks equally shy and uncomfortable. "I suppose you come from below Fourteenth Street too," Spencer says to Gertrude's brother General Cornelius Vanderbilt, as he is called since the war. Neily, who is as shy as Spencer, is so surprised by this opening gambit that he backs into the buffet and picks up a large gob of mayonnaise on his coattail. Still not recognizing the general, Spencer grabs a napkin and wipes off the mess, saying that he does not want the artists to appear in a bad light. Gallantly, Neily thanks him and excuses himself without revealing his identity.

A few days after the opening Harry's lawyer, Frank Crocker, advises Gertrude that he has arranged to have Mayor Walker visit her studio to see the progress on the Union Square Memorial. Jimmy Walker, the enormously popular, celebrated, and corrupt "night mayor," has probably met Gertrude before. As a song writer, he is an "artist." He goes to theater even more often than she. And he is as comfortable with socialites as with Tammany Democrats. Friday morning Gertrude waits for him "from 11 to 1. No Mayor. Evidently he had made a big night of it! Is coming tomorrow." Saturday: "Phil lunched. The Mayor & Mr. Walsh came at 2:30. Stayed 1½ hrs. Very nice talk, he appeared interested. . . ."

In two months Gertrude will receive a letter announcing that Anthony De Francisci has won the competition, but meanwhile they all appear interested—all the politicians in New York, as in Providence, and as in Washington where the Red Cross/Delano commission is still dragging on and where a new commission, celebrating the hundred and fiftieth anniversary of the Declaration of Independence, seems a possibility. Through the spring, despite her frequent colds (and Harry's, when he returns from Aiken at the end of March), Gertrude drives herself relentlessly, compulsively, competitively, going after every commission in sight. . . . She makes two frustrating trips to Washington. In New York she meets several times with Samuel Untermyer and members of his family, before getting approval of the by now elaborate, allegorical gates (on a theme of Man and Woman, Woman and Child, et cetera) for their shrine at Woodlawn. . . . And increasingly she recognizes the great distance between initial interest and final approval, as well as the ratio between acceptance and rejection.

From the end of April on, many items in Gertrude's Line-A-Day and in her scrapbooks and correspondence point toward the *St. Nazaire* unveiling. First is the opening of the Spring Salon in Paris. There, at the Grand Palais, among the works of 3,000 exhibitors, the full-scale plaster model of the monument—standing over thirty feet high on a truncated pedestal, and with the eagle's wings spread about the same distance—dominates all the other sculpture even more than had *Buffalo Bill* in 1924. *St. Nazaire* receives by far the greatest attention in the press. (Only a head of Mussolini, emerging from a huge rough block of marble, is mentioned anywhere near as often.) The American and British reporters are generally descriptive, impressed by the sheer scale of Gertrude's piece, sometimes enthusiastic. The French—often criticis rather than reporters—are occasionally less kind. One writer ridicules the piece as "acrobatic"; another says it represents "an aesthetic closer to that of cinema than of statuary."

But the few negative comments from Paris will reach Gertrude too late to hurt much. By then she will have been given a large St. Nazaire Association testimonial dinner at the Hotel Brevoort, where comments are as comfortable and even as overstuffed as the Victorian décor of the hotel itself—comments from Roynon Cholmeley-Jones, as host; those from generals and admirals; those from American and French diplomats; those even from art critics, on whose behalf Royal Cortissoz speaks. (Henry McBride and Forbes Watson are also present, among about 120 guests, most of them large contributors to the association, some friends and relatives of Gertrude's.) During the evening the praise mounts and broadens, covering Gertrude's patriotism, her internationalism, the universality of her art. And in the echo of the event, in fashion columns, there is nothing but praise for her "gun-metal" shawl and black chiffon dress with short skirt flared toward the hem and with a girdle of two strings of large jet beads at the hipline—all this darkness (probably still mourning dress for

Regi) setting off pearl drop earrings, pearl necklaces, and more pearls wound loosely around the wrist and fastened with a square clasp of diamonds.

The image is right—the sheen and glitter against a dark background—it describes Gertrude's life as well as her dress during the month before her departure for France. Or consider another image: that of the gorgeously balanced and powerful schooner *Vanitie*, seventy-five feet long at the water line, carrying almost 8,000 square feet of sail, which Harry purchases now, announcing that he will race her during the coming season, with Robert W. Emmons II as skipper. Yes, it is nice to read that Harry has "returned to the sport of yacht racing," as it is to study the *Vanitie*'s newspaper photographs and her racing records (some made while chartered to Gertrude's brother Cornelius). But behind the words and the trim image there is darkness too. Harry has not so much returned to yachting as he has left polo, never having completely recovered from his accident and never intending to play again.

≈

JUNE 5: "Flora & I sailed on the *France* 11 o'clock. Was exhausted, Harry came to see us off." Aboard ship there are no entries of interest, except for Gertrude's meeting the drama critic Alexander Woollcott and the playwright Charles MacArthur, with whom she establishes an immediate rapport.

On the Saturday afternoon of their arrival in Paris, Gertrude and Flora stop briefly at the studio and then go immediately to the Salon with Andrew O'Connor, who also has a piece there. "Monument looked impressive. Proportions good," Gertrude writes, but she needs another day to say all she wants to O'Connor. It is obvious that getting *St. Nazaire* into the Grand Palais has been a complicated and expensive undertaking. He gives her photographs of the piece still surrounded by scaffolding and other shots taken earlier in the foundry. There are thanks to be expressed, reimbursements to be made, progress reports on other commissions to be brought up to date. They dine together, and the shop talk goes on and on.

Not until Monday can Gertrude relax. Then, and for the next ten days before leaving for St. Nazaire, she has many informal luncheons in the garden of her studio. Charles MacArthur and Jo Davidson are invited twice together, Jo seemingly hitting it off as well with Charlie as she has. Ambassador Herrick is there at least once. So is Gertrude's friend Mary Harriman Rumsey. So is Noel Murphy, the beautiful six-foot-tall sister-in-law of Gerald and Sara Murphy, who will be immortalized in Scott Fitzgerald's *Tender Is the Night*. So is the artist Marius de Zayas, who organized several shows at the Whitney Studio and Studio Club. . . . Gertrude's brief, hurried scribbles in the Line-A-Day suggest a period of fun, or at least of a good balance between pleasure and business.

JUNE 25: "Left on special train for St. N. Herrick. Pershing. About 35." Among the thirty-five are Flora, Andrew O'Connor, Guy Pène du Bois, and Jo Davidson. The next few days in the book are blank. No wonder. There is hardly time to write—and no need. The unveiling and attendant festivities are presented, day after day for many weeks, by major news media throughout the world, including International Newsreel No. 56, where the event is recorded along with shots of President and Mrs. Coolidge in their Summer White House at White Pines Camp, New York; Take My Tip winning the Paris Grand Prix; and Bobby Jones returning to Atlanta after winning the British Open—winners all.

Not only is this the most international coverage Gertrude has ever received, but the largest crowd (about 30,000) she has ever faced, "more American flags displayed in houses and shops than have been seen in any city of France since 1918," and the greatest number of speeches she has ever heard on a single occasion. The most quoted is by Ambassador Herrick, who commends Gertrude's work and presents it to France while passionately and lengthily defending America's idealism against charges of materialism. Georges Leygues, French Minister of Marine, is the first of several officials to accept the gift, comparing it, as a symbol of friendship between the United States and France, with the Statue of Liberty and the Yorktown Monument. At the close of his speech he approaches Gertrude and pins the medal of the Legion of Honor on her dress. According to some newspaper accounts, her eyes fill with tears. Whatever Gertrude's emotions are at the time, when she returns to Paris and writes Harry an eight-page letter, she treats the decoration and the rest of the ceremony— everything but the work itself—lightly.

. . . Just when I thought I might get a moment's sleep the celebration started, guns, bands, parades. Marie who was pressing my dress for the occasion rushed into my room, very excited. Anyway, as you can imagine, "Une épingle de sûreté, Madame."

All the ceremonies, everything was held up for the moment because Gen. P. had lost a safety pin which held up one of his medals. Finally we all start, visit à la Maire [Mayor], bows, etc. It was a most beautiful day. The Préfet lost his seat because someone pinched it. We had lovely red plush seats & Mr. Herrick was really great. His speech reads better than it sounded. He presented the monument which was really incidental. The response by several Ministers & then its acceptance by the little Socialistic Maire after which we all moved on to the Banquet (400) which lasted for some time. Gen. P. spoke & Mr. H. spoke in words which I did not realize he possessed in his vocabulary. That night I gave a dinner to the officials etc. & we went to three balls. The following day it all began over again only not quite so violently. I was almost surrounded, did my duty in the way of buying some bibelot d'art, contribution to the wounded, listened, by the way, to a very good band, assisted at a dinner which the Americans got up for me, saw a really good show of fireworks, crowned the queens of the country [i.e., beauty queens], received visits from various people & finally at 12 midnight got onto a train.

Flora was fine & very helpful.

What really pleased me was that for once in my life I couldn't have done more [i.e., in connection with the monument itself]. The difficulty of deciding the proportion, the difficulty of standing up against real opposition, and the fact that it is done & over make me much happier than decorations & all the rest of that tomfoolery.

I have never in my life seen so much gold braid, silver galons [military stripes], but the people down there are nice people.

The symbolism only exists as such, but every French paper is publishing articles about the great understanding between the two countries. I am writing in the garden without a table which accounts for my writing.

I wish you could have been here, dearest.

Love G

During Gertrude's final week in Paris, she spends four evenings with Herbert Haseltine, who has just arrived; two with Ambassador Herrick, who on one occasion gives a dinner in her honor at the American Embassy; and the last at a "good-by dinner" for her given by the St. Nazaire Association. On July 7 she and Flora visit Mama and Gladys in Cabourg before meeting the boat train the next day.

Except for a peaceful week's crossing aboard the *Majestic*, the remainder of the summer is restless, without a single week in one place. It begins with the usual shuttlings between Westbury and the city, but even in late July and the first half of August, when Harry is in Saratoga, the movement continues—a few days in Westbury, a few in New York; a trip to Boston to see Barbie and Buz; a visit to a foundry in Queens; another to one in Brooklyn. And as always there are the meetings with Juliana Force—the details and correspondence connected with commissions as well as with the Whitney Studio Club.

This summer the Club is inactive but, mainly at the instigation of Alexander Brook, ads are appearing in and being prepared for *The Arts*.

JULY:

BRING BACK A WORK OF ART FROM YOUR SUMMER TOUR.

This is the season of the year when the artists, like other people, fly to the country. But while others go to play, or sometimes just to get away from the heat of the city, the summer is not the playtime of the artist. It is then that he does much of his best work, then that he is able to concentrate without interruptions upon creative ideas.

Artists have a good eye for the country. Nearly everywhere they go it is pleasant to follow them, whether through the lovely Hudson River country that leads to Woodstock, or along the fine roads of Cape Cod or the North Shore of Massachusetts to Gloucester. Wherever artists congregate in small or large groups, it leads the automobile owner to delightful country. . . .

During the winter season the Whitney Studio Club presents regularly the recent work of vigorous American artists. During the summer, when driving through a village where some artist has his studio, why not alight and make your own discovery? Bring back a work of art from your summer tour!

OCTOBER:

THE SPIRIT OF TODAY

The summer over, the artists who dwell in the city have returned with fresh canvases marking another step forward in their development. Many of these artists made their first bows to the public in the galleries of The Whitney Studio Club. Many will there first present their latest works.

Exhibitions begin in the month of November and follow each other at regular intervals. The increasing public which the progressive artists are winning for themselves will find, in these exhibitions, exceptional opportunities to enjoy works of art by the men and women who are interpreting the spirit of today.

The artists whose exhibitions are being scheduled for the end of the year are all close to Gertrude in different ways, each illustrative of how she expresses her patronage. In November there will be a large show of portraits by her old friend Robert Chanler, to whom she has given sporadic financial assistance and several commissions, surrounding one of sculpture by Reuben Nakian, whom she has never met but has, as we know, supported since 1923. And in December there will be a retrospective exhibition of work by Stuart Davis, who has shown at the Club since April 1921 and who will be indebted to Gertrude and to Juliana Force for subsequently buying two paintings and enabling him, in 1928, to make his only trip to Paris.

One other project being discussed at this time is also explained in an ad.

NOVEMBER:

THE WHITNEY STUDIO CLUB'S SHOP

The Whitney Studio Club opened on November 1st. THE SHOP where water colors, drawings, etchings, woodcuts and lithographs by members of the Club will be sold at Studio Prices [i.e., without commission].

THE SHOP will be open daily until June 1st inclusive. Visitors will find there a constantly changing exhibition showing examples of the works of various members and also portfolios offering to visitors a large selection of prints and drawings. . . .

As to Gertrude's commissions, the most important new one begins in August to grow—only now as an ongoing idea—in the mind of William H. Page, a lawyer who has spent ten days in Palos in 1917 and has thought ever since that this Spanish port from which Columbus sailed to the New World should be commemorated by an appropriate Columbus monument. He explains all this in a long letter to his friend at Harry's office, Thomas J. Regan, who forwards it to Gertrude. Page's letter reads in part:

> Whenever I see a picture of the monument design by Mrs. Whitney at St. Nazaire, I wonder why the American people do not think of some similar conception to Columbus, at Palos. . . .
>
> I enclose a picture of the convent of La Rábida. There appears at the left end of the building, marked with a faint arrow, a shaft or monument to Columbus. It is some fifty feet high, erected in 1892, as I recall. But its condition is so infirm that over the doorway, whence rises an interior spiral staircase, to an outlook, is a sign which reads "Peligroso-Entrada Prohibida" [Dangerous-Entrance Forbidden] . . . .
>
> Certainly the time has come, and appropriately this year, for the commencement of a monument at Palos or La Rábida which will be analogous in thought and parallel in importance to both American and European eyes, to the monument at St. Nazaire.
>
> Miss Ederle, for her swim over the channel to Dover, is to be immediately complimented by a monument. But Columbus for his voyage of seven months to America and opening a new hemisphere, after nearly 500 years, is still on the waiting list.

In addition to the photograph of the convent where, before sailing, Columbus met with Queen Isabella's confessor, Page also encloses an extract from a talk on all of this and particularly the need for a Columbus monument, given in 1919 at the predominantly Catholic New York Athletic Club. Implicit throughout the carefully written—and, indeed, documented—letter are the questions: Might Mrs. Whitney be interested? If so, might she guide me as to procedure? Predictably, she is interested, she will guide Mr. Page. She writes Regan a long letter, outlining each necessary step as to the formation of a committee, the handling of publicity and fund raising ("entirely out of my realm of action"), the commissioning process itself (warning against a competition), and encloses a handsome mounted photograph of the *St. Nazaire* Memorial for Page. At the beginning of September he acknowledges all this and assures her of his intention to pursue the matter at the Columbus Day banquet in Philadelphia. There at the Ritz-Carlton he makes his proposal that a Columbus

Memorial Association be formed to erect a monument at Palos or Huelva as a gift from the citizens of the United States. The resolution is unanimously adopted. Alexander P. Moore, former ambassador to Spain, is elected president and a committee is formed, including Page. By the end of the year the Columbus Memorial Fund, Inc., has been organized by Page as a corporation under the laws of the state of New York, and Moore holds a press conference, announcing that the project has been approved by King Alfonso and Queen Victoria of Spain, that there will probably be a design competition, and that there will surely be a fund-raising campaign "modeled after that in 1886 when $300,000 was raised by popular subscription to erect the Statue of Liberty." By then too, despite the probable competition, Page is sending Gertrude books, articles, maps, and other material relating to Columbus and his voyages.

The Whitney Studio Club and commissions are, of course, but two strands of Gertrude's life—unwound only for narrative convenience. Twist them, now, back in place and in time:

In mid-August, when Harry returns from Saratoga, the rhythm of Gertrude's days changes. Though there is at least as much movement as earlier in the summer, much of it is now on water. For a short time, as she and Harry move back and forth between the comfortable and commodious *Whileaway* and the much trimmer and more spartan *Vanitie*, Gertrude's Line-A-Day makes us almost seasick.

AUGUST 16: Flora, Harry & I went on Whileaway to City Island to see Vanitie. Very bad day, could not put sails up. . . . Sonny lunched with us. Returned Glen Cove.

AUGUST 17: Went to town, returned & went on Whileaway in time for dinner. Stopped to see Sonny. Marie was not well. Sailed for New London. Frank Crocker also.

AUGUST 18: Raced from New London to Newport. Wind died out, only arrived 9:30. . . .

AUGUST 19: Newport on Whileaway. Raced course [Astor Cup] starting light ship along Newport coast, Block Island back.

AUGUST 20: Newport on Whileaway. Got on Vanitie 10. Race [King's Cup] started off light ship 11:30. Won on time allowance by 3 minutes. . . . Heard poor old Ardisson [Gertrude's Westbury studio assistant] committed suicide [by jumping from a water tower near the studio].

AUGUST 21: Westbury. Ardisson was buried. Bad day in country. Heard of Aunt Lulu's [Mrs. Frederick W. Vanderbilt's] death in Paris.

Though the statements concerning Ardisson are brief, like everything in the Line-A-Day, there is no question that his suicide affects Gertrude profoundly. He has been with her since about World War I, assisting her when she is in residence by building armatures and scaffolds, by handing her her tools when she is working up high, by covering her work in clay with wet cloths at the end of the day and by removing them for the next day's work. When she is not in residence, he has supervised routine jobs at the foundry, translated some pieces from modeled materials to carved stone, built packing cases for her exhibitions. And always he has taken care of the many exotic birds roaming in and out of the studio. In short, for all these years he, probably more than Gertrude's other assistants, has been doing the hundreds of odd jobs necessary to her career as a sculptor. Gertrude is so upset that she orders the water tower torn down and remains in Westbury when Harry joins the *Vanitie* for the last three days of the racing reason.

Inevitably there are rumors—some continue to this day—of a romantic liaison between Gertrude and Ardisson: "together so much in the studio . . . modeled for her sometimes . . . lights on and off during all hours of the night . . ." However, there is no evidence that their relationship went beyond the professional one. Furthermore, Ardisson suffered from periods of acute depression, his marriage was unhappy, and his son a "ne'er-do-well."

≈

The previous rhythm resumes—on land. "Came to town." "Back to country." "Day in country." "Night in town."

AUGUST 25: Family arranged anniversary dinner in Westbury. Barbie and Buz came in from Boston.

It is hard to believe that Gertrude and Harry have been married for thirty years, but perhaps no harder than the entry, September 4, commemorating another anniversary: ". . . Regi's death. Went to Staten Island. Took flowers for him, Papa, Bill and Alfred." Long spans of time seem to move as quickly now as short ones. Thirty years require about as many words as one year. A line-a-day becomes a line-a-life.

The fall flashes by: "Worked, went back to country. . . . Ditto. Dined in town. . . . Worked, went to country. . . . Futurity. H's horse Valorous 3rd. . . . Whileaway. . . . Worked, back to country. . . . J. Barrymore in Don Juan. . . . Best sketch I have yet made of Duse. . . . cocktail at Flora's. . . . Aunt Lulu's funeral. . . . Went to studio, worked. Back to Westbury. . . . Opening of Gentlemen Prefer Blondes. . . . Saw Mrs. Force. . . . Gave instructions about enlarging Duse monument. . . . Country. . . . Town. . . ."

The entry of October 11 comes as no surprise: "Saw Dr. James. Not been feeling well for some time." The daily entries change: "Tried to work. . . . Worked a little, felt very shaky. . . . Saw Dr. James. . . . Spent horrid day in country. . . . Went to Harbor Hospital 6 o'clock." She spends a week there being examined and X-rayed every day, unable to visit her fifth grandchild, Sonny's and Marie's daughter Nancy, born October 20. Friday, October 22, she goes "out driving with Mrs. Force, felt very weak and sick." On Saturday, Gertrude leaves the hospital and returns to Westbury. By Monday she is back in town and by Tuesday at the "studio for short time." Wednesday, Thursday, Friday the same: "Studio short time." Gertrude is dizzy. Her vision is unclear. She sees Dr. James again. He recommends a night nurse, then a day nurse, and many specialists. During the remainder of the year there are few days when she is not visited by Dr. James and other doctors—oculists, neurologists, internists, hematologists. The Line-A-Day begins to read like a medical case history. Besides the catalogue of doctors there are those of symptoms and treatments. At least twice Gertrude has her stomach pumped. Frequently she has blood specimens taken and records the red- and white-cell counts. She feels a throbbing pain in the right leg, later in the left, then the right again. Diagnosis: phlebitis. Dr. James's prediction: ". . . no chance of getting out in less than two weeks." A week later: ". . . a long siege."

Through all these depressing weeks Harry and the family are very attentive and obviously very concerned. Harry, whose own health is far from perfect, remains almost always at Gertrude's side. Flora, living nearby, visits frequently, sometimes with her children, sometimes with G. Macculloch Miller, known as "Cully," a charming youthful future architect with whom she is now involved. Mama visits when she can, and Sonny and Marie, Barbie and Buz, Gladys and László, and all their children make several special trips.

However, by late November, despite the devotion of her family and the constant attention of doctors, Gertrude is feeling so helpless and depressed that she turns, as she has several times in the past, to an astrologer for comfort. The need is completely understandable, the method somewhat mystifying. Posing as "Mrs. Thomas White" of 10 West Eighth Street, she has a consultation with John Hazelrigg, president of the American Academy of Astrologians. She tells him she was born January 9, 1877, the false year she has been using since her 1914 passport application. There is no way of knowing what else she tells him, her looks, dress, manners, and speech could not have lied. Anyway, in a twelve-page letter, Hazelrigg tells her mostly what she wants to hear, giving complete credit to the stars for all information. They inform him that in her "the spirit of the muse is very dominant," that hers "is a mixture of the artistic and the executive nature," that "SERVICE [is] writ largely across the scroll," that "there could be interest in both public and official business, though that seems more the province of the sterner sex," that hers "is a mentality that seeks direct results, strong in competition when there is danger of failure, with a blending of the forces of wealth, devotion, and grace," that "the financial side of the chart is very nicely circumstanced," that "while strongly organized constitutionally, you have probably suffered through functional derangements peculiar to your sex." For the coming year, Hazelrigg predicts love, travel, success, better mental and physical health.

≈

During the last weeks of the year Gertrude begins to recover. Several times, after doctors' appointments on Wednesdays and Saturdays, she goes to matinees (*The Constant Wife, The Constant Nymph, The Captive*). One Thursday she sees *The Pirates of Penzance* with Jimmie Appleton. She has "gained 4½ lbs." during this sedentary period and begins walking more and dieting. Slowly: "Lost ¾ lb. . . . Lost ½ lb. . . . Lost ½ lb. . . . ." On December 12 she weighs 112, a day later 110½. By December 20 she is encouraged enough to have "bought some clothes." The next day: "Went down town about passport." The next: "Tried on Frances [a couturière]." December 25: "Flora, Sonny & Marie, Barbie & Buz for Xmas lunch. Cathleen & H. Cushing came in afterward. Rather exhausting." December 29: "Matinee *The Squall* with Mabel [Gerry Drury]. Ambassador Moore came about Columbus statue."

Despite occasional exhaustion, we feel the life coming back into Gertrude, guess that the passport has something to do with the Columbus Memorial, imagine her studying the books and maps from William Page. At the end of the year she is, indeed, strong and undaunted enough almost to ignore a lawsuit started by Katherine Minahan, who claims $80,672 for services in connection with the St. Nazaire-like memorial planned by Gertrude for New York Harbor. Gertrude has more important things on her mind. She does not write a single word about this matter in her Line-A-Day but simply turns it over to Charles Lane, an attorney, who denies all allegations.

≈ *1927*

Between December 21, when she renewed her passport, and the first few days of the new year, Gertrude spends much of her time planning a long trip for her health. Dr. James has said that she must relax, must get away from the strain of work. But by now work is so much of her life that she can never really leave it. Though the trip she plans does not permit studio work, it is surely strenuous and connected with her career. Not only is Huelva on her itinerary, but she plans to spend more than a month in Egypt studying its great sculpture and architecture, and combining that with the marriage of Flora and Cully Miller in Cairo, where he will join Gertrude, Flora, and her children, Pam and "Whitty."

To Harry, the trip sounds exhausting. It is not one he wants to make nor, because of *his* health, can comfortably make. Indeed it is unlikely that he would have accepted Gertrude's going, without Flora and without the reassurances of Dr. James.

To Gertrude, it is another "journey to the East," the first since 1901. For old time's sake, she invites Rollie Cottenet to join her and Flora. He can't, though "it breaks [his] heart." She telegraphs to Jo Davidson in Paris. No reply; it turns out that, by coincidence, he is on his way to Egypt. She writes a note to Bob Chanler, outlining the trip and expressing regret that due to illness she has missed his November show of portraits at the Studio Club. We don't have his response but know that he doesn't appear in Egypt.

All is preparation—family good-bys; final medical examinations; a last visit to the studio; the non-routine part of packing, especially books. From notes, mostly on the back of correspondence, we know that Gertrude takes along a large library—Columbus material, histories of Egypt and its art, at least two volumes of poetry (James Stephens and Walter de la Mare), and many recent books, particularly indicative of her interest in theater, romantic biography, and current fiction (*Best Plays of 1925–1926*; Pirandello's novel, *The Outcast*; George Jean Nathan's *The Autobiography of an Attitude*; Percy Lubbock's *The Region Cloud*; R. M. Werner's *Brigham Young*; Philip W. Sergeant's *Courtships of Catherine the Great*; John Erskine's *Galahad*; Willa Cather's *My Mortal Enemy*; Jay William Hudson's *The Eternal Circle*; Joseph Hergesheimer's *Tampico*; Ernest Hemingway's *The Sun Also Rises*; A. S. M. Hutchinson's *One Increasing Purpose*). We can imagine some of these books piling up on Gertrude's night table during the past two years, others being ordered at the last moment. Finally, there is a note to herself: "*Le Génie d'Edgar Poe*, Camille Mauclair, 10 copies," and we suppose she intends, in the course of her travels, to make gifts of this little book by the man who at the end of 1924 wrote the catalogue introduction for her Durand-Ruel retrospective.

January 5, Harry sees Gertrude, Flora, and her children—accompanied by a maid and a nurse—off on the *Adriatic*. As planned, Gertrude visits or is visited daily by the ship's doctor who, following Dr. James's instructions, is always "jabbing." The days flow by measured in blood specimens taken and books read. The crowd aboard ship is "uninteresting," the sights seen early in the cruise comparatively routine and briefly described in the Line-A-Day: the sled ride down from the Madeira hills, Gilbraltar by moonlight, native dancing in Algiers, gambling at Monte Carlo, the museum in Naples.

We can imagine a limousine meeting Gertrude and Flora at each port and taking them to the local sights. It is luxurious touring but still on January 22: "Had my legs bandaged with bella donna & glycerine. Stayed in bed, read & wrote all day." Much of the writing, besides letters home and bits of fiction and drama, is in a notebook she entitles *Miscellaneous Facts about Egypt,* some seventy-five pages on that country's history, religion, art, architecture, and archaeological sites.

The cruise continues. They anchor off Piraeus. Again there is the rush to see the sights: "Acropolis of course most exquisite. Museum on Acropolis marvelous. Museum in town grand. Returned Adriatic. Sailed." They steam through the Greek islands, arrive at Constantinople, see more sights: "Mosques beautiful. . . . St. Sophia." Again they are at sea, for two days this time, one beautiful, one gray. They anchor off Haifa. Flora and her children go to Nazareth. Gertrude rests, reads, writes. She is saving herself for Egypt. It is as if all the preceding places are hors d'oeuvres— Madeira, Gibraltar, Algiers, Monte Carlo, Naples, Athens, Constantinople, Haifa (untasted).

Saturday, January 28, they arrive at Alexandria after lunch, take a tug ashore, and then get a train to Cairo where they arrive about six. "Bedlam at station. Semiramis Hotel." Sunday: "Lunched Shepheard's Hotel. Museum. Drive." Monday: "Shopped. Saw American Consul Winship & wife afternoon [with whom Gertrude and Flora make arrangements for the wedding.] C[ully] arrived 9." Tuesday: "Went to see Dr. Garry for jab and blood (77) [count]. Mr. & Mrs. Mercer [a "terribly nice couple from Pennsylvania," met aboard the *Adriatic*] lunched. Museum. 6:30 train to Assuan."

After changing trains early the next morning at Luxor, they arrive a little after noon at Assuan where the *Scarab* is waiting, decorated with palm fronds and with the American flag flying above the smokestack. It is Thomas Cook & Son's smallest dahabeah, a double-decker barge, perhaps a hundred feet long, with a crew of nineteen, intended for tourist parties of about two dozen. There is no doubt that Gertrude and her maid, Flora and Cully will all be very comfortable during the next three weeks. Lunch is ready. Afterward Gertrude scribbles, "Scarab perfect."

That will be the last entry so brief until they return to Cairo. Even as the *Scarab* moves slowly through the locks at Assuan, we feel Gertrude's excitement mounting. Suddenly her handwriting becomes minuscule as she tries to cram into the small space allotted for each day too many impressions and too much information (extracted from G. Maspero's *Art in Egypt* and other books she has been reading). Rather than the *Scarab* itself, cities seem to flow by, leaving Gertrude's penciled wake of names: Philae, Amada, Abu Simbel. . . . Ancient rulers flow by: Rameses II,

Nefertari. . . . The trip has a dreamlike quality. Past and present merge into past/present. The *Scarab* passes many feluccas with old patched sails and a Cook's dahabeah carrying thirty tourists. Gertrude rides a donkey to an ancient granite quarry where she sees an unfinished obelisk. Camels and donkeys with their drivers wait for tourists at every important site along the river. Ancient bazaars offer modern wares.

In early February, Gertrude's telegram from New York and a follow-up from Cairo have caught up with Jo Davidson. She learns now that he and Yvonne are in Cairo with the art dealer Dikran Kelekian. She writes, probably from Assuan: "Dear Jo, How very exciting your being in Egypt!" She describes the itinerary, tells him she has been having "a most wonderful trip" and "a tremendous thrill over Egyptian temples and tombs. Do put off going back. I assure you not going to Luxor & Thebes when you are so near will be the regret of your life." Jo says no, his wife has not been well, and besides—we learn from his autobiography—he is very busy buying Egyptian objects with Kelekian.

The *Scarab* moves on. Monday: "Kom-Ombo . . . Gebel-Silsileh . . . crocodile . . . Edfu." Tuesday: ". . . donkeys to temple . . . Ptolemaic Period . . . Children's eyes covered with flies, most unattractive looking people . . . Exneh." Wednesday: "Fine ceilings, signs of zodiac. . . . Luxor . . . Winter Palace Hotel. Met Seton Henry [a writer] who came with a friend, Hungarian Count Redodi, for cocktails on Scarab. Hair washed. Mercers dined with us." Thursday: "Temple of Luxor . . . drove to Karnak . . . Great Temple of Amun . . ." Friday: "Crossed river to Thebes, drove to Temple of Medinet-Habu. . . . Temple of Rameses III . . . Colossi of Memnon . . . Tombs . . . Returned Scarab lunch. Henrys, Hitchins [another writer], Count. All went races, donkey, camel, bullocks. Prince ——, Mercers dined." Saturday: "Temple of Seti I. Beautiful sculptures. Tomb of Tut-ankh-Amun. Outer sarcophagus only thing to be seen. Mummy is there. Tomb Rameses IX, Rameses VI. Fine ceiling. Tomb Amenophis II. Large & deep. Mummies. Rameses III. Seti II (Belzoni discovered). Most beautiful. Lunch Cook's Rest House. . . . Henrys etc. Cocktails Scarab." Sunday: "Drove Karnak morning. Especially saw fine reliefs. Went on donkeys with Henrys, Count & Mr. Taggart to orange grove. Snake charmer. Mr. Hitchins called."

Another week has passed, a week largely of names, ancient and modern; of impressions, quick and general. However, the impressions are supplemented by many sharp and specific photographs. In towns Gertrude most frequently wears comfortable suits that have a Chanel look; for more arduous touring, a belted tunic, knickers, leggings, elegant low French shoes (as opposed to "sensible" English ones). Almost always she carries a cane and wears a pith helmet or cloche, a veil, and sunglasses. Flora, except for the cane (she usually carries a tightly rolled parasol), dresses about like her mother, though in town she often wears chemises and at the sites a shirt and sweater with her knickers. Cully dresses as elegantly as either of them. Except between meals aboard the *Scarab*, he wears a tie and jacket (white linen in town, tweed at the sites) with a handkerchief "casually" placed in the breast pocket. When he is not wearing a helmet or a fedora (with the brim turned down all the way around), we see that his hair is slickly parted. He is as much a model of the twenties as Flora and Gertrude. Despite Gertrude's cane, they all look carefree.

But although dozens of photographs are of these three—posing alone at sites or with the crew of the *Scarab*, with guides, with camel drivers, with Pam and Whitty in sunbonnets and shorts—most are of the monuments themselves, shot after shot of temple or tomb. Individually, these photographs of archaeological fragments, though carefully labeled, become, like the Line-A-Day, a touristic blur, meaningful only to the Egyptologist. Cumulatively, they have impact. We begin to feel, as Gertrude must have, the sculptural power of even the lowest relief; the simplified, stylized strength of this great art. What she is learning—relearning—on this trip cannot easily be found in *Miscellaneous Facts about Egypt*, any more than in the Line-A-Day or the photographs, but it will be found—refound —later in the Columbus monument, about which she is constantly thinking.

Meanwhile, the trip continues—rushed and blurred in Gertrude's notes, even more severely edited now in ours: "Karnak by moonlight. . . . Sailed early . . . donkey ride to Dendera. . . . Fine reliefs but many mutilated. . . . Portrait Cleopatra. . . . Sailed early. Passed home of Sheikh Selim who sat naked on the bank & was given money by all passing ships. Died 1891, son now collects money. [There are several photographs of the short fat son who wears an enormous walrus mustache, a fez, and Western clothes with a heavy gold chain across the vest.] . . . Left on donkeys for Abydos. . . . Seti Temple exquisite reliefs in white sandstone & colored ones also in fine state of preservation. . . . Asyut . . . large, prosperous modern town. Many hideous expensive houses. . . . Beni Hassan . . . rock temple and rock tombs . . . 100 miles today. . . ."

More quickly now they return to comparatively modern, urban life. On Tuesday, February 22—with Washington's birthday far from their minds —they arrive in Cairo, collect their mail, and invite Yvonne and Jo Davidson and Kelekian to dinner, after which Flora and Cully call on the Winships to confirm wedding arrangements. The next day too, still living aboard the *Scarab*, is transitional—a medical examination, minor shopping, arranging tours in the Cairo area with Cook's, taking photographs to be developed. They run into Jim Curtis and Anton Schafer, friends of Cully's, who decide to give him a bachelor dinner. Gertrude and Flora dine alone.

The wedding ceremony the next day at twelve-thirty is short—after the usual vows, Cully puts an elephant-hair ring on Flora's finger—the group which attends almost unlikely, a matter of chance: Consul North Winship and his wife, Vice-Consul Lawton, the Davidsons, Curtis and Schafer. All of them return to the *Scarab* for a wedding breakfast, and then Flora and Cully sail away on their official honeymoon.

The Davidsons and Kelekian join Gertrude aboard the *Homeric*. They make an odd foursome—Yvonne, like Gertrude, elegant and *à la mode*; Jo, burly, bushy, rumpled, animated; Kelekian, suave and sophisticated, his shiny bald head and carefully trimmed white beard and mustache a strong contrast to Jo's dark wild beard and head of hair. For two and a half beautiful days at sea they talk mostly about art. Kelekian has a vast knowledge of the world's antiquities and of the people, like Gertrude herself, who can afford them. The Davidsons know everything that is happening in Paris. They speak familiarly of Picasso, Matisse, Stein, Cocteau, Hemingway, Breton. Gertrude brings Yvonne and Jo up to date on recent exhibitions at the Studio Club (Chanler, Nakian, Davis) and on one that was about to open when she left New York: "Paintings and Drawings of Women by Men." Perhaps she quotes John Sloan's slogan for the show—"Paint Woman 'As Is'"—and recites the names of some of the other artists in it: Demuth, Du Bois, Kuhn, Kuniyoshi, Maurer, Pascin, Man Ray, the Soyer brothers. Perhaps there is criticism of Sloan's theory of "art without idealization," and discussion of this in relation to Egyptian art. . . . Probably one other related topic would have come up: Brancusi vs. the United States, the important case initiated the previous year by the photographer Edward Steichen, and underwritten by Gertrude at his request, after the first bronze version of Brancusi's highly idealized and abstracted *Bird in Space*, purchased by Steichen, was refused tariff-free entry because of the U. S. Customs' contention that it was not a work of art but a utilitarian object. Though the case will not be decided until 1928, during the past few weeks there have been widely reported hearings, a press conference with Marcel Duchamp speaking for Brancusi, and a strong editorial in *The Arts* by Forbes Watson, who will later join Steichen, the sculptor Jacob Epstein, the editor and collector Frank Crowninshield, the critic Henry McBride, and the director of the Brooklyn Museum, William H. Fox, as the experts who successfully defend Brancusi's work as art. . . . The words roll on, the hours pass. . . .

Palermo . . . Naples . . . the train to Rome . . . another to Paris. There, immediately after her arrival on Friday, March 11, Gertrude has a medical examination—"My improvement's very successful"—then is joined in the late afternoon by Andrew O'Connor, who stays for dinner at her studio. As at their last reunion, there is a lot to catch up on. They have "a long talk about everything. Is very keen about my Columbus, says he will go with me to Palos."

As Page has warned Gertrude, Huelva and Palos are competing for the monument. She is careful to spend time with Señor Casto, president of the Huelva Chamber of Commerce; with Señor Albeldo, manager of the port; with Señor Jiminez, ex-mayor of Palos. When she and O'Connor return to Madrid, where he leaves her to go back to Paris, she immediately contacts Ambassador Ogden H. Hammond, then has tea with him and his wife. They invite Gertrude to tea again the following day to meet the Duke of Alba, who is "very interested and helpful," and then arrange a lunch for the next day at which the duke, the great soldier and statesman Primo de Rivera, Prince Alfonso, the Infanta Beatrice, and other powerful Spanish aristocrats will be present. For three days in Madrid, everything revolves around the Columbus monument. Gertrude barely has time to go to the Prado early one morning and to a bullfight late one afternoon. Page has written, "you will of course be functioning not only as sculptor but as a kind of ambassador. The popular approval of your name as the sculptor, since it became known, has been unanimous and enthusiastic." By the time Gertrude leaves Madrid she has the aristocratic approval too. She has been a good ambassador; she has, to use the phrase in a letter to Gladys, "done her business."

As would be expected, Gertrude sleeps well on the train back to Paris. When she arrives early the morning of Tuesday, March 22, she feels sufficiently rested to go directly to O'Connor's studio. He is returning to the States the next day, and once again there is a lot to discuss—his recent work, which she considers "*very* fine"; hers, which he can help her with. They spend the entire day together, first at his studio, then at hers, where she gives him her preliminary sketch of the Columbus monument to take back to New York for enlargement. The basic concept is already established: a heroic figure of Columbus, embracing a shoulder-height cross, as he looks out to sea; a rectangular pedestal about half the height of the figure, with reliefs representing the four hemispheres opened to the world by Columbus, at each of its four upper corners; and, inside the pedestal, a shrine containing statues of Queen Isabella and King Ferdinand. The details—particularly the corner reliefs—will become increasingly "Egyptian" as the design develops.

Once O'Connor has left, Gertrude is free to relax for a week before joining Flora, Cully, and the children in Monaco to sail home on the *Adriatic*. Free to relax!—the phrase, applied to Gertrude, is ironic. Her days are packed. Rollie Cottenet and Jimmie Appleton have arrived in Paris. Jo, Hazy, and another sculptor, Cecil Howard (who has had his first major exhibition, two years ago, at the Whitney Studio Club), are there. She lunches or dines with each of them (twice with Jimmie at Le Caneton); visits each of the sculptors' studios and has each to hers; shops; tries on; receives a visit from Gloria Vanderbilt and Little Gloria; is able to see only one play (Henry Bernstein's *Le Venin*); takes the train to Monaco; boards the *Adriatic* with Pam, Whitty, and their nurse and, not surprisingly, spends the entire first day in bed, feeling "a little shaky."

At first, as three months before, Gertrude finds the "crowd uninterest-ing," but by the third evening she is "in conversation with man at next table who seems nice & is very confiding." From then on she talks almost every evening after dinner with Mr. ———, whom she later calls (filling in the blank with a darker pencil), "Mr. Sterling" or "S." Based on this clue and on subsequent correspondence with Paul Clayton (whom she addresses as "Mr. Velasquez" and "Mr. Partridge" as well as "Mr. Ster-ling"), it is clear that Sterling is a pseudonym for Clayton. The rela-tionship, which begins and ends in this year, is not important or romantic in the same sense as some of Gertrude's other shipboard encounters have been. Rather, this is a situation in which an aspiring artist with a "drink-ing problem" and a "mother problem" needs an older confidante or surro-gate mother and finds, in Gertrude, one who also welcomes the chance to confide without the risks inherent in a relationship with someone of the same age and social background. In theory, the relationship begins as a game, with rules of distance carefully laid out by Gertrude; in fact, as with other young men in the past, Paul Clayton's attachment to Gertrude will become too close for her comfort. However, it is not the familiar case his-tory that is interesting, nor Clayton's many, increasingly embarrassing let-ters, but Gertrude's replies which, related to the Line-A-Day, give us, dur-ing this period, the nearest thing we have to a journal. Even while still aboard ship—along with frequent recordings of massages, jabs, blood counts—there is a new emphasis on drinks ("1 cocktail . . . 2 cocktails . . . 1 cointreau") and then a sudden end to that, as if Gertrude, who, like Paul, is disobeying doctors' orders, has taken a vow, probably with him, to stop—at least temporarily.

⤶

When Gertrude and the children arrive in New York, Gertrude is swamped. Not only is Harry at the pier, as expected; but so are Ex-Ambas-sador Alexander Moore, William Page, and two other members of the Columbus Committee, all unexpected. Collectively, Harry and the com-mittee members are an introduction to what Gertrude must face during the next few weeks: a concentrated catching up with family and commis-sions. The Columbus Committee has good news. The site in Huelva which Gertrude has selected has been informally approved. This very night (April 11) the Duke of Alba expects formal approval by a National Monuments Committee. Page mentions the possibility of a Washington Irving Memorial in Spain, "similar in cut" to Gertrude's studies for Columbus. . . . Page, Moore, and the others talk on—there are hints that Moore doesn't completely approve of the site and doesn't think Ferdinand and Isabella have been given enough prominence. Finally, Harry is able to get his family away from the committee, into his chauffeured car, and off to 871 Fifth. There Mama arrives almost as soon as they do. She hugs her daughter, her son-in-law, her great-grandchildren. Pam looks wonderful, Whitty a bit peaked from a fever aboard ship.

Dozens of questions are being asked about the trip as, late in the afternoon, Gertrude excuses herself to see Juliana Force at the studio. Mrs. Force has good news too. The Daughters of the American Revolution Committee, which first approached Gertrude from Washington in 1924, has the funds now to proceed with a memorial and hopes that Gertrude is still interested. Mrs. Force has replied in Gertrude's absence that, yes, Mrs. Whitney has been working on the design. Now she asks if the $15,000 fee still holds. Gertrude reminds Mrs. Force that costs have gone up and that she is *very* busy. She says the price must be $20,000. Mrs. Force takes all this down and drafts the appropriate letter. (In a few weeks she will receive a confirmation of the new fee and by the end of the year a formal contract). There must also have been conversations about the current shows at the Studio (paintings by children of the Edith King-Dorothy Coit School of Acting and Design) and at the Studio Club (works by members), about another commission called *Pioneer Woman*, and about the $25,000 modernization of 10 West Eighth Street where the Whitney Studio Club will have a new gallery. Mrs. Force bubbles with enthusiasm. There is hardly time for everything that should be discussed. Gertrude must return home to see Sonny and Barbie.

The reunions continue, some pleasant, some not. The next morning Rod comes to pick up Pam and Whitty, whom he has not seen in more than three months. He takes them off to Atlantic City for a few days. Buz arrives from Boston. Sonny and Marie bring Little Harry to visit. Gertrude sees Neily and Grace at Mama's. . . . It takes a week, interrupted by several medical examinations, to settle into the usual routine of "rest" in Westbury and work in New York. O'Connor visits the studio twice and is encouraging about *Columbus*. Several of the committee members come also to see Gertrude's progress. Moore is "rather disagreeable." Page continues to be "enthusiastic." Another committee member, J. P. Morgan's daughter Anne, less visible until now, is as enthusiastic as Page and will, during the coming months, always support Gertrude's design as Moore attacks it. Still another member, Dr. Clarence J. Owens, "falls so violently" for Gertrude that she has "a hard time to get rid of him" (that is, to get him out of the studio) and he, too, will be a strong supporter of her design.

Until almost the end of May she works hard on *Columbus*, on *Daughters of the American Revolution*, and on *Pioneer Woman* (never installed). It is typical that when Charles Lindbergh makes his solo flight from Roosevelt Field, Long Island, to Le Bourget, Paris (May 20–21), Gertrude begins to think almost immediately of a memorial sculpture at Roosevelt Field (one for which she will do many, ultimately abortive, sketches). Besides all this actual studio work, presumably satisfying, there is the irritation of the continuing *Columbus* correspondence, an intrigue in which Gertrude—with the help of Anne Morgan, William Page, and Dr. Owens—overcomes the design and site objections of Alexander Moore; and there is a new action filed by Katherine Minahan in which the former "agent" again asks for $80,672, exclusively now for her assistance in promoting the Providence War Memorial, which leads to a counterclaim by Gertrude for $10,000 lent to Miss Minahan.

Egypt is far behind, Gertrude's blood count is again rising, and Dr. James is beginning to scold Gertrude for driving herself so hard, when suddenly Harry's younger brother Payne dies, at fifty-one, from an attack of acute indigestion, after playing tennis at his country home in Manhasset. Payne's death is a powerful blow and a warning to both Gertrude and Harry. As soon as they receive the news they motor to Payne's house with Harry's doctor, John Hartwell, who has been examining him at the time. There Harry is so upset that Dr. Hartwell must accompany him home. As for Gertrude, from that night on, for a week she records "Legs very jumpy all night. . . . Bad night with legs. . . . Bad night. . . . Legs bothered me at night. . . . Legs bothered a lot at night. . . . I told them wanted nurse at studio & that I thought trouble was legs. . . ." By June 1 there is a nurse at the studio (Miss Hoskins) and a night nurse too, but Gertrude is walking badly and must admit, at least to her Line-A-Day, "Health bad."

Harry, who has been very compassionate and helpful to Gertrude during the weeks following her return from abroad, is now, since Payne's death, as sick as she. Neither of them has any energy to spare. Neither can explain to their doctors in very realistic or specific terms what is the matter. Again and again Gertrude writes, "Studio, very little work" or "Studio, short time." Then on June 9: "Drs. Kennedy, Hartwell, James. Decided I had neuritis. Very nervous. Sick. Judge [Morgan J.] O'Brien [an important member of the Knights of Columbus] came afternoon, liked monument. Stopped all alcohol." "Very nervous" or "jumpy" becomes a frequent entry now. Gertrude asks Dr. Hartwell about going abroad. He thinks it a good idea. Harry agrees. Flora agrees. Arrangements are made for Gertrude to sail in a week on the *Majestic* with her now regular nurse, Miss Hoskins.

In the terse Line-A-Day, it sounds as if Gertrude is at last really planning a rest. However, though that is part of her motivation, another part is, as usual, professional business. Alexander Moore, unwilling until now to approve any site that is not "on the exact spot from which Columbus put his foot on his boat" and still unhappy that Ferdinand and Isabella do not occupy a more prominent position in the design (preferably as prominent as that of Columbus himself), has agreed, if necessary, to reinspect the sites in Huelva and in Palos and to reconsider Gertrude's design in relation to them. He will be aboard the *Majestic,* available for discussion there and, again if necessary, in Paris where Anne Morgan awaits them.

JUNE 22: "Just as jumpy as ever. No drinks since June 9th."

≈

We return to Gertrude's correspondence with Paul Clayton, seemingly initiated by her in late April. In a draft of her first letter Gertrude proposes:

> I) that we just talk in writing to each other (faute de mieux) II) that we amuse each other and ourselves by telling a tale III) that we let our imaginations amuse themselves.

At first, (I) the talk is general, not nearly as revealing as the Line-A-Day, (II) the tales, fables really, are precious and cloyingly encouraging— Gertrude's about a prince with ideals which the world is always "pushing down," Paul's about a fairy who opens a frog's eyes but then disappears; and (III) both imaginations are unamusingly limited—Gertrude's, at this moment, restricted to ironic generalizations about life ("There are such beautiful things to see. Work is such fun. It's grand to be alive!") and Paul's to quoting a passage about a sorceress from the German-American romantic poet George Sylvester Viereck.

Gradually the correspondence warms and becomes more open. Paul's mother wants him put in a sanitarium. Gertrude speaks to the mother, insists that another specialist be called in, lends Paul $2,000 until his plans are resolved. At the same time she encourages him in various rather vague and scattered projects. She reads his "notes on Spinoza." Through Mrs. Force, she has an editor at *The New Yorker* look at his drawings. "He said they lacked humor which was an important asset (I know your state of mind had something to do with that)." Paul goes off to a ranch in Montana. In her letters to him there, she explains *her* state of mind. May 30:

> . . . [Payne's death] was a great shock as we had no idea he had anything at all the matter with him. I have always been really fond of him & Harry simply worshiped him so that I have done nothing ever since except to try & make things a little easier for H.
>
> It is an age since you went away & I feel lost without your visits. I loved hearing about the ranch & wish you needed a maid of all work to look after you! I would be so useful. But you are getting full of health & I am certainly not. I wasn't any too well before this blow came & now the little weight I had is disappearing. Which makes me think I had a funny dream about you too & it was so realistic that I woke up furious with the wicked fairy who only laughed at me. In my dream I gave her my back to give to you & she came to me and said

you didn't want it and I promptly sat down and cried and wondered
what on earth I should do with anything so useless. . . .

Gertrude writes at least six more letters to Paul before her departure. In
the second of these she says of their relationship, "if you think it was just
because I wanted to help, you are wrong. I wanted to be with you, I
wanted to talk to you and have you talk to me. I wanted just you—and
now this letter is getting to be almost a love letter—so I will change the
subject." From then on the subject is never really changed. Paul tells Gertrude he loves her. Gertrude replies that she is "marvelously happy" that
he does and that she longs for him and thinks of him continually.

Aboard ship Gertrude writes Paul every day. The letters are rather arch,
seemingly written as much for her own amusement as his, in a style she
describes as "not my own":

> . . . For minor offenses such as debauch, drunkenness and such like
> peccadillos I am debarred by company [Miss Hoskins] and doctors.
> With incredible irresponsibility I am becoming reconciled to my fate.
> After one anguished glance at the wine list I sip my Poland water in
> comparative calm and the profane thoughts that soil my mind are not
> visible to the most observing.
>
> *Sunday.* Instead of going to divine service this morning, with un-
> swerving devotion to the diversion of my life, I paddled myself about
> in a deliciously cool pool clad in becoming (even if I say it, what
> shouldn't) black silk jersey tights enjoying to the full one of the few
> sensual pleasures left in my repertoire. Under the influence of this
> emotion I became almost human and was able to endure the conver-
> sation of an ambassador [Moore], a trained nurse, and a cousin [Ruth
> Twombly]. Having deeply draughted (don't worry) of a naughty
> book, gazed at a drab colored sea and sky, I am now free to indulge in
> the pleasures of pen and dreams. A veritable avalanche of thoughts
> fill my mind. My thoughts dwell quite simply upon the outrages to
> which I have been subjected during my life and without undue rancor
> I recall effusions and ardor and even violences and I sigh—but so
> complicated is the human mind that I myself do not know if from
> regret or from what emotion. . . .
>
> The poverty of my imagination has never been questioned or chal-
> lenged and I continue to regard the future as excellent. . . .

Friday, July 1, on the way from Cherbourg to Paris, Gertrude meets
briefly at the Caen railroad station with Mama, Gladys, and two of the
Széchényi daughters. By late that afternoon Gertrude is in her Paris studio. By evening Jo Davidson is visiting her there. Saturday she has lunch
with him and Yvonne; in the afternoon has Anne Morgan to the studio,
where they work out their strategy in regard to Moore; in the evening has
O'Connor. Once again there is insufficient time to catch up on everything

that has happened, everything now since the end of March. O'Connor comes back on Sunday for lunch and then they go to the Salon, which is over except for a few remaining large pieces, including a "great monument" of his. Monday, Anne Morgan phones: "Moore will agree to anything." Later in the day: "Flowers from Moore!"

For Gertrude, Paris is not only enchanted but lucky, a city where peace and pace are compatible. We feel her spirits lifting as the next day she sits under a red and white striped umbrella writing to Paul: "Paris and my green bit of garden, my blue room, and the prospect of something new." She tells him that she has had good news about *Columbus* and that she will take O'Connor with her to Spain "to help out with practical questions." She has only one complaint: "I bet you still crave your cocktail, your whiskey, and your stinger—I do. Don't you like to think of me being as good as you are, or are you sorry for me? It's almost four weeks for me & I miss them very nearly as much as I did at the start but I am not quite so cross." And a few days later: "How I wish I could indulge in the cocktails and excellent champagne I am going to watch my guest imbibe. Wouldn't you like to also? Should I not have mentioned the subject? I wouldn't if I had not been in the same predicament myself." The subject is one which she mentions also to Harry: "Naturally I should *love* a drink but tea is becoming second nature."

Harry's health is improving. Flora reports that he has been playing some golf, has been to Belmont Park several times, and is going to referee a polo game in which Sonny and Jock will play. And within a few days, when Gertrude is ready to leave for Spain with Andrew O'Connor, she herself is well enough to take only her maid Marie along and leave Miss Hoskins behind.

This trip is pretty much a repetition of the one in March. Again, William Page has carefully briefed Gertrude as to which officials in Huelva and Palos she must see. However, by now (in a late June letter to Anne Morgan, with a copy to Gertrude) he has "established, beyond a peradventure, that 'the Port of Palos' was a generic term and included La Rábida, the Bar of Saltes, as well as the point at which Mrs. Whitney has advised that the statue be located, which we understand has the approval of the King and the Prime Minister. The Town of Palos was at the head of a very small inlet, from which Columbus' ships did *not* actually sail, and has long since been filled up. In other words, The Town of Palos was one thing, the Port of Palos, another." It is the clearing up of this confusion that so suddenly permits Anne Morgan and Gertrude to persuade Moore to accept the "Palos" site. Now there are only technical problems (having to do mostly with the foundation of the monument) to clear up with O'Connor's help, and final approvals to obtain with Ambassador Hammond's help. All this is achieved quickly and efficiently by Gertrude in an effort to comply with yet another tactical necessity outlined in Page's letter—that is, to be able to present complete plans for the monument to the Supreme Council of the Knights of Columbus which will meet in Portland, Oregon, on August 2, representing some 800,000 Knights, the largest group of potential contributors to the memorial.

In Madrid, on the way back to Paris, Gertrude spends almost a full day having official letters typed and translated by "a busy little Spaniard here at the Ritz." Along with this work she writes by hand to Harry, Paul, and Mrs. Force. These letters, filled with details about the monument, are all cheerful and affirmative except for references to Moore, whom she calls by the code nickname "Mud" in the letter to Mrs. Force. At the end of the day she has time only to "glimpse Velasquez" at the Prado.

About now, though probably not from the Ritz, she also drafts a long letter to Jo Davidson. With him there is no need to concentrate on the Columbus details—she has seen Jo recently and will see him soon again—she can be more broadly "philosophical":

Dear Jo, Life is funny and you are wonderful. We all have, I suppose, a part of us that wants to sing and dance and yet is continually checked by a spun web which we ourselves have spun. The desire to lie flat on the grass and roll like an animal—to have no thought, no consciousness of mystery, to be able to have all our faculties concentrated on just the act of living. And then only too soon time and space and thought start again.

How one imagines! For instance a fairyland—and suppose fairyland were the heart of someone and suppose you were imprisoned in it, but free to go anytime. In my fairyland there would be no walls to keep me in, or shackles to bind my legs and arms, or chains to hold me, but I would not be able to leave for there would be a thousand alluring things to do in fairyland. There would be undiscovered gardens with exotic fruits to taste and wild flowers to smell, and there would be a place with hidden chambers and underground passages in which one would wander and lose oneself. It would be a devastatingly fascinating place!

I don't believe anyone is as lonely as they sometimes feel, for no one is only an individual but is a part of life. He thinks the thoughts of humanity, his visions are part of life's visions. Are you ever worried by feeling how imitative people are, even the people who think for themselves? We answer to the shade and voice of our environment without wanting to. The sun shines and in its radiance we feel peaceful. The rain stills our voices. Why is it that when we are happy we are not conscious of happiness but when we are unhappy it weighs like thunder clouds? I have been going through the process of getting to know myself—a damn uncomfortable experience. It came about I suppose through having been sick and having no false stimulant. It used to be so easy, if you didn't want to face something just exactly as it was to take a cocktail. I wouldn't have missed this facing myself for anything, unpleasant as it often is. It gives one a sort of conceit, doesn't it? A kind of consciousness of power. I can face living with myself, and that is a hell of a lot to be able to say. I think that is the reason you have felt me to be happy. I feel a sort of grasp of things in life, real things. I used to do so many things without knowing why. I thought them inconsequential, they were not. They were the unconscious expression of a development which was going on inside me, and though vacillating, were perfectly direct in getting somewhere which is an island or a stepping stone on the way to a definite end, be it good or bad. And my stepping stone today is a happy island because I see so many more leading to others, so far dreamed of only.

And think of being able to say that at the age of fifty.

Or at fifty-two, which she is.

On her return, Gertrude spends only two days in Paris—the first at Elizabeth Arden's getting her hair done, the next "trying on" and then having dinner with Jo at her favorite Le Caneton, before seeing *Dr. Knock*. During the next ten days—at Cabourg, with her mother, her sister, and Gladys' five daughters ("seven female members of my family!")—she will finally *rest*. There she establishes a routine of massages every morning; short trips, mostly to Deauville, in the afternoon; and letter writing, mostly to Paul, in the evening. Oxymoronically, the days go, at once quick and slow. Gertrude enjoys her nieces (particularly the eldest, Cornelia, nicknamed Giglia, "like me, intelligent, moody, talented, and interesting"), she eats to gain weight, and she returns to Paris feeling good, except "locally" (in the legs). There, after a three-and-a-half-hour drive, she has dinner with Jo again, this time at Fouquet. She writes Paul: "It was a beautiful warm evening so we dined on the sidewalk & I loved it. The people and lights and Champs Elysees all were gay (unlike me) and as Jo and I were both having our troubles he was a sympathetic companion. We talked about everything but unpleasant things and ended up singing songs in the taxi going home."

Gertrude begins the sculptures of Ferdinand and Isabella, which will be within the base of the monument, and gets off to a good start, resting between stretches of work. After three days she motors back to Cabourg with her mother where they receive a wire from Gladys that she has had to go to Pest because László has had a "slight automobile accident." The next day Gladys wires that László "had cut face," and the day after that he "had to have left eye removed." Gertrude can't sleep thinking about Gladys and László. She determines to make the trip to Pest if all is not going well. However, within a few days she receives word that at least László's right eye is all right and that he is recovering.

When Gertrude returns to Paris her work pattern changes, intensifies. At first there are Line-A-Day entries like "Worked on King & Queen" or "Worked half day," but soon, as if emphasizing rushed excitement, the entries become simply "Worked. . . . Worked. . . . Worked. . . .

Same. . . . Same. . . ." In a mid-August letter to Paul she writes: "Work went like wildfire today. A romantic queen emerged in royal regalia, strong, proud and yet feminine too, a king thoughtful yet full of pomp." And a few days later she writes him: "Nothing outside seems to make any difference these last six or seven days. It rains or is cold or the sun shines or it doesn't. I get letters and telegrams; except when they are from you, I forget what they say. The four walls of my being and the four walls of my studio are all I am conscious of. . . . Dinner is over and I am going back for a couple of hours work—to have a whack at my reliefs."

Ferdinand and Isabella are finished August 20, ready to be removed from the studio and cast. Before becoming too deeply involved with the corner reliefs, Gertrude allows herself an abbreviated but expensive, perhaps "economically therapeutic," weekend. With Jo Davidson she takes the Saturday afternoon train to Tours to visit Yvonne and her mother at the Davidsons' nearby country place, Becheron, "an old tower sticking out at one end of an uneven roof, soft-colored stone steps, big shady trees, a courtyard, a high wall, flower garden, vineyards." Sunday, they visit Azay-le-Rideau and some other châteaux, including Le Boulay, a much more elaborate and castellated place than Jo's but with some of the same feeling. Gertrude finds it "enchanting" and decides to buy it, intending to have it used mostly by Flora and Cully, who have expressed a desire to spend more time in France.

During the month following this weekend—that is, until returning to New York—there is hardly an entry in Gertrude's Line-A-Day which doesn't refer specifically to "Reliefs." Immediately upon her return workmen, under Eddy Minazzoli's supervision, begin construction in her garden of a full-scale (44-foot-high) model of the Columbus Memorial pedestal. August 25: "Reliefs. Pedestal finished. Is enormous. Very different anniversary from last year." Then, for the thirtieth, her family had arranged a dinner party in Westbury, an exception among many years of unrecognized anniversaries; now, more typically, she is alone, preparing to study, at the proper height, the reliefs of "hemispheres opened to the world by Columbus."

Each relief, symmetrically wrapped around the corners of the pedestal, is about eight feet square—i.e., four by eight on each of the two faces of each corner. The first, over the door leading to the Ferdinand and Isabella shrine, depicts Europe, the State, the Church, and the Army suppressing the barbarian. Next, to the right: American Indians, Progress, and Labor. Continuing to the right, on the back of the pedestal: Asia, Chinese Mysticism, and Arabs. And on the last corner: Africa and Egypt, the source of learning and art. But, in their stylization, all of the reliefs are "Egyptian." As Gertrude says in a letter to Paul, they are "decorations . . . treated as such, really only light and shade; general character & arabesque will count."

The studio work goes on, barely interrupted by an occasional dinner out with Jo Davidson or Andrew O'Connor or, when Mama is in Paris, with her. Gertrude drives herself terribly, knowing that it will be easier to complete most of the work here than at long distance from New York. The correspondence about the work goes on with Page, with Hammond, with Anne Morgan, with Juliana Force, and others. However, it is only to Paul Clayton that she admits how hard, how exhaustingly and at times discouragingly she is working: "I would like to toss it out of the window—to hell with Columbus, it is keeping me away. I might have had part of the summer with you if it had not been for the miserable creature's discovering America, but then if he hadn't neither of us would have existed, would we? . . . I want to sulk and I do terribly want a drink. A stinger, two stingers, three stingers."

During Gertrude's last weeks in Paris she continues to isolate herself in her work, seeing few people, using her correspondence with Paul Clayton as a safe, long-distance outlet for social and sexual fantasies. Even on the few occasions when she leaves the studio the events seem mostly obligatory—lunch at Jo's with Secretary of the Treasury Andrew Mellon, a "shut-in man" whose bust Jo is doing; a drive with Mama on the second anniversary of Regi's death; frequent discussions with Andrew O'Connor about the reliefs and the length of Columbus' legs in the main sculpture. She permits herself only one evening at the opera—*La Bohème*, with Jo. She hardly has time for dinner at Tour d'Argent with her old friend Charles Draper; she is too busy supervising five workmen, sending drawings and specifications to Spain for cost estimates, corresponding with the Columbus Committee. Afternoons off are the rarest of all—perhaps four or five in a month. Some she spends having tea and shopping with friends or relatives, but one, described in a letter to Paul, seems almost a conscious attempt to recapture childhood: "First I went and had an ice cream soda & some paté, then I got rubbed all over hard & perfumed, powdered & rouged, then I gave the pedestrians on the boulevard a good time, had a sirop at the Café de la Paix, said my prayers at the Madeleine, felt very superior, and am wondering now why I don't spend every afternoon like that."

There is a tone of innocence in Gertrude's letters to Paul as her departure and their reunion near. (He is about to return to New York.) In late August she had written to him about the sensuousness of Indian art, her inability to sleep thinking about it and him. "I am tingling all over. . . . It makes me weak. It is like making love when one loves. You lose yourself in another world where reality touches the limits of unreality." And a few days later: "I wonder and tremble and feel weak and fear change just as you do. And that is the time I want you most. I am going to confess: sometimes even I think it might be better if we never saw each other but just went on writing—always." He complains that she is becoming "unkind and cold." But she avoids a confrontation and pads her letters with impersonal games: "There has been a popular vote taken in England as to who are the six greatest men living today. The most votes were gotten by Mussolini, Einstein, Shaw, Foch, Marconi & Edison. I should leave out Foch. What do you think? Funny, an English vote & not an Englishman! Shaw is Irish. What do you think of Ford or Rockefeller?" Shorter letters follow: "We both seem rather panicky, don't we, about N.Y.? . . . Does distance lend enchantment? Why am I trying to analyze, to ask foolish questions? Is it because you are sending me unconsciously your own fears and doubts?"

No, those sendings are mutual. Though Gertrude has been immersed in her work, one aspect of her real life, she is returning now to other aspects as well—her immediate family, her social circle, the activities at the Whitney Studio Club. Paul is no longer necessary, he might indeed further complicate her already complicated life. As Gertrude sails home on the *Olympic* (bringing Gladys' middle daughter Gladys with her for schooling in the States) there are no letters to Paul. Gertrude's torrent of words—drafted and redrafted nearly every day for almost four months now—reduces, after her return, to the merest trickle: "I am so rushed I am sorry I cannot see you. . . . I was busy with some people or would have chatted longer . . . busy on business. . . ." There is no way of telling how much of this change in tone is willed by Gertrude, how much provoked by Paul. He is drinking again, battling with his mother, in debt, and involved with a "girl" (undoubtedly much younger than Gertrude). By Christmas Eve the relationship is distant. Gertrude writes him a note then explaining that she will not be able to see him the next day, and continues: ". . . I am sorry I have been so busy lately that we could not sit down peacefully and have a more satisfactory talk about your Spinoza or anything else! Now that you are on the right track you must be so much more cheerful in your own mind. I know your Xmas won't be very cheerful, but your mother will get your card and be glad and before long who can tell how things may have picked up. Even if you don't think so—work is a great comfort. With all my best wishes for your happiness." There is no evidence of further communication between Gertrude and Paul. His name appears only once again in her papers—as the central character of a melodramatic short story called "A Star Beyond," probably written in 1928. There "Clayton," a weak, unsuccessful, alcoholic writer-painter in his late twenties, makes forgeries of paintings by a dead friend and is saved finally by the love of an understanding woman.

&

With Ferdinand and Isabella and the reliefs completed, Gertrude concentrates on the refinement and enlargement of the Columbus figure itself, working with the model of it she has had shipped to Westbury. She also continues work on the *Daughters of the American Revolution*. As usual now, she is busy with correspondence concerning these and possible new commissions. And, finally, the suit brought by Katherine Minahan is settled, out of court, for an undisclosed amount.

But despite all this her schedule, compared with that in Paris, is relaxed. She spends a great deal of time with her family, especially with Barbie, who is expecting another child. This time that goes smoothly. On the day that Barbie goes to the hospital, Dr. Owens of the Columbus Committee brings Dr. Belisario Porras, former President of Panama, to Gertrude's studio. Porras wants Gertrude to do a statue in Panama City of Theodore Roosevelt, who in 1904 had recognized (many think too quickly and expediently) Panamian independence from Colombia. "Roosevelt Monument in Panama!" Gertrude writes in her Line-A-Day. Then, later that night: "Buz called me at 3 A.M. to say he had just been telephoned from Dr. Lobenstein's that Barbie had been taken to the delivery room. Baby was born 3:35. Boy [W. Barklie Henry]. 9 lbs. 9 oz. Great rejoicing."

Dr. Owens follows up his visit to Gertrude's studio with several calls urging her to visit Panama City. Little Barklie and the potential Panama commission are a hopeful end to a difficult year. There are no further entries in the Line-A-Day until Christmas weekend when Gertrude and Harry take the midnight train to Boston to visit the Henrys—one reason, anyway, for Gertrude's not being able to see Paul Clayton on Christmas Day.

December 29, Gertrude and Mrs. Force leave for Havana, en route to Panama.

⇜ 1928

They have only New Year's Day in Havana, during which they go to the races at Oriental Park in the afternoon, dine at the Sevilla Biltmore roof, and spend the rest of the evening at the Casino Nationale. The next day they board the *Manchuria* for Panama. Once again Gertrude does her homework aboard ship: "General Information, Notes on a Variety of Subjects, Panama." The notes contain a history of the country and the canal; a description of its geography and topography; an analysis of its ethnic strains as well as other anthropological information; paragraphs on the current political and economic situation. Only once in this sheaf of notes does Gertrude digress from material directly connected with Panama. This digression is, however, surely connected with her reason for going there—fame; more specifically, women's fame:

> The Noble Prize [sic—this time the slip in spelling is revealing enough to record], 1926, has been awarded to Signora Grazia Deledda (only one other woman, Selma Lagerlöf, has won it). Only "La Madre" & one other book have been translated into English. She is a tragic writer, especially fond of describing the wild nature of the people of her own birthplace, Sardinia.
>
> Mazo de la Roche, author of "Jalna," winner of the $10,000 Atlantic Monthly Prize. Born in Toronto, Canada.

Early the morning of January 5 they arrive at Colón and spend the day on deck enjoying the tropical scenery and the activity around the canal locks as the *Manchuria* slowly makes its way to Balboa. There they are met by Mrs. Harry Burgess, wife of the acting governor of the Canal Zone, and members of the Panama-Roosevelt Memorial Association. From then on, for a week, there are only official receptions—a long list of Panamanian and American politicians, ambassadors, generals and admirals, including former President Porras and present President Rodolfo Chiari, who tells Gertrude it was his idea, not Porras', to have a Roosevelt monument: the first hint Gertrude has of political rivalry concerning her project.

In Line-A-Day summary, the visit is a relocated repetition of Gertrude's recent trips to Spain. By the third day she has "Practically decided ledge on Gold Hill for site." By the end of the week everything concerning the monument seems settled, and there is time to see Lindbergh land in Panama on a goodwill flight from Costa Rica, and to go to a reception for *him*. Lucky Lindy! The Bird Man! The Lone Eagle! How Gertrude identifies with him. How, like everyone else, she admires his courage, his youthful good looks, his quiet charm. (He is surely the single greatest national, and probably international, hero of the adulatory twenties.) Lindy! Sailing home, she makes sketches of him, wanting to preserve his soaring qualities, those of a shooting star, in something very permanent, like bronze or stone. Permanence, by now, just now, at fifty-three, is very important. The night after her birthday Gertrude dances on deck, has "great fun," thinks about Lindbergh—"a loner," like herself.

⤙

By the end of the month Gertrude has entered into a contract with the Panama-Roosevelt Memorial Association "to erect and complete . . . on a spot called Gold Hill . . . commemorative monument to Theodore Roosevelt . . . in accordance with a design and plan approved by a Committee of the Association." The price for the monument, including Gertrude's work, is estimated at $250,000. One hundred dollars is to be paid on signing, $5,000 when the design is approved, $50,000 when excavation on Gold Hill is started, $100,000 when the sculpture is ready to be cast, the balance when the monument is completed ("about November 23, 1930").

In effect, Gertrude is acting now as a general contractor, accepting not only the risk of her client's credit (dependent always on the necessary funds being raised) but the risks also of design approval and excess cost (against which she is protected only by the good faith of the committee to pay such excess if "mutually agreed upon by the parties"). Probably no other sculptor of the time would or could accept such conditions. However, Gertrude's financial advantage in competing for commissions is by now matched by experience in completing them and by her familiarity with costs. Her financial stability and experienced speed, along with her help in fund raising, are all as important to her clients—advantages to *them*—as her sculptural talent.

Even as the Panama-Roosevelt contract is being signed, a similar one for the Columbus monument is being prepared. Here Gertrude is taking less risk. The Knights of Columbus, as well as the Spanish government, have endorsed the project; the committee, even Moore, has finally approved the design; and estimates have been obtained; but still there is no certainty that the money will be raised or that the cost won't exceed, in this case, $300,000 (with no provision for review).

As if emphasizing the uncertainties of commissions, a front-page story breaks March 6:

PANAMA PLAN FOR ROOSEVELT SHAFT TOTTERS

Committee Notables, Hearing Politics Backs Project,
Indicate They Will Withdraw Their Names

Promoters Act to Save Their Campaign

Dr. Porras Naming Canal Zone Group
to Assume His Work in Movement

The headlines barely summarize the intrigue behind them. President Chiari has accused former President Porras of using the Roosevelt Memorial to advance his own political aspirations (i.e., in running again for President). Chiari also points out that the Honorary Committee of United States citizens (not to be confused with the Panamanian Committee, headed by Dr. Porras) does not have the endorsement of the Roosevelt Memorial Association (not to be confused with the Panama-Roosevelt Memorial Association), which prohibits the use of Roosevelt's name for personal gain or the advancement of individuals. What is not to be confused *is* confused. In the absence of the Roosevelt Memorial Association's endorsement, members of the Honorary Committee withdraw— first Dr. Owens, as a friend and adviser of Dr. Porras; then such "notables" as General Pershing and Governor Smith. The newspapers get a statement from Gertrude, through Mrs. Force, that "her only interest in the matter is that of an artist employed to perform a task." The decimated Panama-Roosevelt Honorary Committee will struggle on for four more years. This June a bill will be presented to Congress. The next year Dr. Porras will be forced to resign from the Panamanian Committee. And finally, in 1932, a member of the Panamanian Committee will report: "There never was any real interest awakened down here, either among the Panamanians or Americans. A small group of the latter felt a great deal of indignation at what they considered the exploitation of Mrs. Whitney."

When Gertrude resumes her Line-A-Day, the entries are terse: "Went to 'Simba' animal movie. . . . Harry arrived from Thomasville. . . . Toscanini Concert. . . . Paderewski at Carnegie. . . . Flower Show [she wins a gold medal for her garden design]. . . . Mama dined. . . . Barbie, Buz arrived from Boston. . . . Mr. ——— to see Lindbergh sketch." The entries, covering two weeks, flash by as quickly as the preceding two months of blank pages. Then suddenly (March 30): "Harry saw me off Majestic sailing 12 P.M."

Up until almost the moment of departure there is a new flurry of correspondence and meetings concerning yet another commission. A Dr. George Schadt of Springfield, Massachusetts, has formed a committee (again, yet another!) to erect a memorial to the 104th Massachusetts Regiment. The committee has been impressed with the beauty of the St. Nazaire monument, "so much so that we have felt we should like to obtain your interest in our little monument." There is a hurried meeting, a description by Dr. Schadt of the Apremont Triangle site, a promise from Gertrude that she will visit Springfield when she returns.

Though the main purpose of this European trip is to arrange the details for the following year's unveiling of the Columbus Memorial (of which, as she departs, studies are on exhibition at the first Whitney Studio Club Annual devoted exclusively to sculpture), aboard ship Gertrude is already making the first sketches of the Springfield Memorial. She has an idea that will develop through many variations: the contrast between a stark caisson bearing only a coffin with a soldier stretched out on it and, in the background, a more romantic sculpture of a mother offering her child in battle.

Neily and Grace are on the *Majestic*. Except for that notation and the names of mutual friends ("Hoytie [Wiborg, the sister of Sara Murphy], Mrs. [Frank B.] Wiborg etc. etc. on board . . . Dined Mitchels"), the crossing is a blank which can be filled in with the usual massages, walks around the deck, and reading and writing as well as sketching.

In Paris, too, Gertrude sees a lot of her brother and sister-in-law and their friends and, for a week before returning to the States, Flora and

Cully. It is a relaxed period, with no indication of work, during which almost each day bears some such notation as "Everything grand" or "Fine Day" or "Beautiful day again." It is just what we mean by "Paris in the spring." A photograph taken of Gertrude and Cully in the studio garden says it all: the smile on Gertrude's face as she shakes a cocktail, the comfortable knit suit, the dense foliage in the background.

Not until after Flora and Cully leave does Gertrude see O'Connor, and then only briefly before leaving for Madrid. Even her itinerary is more leisurely than usual. "Night Angers. . . . Nantes for lunch, then to St. N[azaire]. Big thrill. On to La Boule. Nantes for night. Movies. . . . Motored to Bordeaux. Musical comedy *Les Trois Vierges Nues.* . . . Motored to Biarritz. . . . Marie [Sonny's wife] met me on Madrid train. . . . Arrived Madrid 9:15. O. Hammond took me to call on the Primo who was most delightful. Said he preferred unveiling to be a few days after opening of Seville Ex[position] March 15 [1929]. He & King would be present. Lunched Embassy. Went to polo. Saw Alba. Americans (2 Hoppings, Schwartz & Sanford) against Spanish. Night in Madrid."

With her mission accomplished, Gertrude returns to Paris for a few days, spent mostly with O'Connor on final details concerning the Columbus Memorial. Then she leaves for Rome with Cecil Howard, who will be her escort for ten days in Sicily. Again, compared with previous trips, the itinerary is leisurely. They join the William Adams Delanos on the boat from Naples to Palermo and, once there, spend most mornings sightseeing, followed by picnic lunches and several afternoons sketching Greek ruins. Besides Bill Delano, architects seem to be everywhere. When Gertrude and Cecil Howard return to Naples, Thomas Hastings and his wife appear as well as an architect named Kendell of McKim, Mead & White, all of whom will be aboard the *Roma* with Gertrude when it leaves for New York on May 3.

Perhaps it is further indication of Gertrude's relaxed mood that four days out, having just passed the Azores, she discontinues her Line-A-Day. There is just one clue concerning the voyage, an unsigned scrap of verse sent to Gertrude on ship's stationery, dated May 11, the last day out:

> A perfect ship.
> A perfect trip.
> A more than perfect woman!
> And yet, because of fam'ly ties,
> By God, we can't be human.

Nor are there many clues about the rest of this year. Gertrude and Harry spend most of the spring in Long Island. In photographs of them walking from the paddock at Belmont (June 6), Gertrude is very thin and drawn, though erect and, as always, elegantly dressed (cloche, drop earrings, pearls, silver fox neckpiece, silk chiffon dress and scarf, small pouch handbag hanging from bony wrist, buttoned pumps. In contrast, Harry appears bloated. His face is puffy; his dark, double-breasted suit baggy. His body seems to be pulled forward by large binoculars around his neck, and his bulging weight leans heavily on a cane in his swollen left hand. From other photographs, we know that much of July and August is spent in Newport, sometimes racing the *Vanitie*, which Harry will sell, because of his health, at the end of this season.

At the beginning of June, Gertrude goes to Springfield and immediately afterward commissions her son-in-law's architecture firm, Noel & Miller, to do drawings of the Apremont Triangle. In July she is working in her Newport studio on sketches for the Springfield Memorial, when she decides to write a fan letter to Struthers Burt about his current short-story collection *They Could Not Sleep*, whose formal aspects she finds analogous to those of great sculpture. "I am struggling with a limited vision and a small vocabulary to do it [i.e., achieve form] in my line—sculpture. Anyway, the monument I am working on now simplifies itself and I seem better able to put the thought behind it in, besides having more courage to risk its unpopularity." (The risk Gertrude is running has to do with the caisson which, through progressive studies on paper and in plasteline, has become not only more simplified but more brutal, especially in contrast to its increasingly softer and more sentimental background.)

From the Bar B C Ranch in Jackson Hole, Wyoming, Burt replies appreciatively:

> . . . I have so long known and admired your work that it was particularly gratifying to have you discover mine. . . . I want so damned much to say things correctly, but life is so intangible. Especially the life of this great, fluid, at times heart-breaking republic. Yet I would rather have a sculptor find something in my attempts than anyone else, because they—sculptors—of all people most appreciate form, and therefore intangibility. . . .
>
> The American writer, for all his cleverness, is still destructive and childish. He takes the toy apart and examines each isolated part and describes it accurately, but he hasn't yet reached the maturity which desires passionately to describe, not the disjointed toy, but a better toy made out of the parts refitted and put together again. The sculptor—at least so it seems to me, although I am quite ignorant on the subject—starts with no such infantile idea as the former; not even Brancusi. He must have as his object the creation of form out of the void—the most primal and fundamental urge there is. The only God, if there is any. . . .

Burt's sympathetic and flattering voice is one to which Gertrude immediately responds in kind:

. . . I don't wonder the writer has difficulty in putting together the toys he has so bravely pulled apart. Writing was surely the devil's own invention. . . . At least in my game I am limited. Form and color, material too, stand as arbiters—saviors maybe. . . .

I often think making a statue (or a book or a picture) is exactly like having a baby. First the ecstasy of conception, then the discomfort, nervousness, fear of the period that follows, culminating in the agony of birth. The child is yours but no longer part of you. You are ready to create again, and so on, always believing that the child to come will more nearly approach your desires. I suppose all arts have truth, or correctness as you call it as their basis. But what is truth? What is true to you is a lie to me. But no matter so long as you tell your truth and I tell mine. It is only insincerity that is odious. . . .

The sketch I was working on when I wrote you I will get a little photograph of to send you, if I may. It's to try its chances with a Mass. Com. soon now. Must American soldiers always wave flags? What about the solemnity of war?

Heavens it's fun to work! . . .

Though Gertrude has previously, in her correspondence and journals, compared making sculpture with having a baby, she may now be thinking too of Flora, who is about to give birth to her third child, Gertrude's seventh grandchild to date, Flora Macculloch Miller, born September 21. On either side of this event—and one more important to Juliana Force, the death of her somewhat estranged husband the same day Little Flora is born—Mrs. Force makes announcements, carefully prepared with Gertrude, of another kind of birth. These describe the penultimate step toward the founding of the Whitney Museum of American Art, the idea which has been in Gertrude's mind and journals since 1904. First, on September 7, there's the simple statement that the Studio Club, which has been closed since May 15, will not be reopened as a club, but will, in November, be used as an art gallery—the Whitney Studio Galleries—directed by Mrs. Force and open to all artists who qualify for exhibits. Two weeks later there's a more detailed statement about the history of the Club and the reasons for closing it:

When the Whitney Studio Club was organized with twenty members in 1914 there were few galleries where liberal American art was welcome. A limited number of Americans were included in the "modern" exhibitions occurring from time to time, but very few artists were enabled to show their work consistently.

In the belief that a useful purpose could be served by opening a gallery devoted to the free expression of non-partisan American artists, the Whitney Studio Club was organized. Many of the artists who showed their pictures and sculpture publicly for the first time at the galleries of the Club have since found the doors of other galleries hospitably open to them.

During the period in which the Whitney Studio Club has aimed to promote liberal American art, the attitude of the public has changed. Art dealers and Directors of great official exhibitions have also changed their point of view. Opportunities for showing work by young American artists have increased tremendously, and academic restraint has become almost insignificant.

The Club, which now consists of four hundred members, is proud to have played its part in bringing about this invigorating change. But this very change makes the Club no longer a pioneer organization. Artists for whom twelve years ago it was necessary to fight are now in high favor. More than this, a general liberal movement in art is in high favor.

The pioneering work for which the Club was organized has been done; its aim has been successfully attained. The liberal artists have won the battle which they fought so valiantly, and will celebrate the victory as other regiments fighting for liberty have done—by disbanding. Believing that the victory which its talented members have helped win for American art will grow greater with the years, the Whitney Studio Club wishes every member success and happiness.

In early November, when the Whitney Studio Galleries open, Mrs. Force is interviewed by the New York *Herald*. She makes three main points: (1) that both native and foreign work will be shown; (2) that no particular school will be emphasized; and (3) that the new galleries will compete with "the Fifth Avenue galleries," with nothing philanthropic about this enterprise. Mrs. Force enlarges upon the last point: "I will show the work of artists whom Mrs. Whitney and I believe in. We are interested from a personal point of view in certain artists, just as we believe other galleries are interested personally in the men they represent. The gallery will revert to and carry on the idea which was originally behind the Whitney Studio Club. That was the idea of an exhibiting gallery for contemporary art rather than an organization of artists philanthropically inspired."

Mrs. Force's points provoke counterpoints. During the brief period that the Whitney Studio Galleries remain open—from November 1928 through March 1930, excluding the summer of 1929—there will be forty one-man exhibitions, of which only two will be devoted to foreign artists, both French, Gerard Cochet and Dujam Penic. Thus, though Mrs. Force's comment is technically accurate, this metamorphosis of the various Whitney exhibition facilities is as basically devoted to American art as its predecessors and its final successor. Indeed, the five one-man shows scheduled for the end of 1928—Glenn O. Coleman, Ernest Fiene, Kenneth Frazier, Reginald Marsh, and Isabel Whitney (no relation)—are a very fair sampling nationalistically, as well as stylistically, qualitatively and sexually (about twenty per cent women) of what the Galleries will show. Another link to the Club is the Christmas Sale this year (and the following year) of small works by members. This had become a tradition at the Club and is announced now as an "annual affair." However, sales cannot support the expense of operating two buildings, installing frequent shows, printing catalogues, paying salaries to Mrs. Force and her small staff, and giving her, rent free, the beautiful duplex apartment above the Galleries. In short, the Studio Galleries, like the Studio Club and Studio, are "philanthropic" and are not really in competition with "Fifth Avenue."

Perhaps financial success for the Whitney Studio Galleries is only a passing fantasy of Gertrude's, encouraged by Mrs. Force—and the times. Everything is booming—the stock market, the nation's business, Gertrude's commissions. . . . Herbert Hoover, running against Al Smith, wins the presidential election in a landslide. . . . It is a period of tremendous optimism and speculation. We can almost hear Juliana Force telling Gertrude that surely, surely there will be lots of money for work by young American artists.

⇌

Meanwhile, the Columbus monument is booming and growing too, and Gertrude, anxious to see the progress, awaits word from Andrew O'Connor as to when she should plan her next trip to Spain. In mid-October she receives a telegram from him bringing her up to date:

NO NECESSITY FOR YOU TO COME NOW STOP PROGRESS SATISFACTORY STONE PEDESTAL TWO THIRDS FINISHED AND WILL BE ENTIRELY FINISHED DECEMBER FIRST WHEN SETTING STATUE IN PLACE STOP TWENTY MEN WORKING ON STATUE STOP SCULPTURE PANELS FINISHED READY TO BE SET TWENTYSIXTH THIS MONTH STONE GROUP INTERIOR IN PLACE NOVEMBER FIFTH STONE INTERIOR CHAMBER BEING EXECUTED IN PARIS READY TO PUT IN PLACE JANUARY ROUGH STONE SEAWALL IS IN PLACE I SHALL BE IN HUELVA NEXT WEEK ADJUSTING STONE PANELS PLEASE CABLE ME THIRTYTHOUSAND DOLLARS IMMEDIATE PAYMENT DUE CONTRACTOR

Gertrude books passage on the *Ile de France* for November 16.

Aboard ship, she writes a long letter to her sister Gladys, in which she thanks her for caviar sent as a bon voyage gift, describes the usual shipboard routine, and highly recommends *Orlando*, the recently published novel by Virginia Woolf, "if you like her books, which I do very much." However, the part of the letter most revealing of Gertrude deals with one of Gladys' daughters:

. . . If only G[ladys, the daughter] could get interested in writing. Try (as an idea) to make her write something about Hungary, get it published, without perhaps her knowing you had had anything to do with it. That might rouse her ambition. . . . There is something about seeing yourself in print, just as in an exhibition, which I am sure to some people means an awful lot. She is such a remarkable kid, has so much in her. Look what having to do something did to L[ászló]. Or maybe if you were very frank with her & told her (which you probably have many times) that she *ought* to write, that it is all wrong for a person with talent to let it go to waste, that people were so much happier in having a resource in themselves, that nothing in life gives one the pleasure which comes from expressing oneself, that at least it is stupid if one can express to give up the chance of having that joy. To try it and if she does not get it, alright then give it up, but not to give herself a chance of happiness entirely outside of anything that may ever happen to her is not intelligent. The outside happiness will come too, but this is something so precious that, if she once knows its fascination, all the trouble and concentration which it takes will be as nothing to her gain. I feel all this strongly and I *know*.

In Paris, Gertrude starts making entries in a new small blue leather-bound notebook. At the beginning ("Paris 2:15 PM") and during the rest of this trip, it is not a Line-A-Day but, as with this first entry, hardly more than a Word-A-Day: a list of undated stops, usually along with the distance in kilometers from one to another as Gertrude again motors through France to Spain, this time continuing by car all the way to Madrid. There, on December 2, a luncheon reception is given for her at the American Embassy before, after only a day, she continues her trip south.

In the blue notebook there is no indication as to whether O'Connor accompanies Gertrude on this trip or meets her in Palos. Nor is there any indication yet of her reaction to progress on the monument. There are only seemingly arbitrary lists of towns visited and kilometers covered—Seville, Córdova, Palos, Málaga, Granada, Palos—which indicate some sightseeing between the last slow stages of construction. There are also seemingly arbitrary lists of useful Spanish words and phrases, though the first list begins with compelling logic: "Que debo? What do I owe? rainy, lluvioso." We can only say with certainty that Gertrude is somewhere in Spain—rainy, winter Spain—at the end of the year.

← *1929*

Early this year, Gertrude receives the following letter on the crested stationery of the Palacio de Liria in Madrid:

My dear Mrs. Whitney,

Your letter of the 22nd. December reached me whilst I was laid up with 'flu in bed, where I still am. I have communicated with General Primo de Rivera and have announced your visit to Huelva for January 9th, asking him to inform the Authorities. I have also communicated with His Majesty about the exact date, as you wish, for the inauguration of your monument. He has not been able to give me any exact date owing to the innumerable occupations that will crop up at that time, but he suggests that you should fix the date any day that suits you best, between the 20th and 30th April, and then he will most certainly attend if he possibly can.

If you come through here and want to see me, please let me know and I shall be delighted to be of use to you if by then I have got rid of my 'flu.

Yours very sincerely,
Alba

This establishes the theme for the first third of the new year, during which Gertrude will devote herself almost entirely to final work on the Columbus Memorial and elaborate preparations for its dedication and unveiling April 20 and 21, the dates (obviously as early as possible) which she sets. We don't know if Gertrude visits the Duke of Alba on her way to Huelva but there, while meeting with local officials, she announces on January 10 that she and several American friends in and/or of Spain will contribute funds for the restoration of the La Rábida Monastery—a suggestion, previously made by William Page and endorsed by Ogden Hammond, intended (successfully, as it turns out) to overcome the last opposition of Huelva in its rivalry with Palos.

Gertrude returns to New York at the end of January and remains just over a month, during which she meets frequently with the Columbus Memorial Committee. They go over invitation lists for the ceremonies; resolve problems of transportation to and housing (ultimately aboard a cruise ship) in Huelva; prepare a brochure, speeches, and publicity. At the same time she fulfills similar obligations to the Daughters of the American Revolution, whose monument will be dedicated just three days before the one for Columbus, and since she cannot be there, arranges for both her daughter Barbara Henry and her sister the Countess Széchényi to represent her at that unveiling. However, although there may be some guilt at not being in Washington, there is no sense of sacrifice. Gertrude has made a choice, even clearer and easier than that, in 1924, between *Buffalo Bill* and *St. Nazaire*. The D.A.R. Memorial—a single, heavily draped female figure with arms outspread—is comparatively small (just larger than life size); conventional (partly because this sponsoring group, like others in the past, has objected to Gertrude's original nude studies); and narrowly national. In contrast, the Columbus monument is colossal, unconventional, and international. There is no doubt about which will get more attention or about where Gertrude wants to be.

In March, before Gertrude departs, Juliana Force is preparing the most lively and popular exhibition done by the Whitney Studio Galleries, "The Circus in Paint." It is the kind of gay theme show in which both women delight. They must chuckle together as Mrs. Force tells Gertrude about Louis Bouché's proposed decorations—sawdust on the floor, an organ grinder (with a monkey) vending peanuts at the entrance, a stuffed horse in the main gallery, circus tubs as seats, lambrequins of vivid scalloped material masking the moldings of the ceiling from which clusters of balloons will hang. The catalogue, designed by Kaj Klitgaard, is equally playful: a circus tent, flying the American flag, and containing a ringmaster and brightly colored animals, all bathed in light from a yellow sun with a smiling face.

Though the show—and especially its trappings—sounds frivolous, it is fundamentally serious. In the catalogue introduction, Lloyd Goodrich (then an editor of *The Arts*; later, a staff member of the Whitney Museum; and still later, its director) traces the circus, as a theme for artists, from the mountebanks of Watteau and Hogarth to the circus figures in Degas, Toulouse-Lautrec, and Picasso, and finally to the artists in this exhibition, for whom, as for their predecessors, "the circus is a gorgeous and richly human spectacle." The thirty-six artists included are all former members of the Whitney Studio Club. Many of the works by those with established reputations are on loan or otherwise not for sale (e.g., Glackens, Marsh, Demuth). Other paintings are offered at prices of less than $100 (e.g., John Steuart Curry, a new "Regionalist" who will here be given his first one-man show the following year) to as much as $2,500 (John Sloan, by now an American Master). But most of the prices are low, and once again it is apparent that the show can't pay for itself. However, it is most unlikely that Gertrude would have brought this up. More likely, she would only have shared Juliana's enthusiasm and filed the economic facts for reference on the future of the Studio Galleries. And surely, once overseas, she would have been very pleased to receive reviews like that by Edward Alden Jewell in the *Times*, affirming "the freshness of the idea, including the peanuts," or that by Murdock Pemberton in the four-year-old but already chic and influential *New Yorker:* "When they come to award shining palms for the art season, we would bespeak one for the enterprise and *joie de vivre* of the Whitney Galleries, which manages to connect art with the ebb and flow of this large town . . . it is a lively exciting show and we hope you have sense enough to see it."

❧

In Huelva, as on her previous trip, Gertrude stays in a small uncomfortable rental room accessible only through the town's largest restaurant. The accommodations are, in addition to being noisy, so stark and drab that when Flora arrives in April she is shocked and photographs the cheap furniture, worn carpet, and bare walls. However, there are no complaints from Gertrude. What complaints she has concern past progress on the monument, but more generally she is elated. Using her small blue book, she drafts a telegram to O'Connor in Paris:

EVERY MAN TURNED UP THIS MORNING ON HIS JOB INCLUDING ME. HOPE FOR SAME TOMORROW. THREE CARLOADS STONE DELIVERED. THREE MORE AT STATION. CHANCES SCAFFOLD WILL BE DOWN END THIS WEEK. MC AULIFFE [the sculptor F. J. McAuliffe whom O'Connor has hired to assist him with supervision] OUT TODAY. MISS YOU BOTH BUT PLEASE DON'T HURRY BACK.

Gertrude's entries expand, beginning March 25:

. . . I was so tired the first days and I did not know why, now I do. It is only now that I realize I was living in emotions. . . . To see suddenly before you the real dream in great blocks of stone is overpowering. The cloud shapes one visualized come down to earth. God. The fascination of building, of creation! Now I see it all more clearly. At first it was just this is to be done, that, how can we get so and so to act, such and such to progress. Where will more stone men be obtainable, how shall cars, dredges, cement come into being—and always back of it the dream come true—the vision materialized.

And now, a week later, the tiredness is gone. . . . why worry that old age has come if it has not come with atrophied mind and energy. The face may fall but the spirit may rise.

Tomorrow I will feel nothing recompenses for youth, but tonight nothing recompenses for expression. . . .

and culminating March 30:

On Thurs. at 12:15 the last stone was fastened in place on the head of Columbus & a white flag hoisted to let us know that the mon. was finished. McAuliffe had ordered some casks of wine and all the work-men on the grounds were given to drink. The inside of the shrine is finished except the ceiling. The King & Queen are not too big as I at first feared.

I came up about 3 & found Seville already en fête. Had to walk from the bridge to the hotel as no cars are allowed in the streets Thurs. or Friday. At seven I went to my seat opposite the city hall to see the procession. Stayed till 9:30 when I came back to telephone O'C. On my arrival in Seville I received telegram about the Com. in N.Y. wanting to change the dedication till Aug. 3!! [Because the Queen Mother has died and therefore King Alfonso will not be able to attend the unveiling.] Was incensed. O'C agreed with me it was absurd. I waited to see Ogden [Hammond] before answering, then quoted him & expressed my own feelings mildly. All the official ar-rangements are well along & what a drop in the interest if it were postponed. Also who knows what will have happened to Spain by au-tumn which would be only possible time in case of postponement.

April 1, Gertrude drafts another telegram to O'Connor in her blue book:

STATUE DOWN TO BOTTOM OF CROSS. EFFECT GRAND. NO LETUP ON WORK. PLENTY STONE. ONLY PART SLOW SUPPORTS FOR IRONS. PLENTY IRONS. PARAPET PLATFORM ADVANCING RAPIDLY.

For a sense of the unveiling and the preparations for it we must rely on a collage of newspaper clippings and photographs, which tell us little about Gertrude; and on personal reminiscences, which contradict each other in many respects, even as to who was there. However, there is basic agreement that Gertrude got her friends to Huelva in great style—first by private train from Paris to Seville, with a day's layover at the Ritz in Madrid; then by chartered cruise ship from Seville, down the Guadalqui-vir River and along the Spanish coast, to Huelva. The passenger list, en-larging at each stop, is incomplete but includes Flora and Cully; Juliana Force, traveling with Josephine Ogden Forrestal, formerly on *Vogue,* the wife of James Forrestal, then with Dillon, Read & Co., later, Secretary of the Navy and then the first Secretary of Defense; Charles Draper; Forbes Watson; Guy Pène du Bois; Jo Davidson; Henry Schnakenberg; Cecil Howard and his French wife; Tommy Slidell, the bachelor and bon vivant who had been on the *Lusitania* with Gertrude's brother Alfred; Ridgeley Carter, head of the Morgan bank in Paris; the beautiful Noel Murphy. . . . It is not clear whether Primo de Rivera, the Duke and Duchess of Alba, and Ambassador and Mrs. Hammond and their daugh-ters (one of whom is now New Jersey Representative Millicent Fenwick) join the group in Madrid or Seville, but surely by Seville all of these and more are assembled on the ship Gertrude has chartered—undoubtedly including some members of the Memorial Committee, probably William Page and R. A. C. Smith, who has by now replaced Moore as chairman, possibly Anne Morgan. . . .

In Seville, just before starting down the Guadalquivir, they are all invited to a dance aboard Vincent Astor's yacht, which is tied up alongside their ship. Du Bois, in his autobiography, comments that the party was "attended by everyone except the Astors. We had the feeling of being guests of the chief steward." The next day the cruise ship, seemingly too large for the river, begins the last stretch of the journey. It moves silently, without engines, preceded and followed by tugboats, ready to pull them off the banks of the sharply turning river. Du Bois remembers the bow "cutting a triangle in a field which was maintained for a hundred or so heavy-shouldered fighting bulls." Millicent Hammond remembers that "in the distance [on land belonging to the Duke of Medina Sidonia] one could see dwarf camels which had been brought over centuries ago from Africa and had gone wild in a climate not suited to them." Flora Miller remembers that Cecil Howard "was wonderful, playing the guitar and improvising songs about the river, the bulls, the camels, whatever was happening." For all of them, one small incident is magnified in memory. The night before reaching Huelva, one or more persons roam through the ship, tying all of the men's pajamas in knots and then soaking them—including the Duke of Alba's! It is their "Rape of the Lock." The Duke of Alba and Ridgeley Carter are outraged. Artists are suspected because they are artists. The Hammond girls are suspected because they are the youngest passengers. Jo Davidson tells Millicent Hammond that Mrs. Murphy perpetrated the crime. Flora Miller says absolutely not, it was Mrs. Forrestal. Everyone is still talking about the pajama scandal when the boat reaches Huelva. There, Millicent Hammond says, "Mrs. Whitney did not seem at all perturbed by the incident," and Du Bois comments on her "constantly calm demeanor, the ease with which she stood being the center of the whole proceeding," meaning of course more than her response to the pajamas.

The exact sequence of "the whole proceeding" is difficult if not impossible to determine. Elements of the collage, mostly from published and unpublished newspaper photographs, refuse to be glued exactly in place and time. April 20, the day before the unveiling, is cold and windy. Gertrude's —and Spain's—inner circle gathers within the cloister of La Rábida. Image: men holding top hats, military hats, helmets; Gertrude, wearing wide-brimmed hat, fur-trimmed coat, and standing as tall as the Duke of Alba, holds a bouquet of daisies; the duke, hair parted down the middle, mustache closely trimmed, stickpin reflecting the sun, cuff links visible on white sleeves under dark sleeves of topcoat and cutaway, spats pristine, reads a dedicatory speech.

The next day it pours. Image: approximately the same group of two hundred or so forming a semicircle at the base of the monument, while hundreds, perhaps thousands, more are being held at a distance by the Guardia Civil; umbrellas everywhere, one being held over Gertrude by an unidentifiable man in a homburg, the Duke of Alba stretching to hold one above the top-hatted head of the much taller Ambassador Hammond, wearing pince-nez now, as he reads a speech, echoing many of the sentiments expressed the previous day by the duke. More images: parades of American and Spanish sailors from the *Raleigh* and *Almirante Cervera,* while in the harbor these warships fire salutes and a replica of the *Santa Maria* sails by; a tremendous lunch under tents; ceremonial visits to the warships for Prohibition loganberry cocktails aboard the *Raleigh* and sherry aboard the *Almirante Cervera.* More words—these, summary and sympathetic, written by Forbes Watson for *The Arts:*

> When ambassadors from various nations meet, politeness is likely to dominate sincerity. That was not true when the Columbus Monument was officially unveiled and officially presented to Spain by the American Columbus Memorial Association. On the afternoon of April 20th, the Duke of Alba spoke in the inner cloister of La Rábida. By every gesture and every sound of his voice one knew that this was not cool official oratory. His tribute was genuine. And on the rainy morning of April 21st when Premier Rivera for Spain and Ogden Hammond, American ambassador to Spain, exchanged official speeches all their listeners knew that they had crossed the cold borders of international courtesy and that they deeply felt the tributes that they paid to the sculptor's achievement. . . .

In a letter to Gertrude he is privately just as enthusiastic:

> I remember the first time you showed me the model and I remember that morning as we approached Huelva getting a first distant glimpse of the accomplished monument. That was the most romantic moment of the entire journey—seeing the achieved monument towering over the sweep of water where the voyage of Columbus started and remembering my first glimpse of your imaginative conception way back there at home. Then, as a background there were all those varied and contrasting people—and your amazing hospitality.

⤞

At her studio home in Paris, with many friends there who were at the unveiling, for two weeks Gertrude digests the excitement of the event, then sails home. She finds Harry unwell and tense but for once receptive, even eager, to return with her to France. Since Flora and Cully have already sailed, Gertrude longs to show Harry, as well as them, the country house near the Davidsons'. It is a short visit—probably, at least from Harry's viewpoint, mostly for the relaxation of the ocean crossings—though he, like everyone else, is charmed by Le Boulay.

Gertrude and Harry are back in Long Island by late spring. June 18, the gossip columnist Cholly Knickerbocker ("Registered U. S. Patent Office" and né Maury H. B. Paul, maybe, if that isn't a pseudonym too) devotes half a column to them:

Mrs. H. P. Whitney Eschews Newport
to Accept Highly Important Art Commission
Art Defeats Society

There is, I hear, a very excellent reason for Mrs. Harry Payne Whitney's decision not to pass the heated months at her Newport villa.

The Bellevue Avenue colony rather hoped Harry and Gertrude would occupy their old-fashioned villa on the cliffs this season, for Mrs. Whitney adds an important sartorial note to any gathering, and as for the jovial Harry, he always can be counted on to stir up some social excitement for his friends.

Mrs. Whitney's devotion to her art work, however, has cheated the Newport set out of a series of Whitney dinners. For, while it is not generally known—in fact, Gertrude believes she is keeping the tidings a deep, dark secret—Mrs. Whitney has already received, or is about to receive, a highly important art commission.

With statues in France, Spain and New York City to her credit, the elder of the dowager Mrs. Vanderbilt's daughters is highly elated over being in a position to do "bigger and better" things, and during the weeks to come, when her intimates are burning social red fire at Newport, Gertrude will be toiling away at her art in the classical marble "studio" which she erected several years ago on the Whitney estate at Old Westbury.

'Tis an ill wind, however, that does not blow some good and the desertion of the Whitneys has made it possible for Mrs. Whitney's sister, the Countess Laszlo Szechenyi, to again occupy the Whitney villa.

No, the studio is not marble and, no, the word should not be placed in quotes but, yes, Gladys will be using the house in Newport and, yes, Gertrude will be working on commissions. However, none of these is more "secret" than any other. The Panama Roosevelt Memorial has received wide publicity and is now barely alive. But since the death certificate won't be delivered until 1932, Gertrude could still conceivably be doing studies for this piece. The Springfield Memorial has been handled more quietly, but a committee and architects have been involved and Hugh Ferriss has been commissioned to do presentation drawings. Again, the commission is no secret. Again, Gertrude could be doing further studies.

And again, to anticipate, this commission will have a lingering death (1933). As to new commissions, not until a few months after Cholly Knickerbocker's "news item" does Gertrude receive the first overtures to do memorials to Marshal Foch, the recently deceased (October 20) supreme commander of the Allied Forces during the war, and to Major L'Enfant, the French architect who fought in the American Revolution and subsequently prepared the basic city plan for Washington, D.C. These projects—finally abortive too—would appeal to Gertrude and she may well be working on them during the late summer.

Harry, meanwhile, is having a very successful racing season. Whichone, a home-bred two-year-old colt wins the Futurity and the Champagne Stakes at Belmont, and the Saratoga Special, and is second in the Hopeful Stakes, also at Saratoga. Whichone is so outstanding that Chaffee Earl, a Texas horseman, begs Harry to put a price, some price, almost any price on him. Harry booms, "A million dollars—and he's not for sale." There is much chuckling and rib-poking. Yet the Saratoga meeting ends sadly. Jimmy Rowe, Harry's trainer for more than twenty years, dies—a great blow to Harry, not surely as profound as the death of his brother two years before but, in its impact on Harry's life, comparable with Ardisson's suicide in relation to Gertrude. Rowe's death, on top of Harry's present poor health, seems in any case to bring Gertrude particularly close to him at this time, and as far as we know this is the only period in which Harry takes part in discussions with Mrs. Force concerning the future of the Whitney Studio Galleries.

By now Gertrude has acquired—directly or through the Whitney Studio, the Friends of the Young Artists, the Studio Club, and the Studio Galleries—more than 600 works of contemporary American art, probably the largest collection of its kind at the time. As Forbes Watson reminisces in *Juliana Force and American Art* (memorial catalogue, Whitney Museum, 1949), the collection "had far outgrown the space for showing it. What to do? After all if one buys an artist's work and puts it in storage it doesn't do him much good. The money is welcome; the result is discouraging. There were two alternatives, to give the collection to a museum with space to show it or to build a museum of one's own." Lloyd Goodrich and Hermon More (then Mrs. Force's assistant) continue the story in the same memorial catalogue:

> Mrs. Whitney . . . decided to offer [the collection] to the Metropolitan Museum. Mrs. Force, who had represented her in many important affairs, was delegated to call on Dr. Edward Robinson, the Metropolitan's director, and not only offer the entire collection but convey to him Mrs. Whitney's willingness to build and endow a wing to house it. The latter subject was never broached because the collection was flatly refused. The next few hours saw the conception if not the birth of the Whitney Museum. When Mrs. Force returned to

Eighth Street with an indignant report of the refusal, a daylong conference ensued between Mrs. Whitney, Mrs. Force and Forbes Watson, at which the plan of the museum began to take shape.

Watson continues:

Before lunch was over Mrs. Force was made director. She was delighted and a little stunned. When she protested Mrs. Whitney said to her, "Either you'll be the director or we won't do it." That was perhaps the happiest second in Mrs. Force's life. Half a dozen artists were suggested as preliminary informal advisers. It is noteworthy that neither Mrs. Force nor Mrs. Whitney thought of getting advice from the officers of established museums. Later they may have. At the moment they only thought of help from the artists. So when the museum was born it was not the ward of committees. Its guardians were two ladies of singularly complementary qualities.

Consider this account of the birth of the Whitney Museum in contrast to that of the Museum of Modern Art, born now also in the climate of a booming stock market and general optimism. The conception of the Whitney stretches back over a period of more than twenty years devoted to helping American artists; its birth, *as a museum*—in any conventional, or perhaps even professional, sense—is almost accidental. In contrast, the Modern is conceived and born quickly *as a museum*. Its "guardians"— Mrs. John D. Rockefeller, Miss Lizzie P. Bliss, and Mrs. Cornelius J. Sullivan, all art collectors—think from the start in terms of art history, art scholarship, internationalism, and collecting. In the winter of 1928–29, as Russell Lynes tells us in *Good Old Modern*, Mrs. Rockefeller and Miss Bliss meet by chance in Egypt and exchange ideas about starting a museum. On the way home Mrs. Rockefeller meets Mrs. Sullivan aboard ship and the ideas are further developed. In New York they add four more to their committee, which will eventually grow into a powerful and fashionable Board of Trustees: as chairman, A. Conger Goodyear, another collector, executive in the family railroad and lumber businesses, and former trustee and president of Buffalo's Albright Gallery, with which he has had a falling out; Mrs. W. Murray Crane, the widow of the president of the Crane Paper Company; Frank Crowninshield; and, perhaps most important to their getting the kind of director they want for their museum, Paul J. Sachs, an apostate from the Goldman, Sachs family banking business and then a professor at Harvard's Fogg Museum, giving his famous "museum course." By summer he persuades Alfred H. Barr, Jr., a brilliant former graduate student of his, then teaching art history at Wellesley College, to accept the job as director. No one could have been more different from Juliana Force than this rather shy, very serious scholar. Nor could any opening show have been more different from the Whitney's series of exhibitions two years later of its permanent collection than the first exhibition at the Modern, a loan show, this November, of work by Cézanne, Gauguin, Seurat, and Van Gogh. The Modern's dream, a collective dream, is based on historicism, impersonality, professionalism, and elitism. Gertrude's is, as always, involved with living artists, a long relationship with them and her personally trained director, amateurism in the root sense as well as the pejorative, and the faith in democracy that led her so long ago to open her studio to one and all rather than to be as selective as, say, Alfred Stieglitz, who is in some ways the spiritual father of the Modern.

꿎

From June on, despite considerable evidence of economic trouble (a billion-dollar drop in housing starts, a tripling of business inventories, a 400 per cent decline in consumer spending, higher interest rates), the stock market booms on. The day after Labor Day the New York *Times* average is 452, up over 200 points since early 1928. ATT is at 304, GE at 396, RCA at 505. Gertrude and Harry, like their counterparts at the Modern—with a board enlarged now to include Stephen C. Clark, Sam Lewisohn, Chester Dale, Duncan Phillips, and Martin A. Ryerson—have plenty of paper profits to invest in a new museum. Flora remembers Mrs. Force coming to Westbury in the fall to present a rough budget for the construction and operation of a new building on Eighth Street. Harry is totally sympathetic to the project, even as he excuses himself several times to take calls from his office and place huge buy orders. Perhaps this meeting occurs during the week of October 23 when, in the first big wave of frenzied selling, J. P. Morgan and Company organizes a group of new York bankers to support the market. In any case, the market can only be supported temporarily. By the end of the month it has collapsed; by mid-November the *Times* average is at 224.

What does all this mean to Gertrude and Harry? We don't know the actual figures, but neither of them (nor any of the wealthy trustees of the Modern) is now poor, just less wealthy, less likely to be expansive. Maybe Harry's portfolio is reduced from $200,000,000 to $100,000,000, Gertrude's from $20,000,000 to $10,000,000—something like that. Probably Sonny's and Marie's divorce, in late September, is more personally saddening. In that, Harry cannot help. Gertrude's dream of a new museum is another matter. He believes in this—in Gertrude herself, really. It is to Harry's credit that he never now withdraws his support, no matter what happens on Wall Street; and it is his good fortune that not long before the market breaks the first hydroelectric plant is completed at Flin Flon and the following year its mines and metallurgical plants are producing and processing ore.

⇜ *1930*

In a general press release, distributed by Juliana Force, January 3, Gertrude announces the new museum. According to the New York *Times*:

. . . the announcement came as a surprise. [Mrs. Whitney's] venture is partly to meet the lack of a museum devoted exclusively to American art. While the new institution, to be known as the Whitney Museum of American Art, plans eventually to acquire works to form a historical portrayal of this country's art, its primary purpose will be "to discover fresh talents and to stimulate the creative spirit of the artist before it has been deadened by old age."

Whether the Whitney Museum, in its emphasis on contemporary art, will overlap the field of the new Museum of Modern Art, only opened last November at 730 Fifth Avenue, could not be learned last night, as all comment was refused by Mrs. Whitney's representative. . . . The Museum of Modern Art has the backing of a board of directors well known socially. . . .

In her announcement Mrs. Whitney aims a dart at the conservatism of older museums:

". . . Not only can the visiting foreigner find no adequate presentation of the growth and development of the fine arts in America under a single roof; the same difficulty faces the native who wants to get what American art is all about. . . ."

Gertrude discusses both the need for historical background in a museum collection and the historical background of the new museum itself. However:

". . . it is not as a repository of what American artists have done in the past that the museum expects to find its greatest usefulness. . . .

"Ever since museums were invented, contemporary liberal artists have had difficulty in 'crashing the gate.' Museums have had the habit of waiting until a painter or a sculptor had acquired a certain official recognition before they would accept his work within their sacred portals. Exactly the contrary practice will be carried on in the Whitney. . . ."

Director Edward Robinson of the Metropolitan Museum, when

notified last night of the announcement, said he thought the new galleries "a very interesting scheme."

Two Sundays later Edward Alden Jewell prods Alfred Barr for his reaction. Barr, like Robinson, is polite. Jewell writes that the "Modern Art's director replies . . . 'The more, the merrier!' Mr. Barr even goes so far as to suggest, with the opulence that momentum nowadays seems to be developing, that 'We could probably have ten museums in New York.' "

Not until March is there another press release, this one announcing that the three buildings on Eighth Street will be extensively remodeled, that completion of this work is planned for November of this year, and that the staff has been selected: Director, Juliana Force; Curator, Hermon More, former director of the Davenport (Iowa) Municipal Art Gallery, and a Woodstock painter; Assistant Curators, Edmund Archer and Karl Free, both artists and alumni of the Art Students League.

While the details leading to this second announcement are being resolved, Gertrude prepares for a trip to Paris, where papers and documents bearing on Foch's life are to be put at her disposal to aid her in choosing, or at least recommending, type and location of the monument. January 7, there is a meeting at her studio of the Memorial Committee, made up mostly of high-ranking World War I veterans, including Major William F. Deegan and Major C. M. Penfield. The next day, following a shipboard party given for her by the committee, Gertrude sails, with her mother, to France.

In Paris, Gertrude concentrates on the Foch papers and does preliminary sketches, in pencil and in clay, from photographs of the general taken during the war, in his sixties but at the height of his powers. She is also in frequent correspondence with Juliana Force and drafts lists of topics for discussion upon her return. One list, headed "Plans for the Museum," contains such notes as "Open Nov. 1930. . . . Present collection—sculpture, paintings, watercolors, drawings, prints. . . . *Rooms* instead of galleries. . . . Acquisitions. . . . Bureau of Information. . . . Lectures. . . ." And, finally, Gertrude is working on some short stories.

"A Machine-Made World" can almost certainly be dated from this period. Mac, its central character, first a farmer and later a successful engineer and the inventor of an unspecified piece of construction equipment— an "Iron Monster"—has succumbed to acute nervous depression and feelings of guilt because of his responsibility for creating an anti-human environment of urban skyscrapers. While watching an automated crane at a construction site, he has an attack of insufferable anxiety and seeks comfort with his friends, the Franks. Mr. Frank, an advertising executive, offers cocktails and his "best champagne" and listens impatiently to Mac's doubts about progress, technology, and success. Mac becomes increasingly depressed and nervous, escapes their large apartment, and steps "from the sidewalk directly into the path of the Iron Monster." The End.

It is a simplistic story, in which the writing is awkward and Mac's point of view poorly controlled. However, it contains a couple of lively, personal non-dictionary words—e.g., "bumpted" and "jumpted"—and, on a deeper, still more personal level, the thematic conflicts between innocence and experience, the farm and the city, nature and technology, old values and new ones. In the Flaubertian sense, Mac *is* Gertrude. Yet, no matter to what extent she gives herself to his characterization, she also uses her experience of other people. Perhaps the specific situation of a man depressed by the implications of his technological invention comes from someone she meets aboard ship, or wherever; another lonely Paul Clayton, or whoever; but much of the more general characterization probably comes from Harry. He, like Mac, is a man of early promise and late disappointment, of increasing discomfort in the city, of intense moods, of resistance to foreign travel. ("People always thought that by going away to some other place they could escape themselves! 'All places are the same,' Mac sulked.") There are many parallels. It may not be stretching them too far to suggest that, after the crash, Harry has expressed some doubts about Flin Flon, his greatest single asset, once thousands of acres of virgin forest, now covered with mining equipment and hydroelectric and metallurgical plants— Harry, who in so many earlier interviews and questionnaires has described himself proudly with the single word *Capitalist!*

Besides her writing and the work on the Foch Memorial, Gertrude is, of course, seeing her friends. In his autobiography Jo Davidson, as always chasing interesting subjects to sculpt, has gotten to D. H. Lawrence through doing a portrait of H. G. Wells, who says to Jo, "I am not doing this for you but for him. You will surely do him good. [Lawrence is dying of tuberculosis.] You can cheer him up." Jo and Yvonne visit, in Lawrence's words, a "sort of sanatorium" outside Vence and Jo begins a bust, first of Lawrence sitting in a chair, later, as Lawrence tires, of him in bed. Jo is at his most ingratiating. He knows Lawrence has painted (the exhibition of his "erotic" paintings, raided by the London police in 1928, has received great publicity), and asks if Lawrence has ever sculpted. The writer replies that "he had once, in plasteline . . . hated the material, its feel and odor, and never touched it again," but that he would like to do some little animals in clay. Jo promises to send some of the kind he has been using, then tells Lawrence he has been experimenting in polychrome sculpture (which may place an undated polychrome bust of Gertrude). Lawrence asks Jo "to do him in color, and not to forget the blue of his dressing gown, of which he is very fond. The bust was finally completed and we got back to Paris. About a week later [March 2], Mrs. Harry Payne Whitney came to lunch. I told her how ill Lawrence was. She was distressed and said, 'Can't you call up Mrs. Lawrence or someone and tell them not to spare any expense?'—she would look after that. When I called H.G. at Grasse, he told me that Lawrence had died that morning."

One other document from this time is specifically dated, an echo from the previous spring:

Particular [Private]   Madrid, March the 10th

Dear Mrs. Whitney:

During my brief passage at the Ministry of Education, I had the honour of proposing to His Majesty the King the concession of an honorific distinction in your favour, and I am pleased to let you know that His Majesty deigned to approve my proposal of the "Gran Cruz de Alfonso XII."

While offering you my best congratulations for this mark of favour conferred on you by His Majesty, I must also congratulate you, personally and on behalf of the people of Spain, on your very active work which you have always developed on behalf of and for the love of Spain, demonstrated only recently by the inauguration of the Columbus Memorial at Huelva and your generous donation to the Monastery of La Rábida, and which I can assure you is greatly and deservedly appreciated in this country, as tending towards the strengthening of the bonds of friendship between our two countries.

Our Ambassador in Washington, Don Alejandro Padilla, will give you your nomination and the insignia of the Order.

With my best regards, I am

Yours sincerely

Alba

During March the Whitney Studio Galleries has its last show, an exuberant "Flower Exhibition" of paintings on this theme by forty artists. As with "The Circus in Paint," the catalogue is large and colorful (all works are reproduced) and contains a scholarly introduction by Lloyd Goodrich. Again, it is the installation which receives most attention. In Forbes Watson's review in *The Arts*, he describes "pictures in painted wood frames, each a color that seemed calculated to harmonize with the picture it was destined to surround . . . an interesting and instructive experiment which dissipated the conventional exhibition atmosphere. The exhibition attracted many visitors. . . ." Again, it is the sort of show Gertrude must have delighted in planning with Juliana Force and, again, as with "The Circus in Paint," she misses it. However, since Mrs. Force is publicly given most of the credit for the show, we turn one last time to Watson's later reminiscence of her: "Only in the last year of her career [i.e., surely after the opening of the new museum and possibly after Gertrude's death] did Mrs. Force play the part of a museum director. I say play the part because in no sense was she a scholastically trained director. She was the dynamo that moved Gertrude Whitney's activities in art forward and Mrs. Whitney controlled the dynamo."

⤚

April 15, Gertrude returns from France on the *Olympic*, accompanied by Sonny. *Their* arrival—only one other passenger's name is mentioned in the newspapers—receives some attention, partly because a strong tide snaps a line as the ship is docking at Pier 59, partly because a dinner at the Plaza in Gertrude's honor has been planned by the Foch Memorial Committee for April 30.

Gertrude writes several drafts of a speech. She reviews the speeches of others referring to her, including the suggestion that when she is introduced the toastmaster "simply say, 'And now, ladies and gentlemen, it is our pleasure to present to you our guest of honor, Mrs. Harry Payne Whitney.' The audience will undoubtedly rise and applaud." And, a few days before the event, when she receives formal confirmation of the Gran Cruz from the Spanish ambassador, she invites him to tea in order to obtain permission to have the honor announced at the dinner.

Gertrude seems to have saved everything pertaining to this dinner: the tasseled program and menu, embossed with the crossed flags of the United States and France; copies of an invocation, many speeches, many messages; seating plans. The program lists eighteen numbered events: "1. Reception of Committee Members by Mrs. Harry Payne Whitney; Mrs. Agnes Peel Hardman, President Pro Tem. 2. National Anthems: *Star-Spangled Banner, Marseillaise.* 3. Invocation by Right Rev. William T. Manning. 4. Dinner. . . ."

She is seated at the speakers' table between New York State Supreme Court Justice Salvatore A. Cotillo, presiding officer, and her old friend, now *ex*-Ambassador Ogden Hammond. Except for Hammond, to her left, and Juliana Force, across the room surrounded by colonels, Gertrude has no close friends among the sixty or more guests. She probably eats her Fruit Supreme Plaza but, watching her diet as always, refuses the Boula Boula and much of the rest of the meal, including sole, squab, tongue, and Fantasie of Billiken Americaine. While her neighbors eat, we can imagine her talking about the death (March 8) of William Howard Taft and the appointment of Charles Evans Hughes as Chief Justice of the Supreme Court; the slightly more recent death (March 16) of Primo de Rivera; hit plays (Anderson's *Elizabeth the Queen*, Barry's *Hotel Universe*, Connelly's *Green Pastures*) and films, (*All Quiet on the Western Front, Hell's Angels, Anna Christie*), all of which she has already seen or plans to see; progress on the Whitney Museum; a flurry of American exhibitions at the Modern (early water colors by Charles Burchfield; a survey of Homer, Ryder, and Eakins); the startlingly contemporary, emphatically vertical News Building, just being completed from a design by Raymond Hood, whose name Gertrude knows because he was a juror in the international competition for the Columbus Memorial Lighthouse at Santo Domingo; the vast popularity of contract bridge, invented by her cousin Harold Stirling ("Mike") Vanderbilt in 1926 but only in the past year or two almost totally replacing auction bridge. . . .

Coffee is served. Judge Cotillo excuses himself to Gertrude, stands, delivers "5. Address of Welcome. 6. Message from His Honor the Mayor, James J. Walker," and presents other messages (7–15)—read by army generals, navy captains, and diplomats (including Hammond, who mentions Gertrude's Gran Cruz)—from General C. P. Summerall, Chief of Staff, U. S. Army; Rear Admiral L. K. de Steiguer; General Weygand, Marshal Foch's Chief of Staff; Madame Foch; et cetera. Word from General Pershing is conspicuously absent. At the press table, Major Penfield, executive vice-president of the Memorial Association, whispers, theoretically off the record, that Pershing never liked Foch. That is not news.

"16. Mrs. Harry Payne Whitney."

Gertrude, in her most public manner, gives the longest speech of the evening. After the usual formalities, she describes Marshal Foch as "one of the greatest geniuses of our times," then describes studying the data made available in Paris ("of real advantage to me in my sketches for your monument") and visits to Ambassador Edge, Madame Foch, and General Weygand. The descriptions are broad, lifeless, undetailed. We have the feeling that from the opening to closing words of thanks, Gertrude is performing a chore, fulfilling a commission within a commission.

"17. Reading Message from his Eminence Patrick Joseph Cardinal Hayes, and benediction by his Representative.

"18. Dancing. Music by Anna C. Byrne."

Only now can we imagine Gertrude having some fun as, one by one, Judge Cotillo, Ogden Hammond, and various high-ranking soldiers and sailors ask her to dance to such new hit songs as "I Got Rhythm," "Body and Soul," "Three Little Words," and "Time on My Hands."

&

Through the spring and summer, work—mostly correspondence—continues on the Foch, Roosevelt, and Springfield memorials, none of which really moves forward. In addion to Pershing's antagonism to Foch, there is, at the beginning of the Depression, a growing resentment toward France for not paying her war debts to the United States. The Panama-Roosevelt Memorial is, as we know, snarled in local politics. And the Springfield monument is, like several other prospective commissions, delayed by lack of funds. In May, President Hoover announces, "We have now passed the worst, and . . . shall rapidly recover," but few believe him.

All the real economic indicators show that the Depression is getting worse. Monuments are fast becoming an unaffordable luxury—for most people.

For the Whitneys and the Vanderbilts and their friends a life of luxury continues. In addition to Whichone, Harry has a new great home-bred two-year-old chestnut colt, Equipoise (nicknamed "The Chocolate Soldier"), who wins the National Stallion and Juvenile Stakes at Belmont, the Great American Stakes at Aqueduct, the Eastern Shore Handicap in Maryland. Between races, Harry is salmon fishing on the Matapedia River in Quebec, while Gertrude does a lavish dinner party in Westbury for Ambassador Padilla, who finally presents her with the Gran Cruz and at the same time tells her that she has been made a Fellow of the Prado Museum (the first woman so honored) and that the city of Huelva has named a street "Calle Mistress Whitney" in her honor. And Mike Vanderbilt's *Enterprise* successfully defends the America's Cup.

All this suggests family business—and/or pleasure—as usual. However, from late August until late October, Harry is continually sick and run down, and his skin is painfully erupted. Understandably, he avoids society, spending most of the time in his room in Westbury, where servants bring him compresses and only Gertrude enters freely and frequently. She avoids going to New York except when necessary and returns always as soon as possible.

Thursday, October 16, there is another Foch Memorial dinner at the Plaza, this one in honor of the French air heroes Major Dieudonné Coste and Lieutenant Maurice Bellonte, who have just been the first to fly non-stop from Paris to New York. The dinner, following a format similar to the previous one but larger and including some of Gertrude's friends and family, moves smoothly from speech to speech (without the pressure of her having to make one) and from Melon Glacé to Bombe Aveline Sauce Caramel. Friday, Gertrude joins Harry in Westbury for what turns out to be an unseasonably cold, damp weekend; no weather in which to enjoy the spectacle of turning and falling leaves. There is winter in the air as Gertrude takes fewer than usual long walks to and from the studio and Harry remains in his room. Nevertheless, Harry comes down with a cold and slight fever. By Tuesday, when his temperature rises, they return to the city and summon Dr. John Hartwell to 871 Fifth Avenue.

"Josh," as Gertrude and Harry call him, is more than the family doctor; he is a close friend and a reassuring presence. Even at sixty-three he is trim and athletic, straight and tall as he was when as a medical student he played end on the unbeaten, untied Yale football team of 1891 and made Walter Camp's All-American team. He has known Harry since then, long before becoming chief of surgery at Bellevue Hospital and president of the New York Academy of Medicine. He has fished and hunted with Harry in Scotland, ridden with him in Westbury and Aiken; he has more recently taken Gertrude through her siege of phlebitis and gotten to know her, too, as a patient as well as a friend.

But now Josh is not reassuring. After examining Harry, he diagnoses the already "heavy cold" as pneumonia, calls in specialists, and confers with Gertrude, trying to explain the seriousness of Harry's condition without unduly alarming her. He reminds Gertrude that Harry has been a sick man for years, very sick during the past two months, what with a chronic liver problem and hardening of the arteries—

Gertrude stops him. Hardening of the arteries? When had that developed? Josh says he is sure he has told her before. She can't believe it, fights against believing what she knows is, in medical parlance, "preparation"— preparation for oxygen tanks; preparation for more specialists; preparation, penultimately, for an ineffective blood transfusion (more than a *reminder* of horrors at the Juilly hospital; the *presentation*—now, still before the existence of blood banks—of an anonymous living donor stretched out beside Harry's bed); preparation, ultimately, for death.

Gertrude calls Flora, Sonny, and Barbie. The children and Cully and Buz gather at 871 Fifth Avenue and wait there anxiously through Saturday night, Sunday morning, Sunday afternoon, Sunday evening. The doctors marvel at the strength of Harry's heart, say they depend more on it than on their medical skills, but at nine thirty-five, unconscious in the huge home that had been his father's, Harry dies at fifty-eight.

PART THREE

"Alone" Again

Gertrude is in a state of shock, but somehow—comforted by her children, sedated by Josh Hartwell—for three days, until Harry's funeral, she holds herself together, even arranges to have a death mask made. No one but she really knows what Harry has meant to her. So often have they been separated, physically and emotionally, since the early years of their marriage—their thirty-fifth anniversary would have been this coming summer—that probably even her immediate family doesn't understand that, despite everything, Harry has been her "big, unselfish love." No doubt, particularly during the three long nights between Harry's death and his funeral, Gertrude painfully recovers memories of Harry: "the boy next door"; the handsome friend at Yale of her brother Bill, dead at twenty-one; the rival of Moses Taylor, Jim Barnes, Esther Hunt, and so many others; the great sportsman; the unfaithful husband; the devoted father . . . .

What does this ellipsis mean? Most important now, that vast, sometimes vague habit of marriage, strung out like insular dots and empty spaces over all those years, and yet a reminder too of many times when Gertrude herself, or Harry, or the children were sick or in trouble and helped one another. What does "unfaithful husband" mean? Probably not as much now as "unfaithful wife." Except for Harry's first breach of faith, Gertrude must think of her own actual, and fantasized, and justifiably rationalized, infidelities. Of course she has feelings of guilt, as he must once have had too, but hers are compounded by doubts about what else she might have done for Harry if she had known, really known, more about his physical condition, and by thoughts about her own death when she "should" be thinking of Harry's.

Another awful reminder of Gertrude's own mortality is a letter she receives shortly before Harry's death from Saxham Drury, the husband of her childhood friend Mabel Gerry:

Dear Mrs. Whitney

Last evening Mabel asked for pencil and paper and tried to write to you but she could not hold the pencil and then asked me to write. The following is as far as I could gather from her somewhat incoherent speech:

"My dear, I always said that when the time came that I should die I would let you know. I am doing so and I am letting you know now.

They give me atropine which upsets my brain & my speech and I cannot speak. It is so horrible that I cannot say what I want. My misery during the last few days has been unthinkable. I send you my dear love. I know you are coming to see me soon. Goodbye dear,

Mabel

Then she added, "You must always love Gertrude."

I am writing this on my knee near her bed so you must excuse untidiness.

Yours v. sincerely, Saxham Drury

Mabel dies October 13. Eleven days later Bob Chanler dies. They—like Harry, like Gertrude herself, like everyone—are too young to die. And now—Monday, October 27—Harry's face is on the front pages of all the major metropolitan newspapers in recent, somewhat puffy photographs, accompanied inside by earlier ones of him at the track with Gertrude or, still earlier, of him playing polo. All of the obituaries—like those of his brother Payne and of Gertrude's brother Regi—emphasize the suddenness and unexpectedness of his death. All of them—and several editorials—extol Harry as "one of America's premier sportsmen" or "America's foremost sportsman." His horse-racing, polo, and yachting accomplishments are listed in paragraphs even longer and denser than those concerning his corporate directorships (at least ten, the number having been reduced by consolidation), clubs (at least twenty, here and abroad), racing associations, trusteeships, charities (with particular emphasis on his having financed American Museum of Natural History ornithological expeditions to the Pacific during the twenties and then a new eight-story wing of the museum, in memory of his father, for the exhibition and study of the bird specimens). And, finally, each obituary devotes a paragraph to Gertrude's background, sculpture, and art patronage and to a guess at the size of the estate that will be left to her. Someone from the *News* reaches Thomas J. Regan at Harry's office and asks the question, "How much?" Regan replies, "The family, I know, hasn't given a single thought to that matter. It is now far from their minds."

On Monday, as the funeral arrangements are being made, a crowd gathers outside 871 Fifth Avenue, and a policeman must be posted there to screen callers. Late in the day Regan announces to the press that the church services—at St. Bartholomew's, 10 A.M. Wednesday—are to be very simple and will be conducted by the Rev. Dr. Endicott Peabody of Groton School, assisted by the Rev. Dr. Robert Norwood, rector of St. Bartholomew's; that there will be no pallbearers; and that interment, at the Whitney family plot in Woodlawn Cemetery, will be private. He hands the reporters a list of those who will be ushers at the church—among them, Harry's cousins Courtlandt Barnes and James Barney; Gertrude's cousin and Harry's close friend William K. Vanderbilt; Harry's former "Big Four" teammates Devereux Milburn and Lawrence Waterbury; his lawyer Frank Crocker and doctor John Hartwell, and half a dozen other old friends, like the rest, almost all dating back to Harry's undergraduate days at Yale.

Letters and telegrams of condolence begin to arrive—ultimately about five hundred of them, not including another two hundred or so addressed to Flora, Sonny, or Barbie. Some are from Gertrude's secret past (e.g., William Stackpole and Captain Guardabassi, both now married), some from Harry's (Mrs. X); some are from the art world (Morgan Russell, John Gregory, Stirling Calder, Varèse, Mary Garden), some from the business and sporting world (Elihu Root, Herbert Bayard Swope, Mr. and Mrs. Harry Sinclair, Bernard Baruch, John Henry Hammond, Lew Thompson, Clarence McCormick); but most are from Gertrude's and Harry's shared, less parenthetical world of relatives and old friends: Adele, Dorothy, Helen, Gladys, Eleo Sears, Jimmie Appleton, Yale Dolan, Phil Carroll, Charles Draper, Frank Polk, Bobby Sands . . . .

Again, that long ellipsis, like a parade of years.

Many of the letters—particularly those from the men Harry knew best, the men least likely to be found in Gertrude's journals and other writings—speak of Harry's generosity, both material and social. He is remembered, in every sense, as a great sport and as one of those men who has many "best friends."

The funeral emphasizes affection for Harry. St. Bartholomew's is filled to capacity (about 1,200) with relatives, friends, servants, trainers, jockeys, even stableboys; and hundreds more—not only the curious but those who have, from a distance, admired him as a sportsman and won on the horses he has raced—stand on Park Avenue in the rain. Despite the family's request that flowers be omitted the chancel of the church and the altar are almost hidden by floral arrangements—dozens from relatives and close friends, a huge horseshoe from the men at the Whitney Stable, and the coffin itself blanketed with pale yellow roses, lilies of the valley, and orchids. However, the service is as simple as announced (and as requested in Harry's will): Handel's *Largo* played on the organ, short prayers by Dr. Peabody and Dr. Norwood, and a few hymns sung by the church choir. Then the funeral cortege, aided by twenty policemen, moves quietly up Park Avenue and north to the cemetery in the Bronx.

The continuing rain, pelting dead and dying leaves, and the dark mud everywhere add to the gloom of the Whitney plot at Woodlawn. It is as if the wet gray granite plinth and surrounding headstones had been bathed in tears. OLIVE WHITNEY 1878–1883, the one sister of Harry's whom Gertrude had not really known, except as the child next door who had died in Paris. FLORA PAYNE WHITNEY 1842–1893, Harry's mother whom Gertrude had never known well but who had done so much to shape the more sensitive and moody side of Harry's personality, the side suppressed most in public. FLORA PAYNE PAGET, Pauline's daughter alive for one day in 1896.

WILLIAM COLLINS WHITNEY 1841–1904, Harry's father whom Gertrude did know well and who had moved through their lives, in two successive homes of his in New York as well as others in Westbury, the Adirondacks, Aiken, October Mountain, Hickory Valley . . . the man who, for better or worse, most influenced Harry's life, leaving him not only the fortune Harry enlarged and the properties he added to but many of the directorships and memberships still held at the time of Harry's death.

PAULINE WHITNEY PAGET 1874–1916 is buried in Esher, Surrey, not at Woodlawn, but her name, her memory, even her dates loom as large as any in this parade of ghosts. Gertrude cannot forget how close they were in their teens and during their courtships and just a little later when Gertrude was Pauline's bridesmaid (as Pauline would have been a matron of honor at Gertrude's wedding had she not been going through the difficult advanced preganancy with the infant buried here). PAYNE WHITNEY 1876–1927, buried in Manhasset but, like Pauline, here now. His terminal date seems like only yesterday; a letter from his wife Helen *is* only yesterday:

> Dearest G, I know so deeply what you are going through. You & Harry were so sweet when I went thro' it, I can never forget & always love you more for it. It is hard to know which is worse, a sudden shock or a terrible big pull such as you have had—but you can always remember that you were there & did a wonderful job. I remember Harry once saying that you & he never had even a small scrap that was not made up, forgiven & forgotten that same night. He adored you so & was so proud of you, that with all his charm for any woman who ever met him you were the one & only woman in his life. Be very full of pride now, lift up your chin—go on with your works as soon as you can & be very sure he is there, closer than ever & understanding everything more perhaps than ever before. Forgive this long letter. I just had to write it & if any moment you want to see me, be sure I'll be there. Your children worship you & that helps a lot. Goodbye dearest Gertrude, with all my love, H.H.W.

At the Whitney plot, perhaps one other message echoes now in Gertrude's mind—a telegram sent from Dartington Hall the day of Harry's death by his sister Dorothy, forty-three now, whom he loved and brought up almost as a daughter:

> MY HEART IS WITH YOU ALL IT HAS BEEN A GREAT EXPERIENCE TO HAVE SUCH A GENEROUS WARMHEARTED AND LOYAL BROTHER MY LOVE TO YOU DEAR GERTRUDE YOU HAVE BEEN A GOOD COMPANION BLESS YOU FOR IT.

With more prayers, the coffin is lowered into its grave. There is the awful echoing plunk of mud, really wet mud. It continues as Gertrude and the children return to their limousine and are driven to Long Island. Not until Westbury, Gertrude's and Harry's favorite home and the one where they have spent the most time together, does Gertrude break down. She goes immediately to Harry's bedroom, closes the door, and settles in there for the next few weeks.

Letters continue to arrive, some from those, like doctors, ministers, lawyers, and the immediate family, who have been so close to Harry's death and funeral that they have had neither a chance nor a reason to write previously; some from those who wrote earlier, shorter, shocked notes or telegrams and want now to say more; some from those, like Rollie, who are abroad and have just heard the sad news.

For Gertrude, each letter is a message of pain as well as comfort. She spends much of November and early December acknowledging, and often responding in detail, to these and the hundreds of other communications and flowers (the particular kind of flower is always specified in her notes). At the same time she receives dozens, possibly hundreds, of condolence calls, thus seeing a great deal of her close friends and immediate family. She also meets several times with Frank Crocker in connection with the estate. And during all these weeks she is anxiously planning to get away to Cuba as soon as possible, surely before the holidays.

Harry's will (dated July 31, 1929—the summer Gertrude was making her final plans for the new museum) is straightforward and simple, especially for one dealing with so vast an estate. Though Frank Crocker and Sonny are named co-executors and -trustees along with Gertrude, whose own inheritance has been substantially increased over the years by Harry's gifts and astute management, the bulk of his real estate and personal property is left to her, and she has broad discretionary powers. For example: "There are many faithful employees and servants for whom I do not make provision in this my will, because my beloved wife, knowing my wishes respecting their remembrance, will provide for them in accordance with our understanding." And: "Without making any specific bequest, I request my wife and children to continue the support which I have given during my life to public institutions and charities." In short, the will is a testimonial to Harry's confidence in Gertrude.

As to specific bequests, Gertrude receives the Westbury property and a life interest in 871 Fifth Avenue; Sonny $2,000,000; Flora $1,000,000; Barbara $1,000,000; Cully $500,000; Buz $500,000; Thomas Regan $200,000; three other office employees and one former valet $65,000. The residuary estate, amounting to about $72,000,000 at the first accounting, is to be divided into four equal trusts, two for the benefit of Sonny and his children, one each for the benefit of Flora and Barbara and their children. Though Sonny receives double what his sisters do, the primogenitary discrepancy is nothing like it was when Gertrude's father died.

The newspapers are surprised by the smallness of Harry's estate. They all compare it with his brother Payne's, valued, in 1927, at about $187,000,000 and then liquidated two years later, at the peak of the market, at $240,000,000. However, there is no doubt that Payne's estate is worth substantially less now. Nor is there any doubt that both estates will decrease far more during the next few years. Indeed, despite Harry's huge holdings in the highest-quality stocks—Standard Oil (of New Jersey, New York, California, Indiana, and Ohio), Guaranty Trust, Bethlehem Steel, Lorillard, Liggett & Myers, Anaconda, Western Union, National Cash Register, et cetera—it is his more speculative 741,500 shares of Hudson Bay Mining and Smelting (the successor to Flin Flon), now valued at $3,560,075, which will make the most spectacular recovery.

≈

Gertrude leaves for Cuba in mid-December. Soon after arriving, she writes to her sister:

Dearest Gladys,

You would be amused to see me quite fairly settled in my little house in Havana [Villa Lewis, Reparto Biltmore]. I wrote Mama some of the harrowing details of water supply, screens with holes, doors that don't close, etc. but really I like it very much and am more than glad I came. I could not have stood N.Y. & here at least there have been so many little things to fuss over and it's so heavenly being out all day in the heat. I moved at once from what was considered the "master's bed room" on the second floor into a medium-sized discarded light room downstairs with a door out to the little cloister & garden, secured the best bed and furniture, a chaise longue just outside my door, some awnings to screen the neighboring house & the heat and am forced to be interested in the butcher, the baker and all the rest of the menage. My butler who is from Czechoslovakia & speaks English & Spanish is a marvel. He works day & night & I feel I can never be parted from him. The chef was a washout & will soon exit from the scene. The maid Carmen (!) has a husband who will & does do anything. My own kitchen maid who came down with me is fine & with Carmen's husband can take care of the kitchen.

My one disappointment was that there was no available room for a studio (no light). I got an architect (builder) from Sonny's friends the Masons [Jane and Grant] & my own studio man has arrived & they promise me to build a little studio in two weeks next to the garage. The whole place is about the size of a ten cent piece but very sweet.

So far I have only been to Havana once which I had to do to get my car out, otherwise not off my place. I was pretty tired when I got here but I don't see how anyone can help getting strong in this country being out all the time.

You must be laughing at me with all these household details but one really can't help it here & I have tried to interest myself in everything. Besides I expected an influx of family & it does become impor-

tant whether anybody is going to have a bath or be eaten by mosqui-
toes. After a great deal of conversation on telephone finally it has
been decided that the Millers (without Pam, she had a bad cold) &
Sonny are arriving tomorrow to stay at the New National Hotel as a
start—later we will see.

You probably heard that Buz's father was very sick in Palm Beach
& he had to come down. Mr. H[enry] was a little better today & Buz
thought there was a possibility of his getting back for Xmas. Barbie
moved back (or was to have) yesterday to Flora's house [in West-
bury] & all the children were to be in our house [ditto].

When once the small things about this house are fixed it will be
very comfortable & really attractive. The sitting room is big, cool &
comfortable. I am longing to have you come down when it works in
with your plans. That is my only regret—being so far away, but I was
not much use to anyone & here I feel sure I will get well much
quicker.

I had my first Spanish lesson today from a nice little man called
Porras & that gives me something to occupy my mind.

Sonny's friends the Masons & [the] Lazos have been wonderful &
without Miss [Claire] Gardner [described in a subsequent letter to
Gladys as "Gardie . . . housekeeper, nurse, staller-off of people, and
major domo in one"] I would have been either exhausted or have
done nothing & lived anyhow.

I hope you are all well & with my very best to you for Xmas & New
Year's.

Heaps of love,
G.

Will you tell [your] kids I am sending them the same Xmas presents
as last year & please be an angel & let me know how much it was as I
have not my old check book here & can't possibly remember.

⤳ *1931*

Soon after the holidays, Gertrude writes again to Gladys:

. . . The weather has been so rotten [Flora, Cully, and Sonny] decided to go back sooner & stay longer when they return. The days slip
by as a week simply disappears into space, so that I don't at all mind
the idea of being alone for a while. Mrs. Force can come down if I
get lonely any time.

The more I think of Mama's coming the more I think it would be a big effort, long trip & I am not at all sure she would like this house. It is far away & in a rather lonely spot & although there is a mounted police & a night watchman I think she might be nervous.

It would not make much sense for her to come & stay at the Hotel, but I have asked F[lora] to call you & tell you all about everything.

You know what this kind of place is like if it rains, blows and is cold. F. had two sunny days, the rest of the time horrible! . . .

That Gertrude does not "at all mind the idea of being alone for a while" is an understatement. Perhaps now more than ever, she *must* be alone for a while and *must* have a studio in which to remove herself from visitors. There, as much as in the charming palm-shaded garden, she will during the next few months spend many hours, at first sketching in pencil and in clay, then mostly in words. It is impossible to know exactly how or when she moves from the habit of almost daily correspondence with her family and friends to renewed efforts at writing short stories, sketches, and personal essays and then on to the larger and more ambitious form of the novel. Perhaps now Gertrude feels cramped in the shorter forms she has previously attempted. Perhaps the experience of creating large-scale monuments, particularly the Columbus Memorial, suggests the possibility of analogous satisfaction in a more sustained and complex work of fiction. Perhaps, at first, even though this novel will ultimately be published under a pseudonym, there is in her mind the possibility, too, of the sort of fame and recognition she has received from her other big works (*Buffalo Bill* and *St. Nazaire* as well as *Columbus*). The only certainty is that sometime during these months in Havana, Gertrude begins to pull together and shape various fragments of her experience, which by late summer will become a full-length novel.

But first—or simultaneously—there are many letters and many visitors. Just before Christmas (the mail is slow) Charles Draper writes a very long letter about parties he has attended and given; Flora's new apartment in New York where "the gold trumpets—or are they lillies?—on her bed do not strike [him] favorably"; a nephew whom he has persuaded "to trustee his small inheritance instead of spending it"; and "companionate marriage & free love" of which he "can't make much sense, not having read *The Revolt of Youth* [though] lots of ladies know it by heart & have plenty to say for the doctrine." Like so many letters Gertrude receives now, this one is intended to cheer and encourage her, but in addition it gives a sense of the times as seen from the viewpoint of an intimate member of her set. Charles continues:

You left town at just the right time, winter stepped in on Monday, stocks fell much farther down and on Tuesday all the telephones got new numbers. Yesterday and today things have improved a bit, warmer weather, Dr. Prosser's Committee reported $8,260,000 collected for the unemployed, Wall St. is feeling better, and the telephone ladies are not so annoyed.

You hear a lot about hard times—I know they are—but there seems to be very little difference in life here, people are entertaining madly, the streets are blocked with new & shiny motor cars, theatres full & so on. . . .

Soon, when Flora and Cully return, Charles will arrive in Havana.

Other frequent correspondents—all, also, before long, visitors to Havana—are Josh Hartwell, Frank Crocker, and Juliana Force. Each mixes professional matters with affectionate encouragement and becomes, through letters and brief visits, closer to Gertrude than ever before. In particular, Juliana Force is working hard on plans for the opening of the new museum which, because of Harry's death as well as various architectural problems, has been postponed for a year—that is, until this coming November.

Gertrude sufficiently enjoys the warmth, restfulness, and privacy of the Villa Lewis to rent it for another year, until April 30, 1932. Before leaving Cuba she receives, among much other correspondence, a flurry of letters from Gladys: happy news of her daughter Alice's wedding to Bela Hadik and thanks to Gertrude for permitting the newlyweds to use her Westbury house before they sail for Italy; sad news of Nicholas Longworth's death ("The whole place is gloomy about Nick. . . . We all feel that a chapter of Washington life which we hoped would go on indefinitely has been closed and that no party can ever possibly be quite the same."

In New York, too, there is an accumulation of many letters. Gertrude barely has time to go over museum matters with Juliana Force, who has been trying on her own to raise $50,000 in order to buy work by American artists hard hit by the Depression. A response from Abby Aldrich Rockefeller is particularly gratifying:

Dear Mrs. Force:-

I have just been over my accounts and I am very happy to be able to say that I find it will be possible for me to join you in the pool which you are getting up. . . .

Whenever you have gotten the other people to join, making up the sum of $50,000, I shall be glad to send you my check for $5,000.

I cannot tell you what a pleasure and comfort it was to me to have you here yesterday. My talk with you has cheered me greatly and has given me confidence to go ahead [with the Museum of Modern Art]. . . .

There is much less mail than in former years concerning commissions: a tentative and preliminary inquiry as to Gertrude's possible interest in doing a monument for the Society of Colonial Dames; a similar though more important and flattering inquiry from the visionary architect Hugh Ferriss in connection with "sculptural opportunities" at a great airport still on the drafting boards, a project "of considerably greater magnitude than 'Radio City' [Rockefeller Center]"; but mostly the commission correspondence now concerns publicity for work done in the past, the rather distant past.

On May 26 the *Titanic* Memorial, erected on the Potomac Parkway in 1930, is finally dedicated, nineteen years after the disaster and Gertrude's preliminary sketches for the commission. Had Gertrude not been in mourning and in poor health, it is the sort of prestigious ceremony she would have enjoyed attending. President and Mrs. Hoover are the guests of honor. Secretary of State Henry L. Stimson presides. The widow of William Howard Taft (President when the *Titanic* sank) pulls the unveiling cord. John Hays Hammond, substituting for his ill wife, the chairman of the Women's Titanic Memorial Committee, dedicates the monument. Massachusetts Representative Robert Luce is the principal speaker, recounting the chivalry shown by the men on the ship. . . . The dedication is widely publicized, Gertrude's absence widely regretted. One correspondent writes that "it was a presentation of *Hamlet* without the Prince."

Three days later she also misses the dedication of her so-called Friendship Fountain (a gift by friends of Canada in the United States to McGill University), which is yet another version of the work designed in 1910 for the Arlington Hotel in Washington; exhibited in the 1915 Panama-Pacific International Exposition; and reproduced in bronze and erected in Lima, Peru, in 1924. . . . Again the years overflow. Again there is a ceremony Gertrude would have liked to attend. (Barbie represents her.) The editor-in-chief of the New York *Times*, Dr. John H. Finley, presents the fountain. The Right Hon. the Earl of Bessborough, Governor General of Canada, accepts it. The sculpture, draped in the Union Jack and the Stars and Stripes, is unveiled. The Royal Montreal Regimental Band plays "God Save the King," "The Star-Spangled Banner," and "O Canada."

In Long Island, stretched out in bed or on a chaise longue, conserving her strength, Gertrude can almost see and hear it all as she reads accounts of the ceremony in American and Canadian papers and, later, listens to reports from Barbie and Buz. No doubt these erections—really resurrections—of past work and past life mean something to Gertrude. No doubt she is pleased to see the stories and pictures in the papers. But still—but still it would mean so much more to be looking at present work, present life.

At Hugh Ferriss' invitation she goes to see the preliminary drawings of his "Air City," which indicate, as he confirms in a subsequent letter, "what will be necessary on the plaza which the main buildings face . . .

two fountains of great magnitude . . . two monumental groups flanking the main stairway . . . several smaller groups, and numerous sculpted panels." Again at Ferriss' invitation, she meets with his associate Otto C. Stephani to discuss more detailed plans and decorative schemes for the modernistic, indeed futuristic, world of "streamlined" buildings, ramps, fountains, statues, and reliefs. She is particularly interested in the fountains which she thinks of as: "1. The Fountain of Youth or El Dorado, the central and highest figure Eternal Youth, call it what you like. 2. The Fountain of Age, the glorification of discoveries, machines—central figure Aviation." In meetings, letters, and telegrams, through the late spring and summer, spent mostly in Newport, Gertrude is in frequent contact with Ferriss and Stephani. She makes dozens of sketches and written suggestions, hoping, always hoping, against the odds of the deepening Depression, for the great commission. At the same time she pursues the lesser but equally elusive commission from the Society of Colonial Dames and another, now, from the Pan American Union. However, mostly she is working on her novel, writing quickly as always, often in her Newport studio overhanging the sea.

In August, Gertrude completes *Diana Opens the Door,* a tentatively titled typescript of some four hundred pages, in which she has somehow forced the sketches of people and places she knows into a tightly constructed, fast-paced mystery story. The situation is simple: Mabel Randolph, a beautiful young woman who has "come out of nowhere to live with Stephen and Katharine Osmund," seemingly commits suicide at the Travers' Fourth of July party, the very day that she has privately announced to a few friends—including Diana, the first-person narrator of the story—that she intends to marry Dick Talbot. The possibilities are many and complex: Is it suicide? If so, what is the motive? Is it possible that Mabel could not face marrying Dick because she is too much in love with Stephen Osmund? Or too much in love with that dark, rootless, intensely intelligent writer, Ronald Gordon? Or if it is not suicide, could one of them or someone else have murdered her?

Diana is obsessed by the possibilities, compulsive about exploring them. Like Gertrude, she is fascinated by detective fiction, puzzles, games, charades. These, along with house parties in Long Island and in the Adirondacks, are part of the texture of the book—these and proplike characters, all reminiscent of Gertrude's circle, a mixture of the very rich and upper bohemia. The recognizability of the characters, plus a subordinate lesbian theme, make Gertrude decide to publish under a pseudonym. Yet in this decision, as in the characterizations of Katharine and Diana, Gertrude refuses to let go completely of her own identity: after first using "Phyllis Lane" she ultimately settles on the Vanderbilt family name "Webb," and sexually neutral initials, "L.J."—another small mystery within the mystery of the novel itself and within the larger mystery of Gertrude's life.

Gertrude sends one rough copy of *Diana Opens the Door* to her sister Gladys and another to Ada Borden Stevens, a Newport writer who has previously worked for Gertrude on shorter pieces, typing them, making mechanical corrections, and offering some criticism. Mrs. Stevens, currently participating in a Bread Loaf Writers' Conference at Middlebury College in Vermont, writes two long letters after transmitting the clean script.

The first, probably written in late August, urges Gertrude to use the title *Walking the Dusk*, one of several alternates suggested by Gertrude. Mrs. Stevens notes that the title *Diana Opens the Door* is close to one already published and that the theme (of opening the door) is not fully carried out, the door never fully opened. On the other hand, *Walking the Dusk* suggests "a story OFF the beaten track." Mrs. Stevens continues: "You did not tell me whether your sister 'got' Katharine. If she didn't, then it is too subtly suggested. . . . The horror of it [Katharine's lesbianism] may make you think it plainer than it is . . . she remains strong, reserved, beautiful. I think it is best she should: the editor may want to 'play up' the unusual note."

The second letter is written September 2, just two days after Flora has given birth to her fourth (and final) child, Leverett. Mrs. Stevens begins on that non-literary note: "Let me too rejoice in the new baby! I am delighted all is well. There is no greater joy for grandmothers than these new, happy homes." Then she quickly returns to the novel and her preferred title, by asking humorously, "They [the Millers] are not letting you name the baby, are they?" The rest of this letter is devoted to a question of Gertrude's: Should she let George Chamberlain—a successful writer, particularly for the *Saturday Evening Post* and Hollywood, and an old acquaintance of hers—read her novel? Mrs. Stevens is wary: "You are not writing the frankly formula popular story which HAS to have obvious things brought to obvious conclusions. I'm a little scared about letting any writer of note see [the book] before the publisher sees it, because of the upsetting effect it may hold for you . . . there might be changes required by the man who knows HIS public. . . . I am especially hesitant because, up here [Middlebury] doctors disagree—*the final doctor is the publisher.*" However, she concedes, ". . . if you can keep your head in spite of what he may say, there would be a tremendous advantage in accepting his very kind offer."

Gertrude prepares a covering letter to Chamberlain, of which only a scribbled draft remains:

> In trepidation I am taking you at your word & sending you my MS of *Diana Opens the Door.*
> I got a kind lady critic to correct punctuation & grammatical errors, otherwise have not changed it inspite of some suggestions on her part

which if you agree with I will change later. Tell me please (truthfully, I need not add, because I trust you as far as that goes!):

1. Are you interested in the story?
2. A reaction or 2 as to clues while in the process of reading.
3. Is it worth sending in search of a publisher? I worked hard over it & with the idea of publishing under a pseudonym.

Its final correcting is only worthwhile from my standpoint if it is worth publishing, & if you don't know now, it is not. Otherwise I have had a hell of a good time & freed my mind to carry on.

It has been interspersed with my own work but has come to assume an almost sculptural form.

I read you with great pleasure. Not only because of its intrinsic value but because I felt myself a little on the inside. . . .

Chamberlain replies in less than a week:

Dear G,

I want to tell you what happened. Yesterday, the hottest Sept. 11 of all time, I was in N. York seeing a dentist. I left at eleven in the morning, motored 150 miles, played 18 holes of golf, got home at seven, bathed, ate and then almost had to call for help to lift yr. MS off my desk! I had no intention of reading it before my own story should be finished in a couple of weeks, but I opened the parcel for a peek and was lost. I laid down the last page at 4:30 this morning.

The above statement of fact is the exact equal of ten pages of superlatives. You have written a corking and brilliant yarn. I wish I could jump in my car (inspite of a record headache) and run up to talk to you for hours but I've simply got to stay here and finish my own story before I do anything else. How much of a hurry are you in?

Here is my snap judgment:

(1.)   Publishers will grab at your book.

(2.)   Properly cut I believe it could be sold as a serial even in these hard times. I'm not sure I would recommend that since you are not out for money.

(3.)   The brilliant conversation is an absolute treat, but every sentence of it that does not advance the story or paint a character should be lifted out and used elsewhere. It's too good to throw away.

(4.)   I criticize the last 10 pages and, if you agree with me, you could do them over at once. . . .

Two pages of suggestions follow for tightening up the story, particularly the end, and another two for marketing it. Chamberlain recommends "that the book be offered through my agent without his knowing who wrote it. After the deal is closed you should change the author's name to

G. V. Whitney—then lie back and keep mumm through thick and thin!" He concludes, "Lock these notes up somewhere in case some dumbbell should someday accuse you of having had help from me."

It is easy to imagine Gertrude's pleasure on receiving George Chamberlain's generous letter, difficult to imagine her reaction to the suggestion that she publish the book under her own name. On the one hand, it is simply a piece of work like any other—sculptural; mind-freeing; handled like a commission, with artisan-technicians to do the final correcting and polishing "only worthwhile . . . if it is worth publishing." On the other hand, the book is so personal, contains so much of Gertrude's own life, that she cannot bear to make the author's identity public. She knows that Chamberlain is right, that if she put her name on the book she would have only to lie back and let it, in all probability, become a best seller. But that is easy for him to say. Despite his having gone to Lawrenceville and Princeton, despite his having a big place in Quinton, New Jersey, and belonging to the right club there, despite, in short, his belonging more or less to her world, he is still a bachelor—like Ronald Gordon in her novel, a rather rootless one who has served in consular posts all over the world, Brazil, Portuguese East Africa, Mexico. . . . He can do what he wants, he can afford risks, he doesn't have a family—a mother who is still a prominent and conservative force in society, an older brother who is a brigadier general in the Reserve Corps, a younger sister who is the wife of the Hungarian ambassador to Washington, three children, eight grandchildren (now, with the birth of Lev). . . .

In the last weeks of September, Gertrude goes through her novel once more, correcting some inconsistencies; then she has Mrs. Stevens put the book in shape for submission to a publisher. We don't know if Gertrude uses George's literary agent. She may have sent the book directly to Thomas ("Tim") Coward, a friend (and suitor between marriages) of Flora's. In any case, the book goes out as *Walking the Dusk* by L. J. Webb, is accepted by Coward-McCann (without a customary advance but with fairly standard royalties of ten per cent), and is scheduled for publication in September of 1932.

While completing the novel, Gertrude continues to do sketches for Hugh Ferriss, to pursue other commissions, and to correspond and talk by phone with Juliana Force about the opening of the museum. Gertrude does not interrupt any of this work until the end of the month when, with the Millers and the Henrys, she travels to Strafford, Chester County, Pennsylvania, to attend the very small and quiet garden wedding of Sonny to his second wife Gwladys Crosby Hopkins at the summer home of her mother, Mrs. Stevens Heckscher. Though the wedding is secluded and attended by only about sixty guests, it is widely publicized—in the society pages, which emphasize the prominence of both families; and in the tabloids, which rehash Evan Fontaine's paternity suit. In bold headlines the

New York *Evening Graphic* asks, "WILL 'SONNY' WHITNEY'S MARRIAGE
LAY GHOST OF HIS FORMER LOVE?" and continues, "Will Sonny's latest
matrimonial venture vindicate the stand made by his mother, Mrs. Harry
Payne Whitney, some ten years ago when a dark horse in the form of
Evan Burrows Fontaine, dancer extraordinary, appeared on the scene and
threatened to run away with the sweepstakes?" Questions, speculations,
innuendoes, half-truths go on for more than a full page. If Gertrude needed
to be further convinced of the desirability of keeping one's private life
private, the *Graphic* does the job. She can imagine what the tabloids would
make of *Walking the Dusk*.

Yes, in fiction one has the advantage of being able to disguise private
subject matter and deep-felt sentiments, but the disadvantage of being
subjected to many plausible interpretations. In autobiography one may
decide to confine and censor oneself, but at least one can say clearly *what
one wants to say*, can interpret oneself and isn't, to the same extent, interpreted, criticized, and analyzed by others. While completing the novel,
or very soon thereafter, Gertrude begins what may be either a straight autobiography or a book-length autobiographical essay, intended for use in
connection with the opening of the museum, when she knows there will
be many requests for statements and interviews. The scribbled, untitled
work begins:

My reason for writing a book is that I have something to say to the
younger generation about the importance I feel should be attached to
the value of study and concentration. It has to do with happiness in
its deepest sense and with the realization that work for the sake of
work is well worth the effort.

I never had much facility in the arts. I had a deep love for them
and a reverential feeling. I never thought of myself as an artist, but I
found a great pleasure in working with a lump of clay. The purely
pleasurable satisfaction I obtained was a selfish indulgence. But it
brought into my life a rare gift and I cling to it as one might to a beacon.

In those days I did not think of it that way, in fact I did not think
of it at all except as being thrilling to try and express what one saw. It
was not till much later that I saw sculpture as sculpture. In the beginning I only loved a piece of clay and delighted in form, and the inadequacy with which I expressed my ideal drove me to frenzy, but somehow I always thought someday I shall be able to approach what is in
me to say.

I think the first time I ever did this (in spite of the many things I
had then done) was in my war sketches. Bad as they were, there was
behind them a driving force which, though inadequately expressed,
soothed my spirit of unrest. They should have been so much better.
With more study I could have made them better, but—and I hated

myself for their inadequacy—these scraps and impressions, unworthy [?] of serious consideration. By myself I should always have considered them as such. But at that time, a great friend, a genius in the realm of decorations, walked one day into my studio and told me to have these all cast. They exist now as a phase of my work. I am grateful to Bob Chanler because his encouragement at that time was what I was least getting and what I most needed.

If one happens to be born rich of a famous family, happens to marry into a rich and famous family, happens to have worked successfully at a profession, one cannot avoid notoriety.

Some people like notoriety and some people don't. It is merely a question of taste. People who get it and like it handle the situation well, people who get it and dislike it handle it badly. Notoriety is merely today getting your name in the newspapers. Or your name being in the newspapers for no matter what reason is notoriety.

This perhaps has nothing to do with writing a book, and my only reason . . .

The autobiographical "book" stops there, as Gertrude is attempting to *decide* (the word, at this moment in her life, seems always to demand emphasis) which facts to include, which to exclude: it is no accident that there are more great works of "fiction" than of autobiography. But, for Gertrude, easier than either of these forms—surely less painfully private and therefore a greater escape from herself—is dealing with the museum's opening, dealing with it as facts are presented rather than selected and as problems are faced rather than created.

The basic problem—the eternal problem of all institutions—is money. For two years, as the Depression has become worse, the plans for the physical museum, as well as its collections and its programs, have grown more ambitious. Where once Gertrude was able to support her benefactions with her own income or with financial help from Harry, she must now dip into or borrow against shrinking capital. Mostly she invades capital, as she answers the demands of Juliana Force and her staff for bigger and better galleries, a more representative collection, enlarged programs in publishing (seventeen monographs, in addition to a catalogue of the collection, will be ready in time for the opening), in lending, in traveling exhibitions, in lectures and symposia.

Whenever Gertrude can, at whatever personal sacrifice, she says yes. The building itself has been the largest immediate drain on her resources. At first, consideration has been given to using just 8 and 10 West Eighth Street, but these are inadequate, and 12 is added. Cully's architecture firm, Noel & Miller, struggles to integrate the buildings and create a reasonably flowing space, despite varying ceiling heights, chimneys and load-bearing walls which cannot be removed economically, differing façades, et cetera.

The interior of the museum's first three floors consists finally of eleven galleries whose sizes and shapes conform to the remaining walls of the old houses. (The fourth floor and a portion of the third are devoted to an apartment and offices for Mrs. Force.) Only at the entrance are there structural modifications: a high hall, a grand stair, an unobstructed sculpture gallery (once the studio of Daniel Chester French).

The three façades are unified by a facing of warm pink stucco, inspired by the typical tone of buildings in Marrakech, "The Rose City." The main entrance is simple—stylistically somewhere between classicism and Art Deco. It is centered, flanked by white marble columns, topped by a low-relief "modern" American eagle. Outer doors are aluminum, with a design of five-pointed stars echoing the modern Americanism of the eagle; inner doors frame sculpted glass panels of animals by the ceramist Carl Walters. A few steps inside, at the bottom of the stair, is a bronze cast of Gertrude's Arlington Fountain and, at the top, two sculptures by John Gregory, *Wood Nymph* and *Bacchante*.

By the end of September the building is substantially completed. Paintings and sculpture are already being placed for the first exhibition. Catalogues and monographs are being printed. Opening-day speeches are being prepared. Invitation lists are being reviewed. And still the demands continue—demands on Gertrude's time, on her money and, ultimately, on her health. Eleanor Lambert, a publicist working for the museum at this time, begs her to write an article called "I Believe in American Art," to supplement Gertrude's speech and be used as newspaper filler. Gertrude writes nineteen typed pages of past history, "The Importance of America's Art to America." Juliana Force needs more furniture here, better lighting there. Gertrude continues to say yes, but the drain on her energy and pocketbook is constant, and one of the most difficult decisions she must make is to discontinue her financial support of *The Arts.* Juliana Force delivers the sad news to Forbes Watson. Then he writes long gracious letters to both of them. Here is most of the one to Gertrude:

> It is a long time since I have seen you and I wish I might tell you in person what I shall attempt to tell you in this letter. Mrs. Force explained to me the other day at tea that, owing to the unexpectedly large cost of the Museum, and to generally unsettled financial conditions, you would be unable longer to contribute to the support of *The Arts.*
>
> I feel that at this time I want to try to express to you my deep sense of gratitude for your generous help to *The Arts* during the past nine years. And I want to discourage any feeling that you may have that, in failing to become self-supporting, *The Arts* has not been a worthwhile venture. To be sure we all agreed in the beginning that although that was not its primary purpose, it would be a welcome achievement and a healthy sign.

I have by no means given up the hope of bringing *The Arts* through its present ordeal. In the month before the "crash" it earned its largest income, an income which if continued, would have supported it; and if I can somehow drag it over the thin ice of present conditions, I feel certain that it will go. But even if it should be compelled, in this difficult year, to suspend publication, I should not feel, personally, that the work had been in vain or that your disinterested generosity had been for nothing.

As I wrote to Mrs. Force, *The Arts* has brought out a group of younger critics, has revived such reputations as that of Thomas Eakins, has promoted the reputations of almost everyone of the independent artists who were formerly unrecognized but are now accepted by a larger public. It has become prescribed reading in several of our leading universities, has changed the course of the public's feeling toward American art—and it has done this thanks to you. In this work it has been doing, through another medium, the printed word, what you have done through your galleries and through other assistance to the American artist. It has added the power of the printed word to the broad-minded and courageous activities that you have supported and sheltered.

I naturally hope that *The Arts* will not go under, but if it does such a disaster will not make me feel any less acutely conscious of your profound generosity to me or of the value of the work which you have accomplished through *The Arts*.

In this critical year I think that the opening of your Museum will prove of inestimable value in encouraging the American artist and in showing the great public that life isn't merely material and that you are not afraid to fight for art as you always have, whatever the world economic outlook may be. At any time what you are about to do would be the most independent and courageous museum undertaking that has ever been attempted in America. But now particularly it is a most splendid act. It is a real raising of the flag of the spirit against material domination. . . .

Gertrude does not return from Newport to New York until mid-October. During the following month her attention is focused almost entirely on the opening of the museum. There, on Monday, November 16, a luncheon is given for professional critics and reviewers, preceding an opening that afternoon for the general press. Mrs. Force presides at lunch, outlining the museum's plans. Royal Cortissoz of the *Herald Tribune* pays homage to the Vanderbilts—William H., William K., George W., and now Gertrude—as patrons of the arts. Hugh Ferriss speaks briefly about the architectural problems in designing a museum. Forbes Watson and the popular and jovial writer Christopher Morley add some historical and congratulatory remarks. Gertrude makes a formal speech of thanks but will be cornered after lunch by an aggressive reporter for the syndicated *Every Week* magazine who asks her mainly about the more abstract paintings in the collection:

Stuart Davis' *Egg Beater, No 1?* "It is an example of a completely abstract modern picture, and it is important as a tour de force in design and color. . . ." (The reporter will have a reproduction of it "printed upside down to prove that it doesn't matter.")

Charles Demuth's *My Egypt?* ". . . neither entirely abstract nor frankly expository."

Max Weber's *Chinese Restaurant?* "The different elements of the place as they affect the artist are . . put together in an artistic chop suey . . . the pattern of the linoleum on the floor, the border of the oilcloth, the motif of the tablecloth."

Georgia O'Keeffe's *Skunk Cabbage?* "[The artist is] a woman who distorts nature in her utter feeling for it . . . you feel as if you could put your face down in its damp green vitality and draw back some of the rankness, some of the wild swampiness of the object."

The questions and answers continue—these particular ones published in a widely circulated, unsigned article called "So This Is Art," others in dozens of newspapers and magazines. Despite Juliana Force "presiding," despite the painters on her staff, despite the presence of the best critics in the country, it is Gertrude's words (even when garbled or misquoted) that are news. She is news. She is the Whitney Museum of American Art, both its mother and its personification.

The official opening of the museum is Tuesday. That day all of the metropolitan papers announce it, along with a history of Gertrude and, almost synonymously, of the museum; list the artists in its collection; and describe its new home. Most detailed, but otherwise typical, is the description in the *Times*:

> . . . the museum differs physically from virtually every other such institution in the country. The severity and bleakness which characterize many such institutions have been done away with in this latest addition to American museums. Instead of the uniform gray or white walls the museum visitor is accustomed to see, he will find here variety of coloring.
>
> The walls of the sculpture gallery are painted powder blue, against which marble and bronze are defined sharply. Two of the picture galleries have white walls and white velvet curtains, but two others have canary yellow walls, carpet and hangings, and furnishings which give it somewhat the effect of a drawing room. Two other galleries have been finished in gray, and two others have cork walls. Except in these two galleries, the sculpture gallery and in the hallways, the wall coverings are of woven paper, painted. The coloring of the walls, nat-

urally, has necessitated careful hanging of the pictures in order to obtain the most harmonious effects.

Another feature of the museum is the generous wall space devoted to each picture. Instead of the crowded walls characteristic of many museums, the visitor finds here each picture isolated from its neighbor by sufficient space to give the effect almost of pictures in a residence rather than a public institution.

Throughout, the museum reflects the personal taste of Mrs. Whitney. In each case final choice of a work of art depended on her, since there is no board of trustees. This is a museum founded, maintained and managed by artists, since Mrs. Whitney, the curator [Hermon More] and his assistants are sculptors or painters.

Shortly before four o'clock Gertrude, Governor Alfred E. Smith, art patron Otto Kahn, and Congressman Robert Low Bacon (the son of Gertrude's old friend Ambassador Bacon) assemble in the powder-blue sculpture gallery with an inner group of Gertrude's friends and immediate family, the museum staff, and technicians from Columbia Broadcasting System. Gertrude, still in mourning, wears a black velvet and chiffon dress, matching hat, jet beads, and a bouquet of purple orchids at her wrist. She stands taller than Al Smith and Otto Kahn in their dark suits, almost as tall as Representative Bacon, very erect in his cutaway. She is tense and tired but happy. Precisely at four the CBS announcer describes the occasion and introduces Bacon, who reads a letter to Gertrude from President Hoover:

"I profoundly regret that the pressure of imperative public duties prevents my accepting your kind invitation to speak at the opening of the Whitney Museum of American Art. It is an enterprise which makes a strong appeal to my own interest and I am sure that this permanent, pioneer museum devoted exclusively to American paintings and sculpture will appeal to the country as a benefaction of nationwide interest. It is a promising step toward placing American art in the position of importance and dignity which its excellence and individuality merit. It should quicken our national sense of beauty and increase America's pride in her own culture. Please accept for yourself my heartiest congratulations on the consummation of your plans and the appreciation which I know every American must feel for so notable a contribution to the nation."

In a strained "reading" voice, Gertrude thanks the President:

"The understanding of my desire to fulfill a public need, so well expressed in his letter, is to me an encouragement and an incentive to further progress. One sentence in his gracious letter is especially significant to me. Let me quote the words: 'It will increase America's pride in her culture.'

"For twenty-five years I have been intensely interested in American art.

I have collected during these years the work of American artists because I believe them worthwhile and because I have believed in our national creative talent. Now I am making this collection the nucleus of a museum devoted exclusively to American art—a museum which will grow and increase in importance as we ourselves grow.

"In making this gift to you, the American public, my chief desire is that you should share with me the joy which I have received from these works of art. It is especially in times like these that we need to look to the spiritual. In art we find it. It takes us into a world of beauty not too far removed from any of us. 'Man cannot live by bread alone.' "

After Gertrude, the strongly contrasting breezy style and heavily New York-accented voice of Al Smith:

". . . Mrs. Whitney is one of the best friends the American artist ever had. . . . I have never been accused of being an art expert. My own collection ranges from pictures of Brown's newsboys to some queer and wonderful creations of amateur artists of every kind of portrait of myself. These are painted, burned or engraved on canvas, wood, leather, glass and almost every sort of material you can imagine. I even saw a photograph the other day of a portrait of myself carefully executed on the face of an egg, and it was not a bad piece of work. Charles Dana Gibson once told me to hold onto these pictures of myself. He said they would make an interesting exhibit. Well, I have plenty of them and maybe someday Mrs. Whitney will lend me space to show them and I, too, will become an art collector. Of course, not all of these works have been frivolous and inconsequential, and I do not mean to belittle the artistic efforts of even messenger boys, elevator operators and streetcar conductors who have taken the trouble to paint my picture. . . ."

And after Al Smith—democratic beyond even the credo of the Whitney Museum—Otto Kahn is another contrast:

". . . the severe and grievously prolonged Depression which has come upon our country has shown all too vividly the hazards and fluctuations to which material possessions are subject. By the same token and by contrast, it has demonstrated the permanency and inviolability of spiritual possessions. That which we have within us in faith, in appreciation and love of art and books and nature, in cultural interests and understanding, no man and no event can take away from us, no income tax can reduce and no stock exchange collapse can diminish."

From four until seven, between 3,000 and 5,000 invited guests (depending upon which paper you read) jam the museum. Henry McBride of the *Sun,* who endorses the 5,000 figure, says that "all of them came in cars" and that the merchants on Eighth Street "gave up all thought of business and simply watched the spectacle." Most of the guests are artists and their mates, certainly hundreds of artists, possibly thousands, many in the collection, many not, some established, some still students, some amateurs, some Village bohemians who surely did not come by car. . . . It is basically an "artists' opening" as openings at the Whitney's predecessor institutions have also been but, milling among the artists and their husbands, and wives and lovers, studying them all more than the paintings which can hardly be seen are "the others," the rest of the art world—patrons, dealers, architects, writers, museum directors and curators, and people who appear on lists. (At random, the newspapers note Mr. and Mrs. Courtlandt Barnes, Mr. and Mrs. Stuart Davis, Mr. and Mrs. Eugene Speicher, Mrs. George Bellows, Mr. and Mrs. Walter Damrosch, Mr. Walter Chrysler, Jr., Mr. and Mrs. John D. Rockefeller, Jr., Mr. and Mrs. Albert Spalding, Mr. and Mrs. Clarence Dillon, Sir Joseph Duveen, Mr. and Mrs. Henry Dupont, Mr. John Sloan, Mr. and Mrs. Grover Whalen, Mr. Felix Warburg, Mr. Adolph Lewisohn, Bishop and Mrs. Manning. . . .)

Gertrude stays close to Juliana Force, greets relatives, friends, and acquaintances; is introduced to strangers, some of whom she knows only by reputation or through works in the collection; escapes finally, at seven, with Juliana Force—first to the director's room on the third floor, with its modern polished steel furniture; then upstairs to Mrs. Force's apartment, with its cozy and fanciful collection of Victorian furniture and bric-a-brac. In both settings the party continues. Gertrude and Juliana are joined by Flora and Cully, Sonny and "Gee" ("Who can say Gwladys without sounding as if he is lisping?"), Barbie and Buz, the curator/painter Hermon More and a dozen or more artists—including those mentioned in the papers, such as Davis, Speicher, and Sloan. It is the continuation of a tradition—an *ambition* for some artists—which will last throughout Juliana Force's life: to be invited to The Apartment after an opening.

The event—the real event, the fact that for the first time the United States has a museum devoted entirely to contemporary American art—is greeted by an enthusiastic press. The very existence of the museum —a "milestone," a "cornerstone," a "steppingstone"—seems an answer to H. L. Mencken's vision of "Boobocracy" and Sinclair Lewis' of "Babbittry." At first criticism of the collection is mild. After the opening Henry McBride writes (*Sun*, November 21):

> In the strict sense, many [items] are not museum pieces. But it is altogether excellent that they were purchased when they were and it is altogether excellent that they are shown now. If one were to wait until an artist becomes an acknowledged master there would be no sense in making the purchase at all—at least for such a museum as this whose business is to make reputations not to embalm them.

And Helen Appleton Read (Brooklyn *Eagle*, November 22):

> The present collection does not pretend to any finality of representation. The story of the 19th Century is only indicated by a few

outstanding figures [Ryder, Eakins, Johnson, Twachtman, Homer, Blakelock—"available" examples bought during the past two years].

Gertrude herself has said as much in "The Importance of America's Art to America":

I don't pretend to have covered anything like the entire field in my collection of American art. There are many gaps. At first I bought with no such idea in mind, just bought a picture because I liked it and thought the artist well worthwhile. In the future I plan to fill in these gaps. . . .

The general public pours into the museum to see for itself. By noon on Wednesday there is a line, swollen by New York University students, extending to Fifth Avenue and around the corner. The *Herald Tribune* estimates 4,000 visitors this day, and there are long lines through the weekend. The museum is a success, as popular and well publicized as Gertrude's greatest creations in bronze and stone. Articles about her, interviews with her, and pictures of her continue to appear in daily newspapers, Sunday supplements, general magazines, fashion magazines, everywhere.

As so often in the past, Gertrude pays a price for all this. The strain of the opening, added to that of Harry's death and the fast compulsive completion of her novel, lead to a severe mastoid infection, an agonizing operation, and postoperative complications. By December 4, having left the Harbor Hospital at 61st Street and Madison Avenue and returned to 871 Fifth, she is so debilitated that Josh Hartwell says she must have a transfusion. Remembering Harry's, and (as Flora recalls) "appalled by the thought of having someone else's blood put in her," Gertrude refuses. Josh says that she must have it within two days unless her condition improves. She fights now, as never before, to get well. In two days her temperature, her blood count, her breathing, her pulse are all back to normal. Josh and the specialists working with him pronounce her recovery "a miracle."

While recuperating she reads a great deal, including the more detailed critical articles on the museum which begin to appear. In the November issue of *Creative Art*, Henry McBride, writing before the opening, predicts one kind of reaction:

There will no doubt be a howl of criticism leveled at the artists that have been included in the fold by the friends of artists who have been left out . . . but all that sort of thing is beneficial and serves the necessary modern purpose of publicity. In fact, a lack of adverse criticism would be almost fatal—it would imply that there was no real public concern in the affair.

But he doesn't recognize—or at least not now, in print—the real schism that has existed in American art since the earliest days of Gertrude's dream of a museum: the conflict, in its simplest terms, between the abstractionists, grouped around Stieglitz and inspired by the European modernists, and the realists, stemming from The Eight. There is no question that, despite Gertrude's defense of Davis, Demuth, Weber, and O'Keeffe in the "So This Is Art" interview, her deepest sympathy (and Juliana Force's, Hermon More's, Forbes Watson's and most of those associated historically with the Whitney) has been with the realists. Now, in the predated December 30 issue of the *Nation,* she reads Paul Rosenfeld, the brilliant author of *Port of New York,* long committed to the Stieglitz group, including such artists as John Marin and Arthur Dove, missing from the museum's collection of paintings; and others, like Demuth, O'Keeffe, and Marsden Hartley, each represented by only one work (as compared with at least five each in the collection by Arnold Blanch, Lucille Blanch, Alexander Brook, Henri Burkhard, Arthur E. Cedarquist, Guy Pène du Bois, Ernest Fiene, Emil Ganso, William Glackens, Harry Gottlieb, Leon Hartl, Max Kuehne, Ernest Lawson, Henry Mattson, Hermon More, Joseph Pollet, Paul Rohland, Katherine Schmidt, H. E. Schnakenberg, Raphael Soyer, Eugene Speicher, and Nan Watson). Rosenfeld writes:

A metal eagle spreads imperial wings over the door of the new museum in Eighth Street. Under the national symbol an inscription specifies the dedication of the building to the arts that have grown from the continental country. Voices even louder than those of metal and engraving have proclaimed the institution a deed in behalf of American art and the American public. At the inaugural a message from the President and a speech from Al Smith figured among many sonorities advertising the museum to the world. Mrs. Juliana R. Force, the director, announced that the purpose of the museum was none other than the acquisition, for the art of America, of "the prestige which heretofore the public has devoted too exclusively to the art of foreign countries and the past." All the papers bruited forth the name and the fame of the donor, Mrs. Gertrude Vanderbilt Whitney. Entering the newly converted building, Mr. Royal Cortissoz, subtle dean of American art critics, saw that it was good. Daily, since the dedication, crowds of people have wandered through the little rooms, "wonders to see." And dismally enough, it appears very possible that only the grace of the gods can prevent the new institution from recoiling upon the prestige of the American art it proposes to enhance.

The collection it houses, all in all, is puny and gray. Few forces, few personalities radiate from the walls. One passes yards of uncreative canvases. The impression of American painting left is extremely disaffecting: that of a matter devoid of large life, of individual charm, of eloquence; and provincial and secondary to a degree. The collection of sculpture is even less attractive. But the fault is the collection's: it is sadly unfaithful to the work it pretends to represent . . .

one does not demand of a museum of American art that it comprise nothing but masterworks. What one does expect, in view of its style, is that it contain good examples of the classics and excellent examples of the work of the significant contemporaries whose best has not yet passed into the safekeeping of museums and large private collections. But the only group thoroughly represented in the Whitney collection is the showy "he-man" generation of the 1900's. . . . And it is precisely the work of Henri, Bellows, Luks, and their school that, of all ambitious recent American painting, seems least deserving of a place in a museum of art. To an eye trained by Manet and Van Gogh and Cézanne, a work like Luks's recent *Mrs. Gamely* appears a mere cavalier evasion of the problems of the painter. . . .

The truth would appear to be that the Whitney collection was formed for purposes other than those of a museum of American art. Unless we mistake, it was originally born of the worthy desire to patronize and support a number of young and struggling artists; and the canvases acquired were bought with an eye bent more to the struggles and promise of the artists than to the completeness of their expressions. Later, when the idea of a museum began to obtain, the collection appears to have rather hastily been augmented to fit the new purpose . . . one could almost wish that the Whitney Museum had never opened its pompous doors.

No doubt the attack hurts Gertrude, as does a less aggressive one by Matthew Josephson, making some of the same points in the *New Republic*. However, although the museum buys three O'Keeffes during the next two years and its first Hartley in 1937, there is no indication that either Gertrude or Juliana is very much influenced by Rosenfeld's and Josephson's criticism. For example, except for one Marin etching, no works by him or Dove will be acquired by the museum until long after both Mrs. Whitney and Mrs. Force are dead. Instead, they continue to rely on the reassuring advice of Nan and Forbes Watson, Eugene Speicher, H. E. Schnakenberg, Allen Tucker, Guy Pène du Bois, Alexander Brook, his wife Peggy Bacon, and others. Nor, during Gertrude's and Juliana's lives, will quality in itself prevail against such human considerations as friendship, need, and encouragement. Indeed, it is rumored that Juliana (acting for Gertrude) sometimes selects weaker works by a given artist in order that the best will be left for him to sell.

Despite all this, it must be said—and no one says it more positively than Stuart Davis (in an interview with Hermon More and John I. H. Baur, September 29, 1953)—that "the Museum in its early days played a unique role in giving the American artist . . . public importance . . . there was no other center where he was given any importance. . . . It not only gave him a place to show his work but also did a great deal in tangible support, in buying paintings and giving money to live on. . . . Nobody else did it."

⪻ *1932*

Though Gertrude must frequently see Josh Hartwell and her other doctors for checkups, she has recovered from her illness and is once more commuting between New York and Westbury—but now in a leisurely way, staying several days at a time in each place.

JAN.1, FRI. Buz stopping in. Bill Delano for lunch. Short drive. Saw M[other].

The entry is typical of the days that follow—days filled, but not overfilled, with family and old friends, all being extremely attentive. At first, except for relatives and doctors, Gertrude sees Charles Draper most frequently. She spends her fifty-seventh birthday with him, often has him to cocktails and dinner, is often taken by him to the movies and theater, almost always matinees. Less frequently, she sees Jimmie Appleton, Adele Burden, Kipp Soldwedel, Phil Carroll, John Gregory, and the Masons, who continue to be as solicitous, to her now as during the previous winter in Cuba. As with Charles, the dates are mostly in the afternoon, mostly to see movies or plays. Only occasionally does the entry "Studio afternoon" appear. Though she is doing some sketching and some studies for Hugh Ferriss' "Air City" (less and less likely to become a reality), it seems that most of her creative energy is now going into writing and that the nights (conspicuously unrecorded in her Line-A-Day) are devoted to short stories and to additional revisions of *Walking the Dusk*, about which she confers several times with George Chamberlain and Tim Coward.

And, of course, there is the museum. Though Juliana Force is its director—"a very autocratic one," as she describes herself in a typical letter of this period, written in response to an artist asking why he is not in the collection—she still confers frequently with Gertrude on all matters of policy and funding. Telephone calls to Long Island and meetings in New York are both frequent, and occasionally Gertrude attends openings and other special events.

FEB. 5th, FRI. Studio, New Society lunch [at museum]. Josh home 4.

The luncheon reception, preceding an exhibition of current work by the American Society of Painters, Sculptors and Gravers, becomes famous for a moment in the art world, not because of the work shown but because of a scene between Gertrude and George Luks. At the reception Luks, a small man, often drunk, as at the "Indigenous" exhibition years before, follows Gertrude around, saying nothing, simply staring up at her. Finally Gertrude asks, "Why are you following me?" Without hesitation, he replies, "Because you're so goddamn rich!"

That's understandable, public, loud. It *is* the lunch. "Josh home 4" is, on the other hand, mysterious, private, quiet. Because of the hour and the lunch just next door, "home" has to be MacDougal Alley, guarded discreetly by Gertrude's studio man, Victor. Only now, by reading between the terse phrases of the Line-A-Day, do we begin to guess that Josh Hartwell's relationship to Gertrude is becoming more than professional. Her references to him change from "Dr. Hartwell" and "Dr. H." in early January to "Josh" and "J." now. Within another month more will change.

March 19, Gertrude, traveling as "Mrs. Austin," leaves on a two weeks' cruise to Cuba with Juliana Force, Charles Draper, and Bobbie Locher, best known as lifelong friend of Charles Demuth but, in his own right, an imaginative decorator who has worked on Mrs. Force's apartment. Letters from Josh follow—long love letters, addressed typically to "My dear, dear person." Here is the beginning of one written at the exact mid-point of the cruise:

> Of one thing, my darling one, I am sure. The week to come cannot be as endless as the week past. Each day then was taking you farther away and added to my pitiful loneliness. Now each day brings you nearer and the aching longing that is so strong knows there will be a compensating joy not too far away. Oh yes, I love you and the sudden cessation of perfect and complete companionship over a month's time left a void that won't be put into words. Your telegrams have been wonderfully helpful and have taken away some of the hurt.
>
> Am I wrong in believing that all the impatience and loneliness have not been mine? And the beauty and memories that come up on reading the morning lines? [Gertrude has left him one loving sentence for each day, without salutation or signature, written on a narrow strip of stationery.] You of course can't remember them day by day but just the same they come to me as though you were just saying them—and you can guess the reaction. For instance Friday: "At least I have time to relive my memories; though they make me restless I float in another world." There is poetry in that. . . .

Though Gertrude is surely responsive to Josh's unequivocal passion, there are hints in her correspondence of tentativeness, defensiveness, flippancy, and an ambivalence which makes her forget (hesitate) to mail a long letter to him and, in a telegram, confuse the date of her return. Like Josh, she is lonely and welcomes a love affair, especially one which, because of his professional relationship to her, can be handled with discretion. However, he is married and has reached a stage in his career from which there is nowhere to go. He is at the top of his profession but dissatisfied by a routine of appointments, teaching, and administrative duties. For him, a virile and handsome man of sixty-five, Gertrude represents escape and hope, an abandonment of his increasingly oppressive practice and stale marriage and, instead, a life of travel, golf, hikes, hunting. Gertrude's situation is different: she is single, free, economically independent, and committed to her career—really two careers now, writing and sculpting.

Gertrude sees Josh briefly the morning she returns ("J. 11:30"), arranges to see him the following day, then has lunch with her mother, dinner with Barbie and Buz. A schedule like the one before the cruise seems about to be resumed. However, the next day's entry ends, "Studio afternoon & dinner. X." There will be many such entries during the following weeks. When Gertrude sees Josh at his office or is visited by him in Westbury or goes out in public with him to theater or a concert he is "Josh" or "J." At the studio he is "X."

The first evening there, while watching the lively flames in Bob Chanler's exotic fireplace and sipping cocktails served by Victor, Josh reads his "almost daily chronicle"—twenty closely written pages, confessing his growing love for Gertrude and his misery during her absence. He recalls every moment he has spent with her, first as her doctor, then as her friend, then as more than her friend during visits to what he calls "the Alley Club," beginning with the first one after the studio New Society lunch. He speaks of questions which "must be decided." He responds to every word of Gertrude's, to every "morning line." He is distressed that she has only received three of his eight letters, the others probably lost forever because addressed to "Mrs. Austin." Finally, on the day before her arrival, he imagines her already "in my arms and every earnest word, every playful thought, every foolish idea, love and fever all come tumbling to the surface—yours and mine, mine and yours, and we are wondrously happy in knowing what it all means. So, my darling, I kiss you. . . ."

The entire chronicle is left with Gertrude in an envelope inscribed by Josh: "An imaginary correspondence, for use in Anne [sic] Webb's first romance. Suggested by her publisher, T.C., Coward-McCann." The inscription is Josh's only attempt at lightness; the rest is heavy, and Gertrude has a lot to think about, perhaps especially his questions which "must be decided." If they include Josh's divorcing his wife, Gertrude is not ready for that. Whatever the relationship with Josh means to her, she still thinks constantly of Harry. Since his death she has contributed over $5,000 each year to one of his favorite charities, Brooklyn's Day Camp Whitney for tubercular children. In January of this year she has been in correspondence with Thomas Regan, carefully seeing to the disposition of Harry's remaining personal effects, including a superb collection of shotguns, mostly in pairs, to be distributed to his close friends. In February and March she has given a total of $230,000 toward the purchase of the Rothschild Collection of Birds—some 280,000 specimens, formerly housed in Tring, Hertfordshire—which will be added to Harry's previous gifts to the American Museum of Natural History as a memorial to him. And now, April 29, there is the short but eloquent entry: "Harry's birthday. Woodlawn."

The affair, however meaningful, continues as an affair: "Studio X. . . . Dined studio X. . . . For tea Dr. Frissell & Josh. . . . Studio dinner X. . . . Went fishing South Side [a fishing club], F[lora] & C[ully] & J[osh]. Returned to dine at studio X. . . . Josh dined, motored to Greenwich to Paderewski concert supper. . . . Josh 2:30. . . . Went to country with J. . . . Dined studio X. . . . Dined & night studio X."

Slightly more than a month has gone by, during which Gertrude has seen more of Josh than of any other friends or members of her family, though she does, of course, see them too. On June 1, only two days after Gertrude has had Adele and J. Burden for lunch in the country, J. dies of an embolism resulting from a hip fracture the previous year. At her studio with Josh the following morning, Gertrude hears of J.'s "sudden death"— a phrase loaded by now with painful irony. She and Josh drive to Woodside, the Burden estate in Syossett, and very late that night Gertrude drafts and redrafts a letter to Adele, along with a eulogy, possibly intended for J.'s funeral but more probably only for Adele. The letter first:

> I know what you face of misery and loneliness. There is only one word of comfort I find to say, but it is comfort. You vaguely suggested the idea yesterday but in another form. Believe me this thought of comfort grows in power and makes life bearable.
>
> Don't let's forget we were both given a rare opportunity. It is true it is cruel that we should not have had J & Harry with us for longer, but we were given the opportunity to prove to them our love. We were able to make life more bearable to them. They had had everything and suddenly were deprived of a great number of things. No more activity, isolated from sport, from club life, from most friends, from their normal pursuits.
>
> Then our function came—to love and cherish them. It wasn't that up to then we hadn't, but now we had to be a thousand more things to them. It wasn't that they had not loved us, but now we had to keep full those hours which other pursuits & friends had kept occupied.
>
> They had always taken & known our love, had received the fullness of life from us but suddenly they wanted more and that we could give it a thousand fold I think of gratefully. And they knew it. It must have been a proof to them of our love. They must have realized that all our lives were given to them and this has been my consolation.
>
> In the ordinary course of life we could not have proved it to them,

not through our lack of love, only because of the stress and distractions of ordinary life.

We had them for our very own in this short space of life.

My, love, G.

And now what seems to be the final version of Gertrude's eulogy, a more public echo of some of her private sentiments:

There are certain men who by their example stand out in the memory of those who have known them. It was my privilege to be a friend of such a man, James A. Burden.

Throughout his business career he stood for integrity, he stood throughout his personal life for high moral standards, and he stood throughout his last illness for real courage.

In saying this it is not only a just tribute to him but must be an inspiration to others.

A high-strung man accustomed to physical exercise and mental activity, he suffered at the age of sixty a fractured hip. For months he was unable to move, then by slow degrees walked on crutches. During all this period at no time did he complain, at no time show anything but the utmost consideration for those about him—his family, his friends, his doctors, his nurses.

Today when we are prone to weep over our material troubles, when we sigh and sob over the ills of existence, it must be, if we think at all about the spiritual, an example to know of a man who having lost the capacity to move, the ability to lead a life of activity, accepted without complaint and with cheerfulness his lot and to the end made all those about him happy.

And soon after the funeral Gertrude writes one more letter to Adele, offering her the Paris studio and the possibility of "getting away completely from hotel life . . . near enough to see the people you want to and far enough away not to have the casual person drop in and disturb you."

But now there is another member of the family who requires Gertrude's time: Regi's daughter, her niece Gloria Vanderbilt. The child is eight—living in New York with her nurse Miss Keislich (known as "Dodo") while her mother is in Europe—when she develops a particularly bad case of tonsillitis. June 9 and 10, Gertrude visits Gloria at the hospital, where her recovery is slow. As soon as she is well enough to be moved, Gertrude brings her to Westbury, and from now on has Gloria with her. It is a period of mounting family resentment at what they consider neglect on the part of Gloria's mother. And they are concerned not only about Gloria's health (at the beginning of July, Gertrude has three doctors, including Josh, in to examine her) but about her safety. Since the kidnapping and murder of the Lindbergh baby in March, no child seems safe, especially none with the name *Vanderbilt*.

Gertrude hesitates to make even a comparatively short trip to Europe but does finally decide to go for about a month, mainly for a cure at the Châtel-Guyon spa. Before leaving, she meets with Frank Crocker to go over a very detailed analysis of her financial situation. In brief, her gross income for this year is estimated to be $797,000 from stocks, $121,000 from tax-exempt bonds, and $175,000 from the Vanderbilt Trust. Frank assumes income taxes of about $300,000, leaving $793,000. This would seem to be an enormous amount of money. However, he then estimates Gertrude's expenditures, based upon past disbursements:

WESTBURY, including taxes $200,000
    Note: This could be substantially reduced

NEWPORT, including taxes   30,000
    Note: This could probably not be reduced very much

FIFTH AVENUE HOUSE, including taxes   90,000
    Note: This could be reduced a little

NEW YORK GARAGE [EAST 66TH STREET]   13,500
    Note: This could be proportionately reduced [i.e., by sharing expenses with other members of the family who use the garage]

STUDIO (NEW YORK) and WHITNEY MUSEUM   160,000
    Note: This could be substantially reduced

STUDIO, PARIS   20,000

OFFICE—247 PARK AVENUE [Thomas Regan]   41,000
    Note: This could and should be substantially reduced

SAFE-KEEPING, GUARANTY TRUST COMPANY   2,500

PENSIONS: Roots   900
             Witte   1,980

INTEREST ON GUARANTY TRUST CO. LOAN   64,000
    $1,600,000 @ 4% (Made to cover capital expenditures and acquisitions at the Whitney Museum)

INTEREST ON $200,000 LOAN @ 4½%, with   9,000
    Goadby & Co. (Made for acquisition of Rothschild Collection)

                                   TOTAL $632,880

Balance applicable to personal expenses, presents, traveling expenses, benefactions, etc. $160,120

Of this, in the opinion of F.L.C., a reserve should be set up for contingencies and for suspension of dividend and bond interest, of $100,000, leaving a net balance for all personal expenses, and unexpected charges and deductions, of . . . . $ 60,120

There is no immediate indication of curtailment in Gertrude's personal spending and none of "substantial reduction" in expenses at the museum where all programs—exhibition, acquisition, publication, loans from the collection, and traveling shows—move forward as planned.

July 8, Josh leaves for Europe. Gertrude spends about a week visiting her mother in Newport, returns to New York by night boat, has dinner the next night with Flora and Cully, Barbie and Buz, and Charles Draper, who drives her to Brooklyn where she boards the *Europa* for a midnight sailing. The Line-A-Day becomes spotty, perhaps purposely so. Though there are blanks rather than Xs, it is almost certain that after landing at Cherbourg, where she is met by her driver Auguste, Gertrude has a rendezvous with Josh in Orléans before visiting the Davidsons in Saché and then rejoining Josh at Châtel-Guyon.

The cure lasts from July 26 to August 5. There is a "nice evening," a "bad day as to weather," a "cloudy day," but mostly blanks, as uninformative as the meteorological comments. After the spa, Josh goes to fish and shoot in Scotland, Gertrude goes to Paris for ten days of fun, shopping, and excursions—perhaps, more simply, all fun—an afternoon at Notre Dame and Sainte Chapelle with the Davidsons; another with them at the new permanent Exposition building; a day at Rheims; lunch one day with Rollie, tea with him another; several dinners with an otherwise unidentified "L." She shops mostly at Ardanse, Yvonne Davidson's shop. The bill, dated August 15, the day before Gertrude returns home, is further evidence of non-curtailment of expenses. It covers thirty-three items—mostly dresses and pajamas, two cloth coats, some nightgowns—at a total cost of 81,528 francs (about $16,300). For the first time since Harry's death, many of the clothes are in bright colors, and the dresses have names that are brighter still: *Pour Georges, Elle Passe, Le Rendez-Vouz, Pour Vous Monsieur, Avec Lui, Half Past Eight, Intrigue Amoureuse.* . . .

⋐

As the previous year, Gertrude spends the late summer and early fall in Newport. She is there, working mostly on sculpture, when her novel is published. Even before publication there are many items in the gossip and book columns about *Walking the Dusk.* Though Tim Coward has contracted to publish the book under the pseudonym L. J. Webb, he and his publicity department are busy creating interest in the mysterious author:

> It is reported that the chief diversion in the Coward-McCann offices these dull August days is in trying to guess the identity of L. J. Webb. . . . T. R. Coward knows . . . he gives the following hints: L. J. Webb is the pseudonym of one of the ten most famous women in the United States. She has for many years been prominently identified with one or more of the following: art, charity, society, the stage, politics. *Walking the Dusk* is her first novel. She is married and

has children. She has written for magazines. A general article by her would command probably $2,500 to $5,000.

And:

> H. Ashbrook of Coward-McCann, the publishers, postcards that a poll of the staff of her firm on the identity of L. J. Webb, author of *Walking the Dusk* . . . picks Ethel Barrymore.

And, after another columnist recites the publisher's hints:

> You are now at liberty to do your own guessing. Unless, of course [the columnist] Walter Winchell or someone gives the show away.

And so forth. The advance publicity is consistently titillating but the reviews are mixed. Despite considerable attention, especially for a first novel, the book doesn't sell at all well. Gertrude, like every author, complains that it isn't being sufficiently advertised; but, unlike most, she offers to have additional advertising charged against royalties. Nothing helps. Perhaps the New York *Times* review has been the kiss of death, since its lead paragraph focuses on "the idle rich" and "bohemians of the more prosperous sort." This is now the depth of the Depression, and as Tim Coward says in a note, "Business is so bad that books have really not much of a chance. It is too bad because *Walking the Dusk* deserves a better fate." He means what he says. Two years later when he sends Gertrude a final royalty statement along with a check for $154 (indicating 770 copies sold at $2.00), he adds, "in view of the fact that the advertising did not pull, I don't feel quite right about charging you for that advertising as agreed. So I am letting the account go through without that charge against it." The check, deliberately uncashed, remains among Gertrude's papers.

≈

About the time of Gertrude's European trip Sonny has been persuaded to run for Congress, as a Democrat, in the First District, against the incumbent Robert Bacon. Like many wealthy men associated with normally Republican Wall Street, Sonny is convinced that, if the economy is to recover, President Hoover's tired reassurances must be replaced by dynamic new programs; and that even if he can't defeat Bacon in Queens, Nassau, and Suffolk counties—also normally Republican—he can cut substantially into his support and thereby help Franklin Delano Roosevelt. Sonny campaigns vigorously and Gertrude supports him—more importantly by coming from Newport to Long Island for several of his political rallies than by making three contributions of $5,000 each, which he appreciates as gestures but doesn't really need, being richer now than she is. At the same time Gertrude, as a Republican, supports Hoover.

Politics is only a small part of this busy fall. Another is resuming the role of mother to a young child, as she gets Gloria ready for school. And still another is posing for many days with Mama and Gladys in front of the huge Renaissance fireplace in the library at The Breakers, while the British painter William Ranken (best known for his interiors) works steadily on the commission so that it will be completed in time for Gertrude to give it to Neily for Christmas. (Though the portraits are poor, the poses are characteristic enough, particularly the willowy one of Gertrude, so that she orders artist's copies for Gladys and herself.) More typical is the resumption of a regular work schedule, though the hours as listed in the Line-A-Day are shorter than in the past, usually "1½ hours morning. 1½ hours afternoon." In early September she writes to Flora at Le Boulay:

> Except for a couple of days, Newport has been lovely and I have enjoyed it. The studio is nice to work in and I see my friends there, now & then having lunch or tea. . . . Mrs. Force came on for a short time to see me, talk business, etc. I go to the beach two or three times a week, lunch out with people I know well . . . enough time to read, write & work.

Later in the month she writes to Flora again:

> Did I tell you that I have decided to work for an exhibition in two or three years time? It is going to be great fun just to do what I want. I am making quick, rough sketches (have done 9 so far). Going to do any old subject that comes into my head and see what the result is. I have even attempted old subjects, a Leda & the Swan, Salome, etc. Then I will take the least bad, do those bigger and just work on to get my hand in again. Am very enthusiastic about it.

At this late stage of Gertrude's life, as one commission after another has aborted, we feel her sense of release from that bondage. Suddenly, despite Sonny's campaign, Gloria's needs, posing for Ranken, and all the usual demands, there is still enough time to read, write, and sculpt, enough time to do what she wants—any old subject that comes into her head. And there is enough time for Josh, enough time for anything—all those refound hours previously spent *around* commissioned works, before and after the actual creation of them.

Gertrude returns to New York October 25. On the twenty-sixth, the second anniversary of Harry's death, she spends part of the day at Woodlawn. The next day she resumes work at MacDougal Alley: "Josh posing." The phrase, which will be repeated in the Line-A-Day, comes as a surprise. We can only guess that Gertrude has suggested this as a way of giving him the amount of time with her that he wants without disrupting her own work schedule. There are no surviving sculptures of hers that look like Josh, who would be easy to recognize because of his striking resemblance to Franklin Roosevelt (they even use the same kind of cigarette holder, held in their mouths at the same rakish angle). However, Josh may have posed—consciously bowing his erect head and squared shoulders—for such a generalized and expressionistic piece as *Unemployed,* a tall, stooped man in a battered fedora and business suit "so tired of life that he will never rise again."

In Gertrude's short stories written in the early thirties the theme of the unemployed man crops up frequently too. Where once in her social circle unemployment itself was desirable, indeed the mark of a gentleman, now it is an economic problem as well as, more than ever, a psychological curse. To Gertrude, the man unable to work, for whatever reasons, becomes an increasingly tragic figure. Salvation—again, more than ever— exists in commitment to a profession, to a *calling,* in the most religious sense. In addition to stories dealing specifically with men out of work, there are at least three dealing with men (two architects, one portrait painter) who betray themselves by doing work (fulfilling commissions) they don't believe in. The theme is large, the writing almost always summary, descriptive, and ultimately self-defeating as Gertrude forces the concept of professional freedom into the shape of slick fiction. As in *Walking the Dusk,* deeper material is smothered by the mechanics of commercial writing. Not only is there a conflict between what Gertrude wants to say and what she thinks the public wants to hear, but the latter is encouraged by critical comments scribbled on her manuscripts, probably by George Chamberlain, less likely by Ada Stevens. These comments are always aimed at what Chamberlain (or whoever) calls "the garden variety reader" who wants characterization absolutely consistent, plot absolutely resolved.

For the moment Gertrude has neither the craft to write successful commercial fiction (none of her short stories is accepted for publication) nor the self-confidence to do what she is again doing in sculpture—that is, just what she wants, for her own sake only. Instead, the subject of professional integrity, as well as infidelity, jealousy, physical desire in old age, parent-child relationships, and many other valid themes are all forced into tight plots with clever or surprising endings, much less interesting and real than the organic flow of Gertrude's own life.

That flow continues—with Josh posing in the studio and often staying on into the night; with Sonny losing to Bob Bacon while Roosevelt defeats Hoover in a landslide; with Jo Davidson completing a polychrome bust of Harry based on his death mask (Gertrude writes to Yvonne that "Dev Milburn just stood and looked at it without saying a word for a long time, a very sad and affectionate expression on his face. Then he turned to me with a smile. 'It is just the way I have seen him look so many times when he was just going to tease someone'"); with a private opening at the museum for the first of what will become traditional biennial (sometimes annual) exhibitions of work by living artists (157 are in this first biennial and $20,000 is allocated for purchases); with the unveiling in the museum's research library of Thomas Hart Benton's murals "The Arts of Life in America"; with the belated, public announcement of the gift of the Rothschild Collection to the Museum of Natural History; with the still more belated private announcement, in a letter from Gertrude to Flora, that "Guardabassi [65] is back & his wife is going to have another baby!"; with dental appointments and eye examinations; with the receipt from the Columbus Memorial Fund of a check for $1,479.69 (again, belated—and uncashed, like the later check from Coward-McCann); with another contribution of over $5,000 to Day Camp Whitney; with a Christmas tree, a pony, and a stocking full of little presents for Gloria; but with none of the neatness of conventional fiction.

Yes, the flow of Gertrude's life is complex. Like many of us, she needs art to simplify it, stylize it, make it concrete and graspable. But how we wish, as she does at times, that she had the genius and took the risks of a Proust or Joyce or Woolf, a Matisse or Picasso or Brancusi, even if knowing that masterpieces, too, are only drops within the endless flow, or specks upon its surface. How we wish that in one finished story or one major sculpture she had gone as far as her talent permitted, at least as far as in some of her journals and sketches. Yet perhaps, given the unusual complexity of her life, there is too great, too irresistible a need for the oversimplifications and facile stylizations of commercial and popular forms and, given her background, too great and irresistible a need also to prove herself in the marketplace.

⇐ *1933*

Work on the "old subjects" is completed—not only *Leda and the Swan* and *Salome*, referred to in the letter to Flora, but an expansive *Daphne* (closely resembling Gertrude), an exhausted *Woman and Child* (later reworked and retitled *Where Is She Going?*—"a woman tired of life, carrying her last child which you know has been one too many"), a *Pan with His Teacher* ("a funny wild group with long lovely lines. . . . A fanatic, inspired but always the fanatic. A god who holds within his clasp two loving creatures who cannot escape their destiny"), and other sculptures and sketches expressive of emotions ranging from lyricism to despondency. The style of this work is no more innovative than the subject matter, but there is a straightforward honesty about it, the presence of Gertrude's hand, and an appropriate scale (usually about three feet high) with no inflated monumentality. As Gertrude says in the March 12 draft of a letter to an unknown recipient (where her comments on *Woman and Child* and *Pan* also appear): "To me, with the return of my health has come a tremendous vigor of creative output . . . I think the best work I have yet done."

When Gertrude finishes one piece she has it cast in bronze, sometimes reproduced in marble by her artisans, and then goes on to the next. Besides the classical subjects she does a sleek, stylized *Nun* and two portraits of blacks, *John* and *Gwendolyn,* the former Rodinesquely (or perhaps Epsteinesquely) textural, the latter as sleek as *Nun* or as typical middle-period works by Nadelman and Lachaise. Gertrude works freely, moving from one subject to the next, from one style to the next, from one mood to the next, never now having to concern herself with the demands of commission committees.

But it is an irony—no doubt, a necessary irony—that at the same time she has freed herself from these demands (or has been freed from them by the Depression), she continues to put a similar kind of pressure on herself, virtually commissioning her own stories, forcing them always into tight, bright little packages. An example of the overplotted, overcompressed story is "The Hand," also in some drafts called "The Scar." It is told from the viewpoint of Mildred Vernon, the wife of a world-famous Parisian doctor who figures in other stories of this period and is probably based on Josh Hartwell. Dr. Vernon, we are told by Mildred, is a genius who has perfected various operations for the transplantation of limbs. Stanley Forrester, a distinguished poet, loses his right hand in an accident. Dr. Vernon is called. He explains to Mildred that he must find someone who is dying who has the same kind of hand as Stanley—someone of his blood type, size, temperament. Conveniently, Egisto, an Italian stone carver, falls from a scaffold. Mildred negotiates with Egisto's wife for his hand, which will live on creatively. The operation is performed, the hand successfully transplanted, but Stanley changes, develops strange violent moods. Both Vernon and Mildred feel responsible. They persuade Stanley and Tony, his mistress, to go with them on a trip through the Italian hill towns. In one of them (indicated by the long mysterious dash of nineteenth-century fiction) Mildred discovers that, as a youth before coming to Paris, Egisto has murdered his mistress. But the discovery is too late. Just as Dr. Vernon is explaining to Stanley the necessity for another operation, Stanley picks up a candlestick and murders Tony with it.

Perhaps Poe could have written this story. Gertrude can't. But what interests us—again, from the biographical rather than the literary point of view—is Gertrude's obsessions. If Vernon is to some extent Hartwell, then Stanley, the moody, maimed poet, is to some extent Harry, for whose condition Gertrude (Mildred) holds herself at least partially responsible. No matter how contrived is this particular fiction, beneath it, visible within its structure, is the theme of castration—Stanley's as well as Egisto's, Harry's as well as Gertrude's. The theme nags like a bad dream, haunts Gertrude like Harry's ghost. Not only will she rewrite "The Hand" many times as a story but, later, as a full-length play.

⤝

The stories and sculptures are now equally important aspects of Gertrude's work; the museum, less important in terms of time given to it, because in effect Juliana Force gives that time for her. However, Gertrude does continue to meet often with Juliana and, for example, spends the afternoon of her birthday at the opening of an acquisitions exhibition.

So much for the flow of work—in clay, in words, in exhibitions—within the larger flow of Gertrude's life. As always, there's the flow of family, dwindling at one end, enlarging at the other. Mama, almost ninety now, has had a bad fall and Gertrude sees her frequently, usually for lunch, many times with Gladys. Less often, again sometimes with Mama, she sees her one remaining brother, Neily, still married to Grace, and still a rather withdrawn and brooding man, distinguished-looking at sixty, with some furrows of fatigue and concern showing in his face, gray dominating his short-cropped beard and mustache. Gertrude thinks about doing a portrait of him—and will in another year.

Gertrude's own children are as attentive to her as she is to her mother. Again and again Flora and Cully, Sonny and Gee, Barbie and Buz visit her, sometimes bringing their children on short visits, sometimes leaving them with Gertrude when the parents go on trips. She is generous to all of them, children and grandchildren alike, giving them much of her time and energy as well as liberal gifts and the use of her homes. A typical queenly gift follows Flora and Cully to Aiken early in the new year, before the repeal of Prohibition:

> Pol Roger 1898—10 magnums
> Cliquot 1904—200 bottles
> Pol Roger 1906—100 bottles
> Chablis—20 bottles
> Claret Pontet-Canet—100 bottles
> Old English Rye—150 bottles
> Brandy—20 bottles
> Bacardi Rum—100 cases

Close as Gertrude is to her immediate family, so is she now to her niece Gloria, whom she has enrolled in the Greenvale School on Long Island

and is bringing up like a daughter, while Gloria's mother remains in Europe. Entries in Gertrude's Line-A-Day are matter-of-fact:

JAN. 8, SUN.: Gloria celebrated my birthday [a day early] with a cake. . . .

FEB. 22, WED.: Went to country for Gloria's party. . . .

APR. 6, THURS.: [Thomas B.] Gilchrist [lawyer, court-appointed guardian of Gloria's property] 5. . . .

APR. 16, SUN.: Gloria & Lady Furness [Gloria's mother's twin sister] afternoon. . . .

APR. 21, FRI.: Went to country 10 to see Gloria & Henry children in French play Greenvale School. . . .

JUNE 2, FRI.: Greenvale School. . . .

JUNE 3, SAT.: Gloria V. [probably the mother] called. . . .

JULY 1, SAT.: Went beach [Newport] to see Gloria

AUG. 12, SAT.: Arrived Racquette Lake. Stayed Camp Togus. Children—Gloria, Emily [probably a friend], & Nancy [daughter of Sonny and his former wife Marie]—at Killoquah.

SEPT. 8, FRI.: [George W.] Wickersham and Gilchrist [partners, Cadwalader, Wickersham & Taft] downtown [14 Wall Street]. . . .

SEPT. 14, THURS.: Gloria (mother) 12. . . .

Until now it would seem that Gertrude has philosophically accepted Gloria's near-abandonment by her mother. However, we can imagine the conversations Gertrude must have had with her own mother and other members of the family about the elder Gloria, running around Europe on Little Gloria's maintenance allowance, income from the child's inheritance. But still, it has been no financial strain for Gertrude to take care of Gloria. It is the least she, as the child's aunt and godmother, can do. It is what Regi would have wanted. And very likely, no matter how hurt and confused and rejected the child feels, Gertrude derives satisfaction from the relationship, enjoys being a mother again after so many years, has a sense of usefulness. (There is no such sense in making sculpture or writing stories.) Besides, allowing for her niece's emotional problems, the child is, even at nine, unusually attractive and intelligent. Gertrude can't help but compare her with Consuelo, until now the greatest beauty the family has produced. Though still plump, Gloria has her coloring and potential physique—the dark hair, the bright eyes, the long neck and torso, as well as a smaller, more beautifully shaped nose and a more sensuous mouth. Yes, ultimately Gloria may be an improvement on Consuelo; she certainly is on Gertrude herself.

We don't know what Gloria's mother says at that noon meeting on September 14. We can only guess that she makes it clear to Gertrude that she likes the present arrangement, likes her own independence, intends to live her own life. Probably, too, financial matters are mentioned and she explains that she can't really live on what Regi has left her, that she must have a reasonably large pied-à-terre in New York for occasional visits from Gloria and her nurse, that she must maintain a certain style for the child's sake as well as her own—she is, after all, *a Vanderbilt*.

Whatever she says, the words are not really necessary. Gertrude sees the fashion magazines, the society and gossip columns, the Pond's Cold Cream ads for which Gloria poses. Gertrude knows all about her sister-in-law's *style*. She has seen enough pictures of her and Lady Furness, both now only twenty-eight, both stunning, always dressed in the newest clothes, accented by the newest accessories, both escorted by the newest names in international society. It is an up-to-the-minute style, an instant style which can be bought and has little to do with personal preferences. Even now she is probably wearing one of those new little hats, a dress with wide shoulders, the latest costume-jewelry clips and rings that cost almost as much as the real things from Cartier.

When her sister-in-law leaves, Gertrude makes an appointment with Frank Crocker to discuss the protection of Gloria and her inheritance. From now on there will be many meetings with Frank, until by the end of the year they are as frequent as those with Josh.

DEC. 25, MON.: Gloria, Henrys for tree at house. Came town 11:45. Lunch M[ama]. Woodlawn. Back country. Gloria [the mother] & Mrs. Morgan [her mother] came for tea. . . .

DEC. 28, THURS.: Hair 9. Frank 10:30. . . .

Again we don't know what is said. Again we can only assume that it is disturbing enough to justify setting up an appointment with Frank. Though Gertrude has the conversations we are missing, it is not certain that even she has at this time a clear understanding that they are leading toward litigation.

December 29, Thomas B. Gilchrist writes to Little Gloria's mother, reviewing the $4,000 monthly maintenance allowance, previously approved by the court:

Schuyler Parsons, rent [sublease, 49 East 72nd Street]	$500
Miss Keislich, nurse	125
Theodore Beasley, chauffeur	160
Personal expenses [Mrs. Reginald Vanderbilt]	750
Allowance to mother [Mrs. Morgan]	250
Butler	150

This much—just under $2,000—though liberal, is acceptable. Gilchrist suggests, even encourages, other expenses that might be presented in court:

Personal maid, cook, kitchen maid, chambermaid, household provisions, elevator [maintenance], garage, Gloria's spending money, Gloria's clothing and personal expenses, doctors' bills, tuition, traveling, entertainment.

Gilchrist's gentle pleading will carry over into the new year. Meanwhile, the flow of Gertrude's friends and relatives, like that of her immediate family, continues to dwindle at one end while enlarging at the other. Harry's best friend, Clarence McCormick, dies at the beginning of the year and Sonny takes Gertrude to the funeral. Dent, her parents' butler, who had been with them "forever," dies too, and Gertrude attends that funeral with her mother. Also early in the year Gertrude is visiting "Gardie" (Claire Gardner) at New York Hospital and Jane Mason at Doctors' Hospital—both of them reminders of their own solicitude to Gertrude during the awful winter 1930–31. In Paris, Gertrude's aunt by marriage, Alva Belmont, formerly the wife of William K. Vanderbilt and since before the war a prominent suffragette, dies, having stipulated that only women shall conduct her funeral. And in the fall Alva's grandson, William K. Vanderbilt III, will be killed at twenty-six in an automobile accident.

The only news seems to be of illness and death. And yet, as with Gertrude's increasing closeness to her grandchildren and niece, she is making new friends and strengthening ties with old ones. George Chamberlain, for example, is not only the writer on whom she depends most for criticism but is now a frequent escort. In January alone he takes her out three times—to the German film *Mädchen in Uniform* ("excellent"), to see Bea Lillie in *Walk a Little Faster*, and to dinner. Nor is George the only literary light. In the spring and summer Gertrude sees Elinor Glyn, the enormously popular British author of such romantic novels as *Three Weeks* (1907), *It* (which made the word synonymous with sex appeal—1927), *Sooner or Later* (currently a best seller), and about twenty others. Mrs. Glyn's productivity and the fact that, though about ten years older than Gertrude, she is still a symbol of glamor, of *it*, are impressive. A mutual interest in the occult is a bond. No doubt Gertrude confides to the famous author that a book of her own has appeared the previous fall and that she has been writing short stories and is thinking about doing another novel. Probably Mrs. Glyn tells Gertrude about the novel she is working on, *Did She?*, a title, a theme, very close to Gertrude's own work and life. Probably, too, Mrs. Glyn tells Gertrude, as she tells us in her autobiography, "On looking back at my life I see that the dominant interest, in fact the fundamental impulse behind every action, has been the desire for romance. I have sought it continuously. . . ." Whatever her exact words to Gertrude, the meetings are encouraging. As we have remarked, more and more now Gertrude respects professionals—in all fields but especially in the arts—and she respects survivors.

⇜ *1934*

> You're the top!
> You're the Tower of Babel.
> You're the top!
> You're the Whitney Stable.
> When folks who still can ride in jitneys
> Find out Vanderbilts and Whitneys
> Lack baby-clo'es
> Anything goes.
> —both from Cole Porter's musical comedy *Anything Goes*, 1934

⇜

During this year, much of 1935, and a little of 1936 (for final revisions), Gertrude is working on her 700-page, never titled second novel. Though the story is ultimately set in 1935, it is fully conceived and outlined in the present year and is based on experiences from 1912 to the present. Indeed, that movement from past to present and from present to past—in the novel itself and more particularly in its creation—is the dominant theme of Gertrude's final years, years less focused on immediate events and goals, more accepting of the slow, circuitous and cyclical, often interrupted but inevitable flow of time.

The novel's protagonist, Sandra Fane, a once wealthy American widow who designs clothes in order to maintain her elegant life style, is in love with Stanley Marston, a powerful and brilliant American lawyer, practicing in Paris and married to a semi-invalid. She is thirty-seven, exactly Gertrude's age in 1912 when she was closest to William Stackpole. As in Gertrude's journals and letters of the following year and as in recent stories, the incident at the *cabinet particulier* is reworked. However, although this pivotal incident is based on a long-past experience involving Stackpole, Marston as a fictional character is much stronger and more direct than Stackpole, a composite of Stackpole himself with Josh Hartwell's ardor and Frank Crocker's professionalism. Now Sandra is followed to the *cabi-*

net particulier not by detectives but by Marston and not because of jealousy but because he has been able unexpectedly to disengage himself from another meeting.

The novel as a whole is Gertrude's best-written work. Not only is Sandra's and Marston's love story convincing, especially the details of carrying on an affair in a close-knit community, but Paris is convincing. The book is as much about Sandra's love for it as for Marston and, again, the details are right, taken from the world of *haute couture* and *haute cuisine* which Gertrude knows so well—the magical time-present and time-past of Paris' ancient narrow streets and wide modern boulevards, its great antique buildings and chic new shops and restaurants, its *fiacres* and fast cars, its river, permanent and in flux, running always through the city. Similarly, Fleuris—the lovers' hideaway, based on Le Boulay—is authentic: its old stonework, irregular beams and floor boards, great hearths and informal grounds and orchards, all nicely contrasted with the need for modern plumbing, bookcases for Marston's work, studio facilities for Sandra's. And, finally, the characters are authentic—not only Marston and Sandra, but her best friend Bea, who reminds us of Helen Whitney and Adele Burden, and an Archie Cummings, who is reminiscent of Jimmie Appleton.

But Sandra now, like Diana in *Walking the Dusk*, interests us most. The styles of the two heroines are similar but Sandra is more "worldly"— worldly, not in the pejorative sense in which Gertrude used the word as a young woman, not as narrowly temporal or materialistic, but rather as broadly experienced and sophisticated. The entire book has the quality of present "worldliness" superimposed on past romanticism; it is oxymoronic, young and old, as is Gertrude herself now and during the remaining years of her life. The second novel serves as psychological background to Gertrude's continuing pursuits of pure love, pure writing, pure sculpture, and pure patronage—pursuits which are, as always, fragmented by interruptions, that are more often choices, and purities that are adulterated by life itself.

Interruptions! In the first few weeks of the new year, Gertrude's relationship with Josh is interrupted, except for his professional care, by a series of colds and sore throats and, at the end of January, by a week's trip to Aiken. And during this month and for several months to come the novel is interrupted by a compulsion (which continues off and on through the rest of Gertrude's life) to make a play out of "The Hand," which she confers and corresponds frequently about now, not only with Ada Stevens and George Chamberlain but with Juliana Force and the artist/architect Paul Chalfin.

Just as Gertrude's play interrupts her novel, both together interrupt her sculpture, and in this, too, old work interrupts new. Though *Nun* and *Gwendolyn* are dated 1934, we know that they have been substantially completed the previous year and need now only to be properly polished. The same is true of *Devotion* ("1934"), the biggest work of this period (65 inches), a sleek enlargement in Tennessee marble of a man embracing a woman from behind, which Gertrude describes in another unaddressed draft of a letter as presenting "no passion—only protection and love." Also, *The Kiss* ("1935") has been sketched (15 inches high) in 1933 but is now and during the coming year being redone (44 inches). In this piece the woman holds herself at a right angle to the man as their lips meet, which Gertrude describes as "a kiss where the woman gives herself with her arms and breast but withholds herself, and yet you feel will soon yield." As in *Devotion*, as in Gertrude's fiction, the eroticism is cool and detached, the emotional content reworked, perhaps overworked, by craft.

Even activities at the museum are interrupted. Beginning in December 1933, the federal Civil Works Administration establishes the Public Works of Art Project, an artists' relief program, to which Juliana Force is appointed New York regional chairman. Working closely with Gertrude and a committee of museum volunteers, including Alfred Barr of the Modern, Bryson Burroughs of the Metropolitan, and William H. Fox of the Brooklyn Museum, as well as members, principally Lloyd Goodrich, paid by Gertrude, Mrs. Force sets up offices at the Whitney. Within a week of the project's establishment she is attacked by the National Academy, which fears she will "favor the modernists," and then defended by the Independent Artists and the National Society of Mural Painters. By March she and her committee and Gertrude, behind the scene, have helped hundreds of artists, but of course hundreds more have been left out of the program. March 17, dissatisfied artists picket the museum, charging that Mrs. Force has favored established artists who have works in the Whitney Collection, especially the painter John Sloan and the sculptor William Zorach. Gertrude writes in her Line-A-Day, "Demonstration by Communists," but it is more complicated than that, as complicated as the Depression itself. During the next week she has four long meetings with Juliana Force, Lloyd Goodrich, and other members of the committee. March 26, Juliana Force issues a public statement:

> Through circumstances beyond its control the identity of the Whitney Museum of American Art has become confused, in the minds of many, with the federal government organization known as the Public Works of Art Project. . . . This confusion has resulted in occurrences which materially interfere with the activities of the Museum and the public use of it.
>
> Lest manifestations of this attitude increase and result in injury to the objects of art in the building, it has been decided, after careful

consideration, to close the Museum Tuesday March 27, six weeks earlier than was originally planned [i.e., for the season].

But this year's two biggest interruptions occur within Gertrude's family. The first is final. From mid-February on Mama is sick and Gertrude visits her more and more frequently—at first every other day or so, between literary and legal conferences, museum and PWAP meetings, inspections at stonecutters', rendezvous with "X," the usual dinner engagements and occasional evenings at the theater or a movie, the opera or a concert. Although there are such notations in Gertrude's Line-A-Day as "M. temperature" or "M. feeling better," more often there is simply the letter "M," which by mid-March occurs almost every day and by mid-April sometimes two or three times a day—M.M.M.—moving like a fever chart:

APR. 16, MON.: M. Studio lunch alone. Chalfin 3–5. Mrs. Force. Drs. Gaston & Davis. Josh 7. M. evening.

APR. 17, TUES.: M. not so well. Studio. [William] Delano for tea. M. Gaston & Davis. Mrs. Short [probably a nurse].

APR. 18, WED.: M. trifle better. Lunch studio X. Mrs. F[orce]. Drs. Gaston & Davis.

APR. 19, THURS.: Hair. M. quite weak. Studio lunch Mrs. Stevens. M. Mrs. S. C[halfin or Charles Draper] cocktail. Dinner J[ames Watson] Gerard [lawyer and diplomat]. Large party. Did not feel like going but Gladys & I decided so as not to make talk about M.

APR. 20, FRI.: Short. M. Studio. Chalfin. M. Dinner home Jimmie [Appleton]. Did not go to play.

APR. 21, SAT.: M. Went to studio. Gladys telephone. M. not so well. Taxi to 67 St. Found both doctors. Breathing bad. Very weak. Stayed 67 St. Dr. Gaston also stayed.

APR. 22, SUN.: M. very weak, pulse better. J[osh] 3 o'clock. About 5 pulse suddenly jumped to 160. Tried various things, injections. Dr. Davis there. At 7 had a stroke. Passed away quietly with no knowledge.

Gertrude and Gladys have already contacted Neily, who has been traveling on the Mediterranean aboard George F. Baker's yacht *Viking*. Their brother will return by early Thursday morning. They decide to have a private funeral service in Mrs. Vanderbilt's home that day and begin making a list. Even keeping it short, there are some three hundred relatives and close friends who *must* be invited. Vanderbilts, Gwynnes, Shepards, Sloanes, Twomblys, Webbs, Burdens begin arriving at 67th Street on Monday. By Thursday virtually the entire family is in New York. At ten Bishop Ernest M. Stires of the Protestant Episcopal Diocese of Long Island and the Rev. Dr. Roelif H. Brooks, rector of St. Thomas' Church (to which Mrs. Vanderbilt has recently switched her allegiance from St. Bartholomew's) conduct the service. Then the immediate family travels to New Dorp, and Gertrude returns at one-thirty, exhausted.

Death is exhausting. Gertrude has no quiet; she does have knowledge— constant reminders in condolence calls and notes and, within two days after the funeral, in the anniversary of Harry's death and the usual trip to Woodlawn. For ten successive days she commutes between New York and Westbury, seeing members of her family—principally her brother and sister and her own children.

During this period, as one of the executors along with Gladys, Neily, and a lawyer, she hears the terms of her mother's will, made in 1928. The three largest bequests are to Gertrude herself, about $7,000,000 which has been held in trust from the sale of the Vanderbilt mansion at 57th and Fifth; to Gladys, The Breakers, the present mansion at 67th and Fifth, and nearly two thirds of another trust of about $7,000,000, established by their father for their mother's support; and to Neily, the Gwynne Building in Cincinnati, leased in its entirety to Procter & Gamble and presumably worth about as much as the inheritance of each of his sisters. Two more gifts are very substantial, almost $1,000,000 each to Regi's daughters Cathleen and Gloria. The rest, typically in amounts of $50,000 to $100,000, goes to more than a dozen other grandchildren and relatives and to St. Bartholomew's, the Newport Hospital, and the Society of St. Johnland in Long Island. Servants receive $1,000 for each five years of continuous employment; $500 for those who have been employed for more than three but not more than five years.

The money, like Mrs. Vanderbilt herself, expires quietly, in small breaths. But for Gertrude, the knowledge of death never dies. Less than two weeks after her mother's funeral another death watch begins. Again we, with her, are witnesses:

MAY 9, WED.: Mr. [Henry B.] A[nderson, estate lawyer], Gladys & me 11. Lunch studio X 1–5:30. Heard Yvonne very ill. Went hotel [where the Davidsons are staying] 8:45. Stayed 11:45. Drs. Goodrich & Foster Kennedy.

MAY 10, THURS.: Hair 10:30. Yvonne better. Hotel morning. Down to see Mrs. Stevens. Lunched 67 St. Hotel. Josh took me to Academy. 4:45 Frank [Crocker] & [Thomas B.] Gilchrist.

MAY 11, FRI.: F[lora], C[ully] & Pam arrived. Y. not so well. Hotel 12:30 to 5. Josh 6. Stayed for dinner. He went back to hotel, returned to report. He spent night in hotel. Only slight hope of recovery.

MAY 12, SAT.: Y. slightly improved. Josh. Went country, returned to find Y. had died. Took Jo, Jacques [Jo's son], & Josh back to 871 for dinner. F[lora] & C[ully] there.

Jo and Jacques spend the three days following Yvonne's death with Gertrude in Westbury, where Yvonne is cremated, then sail to France.

Gertrude receives several very sad letters from Jo mourning Yvonne and his own inability to settle down to work without her. She also receives discouraging letters from Ada Stevens and George Chamberlain about *The Hand*. Chamberlain, though continuing to urge Gertrude to do further rewriting, sends the play at her request to Arthur Hopkins, a producer friend of his, then reports, "I'm sorry, my dear, but Arthur said, 'The author writes beautifully, but I can't believe what happens.' I asked him if there was anything to be done; he said, '*nothing short of another story*' and repeated, 'It's unbelievable.'" Mrs. Stevens writes more enthusiastically about the play but even so suggests that Gertrude "keep it on the shelf a year" and consider taking writing courses at Bread Loaf. Better news arrives from the American Institute of Architects, which elects Gertrude an honorary member; the Architectural League of New York, which has "at last decided to include a limited number of women who are distinguished in the artistic professions, as active members of the League" (besides Gertrude, Gail Sherman Corbett, Laura Gardin Fraser, Malvina Hoffman, and Anna Hyatt Huntington); and Rutgers University, which confers on her an honorary doctorate of fine arts, her third such degree. However, all of these honors relate to the past. None is recorded in the Line-A-Day. There now, part of Gertrude's present life, is only one significant entry:

JUNE 18, MON.: G[loria] made application to be made guardian of child.

That single sentence is like the Act Two curtain line of an Elizabethan tragedy. Recapitulation: in Act One, Scene One (the home of friends, New York, March 6, 1923), Reginald Claypoole Vanderbilt, a rather dissolute Protestant lord, aged forty-two and divorced for four years, has overcome the objections of his family, eluded reporters (court chroniclers, if you like), and married Gloria Morgan, his economic and social inferior, a Catholic, aged seventeen and a half. In Scene Two (the Lying-in Hospital, New York, February 20, 1924), after a Caesarean operation, Gloria gives birth to a daughter. In Scene Three (Reginald Vanderbilt's town house, 12 East 77th Street, New York, May 15, 1924) the child is baptized into her father's faith, Gloria Laura Vanderbilt. Reginald's mother, the dowager Mrs. Vanderbilt, stands in for his sister Gertrude, named as the child's godmother but unable to attend the ceremony. In Scene Four (Sandy Point Farm, Portsmouth, Rhode Island, September 4, 1925), while his wife is in New York, Reginald dies of a hemorrhage. His mother takes charge of funeral arrangements, causing friction between herself and Gloria, who also has a disagreement with Reginald's daughter by his previous marriage, Cathleen, aged twenty-one. In outline, all of this is familiar to us as it has been to Gertrude. Now, from the background of Gertrude's consciousness, it is brought forward and on stage.

Act Two is less dramatic, moves more slowly, has more gaps. After Surrogate Judge Foley approves of the appointment of "Uncle" George W. Wickersham (a friend of Gloria's mother) and his partner Thomas B. Gilchrist as general guardians of Little Gloria's property and approves also of the $48,000 per annum allowance for her maintenance, events are set mostly in Europe. For more than six years while living luxuriously in Paris, Biarritz, and Cannes, in London and Melton Mowbray, in Glion, Switzerland, and Hollywood, California, Gloria sees little of her child, leaving her mostly with her own mother, Mrs. Harry Hays Morgan, and with the nurse hired by Mrs. Morgan, Emma Keislich. In October of 1926, Gloria becomes involved with Prince Hohenlohe, who accompanies her on her travels, seemingly paid for out of the $48,000. In January 1929 her alleged engagement to the prince is broken when the surrogate rules that "no part of the infant's income can be used to finance a second marriage." By June 1932, Gloria—urged by her own mother, by Gertrude, by the nurse and by various doctors—leaves the child, recovering from tonsillitis, with Gertrude. After a year the guardians arrange to pay the child's bills and Gloria's household expenses directly and to give Gloria $1,000 monthly plus any unexpended balance of the annual $48,000. The guardians explain that she is creating a difficult problem by receiving the unexpended balance while the child is with Gertrude and suggest that she might settle in Long Island where her daughter's physical and mental health have improved and where the child has friends and relatives and is enrolled at school. Despite all these arguments the mother prefers to travel again and, only after receiving the guardians' assurance that her allowance will not be further reduced, lets her child remain with Gertrude. During this year she continues to be anxious about her allowance. When she tells one of her friends, a Mr. A. C. Blumenthal, owner of many theaters, about her concern, he introduces her to Nathan Burkan, a capable lawyer who sees immediately that for her financial protection—basically that—she must be appointed guardian of the child's person and co-guardian of the child's estate. This is the action for which Gloria makes application June 18.

What happens between Acts Two and Three is fairly clear, just how it happens is conjectural. Except for the child's mother (to give her the benefit of any doubt), the two people most interested in Little Gloria's welfare are the child's grandmother who, assisted by Nurse Keislich, took care of her from 1924 to 1932 and Gertrude, also assisted by the nurse, who has cared for her since. Mrs. Morgan and Gertrude, both in close touch with Cadwalader, Wickersham & Taft, are immediately informed of Gloria's application. Mrs. Morgan, more emotional and voluble than Gertrude, contacts her and repeats accusations, perhaps previously made, concerning her daughter's selfish neglect of the child and extravagant self-indulgence. She fears for the child's life and is determined to oppose her daughter's application for guardianship, but . . . but can't afford the legal expenses. Given these general circumstances, it is likely that Gertrude would have supported Mrs. Morgan and set up an appointment for her with Frank Crocker.

Act Three begins at the Surrogate Court, before Judge Foley. There, as Gloria recounts in her autobiography *Without Prejudice*, on the uncomfortably hot morning of July 3 she sits in the crowded courtroom with Mr. Burkan and a Mr. Murray of his office. Finally her case is called. Mr. Burkan rises and presents his application, emphasizing that she is now of age, older, wiser, and more competent to be given the guardianship of her child's person and to be made joint guardian, with Mr. Wickersham, of the child's property. For a moment everything seems routine. Then a man behind Gloria rises:

"I object to the petition."

"On what grounds?" asks Mr. Burkan.

"On the grounds that Mrs. Vanderbilt is unfit."

The courtroom buzzes. Judge Foley holds up his hand, announces that court is adjourned, turns to Mr. Burkan and tells him, "I will hear the case in my private chambers after lunch."

"What is it? What does it mean?" Gloria asks Burkan.

He is blunt: "In the last analysis, the allegation means a person is unmoral, immoral—a prostitute."

Murray is sent to find out who is behind the complaint. After lunch he reports that the lawyer is Walter Dunnington, of Dunnington & Gregg, 1 Wall Street. Dunnington arrives in the judge's chambers and begins to recite objections based on neglect of the child.

Burkan interrupts. "I must refuse, your honor, to proceed in this case unless I am informed who is bringing the complaint objecting to the guardianship."

Dunnington whispers to the judge, who asks, "Does Mrs. Vanderbilt insist on knowing?"

Gloria, afflicted by a stutter and shortness of breath anyway and now completely speechless, nods.

"It is her own mother, Mrs. Morgan," Judge Foley says before adjourning the hearing.

Gloria goes immediately to her apartment where her mother is waiting, challenges her, listens to her long reply, which boils down to one defense: "I have done this only for the good of the baby."

"For the child's good, Mama? . . . How will it be for her good when you are trying to destroy her mother?"

"Gloria, I am advising you not to fight this. I have in back of me money, political influence, and the Vanderbilt family."

Mrs. Morgan leaves. Gloria calls Gertrude and arranges to see her at 871 Fifth Avenue. In an understandably excited state, speaking with difficulty, she comes to the point: "Gertrude, do you know what happened today?"

"No. Sit down and tell me."

Gloria tells. ". . . you know my mother has no money but what [my sister Thelma and I] allow her. Someone is back of this case . . . is it you?"

"If you were not so ill, I would ask you to leave my house for the accusation in that question."

In her autobiography, Gloria summarizes: "This interview must speak for itself in duplicity and subterfuge, for I was to learn in a very few weeks that Walter G. Dunnington had been retained by Frank Crocker, Gertrude's attorney. . . ."

As suggested earlier, *Without Prejudice* is hardly *that*, any more than is any other autobiography. When Gertrude first appears in the book, Gloria writes, "Her statue at St. Nazaire and other war memorials serve as reminders in their breadth and granite hardness of what she herself is like." In her description of the immediate interview, Gloria consistently contrasts her own suffering and sincerity with Gertrude's detachment and deceit. However, it is not difficult to imagine either that Frank Crocker has told Gertrude to say as little as possible or that, from Gertrude's point of view, she believes that she is not in back of the case but rather simply shares Mrs. Morgan's desire to protect the child.

Gloria, seeking help, calls her twin sister Thelma in London and their older sister Consuelo in Oslo, where her husband Benjamin Thaw is counselor of the American Legation. Thelma is able to take the first available ship, leaving the next morning, and is with Gloria in a week. The day she arrives, Gertrude calls inviting Gloria for tea to discuss Little Gloria. Tea is served. Conversation is formal until the butler withdraws. Then, in a voice which, according to Gloria, "never separated itself from a toneless note of consistent kindness," Gertrude says:

"I have asked you over to tell you this; that if you go into court and attempt to gain guardianship of the child, I myself will oppose the motion."

Again according to Gloria, Gertrude "sat there and never moved. Behind this unexpressive exterior stood something stony and inexorable . . . a mask of utter stillness—unmoving but living, too, like the sculptured Jo Davidson head in back of her."

Gloria can't speak. Gertrude continues:

"I want you to know, Gloria, it is nothing I have against you personally. There is only one consideration in this, and that is the child's good."

Once more Gloria cannot speak. She can barely get to her feet and shake hands. Only later is she able to write: "Think of it—shaking hands! . . . What a mockery! I wish I might have answered her then: 'You attack my morals, you tear the fabric of my life apart, you intend to crucify me before the world, and you have nothing against me personally!' "

Thelma now speaks to Mrs. Morgan:

"Mothers don't do to their children what you are doing—blacken their characters before the world. Is it for money, or for hatred, you are attacking Gloria? . . ."

Mrs. Morgan weeps and wrings her hands. "You have not been aware of the neglect that has been going on. This unfortunate child has been dying and Gloria has paid no attention to it."

"That is a lie. . . . The child has always come first in Gloria's life. . . ."

"Are you going against me too?"

"If you ask me, am I on your side or Gloria's, I have only to say, I am on the right side. . . ."

From Gloria's and Thelma's viewpoint, their mother, by siding with Gertrude, with "the Vanderbilts," has betrayed not only them but the entire Morgan family. They believe that she is motivated only by money. Thelma never speaks to her again. From Mrs. Morgan's own viewpoint, her motivation is pure, she is only protecting the child. And from Gertrude's viewpoint, we have a long letter written to Gladys soon after the confrontation between Thelma and Mrs. Morgan. The letter is absolutely ingenuous, filled mostly with details about their mother's estate, but with a paragraph devoted to the custody case:

> . . . there will be a hearing & if no settlement is arrived at probably a postponement until Oct. Mrs. M[organ]'s statement is excellent & I am being kept out as much as possible on the grounds that I do not wish to say anything which might hurt the child's future. If it comes up I will only have to testify as to the circumstances under which the child came to me & her condition, which will be substantiated by the doctors. Mrs. G. S. [possibly a housekeeper] fills in things in the past. We are trying to keep out any mention of immorality, but base everything on neglect and indifference. Lady F[urness] is here trying to intimidate her mother but unsuccessfully.

No doubt, Mrs. Morgan is keeping Gertrude informed. But more important is the clear statement of Gertrude's hopes that Mrs. Morgan will do the job which has to be done, that she herself will be kept out of litigation as much as possible, and that the issue of Gloria's immorality can be avoided. In retrospect, it is easy to see that all of these hopes will be frustrated, and easy to say that Gertrude is being naïve in relying too much on her team of lawyers. This is not an aesthetic situation in which talent can be bought to polish the rough edges of a given subject, it is a human situation in which the rough edges are the subject.

By now Consuelo Thaw has arrived. Like Thelma, she has a confrontation with Mrs. Morgan. Gloria writes, "There had been a long estrangement between my eldest sister [Thelma is a few minutes older, Consuelo about two years] and my mother. Consuelo stood close enough to the ugly side of Mamma's calculations to handle her without gloves." Whatever the difference in Consuelo's attitude toward their mother, the result is the same. Mrs. Morgan insists that she will not permit Gloria to neglect the child.

Consuelo replies, "You never considered it neglect when you left *your* children scattered over Europe. For months at a time you never went near Thelma or Gloria when they were little, and at sixteen you left them alone in New York and never came near them. You never thought it neglect to send me to a strange woman I never knew. Neglect! Talk to me of money being the basis of this action but not of neglect."

Consuelo's rhetoric is powerful; her facts, as far as can be ascertained, accurate; but still she is as unsuccessful as Thelma in convincing her mother. She decides to see Gertrude.

"What is behind your opposition?" Consuelo asks her.

"Nothing in the world but the welfare of the child."

"Nothing deeper?"

"No, I have nothing personally against Gloria. . . . But it is my opinion and the judgment of the child's physicians that she will be better off—for the present—with me."

"Perhaps you are basing your opinion on what my mother has told you . . . she is not normal when it comes to the child, nor has she ever been normal on the subject of money. Unfortunately, my niece's money and your own combined must have gone to my mother's head."

"Money, money, money! You sound like newspaper headlines, Mrs. Thaw."

"There is no reason why my mother should say my sister is unfit to look after her own child except money. No doubt you will find she hopes to be appointed guardian herself. She has lived with Gloria all during the child's life. My sister is even now supporting her . . . you will bring down an avalanche of cruel publicity that will harm the child . . . you will ruin my sister . . . you can't touch her without involving us all in the ruins . . . myself . . . my husband . . . possibly yourself. . . . I am here to beg you not to go on with this case."

"It is my intention to oppose it, Mrs. Thaw."

From then on the several attorneys confer frequently, trying to effect a compromise. Finally it is agreed before Judge Foley that the child will remain with Gertrude for the summer, will spend September with her mother, and then return to Gertrude for the academic year at Greenvale. If Little Gloria is healthy and happy and her mother is attentive, it is hoped that they can be reunited permanently at the end of the school year.

At the beginning of August, Gertrude goes with Little Gloria to the Whitney camp in the Adirondacks. They stay with Sonny and Gee and their children at Camp Deerlands. The Millers, the Henrys, the Elmhirsts, and their many children by past and present marriages are scattered among the other camps. There is frequent traffic back and forth by canoe, sailboat, motorboat, and guide boat for picnics, hikes, and overnight camping, and there is the usual swimming, fishing, and boating simply for pleasure, with no other objective and no destination. The days go by quickly. Little Gloria plays with her cousins, reads, and writes letters often illustrated with innocent drawings of the rustic surroundings. Gertrude is happy too. She, like Little Gloria, finds a few hours a day in which to write, returning now from *The Hand* to her second novel. The messy litigation seems behind, although there are two specific reminders of it: a brief visit to New York for meetings with Frank Crocker and an even briefer visit in late August from Gloria and her sister Consuelo to see Little Gloria. The latter is an awkward confrontation at which the child is reluctant to greet her mother. But basically the end of the summer is peaceful. Josh writes frequent loving and supportive letters from London and Juliana Force does the same from the Venice Biennale, despite her own problems there when William Randolph Hearst manages to smuggle a portrait of Marion Davies by a Polish artist into an exhibition at the American Pavilion of paintings from the Whitney Museum collection.

SEPT. 9, SUN.: Henry camp [Killoquah] came to see us [Gertrude and Little Gloria] in the morning. Left on night train from Sabattis 10:16. Buz motored over with me.

SEPT. 10, MON.: Arrived 7:20 daylight saving time. Studio. Dinner X.

SEPT. 11, TUES.: Frank 12:15. Studio 6 & dinner.

SEPT. 12, WED.: Studio 12. Lunch X till 5:30. Dined on Winchester [Neily's yacht] 8. J[ames] Gerard.

SEPT. 13, THURS.: [Thomas] Regan 11:30. [Paul] Chalfin 2:30. X studio 5 & dinner.

SEPT. 14, FRI.: [William C.] Whittemore [lawyer] 10:45. Studio lunch Alice [Nicholas] 1.

SEPT. 15, SAT.: Gloria called me up in country. Had just arrived from abroad. Asked child to lunch next day in town. Dined at Flora's.

SEPT. 16, SUN.: Little G. went to town to lunch with Mrs. V.

SEPT. 18, TUES.: Little G. went to stay with her mother for a few days.

SEPT. 21, FRI.: Little G. at [New York] studio. Mrs. V., Mrs. Thaw, [Dr.] Craig.

SEPT. 22, SAT.: Mrs. V., Mrs. Thaw, Dr. Hunt, Craig. Frank.

SEPT. 23, SUN.: G. came to town with Dodo [Emma Keislich, her nurse]. They spen

The word, probably *spend*, in Gertrude's Line-A-Day is unfinished. The next day, like many of the following days, is blank, left to be filled in, mostly in court.

We return to Friday, September 21. That day Gloria, still staying with her mother in the city and anticipating the start of the fall term at Greenvale the following Monday, is driven to Central Park with Emma Keislich by "her" chauffeur Beasley and, according to the nurse, becomes hysterical in the park, wanting to return to the country. Keislich phones Gertrude at her studio and delivers the child there. Gertrude cannot quiet her and sends for Dr. Craig, who immediately calls for a trained nurse to watch her. At six in the evening Gloria and Consuelo, who have, in Gloria's words, "become lost in a game of bezique," miss the child and call Beasley to find out where she is. He tells them and they go directly to MacDougal Alley. There Gertrude repeats the story.

"I want to see my child at once."

"Of course."

Gertrude and Gloria enter the bedroom, followed by Consuelo.

"Don't let her come near me. She is going to kill me!" the child screams.

Consuelo steps forward: "Hush! It's your mother."

"Don't let them come near me—they are *both* going to kill me!" she screams now, cringing as if expecting to be hit.

The trained nurse tries to calm the child. At the same time Emma Keislich begins talking excitedly, justifying the child's fears. The mother turns to the nurse: "Be quiet—at once." Then to Gertrude: "Ask her to come to your sitting room. I want to question her in your presence."

They go downstairs to the sitting room.

"How did you come to phone Mrs. Whitney and not me?"

Once Miss Keislich has been given permission to talk, she goes on and on about "the child's nervousness" and "the child's neglect" and the way Mrs. Vanderbilt lives and the kind of people who frequent her home.

Gloria tries again and again to stop her. "Control yourself," she says. "Answer my questions quietly," she says. But there is no stopping Miss Keislich. She is by now as hysterical as the child upstairs. She is giving a preview of herself in court.

There can be little doubt in either Gertrude's or Gloria's mind that much of what Miss Keislich says echoes Mrs. Morgan. Gloria probably feels that the nurse is the instrument of her mother's hatred, Gertrude that she is the confirmation of her own worst fears concerning the child's safety. In either case, however the conditioning occurred, the child is frightened, hysterical, perhaps even suicidal, about the thought of returning to her mother.

Gloria discharges Miss Keislich. When the nurse leaves the room Gloria says to Gertrude, "There was nothing left for me to do."

Once again, Gertrude replies, "Of course. . . . She will leave my house this evening."

"I will come back for Gloria in the morning."

"Yes . . . she will be quiet by then."

Gloria and Consuelo return home and begin making phone calls. First, Gloria speaks to Nathan Burkan regarding a court order in case the child isn't available the next day. He explains that the courts are closed on Saturday but that he will try to find a judge to issue a writ. He finds one, tells Gloria to get a doctor she can trust to examine the child the next day, and also to start thinking about witnesses to testify on her behalf. Gloria reaches Dr. Hunt, who has taken care of Gloria some years before. Then she and her sister begin placing overseas calls. Their brother Harry Morgan, Jr., is reached at his home in Paris. Yes, he will take the *Empress of Britain*, leaving Cherbourg the next morning. Thelma is traced to a ball being given at Claridge's by Prince Aly Khan. Yes, she will catch the same ship at Southampton. Prince Hohenlohe, now married to Princess Margarita of Greece, is reached at his family estate at Langenburg. Yes, he and his wife will take the first ship they can. Finally, Consuelo speaks to her husband Ben, in Oslo, to tell him she may be delayed "a short while."

Saturday morning Gloria and Consuelo return to Gertrude's with Dr. Hunt, who examines the child and then confers with Dr. Craig. While they are conferring in Little Gloria's bedroom, the child enters the drawing room, greets her mother, kisses her dutifully, and then asks to be excused. Dr. Hunt reports that the child is "nervously inclined" but "physically sound and sufficiently quiet to go home with her mother." Dr. Craig disagrees. Gloria turns to Gertrude:

"Will you please call the child. I am ready to take her."

"She is now on her way to Westbury."

Gloria is stunned. "All your money, all your position, all the power of your influence—use them, you will find they are not strong enough to kidnap a child from its mother," she says as she leaves. Then she calls Burkan and tells him to serve the papers.

The writ of habeas corpus is returnable in court on Monday. Early that morning Gertrude, the child, Frank Crocker, and three other attorneys appear in the private chambers of Supreme Court Justice John F. Carew along with Gloria and her lawyers. Early on, Judge Carew, the father of five children, announces that his decision will be "largely determined" by the testimony of the child herself. He has her sit in a big swivel chair and, while she rocks with her long legs dangling, questions her for three hours, disguising the examination as a chat. She says that she doesn't dislike her mother but hasn't seen much of her, that they jump around a great deal, that she never has any steady playmates. Judge Carew listens sympathetically, encouraging her, but the more she talks the more apparent it becomes that, although the child obviously has not been kidnapped, she cannot answer the basic question concerning her mother's "fitness." After she has been excused, it becomes equally apparent that the lawyers, speaking for their clients, are in no mood for compromise. The hearing is adjourned for a week.

Though the case has so far been heard "privately," news of it appears in the papers beginning Tuesday. For the rest of this year, whether hearings are private or public, hardly a day will go by without a major story—often, especially in the tabloids, a front-page story—on the "LITTLE HEIRESS" or the "GOLD CHILD."

The following Monday, October 1, public hearings begin without the child present. It is another hot day—Indian summer now—and the courthouse is crowded with reporters, feature writers, reportorial artists, press photographers, motion picture news cameramen, asking questions and taking pictures as Gloria and Consuelo arrive and are seated at a long table at the front of the court with Nathan Burkan and his staff. At a table opposite them sit Frank Crocker and his staff. Gertrude sits at the rear of the courtroom with her daughter Flora. When Mrs. Morgan enters with Emma Keislich and Maria Caillot, a former personal maid of Gloria's, she sits down with them. Gertrude thinks this inappropriate and has one of her lawyers invite Mrs. Morgan to join her and Flora, which Mrs. Morgan does.

Emma Keislich is the first witness. As in private interviews, she tends toward hysteria. She describes a magnificent house rented by Gloria in the best quarter of Paris as "a hovel, unfit for a child." When asked about Consuelo Thaw, she says, "She calls herself Mrs. Thaw." In short, Miss Keislich is such a prejudiced witness that Judge Carew warns the Whitney attorneys that her manner of giving evidence harms and discredits her. Nevertheless, in whatever manner, she does convey the impression that Gloria has led a dissolute life and toward the end of her testimony she speaks at length of Gloria's relationship to Prince Hohenlohe and maintains that she and Mrs. Morgan saw him naked in Gloria's bedroom.

That is the first scandal featured in the newspapers. The next day the second witness, Maria Caillot, presents more sensational scandals. She refers to finding pornography (*The Beautiful Flagellant of New York*) in Gloria's home and also alleges that Gloria was often drunk. Burkan cross-examines her:

"How did you know?"

"She always smiled."

"You see Mrs. Vanderbilt smiling now—would you call her intoxicated?" Mademoiselle Caillot shakes her head. "And so all these months . . . you never once saw evidence of improper conduct?"

"I remember, yes, once—something it seems to me very funny."

"What was that?"

"At the Miramar Hotel in Cannes . . . I served breakfast and I took her things up to my room, pressing them . . . afterwards I came back. . . . Mrs. Vanderbilt was in bed reading a paper, and there was Lady Milford Haven beside the bed with her arm around Mrs. Vanderbilt's neck and kissing her just like a lover."

For a moment the courtroom is silent. Then Judge Carew bangs his gavel. "In the interest of public decency, the press and the public will be barred from this courtroom."

Reporters rush to telephones. When the court is cleared Judge Carew addresses Mademoiselle Caillot: "I want you to tell me the whole thing. I do not want to have to ask you about it. Tell us what you saw."

Mademoiselle Caillot repeats her story. Although no subsequent witnesses can testify regarding this incident with Lady Milford Haven, other servants—"spies," as Gloria characterizes them—do testify regarding her "alleged erotic interest in women" (New York *Daily Mirror*), such as the movie actress Constance Bennett and another less well known actress and model Agnes Horter. They testify, too, regarding the men in her life —not only Prince Hohenlohe, to whom she was presumably engaged, but her friend A. C. Blumenthal (a married man) and a "Mr. Brown," a friend of her brother's whom she knew in England. And they testify to her drinking and to her possessing more pornography (pictures of nuns "doing things" with young girls).

However, surely the most damaging witness is Mrs. Morgan. Holding a crucifix and opposing the writ "as a sacred duty," she speaks of her "daughter's shame," repeating all she has said in previous private meetings and supporting the testimony of Nurse Keislich and the other servants. But there is no point in going on and no space in which to do so (the court transcript fills eleven volumes, about 6,000 pages). Enough to say that by late October, when Gertrude is to be called as a witness, the case has become so messy, so lurid, so grotesque, so much more unpleasant and exhausting than anything she expected, that Gertrude pleads inability to appear as a witness because of illness and instructs Frank Crocker to make one last attempt to settle.

He is unsuccessful, and Gertrude testifies for four successive days, morning and afternoon, in the last week of October. During all these hours her testimony is consistent with the tactics outlined months earlier in her letter to Gladys. She restricts herself to the circumstances under which the child came to her and the child's condition (already substantiated by the many doctors who have appeared as witnesses), and she refuses to discuss Gloria's morality (again, already sufficiently discussed). This exchange between her and Burkan is typical:

"You never saw [Gloria Vanderbilt] under the influence of liquor?"

"No."

"During all the time you have seen her, she acted like a perfectly normal woman?"

"Absolutely."

"In all the time that you have seen her, you saw nothing objectionable about her?"

"Certainly not."

"She always, in so far as you could observe and see, demeaned herself as a perfect lady?"

"Certainly."

In *Without Prejudice* even Gloria admits that Gertrude "made a splendid witness—there was no hesitancy, no blundering, nor was there self-righteousness in her attitude. She just sat there day after day—a brilliantly executed model of restrained and distinguished good manners, finished in arrangement and line . . . the only witness on the opposing side who gave me a clean bill of health."

As to Gertrude's own morality, it is a testimonial to her discretion that the best Burkan can do is exhibit photographs of nude paintings and sculptures in the collection of the Whitney Museum, where on two occasions she has taken Little Gloria. For example, Arthur B. Davies' ethereal *Tiptoeing Youth* is described as "a number of young men in the nude with the penis and testicles being exposed in a very pronounced manner" and Robert Laurent's chaste *The Awakening* as "a woman leaning on her hands in a sitting position, with her breasts highly developed, legs slightly raised but apart, and heavy indentations to show the hair at the very extreme bottom of the abdomen." Burkan reminds the judge that the child's mind was "plastic and immature" when exposed to these influences and that Gertrude herself designs both male and female figures from the nude.

Friday, October 26, is the fourth anniversary of Harry's death, the first on which Gertrude does not visit his grave. She is once again in court early, listening now to the first of Gloria's witnesses, her sister Lady Furness; then her brother Harry Morgan. Saturday Gertrude goes to Woodlawn. Probably never since his death has she needed Harry so much. She is tired and miserable and must, like several members of her family, feel that somehow, if Harry were alive, this whole nightmare would not have occurred and be recurring. There is simply no rest from it. She spends Saturday night reviewing testimony with Cully and Buz. Sunday, as every day, the papers are filled with the case. She cannot help but agree with the *Times* editorial headed "Too Many Innings"—the case has gone on too long, too far—and now Frank Crocker arrives with Mrs. Morgan to discuss further aspects of it.

Day after day and night after night are the same. When Gertrude isn't in court she is with her lawyers, reviewing testimony, planning cross-examination, arranging for witnesses. There is no time to write or sculpt, barely time to live. She can concentrate on nothing but the case. When she is with her family the talk centers on it. With Josh, briefly and infrequently now, she discusses medical witnesses, and with Juliana Force, "pornographic" art at the museum. The days drag on, without real holidays or weekends.

After hearing seven weeks of testimony, Judge Carew announces, November 15, that the child is to have a "new life." However, it takes another six days filled with meetings between lawyers and principals before the final order is signed. The judge rules that Gertrude shall be charged with the child's care and upbringing and that Gloria shall be "given the society of her daughter" on Saturdays and Sundays during the academic year and one full month during the summer, in order that she may be able to win back the child's love if she is inclined and able to do so. Neither the mother nor the aunt may take the child out of New York State without the Court's permission.

From the mother's viewpoint, the decision is a humiliating defeat; from the child's, at best, a compounding of confusion; and from Gertrude's, again at best, a Pyrrhic victory. Some of what Gertrude has won in court she has already lost in the tabloids—there and elsewhere in the popular Depression-oriented press, the Vanderbilt name, which she has sought to protect, along with the child herself, has been besmirched—but beyond that she has lost, and will continue to lose, time, energy, privacy, and freedom. Within a few days after Judge Carew's decision, Gloria announces her intention to "continue the fight." For Gertrude, as for Gloria, this will mean continuing meetings with attorneys, appearances in court, reviews of previous testimony. The child and her potential wealth have been so much publicized by now that for the next several years she will require the protection of detectives against kidnappers, cranks, and relentless journalists. This loss of privacy is one aspect of lost freedom. Another is the court-ordered curtailment of travel, a pleasure surely as meaningful to Gertrude as to her sister-in-law. And finally, ultimately, Gertrude will lose the love of the child herself, who will say later, "The irony . . . was that as soon as my aunt was allowed to take charge of me, she lost interest. . . ." Act Four of this drama will stretch out over many years, in many scenes, with many lawyers.

Once more a thread is torn from the fabric of Gertrude's life and followed into the future. But now, during the final weeks of 1934, that life again becomes almost "normal." There are still some meetings with Frank Crocker and Thomas Gilchrist, but Gertrude is able to spend more time in the country with Little Gloria and with her own children and with their children, all of whom have Thanksgiving dinner at Barbie's. Also, Gertrude is able now for the first time in months to do some work in the studio, to meet there with Josh, and to go from there to the museum where the Second Biennial Exhibition of Contemporary American Painting is installed. The show is very uneven, heavily weighted with social-realistic and regionalistic work, but as always Gertrude's interest, like Juliana Force's, is to some extent extra-aesthetic. With evident pleasure, she scribbles in her catalogue "42 new [artists] out of 153," then writes "PWAP" next to the seventeen works that have come out of that project.

Yes, there is a return to the norm, substantiated too by her going again to the movies and theater, including a Wednesday matinee of *Anything Goes.* However, even that show, which she would have heard a lot about in the two weeks since its opening, must be squeezed in before an appoint-ment with Frank. So there are still those meetings, typically in the middle of the week. The weekends are even more complicated. An isolated Satur-day entry in Gertrude's Line-A-Day is evidence enough: "G. went to town. Terrible scenes." We can imagine ten-year-old Gloria being picked up by her car and chauffeur around noon and being taken, with her nurse and private detectives, to the Hotel Sherry Netherland where she will stay with her mother until returning Sunday evening. In New York the child will, like her "Aunty Ger," see many movies. In *Double Exposure* her mother writes, "To me this interminable movie-viewing had its advan-tages, because in the theaters at least we could sit in happy silence. Yet there was one continuing problem this routine raised: avoiding the press. We were news. Photographers followed us everywhere we went. They would wait for us in theater lobbies; sometimes they would slip into the orchestra and take flash shots of us in our seats. Gloria then would trem-ble and hide her face. Eventually I worked out ways to slip into movie houses . . . through side doors."

If there were some scenes on Saturdays, there were probably scenes, too, on Sunday nights or Monday mornings. Again we find possible evi-dence in an isolated entry:

DEC. 31, MON.: Horrible day.

⇐ *1935*

Though the custody case continues to be a distraction, it is no longer the all-consuming one it has been during the past year. Gertrude is able to resume work—work on her second novel, with its legal background now strengthened by much painful experience; work on her sculpture, particu-larly the larger version of *The Kiss* and the portrait bust of Neily, to whom she becomes increasingly close as she sympathizes with his poor health (angina pectoris) and withdrawal (not only from society in general but from Grace); and work in many areas of patronage (her own museum; the American Museum of Natural History, to which she gives $12,350 to un-derwrite cataloguing the Rothschild Collection; the Buffalo Bill Memo-rial, later a museum, to which she gives land extending far beyond that on which the monument rests; the monastery at La Rábida, for which she designs a plaque in bas-relief commemorating Columbus' voyages; the Cit-izens Welfare Committee, another relief program, to which she gives

$10,000; and surely more gifts of money, time, and energy, the record of many lost among the jumble of papers in her homes and museum).

She also now resumes a more active social schedule, not only seeing her family and Josh frequently but such old friends and escorts as Charles Draper, Jimmie Appleton, Rollie Cottenet, and Bill Delano, and at least one new friend, the famous Philadelphia lawyer and former Pennsylvania senator George Wharton Pepper, whom she meets early in February through her sister Gladys. George Pepper, like Josh Hartwell, is eight years older than Gertrude and, like him, has been a great college athlete, a teacher, and then gone on to become a leader of his profession, receiving the honors in law equivalent to those Josh has received in medicine (e.g., director of the American Law Institute, president of the Pennsylvania Bar Association, chancellor of the Philadelphia Bar Association). Again, like Josh, he is married, vigorous, and handsome.

Though Gertrude's relationship with George will never become as deep as that with Josh, there is clearly the possibility that it could have, had it not been for Josh himself and his proximity. George courts Gertrude from Philadelphia—at first in handwritten letters from his office there:

> When Gladys and I looked in upon you the other day I saw only enough to make me want to see more. I wonder whether you will let me come to see you some afternoon at tea time. I am often in New York—my next visit being scheduled for Thursday February the twenty-eighth. I am sending this note on the bare chance that you may be at home. Almost everybody who is foot-loose is sojourning in sunnier climes. I am tethered and for my own sake I hope you are too. . . .

For Gertrude, February 28 is a busy, carefully scheduled day:

> Return town. Massage 12. Studio Mrs. F. 2:30. X 3:30 (late). Senator Pepper 5.

Presumably she meets the senator at 871 Fifth Avenue. On the train back to Philadelphia he writes:

> I want awfully to see you in your studio and to spend some time in the museum. I am encouraged to believe that this can be arranged.

She sees him again in March, again presumably at 871. Then:

> Apr. 16, Tues: Lunch studio Mrs. F., Senator P. Mrs. F. took him through museum. Then he came to studio.

That night he writes:

> My visit to the museum, to the studio—and to you was, from my angle, a huge success. Moreover, I maintained my record—which appears to be the conversion of visits into visitations. I was particularly

glad that you explained the significance of the Leda group. We men are so unimaginative about things like that. We might easily see a pair in flagrante delicto and suppose they were just talking politics or discussing the New Deal. A woman, on the other hand, takes in the situation at a glance and explanation is superfluous. I was greatly impressed by the Daphne. Of course you are right in your conception of the transformation. When the first Greek artist or poet associated a tree and a young girl it was because he saw the slender trunk against the evening sky, the arms extended and the hair-like foliage blowing in the wind. . . .

Au revoir. You certainly have the divine gift of making life interesting and companionship delightful. Gladys was perfectly right about it.

G.W.P.

The lack of a salutation (formerly he had addressed Gertrude as "Dear Mrs. Whitney"), the initials (he had signed his full name) and, most of all, the tone of the letter are all new. From now on, through the rest of this year and for several years to come, his letters and his visits will become increasingly frequent and intimate. Gertrude, at sixty, is enjoying not only the various aspects of her work but the addition of yet another admirer to an already long list.

≈

Bruno Richard Hauptmann, the Lindbergh baby's kidnapper, finally captured in September of 1934, goes on trial in January 1935. It is by far the most widely publicized civil case of the period. Though behind it in attention, the so-called Gloria Vanderbilt custody case nevertheless appears in the papers almost daily. Every detail of Mrs. Vanderbilt's appeal is reported as well as events in her child's life, such as her eleventh birthday and her first communion (the Court has ordered that she be raised as a Catholic). During the early spring Gertrude reviews much of the previous testimony and then the briefs filed by Nathan Burkan and Frank Crocker, who has had the brilliant trial lawyer Joseph M. Proskauer prepare hers as respondent. She writes to him:

I am afraid I was too emotionally afflicted this afternoon when I spoke to you to tell you how I felt about your presentation of the case. I can't imagine any picture of this child's life shown in a more masterly and truthful way. The picture you gave (from the mother's own evidence supplemented by the child's) of neglect, lack of affection, could not have been more convincing.

Out of 6,000 odd pages of evidence you hit the high spots. You brought out every important point & in just the right consecutive order. Not one too many words, not one too little. You led up to a crucial issue, then left it, just at the critical moment. And always, back of it was the essential truth—the neglect, the lack of affection which the child could not forget.

You got to the essentials and I know you could not have done it if your feeling had not been aroused by the tragedy of this kid. You were inspired by something which made you so eloquent and for that I shall never be able to thank you enough.

I want Gloria to meet you later and realize what you have done for her.

There is not a single mark on Gertrude's copy of Proskauer's brief. Burkan's brief is, however, filled with underlinings, circlings, exclamation points, question marks, and marginal notations, mostly in Frank Crocker's hand, though seemingly his reactions in consultation with Gertrude. Early in the brief, heavily circled, is Burkan's comment: "axiomatic here, that to brand the mother is to brand the child!" (Burkan's exclamation.) When Burkan observes that Gertrude did not visit Gloria in the hospital after her Caesarean operation and later rarely invited her to her home for dinner, Frank scribbles, "What of it?" When Burkan mentions that on one occasion when the child was sick, Gloria stayed up with her till midnight, Frank scribbles even more excitedly, in large letters, "Wonderful for a mother!" (Frank's collaborative exclamation now.) There are many factual corrections and many queries like "Really?" and "Lucid?" But when the "innocence" of Gloria's relationship with Prince Hohenlohe is being defended, Gertrude seems to be asking herself or Frank, in the margin, "Should one admit it?" And similarly the comment regarding Gloria's relationship to Lady Milford Haven seems to be written only for her own amusement and Frank's: "Lesbians always leave doors open. So do f——s, I am told!" On and on the comments run—the product obviously of many hours' study—but it is not till Burkan attacks the Whitney Museum that they become really agitated: "We'll produce them [the paintings]. . . . Only a pornographic mind could compose this [Burkan's description of the art at the museum]. . . . Dirty-minded Burkan. . . . Mrs. V's schooling in dirty books makes all art smut to her!" And finally another heavy circling of Burkan's own words: "There is nothing in the law which warrants the Supreme Court, when it comes to exercise the powers of *parens patriae*, to deprive a mother of her child in favor of a stranger, unless that mother is so unfit that constant association of the child with the mother will prevent the child from growing up a good and useful member of society."

In the midst of Gertrude's collaborative study and commentary, a letter arrives on official White House stationery:

My dear Mrs. Whitney:

Through Mr. [James] Gerard I have learned how much you are interested in Washington.

Would you care to spend the night of June 4 with us and drive around Washington with me and see the new buildings?

We are having Madame Lebrun, the wife of the President of France, for dinner that night.

Very sincerely yours,
Eleanor Roosevelt

Still using the mourning stationery she has for over a year now, since her mother's death, Gertrude writes:

Dear Mrs. Roosevelt,

Thank you so much for your very kind invitation to spend the night of June 4th at the White House and especially for the tempting opportunity of driving around Washington with you. I only wish I could accept but I am involved in a litigation which is coming before the Court the week beginning June 3rd and my attornies have told me I must be in New York that entire week.

With renewed thanks for your thought of me and many regrets, Believe me

Very sincerely yours,
Gertrude V. Whitney

Hearings of Gloria's appeal begin on schedule before Judge Carew and last for a full month, during which Joseph Proskauer carries most of the load of litigation, while Gertrude, though on call and required for some meetings, is able to spend considerable time in her New York studio, which Little Gloria visits frequently now that school is over. Also, during this time and for many months to come, Gertrude entertains Cathleen Vanderbilt, Little Gloria's half sister, twenty years older, who has divorced Harry Cushing in 1932 and married Lawrence Lowman. Burkan in his brief remarked that Gertrude, "who claims this deep affection for [Gloria's] child, has not seen the child's half-sister . . . for 5½ years." Next to that is written, "Good tip." Now Gertrude begins acting on it— not only, we can suppose, hoping to overcome Burkan's criticism but to establish a protective bond between the Lowmans and the child.

The appeal is denied July 3, and Gloria takes her child off to Nissequogue, Long Island, for a month, in accordance with the original decision of the Court. The papers are full of descriptions and photographs of the child's arrival, protected, like the Lindberghs' new baby, by detectives carrying machine guns; and throughout the month there are intrusive stories about the mother and child playing tennis and swimming together, until Little Gloria returns to Gertrude and can be secluded in the total privacy of the Whitney camp in the Adirondacks.

There, Gertrude writes a great deal, working on her second novel but, as usual, interrupting that with frequent letters to family and friends, particularly now to George Pepper and Josh Hartwell. George has a facility for suggestive light verse and, as a Republican, also for attacking the "dictatorial drift" of Roosevelt's New Deal (some of his letters read like drafts of speeches). Josh's letters are much more personal and passionate. One in particular is addressed to "Sandra dearest," indicating that he has read the first part of Gertrude's new novel. Another indicates that Gertrude has by now discussed George with Josh, though possibly as much in a spirit of teasing provocation as of openness. Josh writes: "I am running off with my guns and leaving you to the mercy of all kinds of urging by a Senator with a salacious poetical turn—and with it a burning devotion which was expressed with sufficient heat in a noteworthily short time." Josh's jealousy is playful; he has confidence based on their long relationship. Constantly— in some twenty letters written during this summer—he harks back to their past, giving a better sense of their meetings at the studio than in anything written by Gertrude except for her fiction, especially the relationship between Sandra and Marston.

> . . . You may smile at hearing it again but the things of those days have so permeated my being that they arise to confront me in everything I do. Sitting here in my room thus talking to you I imagine you on the sofa at work on your manuscript or while reading my book I look and there you are doing little touches on the group, or at lunch I must make the champagne cocktail and after clear away the table and at dinner see that you eat something. Then we are talking of the meaning of sculpture and you point out to me the different types and their meanings. It is all so interwoven with you and me that after the thread is cut it goes on circulating—just as I explained the impulse of the heart carries the blood back through the veins even though the pulse itself stops in the capillaries. In all that I read there are things I long to share with you. I want to read to you as we did when Lawrence, Huxley and the others were with us. . . . There is much of Walt Whitman and Oscar Wilde that we left unread—and here [Maine] are such uninterrupted hours in which we might do it all. . . .

Or he pretends to be calling her at the studio:

> RH 4-3926 . . . Ziss . . . Ziss . . . Ziss . . .
> Good morning! You've been a long time "busy" for so
> early. I'm sorry I didn't try sooner but I was afraid

I'd wake you and you're always so pathetic when I do
that.
————————What? You've had six calls
already. My. What popularity.
————————Oh! Only three from beaux.
Well, that isn't so bad. Did you have a good rest?
————————The damn flies. I had only one, the
nasty kind that don't buzz but only let you know he is
there after he has bitten————————I did,
smack on the forehead. What are the plans for today?
————————Not to lunch? Too bad I had hoped for
the whole afternoon and evening too————————Yes,
I know—but if you will let me fall in love with you,
you must bear the consequences.————————Well,
five o'clock then. . . . And remind me there's a story to
tell.————————No not now. It's not a telephone
story————————Yes, it has to do with what we
talked about at dinner and after————————. We
certainly did. But that is nothing new. We always do
————————Yes both of them. I don't know which
I like better————————I know. Half the fun is
reading them together, and there were whole pages which
I wanted to read to you————————Yes, because they
were so apt to us————————I don't know. There never
seems time any more. Either there is too much to talk
about, or you are busy with your writing or on the group.
————————Surely, you've had so much interruption
all winter that I love to see you free and so keen about
it, but just the same I miss the reading. We found such
joy in it. . . . At five o'clock then, and don't forget to ask
for the story. Goodbye, darling————————Whatever
you like. That's more important. You are working too hard
to live on bird food————————And don't forget, a
bottle of champagne on the ice . . . .

Gertrude's letters to Josh are less frequent, less amorous, and less totally
devoted to the consciousness of him. However, they are very affectionate
and intimate and, as in the following draft, give a sense of her life at
Camp Deerlands:

Dear Josh, perhaps I should not mention your name, but I like saying
it, it's like saying something that brings us closer together. I can't tell
you how the days pass here! I always *think*, now today I shall have
hours to write a letter, and lo and behold, before I have a chance to

get out of bed the two little kids [Gloria and probably Gerta] arrive. "Draw me a picture, make me a boat." "Hortense, is my bath ready?" "Oui, Madame." The older batch arrive before I can get into the bath. "May we go to High Pond, may we, etc., etc." "Ask Miss Hill & Mlle. to come & discuss plans." Consultation. Settled at last—sounds of a launch. Advent of some Millers. Pam's voice, "I have brought the Miller twins to see you." [Cully's brother] Larry Miller's kids. "Fine, come in." Discussion of who caught the biggest fish, whether the sound heard in a tent last night was a porcupine, a bear, or a deer. No decision reached. Departure. Conversation about horses, Saratoga gossip. "Please close the door, Sonny, when you go out."

Of course I like it, but it is almost 12 o'clock. In my bath at last, a voice through the door, "Miss Hill says I can only stay in bathing twenty minutes, etc."

Another voice, "Will you come and see how I can swim to the raft?"

I say again to you, of course, I like it.

Lunch at 1.

A slight lull.

Elmhirsts stopping in or something. Arrival of mail, papers. At last a book, a sheet of paper. Mild exercises for me and the return of boats, victory in a sailing contest, a big fish caught, supper for the children. Shall we read or play games. Bedtime for the children. Dinner for the grown ups, early to bed, and practically my only time for uninterrupted work or concentration.

It's my own fault of course, but a matriarch *is* one and prefers to remain one. Next week I go to town for a little attention to my own affairs.

Does this kind of a life make one a very dull person? That's what I worry about sometimes. It's terribly local. I would like to think it was keeping one's finger on the pulse of youth and being a friend, to whom, if I live, all these entities would come & I could somehow feed them, and from whom I would gather more knowledge. For they have so much to give and such a fund of enthusiasm on which to feed, if only one can attune oneself to their vibrations.

These thoughts are far away from what I started to write about. And yet, all fundamental thoughts and emotions are close, whether they are about youth or about age; about personal or impersonal subjects. I bring it back (selfishly) to my greatest interest—creation. Without a vital perception of the emotions of others—plus the ability to depict them—art is a dead thing. As we grow older our powers of emotion decrease and it is only through our ability to perceive through the contact of youth, the freshness of emotion.

(You and I have found that untrue, but as far as the principle is concerned it is correct.)

≈

Gertrude leaves the Adirondacks September 9 to return to New York, and Little Gloria follows three days later to spend her first September weekend in Nissequogue with her mother, just back from England and actively working on her appeal. It is denied October 11, at which time George Pepper writes:

> It was good news when I read in the evening paper that the Appellate Division had refused Mrs. V. leave to appeal from the recent decision sustaining Mr. Justice Carew. I assume that she will try to get a certiorari from the Ct. of Appeals direct: but in this case I should suppose she would certainly fail. I tremendously admire the calm courage with which you have faced—not the music but the discord. Of course it's what I should expect of you—but a woman with less than your spirit would have quailed in anticipation of the sort of warfare which is common in such cases. You are a grand person, Gertrude dear, and I'm proud to be your friend. . . .

The rest of George's letter is about trouble with his knee, foreign politics, and the New Deal's Agricultural Adjustment Act, which he is arguing against, as a test case, before the Supreme Court and which he, with other leading lawyers, will be successful in invalidating. Gertrude replies:

> Thank you for your letter of congratulations. My advisors likewise say they do not think she will get far with her next step, but it keeps the matter in the public eyes, which of course is trying. I am too busy to think much about it these days, and sink myself in an orgy of creation. Finishing statues and books is much like having babies—extremely painful and rather sordid—but at least one hasn't time to think of anything else during the process!
>
> I badly want your advice about some question of French law [for the novel] and I must hear all about your knee, and I have to tell you a funny story, and have you seen the planetarium? and have you read Anne Lindbergh's book? . . .

Besides Gertrude's sculpture and the novel, there is one other aspect to her "orgy of creation." She is more occupied now than for some time past with the museum. Until now, as a completely private enterprise, it has had no legal entity, no tax-deductibility. With these disadvantages in her mind (as well as in Frank Crocker's) and probably with the desire, especially after her sixtieth birthday, to assure the museum's perpetuity, she decides to transform the private institution to a public one. She has many meetings on the subject with Frank Crocker and Juliana Force and seeks the advice too of George Pepper, who sends her a copy of a speech he has made at Lafayette College on the role of the trustee. Frank prepares a Deed of Trust, along with a constitution and by-laws. The Deed reviews the aims of the founder (basically unchanged), names five trustees (Flora Whitney Miller, Cornelius Vanderbilt Whitney, Juliana Force, William Adams Delano, and Frank L. Crocker), and assigns to them a nominal lease at $1.00 a year for ten years) on the real estate at 8, 10, 12, and 14 West Eighth Street; the art contained therein (valued, at cost, in excess of $500,000); 20,000 shares of R. J. Reynolds Tobacco Co. (having a present market value of $1,200,000, the income from which is $60,000 a year); and $100,000 cash.

Juliana Force has already planned a season intended to emphasize the museum's permanent collection, to which about 330 items have been added since 1930. Now she supervises supplementation of the catalogue, which will be attached to the Deed of Trust, and renovation, including better lighting of the galleries, for which part of the $100,000 will be used. She and Gertrude also spend many hours discussing a policy adopted by the Society of American Painters, Sculptors and Gravers under which artists would be paid modest rental fees (one per cent of the price of each work per month) during exhibitions. The two women are sympathetic to this idea and, though they recognize that it will add to their already large overhead, the Whitney, along with just a few other institutions, accepts the policy.

At eleven o'clock Wednesday morning, November 27, the new trustees, except for Flora, who is in Aiken, assemble at 871 Fifth Avenue, where Gertrude executes the Deed in duplicate and conveys the Reynolds stock and a Guaranty Trust check for $100,000. The trustees then have their first meeting. Sonny is elected president; Bill, vice-president; and Frank, secretary and treasurer; after which Juliana Force (not voting) is appointed director at an annual salary of $15,000. Finally it is

> RESOLVED that in due course, the Trustees proceed to memorialize the Legislature of the State of New York or the Regents of the State of New York, requesting an Act of Incorporation, and that the form of the Memorial be prepared by the Secretary and submitted to each of the Trustees in advance, in order that the same may be considered at an early meeting of the Trustees.

No further business coming before the meeting, it adjourned.

"Due course" will run until February 26, 1936, for New York State incorporation and until June 30, 1936, for approval of tax-free status by the Commissioner of Internal Revenue. Meanwhile, at the end of 1935, Gertrude, working closely with Juliana, becomes involved with a project outside of the museum, which will stretch still further into the future: the proposed 1939 New York World's Fair, another attempt to improve business and provide jobs in the city. As so often, Gertrude's concern is both social and selfish. She wants the fair to be "spiritual" rather than "scientific . . . coldly intellectual . . . and commercial." In short, she wants it to be full of art—no doubt, not having received a commission in six years, her own included. As early as the beginning of November— almost two months before the New York Supreme Court approves incorporation papers—she establishes the World's Fair Five Organization, Juliana Force and four architects to whom she feels close: Cully Miller and his partner Auguste Noel, Hugh Ferriss, and Eric Gugler, who has devoted himself primarily to memorials, monuments, and murals. By the end of the month, after much correspondence with Mrs. Force, both Ferriss and Gugler are being retained at $1,000 per month, plus expenses, to work with Noel and Miller on the preparation of a plan for the fair site at Flushing Meadow. The risk of the fair not going ahead is slight. Already it has the endorsement of President Roosevelt, Governor Lehman, and Mayor La Guardia. On December 22, when incorporation is approved, the list of 109 incorporators includes the head of virtually every important bank, insurance company, law firm, retail and real estate business, and giant corporation in New York, along with a token representation of cultural leaders coming from the same high-powered background. The emphasis is surely commercial; the need for the corrective influence of Gertrude's World's Fair Five is valid.

≈ *1936*

The exhibition of recent sculpture which Gertrude has been thinking about since 1933 is scheduled to open March 17 at Knoedler's elegant and prestigious gallery on East 57th Street. Gertrude devotes the first two and a half months of the new year mainly to that show. She supervises the casting and finishing of works already completed in plaster and the cutting and polishing of others in stone, and she creates a 54-inch *Salome* in plaster. Her Line-A-Day continues to be spotty, the most common daily entry being the single word "Work," which includes all the usual details of photographing the sculpture, preparing a catalogue, arranging for shipment to the gallery, making mailing lists and, finally, installation.

In the midst of this Gertrude is still seeing Josh frequently and George periodically. She writes George that she is "frightened that we were trying something impossible . . . which would not make you very happy," and admits that, because of Josh, she does not feel "totally free." Then she asks: "Can there exist an inbetween relation for a man and a woman? The French have a word for it (though I doubt if they ever put it into practice): *amitié amoureuse*. It sounds so lovely but I have never known just how it could be done if the *amoureuse* anywhere nearly compared in strength to the *amitié*." Letters and meetings with George become less frequent during the remainder of this year, and in 1937 stop altogether, though he long outlives Gertrude. The relationship with George, as with Josh, has necessarily been discreet because of his marriage. Gertrude's relationships with bachelor escorts fall into a different category, one which does seem to prove the possibility of an *amitié amoureuse*. Now, of all her close confirmed-bachelor friends, Charles Draper, one of the youngest and most attractive of them, gets married and, like George, though for different reasons, virtually disappears from her life.

However, the life is still very full. Besides Josh, sculpture, writing, the museum, other museums, other "charities," the World's Fair Five, there is the family—and particularly Little Gloria, whose mother begins yet another appeal in February. By now the basic litigation and related issues of allowances, expenses, estate accounting, and so forth have become almost routine. They appear in the papers, as in Gertrude's life, as a chronic irritation. More disturbing is the occasional front-page story prompted by the background of the custody case. Two such incidents occur in February. On Tuesday the fourth, three men attempt to hold up Thomas Griffin, superintendent of the Westbury estate, in his cottage at the entrance. Griffin's daughter screams and the robbers flee. Yet, despite all evidence indicating that there was no intention to kidnap Little Gloria (in the main house with Gertrude), the incident is treated as a kidnapping attempt. On Sunday the twelfth (while the child is with her mother in New York) a suspicious car is seen near the estate. The *Enquirer*, New York's only Sunday afternoon paper, runs a banner headline:

RADIO POLICE CALLED TO FOIL VANDERBILT KIDNAP EFFORT

Monday's papers complete the story:

"KIDNAPPERS" OF GLORIA JUST PETTING

Gertrude is not amused.

⤆

Perhaps because the exhibition at Knoedler's is the first one-person show Gertrude has had in New York since 1923 and because it is small both in number of pieces (fourteen) and in scale (nine are less than three feet high), she invests an unusual amount of time and money in installation. For weeks she confers with the gallery and her friend Paul Chalfin about every detail of placement, lighting, and background, and for two days preceding the opening she is at the gallery morning and afternoon. The exceptional quality of the installation is not lost on the critics. It is, indeed, one of the distractions from the work itself, along with Gertrude's celebrity and her museum and her previous commissions. Henry McBride's review in the *Sun* is the most sympathetic:

> The Gertrude Whitney sculptures . . . are a surprise, and especially a surprise to those who have kept a severe eye upon the artist's career, for they represent not only an increase of command over the medium but an increase in ease of style. Mrs. Whitney's reputation as an artist is much bettered by the event.
>
> This serene growth is all the more astonishing because the times are not especially auspicious for sculptors . . . yet the artist has found it possible to enter quite lightly and blithely and successfully upon the exposition of themes such as "Salome," "Pan" and "Daphne" that used to occupy artists in the remotest pages of history. Obviously, from the point of view of a psychologist, these matters, to her, were "an escape"; but the point is that she did escape. She not only escaped from the present tempestuous era but escaped as well from the domination of the terrible old masters who probably thought that they had made "Salome," "Pan" and "Daphne" theirs forever. Mrs. Whitney makes them hers as well. . . .
>
> It is generally agreed that most sculpture looks its best outdoors, and most sculpture is planned with the dramatic and changing lights of outdoors in mind, but in an enclosed gallery, ordinarily, not much drama is afforded by the lighting, and in fact, generally, the carving is robbed of its vital elements and the emphasis is laid upon some feature that the artist had not wished to be considered at all . . . these difficulties have been ingeniously overcome. The walls have been rehung with a pale gray-blue that is atmospheric, a false ceiling of white still further simplifies the rooms, and in this white ceiling, a few holes have been punched, here and there, to permit a concealed light to shed its rays becomingly upon a carving. . . .

Edward Alden Jewell in the *Times* is more critical, concluding that "most of this work is essentially romantic, often decorative." Emily Genauer in the *World Telegram* echoes him but is more damning. She begins by acknowledging Gertrude's "tremendous contribution to American art" and by tracing the history of her patronage.

> But her contribution has not been a creative one—or perhaps, in fairness, the phrase should be changed to "personally" creative. For while the current exhibition of her own sculpture . . . reveals her as a first-rate technician and a facile modeler, it also, in several instances,

points to a romantic, decorative, conception of sculpture, rather than one springing from a combination of searching expressionism and a formal recognition of masses, rhythms, volumes and their relation to each other. . . .

A large crowd is attracted to the opening, and after it Gertrude has many of her friends and relatives to "tea [as she calls it in her Line-A-Day] at 871." Helen Appleton Read, who is no longer reviewing for the Brooklyn *Eagle*, writes a few days later:

> Ever since your opening last week, I have been meaning to write to you to tell you how much I enjoyed it, and how distinguished and distinctive an exhibition it is. I wish that I might have been able to say what I think in print, but because I am no longer able to do so, I wanted to tell you anyway.
>
> It always gives me a distinct lift to see the work of an artist who still believes that the poetic approach to life and hence to art is the only one that really matters. So few contemporary artists seem to realize this, perhaps because of their preoccupation with problems of form as being more important than ideas or perhaps in the last analysis because there are so few poets among them. . . .
>
> It was also a great pleasure to come to your house afterward for cocktails—thank you so much for asking me.

Mrs. Read's is only one of many congratulatory letters. Another which must have been meaningful to Gertrude comes from Forbes Watson, now in Washington:

> Last Saturday afternoon I went to your beautifully installed exhibition and saw several works which I particularly liked, besides seeing so many friends that the occasion became a regular party. Every artist in town seemed to be there from Allen Tucker to Leon Kroll—that leaves room for all the world. Even our darling Janet Scudder [a commission sculptor, contemporary with Gertrude] was there. Although the others were enthusiastic, I thought dear Janet looked a bit like an onion that had spent the night on an ant hill.
>
> But before I let my friends get me, so to speak, I looked at your sculpture and just let the pieces that particularly wanted to make their impression on me. As a result, I came away enthusiastic about the portrait called "John," the "Daphne" and the "Nun." These were the three that especially hit me.
>
> I enjoyed the exhibition as a whole very much and I am perfectly delighted that you are carrying on so finely. . . .

The split in critical response is equivalent to the split in Gertrude's personality and the artistic expression of it. The exhibition is about one third formal, cool, sleek, and highly stylized (e.g., *Gwendolyn* and *Nun*), about one third "poetic," expressionistic, and/or romantic (e.g., *Mercy, Salome,* and *Daphne*), and about one third somewhere in between, perhaps undecided (e.g., *John* and *Woman and Child*). For no sure reason but possibly at Neily's request, the portrait bust of him, which would fit into the third category, is not included. However, what is sure is that, if it had been, any one of the critics might have liked it or not and called it "romantic" or not. The inconsistent and overlapping judgments of the critics indicate that it is difficult to label individual pieces and still more so to label an entire exhibition like this, containing five years' work and showing all aspects of Gertrude's complex and sometimes conflicted character.

A few days after the opening she receives a letter which means more to her than any review. Harold deWolf Fuller, executive director of the Netherland-America Foundation, asks for an interview concerning the foundation's plan to erect a statue of Peter Stuyvesant in Stuyvesant Square, at Second Avenue and Sixteenth Street, once part of "Stuyvesant Bouery" or farm. The meeting is arranged and Fuller explains that the project has been approved by Park Commissioner Robert Moses but that no sculptor has as yet been selected. He tells Gertrude how much his committee admires her work and likes the idea of the memorial being made by "a member of an old New York family of Dutch descent" —someone, they hope, who might be willing to do the work "con amore and gratis." As much as Gertrude wants the job, she insists that, in accordance with longstanding principle, she cannot forgo a professional fee, that by doing so she might divert the commission from another deserving sculptor. Fuller assures her that it was never the foundation's intention to pay a fee to anyone but only to pay for the cost of casting, estimated at $1,500 to $2,000 for a statue somewhat larger than life size. There is another meeting, another letter, this one containing assurance that "no other sculptor would have been offered a fee," and in a few more weeks Gertrude consents.

Consents!—there is still in her a drive toward public work and recognition that seems to transcend even the greatest satisfactions of private creation. Except for the possibility of work on the 1939 World's Fair, no other major commission appears likely now. Gertrude begins immediately to gather information on Stuyvesant, asking John Gregory's wife Katherine to do some of the basic research with the New York Historical Society, the City History Club, the Museum of the City of New York, and various institutions in Holland. Bit by bit—as with Columbus, Buffalo Bill, and the rest—the facts, more and more specific, are assembled. Birth: 1592. Shot in right leg during the siege of St. Martin: April 16, 1644. Leg amputated and buried in Curaçao: exact date unknown. Return to Holland to recuperate and obtain artificial limb, afterward called his "silver leg" because of its adornments: exact date, in 1645, unknown. Marriage to Judith Bayard, his sister's sister-in-law, sixteen years his junior: August 13, 1645.

Arrival in New Amsterdam, as director general of New Netherland, "like a peacock, with great state and pomp": May 11, 1647. First of two sons born here, baptized Balthazar Lazarus Stuyvesant: May 27, 1647. First ordinance, on the sale of intoxicants: May 31, 1647. Other harsh measures, and some progressive ones, until surrender to the English: August 27, 1664. Eight comparatively quiet years until death at eighty. . . . All this Gertrude learns, along with details about the close cap, the built-out shoulder, the turned-up cuff, the puffed and slashed sleeve, the crushed sash, pantaloons, shoe buckle. . . . Though she has been busy, she needs this project, commits herself to it, thrives on it, and is happy. Her subject *is* "romantic," as much as any in her Knoedler show. Stuyvesant—tough, willful, vital, virile—is Josh Hartwell, George Pepper, and maybe mostly Commodore Vanderbilt, all rolled into one; he is part of her history. Within a year, using a model who wears a period costume made for him in accordance with the research, Gertrude will complete sketches for the most severe sculpture she has ever produced.

⤜

Since the first meeting of the museum's board under the new Deed of Trust, there has been another comparatively routine one, March 10, attended only by Juliana Force, William Adams Delano (superseding Sonny as president), and Frank Crocker at Delano's office. There the museum's incorporation is recorded and the director makes her first report. Because of alterations, the museum has been open only forty-one days since the last meeting. During that period two exhibitions—Shaker Handicrafts and the Second Biennial of Sculpture, Watercolors and Prints (416 works by 257 living artists)—have attracted 17,210 visitors. Of 10,000 catalogues printed, about half have been sold, half given to institutions and artists. Eighty works and 174 slides have been loaned to museums, colleges, and schools across the country. The work of forty-eight young artists has been viewed by the staff "to keep in touch with existing trends . . . and sometimes to discover new talent." Research and the preparation of catalogues is moving forward on the work of David G. Blythe, Winslow Homer, Albert Ryder, and Thomas Nast. . . .

Juliana Force, her eyes bright with pride and excitement, talks on. There are fifteen items of repair, alteration, and decoration, plus a written report by Norman Montforte, superintendent. There are four other written reports—all read or summarized by Mrs. Force—from Hermon More, curator of painting and sculpture; Lloyd Goodrich, curator, research department; Karl Free, curator, graphic arts; Edmund Archer, associate curator, education. We can imagine the impatience of Frank and Bill as the words continue, filling hours, later reduced to "minutes" (eighteen typed pages, plus attached reports). What is missing is the exchange, the informal and enthusiastic dialogue that has for so many years been going on between Juliana and Gertrude. However, on March 11, the day after the meeting, Bill Delano writes a letter "To the Trustees" that will in effect re-establish and more formally restructure the two women's former relationship:

Due to the fact that I am compelled to be absent from New York for a long period, I feel that I should resign from the trusteeship and presidency of the Museum. I do this with regret and beg that you will accept my resignation in the spirit in which it is offered and believe that my interest in the Museum will continue.

A special meeting of the board is called for March 23 at 871 Fifth Avenue, where:

On motion duly made and seconded the following resolution was thereupon adopted:
RESOLVED that the Trustees of Whitney Museum of American Art accept with regret the resignation of their associate Trustee and President of this corporation, Wm. Adams Delano.
Thereupon the Chairman stated that the election of a successor to Mr. Delano was in order and, upon ballots being duly cast, Mrs. Gertrude Vanderbilt Whitney was elected a Trustee of the Whitney Museum of American Art to serve for the remainder of the term for which Mr. Wm. Adams Delano was appointed, and was also elected President of the corporation to hold office during the pleasure of the Board and until her successor shall be chosen. Mrs. Whitney, who was present, then took the Chair and thenceforth participated in the deliberations of the Board.

Except for the approval of an American eagle (designed by Karl Free) on the corporate seal, Gertrude's ultimately inevitable appointment to the board and election as president is the only business done at this meeting. From now until the end of her life she will preside, responding warmly to Juliana Force's long reports and encouraging her as in years past.

⇜

From late February to the end of March, Gloria argues that her daughter has been "shuttled back and forth each week like a tennis ball," that the present arrangement is a "crime against nature and reason" and is "tearing the child's heart in two." But, March 30, her second appeal to the New York Supreme Court is denied. When advised of the decision, she says, "I'll keep on fighting as long as there's a breath left in my body." A reporter asks if she hasn't "reached the court of last resort." "I'll find some way to go on."

Gertrude has no doubt about her sister-in-law's determination. She knows that the case is once again only temporarily behind her and feels that it—the litigation, the newspaper coverage, the whole sorry mess—is endless. She goes to Aiken for a week and a half. Except for that brief rest, the spring is filled with work—specific studies and sketches for Peter Stuyvesant, speculative designs for the World's Fair.

As she did the previous year, Little Gloria joins her mother in Long Island for July. While the child is away, Gertrude spends about half the month working, half with Neily and Grace, aboard the *Winchester*, visiting the Széchényis in Newport. (Because of the court order, she cannot go to Paris for the wedding of Adele Burden to her second husband, Richard M. Tobin, a San Francisco banker.) When Little Gloria returns, Gertrude takes her to the Adirondacks where more of the family awaits—the Millers at Camp Togus, the Whitneys at Deerlands, the Henrys at Killoquah. For greater privacy, Gertrude has had a houseboat fixed up as a studio—named the *Killoquah* because it is docked there. It quickly becomes her favorite place in which to read and write, and she spends much of the month sitting on the afterdeck of the boat doing one or the other but happy to have Gloria, her grandchildren, and their friends come aboard to dive or jump off the high roof and to tell her about the day's activities.

Gertrude writes frequently to Josh, who has been hospitalized in New York. Like last year's, her letters are vivid. In the first, dated August 5, she describes the eight-by-five boat cabin:

> . . . gay and cheery. All white paint, a blue carpet & sofa. Bright red curtains, sort of piazza furniture, white iron or wicker, and a circular open fireplace in the center of the room connected with the smokestack. No fire yet, it has been too warm. Lamps, pictures, cushions complete the picture. How I wish you could see it and above all, how I wish I could have you here to myself. The sofa makes into a bed, our meals could be sent down to us and that would leave only one objection—but we would find a way out of that (there are no lavatory conveniences).

Gertrude intends to visit Josh but can't because her granddaughter Flora Miller must suddenly be operated on for appendicitis and by the time she is recovering Gertrude's old friend Rollie Cottenet is on his way to visit. After his arrival she writes Josh:

> . . . Rollie and I have had two days of talk, talk, talk. It is so long since I have seen him for any length of time that no matter how often I take up a book or a paper to read we get right back to talking. Of course he can't read himself at all [he is now almost blind], but he is wonderful, cheerful, entertaining and to me *very* pathetic. . . . Rollie has said nothing about how long he is going to stay. Of course if it is indefinite I shall leave him for a few days. I am longing to get down & see you, darling, you can't know how much. . . .

I am writing this early in the morning looking out of the big window in my room that faces the lake. The smell of pines comes in through the windows. The lake is so still it looks like oil. A little bed of yellow flowers has been planted right under the window between me & the lake. They stand out against the lake and the trees—the only spot of real color, for the day is dull with a slight mist drooping over the hilltops. . . .

It is no wonder Rollie lingers. He has always enjoyed Gertrude's company and surely prefers the Adirondacks to New York in August. He doesn't leave until the twentieth. Gertrude waits a day, then spends two with Josh at the hospital, then returns to her boat and writing.

Almost certainly she has finished her second novel by now, has probably submitted it to Coward-McCann (pursuant to a standard option clause) and, again probably, has had it turned down. Many typed copies of the book survive but no correspondence concerning it. We can only guess that the copies were circulated to other possible publishers and rejected there too. But as usual Gertrude is undaunted, perhaps even spurred on to fight for acceptance as an author. She returns to writing short stories, some of which will go through many metamorphoses from now until the end of her life.

One called "Crossed Rails" is from the present time and is, in some ways, a distillation and updating of the recently completed novel—which is to say, of Gertrude's own life. The story is told from the point of view of a lawyer, clearly modeled on George Pepper, who has fallen in love with Mrs. Priscilla Leonard, just as clearly modeled on Gertrude herself, a wealthy woman, interested in bookbinding, which she does in a house off Washington Square, identified as "No. 19," the same number as Gertrude's on MacDougal Alley, where "discretion is its essence." Mrs. Leonard believes that she can carry on her relationship with the lawyer while at the same time continuing one with "a big industrialist," modeled, despite his profession, on Josh. Eventually these compartmentalized relationships impinge, the rails cross, just as the rails of Gertrude's own life do when she returns to New York in the fall.

There she visits Josh frequently at the hospital. She meets with Frank several times concerning yet another custody appeal by Gloria. She attends an international polo match at Meadow Brook. She goes for a few days to Newport where the Széchényis have, as the papers say, "more members of the Vanderbilt family at The Breakers than has been the case for years" and where, after dinner on October 1, they listen to radio speeches by Roosevelt and Landon. A few days later in New York she attends the opening of a WPA show at the Whitney at which both Eleanor Roosevelt and Mrs. Henry Morgenthau, the wife of the Secretary of the Treasury, make enthusiastic comments to the press. The same night she goes to a dinner at Grace's for the Queen of Spain. The next evening Jim-

mie Appleton takes her to see Emlyn Williams in his ghoulish thriller
Night Must Fall. This play, in which the psychopathic killer carries his
victim's head around in a hatbox, "works" in a way her own *The Hand*
doesn't. She likes it enough to see it again a week later, taking her sister
Gladys. And there are other evenings with Adele (Tobin now), Rollie
Cottenet, Paul Chalfin, the Delanos, the Lowmans. . . . October rushes
by, to the sixth anniversary of Harry's death, spent again at Woodlawn.

In November there's a slowing down, or at least fewer pleasurable activities. Gladys leaves for England, then Hungary. Neily is in the hospital,
where Gertrude visits him frequently. Frank has received a new petition in
the custody case and must see Gertrude often. The Line-A-Day is sparse,
scattered with hints of a recurring phlebitis: "Foot bothered me. . . .
Bed. . . . Bed. . . . Did not feel well. . . ."

Gertrude and Frank make every effort to avoid further hearings in
court. It takes them until December 8 to work out "an amicable compromise" under which Gloria is to have her daughter with her for longer continuous periods, though fewer total days, during the year—twelve days at
Christmas, six at Easter, and from the close of school in June to mid-
August, until the child graduates from Greenvale in 1938. Gertrude arranges a Christmas party for Little Gloria and Mrs. Morgan on December
24 and the next morning sends them to town. The Line-A-Day entry for
Christmas Day begins "Stockings." These are probably Christmas stockings but it seems almost as likely that they are elasticized surgical stockings for the phlebitis. During the last days of the year the only entries are
"X rays 3 times. . . . X ray once. . . . X ray. Dr. Richards."

⇜ *1937*

When Neily recovers he sails aboard the *Winchester*, accompanied by a
doctor and a nurse, to Miami, Florida. There he has another attack and
Gertrude decides to join him, both to keep him company and to get a
much-needed rest. There is no Line-A-Day for this year or the next. However, from surviving correspondence—mainly with Gladys, Josh, and
Frank—it is clear that she spends about a month with her brother aboard
his yacht, where she continues to work on short stories and to do some
sketching and research for the Stuyvesant monument. Josh, whose handwriting, along with his health, has become shaky, misses Gertrude very
much and teases her because her life "centers around a pencil and pad."

In late February and March, Gertrude completes the Stuyvesant model and goes through the familiar procedures of committee approval, municipal approval (Park Department), and meetings with a consulting architect (Aymar Embury II). For once everything goes smoothly. As planned, the stern but powerful statue will be seven feet four inches high, on a four-foot pedestal of Tennessee pink marble. At the end of March, in a personal note covering copies of his final approvals, Embury writes: "I like this as well as any single figure that I have seen in New York. I think it will rank in public estimation with MacMonnies' 'Nathan Hale.'"

Though enlargement and casting will ultimately take another two years, there is not much more than supervision for Gertrude to do on this comparatively small commission. We can assume that for the rest of the spring she returns to a more active social life, and we know from the minutes and correspondence files of the Whitney Museum that, however far in the background she now keeps her public role, she is privately in constant touch with all major policy matters there. At a trustees' meeting March 9 she states that the museum must have an income of at least $100,000 in order to continue its ever enlarging program of exhibitions and purchases. A week later, so that this can be accomplished, she gives 10,400 shares of Chemical Bank stock, worth about $790,000, a big gift in a big year at the museum. There are five major shows: New York Realists, 1900–1914; Paintings and Prints by Cleveland Artists; Contemporary American Ceramics; Drawings and Small Sculptures by Gaston Lachaise; and Charles Demuth Memorial Exhibition. The first three indicate the museum's continuing interest in Realism, regionalism, and crafts. The last two commemorate the work of one of the best American sculptors and of one of the best American painters of the period between World War I and the Depression. Both artists have died in their early fifties in October of 1935. It is typical of the Whitney—and, more specifically, of Juliana Force and Gertrude—that, although the Modern has had a large Lachaise retrospective just before his death, their own museum can find a theme for another show so soon afterward. This is prompted as much by the financial need of Lachaise's widow (emphasized in letters to Mrs. Force from Lincoln Kirstein, the organizer of the Modern's Lachaise exhibition) as by the quality of the artist's work. In 1936 the Whitney has purchased Lachaise's *Standing Woman,* a major sculpture, and from the present show it will select four drawings.

☙

For the first time in five years Gertrude plans a trip to Europe, now able to under the new provisions of the custody agreement. She misses Paris, Le Boulay, her sister in Pest, and besides she needs a rest. At the final spring meeting of the Whitney's trustees—June 8—there is one agenda item that relates directly to her plans:

The two women sail together, June 11, on the *Bremen*.

Josh is still sick. Gertrude's long, loving, and supportive letters to him
(always sent care of a doctor friend of his—her own penciled drafts are
reproduced below) present a sad summer. About June 25, Paris:

> . . . Jo's beard awaited us. He took us back here [the studio, 49 Rue
> Boileau]. . . . Vines and trees have grown, pink ramblers are in
> abundance, the addition sweet. Your new room & bath white & cerise!
> After lunch in the garden with Jo, I went to bed & slept till dinner
> time. And all the next day I was too exhausted to move. Poor Mrs. F.
> was utterly discouraged with my lack of energy and Hortense [the
> maid] too gloomy for words. But I wouldn't be telling you that if I
> had not quickly (for me) recovered. . . .

About June 29, Paris:

> . . . Mrs. F. was fine on the steamer, but since I have been here she
> has worried so, just because she did not in the least realize how little I
> can do without getting tired. . . .
>
> I told her before I left that I was going to be quiet here and that
> unless she would go ahead and do her own things I didn't want her to
> stay with me. Instead of which she worries all the time (even if she
> doesn't say anything) and appears with red eyes etc. etc. If she isn't
> fussing about me it's about Comet [Gertrude's long-haired dachs-
> hund]! . . .
>
> . . . except on trips with other people, I have never been with her
> for long periods and I am used to jogging along in my own way. . . .

About the beginning of July, Pest:

> Of all the tiresome things to have happen! I arrived here with a
> temperature. Dr. sent for next morning. Have a slight bronchitis and
> must not move for 48 hrs. I was so furious that if I had not been feel-
> ing like hell, I don't know what I would have done. Tem. only 100°
> but had it again last night. Dr. comes at noon tomorrow. Of Pest I
> have seen nothing but the drive down from the station after dark and
> some trees outside my windows! . . . I probably should not have
> come, feeling as I did, but I knew G[ladys] would be so disappointed,
> and now I may be stuck for days. . . . You seem to be able to sit in a

hospital & let your mind wander about perfectly happy among all kinds of things. I know you have made a great effort to do so. My mind is just stuck in the mud. . . .

Later, in the mountains about two hundred miles outside Pest:

. . . My state of health is so much better, just in two days, that I hate more than ever going to a cure. I am coughing less than I have in years (really) and feel much stronger. . . .

The house is a real hunting lodge. Big hall with heads and skins on the walls, all the comforts and at the same time nothing grand or ostentatious. The atmosphere is unlike anything in America. The servants mostly retainers, the village nearby, with a little hospital (built by G.) for the people of the village, a factory (which has existed for years)—things made of the wood on the place. . . .

July 17, Hotel Sarciron, Le Mont-Dore, France:

Here I am back in our part of the world! After five years, and the sad part is without you. But somehow it makes you very close, especially when today I motored up the Puy de Dome. . . .

Dr. Debedour wants me only to take a very mild cure, no baths for the time being and very little water. I told him all I wanted was to gain weight & feel strong! (I don't remember if I told you that before leaving Paris I weighed 91 lbs., which gave me a jar.)

So my regime is breakfast at 8. At nine, dressed in what looks like a white skiing costume—wool trousers covering the feet, wool shirt & coat, muffler and hood! The doctor took me through my paces the first morning, very simple and short. . . .

The cure continues. After the sixth treatment Gertrude writes:

. . . The last few days I have spent my afternoons at the Golf Club. It's on the top of a mountain, air fine & rather nice view and not crowded. Under some trees there are tables, comfortable chairs and with a book of MS [manuscript] and Comet the afternoon slips by. Potbellied men in shirt sleeves, a few women and young men wander by with golf sticks and about twenty people sit about talking, reading, playing bridge and drinking tea or mild refreshments.

I have an intelligent young girl very well educated who comes and talks literature, politics etc. for an hour after massage. . . .

I am glad you liked Hemingway. I wish my writing were like his. . . .

July 30, Paris:

Back again! At last. . . . I have had my sitting room repainted while I was away & it looks lovely. It's pale creamy pink and makes everything in it *beautiful.* The big Chinese screen stands out in all its loveliness, the bronzes and the fine pieces of furniture count for much more—it's perfect & I begin to feel cheerful once more. Also I am stronger. . . .

Adele & Dick [Tobin] are here for a few days. I expect Jo has gone, but I have a few other friends, and you are not going to hear me complain any more. . . .

Gertrude returns to New York on August 16 and has dinner with Josh that night. The remainder of the year is almost without documentation. Probably she and Little Gloria go again to the Adirondacks for a month. Certainly Juliana Force returns from Europe in mid-September and there are subsequent museum meetings. The rest is scraps—the usual checks to charities and two, for $20,000 and $15,000, to Neily, whose medical and yachting expenses have climbed; a note from Royal Cortissoz saying that "The Museum grows more and more to be a tower of strength. The Demuth exhibition warmed my heart"; and a clipping from the *Daily Mirror* of Gertrude on a Monday night at the opera "pictured as she made her way to her box in the parterre row." Even this photograph tells little. In profile we see hennaed waves of hair, heavy brow, strong mouth and nose. But Gertrude is so completely covered by a long bulky mink coat that there is no indication of her present weight and weariness. Even her hand is covered by the silk scarf she carries, and only an orchid suggests her vulnerability.

≈ 1938

Gertrude's World's Fair Five does not seem to have influenced the elaborate plan which has been developed by the fair's own Board of Design. The fairgrounds, some 1,200 acres, are to be dominated by commerce, whether by the exhibitions of the largest American corporations or by those of states and foreign countries interested in trade and tourism. However, thirty-six compensatory commissions, not directly related to specific exhibitions—free-standing sculptures, fountains, and murals—are given to artists and designers. (The most famous of these is the 700-foot-high "World of Tomorrow" *Trylon and Perisphere* created by architects Harrison & Fouilhoux with an interior "Democracity" designed by Henry Dreyfuss.) Gertrude receives a commission from Lee Lawrie, "Consultant in Sculpture," best known for his *Atlas* at Rockefeller Center, to do a monumental fountain, eventually entitled *To the Morrow*, though changed, after the fair, to *The Spirit of Flight*.

There are dozens of pencil sketches dating from early 1938 and possibly late 1937, in which there is an evolution from the conventional style of Gertrude's *Aspiration* (1900) to that of her more dramatic *St. Nazaire* (1924) and from it to the streamlined modernism of Lawrie's *Atlas* and such sculptures as Paul Manship's *Prometheus* (also at Rockefeller Center, dominating its skating rink). From the beginning, each rough pencil sketch might as well be called *Aspiration* as *To the Morrow* or *The Spirit of Flight*. In each, as in *St. Nazaire*, the dominant element is soaring, indeed aspiring, wings. However, in the present work there are three wings and where a bird's head might be emerge the nude bodies of a young man and woman, side by side, leading the wings in flight and simultaneously being lifted by them. As Gertrude simplifies the forms of the wings and the human figures, she simplifies the base. Originally, like that supporting *St. Nazaire*, it is naturalistic; gradually rocky crags are replaced by abstract spirals, zigzags, or arcs, all suggestive of a plane's take-off. Though the symbolism itself is heavy, the conception is remarkably youthful, energetic, and affirmative, especially for an artist of sixty-three whose health has been poor.

A draft of the contract is submitted early in the new year. For a work planned to be about the same height as *St. Nazaire* (70 feet—ultimately reduced to 54), the fee is small: $2,500, plus $30 per day for final supervision and correction, if requested by the World's Fair Corporation. However, Gertrude is required only to design the sculpture and submit a model for approval; all aspects of fabrication and installation are (theoretically) the responsibility of the corporation. Attached as an exhibit to the proposed contract is a map of the fairgrounds. A red dot indicates the site of her sculpture. It is at a dominant location, facing the main entrance of the Flushing stop of the Long Island Railroad, and just to the south of the IRT-BMT subway gate. She is very pleased and asks only that the time for her submission of a finished scale model be extended from sixteen to eighteen weeks, as she has planned to be away during the coming month.

That month—forty days, actually, from late January to early March—is spent on a cruise aboard the *Rex*, mainly to the West Indies and Brazil, with Flora and Cully, who invite their friend Schuyler Livingston Parsons to round out the party. Parsons, a prominent socialite who has lost his money in the crash, is interested in the arts and has for many years been divorced from his wife Betty, later well known as an artist and art dealer. He mentions the cruise briefly in his autobiography *Untold Friendships*, saying it "gave me diversion in my loneliness and it was a great joy to get to know Gertrude Whitney better than I had before. Her kindness and independence endeared her to everyone. . . ." Her independence must, as always, have been expressed in spending part of every day reading, sketching, and writing. We have no letters to Josh from this trip, but three from him to her are loving and are particularly concerned about her getting enough rest and ridding herself of the cough which still bothers her.

Cully, always a camera buff, takes many still and motion pictures of Flora, Gertrude, and Schuyler Parsons. In the shots of Gertrude—aboard ship, at the Union League Club in Panama, at a restaurant in Caracas, on the waterfront in Barbados, on the great boulevards of Rio de Janeiro—she is drawn and emaciatedly thin but still very animated and participative. In one picture taken in Rio, she sits against the rail of a tender, immaculately groomed as always, swigging beer from a large bottle. It is the most unlikely of gestures and in his photograph album Cully labels it "A Joke!" The same label would apply to a scene in which Gertrude pretends to witness a murder in a short silent motion picture, *Sex on the Rex*, made for fun by fellow passenger Harry Rapf, an MGM producer. The scene is captioned, "Society Goes On Dancing."

During the spring Gertrude works steadily. In mid-June her chief studio assistant Salvatore Bilotti delivers a preliminary plaster model to Lee Lawrie and explains that the final piece is to be done in a shining, reflective, modern material—presumably chrome or steel or aluminum—and that Mrs. Whitney hopes that colored lights can be installed in the fountain basin. The model is promptly approved and a final contract, dated July 16, is executed by "Gertrude V. Whitney, Sculptress" and "Grover Whalen, President, New York World's Fair 1939 Incorporated." This contract is substantially the same as the earlier one, except that sometime between the beginning of the year and now the red dot has moved from the location at the public transportation entrances to a less prominent though more open site on the other side of the fairground, in the "Times Square" amusement section across Horace Harding Boulevard. This doesn't seem to bother Gertrude. She believes there is some chance that the piece can remain in the new location after the fair closes. Meanwhile there are more important problems to resolve regarding the sculpture—those having to do with its potential weight, the engineering of its arched base and, as always, *cost*, especially now when that is controlled by a public corporation which may not accommodate her wishes in the way she accommodates her own. Through the rest of the year there will be many conferences and much correspondence—for most of which her old friend, the architect Grosvenor Atterbury, will act as go-between and buffer—while the preliminary model grows to one-quarter scale and the answer (platinum leaf over reinforced hollow plaster) is found to the engineering and economic questions.

☙

July 5, Count Széchényi dies in Budapest. For Gertrude it is a stark and distant fact. She sympathizes with her sister and nieces, but beyond the expression of condolence there is little she can do. Nine days later

William Stackpole dies in New York, but by then Gertrude is in Newport and his funeral, which she would not have attended in any case, might as well have been in Budapest.

In late July and early August, Gertrude shows fifteen pieces of her recent sculpture, first at Cushing Memorial Gallery in Newport, then at Guild Hall in East Hampton, Long Island. Except for two minor substitutions and the addition of the sketch model of *Peter Stuyvesant*, these exhibitions are identical with the one at Knoedler's in 1936; but beautifully installed as that exhibition was, the present installations—arranged with natural vistas and backgrounds of garden greenery—are more beautiful still. The shows are enthusiastically received by these fashionable communities which, of course, pay as much attention to Gertrude's "background" as to her art. In Newport the fact that Miss Gloria Vanderbilt, now fourteen, accompanies her aunt to the opening is news; and in East Hampton so is Gertrude's "short visit" with Rawlins Cottenet and his sister.

Real news will affect both of these communities about a month later. September 21 the most damaging hurricane ever until then strikes the eastern seaboard, and Gertrude's beautiful, seldom-used Newport studio is washed out to sea. The loss is real enough but only a fragment of Gertrude's life, seen by her as that, within the context of people who have lost their homes. She gives $5,000 to the Newport Community Chest and the same to its YMCA before beginning to think about rebuilding the studio with more durable materials.

At the end of the month she enrolls Gloria at Miss Porter's School in Farmington, Connecticut, with which Gertrude has been in correspondence since the spring. From now until the end of the year she writes to Gloria at the school at least seventeen times, drafting and sometimes redrafting each letter and always expressing interest in every detail of her niece's life. The following letter is typical:

Dearest Gloria,

You may take fencing lessons—I thoroughly approve. Also 2 rumba lessons at Arthur Murray. Your box for Thanksgiving is going to-day, I hope you don't have to go to the infirmary afterwards! Better ask for some medicine!

Cathleen and Pam have told me about seeing you. And I hear you had a boy visitor. Why didn't you tell me about that?? I don't disapprove. I like you to have boyfriends so long as you are open about it. I don't remember now what I said about "formal life." I suppose I meant when you went out on parties.

You haven't answered my questions. Is your mother coming back during the holidays? If so when do you want to go to her? (I want to make my own plans for the holidays.)

The parties you go to, you must go to from my house. Just the way your mother does not make plans for you to do things from my house. And that is not because she would not let you, but because we have to keep the two things separate. I insist on that and your grandmother agrees with me. By the way she is coming to see me on Sat. and I am looking forward to a nice talk.

I am working so hard over my Worlds Fair group that I don't do anything else. Am wanting so much to show it to you.

Gloria is writing just as frequently to "Dearest Aunty Ger" or "Aunty Ger Darling," and in the course of these months her handwriting changes from the messiness of a little girl's to the regular and rounded style of boarding school. Though sometimes homesick and sometimes needing reassurance, she feels herself now "grown up to my age." Gertrude responds to that by finding a chaperone for when Gloria is in New York on holidays, someone "sympathetic and enthusiastic rather than the more stereotyped personality"—a Miss Drury from Newport.

≈

In November yet another memorial show is being arranged at the Whitney—this one for William Glackens, one of the first American realists to whom Gertrude committed herself. His widow writes:

Dear Mrs. Whitney,

It won't be possible to tell you all I feel about the Memorial Exhibition you are giving in honor of our beloved William Glackens. You have done so much for American Art in his case alone. His canvas, selected by J. Alden Weir years ago for the Metropolitan was on its way to the cellar when the monograph on William Glackens was published. This brought "Winter in Central Park" back to the line and in time to Paris and the Grand Prix, the last award but one that he received before his death. There are no adequate words to thank you for this.

The exhibition is going to be glorious. And it is just where he would have wanted to have it. It will express eloquently this modest soul who spoke for himself only in the conscientiousness and beauty of his work.

Yours ever gratefully,
Edith Glackens

Except for activities at the museum, really being run now by a newly elected Executive Committee—Gertrude, Juliana, and Frank—which meets about every two weeks, the end of the year is almost entirely focused on the fair. Even *Peter Stuyvesant*, finished and about to be cast in bronze, will go there, to be placed in front of the Netherlands Pavilion until it is permanently installed in Stuyvesant Square. December 7, Gertrude attends a Netherland-America Foundation luncheon in her honor at the Pierre. Sitting at the speakers' table, in front of American and Dutch flags, with Thomas J. Watson, president of IBM and also of the foundation as well as a director of the World's Fair Corporation, to her left and the art critic Royal Cortissoz to her right, Gertrude listens rather stiffly to Watson's tributes to her. (By now how many times has she attended similar affairs, heard similar words?) Watson introduces Cortissoz, who emphasizes the importance of tradition in art: "[Mrs. Whitney] has put character and expression into Stuyvesant's figure and she has done so with an extraordinary integrity of craftsmanship, which is particularly important in times of modernism and cubism, when it is necessary for an artist to stand on the rock of sanity and tradition, profoundly American."

Finally, perhaps wearily, Gertrude says a few words—words, too that are similar to many in the past: "Mr. Watson and Members of the Committee:

"This moment gives me the first opportunity to publicly say how grateful I am to be the sculptor whom you have chosen to make your monument to Peter Stuyvesant. I value the opportunity, as every artist must, to work in his own medium, but I value it also because your idea of making this statue is the embodiment of patriotism and civic pride, which at this moment is more important than ever before in our country's history.

"I believe that your idea of paying tribute to one of the great men of our country will have far-reaching results. A statue is only a milestone, but an idea goes on forever."

Soon after the luncheon Gertrude is interviewed by Kathleen McLaughlin, a "women's page" writer on the *Times* who is doing an article on the four women who have received World's Fair sculpture commissions. Malvina Hoffman, Brenda Putnam, and Augusta Savage are the others, each of whom has, like Gertrude, met her deadline and is now having her one-quarter scale model enlarged. The article, published on Christmas Day, gives Gertrude the most space because her "design is by far the most heroic in size." It is illustrated with a picture of her, looking very gaunt in a pants suit as she works with Attilo Contini, a caster at the Lentelli Foundry, which has been awarded the enlargement contract. McLaughlin reports:

> . . . Mrs. Whitney's statuary idealizes man's future in the sky. The base will be a gracefully curving arc, the section of a rainbow, twenty-six feet in height. A trio of symbolic wings dominates the piece, from the juncture of which, at the tip of the rainbow, rise the figures of a man and a woman, faces uplifted, bodies poised for ascent.
>
> In the finished piece the spread of each wing will be twenty-four feet, and the human figures twelve feet high. The upper half of the statue, atop the rainbow, introduces a novel finish by being coated

with platinum leaf, guaranteed to weatherproof the plaster base for a maximum [sic] of two years, and to hold its gleam innocent of polish which most of such metals require. The expense will not be inconsistent, Mrs. Whitney said.

No decision has been made as to the method by which the rainbow hues may be fused into the base of the monument. Mrs. Whitney cherishes a hope that the necessary prismatic effect might be achieved by covering the arc with accurately tinted glass, with the lighting installed beneath this surface. Especially at night, she believes, the color values will be materially more effective than with paint or colored plaster. . . .

Gertrude confers with the brilliant engineer and inventor Buckminster Fuller about light and color for the base of her sculpture. He is a perfect choice. Already known for his unorthodox and visionary "Dymaxion" cars and homes and later best known for his "Geodesic" domes and world maps—all part of a single "comprehensive design" theory—he now introduces Gertrude to such new materials as neon tubing, lucite, and plexiglass and finally designs for her what may well be the prototype of many subsequent large-size neon-lighted rainbow supports. Gertrude makes notes on the relative merits of the various materials—cost, weight, strength, construction time, weatherability—and simultaneously records her thoughts about the symbolism of her sculpture:

Rainbow = symbol of sun after the storm
Wings = symbol of flight—the air—lofty ideas & ideals—future
Aviation = greatest progress of our day

Many more pages are devoted to catalogues of possible titles:

Outward (Flight), Onward (Flight), Forward (Flight),
New Dawn, New Horizon, New Hopes, Rainbow Dreams,
Tomorrow's Flight, Endless Flight, Eternal Flight,
Something Afar, The Moth for the Star, Excelsior,
Still Higher, Ever Upward, Beyond, Above . . .

And on. Finally, very down-to-earth, she scribbles:

Is it important to ask people to see it?
If so, who?
Publicity?

By the end of the year the questions are answered: Gertrude is preparing more lists—of those, now, whom she wants to see the new work in her studio.

❦ *1939*

Gertrude begins a new Line-A-Day:

JAN. 1, SUN.: Gloria, Mrs. M[organ], Miss Drury & I saw in the New Year. Mrs. M. said a prayer with G. & self. Studio, to see model for World's Fair. Felt very happy.

JAN. 2, MON.: Party at studio to see model for World's Fair. 110 for lunch. About [?] in afterwards. Artists, politicians, friends. Whalen, Moses, Manship, Zorach, etc. Much interest and enthusiasm. Dined at Passy with Jimmie [Appleton].

The five names Gertrude chooses to record are probably a fair sampling—about forty per cent involved with the World's Fair, forty per cent artists, and twenty per cent old friends. A few thank-you notes and regrets echo this distribution. For example, Eric Gugler writes, "*I was delighted.* It's *yours* all over. Every snitch of it and *no one else's.* Poetic and *swell!*" And the sculptor John Flanagan says that "the élan of the figures, the color and metallic effects you intend to introduce and, as an added attraction, the lighting and water reflection effects at night, will make it an extremely exciting work, one of the most effective, I have no doubt, of the Fair decorations." Among the regrets, Christopher Morley writes from Roslyn Heights, New York, that he will be out of town but has done "a little sculpture of my own recently—an attempt at modelling some Future Thinking—though in words, not in your tractable medium! I wish you'd look at it: called *History of an Autumn.*" And Paul Chalfin, in Lantana, Florida, writes:

Gertrude dear—Enfin!

I knew you must be lost in your great undertaking with so long a silence surrounding you. And I made myself strong in determination to let you work on and on without asking even how you were. But I wanted very much to know. I wondered too if a book would come by a new author with a *nom de guerre.*

I think it hasn't, but evidently the other big work went strong, for here you are with a model and a luncheon. And here I am across the lake from the Balsans, doing nothing more than sun bathing for an idle right arm that has a lot of neuritis to excuse my lack of other purpose.

Are you finished and ready for your rest, or just arrived at some stage in your undertaking?

I ask because in the latter case I want to leave you in peace, but in the former I want to tempt you. You remember—we are going some time to the Virgin Islands to look that *fainéant* [do-nothing] paradise over together. And if you are idle, now's the time.

Do not laugh too hard at me. I mean it—and yet—that is because I wish you might play soon, just a bit.

Anyhow, I shall be at Lantana or within reach of it for a month or so.

A world of good to you!

Other correspondents seem to have been asked to suggest a title for Gertrude's sculpture. One that comes up several times is *Evolution*. She writes on a scrap of paper: "Some call it evolution, some call it God."

While Gertrude is resolving the final details for *To the Morrow*, a Dr. Henry Lyle of St. Luke's Hospital contacts Juliana Force about the possibility of Gertrude doing a memorial group dedicated to the doctors from that hospital who died during the war. Within two days after hearing about Lyle's interest, Gertrude is making sketches and notes for a Doctors' Memorial:

Left hand end: doctor examining or operating on a wounded soldier lying on a stretcher supported by boxes.

Center & thinning out: group of wounded soldiers in more or less serious conditions. Ragged uniforms, an officer in the back, French, American, Moroccan, (if desired, German) uniforms. Accoutrements scattered about, knapsacks used to sit on.

Either in gesture or expression of face, all have hope, in spite of suffering and forlorn appearance.

Like so many past potential commissions, this one will be aborted—as much as anything by World War II. But meanwhile, on top of all Gertrude's other activities, it, *To the Morrow*, and the casting of *Peter Stuyvesant*—the model for which is in the present Whitney Annual—keep Gertrude busy. In January the most frequent entries in the Line-A-Day are "Studio" and "Chest Treatment." In the studio, after work—probably some writing as well as sculpture—she is again seeing Josh often. Although he seems to have recovered substantially from his illness, his health, like Gertrude's, is far from perfect, and they spend a great deal of their time together reading. In this month alone Gertrude reads fifteen books—all, except for *Mrs. Warren's Profession*, detective stories or popular novels. Among the latter is *Frost Flower* by Helen Hull, an associate professor of fiction writing at Columbia University, with whom Gertrude will later study.

During the last days of January and the first week in February, Gertrude visits Neily in Miami, where she stays at the Everglades Hotel and has most of her meals aboard his yacht. He is looking and feeling better, and they have a good time dining together, going for occasional drives, visiting Consuelo and Jacques Balsan at Lantana, and watching a tennis match between Don Budge and Ellsworth Vines. The days go quickly, empty hours filled again with light reading. On the train back to New York she finishes Lloyd C. Douglas' "inspirational" best-seller *Disputed Passage*.

Though the omnivorous reading continues, there is little time for other relaxation from now until mid-April when Gloria has her spring vacation just before the opening of the fair. February 7, the night Gertrude returns from Florida, she and Gladys have dinner at Grace's, and Gertrude reports on Neily's seemingly improved health. From the next day on, for over two months—except for one day visiting Gloria at Miss Porter's on her birthday; one visiting Gee at the hospital when Gail, Gertrude's ninth grandchild, is born; and Easter Sunday dinner at Barbie's—every day is spent working at the studio or at the Lentelli Foundry or, toward the end of this period, at the fairgrounds. In her car she crochets in order not to waste time!

Gertrude's schedule is so concentrated and strenuous that it is unlikely she would leave New York now, had she not made promises to Gloria and perhaps to Neily also. The plan is to spend a week in Miami with Neily, a week in Havana with Gloria's half sister Cathleen. Once again there are meals aboard Neily's yacht and drives around the Miami area, but this trip there is less, if any, reading. Gertrude, at sixty-four, is chaperoning a young lady of fifteen. They go to at least four movies, still Gloria's favorite entertainment—*Wuthering Heights*, *The Great Waltz*, and two unspecified. In Havana they see a lot of Cathleen, drive to the house Gertrude had previously rented, and lunch at the American Embassy. Except for three days aboard ship on the way home there seems to have been little rest.

Apr. 29, Sat.: Went to Fair at 12 [noon] with Mrs. Force. Stayed till 3 A.M. working over statue.

Apr. 30, Sun.: Opening of Fair. Did not go.

Gertrude is saving her strength. She has a busy month ahead—not sculpting now but its aftermath, the public side of her work.

May 4, *Peter Stuyvesant* is unveiled at the Netherlands Pavilion. Thomas J. Watson is again the principal speaker and says most of the things said previously at the Pierre luncheon. There are many words; many pictures taken of him with Gertrude; Grover Whalen; Dr. Alexander Loudon, the Dutch ambassador; J. J. Stuyvesant, a direct descendant of

Peter's brought over from the Netherlands for the occasion. The descendant pulls the unveiling cord while Miss Jeanne van Drooge sings the "Hymn of Thanks of the Netherlands." The sculpture appears stern but no more so than the people participating in the ceremony.

Three days after the *Stuyvesant* unveiling and three before the next public event—a dinner of the American Society of Painters, Sculptors and Gravers, prior to an exhibition which includes the model for *To the Morrow*—Gertrude, having been in Westbury for the weekend, writes:

> MAY 7, SUN.: Gloria feeling badly. Returned N.Y. Dr. St. Lawrence & Dr. Weeks met me at house at 10:30. Took her at once to Doctors' Hospital. Operated for appendicitis. Fine. Stayed hospital.

Except for the dinner on the tenth and a brief visit to Central Park on the twelfth to see the completed installation of the gates from her father's Fifth Avenue mansion placed now, at a cost to Gertrude of $15,000, at the entrance to the Conservatory Gardens (105th Street and Fifth Avenue), for the next ten days she dines almost every evening at the hospital.

> MAY 17, WED.: Came down with Gloria in ambulance to country. Glen Cove movie after dinner "The Castles."

> MAY 18, THURS.: Went to town. Dentist. Jab. Josh. Returned country. After dinner went to Fair. Colored fountain beautiful.

Thursday there is also a routine meeting of the museum's Executive Committee. Not until Gertrude knows that Gloria is well does she make detailed arrangements for the dedication, only a week away, of *To the Morrow*. She speaks to Frank Crocker about hiring the Terrace Club, a private club intended for the entertainment of VIPs visiting the fair, of which he is the managing director. On Tuesday the following telegram goes out to another one of Gertrude's long lists:

> WILL YOU COME TO SEE MY SCULPTURE "TO THE MORROW" IN PLACE AT TIMES SQUARE, WORLD'S FAIR, ON THURSDAY, MAY TWENTY-FIFTH, AT 3:30 AND JOIN ME AFTERWARDS AT TERRACE CLUB. PLEASE SEND ANSWER TO MY STUDIO, EIGHT WEST EIGHTH STREET, SO THAT I MAY SEND YOU TICKET OF ADMISSION.
>
> GERTRUDE V. WHITNEY

May 25, the weather is perfect. Gertrude's monumental image of tomorrow shimmers in the sunlight. And more perfect still is the last-minute cancellation of a Florence Crittenton Day celebration, permitting Mayor Fiorello La Guardia to become the principal speaker at the dedication of Gertrude's sculpture. He stands beside her, almost a head shorter, a small man exuding great warmth and vitality. He has spoken once previously today—at the dedication of the Argentine Pavilion—but now he speaks almost extemporaneously (he has, of course, seen the sculpture many times on many visits to the fair), saying that she has "caught the romance of flying . . . has united the motion, the vitality and the emotion of aviation. . . . In the creation of these two youthful, unarmed and unhelmeted figures lies the expression of the hope of all intelligent people that this new destroyer of time and distance, aviation, will be used only for the bringing about of peace in the future." Finally, indicating the three wings, the mayor, himself a wartime flier, expresses appreciation "on behalf of the fliers of the country."

Though La Guardia's interpretation of the sculpture is different from her own, Gertrude is delighted and applauds vigorously when he is through. She mentions that the inspiration for the piece had come as she "passed a book shop and noticed the title *Why Not Try the Sky?*" She is equally unpretentious when Ogden Hammond says that "The statue is a modern version of the *Winged Victory* and the third wing is the Wing of Tomorrow," replying that "it has no particular significance and is included principally to complete the design." Jo Davidson might have settled the matter—"Why shouldn't it have a third wing? Automobiles carry spare tires"—but interpretations, comments, fact pieces, and anecdotes continue to appear for weeks in papers throughout the United States and Canada, some accurate, some not, but all probably ground out by the publicity mills of the fair. Jo Davidson is quoted by the syndicated columnist Louis Sobol. An anonymous reporter quotes an official fair guide who says, "That's silver it's covered with. She did that to show that every cloud has a silver lining." Within a few days there's another story on the Canadian platinum the piece is actually covered with, "pounded to a thickness of 1/250,000th of an inch." The *Times,* which heads its first story "WINGS ON STATUE FOOL THE MAYOR," follows up with an editorial, asking, "Why shouldn't a great piece of sculpture produce a variety of impressions?" and answering "[The Mayor's] opinion is a compliment. A work of art may and should suggest thoughts and dreams that were not in the mind of its maker."

Besides *To the Morrow* and *Peter Stuyvesant,* Gertrude has two earlier pieces at the fair—*Devotion* of 1934, on exhibition at the Contemporary Arts Building; and the Arlington Fountain of 1910, in the Memorial Gardens. In June, given the context of the fair's ongoing publicity, each of these requires another dedication ceremony, more newspaper stories. Gertrude goes to the fair often—both officially and for pleasure. Not until late June, after the last of the dedication ceremonies and after Gloria has gone to California with her mother and Gladys has gone to Hungary, do the entries "Worked" and "Studio" appear in Gertrude's Line-A-Day. Now and for the rest of the year these appear sporadically. It is not clear what Gertrude is working on—possibly on small sculptures (*To the Morrow* is her last major work); possibly on further sketches for the Doctor's Memorial, which has not yet been abandoned; but more probably on short stories and plays; and surely on museum matters, particularly a major exhibition of Twentieth Century American Artists, intended to supplement the one at the fair.

June 30, Gertrude makes one last trip to the Lentelli Foundry, this time for fun—a cocktail party at which the crew gives her a chrome-plated miniature of *To the Morrow* for the radiator cap of her maroon Lincoln. The same day she writes a long letter to Gladys in Hungary, expressing great concern about her sister's safety as the European political situation worsens and then going on to "more happy things";

> . . . Sonny & Gee sailed [sic] on the Dixie Clipper Wed. at 3 [June 28—the first regularly scheduled passenger flight over the North Atlantic]. We saw them off—most exciting—22 passengers. Just under 24 hrs. later they were in Lisbon. . . . Barbie, Buz & family sail for Bermuda next Wed. on the Odyssey. Gloria (after a hectic trip to Hollywood) returns Monday. An interesting evening with Dorothy [Elmhirst], Beatrice & Michael [Straight]. Lovely voices, general interest in all artistic work. Another evening . . . with the Paul Hammonds and a Professor [Samuel Eliot] Morison. They are sailing over some of Columbus' old routes for the latter to write a new book on Columbus. . . .

For the moment Gladys plans to stay in Hungary. There she bases her hope for peace almost entirely on hope itself. She has heard a Goebbels speech on the radio which gave her "a scare, but no one seems to have thought anything of it." She has a Jewish dressmaker where she finds "all going on as usual . . . a very good season." She quotes Hitler as having said, "You can end a war with bread cards but you can't begin one with them," and concludes that "there is a very strong feeling among innumerable people that it isn't going to happen . . . a terribly strong feeling here for neutrality."

With distance, Gertrude is considerably more objective about the situation and yet, though she sends several letters and telegrams urging her sister to come home, she tries not to alarm her:

> I didn't send you another wire as I was thinking of doing, as I could get no more news except what the papers print and that you have and more too. Certainly people who were not worried before are more anxious, but many people are going abroad right now and planning for August trips. Even Roosevelt's mother is sailing soon.
>
> I have been mostly here in the country—working, seeing the family and a few friends, reading. Gloria came back yesterday but as it was [July] 4th and people around all day, we have not yet had a real talk. From my standpoint it was all pretty awful, I gather from Miss Walsh [a trained nurse who took care of Gloria] and the newspapers. A visit to Hearst & Marion Davies among other things!
>
> The family is beginning to separate—Flora & Cully off fishing Sun-

day next for three weeks—the Henry family off tonight for six weeks. As yet I have no plans and may decide to stay right on here. If this weather lasted it would be all right. Gloria has to start regular lessons and I am going to fill up as much of her time as possible. There are always beaches she can go to if it gets very hot. California is now out of the question and she has had a vacation. . . .

Gertrude does "stay right on" in Westbury, with occasional trips to New York, but now her life with Gloria becomes increasingly complicated. Where, during the custody case, the mother could, and did, accuse Gertrude of buying the child with gifts and luxurious surroundings, now Gertrude begins to feel that the mother is buying her back with a permissiveness that undermines Gertrude's strict discipline. It is one thing for a young lady to read about a rich man and his mistress, quite another to visit Hearst and Davies; one thing to be movie-struck, quite another to meet Hollywood stars and producers at the age of fifteen. From Gertrude's point of view, Gloria is becoming as unmanageable as her mother. A few days after Gloria's return from California, Gertrude writes a politic letter to Mrs. Keep, headmistress of Miss Porter's School:

I would have written you about Gloria as soon as your letter came except that when I received it our situation was so thoroughly confused that I did not know what to say.

I was very much distressed because you thought it best for Gloria not to go back to Farmington. I have felt all winter as I feel now that in spite of her having spent so much time in the infirmary and lost the last term, the whole influence and quality of the School as well as your personal touch had given her exactly what I had hoped for—a better comprehension of life and discipline than she had been able to grasp up to that time, by reason of her unusual circumstances. Also she gained companionship and a more understanding attitude towards girls of her own age.

At the moment when your letter came Gloria was in the throes of a number of warring interests. Her mother had arrived unexpectedly from abroad and the child was being pulled in various directions by the people whom I do not consider have her best interests at heart. As a result of those most distressing wire-pullings she told me that she wanted to go to school abroad next winter. Though I would not have insisted on her not going, had I been sure that this was not a passing fancy, I wanted to give her time to think it over from all sides and if possible come to the conclusion herself that she would be much happier at Farmington.

A hastily planned trip by Mrs. Vanderbilt took Gloria away almost immediately. The plan was to go to Catalina but they never got there and stayed in Hollywood for a month getting some rather unpleasant notoriety, from my standpoint.

You will easily understand that I did not want her decision to be made during that time so I delayed writing you until her return. I have been made very happy by her telling me that she would like to go back to Farmington. But I do not know of course how you feel about this, for I do understand how unsatisfactory in some ways last winter must have been for you.

Evidently Mrs. Keep does not feel sympathetic; Gertrude enrolls Gloria at the Mary C. Wheeler School in Providence.

Later in July, Gertrude writes again to her sister:

. . . I am really enjoying L[ong] I[sland]. It is a long time since I have been here for an extended period and the place is lovely, my studio paradise, and enough people around to have friends when I feel like it. Rollie came and stayed for a few days and is his old delightful self. Disagrees with almost everything that is said and has a real point of view of his own. He is pretty blind but, in no way that one can see, discontented or depressed. It's inspiring to see anyone with that kind of courage.

Sonny & Gee went to England, France, Ireland, Denmark, Sweden & Germany! Gee thought England jittery, France sure that trouble was coming but quiet, courageous and resigned. Germany she found absolutely calm & the least troubled. They stayed with Whitney [Straight] & got on *extremely* well. Sonny is working really hard on Pan American. Gee & I are thrilled about it. Harry [Payne Whitney II] has taken a job as a wireless something and is only going to get away now & then for a weekend. Do you suppose our children ever realize that the greatest pleasure we get out of them is their developing themselves? Each, of course, along his own bent, but seeking some kind of goal. Waste! That is what is so horrible and all these children belonging to us have such a wonderful inheritance. Look what you have done. Organized and made possible many constructive works and yourself—your music and what you stand for. I continually meet people who say "Your sister is one of the most marvelous women I know." And it's true. You stand for something and people recognize it. You have developed your talents, your brains, and you have the strength of your convictions. I wish I had half as much. You say I have accomplished something this winter. It's really not much. A certain artistic success which is cumulative. The museum I am very proud of, but without Mrs. Force it never could have been accomplished. Other things are largely a question of money.

I have re-read what I have written and it sounds discouraged. Maybe it is. I am coming to the conclusion that you have to make demands on people. That if you take a back seat you don't accomplish what you set out to do. Then people think you are weak and presume on it.

I did not start out to write this kind of letter—it just developed.

Tomorrow I am meeting the Mayor at the big new Aviation Port [eventually La Guardia Field]. He wants my Rainbow [*To the Morrow*], so it looks good, and Delano who is the architect of the Port & my good friend, I can't trust. He would get me out if he could. I suppose it is these things that discourage me.

My next letter will be more cheerful.

Gen. V. O'Ryan is stopping for me in a few minutes and we are going down to dine with Neily at Port Washington.

August 9, Gladys replies:

Dearest Sister,

Your letter really embarrasses me, for it is the exact reverse of the truth. You have done the big things, and stand out as no one else, and I have done the drudgery, following the line of least resistance, and getting really nowhere. There is not a person who is not filled with admiration and affection for you, while I have succeeded in antagonizing most of the people with whom I have to do. It is probably an over indulgence in criticism, an unfortunate way of saying things, which produces the opposite effect from that desired. . . .

You on the contrary never bear on anything unpleasant, and give everyone the feeling that you think them perfect, which is far nicer, and much more successful, on the honey rather than vinegar system. So that entirely aside from the tremendous accomplishments to your credit, you have filled a unique role among the people who have been fortunate enough to have you in their lives. No one could possibly deny this, and you must know that it is true.

Who is there in your sphere or any other who has risen to the top as you have against those odds? Not only in America, but anywhere, at the present time or any other? To do that and keep up with your, so to speak, inherited life as well, is an amazing feat. Of course you cannot help getting discouraged at times, especially when people are not quite up to appreciating what they owe you, but there must be many moments of compensation, when you cannot help knowing that you have made good to the nth degree. . . .

I wish we could stay on here for a while to see it through . . . but I suppose it is too risky. Although if things get bad, this won't probably be any worse than plenty of other places. . . .

If you had in all your life never been more than what you have been to me, that ought to be enough to make you entirely satisfied.

For the next few weeks Gertrude waits anxiously for Gladys' return:

Aug. 19, Sat.: Bad foreign news.

Aug. 20, Sun.: News of pact between Germany & Russia.

AUG. 24, THURS.: Listened radio most of day. Chamberlain, Halifax, etc. Roosevelt appeals to Italy to intercede. Pope speaks.

SEPT. 3, SUN.: War.

SEPT. 7, WED.: To town. Gladys & Bubbie [her youngest daughter] arrived from Canada.

There are several days of reunion between Gertrude, Gladys, and Neily and then Gertrude plunges back into that "cumulative" success about which she has written to her sister. The Twentieth Century Artists exhibition opens at the Whitney in newly modernized and enlarged galleries the evening of September 11 with a huge artists' party, followed the next day by a trustees' luncheon for about ninety, to which a few artists are invited (e.g., Georgia O'Keeffe, Paul Manship, Stuart Davis, Eugene Speicher, Leon Kroll) to join a representative group of men and women associated with the World's Fair, architecture, museums, art galleries, and the press.

The show contains 288 works, including yet another casting of Gertrude's Arlington Fountain as well as her mysterious 1913 "self-portrait" *Chinoise* and the 1935 *John*. At the luncheon, after greeting everyone, thanking the staff, establishing the relationship between this exhibition and the one at the fair, Gertrude says that because of the war in Europe she had considered canceling the luncheon.

". . . On second thought, however, we decided that it was also important to go forward in our own activities. For it is the business of everyone to keep on with their job. And now when there is at the back of our minds, all the time, one dread thought, we need more than ever to cling to the things of the spirit. In art man has always found the comfort and joy, relaxation and inspiration which helps to take away heartache. It is music, the rhythm of line, color, words, drama, which bring refreshment and which keep alive our trust in human nature and our belief in the future."

Gertrude's conviction that art must go on even in wartime is widely quoted in newspaper stories, editorials, and magazine articles, and the exhibition itself is more widely publicized than any since the opening of the museum. *Life*, then the most popular American publication, schedules a picture story (September 11) to coincide with the new exhibition. It is predictably headlined "THE WORLD'S WEALTHIEST SCULPTOR MODELS MONUMENTS IN HEROIC MOODS." The brief text presents Gertrude's economic, social, and art background, in that order, and then concludes:

. . . A leader in the fight for recognition of American artists, Mrs. Whitney capped her successful battle in 1931 by opening the Whitney Museum of American Art. The most important institution devoted to the work of American artists, it is the sculptor's own fine monument to herself.

The conclusion is one with which many other publications concur. One cannot compare the importance of *To the Morrow* or *Peter Stuyvesant* (both illustrated in *Life,* beside several earlier works) with that of the museum. It has, of course, influenced the history of American art more profoundly than has Gertrude's own work or, for that matter, the work of any single American artist. However, it can be argued that the museum is both strong and weak in the same ways as Gertrude's sculpture—strong in its hopefulness, generosity, and energetic Americanism; weak in its romanticism, permissiveness, and provincialism. Of the many reviews of the current exhibition—substantially, work from the permanent collection, as enlarged—Emily Genauer of the *World Telegram* comes closest to expressing the museum's ambivalent role and her own in response to that:

. . . It is—and we've never made a secret of that fact—our favorite museum in the city. And though every once in a while it shakes our faith a little with the announcement of completely unpredictable— or, if predictable (one does get, after several years, to know something of the private politics and predilections of institutions and individuals), still unjustifiable—purchases it has on the whole done a really enormous work in promoting American art and artists.

Genauer goes on to describe "the 200-odd paintings, water colors, drawings and prints" as "fairly representative." Then, as in the 1936 review of Gertrude's own sculpture, she probes nerves:

. . . But the sculpture section—and we feel so very badly about this because the museum's founder and president . . . is herself a sculptor, and not unnaturally it was to be expected that the museum would be singularly rich in work in this field—is, however, far, far below present standards.

She asks:

why the Whitney should purchase for its permanent collection two such oversized artistic nonentities as Arthur Lee's Rhythm and Ethiopian, or why it was necessary to purchase three pieces by the renowned Jo Davidson (one of them a large, lyric, pretty but utterly unindividual Female Torso and another a portrait of Cecil Howard making him look like a well-fed Roman senator), or why Mario Korbel's Female Torso, or S. F. Bilotti's A Model, were considered indispensable. . . . Not having been given an adequate answer [from Juliana Force], one must then resort to guessing. And among the thoughts that come to us is this: that possibly the very fact that the museum's president is a sculptor, and one who works in a highly competent but usually academic, decorative and unoriginal vein, is directly accountable for the kind of sculpture representation the Whitney Museum has.

Genauer's answer, even as "guessing," is inadequate too. Had she pursued the theme of "private politics and predilections," she might have come closer to the truth. Neither Gertrude's commitments nor Juliana Force's are programmatically aesthetic, but they are personal and not easily swayed by critics.

☙

Many times during this year Frank Crocker calls to Gertrude's attention the high cost of the second major renovation of the museum, combined with increased operating expenses there, in her MacDougal Alley Studio, and in her other homes and studios. And no doubt as her lawyer and closest financial adviser he emphasizes the need for a woman of her age to preserve estate liquidity. Perhaps they discuss the recently filed accounting of the estate of Gertrude's uncle Frederick W. Vanderbilt who, at his death in 1938, left $76,838,530 (an amount comparable with Gertrude's present worth) of which $41,272,109 has now gone to inheritance taxes. As they analyze Gertrude's situation it becomes apparent that 871 Fifth Avenue is her most disproportionate expense—she spends little time there since her New York life is centered in the Village, and besides, in Harry's will, it is to be torn down and sold after her death. Frank suggests that she buy the four-story private house immediately adjoining hers on Fifth Avenue, thus rounding out the property to a hundred feet on Fifth and two hundred on 68th Street, and then sell the enlarged, very desirable plot to an apartment-house builder.

September 25, Gertrude goes to look at two connected carriage houses at 58 and 60 Washington Mews, about a block from the museum and her studio, on a cobblestone alley as charming as MacDougal. She likes the property and during the next few weeks has many meetings with Frank, who works out the details for leasing it while enlarging and disposing of 871 Fifth Avenue. At the same time she has frequent meetings with Juliana Force regarding the decoration of 58–60 Washington Mews, and in Newport Gertrude authorizes the construction of a new studio to replace the one destroyed by the hurricane.

At the fair, at the museum, and now in Newport and Washington Mews, this is a year of construction. It ends with several letters between Gertrude and Park Commissioner Robert Moses concerning the retitled *Spirit of Flight* which she hopes will be shifted after the fair to the new municipal airport. November 24, Moses writes encouragingly:

> . . . We will also be glad to work with you, on the same basis as we did when you generously gave us the fence and gates from your father's house, in obtaining bids for you for the necessary pile foundation. I assume, of course, that you will take care of the actual fabrication of the statue in permanent form.

I am sending a copy of this letter to Mayor La Guardia, whose interest in the matter I appreciate, as well as to Mr. Delano.

Gertrude is at first unwilling to give the new airport a gift of the huge sculpture. She has Juliana Force meet with the commissioner's general superintendent. November 30, Moses writes again:

I am sorry that there was a misunderstanding on my part as to the ways and means of obtaining this statue permanently for the City. Since I wrote you last week I have found out from the WPA authorities that they are prepared to erect the foundation and the base, which of course simplifies the whole matter. I have also found out from the World's Fair that they own the statue at present and that they would be glad to give it to us. With these new developments the sole remaining question is that of permanency, and I am wondering whether there is some way that you can help us out in having the sculpture recast or refabricated in some permanent material?

Silence—at least through the end of the year. And silence, too, in Gertrude's Line-A-Day, which she discontinues with the entry:

Nov 20, Mon.: Lunch studio. New house. Rollie. Home Frank. Country.

≈ *1940*

Early in the new year Gertrude moves to Washington Mews. From there she continues her correspondence regarding *Spirit of Flight* with Robert Moses and other city officials, and by the beginning of April it looks as if a permanent version of the sculpture will be installed at what is now being called La Guardia Airport. However, probably by then Gertrude has agreed privately to pay for most, if not all, of the cost of the permanent casting. It is not difficult to read between the lines of Mayor La Guardia's announcement. He says, "the presentation has been made possible by a group of citizens and organizations, including Grover Whalen, Fair president; Frank Crocker, president of the Terrace Club; and Air Youth of America, Inc." Gertrude is also arranging for a duplicate of her *Peter Stuyvesant* to be erected in Curaçao. But despite obtaining these "cumulative" honors for herself, she is receiving many from others—in March, election as an associate of the National Academy of Design; in

April, the Medal of Honor of the National Sculpture Society and a radio interview as the "Woman of the Week" on General Electric's "Hour of Charm"; and in June, an honorary degree—her fourth—from Russell Sage College.

What she isn't receiving is new commissions—the relief of work into which she can throw herself at a time when both the large world and her private world seem to be falling apart. In less than a year the spirit of optimism symbolized by the New York World's Fair has vanished. Like almost everyone else in the city—and in the rest of the country too—Gertrude is avidly, anxiously, and helplessly reading morning and evening newspapers and listening to the radio as the British evacuate Dunkirk and as Paris falls to the Germans. As far as we know, she is no longer keeping a Line-A-Day but she does frequently scribble notes on current political events and sketch potential monuments on such themes as Victory, Freedom, and Liberty.

As to her private world, we know from questions about her health in letters from Gladys and others that Gertrude is not well and, from her own letters, that Neily may have had a stroke (his memory is wandering); that Josh is terminally ill; that Sonny's and Gee's marriage is breaking up; and that the relationship with Gloria is growing worse as "the child," now sixteen, is understandably eager for independence and Gertrude is, just as understandably, concerned about responsibilities as guardian. As several times in the past when she has been particularly troubled, Gertrude comforts herself by having her palms, handwriting, and stars read—this time by an Austro-Hungarian "analyst" introduced by Gladys.

But more comforting is a trip to Florida from mid-April to mid-May. There Gertrude stays for about a week at the Everglades Hotel in Miami, spending part of every day visiting Neily, part writing, and part looking for a place more private and quiet than the hotel, in which to write. Remembering the peacefulness of writing aboard the *Killoquah* in the Adirondacks, she charters a "barge houseboat yacht named *Shangri-La* . . . overall length of about 67 feet . . . outfitted as a houseboat of her size, type and accommodations . . . fully furnished, including china, linen, glass, and silverware" at $1,100 net (i.e., without operating expenses) for the month. Though the *Shangri-La* is considerably larger than the *Killoquah* and has several guest "staterooms," it is extremely modest compared with the yachts Gertrude has known. Yet, as with the *Killoquah* and Mac-Dougal Alley and Washington Mews and her studios in Newport, in Paris and, to a lesser extent, in Long Island (where the adjoining small garden teahouse satisfies the need), that very modesty and intimacy, plus close contact with nature, lift Gertrude's spirits and, more specifically, her consciousness of self rather than material surroundings. She writes to George Chamberlain from Miami:

It's heaven here as to weather. I am looking over the harbor, with a glimpse of sea beyond, and in the foreground a park spotted with palm trees—lovely. The tropics were made for me (not the real tropics of course). I've never been a cat (I hope) but I'm sure I feel the way it does when it's being stroked. Purr, purr.

My brother lives on a small boat just across the park. He has heart trouble and leads the life of a semi-invalid—doctor, and very little he can do. He is one of the most attractive men I have ever known, with a sense of humor that would delight you, and never a word of complaint, and what terrible suffering when he has attacks! I'm his favorite in the family. He'll be with me most of next summer as he was last, so you will meet him, I hope.

This is really a rather horrid place, but it has sky and water and palm trees, magnolia, bougainvillea and flowing vines so they couldn't spoil it entirely.

Gertrude's writing is going well. She completes enough short stories to invite George down to look at them and she begins now to investigate the possibility of studying with Helen Hull, the novelist teaching at Columbia whom she admires. Gertrude has her friend Alice Nicholas, who is in New York and is also interested in writing, get the information. She reports on two possibilities—an introductory course and an advanced one—and then Gertrude sends examples of her work to Miss Hull.

By the time Gertrude returns to New York there is an acknowledgment but no clear decision, and Gertrude asks her friend and former publisher Tim Coward to intercede. May 21 he writes:

I talked to Miss Hull today. On the whole she was flattering about your work and believed with time and practice you might easily make real progress. She would like to have you in the Seminar Class. . . .

Gertrude writes to George in New Jersey:

Miss Hull said that I had an original point of view in expressing the relationships between men and women. What do you think she meant by that? Perhaps she only thinks so because she is a spinster! . . . And I go in the seminar next Sept.

But how hard it is to do anything or take any interest in one's own life when such desperate things are happening, and the whole world seems crumbling away. In the last war I was able to do something. We may all have a chance of course. I suppose we will adjust ourselves to life and go back to our business, but at present I hang onto the radio and study maps.

The relationship with George becomes increasingly close. He has written in an earlier letter, "Part of the fascination is that I still don't know you and probably never will, which mixes the old charm of variety with the still older lure of exploration. Do you mind my wanting to explore you further?" Now she invites him to Florida for a visit and then writes Gladys that "he fits in perfectly. Everyone likes him. Of course it's wonderful for me. He has friends here and goes off for golf etc."

On their way back to New York they visit Marineland, a commercial aquarium, seventeen miles south of St. Augustine, founded by Sonny and his cousin, Adele's son Douglas Burden, who shows them around. At the porpoise tank, the three of them stand at adjoining portholes. In front of them two porpoises play and then mate. Douglas remembers hearing "Cousin Gertrude's naughtiest giggle" and then her remark, "Now I understand why Marineland is so popular."

By late spring Gertrude and George are visiting each other's country homes for stays of several days at a time, writing letters and verse to one another when they are apart, comparing manuscripts of work in progress, and considering collaboration on a war story. Their growing intimacy is apparent even in fragmentary correspondence. July 8 he writes from New Jersey:

> Do you recognise the paper? [Hers.] You also have a credit with me of $1.20 at backgammon! I have called you up several times at Washington Mews but have not felt like bothering you at the hospital [where probably Neily or Josh is a patient]. Poor girl, I am afraid you are having a very trying time and as long as you are bound to New York there is nothing I can do about it. I do hope things will break so you can come down for a few days' lazy rest and a word or two with poor Pete [his name in several "Pete and Penny" poems they write to each other]. I am making no dates after the weekend of the 12th until I hear from you. In the meantime I am working on the book and have written Jimmie Doolittle to send me an introduction to the Glenn Martin Co. to see a big bomber plane in case you want to do that bomb story with me. The idea is entirely yours and if you don't want to have me use it just say so, but I can still get the technical dope and hand it over to you. The Martin bombers are built at Baltimore, about 80 miles from here.
>
> I miss you terribly and am counting so much on seeing you soon.

⇋

In September, Gertrude begins the course in "Professional Writing"—a two-hour session, one evening a week—with Helen Hull, who is indeed, at the age of fifty-two, an experienced pro. She has come from a writing background and wanted to write all her life, has suffered many rejections until 1915 when her first short stories began to appear, and has since the publication of her first novel *Quest*, in 1922, published thirteen books of fiction, including dozens of short stories. She is a realist and believes that "imagination is the faculty of rearranging the known, of transmuting it into a new and sometimes wonderful piece of creation. Imagination is not, as some writers think, a rocket to a distant star." And yet she loves detective stories, a form in which perhaps "realism" has more to do with the market than with an aesthetic. In classroom discussions, in marginal notations, and in detailed analyses (often a typed page or more attached to each story), Miss Hull's criticism is accurate and helpful. She calls Gertrude's attention to clichés and unnatural or awkward dialogue, suggests ways of clarifying thoughts and character motivation, urges her constantly to rewrite, to probe deeper and present experience rather than describe or summarize it. However, despite the technical advance in Gertrude's work, there is perhaps not enough encouragement of her own voice, which becomes flatter and more vernacular, even if *theoretically*—only that—more popular and marketable.

Though writing is now—and will for the rest of Gertrude's life continue to be—her principal means of creative expression, there is no sharp or complete break with past interests. She continues to meet regularly with Juliana Force and Frank Crocker regarding exhibitions and acquisitions at the museum—a program which now costs about $100,000 a year. When Frank points out that by curtailing purchases the museum could operate without a deficit, he is told by the two women in a report prepared by them that they "feel that the prestige and influence, to say nothing of the reputation, of the Museum make such purchases imperative." He replies:

> Since there appears to be no way to materially increase our income without endangering our principal, and since Mrs. Whitney is our only source of capital, our problem is resolved into the one question: How can Mrs. Whitney finance the Museum's needs with the least possible sacrifice on her part?
>
> The suggestion is: That Mrs. Whitney select from the enormous list of tangible personal possessions which she owns, such as have no sentimental association or value, and present them to the Museum. This gift will be free of taxes, and once the title is vested in the Museum, the Trustees can take their time in selling the articles donated and gradually repay Mrs. Whitney the amount of her [previous] loan, and, if the gift is sufficiently extensive (no objection to jewelry), a fund can be provided for the purchase of securities which will produce an income sufficient to take care of the annual deficit of the Museum which the present high standard of its maintenance makes unavoidable.

The problem is easily resolved, for the time being, by the sale of Chemical Bank stock of no sentimental value. Relocating *Spirit of Flight* is more of a problem. The cost of steel and concrete is rising in what is becoming a war economy. It is estimated that the foundation and support for the monument (without the sculpture itself) will be about $50,000, and no money has come forth from the sponsoring "group of citizens and organizations" which has promised it to Mayor La Guardia. He, Commissioner Moses, and other politicians and bureaucrats are becoming understandably nervous. As so often, Gertrude asks Frank Crocker to help. October 23, he, Gertrude, and Mrs. Force have a morning meeting with the commissioner, after which Frank writes a long, thorough memorandum to Mrs. Force, first reviewing previous correspondence, then the present meeting:

> . . . the Commissioner did not say so but I inferred that the Mayor sought other appropriations which he considered more important, to the neglect of "Spirit of Flight" which he definitely told us the City would erect if Mrs. Whitney would do the casting. . . . Amazed and disappointed as I am at the Mayor's attitude (though perhaps I should not be since he has false-friended everyone who put him into office in opposition to the machine politicians whom he has now chosen as his bedfellows), I feel that we should not allow the perpetuation of this beautiful artistic conception of the influence of flying in our future life to fail because at the last minute Mayor La Guardia, its sponsor and admirer, let us down, and I shall be only too glad, with Mrs. Whitney's permission, to raise the funds necessary to insure the erection of the sculpture.

During November there are more meetings, more correspondence, terminating in an agreement between the mayor and Frank.

The lift Gertrude enjoys at this seeming conclusion is momentary. The relocation of the sculpture continues to be delayed—first by red tape and petty politics, then by war shortages—and the end of the year is filled with even more personal disappointments, none really unexpected but painful nevertheless. First of all, the relationship with Gloria is approaching the breaking point. Now almost seventeen and in her last year at Miss Wheeler's, Gloria is in love with Geoffrey Jones, a junior at Princeton. She writes to Gertrude frequently, wanting her aunt to intercede with the Court so that during the next year while she waits for Geoff to graduate she can have her own apartment with her grandmother, use her own money and, as she says, live in the world for a while before becoming Geoff's wife. Gertrude's reaction, in one of many replies, is predictable:

> . . . For a great many reasons I don't approve of the idea. I think you are in much too prominent a position, I am sure your mother would disapprove and you can have plenty of time living at home to think over all your problems. This—without putting in my own feelings which I think you know well enough for me not to have to repeat. As you say the time is short and to upset the court order

(even if it could be done) might bring down an avalanche of trouble on our heads.

Just by asking for an allowance from the court would mean that they would give you about the same amount I do, $300 a month, unless you specified what you wanted it for.

You will have your own home when you are younger than most girls. A girl in a different position from yours, with a grandmother in a different position—that would be another proposition. The world is still full of vindictive people—and whatever you say, darling, will [be heard?] in the world. If you wanted to go on trips with Nanny [Gloria's grandmother, Mrs. Morgan] that of course you could do, and you know I always try and make it easy for you to see a lot of her. Until the time you get married it is up to me to see that you are protected against evil tongues. I feel sure that G. agrees with me. Stories from Cal. are again appearing in the papers—lies and slander against your family on both sides. The dangers of another case are always hanging over our heads. That's in the background. In the foreground is your own life and, as I said, you are going to have your own home so soon now that for the good of everyone won't you try and see that if you were working and living home you could be getting all the things that you fundamentally want and not be putting yourself and everyone connected with you in a false position.

While she and Gloria are trying each other's patience, Gertrude must face another deep hurt. November 30, Josh Hartwell, recuperating from his long history of phlebitis, dies of a heart attack as he walks in gunning togs from the clubhouse to a nearby duck blind at the South Side Sportsmen's Club on Long Island. Gertrude's grief is private—there is nothing she can write to Josh's widow or to anyone else.

And finally, out of this period of Gertrude's life from which so little besides fiction survives, there is a touching letter to Sonny's wife, who is about to establish legal residence for three months in Florida for her divorce:

Dearest Gee,

Thanks for your remembrance on Xmas.

I have been so horribly unhappy about you and S. Today I got your letter. I'm glad you have a congenial friend to go with you to Hobe Sound.

I admire your courage and spirit. Keep it alive always. I can imagine what you've been through, for facing facts which one hasn't realized is horrible. I hoped all the time that you two would find a new basis on which to build.

I don't think I have to tell you, my dear, but I like to, that my affection for you is lasting and that I shall not forget your devotion to me.

When I come to Miami in Feb. to visit my brother I'd love to stop at Hobe Sound (not according to Hoyle) and you must come over and cheer him up.

Always affectionately,
Mama

⇐ *1941*

Gertrude is now writing "full time"—that is, what most writers would call full time: typically, four or five hours a day of concentrated work on the composition and revision of short stories, hours carefully guarded and separated from family, friends, and museum and other obligations. For the mechanical part of this work she now begins to use Helen Card, a secretary whom she has met through George Chamberlain. Many of the present stories, like a recent one about George, are of course based on characters and situations from Gertrude's life and, as in that story and so many others, the female characters almost always suggest aspects of Gertrude's experience and fantasy. However, whether because of George's influence or Helen Hull's or because of Gertrude's own desire to write something professional and publishable, she forces much of the material into "acceptably"—again, only *theoretically* that—"good stories," neutralizing authentic voice and vision. In other work—blatantly commercial love stories, detective stories, ghost stories, rural stories in which she attempts regional dialect—her voice is altogether lost, as is any concern about authenticity. Early in the year she writes to George:

We have four stories this semester. Mine so far have been:

I. An artist's struggle not to give in to fraud [probably a reworking of a story from the mid-thirties].

II. A woman's decision to take a married man as her lover, in spite of its difficulties, because she knows that they really love each other. [Josh Hartwell?]

III. Three Brothers and a Madonna. (The teaser loses out.)

As a contrast I want IV to be a mystery story & I have a plot, but it all hinges on one point. I wonder if it is possible. If not I won't spend time on it . . . .

While Gertrude is busily creating and revising her stories, she and Commissioner Moses agree to abandon further work on *Spirit of Flight* until "the emergency is over" as casting would require 12,000 pounds of aluminum, already in hand but more necessary "for defense purposes," for which it is released. At the same time, Dr. Lyle's St. Luke's memorial is "temporarily postponed," because many of the doctors involved with it have "already been called into the service." Yet even without shortages of men and materials, it is unlikely that Gertrude's health and flagging energy would have permitted her to work now with real concentration on sculpture as well as writing. The cough that has bothered her for years continues, complicated by an as yet incompletely diagnosed "heart condition." As Paul Chalfin writes during the winter, when Gertrude makes her annual visit to Neily, who is now sicker than ever, "It's a bad winter here [in Florida] for everyone. Everyone is ill, even I—such an oak on the list." But he is exactly the same age as Gertrude and only two years younger than Neily.

Near the end of the spring term at Columbia, Gertrude, having worked hard, if not always successfully, at writing dialogue, once again begins thinking about her play *The Hand*. In May she polishes it and sends it to Richard Myers, a neighbor in Westbury who has with his better-known partner, Richard Aldrich, then recently married to the actress Gertrude Lawrence, co-produced such hits as *My Dear Children* (starring John Barrymore) and Clare Boothe's *Margin for Error* (directed by Otto Preminger and starring him). Toward the end of the month Myers writes:

. . . You have done a fine job with the play. The story line is now, I should say, perfect. The interest and suspense mount as the story progresses. While away I had my partner Richard Aldrich read it, and he is also excited about it.

There is one important point however on which we both agree, and it is this. The dialogue is not right and will have to be gone over with a fine tooth comb. I might almost suggest that you employ a writer of talent and experience to supervise this. In my opinion, it would be very much worth your while as it is vital that the wording and effect of the "speeches" should be sharp, pungent, and to the point. There are many places in the script where this is needed, and it is most important.

In other words, I trust that you gather from this note, that I am definitely interested in your play for production, with this one reservation. If you agree, I should be happy to discuss it with you and perhaps be able to suggest two or three people who would be qualified to do this work with you.

Even before Myers can suggest the writers he has in mind, Flora recommends her friend Major Ronald Victor Courtenay Bodley, educated at Eton and Sandhurst, an officer of the King's Royal Rifles during World War I, and subsequently a great traveler in the Sahara, Asia, and the Pacific islands, the settings of many of his books, a single play, and the 1940 biography of his cousin Gertrude Bell, one of the creators, along with T. E. Lawrence and Sir Percy Cox, of Iraq. Flora has known him in France between her marriages, has corresponded with him about his books, and has seen him a few times since his arrival in New York. In addition to everything exciting and adventurous about the curriculum vitae of this ex-officer, seventeen years Gertrude's junior, Flora can assure her mother that he is very attractive (slim, blond, mustached), very charming, the sort of man with whom Gertrude would be comfortable and enjoy working. And besides he is available and needs money. Gertrude is convinced, and Flora arranges the introduction.

Gertrude and Major Bodley share perfect manners, great style, a romantic outlook; they hit it off immediately. By mid-June, after he has made at least two visits to Westbury, they have progressed from the salutations "Dear Mrs. Whitney" and "Dear Major Bodley" to "Dear Collaborator." Because of Sonny's third marriage (June 18, to Eleanor Searle, in Plymouth, Ohio) and the debutante party of Gladys' youngest daughter Nadine (July 12, Newport), the collaborators cannot begin work until July 15. From then until late August, Ronnie—he is Ronnie now and she is Gertrude—stays much of the time with her in Westbury, working on the play and in leisure hours taking her to see friends and bringing friends of his own down to meet her.

Helen Card types the script in final form, Gertrude and Ronnie reread it, and Ronnie leaves Westbury for New York to deliver it to his literary agent, Alan C. Collins of Curtis Brown. During the last week in August, Ronnie writes:

Dear Gertrude,

I do not think I have spent such a happy ten days as these last with you at Old Westbury. A writing collaboration is a great test to two people's friendship and, although my intuition assured me that I need have no qualms about ours, I hardly expected the complete harmony of thought which we found. But, apart from the work there was such pleasure in being with you and sharing your lovely sense of humor. I felt at home with you, in every sense of the word, and I feel equally homeless and lonely now that I am away. However, what is so attractive in the present outlook is that this, so pleasant, association can continue. As to contract, I will do whatever you like best. I prefer the 50/50 basis for everything, not so much from the point of view of remuneration (though with funds blocked at home this is of great im-

portance to me) but more from the work angle. With a contract of
⅓ or ¼, one somehow feels that this applies to collaboration. I
admit that in the case of "The Hand" you have done more than half
of the work but, if it goes to pictures, I shall catch up with you on the
screen adaptation. *Such thoughts should not come in* and that is why
I am sure that share and share alike, in everything, is the most satisfactory formula for contract. If, however, you do not agree, please say
so, as my main interest, "au fond," is to see the collaboration continue.

I have thought out the whole of the new play and have practically
all the details planned out which I will tell you when we meet on
[September] 28th. I feel satisfied that we have something good
and stageworthy. . . .

A week or so later Ronnie sends Gertrude a letter from Collins to him,
dated September 2:

Dear Bodley,

Here is what my reader said about the play: "The central idea of
this play, dealing with possession [i.e., by another person's spirit], is
not especially new, which is all right if something fresh can be given
to the treatment of it, or some good theatre or characterization can
be extracted from such a situation. But the playwright handles the
plot in a confused and rambling manner. The central situation is
projected by an artificial and extremely unconvincing device, the business of the grafting of a hand transforming an individual's personality, and the loose treatment is even more unconvincing. For a complete act the play is shrouded in an unnecessary fog of mystification
and one is forced to wonder what it is all about. The audience should
be let know right after his operation what has happened to Forrester's
change of personality and the plot should begin to pick up momentum. The epilogue is superfluous and anticlimactic, besides being a
bad scene."

As I told you, I found it unconvincing as a story and although I
don't set myself up as a technician at all, it doesn't have to me the
feel of a methodically written play. I agree with Berman, my reader,
that the epilogue is unnecessary. . . .

to which Ronnie adds:

Dear Gertrude

Here is the report. I don't know if you are accustomed to reader's
reports, but they are usually of this blasting nature. I feel, moreover,
that this one is going to help us a lot to make the play saleable. . . .

Although Gertrude and Ronnie have an idea for another play, they
spend much of the fall fussing with details of *The Hand,* seemingly una-

ble to recognize—as do many others, including Helen Card who is, like Ada Stevens, an aspiring writer as well as a stenographer—that its weakness is more fundamental than that. While revisions, submissions, and rejections of the play continue, Gertrude enrolls again in Helen Hull's class.

It is a gloomy time. Except for the first marriage of a grandchild—Pamela Tower's to Jay Ketcham Secor, December 20, in Aiken—there is little to rejoice about, and even that wedding must bring back many sad memories. Pam wears the heirloom veil of duchess lace worn by Gertrude's mother in 1867 and by Gertrude herself in 1896. There is that continuity but with it the reminder of Gertrude's parents' deaths, of Harry's, of his father's (a founder of this Aiken winter colony), of so many deaths over so many years. Pam is given in marriage by her father, Roderick Tower, and he, too, must remind Gertrude of what became a difficult and ultimately impossible marriage for Flora—a reminder of that divorce and, again, of so many others. But the darkest cloud of all hanging over this wedding is the war. That requires no reminders, but they are there—in absences, such as that of Sonny, who has enlisted in the air corps; as well as in presences such as Rod in his major's uniform and the groom, who is about to enlist in the army.

And there is another dark cloud, another imminent wedding, which Gertrude prefers not to think about but, nevertheless, surely does—that of Gloria, who is just as determined as at the end of 1940 to assert her independence by marrying. The decision seems that abstract: her prospective husband has by now changed several times since Geoffrey Jones. In *Double Exposure*, Gloria's mother summarizes her daughter's adventures after leaving Miss Wheeler's and joining her in California. At first "Gloria had a telephone installed in her bathroom. Lying in luxury in her bubble bath, she would call her friends in New York—or Princeton—and talk for hours. In one month alone she had a phone bill of $900." As she sees more and more of the Hollywood community the calls to New York, and especially to Princeton, dwindle. By early September the current issue of the revived but vulgarized *Smart Set* features Cholly Knickerbocker's "THE STORY BEHIND GLORIA VANDERBILT'S ROMANCE: She's not yet staged her social debut, but still . . . She's already taught wealthy young Geoffrey Jones how to sing a torch song. . . . She knows why Pat Di Cicco, Hollywood dancer from the wrong side of the tracks, dances on air these days. . . . And she's the reason why her guardian Gertrude Vanderbilt Whitney, chafes under a barrage of hated publicity. . . . But Gloria Vanderbilt knows her own mind, and she's a girl to follow wherever her heart may lead! . . . as exciting a drama of the Smart Set as you'll read this year!"

In *Double Exposure*, Mrs. Vanderbilt doesn't get to Pat Di Cicco that quickly. She writes, "One night Gloria came into my room and announced that she wanted to get into bed with me. In my bed, in the dark, she said, 'Mummy, I'm not in love with Geoff any more—I'm in love with Van

Heflin and I'm going to marry him.'" The relationship with the actor lasts about a month, provoking so many items in society columns that Gertrude hires a private detective agency to report to her. However, by the time rumors are confirmed, Gloria is in love with someone else—Howard Hughes, the dashing millionaire (later, billionaire)/flyer/motion picture producer, mysterious even at the age of thirty-six (more than twice Gloria's age). Mrs. Vanderbilt says, "he never lets go of his hat. The butler made the usual effort . . . but he said, 'Oh, no!' and strode into the drawing room with his hat firmly in his hands. . . . There is an old Russian folk tale about a magician whose soul is contained in an egg; Howard behaves as if his were boxed in his hat." They discuss wedding plans and Hughes says they "are entirely up to Gloria. Whatever she wanted was agreeable to him. After Howard left, I asked Gloria if she had written Mrs. Whitney about her engagement. Gloria told me that she had. She added that Howard intended to be in New York in a few days, and that she would like to be there at the same time, to introduce him to 'Auntie Ger.'"

Gloria and her mother fly to New York, bringing a great deal of baggage including Gloria's phonograph and a collection of recent hit records (possibly "Bewitched, Bothered, and Bewildered"; "I Don't Want to Set the World on Fire"; "I Got It Bad and That Ain't Good"; and dozens of other torch songs of the type she had been teaching Geoff Jones to sing). According to her mother, Gloria immediately tells Gertrude "the happy tidings." Though Mrs. Vanderbilt says she "never learned what Mrs. Whitney thought of the marriage," it is not hard to guess—this is the third announcement since summer; like the previous ones, it will become academic. Within a few days Gloria tells her mother she must go to Chicago at once.

"Why? Isn't Howard expected?"

"This has nothing to do with Howard. I want to see Pat."

As Mrs. Vanderbilt continues, "There are limits to the understanding even of a worldly and sympathetic mother." She has known Pasquale ("Pat")Di Cicco as "a pleasant young man who in one vague way or another seemed to be running interference for Hughes." That impression is understandable: he is an actors' agent who has worked with Hughes and is, like him, tall, dark, handsome—and almost the same age (thirty-two). There the resemblance ends. As Cholly Knickerbocker has said, writing from the viewpoint of Café Society, Pat is "from the wrong side of the tracks," Knickerbocker's own side. And as Knickerbocker knows—like Mrs. Vanderbilt, Gloria, Gertrude, everyone who reads society columns—Pat is the son of an Italian immigrant who came to New York in the eighties, established a large-scale truck farm in Queens, and was known, before his death in 1924, as the "Broccoli King." Everyone also knows that Pat has no "real money," that he started his career as an exhibition dancer, and that he was once married to Thelma Todd, a motion picture actress who died, after their divorce, in an unsolved murder at her Hollywood home in 1935.

For once (in these later years) Mrs. Vanderbilt doesn't give in immediately to Gloria's whim. They stay on in New York, Howard Hughes arrives, he and Gloria break up, and Pat arrives. From then on her mother "saw practically nothing of Gloria; she was always out." In November, Gloria tells her she is going to marry Pat.

"You'd better tell your aunt."

Gloria does. "Apparently all hell broke loose, because Gloria came dashing to my room and said, 'Mummy, I want to go right back to California. . . . Auntie Ger doesn't approve at all. But I don't care what she says. After all you are my mother. You have the right to let me marry him."

Mrs. Vanderbilt arranges a meeting with Frank Crocker, who has been kept informed. (Indeed, Gertrude writes a story at about this time called "Mr. Drummond's Client" which clearly shows how completely and continuously informed Eliza Hemingway, the client, a rich widow, keeps Nat Drummond, a lawyer who resembles Frank.) Frank says that Gertrude will not under any circumstances approve of the marriage and that, if Mrs. Vanderbilt approves, it is her own affair.

By the end of November, Gloria has not only persuaded her mother that she must marry Pat but that she cannot wait until her eighteenth birthday in February. Mother and daughter return to Los Angeles to make wedding plans. Though they live in Beverly Hills, Gloria insists on a nuptial mass at the Mission of Santa Barbara—a drive, for most of the guests, of about ninety miles up the coast—but, as Mrs. Vanderbilt reports wearily and resignedly, "possibly . . . more romantic, with the Mission as a stage prop and the ocean nearby, pounding on the rocks." Gloria also wants the wedding to be Christmas Day, but when that can't be arranged she settles for December 28. And finally (as far as Mrs. Vanderbilt reveals), Gloria insists that her childhood nurse Emma Keislich be invited. Facing the most savage of her custody case critics is almost too much for Mrs. Vanderbilt, but once again she goes along with her daughter, "not want[ing] to mar any part of Gloria's happiness on her wedding day." (The happiness of Mrs. Vanderbilt's brother Harry will be marred. Because of Nurse Keislich, he refuses to come to the wedding.)

December 3, Gloria writes a letter from Los Angeles to "Dearest Aunty Ger," telling her about the new happiness with Pat, a love she has never felt before, a love that is *"right"* (her own emphasis). She says that they are coming east the following week, that she wants Gertrude to meet Pat and know him as she does and share their happiness. She knows that Gertrude is "fair" and that, after really meeting Pat, her "prejudices" will be overcome. Finally, she says she will call before they arrive and meanwhile sends all her love.

We can only guess at what that call was like. We do know that Gloria, Pat, and her mother arrive in New York and that, December 11, four days after the bombing of Pearl Harbor, their engagement is announced to the press by Mrs. Vanderbilt before a small dinner at El Morocco. However, two and a half weeks later at Santa Barbara, a thousand glamor-struck fans gather in the mission yard, waiting for glimpses of "the best known of the nation's poor little rich girls" and of such Hollywood stars as Bruce Cabot (Pat's best man) and Errol Flynn (an usher).

All of Gloria's publicity—in which Gertrude's name inevitably appears often—is painful enough to Gertrude, but the year ends with a final cloud darkening her life and her life's work, a literal cloud within the context of the larger clouds of war. The Germans—who have occupied St. Nazaire and use it as a submarine base—are, once the United States enters the war, especially galled by Gertrude's monument to Franco-American friendship. December 13, they build a scaffold halfway up the monument's base, drill into it, and load it with dynamite. The first charge destroys part of the granite shaft supporting the sculpture, which continues to stand. A second charge likewise fails to destroy the sculpture itself. "On the third attempt," according to the official French account, "the bronze sculpture made a fantastic leap up into low clouds and winter haze above the flash and took on the impressive aspect of a legendary eagle carrying on its back a sort of celestial divinity brandishing a cross." The New York *Times* states more flatly (and accurately, judging by photographs), "The third attempt severed the shaft a few yards from its base, toppling the statue."

⇜ 1942

Gertrude quietly spends the holidays until January 7, at Joye Cottage, the old Whitney home in Aiken, with the Millers and the Henrys, enjoying being with her children and grandchildren but partially occupied by various things happening in New York, all of which suggest "intimations of mortality"—her own, that of the museum, that of *The Hand,* and that of 871 Fifth Avenue. This home is now unstaffed except for caretakers, and Gertrude has been stripping it since late December, giving substantial gifts of art, furniture, china, and silverware to her children, before scheduling the auction—at Parke-Bernet, in April of this year—of remaining furnishings.

She has also been having informal discussions with Juliana Force about the future of the museum, expressing the hope that perhaps by consolidation with another institution, less personal but with more public support—a larger board, a greater endowment, and so forth—hers may survive. Near the end of the past year Royal Cortissoz has written:

> . . . when I was calling upon Juliana she told me—in confidence which, knowing me, you will know I will respect—about the idea that had been broached concerning the Whitney. I mean the idea of it being affiliated with either the Metropolitan or the Modern Museum. Dear Mrs. Whitney, I cannot forbear begging you *not* to entertain such fanfaronade [?]. The Whitney has its own roots, its own traditions, and must continue to stand upon its own feet. Let the beautiful work that you and Juliana have been doing go on under your own banner. The Whitney is not so much a museum as it is a studio, with a character, a personality, which must never be changed. You know how I sympathize with it. I would hate to see its individuality lost. I hope I don't seem intrusive to you. Just think of this letter as simply coming from your friend.

Despite this and probably some resistance from Juliana, though assured from the start that the independence of her position and that of other staff members will be protected, discussions of a merger have continued with Juliana and then with Frank and later between them and representatives of the two museums, culminating in a preference for the Metropolitan. It is no accident that at the end of November the lawyer and philanthropist William Church Osborn, then president of that institution, has asked Gertrude to join the board. Nor is it an accident that her reply

> I recognize deeply the honor which you have extended to me, but one fact—that I am president of a museum which has a very definite aim—together with the fact of being occupied with my own profession as a sculptor, firmly convinces me that I must decline to accept.

provokes still further overtures. The declination has been acknowledged by Osborn in a letter of December 8, 1941, which ends, "I trust that you will not hesitate to make such suggestions to us as you may think will forward the purposes of the Museum."

This dialogue continues. Meanwhile, since arriving in Aiken, there is another, also in letters, whch drags on. Before leaving Westbury, Gertrude has been convinced by Ronnie Bodley that *The Hand* can only be saved by buying the talent of John Colton, a highly professional playwright and film scenarist, best known for his work (with Clemence Randolph) on the 1922 production of *Rain*, based on Somerset Maugham's story. He is clearly someone who is used to multiple collaboration. Since Gertrude's departure he and Ronnie have been living at Westbury while working on the play and feeding revisions to Helen Card. Ronnie reports:

> I have never seen a man work so long or so hard as Jack Colton. He is at his desk from 8:30 A.M. till 11 P.M. without moving except to eat.

Wrapped in a scarlet lined kimono he sits at the big table in the drawing room continuously while I remain opposite him, save for my exercise necessary to my clear headedness. I think that Harold [the butler] is shocked at having to wait at meals on one garbed in the robe of the Rising Sun, which he also considers to be a dressing gown, and I am rather sadistically amused by that inimitable British reticence or flinching from the unconventional. But we have done excellent work, kimonos or no kimonos.

The rest of the letter describes changes they have made. January 7, when Gertrude leaves Aiken to be with Neily in Miami, more changes follow her there, along with reactions to the new version from the producer Alfred de Liagre and an agent named Miss Howell. They think that the play is now too macabre, too grim, and Ronnie explains that "it was Colton who brought out all the horror and emphasized it." However, he continues blithely:

. . . On the whole none of this is very discouraging. Rather exciting, I might say for, while we have nothing but praise about the *writing* of the play, we have shocked a hard boiled business woman and an intelligent producer. A little more work, only a little, and we might so shock Broadway that this play might be the hit of the century. Anyway I am going on with this play until I get it produced and I feel sure you will be with me in this. . . . I am more than ever convinced that we have in "The Hand" a valuable piece of property and it needs someone bigger and bolder than a small producer to put it on.

One marvels at Gertrude's patience and wonders what *The Hand* can still mean to her. Like the hand in the play, it belongs by now to someone else, it is a grafting over which she has no control. Besides, Gertrude has other things on her mind, mainly Neily, who is very, very sick. While staying at the Everglades, she spends her sixty-seventh birthday and much of the following month with him, using her free time to write short stories, some explicitly gloomy, some implicitly so but forced into plots which are neater and more cheerful than life. Only one truly optimistic document survives from this period. It is the draft of a telegram to Paul Chalfin in Fort Lauderdale:

AM MAKING SELECTIONS OF SOME OF MY THINGS FROM SIXTY EIGHTH STREET HOUSE WITH WHICH TO FURNISH MY STUDIO IN THE COUNTRY. SHALL NOT MOVE THEM TILL LATER BUT WOULD LIKE TO MAKE CHOICE WITHIN TWO WEEKS. CAN YOU COME NORTH AND HELP ME. HOPE YOU CAN MANAGE IT.

Paul replies, first by telegraph, then in a letter:

I have just wired you, my dear, to say I can come, and that it gives me pleasure to, but what at the moment counts for much more is that I hear from you. I've been worried uncommonly about you. You know the periods of depression you've sometimes had have been also periods of silence, and I have been anxious lest this silence of now months might also cover a time of a like sort. . . .

I'll have much to tell you—all rather good as regards my fortunes. I'm only bored. It is dreadful here [Fort Lauderdale]—empty and shallowed off into countless coctkail lounges and pitiful efforts at exclusive luxury. It needs a wiping up—perhaps all over the country. Anyhow there's nothing for me in it. So. Let's go!

When Gertrude returns to New York in February, she does see Paul at least once at Washington Mews and once at 871 Fifth but, though these appointments with her old friend are cheering, they are inconsequential compared with many she has with doctors, with Frank Crocker, with Juliana Force, and even with Ronnie Bodley. With Frank, in addition to more or less routine legal matters, there is an appeal to take care of from the American wife (since 1928) of Gertrude's old friend Mario Guardabassi, now seventy-five. He has been arrested as an "enemy alien" by the FBI at the Guardabassis' winter home in Tucson, Arizona, and then imprisoned in the Alien Detention Camp at Fort Bliss, Texas. As Mrs. Guardabassi writes, "He may be an 'alien' but he is not an 'enemy.'" Without hesitation Gertrude writes a strong and unequivocal statement regarding her association with Count Guardabassi since "around the year 1912," his "affectionate regard" for the United States, and his "honor and integrity," all of which Frank translates into a sworn affidavit. Later in the month, at the request of Mrs. Guardabassi, Gertrude writes an equally strong letter to Attorney General Francis Biddle, but Guardabassi will not be released until September 20, 1944. With Juliana there are many discussions about the current and well-received "History of American Watercolor Painting" as well as the important exhibitions planned for the rest of the season— "Between Two Wars: Prints by American Artists, 1914-41"; "Contemporary American Sculpture and Sculptors' Drawings"; "Power of American Buildings: Drawings by Hugh Ferriss"; and an Artists for Victory Sculpture Competition. And with Ronnie the revisions to *The Hand* continue along with his reports on the reactions of outside readers—for example:

> . . . I feel too that our characters are not as pleasant as they might be. Mrs. Clarence Day said something to me last Sunday about characterization (quite in the abstract) which gave me food for thought. Incidentally, she partakes entirely now in all the Lindsay & Crouse productions and will be interested to read "The Hand." It took her 2½ yrs. to get "Life with Father" right, but she has just refused a $600,000 film offer for the rights from Goldwyn and expects to sell at the million mark. I will repeat her advice when we meet.

One meeting, perhaps the one referred to in Ronnie's letter, is for the weekend of February 28 in Westbury, to which Gertrude has invited him and the Russian-born pianist Prince George Chavchavadze and his wife. Late that Saturday afternoon Gertrude receives a call from Neily's doctors in Miami saying that he has had a cerebral hemorrhage along with cardiac complications and that they have little hope for his recovery. Having been told that there are no seats on the evening flight, Gertrude nevertheless drives out to the airport and gets one.

On the flight down, despite the opinion of Neily's doctors, she remembers his "wonderful recuperative capacity" and the way he "had come out of several previous attacks," so she is "not without any hope." In Miami, aboard the 100-foot *Ambassadress*, the yacht he has rented this season, Neily, in an oxygen tent, is attended by two doctors and three nurses. After Gertrude's arrival—but before that of Grace, their son and daughter, and Gladys—Neily regains consciousness only once and laughs and talks for a moment. From then on, except for the awful strain of breathing, he is silent until Sunday evening at six when his heart stops beating. "At least," as Gertrude writes to a dear friend of Neily's (along with the other details here), "he had no more to suffer and he died perfectly peacefully."

The newspapers give General Vanderbilt long obituaries, presenting some details of his death and long illness; the saga of his courtship and marriage to Grace; "the good offices of his sister Gertrude" in effecting his partial reconciliation with their parents; the thirty or so inventions he has made or sponsored for the improvement of the locomotive; the royalty his wife and he (mostly she) have entertained; his service as a colonel and then a general in World War I; the score of corporate directorships and another score of club memberships he has held; and the recent sale (like Gertrude's, in anticipation of death) of his Fifth Avenue home.

Gertrude makes the arrangements (and pays the bill, $2,705) for the transportation of his body by private railroad car from Florida to New York. The funeral service is held, March 5, at their mother's last church, St. Thomas' Episcopal. There, about a thousand of Neily's friends and associates—familial, social, corporate, and military—crowd the church, while several hundred strangers wait on 53rd Street to watch the flag-draped coffin leave the side door of the church on its way to the Vanderbilt mausoleum in New Dorp.

Gertrude seems never to have recovered from the death of her last brother. It is a terrible blow to her already weakened body and spirit. During the rest of March she sees few people, mostly her sister and children, and as so many times before she spends much of her time responding to condolence letters. During these weeks there are also many letters and cards from Ronnie, sympathetic and attentive to her in her distress, yet still full of reports on Broadway and Hollywood possibilities for *The Hand*, probably offered with the hope that they will distract and encourage her. But nothing does.

Though her personal physician, Dr. Richards, believes that all Gertrude needs is rest in Westbury, she remains terribly thin and is coughing badly. Finally Flora lectures her about her health, insists that she see another doctor, and selects a Dr. Hinton, a surgeon specializing in gastrointestinal disorders. There is the usual feeling of awkwardness about calling in another doctor but Dr. Richards makes no objection except to recommend that she also see her heart specialist, Dr. Levy. His report is so negative that the three doctors together decide that nothing can be done about Gertrude's other problems until the heart condition is under control; they send her to New York Hospital for a week's rest. On Tuesday, April 7, Gertrude is admitted to the hospital for a general checkup, and on Thursday, Gladys takes a room there to keep her company. There is as yet no indication that Gertrude's condition is critical. Gladys is with her almost all the time, Barbie visits frequently, Flora is sufficiently reassured to go to Aiken, and even Ronnie and a producer interested in *The Hand* meet with her Saturday afternoon. That night she is tired, and the next afternoon she has difficulty breathing. The doctors have another consultation but are now so optimistic about Gertrude's recovery that Gladys returns to Washington. However, as she herself says, she does this mostly to show her sister how satisfied she is with her improvement. Gladys calls several times from Washington and then returns to New York the next day.

During this first week in the hospital Gertrude has been given a great deal of special medication, many lab tests, an electrocardiogram and, no doubt if she were still keeping a Line-A-Day, there would be a record of much "jabbing." But basically the procedures appear to have been routine. By Wednesday all that changes. Special nurses are put on the case, cardiograms become more frequent, X rays and unspecified therapy and infusions begin. Her condition has been diagnosed as bacterial endocarditis, an infection of the heart valves which causes fatal clotting.

Gladys, who has been in constant communication with Flora—Sonny is in India as a major in the air corps—tells her now that she is really worried. Flora speaks to the doctors, who are more reassuring, but she still decides to return from Aiken with Cully the next morning. They arrive at the hospital early but do not visit Gertrude until evening for fear of worrying her, especially since, as Gladys and the doctors report, she is having a better day. Although she is hardly eating and is very weak, she jokes with an intern making his normal round and she listens to the radio for a while. Flora leaves, and Gladys believes Gertrude is better and goes to bed happy. However, at three-thirty in the morning the intern calls her at Dr. Richards' request to say a clot has gone into the upper part of her arm. The doctors confer, decide that an operation to remove the clot is out of the question, and attempt reviving circulation by using suction. Identifying strongly with her sister, Gladys watches in a state of near shock as they place Gertrude's arm in a glass vacuum case, start the pump and give her shot after shot of morphine. Gradually during the morning the arm responds but her general condition grows worse and worse. When Flora arrives at the hospital Gertrude looks weak and can hardly talk. The change from the previous day is terrifying. Flora stays with her mother that night and into the early hours of the following morning, when Gertrude opens her eyes, tries to speak, but can't. Though in one form or another she has written "last words" throughout her life, there are none now. Gertrude dies 2:50 A.M. Saturday, April 18.

Despite the hour of death, her obituaries in the morning papers are as long as Neily's a month and a half before. Indeed, without the arbitrary measurement of column inches, it can be argued that she, more than he, more than any of her other brothers, more than any other Vanderbilt of her generation, has best represented the dynamic and competitive tradition established by Commodore Vanderbilt a century before. Except for the material contained in Gertrude's private and pseudonymous writing, the obituaries recite what we know—her wrong birth date (i.e., 1877) which she has made official; her career as a sculptor and her major commissions in that field; her patronage of American art, culminating in the founding of the Whitney Museum; her marriage to Harry, and her family and social ties, including a lengthy account of the Gloria Vanderbilt custody case; her establishment of the hospital at Juilly during World War I and her many other benefactions. There are brief references to and quotations from published articles, speeches, and statements which reinforce the image of a somewhat fragmented public life devoted largely to art, a life which could only be made coherent by the use of then unknown material, the personal writings that convert public specialization into a richer private complexity.

Gertrude's body is taken to Washington Mews where during all of Saturday and Sunday dozens of relatives and friends congregate to express their love and respect. Outside of the immediate family, none seem more crushed by her death than Juliana Force and Gertrude's personal maid Hortense. They weep freely, expressing their emotion more openly than is permitted by Vanderbilt standards of control. Even Flora, whom Gladys describes as "completely broken" is able to arrange for Salvatore Bilotti to make a cast of her mother's right hand.

The next day Gertrude's funeral, like Harry's almost twelve years earlier, fills St. Bartholomew's to its capacity of about 1,200. As at his funeral, well over a hundred members of the Whitney and Vanderbilt families attend, but in a dozen years this group, seated to the left of the flower-covered coffin, has changed—decimated by death and the absence of so many serving in the armed forces, and replaced by many grandchildren, nieces and nephews who have grown up. Just at eleven-thirty the last family member to arrive at the service is Gloria Di Cicco. The front pews to the right of the coffin are reserved for artists and the representatives of museums and other institutions and organizations with whom Gertrude has dealt professionally and/or philanthropically. Juliana Force, Hermon More, and Lloyd Goodrich are there along with many of the artists they have shown including Jo Davidson (remarried the previous year to Florence Lucius in Venezuela where he has been sculpting the heads of political and military leaders), Eugene Speicher (who has already written a letter to the *Herald Tribune,* accurately stating that Mrs. Whitney has been the "most valued single patron and devoted friend" of the American artist), and too many others to list. With them are representatives of the Metropolitan, Modern, Brooklyn, Natural History, and City of New York museums, the National Academy of Design, the Netherland-America Foundation, physicians and nurses who served at the hospital in Juilly and, again, too many others to list.

The service is simple, lasting about half an hour. Dr. George P. T. Sargent reads the fourteenth chapter of the Gospel of St. John and the Twenty-third Psalm. The choir sings "I Heard a Voice," "Fight the Good Fight," and "Hark, Hark, My Soul." And then the funeral cortege proceeds up Park Avenue to Woodlawn Cemetery where Gertrude is buried beside Harry.

~

A life like Gertrude's doesn't end at the grave. Themes, rhythms, melodies linger—in the museum and sculpture she created, in the family and circle of friends to which she was devoted, in the vast wealth and property she inherited and accumulated. All this has an energy which flows on.

Hortense gives Frank the only papers found posthumously in her mistress' handbag. (*"Lettres et papiers qui étaient dans le sac-à-main de Madame,"* she writes on the envelope.) All of these concern a memorial fund being established for Josh Hartwell by the New York Academy of Medicine, of which he was president from 1929 to 1933 and a director until his death. A draft of a letter of solicitation emphasizes his interest in the library, observes that it "would furnish a splendid setting for a bronze bust of Dr. Hartwell recently done by Jo Davidson [which it presently does]," and notes that such a new memorial room would cost about $50,000.

Two days after the funeral Juliana Force meets with Frank Crocker to discuss an ambitious memorial exhibition of Gertrude's sculpture at the museum, a show far larger than those held elsewhere during her lifetime—ultimately sixty-four pieces, including studies for the major monuments.

~

Editorials, belated obituaries, institutional board resolutions, tributes of all kinds continue to be written for weeks and months after Gertrude's death, many of them by critics such as Helen Appleton Read, Royal Cortissoz, and Henry McBride, who have closely observed her over the years. McBride's "Hail and Farewell" (New York *Sun*, April 24) appears comparatively soon and is typical:

Gertrude Whitney was an artist by vocation and at the same time, by an accident of fate, a very rich woman; but she solved the problems attached to both phases of her career with singular success. Spectacular riches, especially here in America, present so many hazards to character that not all who have been tried in that way have surmounted the test; and the possession of what is known as the artistic temperament is almost as fatal to good citizenship.

But Gertrude Whitney was a good citizen. The mere fact that she chose to be an artist seemed at first, to certain conventional bigots, as a betrayal of the class into which she was born, but as she went resolutely on with the work she had chosen to do, it became apparent that the career of a sculptor, as she understood it, did not necessarily raise any barriers to family life nor entail any separation from her old friends nor, in fact, negate in any way the "noblesse oblige" of her position. On the contrary it raised it to new heights.

For Gertrude Whitney was an artist, and something more. The frank delight she took in her sculpture and her acceptance on equal terms by the leading artists of the day was a pleasant thing to observe. The work itself was a constant surprise, both to laymen and the profession, and chiefly because of the astonishing range of her interests. The first one that attracted me especially was her statue to Buffalo Bill, which was a venture into pure Americanism at a time when the bulk of our men were still looking to Paris for inspiration; and it had its effect in calling attention to our great Mid-West and its traditions.

Then came the lofty monument that rose above the waters of St. Nazaire harbor to commemorate the landing spot in France of our soldiers in that other war, and this was followed by the equally daring memorial at Palos, Spain, to mark the point of departure from the old world of Columbus. Both these startling enterprises testified to a cosmopolitan, wide-world vision that linked the artist, in the public mind, to Bartholdi [the French sculptor, 1834–1904, of the Statue of Liberty]. In both cases the gesture, like his, was that of world friendliness.

But Mrs. Whitney, as I have said, was an artist and something more. It was not enough to put her thoughts into concrete, stone and bronze, she wished the entire country to share her pleasure in the arts, and from the moment of her first emergence into public life she began a system of philanthropies that finally placed the entire country in her debt. It is not an exaggeration to say that there is not a contemporary artist of note in America who has not been helped by her. Her collection contains something by all of them, and it is constantly growing. Although I was probably its most jealous critic, due to my high ambitions for it, I never detected any arbitrary leanings on Mrs. Whitney's part, toward any special schools. She was completely liberal, completely open-minded and never demanding. Life to her, apparently, was an uncharted stream, and the artist-explorers upon it who returned with what John Masefield called "cargoes" were gratefully received "and no questions asked."

When her collection finally crystallized into the Whitney Museum of American Art it was definitely felt in all our art circles that at last we were on our own, that we had cut loose from the apron-strings of Europe and had become adult. It is still too soon to measure its contribution. These recent years since its establishment have been lean years. Just at present we have a war on our hands and pictures and statues are not so much in our thoughts as they used to be, and somehow a chapter in life seems to have been closed. But some day the book will be re-opened, life will be resumed at the old stand, our present story will be found interesting and Gertrude Whitney will be a shining figure in it.

≈

Gertrude's will—dated June 11, 1938, when she was hard at work on *Spirit of Flight*—is made public May 4. The estate, estimated at only $11,000,000—after Harry's bequests to their children and Gertrude's many gifts to them and others during her lifetime—is divided mostly among the three children. Flora and Barbie are to share the pearl necklace given to Gertrude as a wedding gift by Oliver Payne. Sonny is to receive the large ruby set in a circle of diamonds given to her—as part of another necklace, a wedding gift—by William C. Whitney. Gertrude's nieces Cathleen Lowman and Gloria Vanderbilt are each left "one of the two pearl and diamond bracelets which I almost always wear." This gift is the only one to Gloria, except for "the trophies and other mementos of her father which I have collected and preserved for her." Other nieces and grandchildren receive specific pieces of jewelry, a long list ending with the gift of Harry's gold watch to Harry Payne Whitney II, and the stipulation that the rest of the jewelry be divided between Flora and Barbie.

All the domestic real estate and the contents of the many buildings in Westbury, in New York, in Newport, and in the Adirondacks are left in equal parts to the children, except that Flora receives 8–14 West Eighth Street (subject to the Whitney Museum leases), and the properties in France—the Paris studio and the country house known as Le Boulay—are also left to her; and Gladys receives those paintings, tapestries, rugs, and other furnishings left to Gertrude at the time of their mother's death but still remaining in 1 East 67th Street where Gladys lives.

The three most valuable paintings in 871 Fifth Avenue are left to the children in accordance with their preferences—the Venetian Turner to

Flora, a Reynolds portrait of a lady to Barbara, and a Van Dyck portrait of William Villiers to Sonny—all removed from the auction, scheduled before Gertrude's death and occurring just after it.

Finally, among the major bequests is a gift of $2,500,000 outright to the Whitney Museum, plus the forgiveness of all its outstanding debts to Gertrude, and a general instruction that the "remaining estate shall be devoted to such charitable and educational purposes, including the encouragement of art, as my children shall determine to be most worthy and deserving."

Smaller gifts include $50,000 to Juliana Force; $15,000 to Marie Pfitzer, Gertrude's personal maid before Hortense; $10,000 to her chauffeur, Fred Stone; and $20,000 to be divided among other servants, including Hortense. However, although some of these details, along with major bequests, are recorded in the *Times*, the *Herald Tribune*, and the *Sun*, the New York tabloids and sensational papers there and outside the city focus on one item: "No CASH FOR GLORIA" (New York *Mirror*). And for whatever reasons there and elsewhere, the bracelet grows: "GLORIA GETS ONLY PEARL NECKLACE BY WHITNEY WILL." (New York *Journal-American*).

❧

One of the institutions which commemorates Gertrude's death with a board resolution (May 18) is the Metropolitan Museum:

> The Trustees . . . wish to mark with the deepest regret the death of Gertrude Vanderbilt Whitney.
>
> For a period of twenty years her active interest in the field of American art bore fruit of inestimable importance. Her general attitude towards the contemporary artist transformed his outlook; and though there will not be forgotten her own admirable achievements as a sculptor, the exhibitions and purchases she sponsored and the great museum she founded, it is the unbounded enthusiasm she engendered for every cause she undertook that her city will long remember and deem itself the richer for having enjoyed.
>
> She would not have wished the Trustees of the Metropolitan Museum of Art, we feel, to extend to the Trustees of the Whitney Museum of American Art their expressions of sorrow at her death, but rather their expressions of high satisfaction that Gertrude Vanderbilt Whitney should have been among us and that the institutions of her city should have shared so greatly of her spirit.

Though there is no reason to doubt the sentiments expressed by the Metropolitan trustees, these must be placed within the context of ongoing negotiations between the two institutions. From now until July 21, 1943, when these negotiations are "temporarily" abandoned, Frank Crocker is in frequent communication with William Church Osborn, president of the

Metropolitan; Francis Taylor, its new director; and Roland Redmond, counsel. It is clear from the start of over a hundred pages of correspondence and memoranda during this period that Frank, Flora, and Juliana have come to accept the advantages of being associated with the Metropolitan, *if* the separate identity and autonomy of the Whitney can be retained. It is just as clear that the Metropolitan is attracted to the Whitney's endowment, some but not all of its collection, and the likelihood of a new wing being built out of funds from Gertrude's residual estate, *but* it is determined to absorb the Whitney into its staff structure and into a wing with functions shared by the two institutions.

June 4—long before negotiations break down (they will drag on, less actively, until 1948)—the first meeting of the Whitney trustees since Gertrude's death is held. It is in Flora Miller's apartment at 544 East 86th Street. There, high above the East River, Flora is appointed "temporary chairman" and calls the meeting to order. She tells Frank and Juliana that "the immeasurable loss sustained by the Museum . . . requires no formal eulogy to be spread upon the minutes . . . because the greatest tribute the Trustees can pay to [Gertrude's] memory is their endeavor to carry out her aims and aspirations for the future of the Museum." Flora wishes only to present to the meeting for incorporation in the minutes the May 18 resolution she has received from the Metropolitan. It is duly recorded and then the formalities are performed of electing Cully to fill the vacant seat on the board and Flora to become its president. Much of the rest of the meeting is devoted to Mrs. Force's report on the program for the coming season, which includes the "Exhibition of Mrs. Whitney's work." And finally, as if in economic counterpoint, her salary is raised to $30,000 a year and Flora indicates willingness not only to renew the lease on 10–14 West Eighth Street at a dollar per year but to include number 8, formerly occupied by her mother.

A few days after the meeting Flora receives a letter from Helen Card, now in Woonsocket, Rhode Island:

. . . Apart from my personal sorrow, her passing was a great blow to me, as my work was all planned around the play she was doing. It looked then as though Ben Boyar would produce it, etc., and I was to go on working on it.

When she began to be ill, she would say that the play would be along in a day or two—and I would count on it. There was no warning of what was to become of me, and when she did not recover there was simply a terrifying blank for me. I finally decided to leave the city and get some rest—I sold my bracelets and a gold cross and a few books, took dictation at the Swiss Consulate for a time, and thus managed to pay off my obligations and get away.

I'm having fresh air and a rest now, but it will be necessary for me to return to New York for work in a few weeks—which will be easy, as stenographers are practically lapped up at sight nowadays. But it would help me if you would give me some hint as to whether you really intend having the play produced and having me work on that again.

As I'm a writer as well as a stenographer—which is why George Chamberlain recommended me to Mrs. Whitney in the first place—I'll be trying to finish stories—hoping to bail myself out of the much-hated office work. I don't want to count hopelessly on the play—but I'd hate to miss it, after doing so much on it.

Of course, while doing so much work for her for almost two years, I knew no members of the family, and to her I was only the stenographer she could always count on not to fail her when she phoned unexpectedly or in a rush—

But to me she was a sort of Great Lady, and there will always be a charm to me about those long afternoons and sometimes evenings, when she had me sitting there to straighten out manuscript while she worked out her short stories. It was a job very different from any I had ever held. No one ever was quite as tactful and gracious, that I had worked for! Then she had a kind of charming and lightning-quick understanding, and a terrific sort of nonchalance which I admired extravagantly—so that I can only imagine how those who really were close to her feel now.

Now Major Bodley said you had been extremely busy lately—and if I have added to this, I do apologise. I'm not writing to urge you in some way, I only wanted you to know about me and my address, and ask about the play, and thank you for the clothes [given to her by Gertrude when she went into mourning for Neily].

And still in 1942, during the summer, there is an obituary that would have touched Gertrude, that of Jimmie Appleton—dead at seventy-five, never married—who many friends say remained single because of his love for her. . . .

⇜ And On

Gertrude's energy flows on, affecting the thousands of people each year who visit the Whitney Museum of American Art, the Whitney Wing of the American Museum of Natural History, the Cushing Memorial Gallery of the Newport Art Association, her bedroom at The Breakers (recently restored by her niece, Countess Anthony Szápáry); and those who respond to her monuments; and those who come in contact with her children, grandchildren, and posthumous great-grandchildren; and perhaps those, too, who for the first time read here a small fraction of the words she used to record a life, aristocratically privileged but democratically human.

Surely the most lasting of all her different kinds of monuments—especially given the deterioration of the *El Dorado* frieze, the relocation to a more obscure site of the *Titanic* Memorial, the destruction by the Germans of the *St. Nazaire* Memorial, the neglect of the Columbus Monument in an area which has become increasingly industrialized, and the abandonment of *Spirit of Flight*—is the Whitney Museum itself. That small dream, going back now three quarters of a century, has grown from the cozy galleries on MacDougal Alley and then on West Eighth Street to the impersonal ones on the north side of the Museum of Modern Art (1954–66) to the distinguished present building at Madison Avenue and 75th Street, designed by Marcel Breuer. A collection, which really began in 1908 with the purchase of four paintings by The Eight, has grown to one containing over 6,000 works, including the bequest of more than 2,000 by the great American realist Edward Hopper, given in appreciation of the Whitney's early exhibition and acquisition of his work. A staff of half a dozen or so has grown to about 120. Annual attendance in the low thousands has grown to about half a million (including, now, that of a Downtown Branch). And openings such as biennials, once attended by a few hundred artists and their friends, are now art world events attracting as many as 3,500.

Gertrude's dream has become institutionalized, her shadow has lengthened—lengthened far beyond the walls of the museum which she founded. It now influences hundreds of newer museums, as well as patrons, collectors, and dealers. With mass media and mass marketing, everything about her dream has become enlarged, extrapolated, exaggerated and, at times, caricatured. Partly because of Gertrude's pioneering, art in general, American art in particular, has become chic. Jackson Pollock's large paintings have twice brought prices of $2,000,000. Litigation surrounding the multimillion-dollar Mark Rothko estate has been front-page news. Alexander Calder has decorated commercial airplanes. Robert Indiana's $\frac{LO}{VE}$ love image has been "ripped off" by a thousand novelty companies. Jasper Johns's beer and coffee cans, targets, numbers and letters, maps and flags are as familiar as trade marks. The face of Larry Rivers, since it appeared on "$64,000 Question," is as recognizable as the style of his work. Andrew C. Wyeth has reached a nostalgia market almost as large as that to which Norman Rockwell's *Saturday Evening Post* covers appealed. Andy Warhol's "factory" has turned out fast-selling silk-screen prints and films that are box-office hits. Artists such as these—and a few "discovered" or "rediscovered" women (e.g., Louise Nevelson and Georgia O'Keeffe)—now have the celebrity once enjoyed by society figures, opera singers, athletes, and movie stars. They, as much as their work, are the raw material for magazine cover stories and TV talk shows.

Once Juliana Force conferred intimately with Gertrude about comparatively small public relations matters or the details of a traveling exhibition. Now Thomas Newton Armstrong III, the fifth director of the museum, reports to thirty trustees. Five of Gertrude's relatives, including her daughter Flora Whitney Miller, honorary chairperson, and granddaughter Flora Miller Irving, president, still represent the family—and, indeed, eight board members are women—but the board is dominated by bankers and businessmen. They all listen as Armstrong reviews the cost of sending an exhibition—fully insured and accompanied by a registrar—on a jet plane to England, France, Germany, and Japan. It will be expensive—perhaps $400,000. But attendance is growing. Interest in American art is growing. Corporate and foundation grants are growing. Financial support from federal, state, and city agencies is growing. And now support from foreign governments is also growing. Everything is growing.

Yes, with growth, with the qualitative change that accompanies quantitative change, Gertrude's museum has become democratized, popularized, even inflated, beyond her dream.

Index

T3

THE VANDERBILTS *

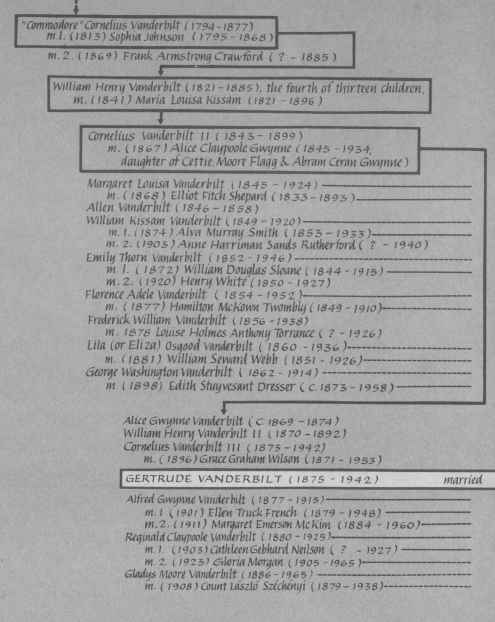

Jan Aertsen van der bilt (? – 1705)

"Commodore" Cornelius Vanderbilt (1794 – 1877)
  m.1. (1813) Sophia Johnson (1795 – 1868)

  m. 2. (1869) Frank Armstrong Crawford (? – 1885)

William Henry Vanderbilt (1821 – 1885), the fourth of thirteen children,
  m. (1841) Maria Louisa Kissam (1821 – 1896)

Cornelius Vanderbilt II (1843 – 1899)
  m. (1867) Alice Claypoole Gwynne (1845 – 1934,
    daughter of Cettie, Moore Flagg & Abram Ceran Gwynne)

Margaret Louisa Vanderbilt (1845 – 1924) ——————————————
  m. (1868) Elliot Fitch Shepard (1833 – 1893) —————————
Allen Vanderbilt (1846 – 1858)
William Kissam Vanderbilt (1849 – 1920)—————————————
  m.1. (1874) Alva Murray Smith (1853 – 1933)—————————
  m. 2. (1903) Anne Harriman Sands Rutherford (? – 1940)
Emily Thorn Vanderbilt (1852 – 1946) ——————————————
  m. 1. (1872) William Douglas Sloane (1844 – 1915) —————
  m. 2. (1920) Henry White (1850 – 1927)
Florence Adele Vanderbilt (1854 – 1952)———————————
  m. (1877) Hamilton McKown Twombly (1849 – 1910)—————
Frederick William Vanderbilt (1856 – 1938)
  m. 1878 Louise Holmes Anthony Torrance (? – 1926)
Lila (or Eliza) Osgood Vanderbilt (1860 – 1936)——————
  m. (1881) William Seward Webb (1851 – 1926)——————
George Washington Vanderbilt (1862 – 1914) —————————
  m. (1898) Edith Stuyvesant Dresser (c. 1873 – 1958)———

Alice Gwynne Vanderbilt (c. 1869 – 1874)
William Henry Vanderbilt II (1870 – 1892)
Cornelius Vanderbilt III (1873 – 1942)
  m. (1896) Grace Graham Wilson (1871 – 1953)

GERTRUDE VANDERBILT (1875 – 1942)   married

Alfred Gwynne Vanderbilt (1877 – 1915)—————————
  m.1 (1901) Ellen Truck French (1879 – 1948) ——————
  m.2. (1911) Margaret Emerson McKim (1884 – 1960)————
Reginald Claypoole Vanderbilt (1880 – 1925)——————
  m.1. (1903) Cathleen Gebhard Neilson (? – 1927) ————
  m. 2. (1923) Gloria Morgan (1905 – 1965)——————
Gladys Moore Vanderbilt (1886 – 1965) ————————————
  m. (1908) Count László Széchényi (1879 – 1938)—————

* Genealogies are abbreviated.
  Broken lines, both vertical and horizontal, indicate generations not shown.